The Position of Dutch Works Councils in Multinational Corporations

The Position of Dutch Works Councils in Multinational Corporations

Marcus Meyer

eleven international publishing

Published, sold and distributed by Eleven International Publishing
P.O. Box 85576
2508 CG The Hague
The Netherlands
Tel.: +31 70 33 070 33
Fax: +31 70 33 070 30
e-mail: sales@elevenpub.nl
www.elevenpub.com

Sold and distributed in USA and Canada
International Specialized Book Services
920 NE 58th Avenue, Suite 300
Portland, OR 97213-3786, USA
Tel: 1-800-944-6190 (toll-free)
Fax: +1-503-280-8832
orders@isbs.com
www.isbs.com

Eleven International Publishing is an imprint of Boom uitgevers Den Haag.

ISBN 978-94-6236-848-4
ISBN 978-94-6274-872-9 (E-book)

Printed in The Netherlands

Table of Contents

Acknowledgements

This research project has by no means been a lonely endeavour and would not have been possible without the invaluable input from many colleagues and friends. I first would like to thank prof. Saskia Klosse and prof. Ferdinand Grapperhaus for having advised and supported me throughout this project. Their guidance on the combination of legal and empirical research elements has been very helpful in carrying out the quantitative and qualitative research for this study. I would further like to thank prof. Mieke Olaerts, prof. Evert Verhulp, dr. Robbert van het Kaar and dr. Anne Pieter van der Mei for their constructive and thoughtful feedback on my research, and all others that gave me the opportunity to discuss my research with them.

This project would not have been possible without the financial contribution by the MNO Foundation (*Stichting MultiNationale Ondernemingsradenoverleg*), who approached prof. Grapperhaus in the fall of 2013 leading to the start of this project. The Foundation and, in particular, Mathi Bouts opened their network to me, without which this project could not have been carried out so swiftly. The MNO conference '*Grenzeloze Medezeggenschap*' in November 2015 was an important milestone for the project and allowed me to engage with the stakeholders involved in this area, namely Dutch works councils, managers, supervisory board members and governmental institutions, such as the Social and Economic Council. The continued exchange with the field through the Foundation was an invaluable asset for me, for which I am thankful. I also gratefully acknowledge the financial contribution of the Ministry of Social Affairs and Employment (*Ministerie van Sociale Zaken en Werkgelegenheid*), which allowed me, through its '*Subsidieregeling kwaliteit arbeidsverhoudingen* (3213-0001)', to expand the research project and include substantially more interviews through which the project has gained added value and received significantly more input from stakeholders involved in employee participation.

Important was also the input of Jan Heijink and prof. Jan Kees Looise of *Stichting Onderzoek Medezeggenschap* (SOMz) for the conceptualisation of the questionnaire used in this study. I would further like to thank the Social and Economic Council, in particular Sophia Geelkerken, for kindly allowing me to draw a sample of works councils from its Mezzo-database for the quantitative part of this study.

My dear colleagues of the Social Law Department have helped to make this project a positive endeavour and I am grateful to be able to work with Malva, Nicola, Rankie, Renate, Saskia and Suzanne. Many thanks also go to Antonia, Giulia, Kim, Chris, Constantijn, Sascha as well as to my family for all their support. And to Alexander for the editing of the manuscript and Jean and Yoram for their assistance with the transcriptions.

Finally, I would like to thank Annika, who has put up with me through the entirety of this project. Without you, it would not have been possible.

Chapter I: Introduction

1 Background of the study

Employee participation, through the collective exercise of this fundamental right of employees,[1] has been the subject of academic debate for decades. In the Netherlands, after the introduction of the Works Council Act[2] in 1950 (hereinafter: WCA), the debate has primarily focused on the black letter analysis of the rights and duties conferred upon the works council by the WCA. This study will adopt an evidence-based approach and will combine a legal dogmatic with an empirical analysis, on the use of employee participation rights.

Due to increasing globalisation and the growing internationalisation of the Dutch economy, more and more multinational corporations (hereinafter: MNCs) are economically active in the Netherlands. MNCs are nowadays operating across borders and along functional decision-making and operating lines. Employee participation law is, on the other hand and to a large extent, limited to national legal frameworks (with the exception of some EU legislation such as the Directive on European Works Councils). Therefore, MNCs and their decision-making structures are, to a large extent, global whereas employee participation has overwhelmingly remained anchored at the local level.

Because of the limitations of the Dutch employee participation framework in light of the principle of territoriality, which limits the applicability of the framework to the territory of the Netherlands, a tension exists between these statutory rights and the practical application thereof, because of the globalised decision-making structures that exist in MNCs. The duty to consult the Dutch works council at a time when it can still significantly affect the prospective decision (article 25(2) of the WCA) is becoming increasingly difficult to adhere to in transnational corporations as a result of this. The case law on this core problem of timely and effective works council influence on the decision-making process, specifically on the concepts of attribution of (intended) decisions and co-entrepreneurship, is one of the many issues that are addressed in this study.

Another example of the tension between 'internationalised' decision-making in MNCs and employee participation, is the possibility for international corporate groups to apply the so-called mitigated structure regime (*verlicht structuurregime*). Under this mitigated regime, the parent company of the group can be exempted from applying the regime under certain conditions, but instead the duty to comply with the structure regime

1 Article 19 of the Constitution of the Kingdom of the Netherlands [*Grondwet*].

2 *Wet van 28 januari 1971, houdende nieuwe regelen omtrent de medezeggenschap van de werknemers in de onderneming door middel van ondernemingsraden*, *Stb.* 1971, 54.

applies to the Dutch sub-holding of the company group. This splitting of the international activities of the group from the obligation to apply the structure regime is referred to as the 'Netherlands construction' (*Nederland-constructie*). One can argue that multinational corporations have adapted to internationalisation whereas the Dutch employee participation regime has not. The legal dogmatic analysis of these topics can be found in chapter III of this study.

2 Relevance of the study

Much research has been carried out on the Dutch works council in general, mostly by means of an analysis of the appropriate legal framework.[3] The multitude of dissertations on the topic in recent years as well as articles on topics such as the role of works councils in the case of a share transaction at a higher level within the corporation[4] or pre-packs in the case of insolvency proceedings,[5] naturally highlight the importance of this topic. The topic is therefore still very relevant and it is increasingly important in light of the internationalisation of the Dutch economy. Due to this increasing internationalisation and given the fact that 80% of the global value chain is generated by multinational organisations, research on employee participation mechanisms in such corporations is of especially high societal value.[6]

Little research, however, has hitherto been conducted on the position of works councils in multinational corporations, and no empirical data have been collected yet for the Netherlands.[7] While the approximate number of active multinationals[8] in the Netherlands is relatively small (circa 635 in 2014) compared to the number of companies having a works council in the Netherlands (circa 12.000-14.000), the impact of these

3 See *inter alia* the most recent dissertations on the topic; I. Zaal, *De reikwijdte van medezeggenschap* (Kluwer, Deventer 2013); J.J.M. van Mierlo, *Medezeggenschap en de spanning tussen WOR en ondernemingsrecht* (Kluwer, Deventer 2013); M. Holtzer, *De invloed van werknemers op de strategie van de vennootschap* (Kluwer, Deventer 2014); see also L.G. Verburg, *Het territoir van de (Nederlandse) ondernemingsraad in het internationale bedrijfsleven* (Kluwer, Deventer 2007).

4 See J. Lamers (*red.*), M. van Kempen, M. Meyer, K. Wiersma and P. Witteveen, 'De OR en aandelenoverdracht in internationale concerns', in R. Houweling and L. Sprengers (*eds.*), *70 jaar VvA: einde van het begin (lustrumbundel VvA)* (Wolters Kluwer, Deventer 2016); I. Zaal, 'De rol van de OR ten aanzien van aandeelhoudersbesluiten', 10 *ArbeidsRecht* 2 (2015); see also OK 19 October 2016, JAR 2016/278, TRA 2017/9 m.nt. I. Zaal (*OR SHL Cyprus Holding*).

5 In light of the recent judgement of the Supreme Court of the Netherlands (HR 2 June 2017, RO 2017/59 (*OR/DA Retailgroep B.V.*));

6 Statistics Netherlands, *Internationalisation Monitor 2013* (Statistics Netherlands, The Hague 2013), p. 67.

7 One study outlined four scenarios for the future of employee participation in the Netherlands; see R.H. van het Kaar en E. Smit (*eds.*), *Vier scenario's voor de toekomst van de medezeggenschap* (Eburon, Delft 2007).

8 I.e., having more than 1000 employees and fulfilling the criteria applied in this study; see section 1.2.1.3 in chapter II for a detailed over view of the methodology that is applied in this study.

corporations on the Dutch economy is considerable. The works council representatives, whom filled in the questionnaire for this study, represent some 426.084 employees – 5,9% of the total Dutch labour force in 2014 at the time the survey was carried out.[9] By employing quantitative and qualitative research methods, trends and examples of good practice on employee participation in multinational corporations can be identified and recommendations for improving the status quo can be put forth.

The results of this study are primarily focused on the position of Dutch works councils in multinational corporations. However, the results and examples of good practice are certainly also relevant for works councils that are located in smaller companies. By means of the mixed-methods approach used in this study, and through a thorough sampling process, the results should be reflective of the position of works councils in the decision-making process in MNCs in the Netherlands. Access to the unit of analysis – Dutch works councils of MNCs exercising participation rights at the highest possible level within the Netherlands – was sought through existing networks (SER Mezzo database and MNO Foundation). An advisory council consisting of researchers, the SER *Commissie Bevordering Medezeggenschap* as well as *Stichting Onderzoek Medezeggenschap* (SOMz) and members of the board of the MNO-Foundation were consulted to ensure a high level of scientific rigour of the data collected.

3 RESEARCH OBJECTIVE

In light of the background described above, the aim of this study is to examine the position of Dutch works councils in multinational corporations in the context of the tension between globalised decision-making by MNCs, on the one hand, and employee participation at the local level in the Netherlands, on the other. The objective is to enhance the body of knowledge on the position of Dutch works councils within MNCs, both by examining the applicable legal framework and through the collection of empirical data.

The Dutch regime is a highly relevant unit of analysis for two reasons. Firstly, the Dutch economy is highly internationalised and much of the value chain is controlled by or linked to the activities of MNCs, which is linked to the statistics presented in section 2 above concerning the relevance of this study. Secondly, the Dutch regime is unique in the application of the structure regime which allows a differentiation between national (Dutch) activities of corporations and their international activities.[10] Given the high

9 The total labour force of the Netherlands in May 2014 was 7,198 million (8,287 million in 2016) according to Statistics Netherlands (CBS); Statistics Netherlands, 'Werkzame en totale beroepsbevolking', <https://www.cbs.nl/NR/rdonlyres/9278A94C-243D-4FEA-B61F-57BF68E6F479/0/pb14n041.pdf> (last accessed 23 August 2017).

10 See section 3.2 in chapter III, section 4 in chapter IV, section 3.4 in chapter V and section 3 in chapter VI for further analyses on this topic.

societal relevance of this topic, the (former) Minister of Social Affairs and Employment (*Minister van Sociale Zaken en Werkgelegenheid*), Lodewijk Asscher, wrote in a letter to the Second Chamber of the Dutch Parliament in 2013 that he is looking forward to receiving recommendations on the basis of examples of good practice concerning employee participation in internationally operating corporations.[11] This study's objective is to contribute to the body of knowledge – both from a legal dogmatic and an empirical point of view – and to provide such examples of good practice.

A multinational corporation, in the context of this study, is a group of undertakings with subsidiaries, branches, factories or sometimes only with assets in one or more countries other than its home country.[12] The concept of employee participation is circumscribed by some authors as 'difficult to define' or as a catch-all term.[13] At the same time, it is undisputed that the point of departure with regard to the legal basis of employee participation is article 19(2) of the Constitution of the Kingdom of the Netherlands (hereinafter: *Grondwet*, GW).

By virtue of article 19(2) of the GW, the right to employee participation is a basic, civil right of employees and, therefore, prevails over any rights of undertakings stemming from secondary law such as the freedom of establishment. Employee rights are also codified at the European level in article 27 of the Charter of Fundamental Rights of the European Union (hereinafter: the Charter) as well as in article 21 of the European Social Charter. The Charter of Fundamental Rights has the status of primary EU law pursuant to article 6 TEU and the rights stemming therefrom enjoy supremacy over secondary (EU and national) law and thus prevail over the secondary rights of undertakings as well. Works councils in the Netherlands have a dualistic mandate, namely the representation of the employees as well as a duty of care with regard to the well-functioning of the undertaking for which the works council is established (article 2(1) of the WCA).[14] In light of this dualistic mandate, the notion of employee participation, as such, needs to be defined as well.[15] The position of the Dutch works council is thereby deeply rooted in the

---

11 *Brief van minister Asscher (SZW) aan de Tweede Kamer over de stand van zaken van de medezeggenschap in Nederland van 7 maart 2013, Kamerstukken II* 2012/13, 29818, no. 36, p. 6.

12 MNCs are also referred to, in the literature, as multinational enterprises (MNEs), multinational organisations (MNOs) or transnational corporations; the 'home country' is referred to as the country in which the corporation has its registered office; see also section 1.1 in the methodological chapter II for the conceptualisation of the concept of registered office.

13 W.F. De Nijs, 'Medezeggenschap', in W.H.J. Reynaerts (eds.), *Arbeidsverhoudingen: Theorie en Praktijk* (Stenfert Kroese, Leiden and Antwerp 1987), p. 81-150; See also R.H. van het Kaar en E. Smit (eds.), 'Vier scenario's voor de toekomst van de medezeggenschap – Een onderzoek in opdracht van het Ministerie van SZW', (2006), p. 44.

14 See for an overview L.G. Verburg, *Het territoir van de (Nederlandse) ondernemingsraad in het internationale bedrijfsleven* (Kluwer, Deventer 2007), p. 38 et seq.

15 See section 1.1 in chapter II for a conceptualisation and operationalisation of the main concepts used in this study.

notion of employee participation and the stakeholder approach based on the so-called Polder-model that lies at the core of the Dutch society.

Against the background of increasing globalisation and internationalised trade and decision-making, the following research questions have been formulated:

1. What is the status quo of the position of Dutch works councils in multinational corporations?
2. Is there a need for an improvement of the position of Dutch works councils in MNCs? And which tools within the Dutch legal framework can be utilised in order to secure the successful involvement of the works council in light of the increasingly globalised economy?

By means of an empirical legal research approach, a comparison between the company and labour law tools available to Dutch works councils and the practical application thereof is made. By employing quantitative and qualitative research methods, trends and examples of good practice will be identified and recommendations will subsequently be made in order to contribute to the improvement of the position of the Dutch works council in the globalising economy. The sub-question for the quantitative analysis is therefore:

3. To what extent are the rights identified in the legal dogmatic analysis applied in practice and can differences between Dutch and foreign MNCs be observed?

The sub-question for the qualitative analysis is formulated as:

4. To what extent exist examples of good practice that are aimed at facilitating the employee participation process in MNCs?

4 RESEARCH APPROACH

The approach taken in this study is twofold.[16] In the first step, the current legal framework applicable to Dutch works councils will be examined. The focus lies on the statutory rights that are especially relevant in the context of employee participation in multinational corporations. Notably, the rights stemming from the Works Council Act and the structure regime applicable to large undertakings are taken as a starting point for an inventory of the rights of the Dutch works councils. The extent to which tensions in the legal framework on employee participation also exist in practice, is examined in the second step by means of a quantitative and qualitative approach. A questionnaire

16 See chapter II for a detailed overview of the methodology that is applied in this study.

was sent out to Dutch works councils in multinational corporations in order to assess whether the potential issues regarding the use of employee participation, which were identified in the legal dogmatic analysis, were taking place in practice. By using a questionnaire, the respondents were asked to indicate the position of their works council on the topics identified in the prior analysis of the legal framework.[17] These quantitative findings are reported in greater detail in chapter IV. Based on the quantitative analysis, semi-structured interviews with works council representatives as well as management and supervisory board members were conducted in 24 multinational corporations (58 interviews were carried out in total).[18] These interviews were based on the questionnaire responses and were used to scrutinise the reasons as to why certain rights were not being used by works councils and more importantly, which steps the works council, the management and also the supervisory board had taken to overcome the legal and practical problems identified in the quantitative analysis. These solutions were reported as examples of good practice of employee participation in MNCs and were used to devise a toolbox for the effective participation of Dutch works councils in a multinational setting. The results of the qualitative analysis are reported in chapter V of this study.

This study has focused on the works councils in MNCs that exercise participation rights at the highest possible level within the Netherlands. Excluded from the scope of this study were works councils at lower levels within the corporations, employee representation bodies in entities with fewer than 50 employees (*personeelsvertegenwoordiging*) and other forms of direct participation. This was due to the infeasibility of an empirical analysis of all these forms of employee participation.

It is important to further point out that not all of the rights and duties of Dutch works councils are included within the scope of this research. Parts of the Works Council Act, some rights under the Dutch Civil Code and in EU law were excluded from the scope, due to this study's focus on rights that are (potentially) affected through the multinational nature of the corporations studied. Amongst others, EU legislation such as Directive 2005/56/EC on cross-border mergers,[19] the SE Regulation (EC) 2157/2001[20] and SE Directive 2001/86/EC,[21] Directive 2001/23/EC on the transfer of undertakings

17 See section 1.2.1 in chapter II for a detailed overview of the methodology that is applied in the quantitative analysis.

18 See section 1.2.2 in chapter II for a detailed overview of the methodology that is applied in the qualitative analysis.

19 Directive 2005/56/EC of the European Parliament and of the Council of 26 October 2005 on cross-border mergers of limited liability companies [2005] OJ L 310/1.

20 Council Regulation (EC) No 2157/2001 of 8 October 2001 on the Statute for a European company (SE) [2001] OJ L 294/1.

21 Council Directive 2001/86/EC of 8 October 2001 supplementing the Statute for a European company with regard to the involvement of employees [2001] OJ L 294/22.

and Directive 2002/14/EC[22] – while being relevant for the position of works councils – will not be examined in this study due to the focus on empirically analysing the position of Dutch works councils.

5 STRUCTURE OF THE STUDY

The research is divided into three parts. Following this introductory chapter, a methodological chapter provides a detailed overview of the quantitative and qualitative research methodology that was applied in this study (Chapter II).

The first substantive part of this study concerns the legal dogmatic analysis of the Dutch employee participation framework that is applicable to works councils in multinational corporations. The legal dogmatic chapter is further divided into subsections. In the first part of the chapter (Chapter III, sections 1.1 – 1.3), the Dutch legislative framework on employee participation is introduced, including different forms of employee participation and the institution of the Dutch works council as such. In the following part (Chapter III, sections 1.4 and 1.5), the most important rights and duties of Dutch works councils that are relevant, especially in the context of multinational corporations, are examined.

Given the long-lasting debate on the added value of employee participation and works councils as part of the company, a brief analysis of the possible contributing factors of works councils is carried out in the section 2 of chapter III. Section 3 then examines multinational corporations vis-à-vis national undertakings as well as references to multinational corporations in the Dutch Works Council Act and the definition of company groups pursuant to the Dutch Civil Code (Chapter III, section 3.1). The specificities of the structure regime are also examined in the third section of the chapter due to the importance of this regime on the position of Dutch (central) works councils in MNCs (Chapter III, section 3.2). The chapter, finally, concludes, with an examination of the concepts of attribution of (intended) decisions (*toerekening*) and co-entrepreneurship (*medeondernemerschap*) in section 4 thereof. The Enterprise Chamber of the Amsterdam Court of Appeals (*Ondernemingskamer*) has developed these concepts because of the aforementioned tension between the application of statutory rights – in this case the right of timely consultation and access to relevant information – and the practical application thereof. These concepts are therefore important examples of the tension between

22 Directive 2002/14/EC of the European Parliament and of the Council of 11 March 2002 establishing a general framework for informing and consulting employees in the European Community – Joint declaration of the European Parliament, the Council and the Commission on employee representation [2002] OJ L 80/29.

the Dutch legislative framework and the internationalised decision-making processes that are present in MNCs.

The legal dogmatic analysis located in Chapter III is the foundation for the empirical analysis in the following (second) part of this study. The practical application of the legal framework is examined by means of a quantitative (Chapter IV) and qualitative analysis based on semi-structured interviews (Chapter V). Chapter IV focuses on the examination of the use of rights and the occurrence of legal issues in practice, based on the findings of the legal dogmatic analysis carried out in the first part of the study. The follow-up interviews were conducted on the basis of the findings of the quantitative analysis and in light of the legal dogmatic analysis.

The qualitative findings are grouped according to the clusters of issues identified in the quantitative analysis and in light of the employee participation process *de lege lata*, based on the WCA. The first cluster concerns examples of good practice regarding access to information (Chapter V, section 3.1), the second contains practices regarding consultation meetings (Chapter V, section 3.2) and the third addresses access to and the use of facilities (section 3.3).

The important relationship between the works council and the (Dutch) supervisory board and the effect that this has on corporate governance issues is discussed in the following section (Chapter V, section 3.4). Dutch works councils have developed a number of examples of good practice to ensure communication with the supervisory board and, in some cases, even with the top-management through the Dutch supervisory board. The chapter also examines examples of good practice on the topic of professionalism within the works council itself (Chapter V, section 3.5), the relationship with the European works council (section 3.6) as well as the soft skills that are an important prerequisite for many of the other examples of good practice (section 3.7).

In the third and final part of this study (Chapter VI), a bird's eye view on the topic of this study is provided. The main findings of this study are analysed in this chapter with an emphasis on the quantitative and qualitative findings. In the first substantive part of the chapter (Chapter VI, section 2), the main differences between Dutch and foreign MNCs based on the quantitative analysis are discussed. The second part of the chapter addresses another main issue that impacts the position of Dutch works councils in MNCs, namely corporate governance-related issues (Chapter VI, section 3). The final part of the chapter provides a potential, evidence-based approach towards improving the position of works councils through the use of process-oriented employee participation mechanisms (Chapter VI, section 4).

The concluding Chapter VII, finally, summarises the findings of all parts of this study and provides an outlook for possible future research on the topic and the challenges that may potentially lie ahead.

6 Transparency disclosure

This research project has been supported by the MNO Foundation (*Stichting MNO*) as well as through an additional grant by the Ministry of Social Affairs and Employment (*Ministerie van Sociale Zaken en Werkgelegenheid*) through its '*Subsidieregeling kwaliteit arbeidsverhoudingen (subsidienummer 3213-0001)*'. The MNO grant was awarded prior to the start of the project in October 2013. The additional grant by the Ministry of Social Affairs and Employment, which was awarded in December 2014, allowed for a substantive expansion of the qualitative (interview) phase in this study. The author hereby declares that no conflict of interest exists.

Neither the MNO foundation nor the Ministry of Social Affairs and Employment had any influence on the data collection and data analysis conducted in this study. The MNO Foundation's network of central works councils was used to get in contact with members of these central works councils for the empirical phase of this study. Works council representatives did participate in the quantitative phase of this study by filling in the online questionnaire, which was anonymous, and could voluntarily participate in the qualitative (interview) phase of this study. To ensure that no sampling bias in favour of MNO Foundation members occurs, a second sample of works councils was drawn from the Mezzo database of the Social and Economic Council of the Netherlands. This Mezzo sample constitutes two-thirds of the overall sample used for the quantitative phase of this study (see further section 1.2.1.1 in chapter II on the sampling for the empirical part of this study).

To ensure that the research is carried out in an ethical manner, an advisory board was formed which was comprised of representatives from the Social and Economic Council's *Commissie Bevordering Medezeggenschap*, board members of the *Stichting Onderzoek Medezeggenschap* (SOMz),[23] professor Grapperhaus and professor Klosse as well as the chairperson of the MNO Foundation, Mathi Bouts.

23 Professor Jan-Kees Looise and Jan Heijink participated in the meeting on behalf of the SOMz-Foundation.

Chapter II: Methodology

1 Introduction

This chapter will provide an overview of this research project's structure and the methods that were applied throughout this study. This chapter follows up on the research question that was formulated in chapter I and the research objective that was also outlined in that chapter. This chapter focuses on the legal-analytical and empirical research methods that were applied to answer the research question and the research design used to formulate recommendations on how to improve the position of Dutch works councils in multinational corporations. Before discussing the applied legal-dogmatic, quantitative and qualitative research methods in more detail, a brief overview of the general research design will be provided.

There is a twofold structure to the research conducted. Firstly, a legal analysis of the rights and duties of Dutch employee participation law is carried out.[1] By doing so, it is then possible to identify issues regarding the applicability of employee participation law in a multinational and therefore cross-border setting. By examining the main rights and duties of Dutch works councils in the context of multinational corporations' operations, a number of (potential) issues and gaps in the legal framework can be identified. The research approach on the legal dogmatic analysis is further elaborated upon in section 1.1 below.

Secondly, and based on this analysis, a questionnaire was prepared, which reflects the potential issues of using these employee participation rights in practice. Core legal provisions conferring crucial employee participation rights on Dutch works councils in particular were incorporated into this questionnaire. The questionnaire is therefore not exhaustive in its scope and is limited to the main rights and duties of Dutch works councils in MNCs. The empirical research – both quantitatively and qualitatively – is therefore based on the analysis of the legal, dogmatic analysis carried out in the first part of the study. The quantitative research was formulated by means of a questionnaire to ascertain whether the (lack of) rights and duties identified in the legal analysis (chapter III) was also evident in practice. Furthermore, it was scrutinised whether rights were actually used in practice and whether there was room for improvement for the legislator as well as works councils and the management when it comes to adopting rights (legislator) or applying rights (works councils and management). The quantitative findings will be reported in chapter IV.

1 Reference to the relevant and applicable EU legislation is made as and when it is appropriate to do so.

As a next step, semi-structured interviews were used to further scrutinise why certain rights are not utilised by works councils – as indicated in the questionnaire – and more importantly, which steps the works council, the management and also the supervisory board had taken to overcome the legal and practical problems that were identified. Therefore, the interviews were used to identify examples of good practice of employee participation in MNCs and to devise a toolbox for the effective participation of Dutch works councils in a multinational context.

Altogether, the quantitative and qualitative elements of the empirical part of the research are used to shed light on the same topic of employee participation practices in multinational corporations. This technique is referred to as the data triangulation method through which findings of both quantitative and qualitative nature are combined for validation purposes and to provide a broader picture of the research topic.[2]

The research method used for the empirical part of this study constitutes a mixed methods research design.[3] The research design can be further described as a sequential explanatory design.[4] In this design, quantitative data are collected and analysed in phase one and qualitative data are subsequently collected that build upon the results produced by the quantitative phase. While the two forms of data are separate – and will be analysed in chapters IV and V respectively – they are nevertheless connected. The analysis of the quantitative data resulted in the identification of issues concerning the non-use of rights or the lack of knowledge of certain works council rights.[5] Based on these findings, the interview questionnaire was prepared and interviews were conducted with works council, management and supervisory board representatives. The sampling criteria for the quantitative part of this study are further elaborated on in section 1.2.1.1 below. It is worth noting that a sequential sampling technique was applied,[6] which means that works councils were selected according to the selection criteria for the quantitative part

2 See C. Seale, *The Quality of Qualitative Research*, (SAGE, London 1999), p. 53-59; U. Flick, *An Introduction to Qualitative Research*, (SAGE, London 2009), p. 25 and 31-33; U. Kelle and C. Erzberger, 'Qualitative and Quantitative Methods: Not in Opposition', in U. Flick, E. von Kardorff and I. Steinke (eds.), *A Companion to Qualitative Research* (SAGE, London 2004), p. 172-173; U. Flick, 'Triangulation in Qualitative Research', in U. Flick, E. von Kardorff and I. Steinke (eds.), *A Companion to Qualitative Research* (SAGE, London 2004), p. 178 et seq.

3 A mixed methods design is defined by Johnson (et al.) as a "type of research in which a researcher or team of researchers combines elements of qualitative and quantitative research approaches (e.g., use of qualitative and quantitative viewpoints, data collection, analysis, inference techniques) for the purposes of breadth and depth of understanding and corrobation", R.B. Johnson et al., 'Toward a Definition of Mixed Methods Research', 1 *Journal of Mixed Methods Research* 2 (2007); see further J.W. Creswell and V.L. Plano Clark (eds.), *Designing and Conducting Mixed Methods Research* (2nd edition, SAGE, London 2011).

4 Cf. J.W. Creswell, *Research Design: Qualitative, Quantitative and Mixed Methods Approaches* (3rd edition, SAGE, London 2009), p. 209 and 211.

5 See section 1.2.2 below for a detailed discussion of the findings that were used as starting point for the qualitative analysis.

6 J.W. Creswell, *Research Design: Qualitative, Quantitative and Mixed Methods Approaches*, p. 217.

of this study and subsequently, the same works councils were contacted for the qualitative (second) phase.

Both the quantitative and qualitative data analysis are descriptive in nature, which is primarily a result of the limited sample size (quantitative part) and the nature of the data provided (qualitative part). The quantitative sample of 56 responses and an even smaller sample size for some questionnaire items only allows for a descriptive analysis. Where possible, a comparison of the sub-samples of Dutch MNCs and foreign MNCs is made.[7] The qualitative data analysis is aimed at inventorying of examples of good practice that aim to improve the position of Dutch works councils in MNCs. Due to the nature of the data (interview transcripts) and the aim of compiling an inventory, a descriptive analysis must be regarded as the most purposeful means of doing so. Finally, it should be noted that the reporting of the results is also done in a sequential manner with the quantitative findings being reported in chapter IV and the qualitative findings being reported in chapter V. An overall discussion of the findings and the identification of trends based on the quantitative and qualitative findings, as well as the legal dogmatic analysis (chapter III), will be provided in chapter VI.

In the following sections, the specific methodology that was applied in the legal and empirical parts of the study will be discussed in detail. Moreover, the approach to data collection and data analysis for the quantitative and qualitative parts will be further elucidated upon.

1.1 Conceptualisation and operationalisation

Before turning to the methodology that was applied in the legal dogmatic chapter, one must conceptualise the objective of this research, namely the examination of the position of Dutch works councils in multinational organisations. For this purpose, a conceptualisation of the '*position*' as well as '*Dutch works councils*' and '*multinational organisations*' must be made. Only after these concepts have been clearly defined, can a sampling of the participants for the quantitative and subsequently the qualitative parts of the study be made.

Firstly, *Dutch works councils* are defined in accordance with the Works Council Act (hereinafter: WCA) that was examined in detail in chapter I above. For the purposes of this study, only Dutch central works councils, which exercise employee participation rights at the highest possible level within the corporation in the Netherlands, or an equivalent works council, were examined. Therefore, central works councils within the meaning of article 33(1) of the WCA were selected or, in the absence of a central works

7 See section 1.2.1 below for a further elaboration in this regard.

council, a works council that exercises employee representation at the highest possible level in the Netherlands.[8] Thus, when referring to central works councils in the remainder of this chapter, equivalent employee representation bodies exercising participation rights at the highest possible level within the Netherlands were also included.

Secondly, *multinational corporations* were operationalised on the basis of three criteria, namely size, turnover and transnationality. Size is thereby measured by a minimum of 1000 employees within the entire corporation and transnationality by a minimum of 150 employees in at least two countries. These two criteria constitute the same thresholds that are applied in Directive 2009/38/EC on European works councils with regard to the definition of Community-scale groups of undertakings. By applying the same thresholds, the questions on European works councils can be posed in the quantitative part of the empirical section and allow for a comparison of the results with earlier studies. In addition, turnover was used as a third criterion to ensure that sufficiently large corporations were indeed included in the sample. Size is measured on the basis of the criteria of the structure regime, namely an equity capital of at least 16 million EUR. Multinational corporations are further classified as either being 'Dutch MNCs' or 'foreign MNCs'. Dutch MNCs are defined as having their registered office of the top-holding of the group within the Netherlands. Foreign MNCs are defined as having their registered office of the top-holding of the group outside of the Netherlands. The registered office is thereby defined as the official address that is registered with the company registry of that country.[9]

Thirdly, the *position* is conceptualised through the use of four dimensions, namely the 'use-of-rights dimension', the 'participation dimension', the 'facilities dimension' and the 'cooperation dimension' (see Figure 1.1 below).[10]

8 This is particularly important for the sampling in the quantitative part of this study, discussed in section 1.2.1.1 below; such as group works councils within a division (pursuant to article 33(2) of the WCA) or a regular works council that is competent to exercise participation rights for the Dutch activities of the MNC at the highest possible level.

9 There has been a longstanding discussion in the literature about the application of the real-seat versus the incorporation doctrine (especially in light of the CJEU case law in *Centros* (Case C-212/97, *Centros Ltd v. Erhvervs- og Selskabsstyrelsen* [1999] ECR I-1459) and *Überseering* (Case C-208/00, Überseering BV v Nordic Construction Company Baumanagement GmbH (NCC) [2002] ECR I-9943) and *Inspire Art* (Case C-167/01, *Kamer van Koophandel en Fabrieken voor Amsterdam v. Inspire Art Ltd*, [2003] ECR I-10155)), which will not be revisited in this study; see *inter alia* J. Armour and W.G. Ringe, 'European Company Law 1999–2010: Renaissance and crisis', 48 *Common Market Law Review* 1 (2011), p. 131 et seq. for an overview of this discussion.

10 Dimensions are specific aspects of a concept; Cf. E. Babbie, *The Practice of Social Research* (12th edn., Wadsworth, Belmont 2010).

The 'use-of-rights dimension' was assessed by measuring the use, non-use or only partial use of works council rights pursuant to the WCA as well as other rights of particular importance and relevance to the position of Dutch works councils in MNCs.[11] The questions were thereby specifically linked to the previous surveys that were conducted in 1999 and 2009 as well as the literature that will be examined in chapter III. To this end, the works councils were asked to indicate whether they have exercised a right and if so, how frequently they did so. The questioning format used in the online-questionnaire was, furthermore, scaled by means of three-point or five-point Likert scale or via dichotomised (i.e., yes or no) answers. Due to the fact that the Likert-scale answer format allows for unambiguous answer categories on an ordinal level, response categories are mutually exclusive and standardised answer categories could thereby be uniformly applied throughout the questionnaire.[12]

The 'participation dimension' aimed at ascertaining the participation of the Dutch central works council in the organisational and strategic decision-making process. In light of the consultation rights of the works council pursuant to article 25 of the WCA and given the fact that the works councils' "*advice shall be requested at a time when it can still significantly affect the decision to be taken*" (article 25(2) of the WCA), the position of the works council in MNCs is particularly affected by the timing and frequency of the involvement in the decision-making process.[13] Furthermore, the position of the work councils' consultation partner as well as the level at which the works council is maintained, affects the position on the participation dimension (i.e., whether the CEO of the parent company or rather the Dutch country manager or HR manager is designated as the work councils' consultation partner).

Furthermore, the 'facilities dimension' is important for the position of the works councils insofar as access to training and development enables them to effectively and efficiently fulfil their duties as employee representation bodies. Further to this, an adequate balance between the duties as an employee representative and work obligations affects the individual employee representative and might also have possible negative ramifications for the career prospects of employees on account of their membership of a works council.

11 The relevant rights were identified and examined in chapter III of this study.

12 See E. Babbie, *The Practice of Social Research*, p. 179-180.

13 This is also noted in the literature; see I. Zaal, *De reikwijdte van medezeggenschap* (Kluwer, Deventer 2014), p. 87-89; M. Holtzer, *De invloed van werknemers op de strategie van de vennootschap* (Kluwer, Deventer 2014), p. 60 et seq.

Finally, the cooperation dimension was incorporated in this analysis due to the importance of cooperation between the Dutch works council and the European works council, if such a EWC is maintained within the corporation. Thereby, the exchange of information between the two employee representation bodies as well as the supportive role that the EWC can fulfil for the Dutch works council are factors that can positively influence the position of Dutch works councils in multinational corporations.[14] Moreover, contacts with other employee representatives (outside the EWC structure) can positively influence their position due to the exchange of information on the overall corporate policy (in case foreign subsidiaries are concerned). Due to the fact that the consultation of the Dutch works council is almost exclusively limited to (intended) decisions affecting the Dutch subsidiaries of the MNC, contacts with employee representatives abroad can provide valuable insights into the corporate strategies that are applied in other countries. Contacts with employee representatives outside their own MNC can, furthermore, facilitate the exchange of best practices that are applied in other corporations.

In order to measure the four dimensions that influence the *position* of Dutch works councils in multinational corporations, the focus was placed on the following topics in the quantitative analysis. Firstly, the general characteristics of the corporations examined in the sample were analysed (chapter IV, section 2) as well as the level at which employee representation takes place and with whom (chapter IV, section 3). Secondly, the role of the works council within the corporate structure and the influence of the parent company in particular concerning the structure regime were examined in chapter IV, section 4. Subsequently, the work councils' use of rights was addressed in chapter IV, section 5. Finally, in chapter IV – sections 6 and 7, the relationship with foreign employee representatives and the relationship with the European works council was addressed. The concluding remarks and main findings of the quantitative analysis are reported in section 8 of that chapter.

14 J. Waddington et al., 'Managers, BusinessEurope and the development of European Works Councils', *ETUI Research Paper* 6 (2016), <https://ssrn.com/abstract=2792020>, p. 9-12 and 44-50; at the same time, dissatisfaction with the lack of support from the EWC can also be a potential outcome; see J. Waddington, 'What do Representatives Think of the Practices of European Works Councils? Views from Six Countries' 9 *European Journal of Industrial Relations* 3 (2003), p. 320 et seq.

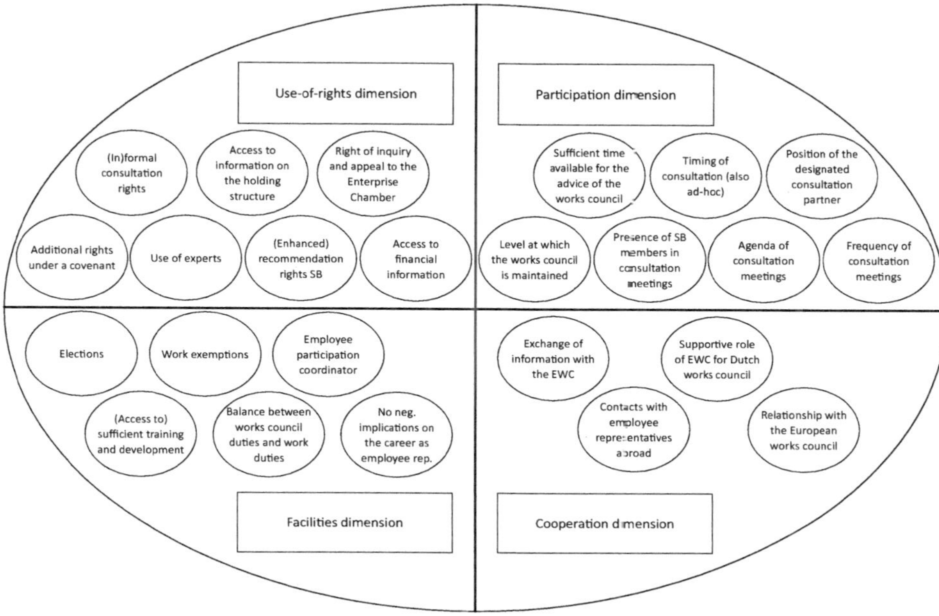

Figure 1.1 *The concept of the 'position' and the dimensions used as level of measurement*

In the qualitative part of this study, these dimensions were also applied, but were rather clustered around seven categories, which constitutes a more detailed application thereof.[15] The 'use-of-rights dimension' is operationalised into the categories of 'information rights' (chapter V – section 3.1) and 'consultation rights' (chapter V – section 3.2), with the latter falling partially under the 'participation dimension' as well. The categories of 'relationship with the supervisory board' (chapter V – section 3.4) and 'professionalism of the works council' (chapter V – section 3.5) can also be placed under the 'participation' and 'use-of-rights' headings. The facilities dimension is examined in the 'facilities' category in chapter V – section 3.3. Finally, the relationship with the European Works Council, falls within the 'cooperation dimension' (chapter V – section 3.6).

1.2 Empirical analysis

Based on the analysis of the rights and obligations of the Dutch works councils in chapter III, a number of topics were identified that could have a particular impact on the works councils' position in a multinational corporation. It is further argued in chapter III that

15 See section 1.2.2.4 below.

the timely access to information in particular, the level at which the (central) Dutch works council is maintained in a MNC and on which topics consultation takes place, has an impact on the position of employee representation. Moreover, the relationship between the works council and the supervisory board, and the influence of the works council on the composition of the supervisory board can improve the position of employee representation within MNCs.

The degree to which these rights are available to Dutch works councils and are used by them in practice was examined through an online-questionnaire that was sent to 185 Dutch central works councils. They were asked to answer the research (sub-)question: 'how far are the rights identified in the legal dogmatic analysis applied in practice and can differences between Dutch and foreign MNCs be observed?'.[16] Subsequently, 58 interviews were conducted with members of the management, supervisory board and the central works councils of MNCs in order to identify examples of good practice regarding the application of these rights in practice. This was linked to the research (sub-)question 'how far do examples of good practice that are aimed at facilitating the employee participation process exist in MNCs?'.

Both the questionnaire responses and the interview recordings were recorded on the premise of anonymity and the results are reported in an aggregated manner to ensure that no individual responses can be traced back to a specific corporation.

Research objective and timeframe	**Number of contacted persons / responses**
Questionnaire sent (May 2014)	185
Questionnaires returned (May-June 2014)	56
Response rate	30,3%
Interview requests sent to works councils, incl. interview requests with management and supervisory board members (October 2014)	30
Interviews with Dutch works council representatives	25
Interviews with members of the board of management	19
Interviews with members of the supervisory board	14
Interviews in total	58

Figure 1.2 Overview of the conducted empirical research

16 See section 2 in chapter VI for an overview of the main differences.

1.2.1 Quantitative analysis: online-questionnaire

It is worth noting that the previous quantitative analysis concerning the use of rights by Dutch works councils in large Dutch undertakings was conducted in 2009 and focused exclusively on the use or non-use of rights by central works councils.[17] Furthermore, the last comprehensive analysis on the position of Dutch works councils in the Netherlands by means of a questionnaire, which included works councils of small- and medium-sized as well as large undertakings, was conducted in 1999.[18] Therefore, empirical data on the position of Dutch works councils in multinational corporations are absent and the existing data are limited to the overall position of works councils in Dutch undertakings, irrespective of the size of the undertaking. The limitations of the existing empirical data, therefore, created the need for the quantitative aspect of this study.

The analysis of the legal framework applicable to Dutch works councils in multinational corporations has shown that, in particular, the corporate structure applied within MNCs and the Dutch works councils' limited influence on the parent undertaking and the use of rights attached thereto, have a substantial influence on the works councils' position. Moreover, topics falling within the scope of the consultation right that is located in article 25 of the WCA, such as major investments or granting substantial credit to another entity within the corporation, are of greater importance in such multinational corporate organisations when compared to smaller (regular) Dutch undertakings. Therefore, an empirical analysis of the current position of Dutch works councils in multinational corporations is made in order to obtain insights into the *status quo* anno 2014/2015 and to ascertain whether the legal framework identified in the first part of the study is applied in practice, and furthermore to answer the research question that was outlined above.

To this end, an online-questionnaire was sent to 185 Dutch central works councils, whom fulfilled the selection criteria, in May 2014.[19] The quantitative research thereby builds on the earlier studies that were conducted in 1999 and 2009 in order to be able to compare, where possible, the current results with the data that was obtained in these questionnaires. By doing so, trends concerning the position of Dutch works councils on specific topics such as the application of the structure regime, the agenda priorities of the works council and the agenda in consultation meetings with the designated management could be identified.

---

17 R. Goodijk, P. van Beurden and H. van Ees, 'Gebruik, niet-gebruik of onderbenutting? Onderzoek naar de mogelijke onderbenutting van bevoegdheden en mogelijkheden door de (Centrale) Ondernemingsraad in grote Nederlandse ondernemingen' (Ministerie van Sociale Zaken en Werkgelegenheid, 2009).

18 R.H. van het Kaar and J.C. Looise, *De volwassen OR – Groei en grenzen van de Nederlandse ondernemingsraad: Resultaten van het grote OR-onderzoek* (Samsom, Alphen aan den Rijn 1999).

19 See section 1.2.1.1 below for an explanation of the sampling criteria.

Therefore, several of the questions that were posed in the earlier studies were incorporated into the online-questionnaire that was used in this study in order to allow for a benchmarking of the results with the results of the 1999 and 2009 studies. Where such a comparison was possible, explicit reference was made to the respective question posed in the earlier study in the corresponding section of chapter IV on the quantitative analysis. Furthermore, in addition to the questions posed in the earlier studies that were incorporated in this questionnaire, additional questions were incorporated to reflect the recent changes to the legal framework as well as to examine the specificities of the position of Dutch works councils in multinational corporations and the interplay between the subsidiary and top-holding level within multinational corporations. To this end, questions on the level at which the works council is maintained, the consultation partner of the works council, the presence of corporate representatives on the supervisory board (so-called *concernfunctionarissen*), the timing of the works councils' involvement, the access to information (specifically financial information and information on the corporate structures), the use of covenants and contacts with employee representatives in subsidiaries of their MNC abroad were included in this study's questionnaire.

Finally, in the reporting of the questionnaire results, a general distinction is made between the overall results based on all responses ('Full sample'), the responses by works councils in Dutch MNCs ('Dutch MNCs') and responses from works councils in foreign MNCs ('Foreign MNCs'). This distinction was made to check whether a difference in the position of works councils in Dutch and foreign multinationals could be observed. It is important to note that due to the small sample size and the even smaller sub-samples of responses from Dutch and foreign MNCs, the results must be treated with a degree of caution. A statistically significant difference could not be determined for most of the topics and no generalisation from these results is therefore possible. The differentiation between Dutch and foreign MNCs was nevertheless reported in order to examine whether divergent trends between the sub-samples could be seen. This hypothesis is based on the findings of Looise and Drucker, who examined the effects of internationalisation on the position of Dutch works councils.[20] They concluded that "*the further away the company is from the national context, from national concern to Dutch MNE and to foreign MNE, the less influence the works council will have and the less serious its role will be*".[21] An effect on the position of works councils in foreign MNCs compared to Dutch MNCs should also be visible in this study. Therefore, the differences in responses between the two sub-samples will be reported throughout the quantitative chapter.

20 J.K. Looise and M. Drucker, 'Employee participation in multinational enterprises: The effects of globalisation on Dutch works councils', 24 *Employee Relations* 1 (2002).

21 *Ibid.*, p. 37.

1.2.1.1 Sampling

In order to identify problematic topics and trends by which Dutch works councils in MNCs are affected and to formulate recommendations that are capable of solving such issues, obtaining a sample that is representative of Dutch works councils in MNCs was of particular importance. Based on the conceptualisation of Dutch works councils and multinational corporations that was introduced in section 1.1 above, as well as in the introductory chapter I, Dutch works councils had to be selected based on the criteria concerning the size of the undertaking, turnover and transnationality and had to constitute the highest employee representation body of the MNC in the Netherlands. Central works councils were selected, on the one hand, for practical reasons, as access to the contact information for all works councils within such MNCs was not possible due to the lack of a database. Due to the unique access to central works councils via the MNO Foundations member list as well as the Social and Economic Council's Mezzo-database, a comprehensive set of contact information was only available for central works councils. One the other hand, central works councils are in a position to assess the overall position of the employee representation bodies within their corporation due to their overarching role. Moreover, central works councils are entrusted with rights, such as the enhanced right of recommendation for one-third of the supervisory board members, which can only be exercised by a single works council of the MNC. Certain questions in the questionnaire could, therefore, only be addressed to central works councils due to the fact that the exercise of certain rights are limited to them and once the central works council has exercised a particular right, such a right can no longer be exercised by another works council within the corporation pursuant to the principle that the central works council is maintained in the interests of the proper implementation of the WCA.[22] Hence, central works councils are the most suitable unit of analysis and are furthermore conducive to producing accurate research as a result of the fact that they are listed on the existing networks (SER Mezzo database and MNO Foundation).

Due to the lack of a comprehensive database on Dutch central works councils in multinational corporations, which would have permitted a probability sampling, a nonprobability sampling technique was applied instead.[23] The MNO Foundation's list of members was taken as a starting point due to the fact that the works councils represented in the Foundation had already identified themselves as being set up in a multinational corporation. Subsequently, the list of members was checked to ensure that indeed all MNO members fulfilled the above-mentioned criteria, which was indeed the case. The central works councils organised in the MNO Foundation represent the largest multinational organisations that are active in the Netherlands. The advantage of using the MNO members list lies in the access to a substantial group of central works councils, which are

22 Cf. J. van Drongelen and S.F.H. Jellinghaus, *Collectief Arbeidsrecht – Deel 1: Wet op de ondernemingsraden* (2nd edn., Uitgeverij Paris, Zutphen 2010), p. 89 and 232-233.

23 Cf. E. Babbie, *The Practice of Social Research*, p. 192.

active in all private sectors throughout the Netherlands.[24] The disadvantage lies in the fact that such works councils had already organised themselves to exchange knowledge and to serve as a platform for works councils in MNCs. These works councils, therefore, were likely to be more active compared to works councils in MNCs that were not linked to the MNO Foundation.

In order to safeguard the representativeness of the obtained sample, a second (sub)sample of works councils was obtained that consisted of central works councils that were not a member of the MNO Foundation, but fulfilled the above-mentioned selection criteria. In order to obtain the contact information for such a (sub)sample, the Social and Economic Council's committee for the promotion of employee participation (*Commissie Bevordering Medezeggenschap*, hereinafter: CBM) was contacted in order to draw a sample from the large Mezzo database, which in turn contained the contact details of most works councils in the Netherlands. Due to privacy and data-protection constraints, the sampling was carried out by the CBM by applying the already formulated criteria of size, turnover and transnationality.

Firstly, the CBM only selected central or group works councils registered in the Mezzo dataset, which yielded a total of 320 entries. Secondly, only large undertakings having more than 1000 employees were selected and Dutch hospital groups were excluded due to the fact that they could not fulfil the transnationality criterion. This led to a remaining sample of 159 undertakings. Thirdly, a comparison was made with the already obtained sample among the MNO Foundation members in order to prevent double selections, which led to a final (sub)sample size of 123 additional works councils. The overall sample was therefore comprised of all MNO Foundation members, which was 63 works councils, and the 123 works councils registered in the Mezzo database that fulfilled the pre-formulated criteria.[25] The total sample size was therefore 186 Dutch central works councils. After emailing the invitation letters, one works council could not be contacted due to outdated contact details, resulting in 185 works councils being successfully contacted in total.

Considering the official status of the Mezzo database, which is the largest comprehensive database on works councils in the Netherlands, the representativeness of the sample was considerably increased. Not only could a large number of central works councils be contacted, but also works councils of large undertakings that fulfilled the criteria formulated in this study, albeit not being a member of the MNO Foundation, could also be included in the sample. Through this two thirds increase of the sample size, a potential bias could be avoided since it was not only members of the organisation that funded the

24 Which avoids a bias regarding the overrepresentation of specific industrial sectors.

25 The MNO Foundation has 51 members, but contact information for 12 additional central works councils was obtained via the MNO Foundation in the sampling process.

research that participated in the questionnaire. Furthermore, an oversampling of works councils in very large MNCs was avoided by including works councils that were not a member of the MNO Foundation. The sample was therefore considered to be representative of the population of (central) works councils in MNCs. That being said, the sample was not intended to be representative of the overall population of works councils in general and no conclusions as to the overall position of works councils in the Netherlands can be drawn from this study as a result.

1.2.1.2 Pretesting

In order to ensure that the topics identified and the questions formulated in the questionnaire were sufficiently suitable for the measurement and in order to also safeguard the exhaustiveness of the topics, the questionnaire was presented to a panel of experts and a pre-test was conducted. The three pilot participants were contacted via the MNO Foundation and were selected to reflect the different types of multinational corporations, namely a Dutch multinational corporation, a foreign multinational corporation with their headquarters outside of Europe and one MNC with a particularly complex corporate structure. This pilot was conducted because it had to be ensured that a clear and unambiguous wording was used throughout the questionnaire in order to permit respondents to answer the questions that were being asked.[26] The pilot participants were furthermore asked to pay particular attention to potential issues concerning the formulation of questions such as the corporate structures applied within their undertaking and whether or not the questions were comprehensible. In addition, the pilot participants were asked whether topics were missing according to their situation and how much time they spent on completing the questionnaire. The feedback from the pilot participants was obtained through telephone or face-to-face interviews where possible (exit-interviews).

The questionnaire was subsequently updated to incorporate the feedback provided by the pilot participants, with particular attention being paid to additional answer categories reflecting organisational structures applied within the MNCs such as divisions, matrix structures or a geographical grouping of subsidiaries. Additional explanatory statements were added to the questions that were difficult to comprehend and the wording of questions was changed in order to remove ambiguities.

1.2.1.3 Representativeness of the questionnaire

The sample of 185 MNCs is relatively small in terms of absolute numbers, which already limits the representativeness of the questionnaire. At the same time, however, one must point out that the overall population of multinational corporations active in

26 Cf. R. Czaja, 'Questionnaire Pretesting Comes of Age', 9 *Marketing Bulletin* (1998), p. 52-66.

the Netherlands is already limited. In 2014, approximately 635 companies fulfilled the threshold criterion that were applied in this study, i.e., of having at least 1000 employees in total.[27] No information, however, exists as to whether these companies also employ at least 150 employees in two EU Member States (i.e., the transnationality criterion). Due to the lack of data, no more precise data on the overall population of MNCs can be provided. Unfortunately, no additional data on active multinational corporations in the Netherlands are available, at least data that are precise enough. In a Statistics Netherlands study that was published in 2015, 1086 Dutch and foreign multinationals were identified.[28] This study, however, applied a threshold of 250 employees for 'large' corporations, which resulted in a considerably higher number of companies falling within its applicable scope. The sample drawn is therefore at least 30% of the overall population when one takes 635 MNCs as reference point. It must also be pointed out that the largest possible sample was drawn from the Mezzo database by the CBM and no contact details for the (central) works councils of other multinationals could be obtained.

With 56 returned questionnaires out of 185 invitations to participate in the study, the percentage return rate of 30,3% can be considered as satisfactory. Given the fact that the online questionnaire yielded a lower response rate than (paper) mail or researcher-instructed questionnaires, and due to the fact that the estimated time of completion was relatively long (30 minutes), the net response can therefore be regarded as being above average.[29] Moreover, the net response rate of this questionnaire was considerably higher than the response rate for the large-scale study that was conducted in 1999 (12% for works councils).[30] Nevertheless, the sample size of 56 responses is still too small in terms of its statistically significant size and it does not allow for a generalisation of the results with regard to the situation in Dutch works councils in multinational organisations in general.

Another threat to the generalisability and hence the validity of the results lies in the number of missing answers (see below). Descriptive and especially explanatory analyses are only possible to a limited extend when the sample size is too small, and the analyses is further diminished if answers to the variables are lacking, particularly when a cross-tabulated analysis on the basis of two or more questionnaire items is computed. But due to the fact that the sample is overall representative of the total population (i.e., Dutch works councils in multinational organisations), the results from the questionnaire are

27 See Centraal Bureau voor de Statistiek (CBS), 'Bedrijven; bedrijfsgrootte en rechtsvorm', <CBS data catalogue> (last accessed 24 October 2017).

28 Centraal Bureau voor de Statistiek (CBS), *Internationaliseringsmonitor 2015 – Derde kwartaal* (CBS, Den Haag 2015), p. 48.

29 Research on the average response yielded responses between 17% and 20%; E. Deutskens (et al.), 'Response rate and response quality of internet-based surveys', 15 *Marketing Letters* 1 (2004), p. 28 and 33.

30 Cf. R.H. van het Kaar and J.C. Looise, *De volwassen OR – Groei en grenzen van de Nederlandse ondernemingsraad: Resultaten van het grote OR-onderzoek*, p. 26.

nevertheless a strong indicator of the actual position of Dutch works councils in multinational organisations. While the results thus have to be examined with some degree of caution concerning the overall generalisability, they nevertheless provide an overview of the current situation in multinational corporations in the Netherlands *anno* 2014/2015.

Whenever the sample size is particularly small (such as in the case of contingency questions) or where the number of missing answers exceeds the number of responses to a question, this is explicitly stated in the respective section.

In order to determine whether the questionnaire sample was representative of the overall population (i.e., Dutch works councils in multinational corporations), a comparison of the sample with the reference data available from the official Dutch statistical service was made. Hence, by comparing the sample distribution among the different industrial sectors with the reference data available from Statistics Netherlands (hereinafter: CBS), it could be determined whether or not the sample drawn and the responses received were representative of the overall population. To this end, the participants were asked in which sector their undertaking operates in (question 1).[31]

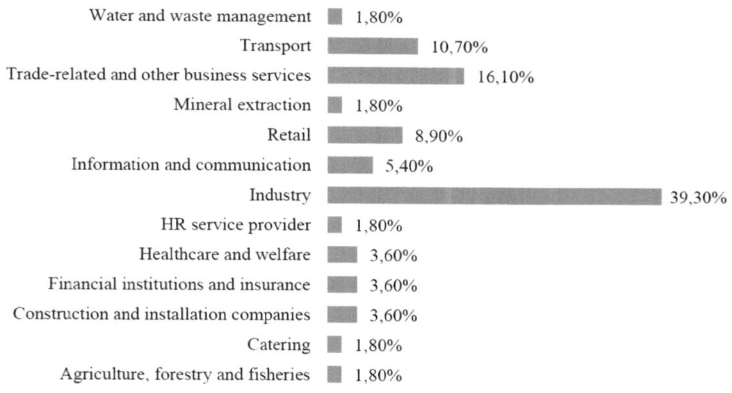

Figure 1.3 Responses by sector (N = 56)

The categories used in this question were based on the official CBS categories in order to be able to compare the results. Furthermore, by applying the same set of categories, the reliability of the categories used can be considered to be very high. At the same time, the comparison can only be indicative of the overall representativeness of the sample, since companies that did not fulfil the three selection criteria for multinational corporations

31 See Table 1.2 below.

(size, turnover and transnationality) were included in the CBS reference data as well. The categories, as well as the reference data by the CBS, are reported in in annex V.

The comparison of the two datasets in Figure 1.4 below shows that the distribution of respondents with regard to the sectors is overall consistent with the actual distribution according to the CBS reference data. Four differences in distribution can be highlighted, however.

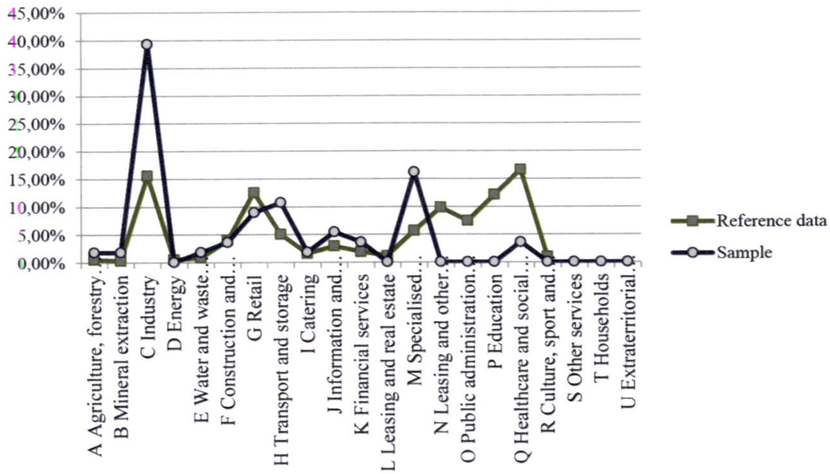

Figure 1.4 Frequency of undertakings by sector (questionnaire data and CBS, 2014)

Firstly, the industrial sector was overrepresented in the response set with 39,3% of all respondents having indicated that their works council was maintained for an undertaking in this sector. This overrepresentation is rather unsurprising given the fact that this sector is particularly dominant in the context of Dutch international trade.[32] Therefore, multinational organisations are more likely to fall under this sector and hence the number of respondents selecting the industrial sector was higher than the Dutch national average.

Secondly, no differentiation in the questionnaire categories was made between specialised and other trade-related services, whereas the CBS dataset distinguishes trade-related and business services belonging to higher educational training and such services for which no higher education is necessary. The questionnaire respondents indicated in 16,1% of the cases that their undertaking belonged to the "trade-related and other

32 Cf. M. Jaarsma and F. van Berkel, 'Trends in Dutch international trade' (Internationalisation Monitor, Statistics Netherlands, The Hague 2013), p. 41.

business services" sector, while the CBS data report mentioned 5,63% for specialised and 9,8% for other trade-related services. Although no distinction between specialised and other trade-related services was made in this study, the sample of 16,1%, is to a large degree, representative of the general population due to the fact that in total, 15,43% of all undertakings fall under one of the business services sectors according to the CBS data.

Thirdly, the healthcare and welfare sector was underrepresented in this study. Only 3,6% of the respondents selected this sector, whereas the national average lies at around 16,58%. This difference in distribution can be explained by the fact that this questionnaire was distributed among Dutch works councils, which are maintained in *multinational* organisations. This transnationality criterion excludes the hospital sector in particular due to the fact that hospital groups do not operate in a cross-border or even multinational group, as a consequence of significant differences in the healthcare and social security legislation that is applicable throughout the Members States of the European Union. Legislation in such matters is still, to a large extent, an exclusive competence of the EU Member States with little harmonisation at the EU level. Consequently, hospitals were excluded from this analysis due to the fact that they could not satisfy the transnationality criterion, which consequently causes the underrepresentation of this sector in the sample drawn.

Fourthly, the educational sector was also underrepresented in the sample. While the national average is 12,10%, no respondents selected this sector as being applicable. The reasons are similar to the healthcare and welfare sector due to the absence of a cross-border element in education and, therefore, the lack of fulfilment of the transnationality criterion. The same holds true for public administration, which is inherently national and does not have a transnational dimension and was hence excluded from the sample.

No comparison in terms of the size of the undertakings with the CBS data is possible. A comparison in this regard with the large-scale study conducted by van het Kaar and Looise is also not possible due to the difference in units of analysis. It should be further noted that when comparing the distribution of the sample obtained in this study with the earlier research carried out by van het Kaar and Looise, it becomes apparent that the two samples are very different from the outset.[33] Whereas the public sector and the healthcare sector were overrepresented in the 1999 survey, these sectors were not included in the sample for the present questionnaire as will subsequently be explained. Rather, the industrial sector is stronger represented in the current sample compared to the 1999 study. Therefore, while the broad study conducted in 1999 examined Dutch works councils in general, this study only examines the specific subgroup of Dutch works councils in multinational organisations in order to answer this study's research question.

33 Cf. R.H. van het Kaar and J.C. Looise, *De volwassen OR – Groei en grenzen van de Nederlandse ondernemingsraad: Resultaten van het grote OR-onderzoek*, p. 26-28 and 261.

Yet, the overall consistency of the sample drawn in comparison with the CBS reference data gives no indication, as such, to presume a threat to the representativeness of the sample.

1.2.1.4 Validity and reliability of the sample

While the sample of works councils was selected with the utmost care and according to pre-formulated criteria, a number of threats to the validity of the sampling nevertheless remain given the fact that it is impossible to conduct such empirical legal research in a controlled experiment (i.e., through a controlled, randomised laboratory experiment).[34]

Firstly, researcher bias could potentially negatively affect the sample by neglecting the predefined selection criteria and due to the fact that no random sampling was feasible, as was elaborated upon in the previous section. Researcher bias was avoided as much as possible by uniformly applying the criteria formulated in the EWC Directive as well as by relying on official data produced by the Dutch Chamber of Commerce with regard to the size of the MNCs included in the sample.

Secondly, sampling errors could potentially impact the sample's validity and hence adversely affect the representativeness of the conclusions drawn from the empirical analysis.[35] Due to privacy and data-protection constraints, no direct sampling of Dutch works councils within the (sub)sample derived from the Mezzo database was possible. Rather, the selection was made by the CBM staff on the basis of the criteria formulated by the author. Therefore, a number of control questions were incorporated in the questionnaire in order to safeguard that only responses by members of Dutch central works councils maintained in MNCs, which fulfil the predefined criteria outlined above, were used in the subsequent analysis of the empirical research.[36] Moreover, the increase in the sample size by including a (sub)sample derived from the Mezzo database in addition to the members of the MNO Foundation decreased the sampling error.[37]

Lastly, measurement validity can be problematic due to a difference of understanding by the individual respondents of the terms used in the questionnaire. In order to ensure that terms such as 'structure regime' or 'covenant' were understood as uniformly as possible by all participants, a pilot was conducted.[38] Moreover, explanations based on

34 See in a similar vein C. Coglianese, 'Empirical analysis and administrative law', *University of Illinois Law Review* (2002), p. 1116.

35 Cf. M.B. Brewer, 'Research design and issues of validity', in H.T. Reis and C.M. Judd (eds.), *Handbook of research methods in social and personality psychology*, (Cambridge University Press, Cambridge 2000), p. 12 et seq.; see also section 1.2.1.4 below regarding the representativeness of the sample drawn.

36 Questions 2 – 6 of the questionnaire; see Annex II.

37 Cf. E. Babbie, *The Practice of Social Research*, p. 219.

38 See C. Seale, *The Quality of Qualitative Research*, (SAGE, London 1999), p. 35.

the legal basis of these items was included as a sub-heading under the respective questions to ensure that words possessed a common currency. In addition, the use of every-day-language was employed as much as possible so as to avoid confusion amongst the participants.

1.2.1.5 *Scope of the Dutch works councils included in the sample*

Another characteristic of central works councils concerns their scope. Whereas some central works councils are maintained for a large number of entities within their corporation, others are limited to very few entities, which is largely dependent on the corporate structure that is applied within a given MNC.[39] The participants were therefore asked to indicate for how many establishments their (central) works council was maintained.[40]

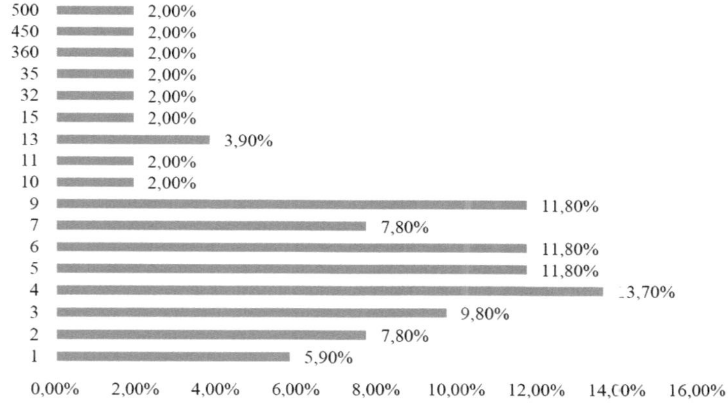

Figure 1.5 Number of establishments represented by (central) works councils (N = 51)

The results displayed above show that a large divergence concerning scope exists between the works councils that responded to the questionnaire. Although most (central) works councils represent between one and nine establishments (80,4%), some central works councils are maintained for several hundred entities.

Yet, the difference in scope is not correlated with the importance of the respective works council due to the fact that the number of entities rather results from the corporate structure and financial considerations rather than from the importance of the employee participation structure that is applied.

39 See A. Cahn and D.C. Donald, *Comparative Company Law* (Cambridge University Press, Cambridge 2010), p. 677 et seq.

40 Question 9 of the questionnaire; see Annex II.

1.2.1.6 Position of the individual respondents within their works council

Whereas the sectorial distribution of the responses and the scope of the participating works councils was addressed in the previous sections, the position of the individual respondents was also checked with recourse to a number of control questions.

Due to the fact that the scope of the questionnaire was limited to the central works councils in multinational corporations (or an equivalent works council that is exercising employee participation rights at the highest possible level within a MNC), only members of such a central works council were supposed to fill out the questionnaire. Therefore, the respondents were asked to indicate, on the one hand, whether they were, aside from their membership in a works council, also a member of the central works council or an equivalent employee representation body.[41] On the other hand, the participants were asked to indicate their position within their (central) works council.[42] By means of the answers to these control questions, it could be determined whether the participants were indeed in a position to fill in the questionnaire and to provide meaningful answers on the position of Dutch works councils in multinational corporations.

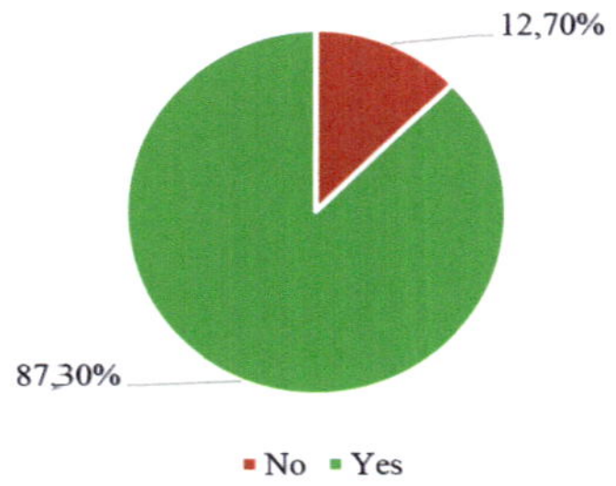

Figure 1.6 Membership of the central works council or equivalent employee representation body (N = 55)

As the responses to question five show, the majority of respondents were a member of both a works council as well as a central works council within their MNC or an equivalent employee representation body (87,3%). Although seven respondents indicated that they were not a member of a central works council and a regular works council, their responses were not excluded from the analysis. When examining the seven cases individually, it must be concluded that in three cases the official secretary of the central works council responded to the questionnaire and in the remaining four cases, a member of the executive committee or the chairman of the central works council filled in the

41 Question 5 of the questionnaire; see Annex II.
42 Question 6 of the questionnaire; see Annex II.

questionnaire and are hence also works council members that fall within the questionnaire's target group.

Because the official secretaries are not necessarily elected for another (ordinal) works council, the responses to question five were necessarily negative, although the responses to the subsequent questions were still valid due to the fact that the official secretaries are considered to have sufficient insight into the functioning of the (central) works council concerned. The other four respondents that responded negatively to question 5 did, at the same time, respond to question 6 by stating that they were either the chairman of their central works council or a member of the executive committee. Therefore, these responses were also regarded as valid in light of their insights into the functioning of their works council as a member of the executive committee or in their capacity as chairman. It is, therefore, dubious as to whether their responses accurately reflect the current situation. In such a case a bias can be created by the respondents answering questions incorrectly, because they misunderstood the question, believed to "know" the wrong answer or had forgotten the answer.[43]

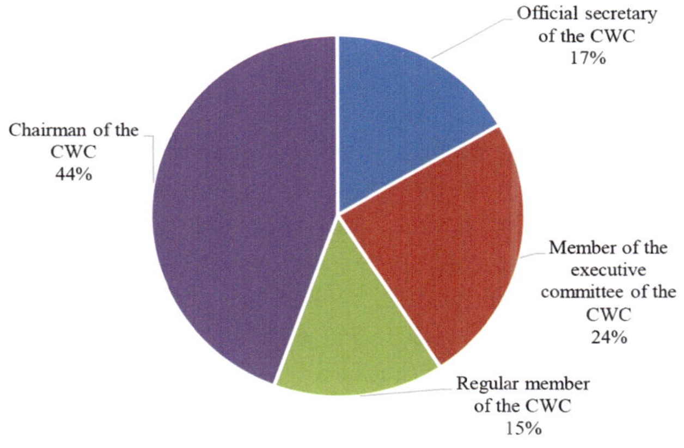

Figure 1.7 Position of the respondents within the (central) works council (N = 54)

When examining the position of the respondents, as is shown in Figure 1.7 above, it becomes apparent that the majority of the participants were also the chairmen of their central works council (44,4%) or a member of the executive committee (24,1%). This certainly contributes to the validity of the questionnaire insofar as the chairman is in many cases an employee representative with ample experience and substantial insight into the functioning of the employee representation body within the given corporation.

43 Cf. O. Sjöström, D. Holst and S.O. Lind, 'Validity of a questionnaire survey: the role of non-response and incorrect answers', 57 *Acta Odontol Scand* 5 (1999), p. 242-243.

1.2.2 Qualitative analysis

The quantitative analysis that was carried out by means of an online questionnaire was completed in September 2014 and it revealed that problems with the use and/or application of participation rights exists in practice. Shortcomings could be identified in the areas of (i) information rights (access to financial information and information on corporate structures), (ii) consultation rights (discrepancy between Dutch and foreign corporations and the use of covenants) and (iii) corporate governance (presence of the supervisory board, use of recommendation rights and the presence of supervisory board members at consultation meetings).[44]

Answering why these shortcomings exist and, more importantly, how these shortcomings are overcome in practice, had to be analysed by means of explorative, qualitative research on account of the close-ended nature of the quantitative research. This was necessary, because "[q]ualitative investigations [...] often yield this type of information, which could not easily have been obtained using a quantitative research design".[45]

The main stakeholders in this decision-making process were included in the interview phase, namely the management (CEO, Dutch country director or HR representative), the Dutch works council (chairman or member of the central works council) and the supervisory board.[46]

All three stakeholders ought to be taking part in consultation meetings on the general operation of the enterprise (as per article 24 of the WCA). Moreover, the works council has both a regular recommendation right for the entire supervisory board (as per article 2:158/268(5) of the DCC) as well as an enhanced recommendation right for one-third of the supervisory board members (as per article 2:158/268(6) of the DCC).[47] The agreements made between the three actors on the matters of employee participation and board level representation in the supervisory board thus clearly influence the position of the works council and all three stakeholders therefore had to be included in the interview phase. Three interviews, if this was possible, were therefore conducted for each MNC. No additional criteria for the selection of multinational corporations were applied other than those that were used in the quantitative part of this study.[48]

---

44 See chapter IV for a detailed analysis.

45 U. Kelle and C. Erzberger, 'Qualitative and Quantitative Methods: Not in Opposition', in U. Flick, E. von Kardorff and I. Steinke (eds.), *A Companion to Qualitative Research* (SAGE, London 2004), p. 175.

46 The 'management representative' is thereby defined as the director within the meaning of article 1(1)(e) of the WCA or the designated director (article 24(2) of the WCA), who is the interlocutor of the central works council (i.e., the management representative present during the consultation meetings). The supervisory board members are defined within the meaning of article 2:158/268 of the DCC.

47 Information rights of the works council (articles 31-31b of the WCA) and the supervisory board's rights vis-à-vis the management also have an impact on the employee participation process.

48 See section 1.2.1.1 above for a description of the selection criteria applied.

The interview participants were identified as follows. The works council members, whom filled in the questionnaire, were asked at the end to indicate their willingness to participate in follow-up interviews. 30 works council representatives answered this request in the affirmative. The 30 works council representatives were contacted in October 2014 and were asked to contact their management and supervisory board regarding the request to participate in the interviews. 25 works councils responded positively to this request and interviews were scheduled in the period from January to October 2015.[49] 19 members of the management and 14 supervisory board members also agreed to an interview after being contacted by the respective works council members on the author's behalf.[50] Therefore, a total of 58 interviews were conducted with interviewees from 24 different corporations.

Initially, it was aimed to conduct a total of three interviews per MNC. Unfortunately, members of the management were not in all cases willing to participate in an interview due to various circumstances. The even smaller number of interviews with supervisory board members was caused by two factors. First, one in six corporations maintains no supervisory board at the level of the Dutch entity, which is on its own a quite surprising finding of the quantitative research conducted.[51] Second, supervisory board members often have multiple mandates and furthermore often reside outside of the Netherlands and could therefore not be interviewed due to practical reasons. This was especially the case when most or all of the members of the supervisory board were also managers at a higher corporate level or even the CEO or CFO of the parent company (so-called *concernfunctionarissen*).[52]

In order to receive as much feedback as possible on examples of good practice implemented in MNCs in the Netherlands, additional representatives of Dutch works councils and management from other corporations were interviewed. Therefore, it was not possible to conduct three interviews per corporation. This certainly introduced a selection bias due to the overrepresentation of interviewees from Dutch works councils (25 responses) compared to management (19 responses) and supervisory board (14 responses) respondents. At the same time, the qualitative research was designed as explorative research with the aim of identifying as many examples of good practice applied in practice as possible. The impact of the selection bias in the interview phase was significantly limited, since

49 23 of the 25 works councils indicated their willingness to participate at the end of the questionnaire and 2 works councils indicated their willingness to be interviewed via e-mail.

50 An email containing information on the structure and objective of the interviews was send to all works councils. The email also contained a summary of the entire research project and information on how the data obtained in the interview were to be used.

51 See section 4.1 in chapter IV and section 3 in chapter VI for the quantitative findings regarding corporate governance.

52 See figure 1.12 in section 4.2 of chapter IV.

no generalisation of these findings vis-à-vis the general population of works councils in multinational corporations is being distilled.

1.2.2.1 Structure of the interviews

A semi-structured interview format was chosen in order to predetermine a number of topics to be addressed on the basis of the quantitative research and to be able to ask follow-up questions on important aspects that were raised by the interviewee. Semi-structured interviews allow for an exploration of the interviewees' perceptions and opinions and the researcher can probe for more information or a clarification of given statements. The latter aspect is of particular importance for this study, because examples of good practice should be explained by the respondents in as detailed a manner as possible to allow for a precise reporting of them in the analysis of the interview recordings. Moreover, different interpretations of principles and legal terms could result in misunderstandings or irritations on the side of the participants. The researcher can overcome this by immediately clarifying unclear terms and, therefore, ensure that the responses accurately reflect what the participants mean.[53]

The interview-protocol can be found in Annex VI. On the basis of the questionnaire results, the following topics were identified as possible issues in the participation process:

1. Who actually conducts the consultations on behalf of the management?;
2. The perception of the Dutch works council from the management's and supervisory board's perspective;
3. The discrepancy between Dutch and foreign MNCs regarding the consultation of the works council on the future strategy of the MNC and trends;
4. The dispute resolution mechanisms used when a disagreement between the management and the works council arises on the question of whether or not a topic falls within the scope of article 25 of the WCA;
5. The presence (or absence) of supervisory board members at consultation meetings between the management and the works council;
6. The independence of supervisory board members vis-à-vis the presence of corporate executives on the board of the Dutch sub-holding;
7. The use of experts, in particular internal experts, by the works councils;
8. The relationship between the Dutch works council and the EWC as well as other foreign employee representatives and;
9. Other forms of employee participation used alongside the more formal works council structure.

53 The ambiguity of terms and difference in understanding is referred to as Lazarfeld's principle of tacit assumption; Cf. K.L. Barriball and A. While, 'Collecting data using a semi-structured interview: a discussion paper', *Journal of Advanced Nursing* 19 (1994), p. 331.

Based on these topics, the following structure for the interviews was formulated:

1. Introduction of the researcher and the study; structure and purpose of the interviews
2. Position of the interviewee vis-à-vis the corporation
   a. Works council and management: what is your position within the MNC?
   b. Supervisory Board: what is your position towards the undertaking (external or corporate supervisory board member)?
3. What is your position within the works council/management/supervisory board?
4. Consultation process within the corporation
   a. Works council and management: how does the consultation of the management with the central works council take place?
   b. Supervisory board: consultation of the management with the central works council.
5. Relationship with other stakeholders in the corporation
   a. Works council and supervisory board: what is the relationship with the supervisory board?
   b. Works council: what is the relationship with the European works council and how are contacts with foreign employee representatives maintained?
   c. Management: what is the role of the central works council from the management's perspective?
6. Are other forms of employee participation used within the undertaking?

1.2.2.2 Ethical considerations

All interviews were conducted by the author under the premise that the results would be reported anonymously. Furthermore, it goes without saying that prior consent for an audio recording of the interviews was obtained by the interviewees and responses were reported or quoted as such that these could not be linked back to the MNC in question. In cases whereby the participants did not wish to be recorded, the interview notes were used for the analysis of the data obtained.

The length of the interviews ranged from around 60 to 90 minutes. The audio recordings were subsequently transcribed for the purpose of further analysis and the recordings were, thereafter, erased.

1.2.2.3 Validity and reliability

In this section, a short explanation is given pertaining to the effect of using a semi-structured interview method on the validity and reliability of the findings.

A first threat to the validity is a high non-response rate and the resulting oversampling of a specific group of respondents. This was not the case in this study. Of the 30 corporations that were contacted, 24 participated in the interview phase (80% response rate). Moreover, both Dutch (7) and foreign corporations (10) as well as MNCs of Dutch origin that are now of foreign origin (7) participated in the interview phase. The fact that a total of 17 foreign corporations and only seven Dutch corporations participated should not be regarded as having a negative impact on the study. On the contrary, the participation of corporations of Dutch origin that are now part of a foreign MNC allowed for questions on the possible change of position of the works council before and after the takeover. One point of concern is the relatively small number of supervisory board members (14 participants) in comparison to the number of employee representatives (25 respondents) and management representatives (19). The fact that supervisory board members in MNCs are in many cases managers at the top-holding-level (e.g., the CFO or CEO of the parent company) thereby made it impossible to interview them owing to time-constraints and the physical distance from the Netherlands. Furthermore, a number of the MNCs are (partly) controlled by private equity firms, which are also located outside of the Netherlands and were, as a result, not available for an interview. Finally, the questionnaire revealed that one in six (16%) corporations do not maintain a supervisory board at the level of the Dutch entities, which means that no supervisory board members could be interviewed in these cases either.

Type of corporation	Participants	Number of responses
Dutch corporations		7
	Works council	7
	Management	6
	Supervisory board	7
Foreign corporations		10
	Works council	10
	Management	8
	Supervisory board	3
Foreign corporations with Dutch origin		7
	Works council	8*
	Management	5
	Supervisory board	4
Interviews in total		58

Figure 1.8 Number of interviews conducted per corporation[54]

54 In one case, two interviews with works council representatives were conducted. Yet one of the two interviewees was also one of the top-70 managers within the corporation and could provide insights from a management perspective as well.

A second threat to the validity is the possible researcher bias due to the use of different words in the interviews. Therefore, the stimulus to the participants differs.[55] But in light of Lazarsfeld's principle of tacit assumption,[56] every term or concept has a different meaning to the respondents and semi-structured interviews provide the necessary flexibility to achieve a uniformity of meaning during the interviews rather than a uniform wording of questions.

Furthermore, probing allows the researcher to validate the participant's answers. Probing therefore also enhances the reliability of the answers. Barriball and While correctly point out that probing (i) allows for a clarification of important points raised by the participants, (ii) permits the researcher to explore sensitive issues, (iii) allows the collection of complete information and to (iv) address and subsequently clarify inconsistencies within responses.[57] Moreover, the interviews allow for a follow up on issues raised by employee representatives in the questionnaire.

Thirdly, the use of audio tapes allows for an identical replication of the contents of the interviews, which significantly improves the accuracy of the data and the subsequent interpretation of the findings.

1.2.2.4 Analysis of the qualitative results in ATLAS.ti

The interview recordings were transcribed in a literal, verbatim, manner.[58] The only exception concerned interruptions in the recording due to breaks or other circumstances. The interview transcriptions were carried out by the author and student assistants. The transcripts were checked by the researcher in a second reading to ensure that the interview recordings were transcribed correctly.

Subsequently, the transcripts were imported into ATLAS.ti for further analysis. Every imported transcript receives a unique document number in ATLAS.ti, which is also used for the referencing of interviews in chapter V. Based on the legal dogmatic analysis carried out in chapter III and the quantitative analysis in chapter IV, a number of categories were identified, which were used to establish initial coding categories.[59] These initial categories were closely linked to the employed interview structure (see section 1.2.2.1 above), which was also based on the legal dogmatic and the quantitative

55 K.L. Barriball and A. While, 'Collecting data using a semi-structured interview: a discussion paper', *Journal of Advanced Nursing* 19 (1994), p. 330.

56 *Ibid.*, p. 331.

57 *Ibid.*

58 Cf. C. Schmidt, 'The Analysis of Semi-structured Interviews', in U. Flick, E. von Kardorff and I. Steinke (eds.), *A Companion to Qualitative Research* (SAGE, London 2004), p. 254 et seq.

59 Cf. H. Hsieh and S.E. Shannon, 'Three Approaches to Qualitative Content Analysis', 15 *Qualitative Health Research* 9 (2005), p. 1281-1283.

parts of this study. In total, eleven code groups, which are an umbrella for specific codes, were established. Of those eleven code groups, four were used for general identifiers such as the 'Organisation of the MNC'[60] (code group 1), the 'Organisation of the (central) works council'[61] (2), 'General Characteristics of the interviewees'[62] (10) and a category for 'Other' (11), whereby codes were grouped that could not be linked to another code group. The other seven code groups were used for the coding of examples of good practice that could be linked to one of the following categories:

- Information rights and the exchange of information between the works council, the management and the supervisory board (code group 3)
- Consultation rights (4)
- The relationship between the works council and the supervisory board (5)
- Professionalism of the works council (6)
- The relationship of the works council with the European Works Council and transnational contacts (7)
- Facilities by the MNC for the works council (8)
- Soft skills (9)

These categories were identified as important aspects that influence the position of Dutch works councils in MNCs. Based on these categories, a directed content analysis method was applied to the interview transcripts.[63] The categories were used to formulate the open-ended questions used in the semi-structured interviews, as was discussed in section 1.2.2.1 above.

The interviews were then coded according to these pre-defined code groups. The focus thereby lay on the identification of examples of good practice that were developed in practice. Any interview passages that contained useful insights into the successful realisation of, for instance, timely access to information by a works council were coded with a code that was linked to the code group 'information rights'. To ensure the exhaustiveness and mutual exclusiveness of the codes used, while at the same time being specific about the nature of an example of good practice, prefixes were used in this regard. For the example of timely access to information, one works council may receive a monthly information dossier from the management. To ensure the consistency and accuracy

60 This code group also includes an identifier-code as to whether the MNC is foreign or Dutch and how the general structure of the MNC is established; see Annex VII for the code book that was applied in this study.

61 This group includes identifier-codes on the status as central or regular works council as well as the level at which the works council is maintained; see Annex VII for the code book that was applied in this study.

62 This group includes identifier-codes on the position of an interviewee within either the management, the works council or the supervisory board; see Annex VII for the code book that was applied in this study.

63 Cf. H. Hsieh and S.E. Shannon, 'Three Approaches to Qualitative Content Analysis', 15 *Qualitative Health Research* 9 (2005), p. 1281-1283.

of coding of such a good practice, the practice was coded as "3 Access to information: monthly information dossier".[64] The code book that was used in this study can be found in Annex VII.

Quotations that fitted into one of the existing codes, were coded with the same code. But quotations that did not fit into one of the codes, were coded with a new code in order to ensure the completeness of the qualitative analysis.[65] Furthermore, while the identification of examples of good practice was the primary objective of the analysis, negative examples were also coded. This was done to provide both a more complete picture of the works councils' position in the MNC in question and to identify reasons for the non-use of rights of Dutch works councils.

After the coding of ten interviews, the codes used were then examined to ensure that no ambiguous or overlapping codes were used. This was done to ensure the mutual exclusiveness of codes, while at the same time ensuring exhaustiveness. Once all interviews were coded, the code book was examined once again to combine overlapping codes and to sort the codes according to existing prefixes such as 'access to information' or 'process-oriented consultation'.

The seven code groups used to code the examples of good practice were subsequently used as a general framework for the qualitative chapter V. The practices were reported according to these categories and more specifically according to the prefixes described above. This ensured that similar examples of good practice were reported together in a structured way so as to provide clarity and to contrast potentially diverging practices. Due to the qualitative nature of the data, no in-depth analysis of the data or quantification of the results was possible. The examples of good practice are therefore reported in order to provide examples of potential practical solutions on information, consultation and other rights of Dutch works councils. The reported examples of good practice are therefore not an exhaustive list of practices and are not representative of employee participation in MNCs. Nevertheless, the 143 examples of good practice provide an insight into potential solutions on the issues surrounding works council involvement that were identified in chapters III and IV.

The results of the quantitative and qualitative parts of this study are therefore complementary to each other. The results of the quantitative part were furthermore aimed at identifying and quantifying the problems associated with the application of the legal

---

64 The '3' refers to the code group for information rights. 'Access to information' is used as prefix for a sub-category of information rights, which is used to cluster examples of good practice linked to information access; see Annex VII for the code book that was applied in this study.

65 See C. Schmidt, 'The Analysis of Semi-structured Interviews', in U. Flick, E. von Kardorff and I. Steinke (eds.), *A Companion to Qualitative Research* (SAGE, London 2004), p. 255.

framework, which was previously analysed in the legal dogmatic part of this study. The qualitative part then aimed to contribute potential solutions to a number of the identified issues regarding the involvement of Dutch works councils in MNCs.

The study is, at the same time, also limited. The focus clearly lies on the position of *Dutch* works councils in MNCs. Yet, further research into the position of works councils in MNCs in other (EU) countries is necessary to establish a more comprehensive picture of the overall employee involvement in multinational corporations. Moreover, in the Netherlands, further research – both empirically and legal dogmatically – is necessary in order to ascertain the position of works councils in MNCs in general. While this study has focused on the position of those works councils that exercise employee participation at the highest possible level, the position of the underlying works councils were excluded from the scope of this study. But this "works council base" within MNCs also plays a role in the employee participation process, which is worth examining. Moreover, this study has touched upon the topic of supervisory boards in the Dutch subsidiaries of MNCs and a number of issues were identified in this regard.[66] Furthermore, this topic and the position of board members especially, whom are recommended by the works council, as well as the role of so-called corporate representatives are avenues for potential future research in this field.

66 See section 4 in chapter IV, section 3.4 in chapter V and section 3 in chapter VI.

Chapter III: The Dutch legal framework

1 The Dutch legislative framework on employee participation

The position of Dutch works councils in multinational corporations is a multi-faceted concept, which naturally warrants a systematic analysis of the various elements attached thereto. This chapter will provide an analysis of the legal framework that is applicable to Dutch works councils in multinational corporations in accordance with the methodological framework of this study, which was outlined in the previous chapter II.

The position of Dutch works councils will be initially analysed from a legal dogmatic perspective in order to provide an inventory of the rights and duties of Dutch works council and to serve as starting point for the subsequent empirical analysis. The structure of the chapter is further outlined in the following section.

1.1 Introduction

The current legal framework that is applicable to Dutch works councils is examined in this first substantive chapter of this study. The focus lies on statutory rights that are especially relevant in the context of employee participation in multinational corporations. The inventorying and analysis of these rights in the following sections is taken as point of departure for the empirical analysis in the subsequent chapters IV and V of this study. In the first section of this chapter, the concepts of 'employee participation' and the Dutch works council are the subjects of analysis. Firstly, a brief overview of the historical developments is provided in order to highlight the developments towards the current status quo (section 1.1.1) and a conceptualisation of the notion of employee participation as such is also provided (1.1.2). Following the conceptualisation of employee participation, different forms of employee participation (section 1.2) will also be briefly discussed in order to provide a general overview before turning to the analysis of the Dutch works council (section 1.3). It must be noted that works councils in the Netherlands have a dual mandate, namely the representation of the employees as well as a duty of care towards the well-functioning of the undertaking for which the works council is established (article 2(1) of the WCA).[1] This dual mandate is reflected in the various rights and duties of Dutch works councils, which are discussed in detail in the following sections 1.4 and 1.5 of this chapter. These rights stem not only from the Works Councils Act (hereinafter: WCA) but also from the Dutch civil code and (implementing legislation of) EU law.

1 See for a detailed overview L.G. Verburg, *Het territoir van de (Nederlandse) ondernemingsraad in het internationale bedrijfsleven* (Kluwer, Deventer 2007), p. 38 et seq.

The second section of this chapter is related to the first one and reflects on the question of whether or not (Dutch) works councils have an added value for (decision-making in) multinational corporations.[2] It is generally accepted in the Netherlands that works councils may participate in the decision-making process of undertakings on behalf of employees, but this is not always the case in other jurisdictions. Multinationals from an Anglo-Saxon background may not have the same longstanding history of employee involvement and may therefore question the added value of works councils. The qualitative analysis in chapter V below reveals that 'soft factors' such as trust and regarding the works council as valuable are important linking pins for the successful application of employee participation in the decision-making process. The added value of works councils on a more general level is therefore addressed in section 2 below.

The third section of this chapter concerns the legal notion of multinational corporations and specifically focuses on the application of the structure regime in such multinational corporations. The first part of the section concerns the notion of groups of companies within the Dutch legal framework (section 3.1). The second part of the section focuses on the application of the structure regime, which is unique in its form and in the exceptions that are available to 'international' corporate groups (section 3.2).

The fourth section, which is related to the third section, concerns the concepts of attribution of (intended) decisions and co-entrepreneurship. The Enterprise Chamber of the Amsterdam Court of Appeals has developed these concepts due to the inherent tension between decisions being taken at an international level – which fall outside the scope of Dutch employee participation – while such decisions naturally have an impact on the Dutch activities of that company (group). The structure regime and the possibility to apply the so-called mitigated structure regime discussed in section 3.2 are therefore a contributing factor to this tension. In this section, the concepts as well as their development through the case law of the Enterprise Chamber and the Supreme Court of the Netherlands are therefore discussed due to the importance of these concepts for the position of Dutch works councils in MNCs.

1.1.1 Brief overview of the historical development of works councils in the Netherlands and Western Europe

The Dutch employee participation framework has a longstanding history, which has a profound impact on the regime that is still applicable today. The historical development will therefore be briefly introduced before then turning to the substance of the legal framework in the subsequent sections.

2 Such added value should be seen in addition to the fundamental nature and statutory obligation of employee involvement in the decision-making process in the Netherlands (article 19 of the GW).

While no tradition of employee representation by means of works councils existed prior to the Second World War in the Netherlands, some earlier forms of representation nevertheless existed within Dutch undertakings.[3] Following the Second World War, legislation on works councils was passed in all Western European countries, which was from the outset characterised by consultation rather than employee codetermination, with the exception being (to some extent) the West German works council which since the *Weimarer Verfassung* was based on economic democracy and co-determination by means of works councils.[4]

The earliest forms of employee participation were first introduced in the Netherlands in the late 19th century in the form of so-called "core committees" (*kernen*) or "factory councils" (*fabrieksraden*), and they were regarded as an attempt to prevent union influence in the undertakings.[5] Such core committees were, due to their establishment by the owner of the undertaking, characterised as paternalistic and rather aimed at preserving the position of the management as the sole decision-making power rather than introducing a genuine institution for worker representation. Trade unions warned their members in the 1910s not to participate in elections or to join such core committees.[6]

With the adoption of the Collective Agreements Act (hereinafter: CAA) [*Wet op de collectieve arbeidsovereenkomst, Wet CAO*] in 1927, which was adopted as a response to issues regarding working conditions, such paternalistic core committees no longer constituted a threat to the unions. By means of the CAA, the labour unions were granted the exclusive right to engage in collective bargaining and, thus, employers lost interest in establishing core committees.[7]

3 Cf. J. Visser, 'The Netherlands: From Paternalism to Representation', in J. Rogers and W. Streeck, *Works Councils: Consultation, Representation, and Cooperation in Industrial Relations* (University of Chicago Press, Chicago 1995), p. 100.

4 W. Streeck,'Works Councils in Western Europe: From Consultation to Participation', in J. Rogers and W. Streeck, *Works Councils: Consultation, Representation, and Cooperation in Industrial Relations* (University of Chicago Press, Chicago 1995), p. 316 and 320; following the *Weimarer Verfassung* of 1919 the *Betriebsrätegesetz* of 1920 was adopted, which was then revised in 1952 to become the *Betriebsverfassungsgesetz* of 1952; see Österreichische Nationalbibliothek – ALEX Historische Rechts- und Gesetzestexte Online, 'Deutsches Reichsgesetzblatt Jahrgang 1920', <http://tinyurl.com/p9jh7n8> (last accessed 30 September 2017).

5 Cf. J.A.M. Cornelissens, 'Enkele beschouwingen bij het 10-jarig bestaan van de Wet op de ondernemingsraden', 14 *Katholiek Staatkundig Maandschrift* 2 (1960), p. 42.; see also J. Visser, 'The Netherlands: From Paternalism to Representation', in J. Rogers and W. Streeck, *Works Councils: Consultation, Representation, and Cooperation in Industrial Relations* (University of Chicago Press, Chicago 1995), p. 100.

6 *Ibid.*

7 *Ibid.*; see also W. Streeck, 'Works Councils in Western Europe: From Consultation to Participation', in J. Rogers and W. Streeck, *Works Councils: Consultation, Representation, and Cooperation in Industrial Relations*, p. 314.

Shortly after the Second World War, the first Works Council Act of 1950 was adopted, which constituted a legislation-based approach to employee representation similar to schemes that were enacted in other Western European countries such as in Germany, Italy and Spain.[8] Nevertheless, the works councils pursuant to the 1950 WCA were still characterised as 'pseudo-democratic'[9] due to the fact that the managing director was also the chair of the works council. The works council was seen, at that time, as a pooling of the management's common interests as well as the workforce and not as an independent institution within the undertaking.

Due to the tensions that existed in the 1960s, which took place across Europe, stronger works council legislation was sought in order to increase the representativeness of works councils.[10] As a response to the strikes in 1968 and 1969, the 1971 and 1976 revisions of the WCA introduced *inter alia* a better representation of workers by means of the central works council and endowed councils with enhanced information, consultation and co-determination rights.[11] Furthermore, the greater involvement of the labour unions by facilitating access of the unions to works councils was introduced by the 1971 revision.[12] Another crucial amendment of the 1971 revisions was the notion of the dualistic character of the works council, which was introduced by virtue of this revision in the WCA.[13]

Whereas the works council of the period from 1950 to 1970 could be characterised as a dependent council, it could be noted that in the 1980s it had developed towards an independent institution within the undertaking.[14] Such independence was particularly the result of the subsequent 1979 revision of the WCA, which removed the managing director from the position of chairman (or chairwoman) of the works council. Instead, the chairperson would be chosen among the members of the works council.[15] Moreover, the works councils were granted more extensive consultation as well as co-determination rights. Overall, the post-1979 works council was perceived as "an established institution, that council-employer relations have become more professional, and that there was

8 *Ibid.*

9 J.K. Looise and M. Drucker, 'Dutch Works Councils in Times of Transition: The Effects of Changes in Society, Organizations and Work on the Position of Works Councils', 24 *Employee Relations* 3 (2003), p. 382.

10 W. Streeck, 'Works Councils in Western Europe: From Consultation to Participation', in J. Rogers and W. Streeck, *Works Councils: Consultation, Representation, and Cooperation in Industrial Relations*, p. 321 et seq.

11 *Wet op de ondernemingsraden 1971, Stb.* 1971, 54; *Wet op de ondernemingsraden 1976, Stb.* 1976, 225.

12 W. Streeck, 'Works Councils in Western Europe: From Consultation to Participation', p. 323.

13 Cf. J.K. Looise and M. Drucker, 'Dutch Works Councils in Times of Transition: The Effects of Changes in Society, Organizations and Work on the Position of Works Councils', p. 383; see also J. Visser, 'The Netherlands: From Paternalism to Representation', in J. Rogers and W. Streeck, *Works Councils: Consultation, Representation, and Cooperation in Industrial Relations*, p. 91.

14 J.K. Looise and M. Drucker, 'Dutch Works Councils in Times of Transition: The Effects of Changes in Society, Organizations and Work on the Position of Works Councils', p. 384.

15 J. Visser, 'The Netherlands: From Paternalism to Representation', in J. Rogers and W. Streeck, *Works Councils: Consultation, Representation, and Cooperation in Industrial Relations*, p. 79.

no polarization of interests or much less than had been expected".[16] The works council developed by not only becoming more independent, but also transitioned from a mere information exchange body to a mature and widely accepted consultation body.[17]

With the codification of the employee participation rights into article 19(2) of the Constitution of the Kingdom of the Netherlands in 1983, the employee participation by means of the works council was further substantiated.

The fact that the WCA has never been subject to deregulation since the 1980s (contrary to deregulation trends in other areas of labour law, such as working times and labour conditions) shows the acceptance that works council legislation in the Netherlands has received.[18]

More recent developments with regard to employee participation legislation concerned the extension of the WCA to the public sector in 1995 through a revision of the WCA that introduced section VII-B regarding special provisions for works councils in the public sector.[19] Moreover, the distinction between small undertakings with less than 100 employees, for which a lighter works council regime was applicable, and undertakings with more than 100 employees was amended in the 1998 revision. After the revision, works councils have to be installed in undertakings having more than 50 employees and a lighter regime is applicable to smaller enterprises since then (article 35b WCA et seq.).[20] Also the possibility to conclude individual agreements between the works council and the management of the particular undertaking (the so-called covenants pursuant to article 32 of the WCA) was introduced in 1998.

A more recent proposal for a revision of the WCA, the Employee Participation Act of 2004 [*Wet medezeggenschap werknemers, Wmw*], was withdrawn by the Minister for Social Affairs in October 2005 due to the lack of a majority in favour of the proposal before the Parliament.[21] While the proposal would have given the concerned parties,

16 *Ibid.*, p. 92.

17 J.K. Looise and M. Drucker, 'Dutch Works Councils in Times of Transition: The Effects of Changes in Society, Organizations and Work on the Position of Works Councils', p. 385.

18 *Ibid.*, p. 385-386.

19 Social and Economic Council, 'English translation of the Dutch Works Councils Act', <http://tinyurl.com/lzhw4uz> (last accessed 29 September 2017), p. 34 et seq.

20 The lighter regime laid down in article 35b(1) stipulates that "*[i]n the case of an enterprise in which there are normally at least 10 and fewer than 50 persons working and for which no works council or employee representative body has been established, the entrepreneur shall give the persons working in the enterprise an opportunity of meeting with him at least twice each calendar year.*" Alternatively, the undertaking can establish an employee representative body (*personeelsvertegenwoordiging*) pursuant to article 35c WCA.

21 Eerste Kamer der Staten-Generaal, '29.818 Wet medezeggenschap werknemers', <http://www.eerstekamer.nl/wetsvoorstel/29818_wet_medezeggenschap> (last accessed 29 September 2017); see also Minister van Soziale Zaken en Werkgelegenheid, 'Brief van 5 oktober 2005', <http://tinyurl.com/pym5u9g> (last accessed 29 September 2017).

namely the works councils, the management of the undertaking and the unions, more freedom with regard to the establishment of employee participation rules based on a contractual model, the Minister concluded that the proposal for an Employee Participation Act would not encompass all developments in the field of employee participation against the background of the economic development in the Netherlands (such as increasing globalisation).

Rather than replacing the WCA altogether by means of an Employee Participation Act, the WCA was revised incrementally in 2013,[22] which addressed works council elections and the training and development facilities for works council members. More specifically, article 8 of the WCA was amended and no longer mandates works councils to send a copy of the (amended) rules of procedure of the council to the competent joint sectorial committee [*bedrijfscommissie*].[23] The *bedrijfscommissie* no longer has to be called upon by works councils and management for mediation prior to an article 36 WCA procedure on non-compliance with the Act, but can be requested to mediate on a voluntary basis and is still used by works councils and management. Furthermore, the minimum requirement of 30 signatures for candidate lists for works council elections was omitted, which concerned article 9 of the WCA.[24] Moreover, a provision regarding information rights of the works council in corporations was added to the WCA, which is subsequently discussed in section 1.4.1 regarding information rights of the works council.

Another revision that was carried out in 2013 made significant changes to the funding of the training and development of works council members.[25] Rather than a levy being paid by all undertakings for the institution tasked for the supply of training and development,[26] the so-called "training-levy" [*scholingsheffing*], the undertakings must pay for the training directly while such training must also be of *sufficient quality*.[27] Finally, a 2016 amendment of the WCA concerned the works council's codetermination right (*instemmingsrecht*) with regard to pensions and extended the works council's codetermination right by specifying that the council's right covers pension agreements concluded with both pension funds and so-called premium pension institutions (*premiepensioeninstellingen*, PPIs).[28]

---

22 Another change concerned the scope of pension agreements stipulated in article 27 of the WCA, which is not further examined in this study; see *Wet van 22 juni 2016 tot wijziging van de Wet op de ondernemingsraden en de Pensioenwet in verband met de bevoegdheden van de ondernemingsraad inzake de arbeidsvoorwaarde pensioen*, *Stb.* 2016, 249.

23 Cf. Bedrijfscommissie voor de Overheid, 'Gevolgen WOR-wijzigingen 19 juli 2013', <https://www.bedrijfscommissieoverheid.nl/actueel/2013/gevolgen-wor-wijzigingen-19-juli-2013/> (last accessed 29 September 2017).

24 *Ibid.*

25 *Ibid.*

26 The *Gemeenschappelijk Begeleidingsinstituut Ondernemingsraden* (GBIO) [MM, Joint Training and Development Institute for Works Councils].

27 Article 18(2) of the WCA.

28 *Wet van 22 juni 2016 tot wijziging van de Wet op de ondernemingsraden en de Pensioenwet in verband met de bevoegdheden van de ondernemingsraad inzake de arbeidsvoorwaarde pensioen*, *Stb.* 2016, 249.

It remains to be seen in the empirical section of this study whether the changes through these revisions of the WCA impact the position of the works council in MNCs.

Other acts applicable to Dutch works councils

Several other Acts have been enacted over the course of the last few decades, which include provisions on employee participation or that (indirectly) affect the position of the Dutch works council. Firstly, the Social and Economic Council Merger Code [*SER fusiegedragsregels*] of 1970 must be mentioned in this regard. This Code of Conduct was successfully revised in 1971, 1975, 2000 and most recently in 2015.[29] The main purpose of the Code is to lay down the rules for the protection of employees (and the notification of employee representation bodies) in case of an (intended) merger.[30]

Secondly, the introduction of the Dual-Board Company Structure Bill [*structuurregime*] of 1971[31] – which is referred to as the 'structure regime' throughout this study – as well as the introduction of group works councils in 1976, further enhanced the representativeness and influence of works councils. The structure regime mandates the establishment of a supervisory board – or alternatively the establishment of a one-tier board[32] – in large undertakings while prescribing information and voting rights of the works council for the election of such a supervisory board. The regime was revised in 2004 and now has an increased emphasis on shareholder rights, which will be further discussed in section 3 below.

Thirdly, the Dutch Corporate Governance Code[33] was adopted in 2003, which is applicable to all companies listed on the stock exchange. The Code was revised in 2008 and most recently in 2016.[34] The Corporate Governance Code (hereinafter: CGC 2016) has been applicable, by means of the "comply or explain-principle", since 1 January 2017 and it has its legal basis in article 2:391(5) of the DCC.[35] The preamble to the CGC specifies that

29 *SER Fusiegedragsregels 2015* <https://www.ser.nl/~/media/files/internet/publicaties/overige/2010_2019/2015/fusiegedragsregels/fusiegedragsregels.ashx > (last accessed 15 January 2018).

30 *SER Fusiegedragsregels 2015*, p. 25 et seq.

31 Replaced by the *Wet van 9 juli 2004 tot wijziging van boek 2 van het Burgerlijk Wetboek in verband met aanpassing van de structuurregeling* (*Wet aanpassing structuurregeling*), Stb. 2004, 370.

32 The same regime also applies to one-tier boards with non-executive directors; Article 2:164a (1) of the DCC stipulates that "what is provided in Article 2:158 paragraph 2 up to and including 12, 2:159, 2:160, 2:161 and 2:161a on the Supervisory Board, respectively, on the Supervisory Directors shall then apply accordingly to the non-executive Directors of the Open Corporation". The same applies to private limited liability companies (B.V.) pursuant to article 2:274a (1) of the DCC.

33 The so-called *Code Tabaksblat*, <http://www.mccg.nl> (last accessed 30 September 2017).

34 Recast of the Dutch Corporate Governance Code (December 2016), available at: http://www.mccg.nl/download/?id=3364 (last accessed 30 September 2017), p. 11.

35 The recently adopted CGC 2016 has to be taken into account in the drafting of annual accounts from 1 January 2018 onwards; *Besluit van 29 augustus 2017 tot wijziging van het Besluit van 23 december 2004 tot vaststelling van nadere voorschriften omtrent de inhoud van het jaarverslag* (*Stb.* 747), *Stb.* 2017, 332.

"[t]he relationship between the company and its employees (representatives) is regulated by law". However, at the same time, the "Code is based on the notion that a company is a long-term alliance between the various stakeholders of the company".[36] The latest recast of the CGC in 2016 also puts specific emphasis on long-term value creation [*langetermijn waardecreatie*] and the involvement of all stakeholders in this process.[37] It is worth noting that this Code only applies to MNCs that are listed on the stock-exchange, which thus limits its scope and is therefore not applicable to all of the corporations included in this study in chapters IV and V below.

Fourthly, the Act of the 30th June 2010 is noteworthy as it introduced a right to speak for the works council at the General Meeting of shareholders on matters such as the dismissal of members of the management or supervisory board or the payment policy of members of the company boards.[38] This act is applicable to public limited companies (*naamloze vennootschappen*).[39]

Finally, the Act of 6 June 2011 with regard to the applicability of enhanced voting rights of the works council in case of one-tier boards must be mentioned.[40] While the works councils' position is not explicitly mentioned in the Act, it can be concluded that the enhanced voting right is nevertheless applicable to one-tier boards. Moreover, such a change in the board structure of an undertaking constitutes a significant organisational change or alteration of the distribution of powers within the meaning of article 25(1)(e) of the WCA. Therefore, the works council must be consulted prior to any such change from a dualistic to a monistic board structure.

1.1.2 Conceptualisation of employee participation

When examining employee participation (in Dutch '*mede-zeggenschap*') semantically, one must note that participation cannot exist prior to any decision-making within an undertaking (in Dutch '*zeggenschap*'). Therefore, the concept is based on the involvement of the employee in the employer's decision-making process by means of consultation and on some topics by means of co-determination. Thus, the decision made by the management of the undertaking, which in the case of MNCs is mostly the board

36 *Ibid.*, p. 8.

37 Principle 1.1. of the 2016 Dutch Corporate Governance Code.

38 *Wet van 30 juni 2010 tot wijziging van Boek 2 van het Burgerlijk Wetboek in verband met de invoering van een recht voor de ondernemingsraad van naamloze vennootschappen om een standpunt kenbaar te maken ten aanzien van belangrijke bestuursbesluiten en besluiten tot benoeming, schorsing en ontslag van bestuurders en commissarissen alsmede ten aanzien van het bezoldigingsbeleid*, *Stb.* 2010, 250; this newly introduced right will be further examined in section 1.4.5 below.

39 Articles 2:107a, 2:134a, 2:135, 2:144a and 2:158 of the DCC.

40 *Wet van 6 juni 2011 tot wijziging van boek 2 van het Burgerlijk Wetboek in verband met de aanpassing van regels over bestuur en toezicht in naamloze en besloten vennootschappen*, *Stb.* 2011, 275.

of directors and the board of supervisors, is influenced by means of the involvement of employee representatives in the decision-making process.

The participation of employee representatives in the MNCs decision-making process can thereby be defined as strategic employee participation due to the fact that a direct influence on the undertaking's strategy can be achieved.

What is predominantly mentioned in the management literature, however, is that the participation is seen as a more direct form of employee participation through employee voice.[41] According to Human Resource Management (HRM) theory, this participation is considered to be a utilisation of the human capital of the undertaking through which a learning process within the organisation can take place. This learning process, in turn, then leads to a higher level of productivity and greater innovative capital within the organisation, which leads to greater continuity and economic success in the long run.

Lammers, finally, has defined the participation of employees as a "bottom-up expression of power of subordinates within the organisation which is deemed to be legitimate according to their superiors and themselves".[42] This bottom-up approach of employee participation is an important characteristic of the Dutch participation system.

Another approach is taken from the so-called 'industrial relations theory', whereby the balance of powers within the undertaking is the centre of gravity of the participation mechanism.[43] Within this theory, the focus rather lies on the aspect of the democratisation of the workplace by means of the participation of *all* actors within the undertaking. The industrial relations theory is important insofar as it explains the fundamental value of works councils, whereas the notions of participation and utilisation by themselves fall short in this regard.

Already in 1960, the Verdam Commission was tasked with answering the question of whether or not employees should be formally included in the decision-making process. The Commission came to the conclusion that, as a result of the concentration of power in the hands of the management of undertakings, a representation of employees by means

41 See *inter alia* P. Boxall and J. Purcell, 'An HRM Perspective on Employee Participation', in A. Wilkinson et al. (eds.), *The Oxford Handbook of Participation in Organizations* (Oxford University Press, Oxford 2010).

42 C.J. Lammers, *Organiseren van bovenaf en van onderop. Een beknopte inleiding in de organisatiesociologie* (Het Spectrum, Utrecht 1993).

43 See *inter alia* P. Ackers, 'An Industrial Relations Perspective on Employee Participation', in A. Wilkinson et al. (eds.), *The Oxford Handbook of Participation in Organizations* (Oxford University Press, Oxford 2010); A. van den Berg, Y. Grift and A. van Witteloostuijn, 'Managerial perceptions of works councils' effectiveness in the Netherlands', 50 *Industrial Relations* 3 (2011).

of a works council would be advisable in order to sufficiently safeguard the interests of employees.[44]

Verburg cited the report of the Verdam Commission as follows: "Employee participation can be defined as the participation of employees by means of advising as well as being consulted on issues on the agenda, whereby the employee against the background of his position and task within the organisation and with his knowledge of the internal organisational structure has to be aware that the final decision-making power lies with the management of the organisation".[45]

The right to give advice as well as the co-determination rights and also the right to information for the works councils will be addressed, in greater detail, in section 1.4 below.

However, before turning to the rights of works councils, one must briefly discuss the possible forms of employee participation that exist in general.

1.2 *Forms of employee participation*

Employee participation, as was conceptually introduced in the previous section, can be applied in practice through different means, which can be distinguished as indirect (or collective) or direct (or individual) forms of participation as well as formal or informal means of employee participation.[46]

Firstly, one must mention direct forms of participation, which include workers' assemblies and team discussions that are thus a form of "immediate personal involvement of organization members" on an individual level.[47] In times of the increased reliance of companies on the independence of their employees, direct consultation of subordinates by their superiors is gaining importance in practice. The increased access to education and the resulting diversity of the workforce further increases the level of employee independence. In particular, the HRM approach of utilising employees' participation to increase efficiency and effectiveness as well as the level of innovativeness has led to a greater reliance on more direct forms of employee participation over the last few decades.

44 P.J. Verdam et al., *Herziening van het ondernemingsrecht* (Staatsuitgeverij, 's-Gravenhage 1965), p. 24 et seq.

45 L.G. Verburg, *Het territoir van de (Nederlandse) ondernemingsraad in het internationale bedrijfsleven* (Kluwer, Deventer 2007), p. 21; see also P.J. Verdam et al., Herziening van het ondernemingsrecht, p. 88 et seq.

46 A detailed analysis of the different forms can be found in J.L. Cotton et al., 'Employee Participation: Diverse Forms and Different Outcomes', 13 *The Academy of Management Review* 1 (1988); see also R.H. van het Kaar and E. Smit (eds.), 'Vier scenario's voor de toekomst van de medezeggenschap – Een onderzoek in opdracht van het Ministerie van SZW', (2006), p. 44 et seq.

47 J.L. Cotton et al., 'Employee Participation: Diverse Forms and Different Outcomes', p. 9.

This tendency thereby goes hand in hand with the growing globalisation of the international economy.

While direct participation is beneficial insofar as the distance between the decision-making process and the individual employee affected by the outcome of that process is as short as possible, direct participation is less representative when compared to the organisation as a whole. Moreover, direct participation in MNCs, which are the subject of this study, cannot feasibly be applied on a large scale due to the costs and time resources that are necessary for such a form of participation to be applied throughout all the levels of the corporation. Furthermore, a greater degree of plurality of the workforce, different socio-cultural backgrounds and thus the heterogeneity of the workforce makes the application of direct participation unlikely. Accordingly, direct forms of participation will not be examined any further in the course of this study.

Secondly, and by way of contrast to direct participation, indirect participation lies at the opposite end of the continuum and always involves a certain form of employee representation. Rather than being comprised of the individual employees participating in the decision-making process, this indirect form of participation is aimed at a collective representation of the workforce.

The works council is thereby the most common form of indirect employee representation that exists in the Netherlands, with the overall workforce of an undertaking being represented by the works council in companies having 50 or more employees pursuant to article 2(1) of the Works Council Act (hereinafter: WCA) [*Wet op de ondernemingsraden*, WOR].[48] While a works council is present, on average, in 67% (71% in 2011) of the undertakings with 50 or more employees, in undertakings with 200 or more employees a works council has been set up in 95% of the cases (94% in 2011), which further underlines the representativeness of this form of employee representation.[49]

Other forms include the unions, workers' assemblies and personnel representation, which are similar forms of representative participation. Yet, personnel representation

48 The most recent research shows that 67% of the companies having 50 or more employees set up a works council; see I. Wajon, P. Vlug and E. Enneking, 'Naleving van de Wet op de Ondernemingsraden: Stand van zaken begin 2017', < https://www.rijksoverheid.nl/binaries/rijksoverheid/documenten/rapporten/2017/10/17/onderzoeksrapport-naleving-wor/Eindrapport+Onderzoek+Naleving+WOR+juni+2017.pdf> (last accessed 15 January 2018), p. 3; the percentage was slightly higher in 2011 with 71% of the companies having reported the presence of a works council; see Regioplan, 'Nalevingsonderzoek van de Wet op Ondernemingsraden 2011', <http://tinyurl.com/n58duhc> (last accessed 31 October 2017), p. 6.

49 I. Wajon, P. Vlug and E. Enneking, 'Naleving van de Wet op de Ondernemingsraden: Stand van zaken begin 2017', p.13; this tendency towards significantly higher coverage of large companies by works councils can also be found in other European countries; Cf. W Streeck, 'Works Councils in Western Europe: From Consultation to Participation', in J. Rogers and W. Streeck, *Works Councils: Consultation, Representation, and Cooperation in Industrial Relations*, p. 340.

is less formalised than works councils and takes place on a much smaller scale and is usually adopted for use in smaller companies.

Due to the fact that personnel representation and workers' assemblies are seldom applied in MNCs, with about 4% of large undertakings having set up such a form of representation, these forms will not be examined any further in the remainder of this study.

The topic of trade union representativeness has been the subject of the academic discourse for decades. This debate has substantiated the fact that representativeness is questioned when the number of workers in trade unions is decreasing and as to how far the unions are still legitimised to conclude collective bargaining agreements [*collectieve arbeidsovereenkomst*, CAO]. It suffices to note that unionism in the Netherlands can be described as weak.[50] For a detailed analysis of this topic, a referral should be made to the existing literature.[51]

Thirdly, one must distinguish formal and informal modes of employee representation. While informal forms are a non-statutory and consensus driven mode of participation, formal participation is based on a system of rules that are either imposed by (public) law or laid down in the company's statutes and agreements with the works council.[52] The Dutch works council is codified in the Works Council Act, as will be discussed in detail in section 1.4 below, and can hence be characterised as formal mode of employee representation.

In conclusion, when examining employee representation and in particular employee representation in MNCs, the Dutch works council is not only the most common form of employee representation in the Netherlands, but is also an institutionalised, formal method of indirect employee representation with the highest degree of representativeness among the available modes of employee representation. However, it should be borne in mind that individual forms of employee participation are gaining traction, due to the increased level of the independence of workers, especially in lower and higher management positions and in times of a greater variety of flexible employment contracts. Short term contracts are adversely influencing the support for works councils within companies since employees, who have been employed for less than one year within the

50 J. Visser, 'The Netherlands: From Paternalism to Representation', in J. Rogers and W. Streeck, *Works Councils: Consultation, Representation, and Cooperation in Industrial Relations*, p. 80.

51 See *inter alia* R. Beltzer, 'Vakbonden en collectieve arbeidsvoorwaardenvorming: de juridische legitimatie erodeert', *Nederlands Juristenblad* (2010); F.B.J. Grapperhaus, 'Over legitimatie en rol van de vakbond', *Ondernemingsrecht* 83 (2011); A dissertation is currently being written on this topic by N. Jansen, *Legitimiteit van de vakbond als (mede)ontwerpers van collectieve arbeidsvoorwaarden*, forthcoming.

52 Cf. J.L. Cotton (et al.), 'Employee Participation: Diverse Forms and Different Outcomes', p. 9; article 32 of the WCA provides for the possibility of additional employee participation rights through company-level agreements (covenants).

organisation are not eligible for election to the works council[53] and given that only employees that have been employed longer than six months are entitled to vote.[54] In an even weaker position are agency workers (*uitzendkrachten*), who must work for 24 months at the undertaking in order to be regarded as employees for the purposes of the WCA.[55] Temp-workers, who are posted for a period shorter than six months within a company that belongs to the corporation and agency workers, who were working less than 24 months at the company, are therefore at risk of being excluded from the elections to the works council.

Nevertheless, the overall representativeness of works councils is undisputed and it is consequently the forum that is conducive to employee participation within companies. By taking, therefore, works councils as starting point for the examination of employee participation within MNCs, one can address the means by which a works council can be set up as well as the topic areas for which consultation and co-determination by a works council is mandatory.

1.3 The Dutch works council

This study aims to assess the position of the Dutch works council within multinational corporations. It is therefore necessary to operationalise the unit of observation, which will thus be this study's subject of analysis. After having addressed the forms of employee representation in the previous section and having identified the works council as the most appropriate forum in this context, the following section encompasses the different forms of works councils and how they are established, before then turning towards the actual rights and duties of the Dutch works council in the subsequent section.

The establishment of a works council is mandatory for any entrepreneur who maintains an undertaking in the Netherlands with at least 50 employees, pursuant to article 2(1) of the WCA. Thereby, the works council must be set up in the interest of a "proper functioning of the enterprise [...] in order to ensure the proper consultation and representation of the persons working in the enterprise, and in order to be able to comply with any requirements of [the WCA]".[56]

When speaking of the Dutch works council, this encompasses the works council (article 2(1) of the WCA), but also the joint works council (hereinafter: JWC) [*gemeenschappelijke ondernemingsraad*] (article of the 3 WCA), the central works council (hereinafter:

53 Article 6(3) of the WCA.
54 Article 6(2) of the WCA.
55 Article 1(3)(a) of the WCA.
56 Social and Economic Council, 'English translation of the Dutch Works Councils Act', p. 5.

CWC) [*centrale ondernemingsraad*] (article 33(1) of the WCA) and the group works council (hereinafter: GWC) [*groepsondernemingsraad*] in accordance with article 33(2) of the WCA.

At the same time, works councils that are set up in public administration organisations are excluded from the scope of this study, even although the WCA was declared to be applicable to the public sector following the 1995 revision of the WCA.[57] Moreover, the participation rights of pensioners and clients will not be analysed in this study.

A works council must be set up as soon as 'normally' more than 50 persons are employed within the undertaking as specified by article 2(1) of the WCA. Normally is defined as more than 50 employees being employed, on average, within the undertaking.[58] If for a short period of time, fewer than 50 persons are employed within the undertaking, the works council can nevertheless continue to operate as long an average of at least 50 persons work in the undertaking and the existence of the works council is beneficial for the proper functioning of the enterprise. If the threshold of 50 employees is no longer fulfilled, the works council will cease to exist at the end of its current term of office.[59]

Once the entrepreneur or a group of associated entrepreneurs maintains two or more undertakings, a joint works council can be set up if the establishment would be beneficial for the proper functioning of the enterprises.[60] In the case of a group of associated entrepreneurs, they shall designate one of themselves to act on behalf of the group as the entrepreneur within the meaning of the WCA.[61] While the notion of a group of associated entrepreneurs will be discussed in further detail in section 1.4.1 along with the definition of a multinational corporation, one can note that the members of the group can decide who will be designated as the entrepreneur vis-à-vis the works council. What is questionable, however, is why the legislator has chosen a different wording in the applicable laws with regard to a network of companies (such as corporations).

For the sake of completeness, one must also mention the possibility to establish a separate works council for any undertaking in which more than 50 persons are employed, as

57 See for a detailed analysis of the application of the WCA for employees in the public sector; L. Sprengers, *De wet op de Ondernemingsraden bij de overheid. Op weg naar een arbeidsrecht voor ambtenaren en werknemers* (Kluwer, Deventer 1998).

58 As a side note, it must be mentioned that the bipartite regime, comprised of a lighter works council regime for companies having less than 100 employees and the fully applicable regime applicable to companies having more than 100 employees, was removed in the 1998 revision of the WCA (the so-called *Knelpuntenwet* which addressed bottlenecks in the WCA). Since then, the general threshold of 50 employees is applicable to all companies within the Netherlands; see for a detailed overview of all revisions of the WCA in the *Knelpuntenwet*; L.G. Verburg, *Rood's Wet op de ondernemingsraden* (2nd edition, Kluwer, Deventer 2013), p. 20 and 51-57.

59 Article 2(2) of the WCA.

60 Article 3 of the WCA.

61 Article 3(2) of the WCA.

is codified in article 4 of the WCA. This allows for the establishment of works councils in smaller entities within a corporation alongside a central or a group works council.

In the 1976 revision of the WCA,[62] section V was added to the Act following a recommendation of the Social and Economic Council (hereinafter: SEC) [*Sociaal-Economische Raad*, SER], which introduced *inter alia* provisions with regard to the establishment of central works councils and group works councils. This revision was recommended by the SEC in order to minimise delays in the decision-making process.[63]

Pursuant to article 33(1) of the WCA, entrepreneurs shall establish a central works council if two or more works councils are established within the corporation and insofar as the establishment of a CWC is beneficial to the implementation of the WCA. A group works council can, furthermore, be established if two or more works councils are already set up within the corporation and if the GWC would be beneficial for the implementation of the WCA.[64]

The difference between the central and the groups works council lies in the difference of the position of the council within the corporation. While the central works council overarches *all* other works councils and is situated at the highest possible level within the corporation to ensure that employee participation is carried out at the top management level (within the territory of the Netherlands), the group works council is usually located at the division level and is thus connected to the management of a certain division or country branch of the corporation.[65] While the central works council should be linked to the top management level, the CWC is in practice connected, in the majority of MNCs, to the holding company of the Dutch entities due to the so-called "Netherlands construction", which will be discussed in further detail in section 3 below. Thereby only one central works council can be established, but several group works councils can be set up for each individual division.

While the WCA institutionalises the works council, the council does not possess a legal identity as is repeatedly emphasised in the legislative history,[66] the literature[67] and the relevant case law.[68] The works council may, however, lodge an appeal in the case of an infringement of the entrepreneur's duties under the WCA with the Enterprise Chamber [*Ondernemingskamer*] of the Amsterdam Court of Appeal [*Gerechtshof*] pursuant to article 26 of the WCA. An appeal against a decision made by the entrepreneur can be

62 *Wet van 24 maart 1976, houdende regelen inzake melding van collectief ontslag, Stb.* 1976, 225.
63 SER Advies 1973/14, 'Inzake wijziging van de WOR tot de instelling van groepsondernemingsraden', p. 3.
64 Article 33(2) of the WCA.
65 Cf. SER Advies 1973/14, p. 3; see also H.J.M.N. Honée, *Concernrecht en medezeggenschapsregelingen* (Kluwer, Deventer 1981), p. 159.
66 Cf. SER Advies 08/01, *Evenwichtig Ondernemingsbestuur*, p. 91.
67 See for an overview, L.G. Verburg, *Rood's Wet op de ondernemingsraden*, p. 61.
68 OK 13 November 1980, nr. 100; Hof Arnhem, *JAR* 2008/314 and *ROR* 2009/15.

lodged if the works council had rendered opposing advise on the matter or "if facts or circumstances have become known which, if they had been known to the [w]orks [c]ouncil at the time of rendering its advice, could have been grounds for not rendering the advice as rendered" (article 26(1) of the WCA).[69]

According to Verburg, such an appeal becomes possible only in cases (i) where the advice of the works council on an (intended) decision [*voorgenomen besluit*] and the final decision made by the entrepreneur are not identical or (ii) where both the advice of the works council and the final decision are in conformity, but the facts or the situation in light of article 26(1) of the WCA have changed.[70] The key criterion for rendering the decision made by the entrepreneur unlawful is found in article 26(4) of the WCA, which stipulates that "appeals may be lodged only on the grounds that the entrepreneur, in weighing the interests involved, could not in all fairness have arrived at the said decision".[71] If the entrepreneur does not follow the advice of the works council, the works council may appeal this decision, but is unlikely to win the procedure.

Due to the fact that the works council does not possess legal personality, all the costs of legal proceedings incurred by the works council, such as attorney fees and expert opinions, and the litigation costs [*proceskosten*] are to be borne by the entrepreneur.[72]

After having introduced the Dutch works council in general, the rights and duties thereof will be further discussed in more detail in the following section.

1.4 Rights of the Dutch works council

The WCA confers several rights on the works council, which can be summarised as information, consultation and codetermination rights. In the following section, these rights will be addressed as well as the duties that are attached to the various rights, such as the duty of strict confidence.

Before examining these rights, however, one should bear in mind that from an organisational perspective, a differentiation must be made with regard to strategic management decisions and those with regard to the organisational structure of the corporation. While decisions concerning the organisational structure are made closer to the "work floor level" and are therefore taken at the subsidiary level of the undertaking, strategic

69 Social and Economic Council, 'English translation of the Dutch Works Councils Act', p. 19.
70 Cf. L.G. Verburg, *Rood's Wet op de ondernemingsraden*, p. 322-323.
71 Social and Economic Council, 'English translation of the Dutch Works Councils Act', p. 19; the official Dutch version reads *niet in redelijkheid tot zijn besluit had kunnen komen*.
72 Articles 22(2) and 22a of the WCA.

decisions in MNCs are taken at a higher organisational level. Strategic decisions are thereby taken at the level of the respective holding company as well as at the central management level, which is thus further away from the Dutch workforce, from an organisational perspective at least.

Information rights are thereby the starting point of the section (paragraph 1.4.1) due to the fact that access to information regarding (intended) management decisions is a crucial prerequisite for subsequent consultation and codetermination rights of the works council. The timing of access to information is, in this regard, the most important aspect of the works council's work and especially in the case of MNCs.

The following paragraphs regarding consultation (1.4.2) [*adviesrecht*] and codetermination rights (1.4.2.1) [*instemmingsrechten*] as well as the right to appeal [*beroepsrecht*] (1.4.4) and the right to speak at the general meeting of shareholders [*spreekrecht*] (1.4.5) will provide an overview of the rights of the works council *after* being informed of an (intended) management decision. Examining the added value and critique of employee participation will then conclude this section (1.5).

In addition, the "enhanced right of recommendation" [*versterkt aanbevelingsrecht*] of members of the supervisory board (3.2) will be addressed in the context of the so-called structure regime, since it gives the works council the opportunity to establish links with the management of the undertaking and to possibly influence future decision-making.

1.4.1 Information rights of the Dutch works council

The notion of information rights encompasses a number of provisions on information rights that are codified in articles 31-31f of the WCA.[73] One can distinguish between the *ad hoc* communication of information and the communication of information at fixed intervals. The provisions on information rights are thereby aimed at providing access to information for the works council in situations where such access is of the utmost importance for the attainment of the consultation and codetermination rights of the works council. The access to information is, therefore, an essential prerequisite for effective employee participation through the works council as was already concluded by the Social and Economic Council of the Netherlands (hereinafter: SER) back in 1976.[74] According to the SER, the works council must be put in a position where it can acquire background information and motives for (intended) decisions in order to assess the possible consequences of the management's decision for the entire workforce. Without

73 The communication of information to the works council was already included in the first WCA of 1950 in articles 6(2) and (5) thereof; see for a detailed analysis of the history of the information rights of the works council L.G. Verburg, *Rood's Wet op de ondernemingsraden*, p. 407 et seq.

74 Social and Economic Council Advies 1976/20, Verstrekking door de ondernemer van informatie aan de ondernemingsraad, p. 9.

access to such information, the works council has a very little chance of effectively influencing any decision-making process within the organisation.

As a general rule, the entrepreneur must supply the works council with all the necessary information for the fulfilment of the council's duties.[75] Moreover, the management must provide the information in a timely manner so as to make an effective fulfilment of the works council's duties possible.[76]

The right to information pursuant to article 31 of the WCA can, furthermore, be described as an *active* right to information due to the fact that the works council may request the information that it deems necessary for the fulfilment of its tasks.[77] Thus, the council may request information and data on an *ad hoc* basis, but it must sufficiently motivate this request with regard to how far this information is necessary for the fulfilment of its duties.[78]

The works council also has a right to receive information periodically, which can be described as *passive* right to information.[79] For this periodical communication of information, a further distinction between *ex post* and *ex ante* information should be made.

Ex post information is to be provided to the works council at least twice a year in so-called consultation meetings [*algemene gang van zaken bespreking*] pursuant to article 24 of the WCA. Further to this, "general information concerning the activities and financial results of the enterprise relating to the preceding period and in particular regarding the matters mentioned in [a]rticle 25"[80] must be provided at least twice a year as per article 31a of the WCA. Of particular importance for this study is thereby the provision contained in article 31a (6) of the WCA, due to the fact that it specifically addresses undertakings that are part of a MNC, and which reads:

> *"At least twice a year, for the purposes of discussing the general operation of the enterprise, the entrepreneur shall inform the Works Council orally or in writing of his expectations with respect to the activities and the financial results of the enterprise in the coming period, in particular with regard to such matters as mentioned in Article 25, and to all investments at home and abroad."*

---

75 Article 31 of the WCA.

76 The original text holds that the information has to be provided '*tijdig*' (in good time); see article 31(1) of the WCA.

77 Cf. P.P. van Schaik, *De adviesplichtige intentieverklaring: Het adviesrecht van de ondernemingsraad bij een overname* (Celsus juridische uitgeverij, Tilburg 2010), p. 8.

78 Ktg. Rotterdam 24 November 1995, *JAR* 1996/4.

79 *Ibid.*, p. 9.

80 Social and Economic Council, 'English translation of the Dutch Works Councils Act', p. 23.

While this provision, read on its own, would prescribe access to information concerning *all* financial activities of the undertaking, in which the works council is set up, at home and abroad; the specific holding structure applied in MNCs nevertheless limits the works council's access to information of the MNC's activities within the Netherlands, although more information may be provided by the management.[81]

The specificities of the holding structure applied in MNCs is addressed in section 3 below. Therefore, the entrepreneur within the meaning of the WCA, which is not the central management of the corporation, but the management of the Dutch holding company, must only provide information with regard to the holding's (intended) investments.[82]

Furthermore, a new provision was added during the latest revision of the WCA,[83] which is laid down in articles 31(2)(d) and (e) of the WCA. This provision specifically addresses the power structures [*zeggenschapsverhoudingen*] and the linkages within a network of companies. Of particular importance is therefore that the WCA provision explicitly includes the duty to provide the works council with basic information regarding the international power structures as well as the names of key personnel and, thus, it does not limit the right to information to the undertakings within the MNC that are situated in the Netherlands. To underline the extension of the scope of this provision, article 31(3) of the WCA was added during the 2013 revision to the WCA, which explicitly mentions the applicability to international corporations.[84] According to the motion of the Dutch MP Hamer, the works councils should be put in a position where they have more clout over reorganisations, such as issues pertaining to takeovers, mergers, demergers or outsourcing, within the corporation. The SER explicitly mentioned, already in 1992, that the works council should have periodical access to such general information regarding the corporation as a whole.[85]

The question of whether this access to information regarding the structure of the corporation is used in practice by the works council and in how far it is beneficial for the position of the works council, will be addressed in the empirical part of this study.

---

81 See section 5.4 in chapter IV and section 3.1 in chapter V for further details.

82 See also the *Ford* case of 1983 in this regard; OK 10 December 1981, *NJ* 1983/24 (*Ford*); in *Philips/Glas* the Council of State [*Raad van State*] adjudicated that the works council clearly has to motivate for which of its tasks the requested information is necessary; cf. R.H. van het Kaar, 'GS Rechtspersonen, artikel 31 WOR, aant. 1', <http://deeplinking.kluwer.nl/?param=00C4AF50&cpid=WKNL-LTR-Nav2> (last accessed 30 September 2017); see also L.G. Verburg, *Het territoir van de (Nederlandse) ondernemingsraad in het internationale bedrijfsleven*, p.119 et seq.

83 *Wet van 26 juni 2013 tot aanpassing van de Wet op de ondernemingsraden in verband met wijziging van de financiering van het scholingssysteem voor leden van de ondernemingsraad en enkele andere wijzigingen van deze wet, Stb.* 2013, 296.

84 The Minister of Social Affairs Kamp has introduced the provision in 2013, following the motion of the *Tweede Kamer* [Second Chamber of the Dutch Parliament] by Member Hamer in order to improve the information rights of works councils (the so-called "motion Hamer").

85 Social and Economic Council Advies 1992/07, *Knelpunten Wet op de ondernemingsraden*, p. 55.

Moreover, information regarding the undertaking's social policy as well as the number of employees, information on staffing and employment schemes or agreements must be provided at least once a year by the entrepreneur pursuant to articles 31b and 31d of the WCA.

Furthermore, the entrepreneur must provide *ex ante* information regarding the decisions that (s)he is considering taking and which fall within the scope of the work councils' article 25 WCA consultation or the article 27 WCA codetermination rights.[86]

Finally, the entrepreneur must provide a summary (including all relevant information) of the grounds when taking an (intended) decision that requires the prior consultation of the works council as stipulated in article 25(3) of the WCA. A similar provision can be found with regard to codetermination rights in article 27(2) of the WCA, with the caveat that the expected consequences for the employees in the undertaking in question must also be submitted. Yet another provision along the same lines is article 30(3) of the WCA, which holds that in the case of the appointment of a director, information must also be provided to the works council.

1.4.1.1 The Harrewijn Act of 2006

In the context of the work's councils' information rights, it must be noted that the 'Harrewijn Act' of 2006 has extended the information rights of the Dutch works council.[87] The Act introduced a right of information for the works council with regard to the incomes of the top-management, board of management and supervisory board members, but also information rights with regard to the remuneration of all other employees of the undertaking. These information rights are now incorporated in articles 31d and 31e of the WCA. The Act must therefore be seen in the context of the previously enacted Law on the disclosure of the remuneration and the share ownership of members of the management and supervisory board as incorporated in article 2:383b et seq. of the DCC.[88] The "Executives' Pay Financed from Public Funds (Disclosure) Act" also must be mentioned in this context.[89]

The Harrewijn Act, therefore, serves as an additional source of information for the works council with regard to the general remuneration policy within a given undertaking and

86 Article 24(1) of the WCA.

87 *Wet van 14 juni 2006 tot wijziging van de Wet op de ondernemingsraden in verband met het verschaffen van informatie over de hoogte van inkomens van topkader, bestuurders en toezichthouders van ondernemingen aan de ondernemingsraad* (Wet Harrewijn) [MM, Harrewijn Act], *Stb.* 2006, 286.

88 *Wet van 18 april 2002 tot wijziging van boek 2 van het Burgerlijk Wetboek alsmede enige andere wetten in verband met de openbaarmaking van de bezoldiging en het aandelenbezit van bestuurders en commissarissen, Stb.* 2002, 225.

89 *Wet openbaarmaking uit publieke middelen gefinancierde topinkomens, Stb.* 2006, 95; the law was abolished as of 1 January 2013.

also with regard to the remuneration policy and possible differences in the payment of the individual employee-groups within the company. The explanatory memorandum [*memorie van toelichting*] also addresses the importance of the information right with regard to income differences between men and women, as well as any differences in pay with regard to minority groups in conjunction with article 28(3) of the WCA.[90] The Act thus introduces, on the one hand, access to information concerning the remuneration of the management of the undertaking, but also addresses the general remuneration policy and remuneration differences that exist within the company.[91]

The Harrewijn Act initially foresaw a general right of information for the works council, irrespective of the size and revenue as well as the company form of the undertaking, but the first proposal was rejected following the negative advice of the Social and Economic Council, which led to an amendment of the proposal by the initiators of the Act.[92] The amended Act, which was ultimately adopted, now stipulates that only undertakings employing (normally) at least 100 employees must provide information regarding the remuneration policy.[93] The Act does not apply to "*a private limited liability company in which one of the managers or supervisors is a natural person with a direct or indirect interest in the legal entity, pursuant to Article 4.6 of the Income Tax Act 2001 [Wet inkomstenbelasting 2001]*"[94] or to small and medium sized enterprises (SMEs).[95] These amendments considerably restrict the scope of the Act and it excludes half of the undertakings with a works council from the duty to provide information on their remuneration policy.[96]

With regard to the position of the works council in MNCs, the remuneration of the top-management and supervisory board is, also in light of the right to speak at the general meeting of shareholders, of particular importance. The remuneration of the top-management is certainly an integral part of the appointment or dismissal of members of the management and the prior access to such information for the works council is therefore of significant importance.

The Harrewijn Act stipulates that information on the remuneration policy must be provided for each *group* of employees. While the Act does not further stipulate what is meant by the term *group*, the term 'function groups' is used in the explanatory memorandum of the Act.[97]

90 *Kamerstukken II* 2001/02, 28163, no. 5, p. 7.
91 The first aspect on the remuneration of the management is furthermore closely connected to the works councils' right to speak at the general meeting of shareholders in listed corporations, which is further addressed in section 1.4.5.
92 Cf. second letter of amendment, *Kamerstukken II* 2001/02, 28163, no. 16, p. 2.
93 Article 31d(6) of the WCA.
94 Article 31e(a) of the WCA.
95 Article 31e(b) of the WCA.
96 Cf. M.C.T. Burgers, 'Wet Harrewijn; (hoe) werkt het in de praktijk?', 20 *ArbeidsRecht* (2008), p. 2.
97 *Kamerstukken II* 2001/02, 28163, no. 5, p. 9; the term used is '*functiegroepen*'.

While the individual remuneration of members of the board of management or the supervisory board of the undertaking might be of particular interest to the works council, such disclosure is precluded pursuant to article 31d(4) of the WCA, which stipulates that "two or more functions may be combined for the purposes of the application of [...] [the Act], so that a group of at least five persons is created".[98] It is therefore unlikely that the remuneration of only the supervisory board members is disclosed and such information is rather combined with those of the management board so that the clustered information are not retraceable. Since the entrepreneur is free in his or her choice as to which groups and functions to cluster, the goal of access to information on the remuneration policy of the top-management can be questioned in this context.[99] At the same time, it can be noted that the term *remuneration policy* is construed broadly so as to include all forms of compensation. Therefore, so-called executive compensation packages, which typically include bonuses and stock options alongside the base salary, fall under the Harrewijn Act and must be reported to the works council.

The information must be provided at least once a year to the works council,[100] save for any *significant* changes to the remuneration policy, which must be provided as soon as possible.[101] The term significant is not further defined and therefore, similar to the provisions found in article 25 of the WCA, leads to disputes in the undertaking between the works council and the management as to how far an alteration can be considered as significant.[102]

Analogous to the application and interpretation and the case law on the term *significant* with regard to article 25 of the WCA, any extraordinary measure that has a certain gravity in terms of its nature and impact on the undertaking and particularly its employees must be regarded as significant.[103] Any failure to fulfil the obligation to provide information on behalf of the management can be enforced by the works council with recourse to the general dispute mechanism located in article 36 of the WCA.

98 Article 31d(4) of the WCA; a majority of votes was not feasible to introduce information rights on individual remuneration schemes; Cf. P.F. van der Heijden, 'Harrewijn revisited', *OR Informatie* 4 (2014), p. 8.

99 Cf. M.C.T. Burgers, 'Wet Harrewijn; (hoe) werkt het in de praktijk?', 20 *ArbeidsRecht* (2008), p. 3.

100 Article 31d(1) of the WCA.

101 Article 31d(5) of the WCA.

102 See further section 1.4.2 on the matter of *significant* matters within the context of article 25 of the WCA.

103 Cf. R.H. van het Kaar, 'GS Rechtspersonen, artikel 25 WOR, aant. 4', <http://deeplinking.kluwer.nl/?param=00BFDF2F&cpid=WKNL-LTR-Navigator> (last accessed 29 September 2017); see for a 'non-significant measure' OK 29 September 2003, *ROR* 2003/33 (*Top Craft*); agreements between the management and the works council have a binding effect and have to be complied with as adjudicated in the case HR 17 March 1993, *ROR* 1993/16 (*Smit Vlootbeheer*); the covenant clause, as was introduced at by the 1998 amendment, incorporated in article 32 of the WCA.

1.4.1.2 The entrepreneur *within the meaning of the WCA*

At this point, the 'entrepreneur' within the meaning of the WCA must be briefly addressed. When examining the position of the works council within MNCs, the aspect of identifying the entrepreneur becomes central when determining the level of the corporation at which information has to be provided to the works council. Due to the fact that the so-called 'Netherlands construction' is applied in the vast majority of corporations, a holding company with the sole purpose of holding all shares of the Dutch undertakings of the corporation is placed between the international topholding and the Dutch undertakings. Instead of the topholding with the central management of the corporation – which may also be located outside the Netherlands and often a foreign entity – the Dutch subholding holds the shares of the Dutch undertakings, and the central works council is set up at the level of the Dutch subholding instead of at the top-holding level.[104] The definition contained in article 1(1)(d) of the WCA, which defines the term 'entrepreneur', then has to be seen in the light of this holding structure. Article 1(1)(d) of the WCA defines an entrepreneur as "[a]ny natural person or legal person carrying on an enterprise".[105] Against the background of the holding structure applied in MNCs, the legal person carrying on the Dutch enterprises is no longer the central management of the top holding, but the management of the Dutch subholding that holds all the shares in the Dutch undertakings.

When reading article 1(1)(d) of the WCA in conjunction with articles 2-4 and 33 of the WCA, which specify the establishment of a works council, it is the Dutch holding that is the entrepreneur within the meaning of the WCA that must establish the works council. With regard to the information rights of the works council, one should conclude that these rights are, due to the holding structure applied in MNCs, significantly limited to the Dutch undertakings of the corporation with the exception of the information on power structures that was addressed above.

1.4.2 Consultation rights of the Dutch works council

From the outset of article 25 of the WCA, the entrepreneur shall, before taking a decision that affects the undertaking as a whole, give the works council the opportunity to render its advice on the matter, if the decision falls under one of the categories that are stipulated in article 25(1) of the WCA.[106]

104 See section 3 for a detailed examination of the holding structure applied in MNCs.

105 Social and Economic Council, 'English translation of the Dutch Works Councils Act', p. 5.

106 Such provision regarding consultation rights of the works council was already included in the first version of the WCA of 1950 and was originally laid down in article 6(2)(f) of the WCA; see P.F. van der Heijden, *Rood's Wet op de Ondernemingsraden*, p. 273 et seq. for a detailed analysis of the history of the consultation rights of the works council.

The article was introduced at the 1971 revision,[107] while article 25(1)(b) was added in the important 1979 amendment[108] and subparagraph (j) in 1998.[109] The entrepreneur must ask for the council's advice as soon as the internal decision-making process of the management of the undertaking has advanced far enough to be able to present the expected consequences of the (intended) decision.[110] This obligation to provide a statement of reasons falls on the entrepreneur of the undertaking for which the works council is established as was held by the Enterprise Chamber in the *OR Security Services Holding B.V.* (SSH) case in 2005.[111]

Important to note is, first, that an *opportunity must be given* to the works council to render its advice.[112] This implies that the works council does not have to render its advice *per se*, but can do so after a consultation meeting on whether or not the works council is going to render advice on a particular matter.[113]

A second important aspect is the fact that the entrepreneur must give the works council the opportunity to render its advice, but it is not bound by the works council's advice. Rather, the entrepreneur can implement its (intended) decision one month after having notified the works council of doing so, while providing reasons in writing in cases when the entrepreneur does not follow (or only partially follows) the advice of the works council.[114]

Of particular importance for this study and therefore of interest with regard to works councils in international corporations are the following provisions contained in article 25(1) of the WCA:[115]

i. Transfer of control of the enterprise or any part thereof;
ii. The establishment, take-over or relinquishment of control of another enterprise, or entering into, making a major modification to or severing a continuing collaboration with another enterprise, including the entering into, effecting of major changes to or severing of an important financial holding on account of or for the benefit of such an enterprise;

107 *Wet op de ondernemingsraden 1971*, *Stb.* 1971, 54.
108 *Wet op de ondernemingsraden 1979*, *Stb.* 1979, 448,
109 *Wet op de ondernemingsraden* 1998, *Stb.* 1998, 107.
110 R.H. van het Kaar, 'GS Rechtspersonen, artikel 25 WOR, aant. 14', <http://deeplinking.kluwer.nl/?param=00BFDF3A&cpid=WKNL-LTR-Navigator> (last accessed 29 September 2017).
111 OK 20 October 2005, *ARO* 2005/191 (*OR Security Services Holding B.V.*); the obligation to provide a statement of reasons was also addressed in the *VLM Nederland* case; OK 14 October 2010, *RO* 2011/11 (*VLM Nederland*); here the Enterprise Chamber regarded the (intended) decision to be sufficiently motivated by the entrepreneur.
112 Article 25(1) of the WCA, first sentence.
113 Article 25(4) of the WCA.
114 Article 25(5) of the WCA with regard to the duty to give reasons and article 25(6) of the WCA with regard to the one month standstill period.
115 Social and Economic Council, 'English translation of the Dutch Works Councils Act', p. 18.

iii. Termination of operations of the enterprise or a significant part thereof;
iv. Any significant reduction, expansion or other change in the enterprise's activities;
v. Major changes to the organisation or to the distribution of powers within the enterprise;
vi. Making major investments on behalf of the enterprise;
vii. Taking out major loans for the enterprise and
viii. Granting substantial credit to or giving security for substantial debts of another entrepreneur, unless this is normal practice and part of the activities of the enterprise;

These areas will be considered in further detail in the remainder of this section, while a detailed analysis of all that fall within the scope of article 25 WCA can be found in the existing literature.[116]

The provisions introduced above are of particular importance for this study insofar as the holding structure applied in MNCs is creating an inherent tension with regard to the position of the works council, which becomes visible when examining these subjects. The tension arises in situations where a strategic decision is taken at the top holding-level,[117] while the implementation of such decision directly affects the Dutch undertakings that are situated at the sub-holding level. The emerging tension between decision-making at the top-holding level and employee participation rights at sub-holding level in the Netherlands becomes visible especially with regard to the consultation rights pursuant to article 25 of the WCA.[118]

1.4.2.1 Article 25(1)(a) WCA

Within a corporate setting, the following situation is problematic with regard to the transfer of ownership pursuant to article 25(1)(a) of the WCA: the top-holding sells all or part of its shares in its subsidiary, which was previously wholly-owned by the top-holding. Due to the holding structure applied in the corporation, the works council is established at sub-holding level, while the decision to transfer all or part of the control over the subsidiary is taken at the top-holding level.

The debate therefore concerns the issue of whether the entrepreneur within the meaning of the WCA (thus the management of the Dutch holding) has to give the works council the opportunity to render its advice in case the top-holding transfers part of

116 See *inter alia* R.H. van het Kaar, 'GS Rechtspersonen, commentaar op artikel 25 WOR', <http://deeplinking.kluwer.nl/?param=00BFDF2A&cpid=WKNL-LTR-Navigator> (last accessed 29 September 2017); H.J.M.N. Honée, *Concernrecht en medezeggenschapsregelingen* (Kluwer, Deventer 1981), p. 141 et seq.
117 Cf. M. Holtzer, *De invloed van werknemers op de strategie van de vennootschap* (Kluwer, Deventer 2014).
118 See also the Social and Economic Council members commentary by P.F. van der Heijden et al., 'Medezeggenschap: Ontwikkelingen in de 21e eeuw', p. 31-32.

its shareholdings in the subsidiary and thus a change in control consequently occurs.[119] According to Honée, a consultation of the works council has to occur whenever a change of control over the undertaking takes place.[120]

Furthermore, it is difficult to determine at which point in the merger (or takeover, etc.) negotiations that the consultation of the works council has to take place, because the advice "*shall be requested at a time when it can still significantly affect the decision to be taken*"[121] while the (intended) decision must be concrete enough before the works council is consulted.

The issue of declarations of intent is central to the question of when a (intended) decision is concrete enough to consult the works council with regard to decisions falling under subparagraph (a).[122]

In this context, one should mention the *NS Reizigers* case, in which the Enterprise Section of the Amsterdam Court of Appeal ruled that under certain circumstances such a declaration of intent could be sufficiently concrete to make the consultation of the works council necessary.[123]

NS Reizigers (hereinafter: NSR) and NZH Vervoermaatschappij [MM, carrier company] (hereinafter: NZH) signed, on 10 March 1997, a declaration of intent to establish a partnership regarding a railway network in the Northwest of the Netherlands (the 'NoordWest Net'). The declaration *inter alia* included a provision stating that both parties would establish a business plan prior to October 1997. In addition to signing the declaration of intent, both parties issued a press release on March 10 to make the future cooperation public and the director of NZH gave an interview on March 11, in which he further explained the cooperation. The group works council of NSR, however, was not consulted on the matter.

The partnership was finally established in 1998 without seeking the prior consultation of the GWC, following which the GWC lodged an appeal with the Enterprise Section claiming that prior consultation to the declaration of intent, which was signed on March 10 1997, was necessary. The Enterprise Chamber ruled that NSR could not in all fairness

119 Cf. R.H. van het Kaar, 'GS Rechtspersonen, artikel 25 WOR, aant. 3A', <http://deeplinking.kluwer.nl/?param=00BFDF2C&cpid=WKNL-LTR-Navigator> (last accessed 29 September 2017).

120 H.J.M.N. Honée, *Concernrecht en medezeggenschapsregelingen*, p. 150 et seq.

121 Social and Economic Council, 'English translation of the Dutch Works Councils Act', p. 19.

122 P.P. van Schaik, *De adviesplichtige intentieverklaring: Het adviesrecht van de ondernemingsraad bij een overname* (Celsus juridische uitgeverij, Tilburg 2010), p. 28 and p. 40 et seq.; Schaik argues that once certain elements are included in a declaration of intent, such a declaration can become sufficiently concrete in light of article 25(1)(a) of the WCA in order to trigger the duty to consult the works council.

123 OK 10 July 1997, *JAR* 1997/164 (*NS Reizigers*).

have arrived at the said decision. This judgment was later confirmed on appeal before the Dutch Supreme Court [*Hoge Raad*, HR].[124]

While the Enterprise Chamber held that a declaration of intent constitutes merely an envisaged policy, which does not trigger the duty to consult the works council, the Chamber also held that the circumstances surrounding the signing of the declaration had to be taken into consideration.[125]

The fact that a press release was issued on March 10 and against the background of previous agreements entered into by NSR by means of a declaration of intent, the Court held that, in light of such circumstances, it was out of the question that the (intended) decision was concrete enough to make the prior consultation of the works council necessary.

For the purposes of this study, it can therefore be concluded that the content as well as the circumstances leading up to the signing of a declaration of intent can be crucial for the determination of the duty to consult the works council. It must be further noted that under certain circumstances a business plan can also constitute an (intended) decision within the meaning of the WCA, as was adjudicated upon by the Enterprise Chamber.[126]

1.4.2.2 Article 25(1)(b) WCA

A second area for which the consultation of the works council is mandatory is concerned with changes in the ownership of the undertaking (for which the works council is established) over *another* undertaking or a change in collaboration with another undertaking. By way of comparison to the situation under subparagraph (a), article 25(1)(b) of the WCA is triggered in situations whereby an undertaking, other than the one for which the works council is established is concerned and such situation can be regarded as "major modification" or a "major change".[127]

This subparagraph concerns the take-over of other companies as well as the establishment or relinquishment of control over another undertaking and also the change in the financial holdings of another undertaking.[128] Furthermore, a consultation of the works council is mandatory in case of a major cooperation (i.e., joint venture) with another undertaking.[129]

---

124 HR 7 October 1998, *NJ* 1999/778.

125 Cf. P.P. van Schaik, *De adviesplichtige intentieverklaring: Het adviesrecht van de ondernemingsraad bij een overname*, p. 28.

126 OK 30 May 2003, *ARO* 2012/94 and *JAR* 2012/181 (*Stichting Het Brabants Orkest*).

127 Social and Economic Council, 'English translation of the Dutch Works Councils Act', p. 18.

128 *Ibid.*

129 Cf. L.G. Verburg, *Rood's Wet op de Ondernemingsraden*, p. 295.

Strikingly, neither a *major modification* nor a *major change* is further defined within the WCA. The Enterprise Chamber ruled in this regard that the *major*-criterion is dependent on the nature of the operations in which the undertakings are involved and the nature of their cooperation and is, therefore, to be assessed on a case-by-case basis.[130]

This provision is important in the light of the corporate structures insofar as major changes in control over another undertaking could have considerable effects on the position of the Dutch undertaking, for which the works council is established. Yet, the consultation rights of the works council are confined to the Dutch undertakings of the corporation following the principle of territoriality. Therefore, decisions are not subject to the consultation of the Dutch works council, if these are taken outside the Netherlands without the involvement of the Dutch subsidiaries of the corporation. An exception is a situation in which it is 'reasonably foreseeable' that the employment situation in the Netherlands would be affected by such a decision.[131] The minister further elaborated that the 'reasonably foreseeable' criterion is fulfilled once the Dutch undertaking engages in cooperation of considerable scale with a foreign undertaking that is engaged in economic activities in the same or almost the same market or belongs to the same sector.[132] This criterion can certainly be regarded as fulfilled in cases of undertakings belonging to the same division of a MNC.

Whether the subjects pursuant to article 25(1)(b) of the WCA are submitted to the Dutch works council for consultation, will be considered in the quantitative analysis in chapter IV of this study.[133]

1.4.2.3 Article 25(1)(c) and (d) WCA

Within the meaning of article 25(1)(c) of the WCA, the Dutch works council must be consulted in cases concerning the termination of operations of the enterprise or a significant part thereof.[134] Reorganisations occur relatively often within international corporations and subsidiary activities are often subject to outsourcing or external contracting. While such matters are indisputably to be submitted to the works council for consultation, the timing of the consultation is problematic from the perspective of the works council. The consultation rights of the works council exist vis-à-vis the management of the undertaking for which the council is established, as it is the case with all consultation rights of the works council pursuant to article 25 of the WCA. If, however, the reorganisation is planned by the central management at top-holding level, no consultation right

130 HR 11 July 1984, *NJ* 1985/212 (*Howson Algraphy*).

131 L.G. Verburg, *Rood's Wet op de Ondernemingsraden*, p. 305-306; the explanatory note by the minister reads '*redelijk te verwachten*'.

132 *Ibid.*, p. 306.

133 See section 5.2 in chapter IV.

134 Social and Economic Council, 'English translation of the Dutch Works Councils Act', p. 18.

of the works council arises up until the moment at which the subsidiary undertaking becomes involved in the decision-making process. This involvement only occurs at a very late stage in the decision-making process, namely the implementing phase, once the central management has instructed the management of the subsidiary by means of their implementing decision.

The Court of Justice of the European Union (hereinafter: CJEU) had to rule on such a reorganisation decision in the *Akavan* case.[135] Due to the fact that reorganisations often go hand in hand with collective redundancies, Council Directive 98/59/EC is applicable if the reorganisation includes measures for the termination of more than 20 employee contracts.[136] It can be concluded on this matter that in order to safeguard the effective application of Council Directive 98/59/EC "the consultation procedure must be started by the employer once a strategic or commercial decision compelling him to contemplate or to plan for collective redundancies has been taken".[137] Therefore, the consultation must take place prior to the implementation of the decision of the central management by the subsidiary in case of imminent collective redundancies. The timing of the consultation will also be the subject of the empirical part of this study, since the effectiveness of employee participation and thus the position of the works council is highly dependent on the timing of the council's participation in the decision-making process.

Significant reductions, expansions or other changes in the activities of the undertaking are also subject to the prior consultation of the Dutch works council pursuant to article 25(1)(d) of the WCA.[138] While such prior consultation can be necessary for positive developments in the undertaking's activities (i.e., expansions), the most controversial are (intended) decisions regarding significant reductions in the activities of the undertaking. It is particularly questionable, therefore, as to what constitutes a *significant* reduction.[139] A difference in interpretation between the central management and the subsidiary management can therefore become a source of conflict, such as was the case in the *Shell Research* case.[140]

In the *Shell Research* case, a decision with regard to the annual budget for 1987 was taken in August 1986 by the holding company of the Shell Group, namely the Shell Internationale Research Maatschappij BV (hereinafter: SIRM). SIRM was, at the same time, the sole owner of all of the shares in Shell Nederland BV, which in turn held all

135 Case C-44/08 *Akavan Erityisalojen Keskusliitto AEK ry e.a. v. Fujitsu Siemens Computers Oy*, EU:C:2009:533; see also the more recent confirmation in Case C-429/16 *Ms Ciupa and Others v. Łódź Hospital*, EU:C:2017:711, para. 32-38.

136 Article 1(a) of Council Directive 98/59/EC of 20 July 1998 on the approximation of the laws of the Member States relating to collective redundancies [1998], OJ L 225/16.

137 Case C-44/08 *Akavan*, para. 48.

138 Social and Economic Council, 'English translation of the Dutch Works Councils Act', p. 18.

139 L.G. Verburg, *Rood's Wet op de Ondernemingsraden*, p. 297.

140 OK 2 April 1987, *NJ* 1988/382 (*Shell Research*).

of the shares in Shell Research BV (hereinafter: SR). Two members of SR's management took part in the SIRM meeting that led to the establishment of the 1987 annual budget. A significant decrease in the research budget for SR by at least 20% with a desired reduction target of 25% was then decided in the said meeting. Since no prior consultation of the works council of SR took place with regard to the significant decrease of the research budget, the works council subsequently appealed this before the Enterprise Chamber.

While the decision was taken by SIRM and thus on a level outside the influence of article 25(1)(d) of the WCA, which would have barred SR's works council consultation right, the Enterprise Chamber considered in its decision that both SIRM and SR (as well as Shell Nederland BV as an intermediary) were part of the Shell Group. Due to the fact that the two members of SR's management, whom were also members of the SIRM management, were present during the SIRM meeting and had a significant impact on the decision that was taken, the decision had to be attributed to SR's management. By attributing the decision to SR's management, the Enterprise Chamber therefore set aside the corporate structure of the Shell Group and held that the decision was subject to the mandatory consultation of the works council, especially given the fact that members of the SR management were present during the meeting and had a decisive influence over the decision-making process.

The attributability[141] of decisions in court proceedings in order to set aside the corporate structures that prevent the invocation of the works councils' participation rights pursuant to the WCA will be discussed in greater detail in section 4 below.

1.4.2.4 Article 25(1)(e) WCA

Article 25(1) subparagraph (e) WCA concerns "major changes to the organisation or to the distribution of powers within the enterprise".[142]

Again, no definition of *major* changes exists in the legal provision. The Minister of Social Affairs, when asked in Parliament during the legislative process, stated that "decisions that are not part of the daily decision-making process of the undertaking and are hence extraordinary" are to be regarded as major changes.[143]

141 The Dutch courts have developed the concepts of *toerekening* [attribution] and *medeondernemerschap* [co-entrepreneurship] in this regard; see section 4 for an examination of these concepts.

142 Social and Economic Council, 'English translation of the Dutch Works Councils Act', p. 18.

143 Cf. L.G. Verburg, *Rood's Wet op de Ondernemingsraden*, p. 287-288.

A matter falls within the scope of subparagraph (e) once a change in the management structure is decided, such as an alternation of the number of persons that comprise the management board or the supervisory board.[144]

It must be reiterated that within international corporations, the entrepreneur within the meaning of the WCA is the Dutch management. Therefore, changes in the organisational structure outside the Netherlands that are made by the international top-holding do not fall within the scope of article 25(1)(e) of the WCA and are accordingly not subject to prior works council consultation.

1.4.2.5 Article 25(1)(h) and (i) WCA

The provisions under subparagraph (h) and (i) were the result of a lengthy discussion in the Dutch Parliament, due to the fact that no separate provision with regard to investments was included in the WCA prior to the 1979 revision.[145]

While subparagraph (h) concerns major investments on behalf of the undertaking, subparagraph (i) stipulates that the taking out of major loans on behalf of the undertaking are also subject to the prior consultation of the works council.

What is important to note regarding subparagraph (h) in relation to major investments is that by way of contrast to the provisions discussed above, the principle of territoriality is *not* applicable to decisions that fall within the scope of this provision. Therefore, investments by the Dutch subsidiary made abroad are subject to the prior consultation of the works council. If, however, the corporation makes the investments via a foreign (read not Dutch) subsidiary, the matter falls within the scope of article 25(1)(b) of the WCA, for which the "overseas clause" [*buitenlandclausule*] is applicable again, which precludes the right to prior consultation for the works council (the overseas clause implies that all decisions that are made outside the Netherlands fall outside the scope of the WCA due to the *lex loci* which confines the applicability of the WCA to Dutch territories pursuant to the principle of territoriality).[146]

A similar rationale is applied in relation to major loans pursuant to subparagraph (i). The works council retains a right to consultation as long as the loan is taken by the Dutch subsidiary, while the right to consultation is precluded as soon as the loan is taken by a foreign subsidiary instead, which brings the matter within the scope of article 25(1)(b) of the WCA.[147]

144 See case OK 30 December 2003, *JOR* 2004/102 and *JAR* 2004/45 (*Intergas*).
145 Cf. L.G. Verburg, *Rood's Wet op de Ondernemingsraden*, p. 301.
146 *Ibid.*
147 *Ibid.*

1.4.2.6 *Article 25(1)(j) WCA*

Finally, the provision under subparagraph (j) was included in article 25 of the WCA in the 1998 revision of the WCA; the so-called *Knelpuntenwet* addresses bottlenecks within the meaning of the WCA. While sub-paragraph (i) concerns the taking out of loans, the provision under (j) is concerned with the *granting* of substantial credit or giving securities. The credit must be granted, therefore, to another entrepreneur and thus does not give rise to the works councils' consultation rights with regard to securities for the own undertaking.[148]

The final sentence of sub-paragraph (j), "unless this is normal practice and part of the activities of the enterprise",[149] is a possible source of conflict as to the interpretation of what is regarded as *normal practice*, since the central management of the corporation can burden the undertaking with loans or securities for other subsidiaries. When such securities are declared to be normal practice, the consultation rights of the works council are not applicable, while the effects on the workforce in the Dutch undertaking are potentially significant.

1.4.3 Consultation right on the appointment or dismissal of the management

The works council also has consultation rights over important (intended) management decisions falling within the scope of article 25 of the WCA, as was discussed in the previous section.

In the case of the appointment or dismissal of a director of the undertaking, the works council also has a consultation right that is laid down in article 30 of the WCA.[150] The rationale behind this provision is that the appointment or dismissal of the directors of the undertaking is of significant importance for the employees of the undertaking and they should therefore have a right to be consulted on this issue. The right of consultation on any appointment or dismissal of the director was introduced following the 1979 recast of the WCA.[151]

With particular regard to MNCs, it is important to note that the director within the meaning of the WCA is not necessarily the director within the meaning of articles 2:132/242 – 2:134/244 of the DCC. Rather, the works council enjoys a consultation right on the appointment or dismissal of "*an individual who, alone or jointly with others, exercises the highest direct authority in managing work within an enterprise*". Thus, when the management and the 'exercise of the highest direct authority in managing work within

148 *Ibid.*, p. 302.
149 Social and Economic Council, 'English translation of the Dutch Works Councils Act', p. 18.
150 Any director within the meaning of article 1(1)(e) of the WCA.
151 *Wet van 5 September 1979, Stb.* 448.

an enterprise' is divided amongst a number of statutory directors (this may include next to the Chief Executive Officer (CEO) also the Chief Financial Officer (CFO) and Chief Information Officer (CIO)), any appointment or dismissal of one of the statutory directors can fall within the scope of article 30 of the WCA in conjunction with article 1(1)(e) of the WCA. Also an interim manager can fall under this provision in conjunction with article 1(1)(e) of the WCA.[152] Nevertheless, uncertainties as to whether or not a person exercises the highest direct authority within an undertaking can arise. By means of a covenant, the consultation right of the works council can be further extended to include persons other than those falling within the scope of article 1(1)(e) of the WCA.[153]

The works council must be informed of any such appointment or dismissal in a timely manner in order to render its advice *"at a time when it can still significantly affect the decision to be taken"*.[154] Due to the unique twofold contractual relationship of the director under Dutch law, namely the one under labour law concerning the employment contract and the other under company law regarding the appointment as statutory director of the undertaking, the consultation right of the works council must be safeguarded under the following circumstances.

The works council's advice must be obtained before the general meeting of shareholders (which is often the parent company in MNCs) may appoint or dismiss a director. Although the parent company may be situated outside of the Netherlands and would therefore fall outside the scope of Dutch law due to the principle of territoriality, the Dutch works council must nevertheless be consulted due to the fact that the appointment concerns the Dutch subsidiary and the director thereof, and especially given the fact that the parent company is acting in the capacity of (majority) shareholders of the *Dutch* undertaking, which falls under the scope of the WCA.[155]

A resignation of the director, however, does not fall within the scope of article 30 of the WCA, although it is discussed in the literature whether or not an (involuntary) resignation on the initiative of the undertaking is subject to the prior consultation of the works council.[156]

In a number of cases, directors that were dismissed argued that the absence of the prior consultation of the works council prior to the dismissal would render the dismissal unlawful. The courts, however, held that only the works councils could invoke the rights stipulated in the WCA.[157]

152 See also L.G. Verburg, *Rood's Wet op de ondernemingsraden*, p. 397.

153 See also Bedrijfscommissie voor de Overheid 20 June 1997, *JAR* 1997/155 and *ROR* 1997/28.

154 Article 30(2) of the WCA.

155 Cf. R.H. van het Kaar, 'Artikel 30 WOR', in *Ondernemingsraad* (Kluwer, Deventer 2011).

156 R.H. van het Kaar, 'Artikel 30 WOR', in *Ondernemingsraad* (Kluwer, Deventer 2011).

157 Amsterdam Court of Appeal 20 May 1999, *JAR* 1999/146; and President of the District Court of Arnhem 4 May 1995, *KG* 1995/247.

Once the works council has been consulted on the appointment or dismissal of the director, the undertaking "*shall inform the Works Council of the reasons for his decision and in the event of an appointment shall also provide information on the basis of which the Works Council can form an opinion of the individual in question in relation to his or her future position in the enterprise*".[158]

By way of contrast to the consultation procedure laid down in article 25 of the WCA, the works council cannot appeal against a decision to appoint or dismiss the director following a procedure such as the one under article 26 of the WCA. The entrepreneur does not have to adhere to a standstill period, as stipulated by article 25 of the WCA, in cases where the advice of the works council is not followed. Only in cases where the consultation right of the works council is infringed, can the works council then demand compliance with article 30 of the WCA pursuant to article 36(2) of the WCA and request the District Court to order the entrepreneur to comply with the said provision.

1.4.4 Right to appeal pursuant to article 26 WCA

After having introduced the consultation rights of the works council in the previous sections, the right to appeal pursuant to article 26 of the WCA will be examined in the following section.

Such a right of appeal arises in cases where a decision of the management as per article 25(5) WCA "*does not accord with the advice of the Works Council or if facts or circumstances have become known which, if they had been known to the Works Council at the time of rendering its advice, could have been grounds for not rendering the advice as rendered.*"[159]

Thus, once the works council renders its negative advice on an (intended) decision of the management and the management nevertheless carries out the decision, the works council may lodge an appeal before the Enterprise Chamber. The works council can also lodge an appeal in cases where crucial information was not available at the time of the advice being rendered and which could have altered the advice of the works council. However, an appeal can only be successful if "*the entrepreneur, in weighing the interests involved, could not in all fairness have arrived at the said decision*".[160]

Furthermore, an appeal by the works council against a decision must be lodged within one month of the council being informed of such decision (article 26(2) of the WCA) and the entrepreneur must be informed of any appeal lodged by the works council (article 26(3) of the WCA).

158 Article 30(3) of the WCA.

159 Social and Economic Council, 'English translation of the Dutch Works Councils Act', p. 19.

160 *Ibid.*; article 26(4) of the WCA.

In the very first appeal case, another important question arose with regard to situations in which the management did *not* consult the works council prior to a decision being taken. Specifically, the question arose as to whether the Enterprise Chamber was competent to hear cases where no prior consultation of the works council took place and the works council brought an appeal pursuant to article 26 of the WCA rather than article 36 of the WCA. While the Enterprise Chamber is competent to rule in cases concerning article 26 of the WCA and must adjudicate such cases "with the utmost urgency" (article 26(5) of the WCA) and can even take provisional measures after a petition has been lodged (article 26(8) of the WCA), cases concerning article 36 of the WCA must be lodged before the judge of the sub-district sector.

In this first appeal case lodged before the Enterprise Chamber, the *Linge Ziekenhuis* case,[161] two hospitals intended to merge and in the process sent a letter to the competent State Secretary at the Ministry of Health and Environmental Protection, which stipulated the consequences of the merger – namely that the Linge hospital was to be closed within two years and the activities were to be relocated to the location of the other hospital. No prior consultation with the works council of the Linge hospital took place prior to the sending of the letter to the Secretary of State.

The question for the Enterprise Chamber then related to whether it was competent to hear such cases where no prior consultation of the works council in cases falling within the scope of article 25 of the WCA (in the case at hand, this was article 25(1)(c) of the WCA) had taken place. In what is known as the *Linge Ziekenhuis-doctrine*, the Enterprise Chamber ruled that it was indeed competent and thus allowed for a majority of all appeals to be made before the Enterprise Chamber. The court then held that in situations where the procedural aspects of the consultation procedure are not upheld and thus the consultation rights of the works council are being undermined, then these are *per se* invalid and must be annulled in accordance with the *Linge Ziekenhuis*-doctrine.

By doing so, the works councils also have access to the highest instance of appeal, the Dutch Supreme Court [*Hoge Raad*] and this therefore allows for a more effective and practical application of the right to appeal for works councils.

After a petition is lodged, the Enterprise Chamber firstly checks whether the procedural requirements have been fulfilled by the parties, in particular by the management with regard to the consultation procedure, and is otherwise annulling the (intended) decision in its entirety.[162]

161 OK 1 May 1980, *NJ* 1981/272 (*Linge Ziekenhuis*).

162 L.G. Verburg, *Het territoir van de (Nederlandse) ondernemingsraad in het internationale bedrijfsleven*, p. 70.

If the consultation procedure was carried out in accordance with the procedural requirements, the Enterprise Chamber applies a marginal test to the final decision made by the management. By doing so, the Enterprise Chamber takes into consideration two aspects of the management's duty to explain [*motiveringsplicht*]. On the one hand, the management must give reasons for the (intended) decision as such and what the consequences of such a decision for the undertaking and the workforce would be. On the other hand, the management must also state reasons in cases where the (negative) advice of the works council is not followed by the management. One can, therefore, speak of a dual duty for the management to state reasons in order to comply with its obligations pursuant to the WCA.[163]

1.4.5 The right to speak at the general meeting of shareholders

The Dutch works council received extended information rights regarding the remuneration policy within the undertaking pursuant to the Harrewijn Act of 2006 as was examined in section 1.4.1.1 above. These information rights are closely linked and are a prerequisite for the speaking rights of the works council at the general meeting of shareholders on a number of important issues as was introduced shortly thereafter in 2010 by virtue of the Act of 30 June 2010.[164]

Prior to the introduction of the right to speak in 2010, works councils of large corporations could gain a right to speak at the general meeting by buying shares in the undertaking as was exemplified by the central works council of Stork in 2006.[165]

The Act does not refer to a right to speak as such, but rather introduces the rights *(i)* to be informed of any such general meeting in a timely manner in order to prepare its standpoint [*kennisnemingsrecht*], *(ii)* to subsequently determine the works council's point of view [*standpuntbepalingsrecht*] and *(iii)* having the right to elucidate its standpoint at the general meeting of shareholders [*toelichtingsrecht*]. These rights are, in the literature, altogether referred to as the works councils' right to speak.[166] This right to speak,

163 *Ibid.*

164 *Wet van 30 juni 2010 tot wijziging van Boek 2 van het Burgerlijk Wetboek in verband met de invoering van een recht voor de ondernemingsraad van naamloze vennootschappen om een standpunt kenbaar te maken ten aanzien van belangrijke bestuursbesluiten en besluiten tot benoeming, schorsing en ontslag van bestuurders en commissarissen alsmede ten aanzien van het bezoldigingsbeleid*, *Stb.* 2010, 250.

165 Cf. P. van Beurden, H. van Ees and R. Goodijk, 'Gebruik, niet-gebruik of onderbenutting? – Onderzoek naar de mogelijke onderbenutting van bevoegdheden en mogelijkheden door de (Centrale) Ondernemingsraad in grote Nederlandse ondernemingen', p. 25.

166 Cf. R.G.J. Nowak, 'Het wetsvoorstel spreekrecht OR bij belangrijke ava-besluiten', *Ondernemingsrecht* 59 (2009); I. Zaal, 'Spreekrecht voor de ondernemingsraad', *Tijdschrift Recht en Arbeid* 17 (2009); P.J. Dortmond, M.J. Kroeze and R.G.J. Nowak, 'De aangenomen amendementen bij de wetsvoorstellen bestuur en toezicht, flexibilisering bv-recht, spreekrecht OR, uitvoeringswet aandeelhoudersrichtlijn en invoeringswet titel 7.13 BW', *Ondernemingsrecht* 9 (2010); P.J. Dortmond, 'Toegang tot de algemene vergadering en besluiten buiten vergadering', *Ondernemingsrecht* 45 (2010); M. Holtzer,

however, is not a general right but is rather limited in its scope and applies only with respect to certain important issues, which will be addressed in the following section. By means of this right to speak, the shareholders should be put in a position whereby all of the opinions of the various stakeholders within the undertaking are taken into consideration before taking a decision and should, therefore, include the standpoint of the works council alongside the position of the board of management and the supervisory board.

From the outset, the Act confers a right to speak on the works council in cases concerning major (intended) management decisions[167] and on the subject of an appointment, suspension or dismissal of a director pursuant to article 2:134a of the DCC and article 2:144a of the DCC for supervisory directors. Furthermore, the works council has obtained this right to speak on the remuneration policy of the undertaking by virtue of article 2:135(2) of the DCC and with regard to the nomination of the supervisory board under the structure regime by virtue of article 2:158(4) of the DCC.

Measures falling under the *ratione materiae* of the Act must be submitted to the works council in a timely manner before the general meeting where such a measure will be addressed. The notion of *timely* was further concretised in the explanatory memorandum to entail a period of 30 days.[168] In conjunction with the so-called shareholder rights directive,[169] the works council is informed of any such measures 45 days prior to the general meeting, due to the fact that the shareholders are to be informed of the convocation at least 15 days before the general meeting.[170]

The Act furthermore only applies to public limited liability companies [*naamloze vennootschap*] and therefore not to private limited liability companies [*besloten vennootschap*]. The preceding advice of the Social and Economic Council even recommended a further limitation of the scope by granting the speaking right only to works councils located in public limited liability companies that are listed on the stock exchange [*beursvennootschappen*].[171] This advice was, however, not followed.

Furthermore, the Act includes the right of the works council to speak at the general meeting with regard to the remuneration policy within the undertaking.

'Het spreekrecht van de ondernemingsraad van de naamloze vennootschap bij belangrijke besluiten', *Ondernemingsrecht* 114 (2010); C.W.P. Ommeren and D.J.W.M. Kemperink, 'Het spreekrecht van de ondernemingsraad', *ArbeidsRecht* 5 (2011).

167 Article 2:107a(3) of the DCC.

168 *Kamerstukken II* 2008/09, 31877, nr. 3, p. 10.

169 Directive 2007/36/EC of the European Parliament and of the Council of 11 July 2007 on the exercise of certain rights of shareholders in listed companies [2007], OJ L 184/17.

170 Article 2:115(1) of the DCC; the convocation deadline is 42 days (pursuant to article 2:115(2) of the DCC) for publicly traded corporations within the meaning of article 1(1) of the Financial Markets Supervision Act (*Wet op het financieel toezicht*).

171 Cf. R.G.J. Nowak, 'Het wetsvoorstel spreekrecht OR bij belangrijke ava-besluiten' *Ondernemingsrecht* 59 (2009), p. 1; see also the SER Advies 2008/01, *Evenwichtig ondernemingsbestuur*.

Turning to the procedural requirements, it must be noted that the works councils' standpoint is presented to the general meeting of shareholders simultaneously with the request for an approval of an intended decision to the general meeting.[172] Furthermore, (intended) decision falling under the scope of the aforementioned provisions may not be approved by the general meeting of shareholders before the works council is put in a position to make use of its right to speak.[173]

Moreover, the right of the works council may be exercised in situations whereby the decision of the shareholders is taken outside the general meeting of shareholders. Such a situation is possible in cases where only one shareholder (for instance the top-holding) lays down in the statutes that another forum is chosen.[174] According to Dortmond, and in light of the explanatory memorandum of the Act, the works council must then still be allowed to explain its point of view to the (sole) shareholder before the decision is taken.[175]

The absence of the works councils' point of view, however, does not affect the decision-making over the request for an approval.[176] Therefore, the Act does not limit the exclusive power of the general meeting to take decisions that fall within its competence by virtue of the undertaking's statutes.[177]

A discussion in the literature concerns the issue of whether a frustration of the works councils' right on the contrary leads to the annulment of a decision on the grounds of reasonableness and fairness pursuant to article 2:8 of the DCC in conjunction with either article 2:14 or article 2:15 of the DCC. The majority of authors, *inter alia* Novak and in a similar vein Holtzer, argue that an annulment of a decision without the prior observance of the works councils' right to speak is *not* possible on the grounds of reasonableness and fairness.[178] Due to the fact that the provisions explicitly exclude the possibility of an annulment of a decision of the general meeting and given the fact that this argumentation is also reflected in the reply to the statement of objections [*memorie van antwoord*],[179] one can conclude that the non-compliance with the works councils' right to speak has no consequences insofar as an annulment is not possible. With the absence of

172 See article 2:107a(3) of the DCC, article 2:134a(1) of the DCC, article 2:135(2) of the DCC, article 2:144a(1)of the DCC and article 2:158(4) of the DCC.

173 *Ibid.*

174 Article 2:128 of the DCC.

175 P.J. Dortmond, 'Toegang tot de algemene vergadering en besluiten buiten vergadering', *Ondernemingsrecht* 45 (2010), p. 5.

176 *Ibid.*, last sentence.

177 Cf. M. Holtzer, 'Het spreekrecht van de ondernemingsraad van de naamloze vennootschap bij belangrijke besluiten', *Ondernemingsrecht* 114 (2010), p. 1.

178 Cf. R.G.J. Nowak, 'Het wetsvoorstel spreekrecht OR bij belangrijke ava-besluiten', *Ondernemingsrecht* 59 (2009); M. Holtzer, 'Het spreekrecht van de ondernemingsraad van de naamloze vennootschap bij belangrijke besluiten', *Ondernemingsrecht* 114 (2010).

179 *Kamerstukken I* 2009/10, 31877, C, p. 4-5.

jurisprudence on this matter, it remains to be seen whether an annulment of a decision is possible.

Nonetheless, the non-compliance of an undertaking with the right of the works council to speak in the general meeting can be an indication of mismanagement [*wanbeleid*]. This in turn can be taken into consideration once the unions make use of their right of inquiry [*enquêteprocedure*] by filing an application before the Enterprise Chamber.[180]

Another contested aspect of the right to speak is the question of whether or not the Dutch (central) works council has such a right when it is part of an international corporation, and if so, under what circumstances. In the explanatory memorandum to the Act, the government emphasises the principle of territoriality that limits the application of *any* Dutch legislation.[181] Accordingly, the right to speak is only applicable to public limited liability companies provided that the majority of the employees in the service of the undertaking and the group companies are working/operating within the Netherlands.[182] The right to speak in such cases is exercised by the central works council; in cases where no central works council is maintained, a common position of the works councils of the subsidiaries must be formulated and subsequently presented before the general meeting of shareholders.

Such a limitation is reasonable and in line with the earlier legislation with regard to the structure regime.[183] As will subsequently be outlined in section 3.2, the Dutch structure regime limits the exercise of the works council's right of recommendation in relation to the supervisory board insofar as the international holding can be exempted from the regime once the majority of employees work outside of the Netherlands. The scope of the structure regime and the scope of application of the right to speak at the general meeting, therefore, closely correlate and avoid legal uncertainty and an extraterritorial application of Dutch law outside the Netherlands and with regard to foreign corporations.

The right to speak is not permitted at the level of the holding once the majority of the employees of the undertaking work outside the Netherlands, but it can nevertheless be exercised at the level of the Dutch subsidiary provided that the majority of employees of such a subsidiary work within the Netherlands.[184]

180 The works council can become an intervening party in such inquiry proceedings; see also M. Holtzer, 'Het spreekrecht van de ondernemingsraad van de naamloze vennootschap bij belangrijke besluiten', *Ondernemingsrecht* 114 (2010), p. 4.

181 *Kamerstukken II* 2008/09, 31877, nr. 3, p. 5.

182 See article 2:107a(4) of the DCC, article 2:134a(2) of the DCC, article 2:135(2) of the DCC and article 2:144a(2) of the DCC.

183 See also in the affirmative: C.W.P. Ommeren and D.J.W.M. Kemperink, 'Het spreekrecht van de ondernemingsraad', *ArbeidsRecht* 5 (2011), p. 3.

184 Cf. *Kamerstukken I* 2009/10, 31877, E, p. 2.

In conclusion, one can welcome the introduction of such a right to speak at the general meeting of shareholders for the works council. It introduced the possibility of formulating the workforce's position and to explain such a position at the general meeting. No other right of the works council permits a direct influence of the works council vis-à-vis the shareholders of the undertaking. At the same time, however, genuine influence can be questioned given the fact that the general meeting can set aside the work councils' standpoint without any consequences.[185] Contrary to the consultation rights pursuant to article 25 of the WCA, no standstill period of 30 days must be observed and it is not possible for the works council, as is the case under the co-determination procedure pursuant to article 27 of the WCA, to veto such a decision.

Nonetheless, the right to speak can be regarded as an opportunity for the Dutch works council to formulate a position with regard to the corporate structure and concerning the group's strategic decisions in light of the speaking right of article 2:114a of the DCC. As Holtzer rightly points out, the right does not lead to an improved position of the works council with regard to the actual decision-making process because of the absence of sanctions in cases of non-compliance with the works councils' right.[186] Yet, it enhances the position of the works council in general due to increased access to information on strategic management decisions – such as the decision to sell all or the majority of shares in the corporation – and expertise on the subject matter due to the necessity of formulating a standpoint on behalf of the works council. Another possible solution can be the relinquishment of this right by the works council in exchange for another right, which can be granted to the works council by means of a covenant.[187]

It remains to be seen in the empirical section of this study whether the works councils are actually making use of this right in practice.

1.4.6 The (possible) right of inquiry

The right of inquiry [*enquêterecht*] is a general dispute resolution mechanism pursuant to section 8 of book 2 of the Dutch Civil Code. While the Dutch works council can already make recourse to the appeal procedure pursuant to article 26 of the WCA with regard to individual management decisions[188] the inquiry procedure [*enquêteprocedure*] is aimed at settling disputes on the general policy and state of affairs of the undertaking.

185 Cf. M. Holtzer, 'Het spreekrecht van de ondernemingsraad van de naamloze vennootschap bij belangrijke besluiten', *Ondernemingsrecht* 114 (2010), p. 4.

186 *Ibid.*

187 C.W.P. Ommeren and D.J.W.M. Kemperink, 'Het spreekrecht van de ondernemingsraad', *ArbeidsRecht* 5 (2011), p. 7.

188 See section 1.4.4 above.

The starting point is that the management of the undertaking is entrusted with the decision-making process in the undertaking.[189] The works council and other stakeholders can influence the decision-making process by means of the legal tools available to them, which were outlined in the previous sections of this chapter.

If the management is taking decisions (or refuses to do so), stakeholders can ask the Enterprise Chamber to appoint one or more persons to conduct an inquiry procedure in order to determine whether or not the policy and the state of affairs of the legal person is such that mismanagement [*wanbeleid*] can be established.[190] Once such a procedure is initiated, the Enterprise Chamber can order provisional measures[191] as well as further measures in its judgement on the merits.[192] Particularly, the application of provisional measures and the swift adjudication of cases make the inquiry proceedings very important in practice and arguably the strongest corporate litigation tool.[193]

A number of stakeholders may start such an inquiry procedure, which was introduced in 1971.[194] The right of inquiry was therefore introduced alongside the structure regime and following the Verdam report of 1964.[195] Firstly, shareholders of a public or private limited liability company with an issued capital of less than 22.5 million EUR must represent (together) at least 10% of the share capital with a nominal value of 225.000 EUR to be eligible to start such a procedure.[196] Secondly, shareholders of a public or private limited liability company with an issued capital of more than 22.5 million EUR must hold (together) at least 1% of the shares with a nominal value of at least 20 million EUR to start the procedure.[197]

Thirdly, in the case of an association, a cooperative or mutual insurance society, the members of the legal person can exercise this right, provided that they "number at least 300, or at least one tenth of the total number of members or at least representing one tenth of the votes that may be cast at the General Meeting".[198] Fourthly, for public interest

189 The scope of the inquiry procedure applies to all company forms stipulated in article 2:344 of the DCC.

190 Article 2:345 of the DCC; the most prominent cases of (alleged) mismanagement in the recent jurisprudence are the *ABN AMRO* cases; OK 03 May 2007, *JOR* 2007/143 and *ARO* 2007/80 (*ABN AMRO*); and HR 13 July 2007, *JOR* 2007/178 (*ABN AMRO*); see also OK 24 November 2008, *JOR* 2009/9 (*Fortis*).

191 Article 2:349a of the DCC.

192 Article 2:356 of the DCC.

193 Cf. P.A.M. Witteveen et al., '9 Ondernemingsraad en enquêterecht', in L.C.J. Sprengers and G.W. van der Voet (eds.), *De toekomst van de medezeggenschap: Aanbevelingen aan de wetgever* (Kluwer, Deventer 2009), p. 120; and with regard to the scope of the provisional measures see OK 25 February 2011, *NJ* 2011/335 (*Marigot c.s./IA groep en Rapar*).

194 *Wet van 10 September 1970*, *Stb.* 1970, 414 [Act on annual accounts of enterprises: Act of 10th September 1970, Gazette 414].

195 P.J. Verdam et al., *Rapport herziening van het ondernemingsrecht* (Staatsuitgeverij, 's-Gravenhage 1965).

196 Article 2:346(b) of the DCC.

197 Article 2:346(c) of the DCC.

198 Dutch Civil Law, 'Section 2.8.1 Rules for resolving disputes between shareholders', <http://www.dutchcivillaw.com/civilcodebook022.htm> (last accessed 29 September 2017).

reasons, such an inquiry procedure can be also requested by the Advocate-General at the Amsterdam Court of Appeal.[199] This, however, is rarely used and has been the subject of criticism in the literature.[200] Fifthly, the undertaking itself (or in case of bankruptcy proceedings, the trustee)[201] also has a right of inquiry as is laid down in article 2:346(d) of the DCC, which can also be exercised by the supervisory board or the non-executive members of a one-tier board from 1st of January 2013.[202]

The labour unions, finally, may also file such a request for an investigation as is stipulated in article 2:347 of the DCC. The labour union must be established for a period of at least two years, must have laid down in its articles of incorporation that it is actively looking after the interests of its members in the concerned economic sector and must have members in the undertaking in question.[203] Notably, it follows from the case law that the labour unions can also exercise their right of inquiry vis-à-vis the international top-holding and can therefore challenge decisions that are taken outside the scope of Dutch law.[204] In the *Landis* case, the Dutch Supreme Court further held that the *de facto* economic reality is decisive when considering a request for an inquiry procedure that concerns the MNC as a whole.[205] While the labour unions could thus play a significant role in such inquiry proceedings, the right of inquiry was only used 15 times throughout the period from 1971 – 2007 and only five times in more recent years.[206] The number of inquiry procedures overall, however, is increasing and amounted to 510 applications in the same period.[207] However, it has to be noted that the last empirical analysis of such inquiry procedures was done ten years ago. The Enterprise Chamber adopted in 2010 a new calculation method for the number of inquiry procedures, which does not allow for a comparison with the figures prior to that.[208] Inquiry procedures pursuant to articles 2:345 – 2:347 of the DCC are not individually reported by the Enterprise Chamber in its annual reports.[209]

199 Article 2:345(2) of the DCC.

200 See *inter alia* S.M. Bartman and M. Holtzer, 'Enquêterecht voorzichtig onder het mes', *Ondernemingsrecht* 14 (2010), p. 4; E. Schmieman, 'De bevoegdheden van de advocaat-generaal bij het Gerechtshof Amsterdam in het enquêterecht (art. 2:345 lid 2 en 2:355 lid 1 BW)', in G. van Solinge and M. Holtzer (eds.), *Geschriften vanwege de Vereniging Corporate Litigation 2003-2004, Serie vanwege het Van der Heijden Instituut, deel 75* (Kluwer, Deventer 2004), p. 359 et seq.

201 Article 2:346(3) of the DCC.

202 Article 2:346(2) of the DCC.

203 OK 16 April 1987, *NJ* 1988/183 (*Stolk*); OK 17 March 1994, *NJ* 1995/408 (*Janssen Pers*); OK 10 September 1999, *Ondernemingsrecht* 1999/83 (*IJsselwerf*); OK 18 May 2004, *ARO* 2004/74 (*Esteves*); OK 27 May 2010, *JOR* 2010/189 (*PCM*).

204 Asser 2-II*, '742 Enquêtebevoegdheid vereniging van werknemers in concernverhoudingen', p. 1.

205 HR 4 February 2005, *NJ* 2005/127 (*Landis*); cf. P. Ingelse, 'Mede-ondernemen en concernenquête', *Tijdschrift voor Arbeid & Onderneming* 1 (2012), p. 31 et. seq.

206 K. Cools et al., *Het recht van enquête: Een empirisch onderzoek* (Kluwer, Deventer 2009), p. 79.

207 *Ibid.*

208 See Enterprise Chamber of the Amsterdam Court of Appeal, 'Jaarverslag Ondernemingskamer 2016', <https://www.rechtspraak.nl/SiteCollectionDocuments/Jaarverslag-ondernemingskamer-2016.pdf> (last accessed 29 January 2018), p. 7 et seq.

209 *Ibid.*, p. 9-13.

Overall, it can be assumed that neither the labour unions nor the Advocate General make frequent use of their right. Therefore, the potential access of the works council as an intervening party is considerably limited.

The Dutch works council is not allowed to request an inquiry procedure individually unless such right is granted voluntarily in the articles of association. While the question of granting the works council a statutory right of inquiry was frequently addressed in *inter alia* the Verdam report and the subsequent advice given by the Social and Economic Council,[210] the right was not granted on the basis of a number of arguments as will subsequently be addressed.

i. The entrepreneur as chairman of the works council

Firstly, it was held that the works council could not take an objective position in such an inquiry procedure given the fact that the entrepreneur himself had the function of the chairman of the works council.

It was concluded in the Verdam report that a right of inquiry was not in line with the objectives of the works council, namely to be a forum of consultation of which the entrepreneur is the chairman. If the works council would have been granted the right of inquiry, the Verdam Commission noted, this would have opened up proceedings against the own chairman of the works council. Therefore, such a right was not deemed to be acceptable.

It must be noted, however, that pursuant to the recast of the WCA in 1979, the entrepreneur is no longer part of the works council. Consequently, this argument can be disregarded in the context of the current debate. Moreover, it can be noted that the works council, since 1979, has developed into a mature consultation organ of the undertaking, which adopts a professional stance towards its dual mandate of representing the employees of the undertaking as well as the economic well-being of the undertaking as such.[211]

ii. The absence of the works councils' legal personality

The main argument used against the introduction of the right of inquiry for the works council is the fact that the works council has no legal personality.[212] According to those

210 Social and Economic Council, Advice 1967/5; the question of granting the works council such right was also addressed in subsequent Social and Economic Council advices 1976/5, 1988/14 and 08/01.

211 Cf. R.H. van het Kaar and J.C. Looise, *De volwassen OR – Groei en grenzen van de Nederlandse ondernemingsraad: Resultaten van het grote OR-onderzoek* (Samsom, Alphen aan den Rijn 1999), p. 257 et seq.; see also L.G. Verburg, *Het territoir van de (Nederlandse) ondernemingsraad in het internationale bedrijfsleven*, p. 366.

212 See *inter alia* the explanatory memorandum of the amendment of the right of inquiry; *Kamerstukken II* 2010/11, 32887, No. 3, p. 13.

critics, the absence of legal personality would prevent the works council from being ordered to pay the costs of the inquiry procedure.[213] This in turn could lead to a lightly use of the right of inquiry of the works council as will be subsequently addressed below.

Although it is true that the works council does not have legal personality, it must be constituted that the absence of legal personality does not preclude the attribution of other rights to the works council and the recourse to legal proceedings once such rights have been infringed. In addition to the rights under the structure regime, the works council has a right to speak at the general meeting of shareholders as was discussed in the previous section 1.4.5 and can, under the current regime, intervene in inquiry proceedings that are already started by another stakeholder mentioned in article 2:346 of the DCC. Due to the fact that the works council is closely connected with the day-to-day proceedings within the undertaking, it is the works council who urges the labour unions to initiate an inquiry procedure and can only take part in the proceedings as intervening party.[214]

Moreover, the works council is permitted to submit a statement of opposition [*verweerschrift*] in an inquiry procedure when it is acting in its capacity as an intervening party.[215] The works council, therefore, comes very close to being a fully recognised party in the inquiry proceedings with regard to the legal personality.

Finally, in light of the *Batco* case it can be concluded that the works council has legal standing for the fulfilment of its tasks as laid down in the WCA and any other legal provision.[216] Legal personality, therefore, cannot be regarded as *conditio sine qua non* for granting the works council a right of inquiry.

iii. The works council may use the right of inquiry lightly

Firstly, due to the fact that the works council does not have legal personality, the argument is put forward that the works council may use the right of inquiry lightly. As a result, the work council may use the inquiry procedure too early and/or too frequently, which will naturally be to the detriment of the undertaking due to the reputational loss and costs of the procedure.

213 P.A.M. Witteveen et al., '9 Ondernemingsraad en enquêterecht', in L.C.J. Sprengers and G.W. van der Voet (eds.), *De toekomst van de medezeggenschap: Aanbevelingen aan de wetgever* (Kluwer, Deventer 2009), p. 120- 121.

214 *Ibid.*, p. 122.

215 HR 6 June 2003, *NJ* 2003/486 (*Pich/Scheipar*); OK 13 March 2003, *JOR* 2003/85 (*Corus*); and OK 10 December 2003, *ARO* 2003/186 (*ERU Beheer*); cf. L.G. Verburg, *Het territoir van de (Nederlandse) ondernemingsraad in het internationale bedrijfsleven*, p. 367.

216 OK 13 November 1980, *NJ* 1981/258 (*Batco*); see also S.M. Bartman and M. Holtzer, 'Enquêterecht voorzichtig onder het mes', *Ondernemingsrecht* 14 (2010), p. 8.

Secondly, it is argued that the works council is an internal and therefore not neutral party compared to the other stakeholders that are external parties, such as the labour unions. Therefore, the works council may use the inquiry procedure to object an (intended) decision after having been consulted on the subject matter pursuant to article 25 of the WCA. Not only would such a repeated objection to an (intended) decision considerably delay the decision-making process, but it could also lead to the distortion of the relationship of the works council vis-à-vis the management of the undertaking.[217] A practical solution would be to declare a works councils' request for an inquiry procedure inadmissible as long as the works council, prior to filing such a request, does not exhaust all other legal means available.[218]

The third and main objection raised in this regard, however, is the fact that the works council cannot be ordered to pay the costs of the inquiry procedure. The Minister of Social Affairs has reiterated this argument in the context of the amendment of the right of inquiry in 2010.[219] According to the Minister, the possibility to order a party to pay the costs of the procedure is the single most important safeguard to prevent a light use of the inquiry procedure and such a possibility is therefore absent for the works council.

While it is true that the possibility to order a party (i.e., the works council) to pay the costs of the procedure is having a preventative effect, the Enterprise Chamber has so far never made use of it.[220] Therefore, it can be held that the misuse of the procedure is rather a theoretical possibility rather than actually being the case in practice.

Moreover, the Social and Economic Council held in this regard that the works council is, due to its close ties with the undertaking, well aware of the possible detrimental effects of an inquiry procedure for the undertaking and of the consequences this may have for the employees of the company.[221] In order to prevent a light use of the inquiry procedure, Grapperhaus proposed that a qualified majority among the workforce must be obtained by the works council prior to starting such a procedure (in case such a right were to be awarded to the works council). In addition, the employees could contribute a small percentage of their salary as a guarantee.[222]

217 Cf. L.G. Verburg, *Het territoir van de (Nederlandse) ondernemingsraad in het internationale bedrijfsleven*, p. 366.

218 Cf. P.A.M. Witteveen et al., '9 Ondernemingsraad en enquêterecht', in L.C.J. Sprengers and G.W. van der Voet (eds.), *De toekomst van de medezeggenschap: Aanbevelingen aan de wetgever* (Kluwer, Deventer 2009), p. 125.

219 *Kamerstukken II* 2010/11, 32887, No. 3, p. 13.

220 SER Advies 2003/12, *Aanpassing van de Wet op de ondernemingsraden*, p. 68.

221 *Ibid.*; see also P.A.M. Witteveen et al., '9 Ondernemingsraad en enquêterecht', in L.C.J. Sprengers and G.W. van der Voet (eds.), *De toekomst van de medezeggenschap: Aanbevelingen aan de wetgever* (Kluwer, Deventer 2009), p. 126.

222 F.B.J. Grapperhaus, 'Medezeggenschap, onderneming en evenwicht', *Ondernemingsrecht* 31 (2009).

Furthermore, the cases whereby the right of inquiry is awarded to the works council pursuant to article 2:346(e) of the DCC shows that the use of this right of inquiry is only made in situations, in which no other solution was viable. Although it was questioned whether the works council abused its right of inquiry in these cases, the Enterprise Chamber did not come to such a conclusion.[223]

iv. The costs of the procedure (and the possible abuse thereof)

Resulting from the absence of a legal personality of the works council, as was discussed above, it is not possible to order the works council to pay the cost of the procedure. It was therefore held by the minister that the works council might not only use the inquiry procedure lightly, but also that other parties may potentially take advantage of this lacuna. It was argued that other stakeholders would potentially refrain from starting an own procedure and rather participate as an intervening party in a procedure started by the works council.[224] Other parties may therefore avoid the financial risks when participating in an inquiry procedure that is initiated by the works council, due to the fact that the works council cannot be ordered to pay the costs.

The starting point is thereby that the legal entity has to pay the costs of the inquiry procedure pursuant to article 2:350(3) of the DCC in any case. This holds true except for situations in which the procedure is started contrary to the principles of reasonableness and fairness and is therefore considered to be unjustified. Therefore, while the argument of an abuse of the procedure in theory can be made, it has to be noted that a compensation of damages due to the unjustified initiation of an inquiry procedure pursuant to article 2:350(3) of the DCC has so far never been ordered by the court.[225]

This is different with regard to the costs of legal assistance and experts in the procedure. The works council may hire lawyers and experts to assist them in the procedure, while the costs are to be borne by the legal entity itself. Other stakeholders, therefore, could attempt to shift their own litigation costs by urging the works council to initiate the inquiry procedure with the result that the litigation costs are ultimately borne by the undertaking. Although such an abuse is possible, the overall cost of the procedure can also be *decreased*. This can be achieved due to the fact that one instead of two procedures, namely the appeal procedure pursuant to article 26 of the WCA as well as the inquiry procedure, might be necessary to resolve a dispute once the works council is granted the right of inquiry.

223 OK 5 October 2005, *ARO* 2005/186 (*Smit Transformatoren*); and OK 10 December 2008, *ARO* 2009/1 (*AHAM*).

224 *Kamerstukken II* 2010/11, 32887, No. 3, p. 13.

225 Cf. P.A.M. Witteveen et al., '9 Ondernemingsraad en enquêterecht', in L.C.J. Sprengers and G.W. van der Voet (eds.), *De toekomst van de medezeggenschap: Aanbevelingen aan de wetgever* (Kluwer, Deventer 2009), p. 126.

Possible overlaps with the procedure under article 26 of the WCA and the inquiry procedure can be avoided by dismissing applications for an inquiry procedure initiated by the works council, so long as an article 26 WCA procedure is feasible.[226] Furthermore, such overlap is only expectable in very limited circumstances due to the different nature of the two procedures. While the article 26 WCA procedure concerns appeals regarding an individual management decision, the inquiry procedure is rather aimed at addressing the overall (mis)management of the undertaking in question.

1.4.6.1 Conclusion

In the foregoing section, a possible right of inquiry for the works council was addressed. The right of inquiry is the most effective litigation tool with regard to possible mismanagement within an undertaking and can even be applied with regard to corporate structures, as was held in the *Landis* case. Consequently, stakeholders increasingly apply the inquiry procedure in practice. Furthermore, the number of stakeholders having the right of inquiry was further extended very recently in 2013 and it now also includes the legal entity itself.

The works council, however, is not permitted to start such an inquiry procedure on the basis of the arguments that were introduced above, namely the absence of independent legal personality and the fact that the works council cannot be ordered to pay for the costs of the procedure. The works council is, therefore, assumed to use the right of inquiry lightly and other stakeholders can take advantage of that latter possibility.

The arguments that are extensively discussed in the literature are, however, out-dated and also to a certain extent unfounded against the background of the status quo of the regime applicable to works councils. The absence of a legal personality does not constitute an obstacle for the attribution of other rights such as the right to speak at the general meeting, but thresholds could be applied in order to prevent a lightly use of the inquiry procedure. In the literature, a coordinating mechanism similar to article 2:349(2) of the DCC or a right of inquiry only in case of specific circumstances such as the danger of bankruptcy are introduced as possible solutions.[227] Another solution is the aforementioned proposal by Grapperhaus to require a qualified majority-threshold among the workforce in favour of initiating such a procedure.

226 Cf. B. van Duren-Kloppert, 'Enquêterecht en medezeggenschap: tijd voor Doornroosje om te ontwaken?', *ArbeidsRecht* 36 (2004), p. 6.

227 Cf. P.A.M. Witteveen et al., '9 Ondernemingsraad en enquêterecht', in L.C.J. Sprengers and G.W. van der Voet (eds.), *De toekomst van de medezeggenschap: Aanbevelingen aan de wetgever* (Kluwer, Deventer 2009), p. 127.

The amendments to the structure regime, as will further be discussed in section 3.2, has led to a shift in the balance of powers within the undertaking in favour of the shareholders. The Dutch stakeholder-model or *Poldermodel*, however, emphasises the importance of the long-term strategy of the undertaking and the important role of all stakeholders including the works council. By virtue of a right of inquiry, the works council would be put in a position to fulfil an important role in order to safeguard the long-term economic well-being of the undertaking and the power balance within the Dutch regime could be restored. This would also be in line with the recent developments in the area of corporate governance.[228]

Concerning the position of the works council in a MNC, the attribution of the right of inquiry would considerably elevate the works council's influence, especially on matters of strategic decision-making and the overall position of the Dutch subsidiaries of the corporation. At the same time, the right of inquiry should be limited to matters that directly and immediately have an impact on the Dutch subsidiaries. Therefore, the right should be conferred to the works council for situations in which the decisions of the top-holding can be qualified as mismanagement and which have an impact on the state of affairs of the Dutch subsidiaries. This could prevent an unwarranted impact of the Dutch regime on foreign legal systems in light of the principle of territoriality.

1.4.7 Other rights of the Dutch works council and its members

When examining the rights of the Dutch works council, one has to consider several further rights that can prove crucial for the effective and efficient work of the works council in practice.

While the rights discussed above are concerned with participation rights of the works council and the right to appeal if such participation rights were unlawfully denied, the rights addressed in the following section are concerned with the means of the works council to effectively work in the undertaking.

1.4.7.1 The right to set up committees

Firstly, the works council may set up committees pursuant to article 15 of the WCA, if such a committee is deemed necessary for the performance of the council's duties (article 15(1) of the WCA). With regard to the empirical research conducted in this study, such committees are interesting insofar as the effectiveness of works councils can be partially dependent on an efficient delegation of tasks between the works council as such (including the chairman and his deputy) and the respective committee's in place within

228 Cf. I. Zaal, *De reikwijdte van medezeggenschap* (Kluwer, Deventer 2013), p. 79-80.

the undertaking. On the other hand, it is noted in the literature that by establishing committees such as an administrative board [*dagelijkse bestuur*] the works council and particularly the administrative board becomes further detached from the workforce.[229] Yet, the administrative board also is more professional and has ample experience with regard to employee participation through works councils, which particularly holds true for MNCs.[230]

It remains to be seen in the empirical analysis whether the reliance on committees and a coordination with as well as a delegation of tasks to such committees is in fact improving the position of the works council in practice.[231]

1.4.7.2 The right to consult internal and external experts

Secondly, the works council has the right to consult both external as well as internal experts, such as company directors or expert staff employed in the undertaking, whom are competent on the subject for which advice of the council is to be given (article 16 of the WCA). As will be further discussed below in section 1.5.4 regarding the duty of confidentiality, any expert can be bound by the duty of confidentiality pursuant to article 20 of the WCA. Recourse to expert consultation is increasingly made by works councils and particularly in larger undertakings, according to a study that was conducted in 2009.[232] Nevertheless, it remains to be seen in the empirical part of this study as to how far such recourse is actually made and whether such expert advice is seen as a positive influence on the position of works councils, both from the perspective of the works council with regard to access to valuable information and from the undertaking's perspective concerning the degree of professionalism of the works council.[233]

1.4.7.3 The right of access to facilities of the undertaking

Thirdly, the works council, its committees as well as the secretariat, if established, are to be allowed to "*use any facilities that [the entrepreneur] may have at his disposal [...] and which the Works Council and its committees may reasonably be deemed to require in order to perform their duties*" while retaining full pay during their meetings (article 17 of the WCA).[234] This also includes expenses incurred by the works council or one of the

229 See P.F. van der Heijden et al., 'Medezeggenschap: Ontwikkelingen in de 21e eeuw', p. 23 and 68.

230 Cf. P. van Beurden, H. van Ees and R. Goodijk, 'Gebruik, niet-gebruik of onderbenutting? – Onderzoek naar de mogelijke onderbenutting van bevoegdheden en mogelijkheden door de (Centrale) Ondernemingsraad in grote Nederlandse ondernemingen', p. 76.

231 See section 3.5.3 in chapter V.

232 P. van Beurden, H. van Ees and R. Goodijk, 'Gebruik, niet-gebruik of onderbenutting? – Onderzoek naar de mogelijke onderbenutting van bevoegdheden en mogelijkheden door de (Centrale) Ondernemingsraad in grote Nederlandse ondernemingen', p. 14, 33 and 42.

233 See section 5.6 in chapter IV and sections 3.3 and 3.5 in chapter V.

234 Social and Economic Council, 'English translation of the Dutch Works Councils Act', p. 12-13.

committees, provided that such expenses were communicated to the management in advance (article 22 of the WCA). Possible litigation costs as well as the costs of expert consultations are also to be borne by the entrepreneur (articles 22(2) and 22a of the WCA). Furthermore, an annual expenditure budget may be agreed upon between the entrepreneur and the works council (article 22(4) of the WCA). The condition of costs being *reasonable and necessary for the fulfilment of the works council's tasks* is thereby construed broadly. The most recent monitoring of works councils (*nalevingsonderzoek*) in 2017 showed that agreements on support of the works council have been made in 54% of undertakings.[235] But it has to be noted that the recent survey only covered internal support and not external support such as external experts.

1.4.7.4 The right of access to training

Fourthly, the members of the works council must have access to training and the ability to consult with others persons within the undertaking, while retaining full pay, for a certain amount of hours per year, which must include at least five workdays for training and development pursuant to article 18(3) of the WCA.[236] While training and development is considered to be very beneficial for the degree of professionalism with which works council members are participating in consultations with the management of the undertaking,[237] studies have shown that in some works councils, members are not using the minimum amount of sixty hours a year for training and development.[238] The use of training facilities is also revisited in the empirical part of this study.[239]

1.4.7.5 Protection from unfair treatment resulting from the works council membership

Fifthly, works council members (as well as former members) and persons that were on the lists for works council elections are to be protected from being "*placed at any disadvantage with respect to his or her position in the enterprise on the grounds of any candidature for or membership of the Works Council or a Works Council committee*" pursuant to article 21 of the WCA.[240] This protection also applies to any staff member of the works councils' secretariat, if applicable. Moreover, members of the works council, members of

235 I. Wajon, P. Vlug and E. Enneking, 'Naleving van de Wet op de Ondernemingsraden: Stand van zaken begin 2017', <https://www.rijksoverheid.nl/binaries/rijksoverheid/documenten/rapporten/2017/10/17/onderzoeksrapport-naleving-wor/Eindrapport+Onderzoek+Naleving+WOR+juni+2017.pdf> (last accessed 15 January 2018), p. 34.

236 Article 18(2) of the WCA concerning training and development.

237 Cf. R.H. van het Kaar and E. Smit (eds.), 'Vier scenario's voor de toekomst van de medezeggenschap – Een onderzoek in opdracht van het Ministerie van SZW', p. 196.

238 H. van den Tillaart and J. Warmerdam, *Ontwikkelingen in scholing van ondernemingsraden: Terugblik op de afgelopen jaren en verwachtingen voor de toekomst* (ITS, Nijmegen 2016), p. 20-22.

239 See section 5.7 in chapter IV as well as sections 3.3.2 and 3.5.4 in chapter V.

240 Social and Economic Council, 'English translation of the Dutch Works Councils Act', p. 14.

one of its commissions and staff of the secretariat are protected from dismissal by means of a statutory protection as laid down in article 7:670(4) of the DCC. However, it remains to be seen whether the members of the works council nevertheless experience a negative implication on their career as a result of their involvement in the works council.[241] This subject will be further addressed in the empirical section of this study.

1.4.7.6 *Additional rights through covenants*

Finally, further rights can be given to the works council pursuant to article 32 of the WCA by means of provisions that are stipulated in a collective bargaining agreement (article 32(1) of the WCA) or by means of a so-called covenant between the entrepreneur and the works council (article 32(2) of the WCA).[242] By means of such a (written) covenant, further rights and powers can be attributed to the works council such as access to further information, the right to render advice on additional subjects[243] or meetings with the central management in corporations in which a holding structure is applicable, which would normally preclude access of the works council to the central management and rather only access to the management at sub-holding level. It must be noted, however, that additional powers granted to the works council are precluded if such a matter has already been addressed by a collective labour agreement or another arrangement relating to terms of employment (article 32(3) of the WCA).

1.5 *Duties of the Dutch works council*

While the WCA contains ample rights for the Dutch works council, it also stipulates certain duties for the members of the works council. Such duties include adherence to the own statutes of the council, particularly with respect to works council elections, the composition of the council regarding the number of members and possible union affiliation and the *modus operandi.*

Other duties are specifically formulated in the WCA on issues such as consultation meetings with the management of the undertaking and, finally, the duty to be transparent vis-à-vis the employees that the council is representing and the duty of confidentiality. These duties will be examined in the following paragraphs.

241 See section 5.7.2 in chapter IV; see also E. van der Cruijsen and J. Warning, 'De ondernemingsraad: een stap in de goede richting? – Een onderzoek naar de loopbaan van OR-leden', p. 7; see also R.H. van het Kaar and E. Smit (eds.), 'Vier scenario's voor de toekomst van de medezeggenschap – Een onderzoek in opdracht van het Ministerie van SZW', p. 74-75.

242 See for the empirical results on the use of covenants section 5.3 in chapter IV.

243 Article 32(4) of the WCA.

1.5.1 The composition of the works council, elections and terms of office

The starting point for the provisions on the composition of the works council can be found in article 6(1) of the WCA. It is stipulated that members (i) are directly elected, (ii) by persons working in the undertaking and (iii) must be employees of the undertaking ("from their own ranks").[244] What is also important to note here is that the elections have to take place by secret written ballot from one or more lists of candidates pursuant to article 9 of the WCA.[245]

Those whom are eligible to vote are those employees that have been working in the undertaking for at least six months.[246] Furthermore, all employees that have been working for at least one year within the undertaking can be elected to the works council via these elections.[247] As was pointed out in section 1.2 above, the term 'working' includes all employees that are posted in the undertaking rather than only those that have an employment contract with the undertaking, but agency workers and temp-workers are in a weaker position due to the requirement to work 24 months for (agency workers) or be posted longer than 6 months (temp-workers) to the undertaking. Yet, differing regulations with respect to the period of service of the workers that are used as a requirement to become eligible to vote or to be elected in the elections can be laid down in the works councils' rules of procedures.[248]

The number of members to be elected depends, thereby, on the number of persons working in the undertaking and this typically ranges from at least 3 works council members (in undertakings with less than 50 employees) to a maximum of 25 members.[249] The works council may, however, lay down in its rules of procedure [*reglement*] a different number of members to be elected as well as the possibility to elect deputies, which is subject to prior consent of the entrepreneur.[250] Once the works council is established, the council itself shall elect the chairman of the works council as well as a deputy pursuant to article 7 of the WCA.

The results of the works council elections have to be submitted to the entrepreneur, the persons working in the undertaking and also to any person that has submitted a list of persons for election.[251] Lastly, additional rules on matters such as elections, candidature and vacancies can be included in the rules of procedure of the works council.[252]

---

244 Social and Economic Council, 'English translation of the Dutch Works Councils Act', p. 8.
245 *Ibid.*
246 Article 6(2) of the WCA.
247 Article 6(3) of the WCA.
248 Article 6(5) of the WCA.
249 Article 6(1) of the WCA, second sentence.
250 Article 6(1) of the WCA, last sentence.
251 Article 11 of the WCA.
252 Article 10 of the WCA.

Regarding the terms of employment of the works council, it is stipulated in article 12(1) of the WCA that the works council shall be elected for a period of three years and that the members will simultaneously resign after such period, but variation is possible (article 12(2) of the WCA). It may be laid down in the rules of procedure of the works council that the members of the council have to resign simultaneously after two or four years, or rather that half of the members are to be replaced every two years.[253] Members of the works council are, as a starting point, immediately eligible for re-election, but can also be subject to alternate arrangements pursuant to the rules of procedure. While members of the works council may resign at any time,[254] their membership automatically ends once the person is no longer working in the undertaking.[255]

Whereas the employees working in the undertaking elect the regular works council members, the central works council as well as the group works council are to be made up by members of the (already elected) regular works councils pursuant to article 34(1) and article 34(7) of the WCA with regard to the groups works council. Examples of good practice regarding the internal structure and practical application of the legal framework are further discussed in section 3.5 of chapter V.

1.5.2 The mode of decision-making in the works council

The works council must further establish rules regarding its internal decision-making process, which has to be laid down in its rules of procedures.[256]

From the initial establishment of a works council within an undertaking and up until the moment at which the works council has drawn up its rules of procedure, the entrepreneur has to establish provisional rules of procedure provisions pursuant to article 48 of the WCA. Once the works council is able to exercise its rights and has drawn up its own rules of procedure, the provisional rules cease to be effective.

While the list of matters to be covered by the rules of procedure is not exhaustive, at the very least, the following matters should be codified: the intervals at which meetings are convened (article 14(2)(a) of the WCA), how the meetings are convened (subparagraph b), rules regarding a necessary quorum (subparagraph c), voting procedures (subparagraph d), the provision of a secretariat (subparagraph e), how the agenda setting is conducted and the notification of the entrepreneur thereof (subparagraph f), the timing of notifications of the entrepreneur as well as the workforce (subparagraph g) and,

253 Article 12(2) of the WCA.
254 Article 12(4) of the WCA.
255 Article 12(3) of the WCA.
256 Pursuant to article 14(1) of the WCA; article 8 of the WCA further prohibits any rules that conflict with the WCA.

finally, provisions on the establishment of minutes of the meetings and of the annual report of the council (subparagraph h).

Another important procedural obligation is stipulated in articles 25(4) as well as article 27(2) of the WCA, namely the obligation to render advice or give consent only after the matter "has been discussed at least once in a consultation meeting".[257] These provisions are in alignment with the Dutch consensus-oriented '*polder model*', which is aimed at cooperation despite differences and thus is regarded as a problem-solving approach.[258] By obliging the works council to meet at least once with the management, an opportunity to motivate decisions as well as to give reasons for a particular decision can be given and a dialogue between the parties is obligatory. Moreover, the works council is obliged, as a result of its dual mandate, to bear in mind the well-being of the undertaking as a whole.

1.5.3 Duties regarding meetings with the management

The provisions regarding consultation meetings are laid down in articles 23 to 23c of the WCA, while articles 24, 25, 27 and 30 of the WCA, which have already been discussed in this chapter, govern the content of such meetings.

Firstly, consultation meetings shall take place within 14 days of a request for such a meeting being put forward by either the works council or the entrepreneur pursuant to article 23(1) of the WCA. Such consultation meeting can concern either matters that are regarded as desirable by one of the parties or is a mandatory requirement of the WCA, such as the provisions found articles 25(4) and 27(2) of the WCA that prescribe at least one consultation meeting for matters falling within the scope of articles 25 and 27 of the WCA.[259]

Secondly, all consultation meetings must take place in accordance with the rules of procedure of the works council and all works council members are permitted to speak during the meeting.[260] Moreover, the member of the management, who is designated to attend the consultation meetings on behalf of the undertaking, and the chairman of the works council are chairing the meetings alternately with a possibility of variation.[261]

257 Social and Economic Council, 'English translation of the Dutch Works Councils Act', p. 20.

258 See J. Visser, 'The Netherlands: From Paternalism to Representation', in J. Rogers and W. Streeck, *Works Councils: Consultation, Representation, and Cooperation in Industrial Relations*, p. 82.

259 Article 23(2) of the WCA.

260 Article 23a(1) of the WCA.

261 Article 23a(2) of the WCA.

Thirdly, both the entrepreneur and the works council are in a position to take decisions during such meetings.[262]

Finally, the works council may grant authority to a committee to take part in consultation meetings on behalf of the works council, but such meetings cannot deal with matters that have been already subject to prior consultations between the works council and the entrepreneur.[263]

The practical application of these provisions is further examined in the quantitative (sections 5.1 and 5.2 of chapter IV) and qualitative analysis (section 3.2 of chapter V) below.

1.5.4 Confidentiality

Another crucial duty concerns the duty of confidentiality of the works council pursuant to article 20 of the WCA. This aspect is of particular importance in corporations that are listed on the stock market due to the fact that the premature disclosure of information can have a negative impact on the corporation's share value or its competitive position on the market.[264] Especially with regard to matters that fall under the scope of article 25 of the WCA, like financial information, such sensitive information can be given. A particular obligation of confidentiality is given in cases where the member of the management, who is present at the consultation meeting, expressly communicates the confidentiality of a matter.[265]

While such strict confidentiality shall not be used excessively,[266] it applies to the entire works council as well as to its secretarial staff and council committees.[267] Moreover, such a duty of confidentiality can be extended to experts or any other person that are consulted on matters for which confidentiality is prescribed.[268] Lastly, the confidentiality requirement does not cease to be applicable at the end of the works council membership or upon the cessation of the employment of the person in the undertaking concerned.[269] Such a duty of confidentiality can also be found in section 4(4) of the European Works Council Directive.

262 Article 23b of the WCA.
263 Article 23c of the WCA.
264 Cf. L.G. Verburg, *Het territoir van de (Nederlandse) ondernemingsraad in het internationale bedrijfsleven*, p. 127 et seq.; see also E. Verhulp, *Vrijheid van meningsuiting van werknemers en ambtenaren* (Sdu, The Hague 1997).
265 *Ibid.*
266 Article 20(7) of the WCA.
267 Article 20(2) of the WCA.
268 Articles 20(1) and (4) of the WCA.
269 Article 20(6) of the WCA.

1.5.5 Other duties

To conclude the section on the duties of the Dutch works council in light of the WCA, one must mention the duty to observe the regulations that are applicable to the undertaking in terms of working conditions, working time as well as equal treatment, non-discrimination and sustainability, as are down in article 28 of the WCA. While the works council is obliged to do all within its power to observe such regulations, this provision does not allow the works council to engage in collective bargaining on behalf of the employees as has been argued in the literature and by the Dutch legislator.[270]

A final aspect concerns article 13 of the WCA. Even although members of the works council shall not be subject to any disadvantage by the employer as a result of the person's membership in the works council (article 21 of the WCA), an application to the subdistrict court can be made by the entrepreneur or the works council in cases where a member of the council is "seriously hindering consultation meetings between the Works Council and the entrepreneur".[271] This provision can be regarded as placing further emphasis on the duty of the works council and its members to participate in a constructive manner in consultation meetings with the management of the undertaking.

2 The added value of works councils in multinational corporations

When examining the position of works councils in multinational corporations, the question arises as to whether or not works councils are a necessary stakeholder and how the presence of a works council contributes to the performance of the corporation as a whole. The question is, therefore, what the added value of works councils is.[272]

Is the institutionalised and statutory mandatory presence of a works council *per se* inefficient given the fact that the market itself has not adopted such an employee participation mechanism itself?[273]

The rights of the Dutch works council, as were examined in the sections above, are far reaching and could constitute a burden for the performance of the undertaking, in which a works council is maintained. On the other hand, the rights of the works council could

270 See W. Streeck, 'Works Councils in Western Europe: From Consultation to Participation', in J. Rogers and W. Streeck, *Works Councils: Consultation, Representation, and Cooperation in Industrial Relations*, p. 314 and 347; the collective bargaining agreement has an overriding effect on works council rights, which precludes council action where a matter is regulated in a collective bargaining agreement.

271 Social and Economic Council, 'English translation of the Dutch Works Councils Act', p. 11.

272 While a more democratic rights approach was chosen in section 1.1.2, here an efficiency-based approach is adopted.

273 U. Jirjahn, 'Ökonomische Wirkungen des novellierten Betriebsverfassungsgesetzes – Was können wir vor dem Hintergrund zunehmender Globalisierung und veränderter arbeitsorganisatorischer Bedingungen erwarten?', *ZAF* 2 and 3 (2005), p. 242.

contribute to the efficiency of the human factor as Freeman and Lazear exhibited in their theoretical model.[274] The impact of the works council on the undertaking will, therefore, be analysed in the following section in order to examine the added value of works councils in general and in international corporations specifically.

The majority of existing research on this point has been conducted within the context of the impact of the German works council,[275] although more recent studies have also examined the Dutch regime.[276] While the results of the empirical studies were mixed, more recent studies have reported a positive impact of the works council on the performance of the undertaking, as will subsequently be addressed in greater detail.

2.1 *Less labour fluctuation*

The first aspect related to the performance of the undertaking is the amount of labour fluctuation within the firm. The undertaking as well as the employee is investing in the employment relationship and a high fluctuation in the workforce is therefore perceived as being negative due to the reoccurring 'investment-costs' in new employment relationships. The impact of a high level of fluctuation on the undertaking's performance is even greater, the higher skilled the employee is. Once an employee is dissatisfied with his or her situation within the undertaking, this dissatisfaction is expressed in the act of exiting the undertaking. The exit of dissatisfied employees, in turn, necessitates the employment of new staff and therefore causes an increased labour fluctuation. The presence of a works council can overcome such problems and serve as collective voice mechanism, which offers an alternative means of expressing the employees' dissatisfaction with a situation other than through exiting the undertaking.[277] Due to the fact that works councils are not perceived as hindering the hiring of personnel while at the same time

274 R.B. Freeman and E.P. Lazear, 'An Economic Analysis of Works Councils', in J. Rogers and W. Streeck, *Works Councils: Consultation, Representation, and Cooperation in Industrial Relations* (University of Chicago Press, Chicago 1995).

275 J.T. Addison, C. Schnabel and J. Wagner, 'Works councils in Germany: their effects on establishment performance', *Oxford Economic Papers* 53 (2001); U. Jirjahn, 'Ökonomische Wirkungen des novellierten Betriebsverfassungsgesetzes – Was können wir vor dem Hintergrund zunehmender Globalisierung und veränderter arbeitsorganisatorischer Bedingungen erwarten?', *ZAF* 2 and 3 (2005); J.T. Addison and P. Teixeira, 'The Effect of Works Councils on Employment Change', 45 *Industrial Relations* 1 (2006); U. Jirjahn, 'Works councils and employment growth in German establishments', 34 *Cambridge Journal of Economics* (2010).

276 A. van den Berg, Y. Grift and A. van Witteloostuijn, 'Works Councils and Organizational Performance: The Role of Top Managers' and Works Councils' Attitudes in Bad Vis-à-vis Good Times', *Journal of Labor Research* (2011); A. van den Berg, Y. Grift and A. van Witteloostuijn, 'Managerial Perceptions of Works Councils' Effectiveness in the Netherlands', 50 *Industrial Relations* 3 (2011).

277 Cf. J.T. Addison, C. Schnabel and J. Wagner, 'Works councils in Germany: their effects on establishment performance', *Oxford Economic Papers* 53 (2001), p. 669.

reducing the number of exits, the works council positively affects the labour fluctuation in undertakings.[278]

Moreover, some studies have reported that works councils are contributing to an increased internal flexibility of the workforce.[279] Works councils can engage in consultations with the management in order to prevent forced redundancies in exchange for a greater flexibility of the staff regarding replacement within the undertaking and to participate in training to become suitable for such new placements. Such internal relocation mechanisms generate "win-win" outcomes for both the employees – due to an avoidance of dismissals – as well as for the undertaking, which can adjust the production of the undertaking more flexibly and without the need for (often costly) dismissals. Such "work to work (mobility) arrangements" [*van werk naar werk trajecten*] are also reflected in the recently amended Dutch Labour Code (*Wet Werk en Zekerheid, WWZ*).[280]

Finally, the co-determination rights of the works council (article 27 of the WCA) allow the works council to incorporate employees' preferences regarding working conditions, which thereby increases the loyalty of the workforce due to an elevated level of inclusion of employee interests.[281]

2.2 *Enhanced trust*

A second factor that increases the overall productivity of the undertaking due to the presence of a works council is the enhanced trust of the workforce in the management. The management must inform and consult the works council and must obtain their consent on a number of topics pursuant to articles 25, 27 and 31-31e of the WCA.[282] Due to the involvement of the works council in the decision-making process, the management decisions become indirectly known to the employees via the works council and as such can be validated. This, in turn, increases the overall credibility and trust in the

278 *Ibid.*

279 U. Jirjahn, 'Works councils and employment growth in German establishments', 34 *Cambridge Journal of Economics* (2010), p. 480.

280 The WWZ has been applicable since 1 July 2015 and contains a duty to provide training for employees (article 7:611a of the DCC) as well as the duty to pay a "transitional or bridge compensation" (*transitievergoeding*) pursuant to article 7:673 of the DCC; *Wet van 14 juni 2014 tot wijziging van verschillende wetten in verband met de hervorming van het ontslagrecht, wijziging van de rechtspositie van flexwerkers en wijziging van verschillende wetten in verband met het aanpassen van de Werkloosheidswet, het verruimen van de openstelling van de Wet inkomensvoorziening oudere werklozen en de beperking van de toegang tot de Wet inkomensvoorziening oudere en gedeeltelijk arbeidsongeschikte werkloze werknemers (Wet werk en zekerheid)*, *Stb.* 2014, 216.

281 Cf. A. van den Berg, Y. Grift and A. van Witteloostuijn, 'Works Councils and Organizational Performance: The Role of Top Managers' and Works Councils' Attitudes in Bad Vis-à-vis Good Times', *Journal of Labor Research* (2011), p. 139.

282 See on the specific rights of the works council pursuant to the WCA, section 1.4 above.

management.[283] Furthermore, the works council can communicate the outcome of the information and consultation procedure, which then increases the acceptance of individual management decisions among the workforce.[284]

Moreover, co-determination rights (article 27 of the WCA) prevent the management from engaging in opportunistic behaviour, which serves as another pillar of trust in the management.[285]

2.3 *Greater labour productivity and incremental product innovation*

A third factor justifying the presence of works council is the increase in labour productivity, which results from the decreased labour fluctuation and the increased trust in management decisions.

The works council serves as collective voice institution and, therefore, information on inefficiencies within the undertaking can be communicated to the management via the consultation process.[286] In a study on the Dutch regime, it was reported that the more the management is willing to adopt an open attitude to the works council and involves the latter in an early stage, then the greater the productivity benefit is.[287]

This is reflected by the 2017 survey on works councils in the Netherlands (*nalevingsonderzoek*), in which 94% of the respondents indicated that their own works council serves as a valuable information channel from the work floor to the management.[288] The management, therefore, sees the works council as an important channel of communication of the day-to-day operations as well as a gauge as to the attitude of the workforce towards the management in general. Accordingly, this leads to increased productivity due to the removal of such inefficiencies. While earlier studies reported the opposite, namely a

283 The 2017 monitoring report on works councils stated that employers valued the quality of employee participation with a 7 out 10 ('good'), whereas works councils valued the participation in the consultations with a 6.3 of 10 ('just sufficient'); I. Wajon, P. Vlug and E. Enneking, 'Naleving van de Wet op de Ondernemingsraden: Stand van zaken begin 2017', p. 56.

284 Cf. A. van den Berg, Y. Grift and A. van Witteloostuijn, 'Works Councils and Organizational Performance: The Role of Top Managers' and Works Councils' Attitudes in Bad Vis-à-vis Good Times', *Journal of Labor Research* (2011), p. 138-139.

285 U. Jirjahn, 'Works councils and employment growth in German establishments', 34 *Cambridge Journal of Economics* (2010), p. 479.

286 Cf. J.T. Addison, C. Schnabel and J. Wagner, 'Works councils in Germany: their effects on establishment performance', *Oxford Economic Papers* 53 (2001), p. 671.

287 Cf. A. van den Berg, Y. Grift and A. van Witteloostuijn, 'Works Councils and Organizational Performance: The Role of Top Managers' and Works Councils' Attitudes in Bad Vis-à-vis Good Times', *Journal of Labor Research* (2011), p. 140 and 155.

288 I. Wajon, P. Vlug and E. Enneking, 'Naleving van de Wet op de Ondernemingsraden: Stand van zaken begin 2017', p. 45.

negative impact of works council presence on productivity, more recent studies come to a positive conclusion on the works council-increased productivity relationship.[289]

Furthermore, an empirical study established a linkage between works council presence and incremental innovation within a given undertaking. Due to the employees' long-term view and willingness to invest in the undertaking as a result of a higher morale of the workforce, as well as the communication thereof via the works council, this can lead to incremental product innovations.[290]

2.4 *Direct and indirect costs of employee representation*

Whereas the presence of a works council is overall associated with a positive impact on labour fluctuation, credibility of the management and greater labour productivity, a number of negative aspects are nevertheless mentioned in the literature.

The costs of the presence of the works council can be distinguished between direct costs as well as indirect costs. The direct costs thereby relate to the work of the works council as such and includes the costs of the facilities, the loss of working hours of the works council members, the costs for schooling, the costs for outside professionals assisting the works council and the litigation costs. While such costs can be substantial for smaller undertakings, the impact of these costs in MNCs is significantly smaller. The direct costs explain to a certain extent, however, the lower ratio of works councils in smaller undertakings due to the fact both the employees and the employer could agree that the added value of a works council does not outweigh the costs in such circumstances. Accordingly, the coverage by works councils in undertakings increases with the number of persons employed.[291]

The lack of know-how of works council members, the slowing down of the decision-making process by the works council and the rent-seeking behaviour resulting in higher wages of the workforce are referred to as indirect costs. These aspects will be addressed in the following paragraphs.

289 J.T. Addison, C. Schnabel and J. Wagner, 'Works councils in Germany: their effects on establishment performance', *Oxford Economic Papers* 53 (2001), p. 674; U. Jirjahn, 'Works councils and employment growth in German establishments', 34 *Cambridge Journal of Economics* (2010), p. 479.

290 U. Jirjahn and K. Kraft, 'Do Spillovers Stimulate Incremental or Drastic Product Innovations? Evidence from German Establishment Data', 73 *Oxford Bulletin of Economics and Statistics* 4 (2011).

291 Cf. J.T. Addison, C. Schnabel and J. Wagner, 'Works councils in Germany: their effects on establishment performance', *Oxford Economic Papers* 53 (2001), p. 667.

Firstly, works councils are associated with rent-seeking behaviour.[292] The works council, as collective voice mechanism and being entrusted with far-reaching rights, could leverage higher wages in exchange for the support of (intended) management decisions. As the study by Addison (et al.) reports, wages are approximately 15% higher in undertakings that have a works council present.[293] The results, however, concerned German works councils, which are dominated by labour unions and whom routinely pressure the management to agree on higher wages in order to prevent strikes from taking place. Although German works councils have a so-called peace obligation (i.e., works councils may not strike), German works councils do not have the same dual mandate that is codified in the Dutch regime. Accordingly, van den Berg (et al.) rightly note that such rent-seeking behaviour is curtailed under the Dutch regime due to the fact that works councils are obliged to act in the interest of the undertaking as well as to protect the interests of personnel.[294] Moreover, collective bargaining is a clear competence of labour unions in the Netherlands, although works councils are to a considerable extent comprised of labour union representatives. The ties between the works councils and the unions are, however, not that strong in practice.[295]

Therefore, works councils could potentially negatively affect the performance of the undertaking by engaging in rent-seeking behaviour and thus reap the majority of the firm's profits. But such behaviour is less likely to occur under the Dutch framework. Furthermore, a difference between the private and the public sector is reported in the Dutch study that was carried out by van den Berg (et al.).[296] The authors concluded, "works councils in the private sector primarily focus on the firm's overall interest, whereas works councils in the public sector tend to be more oriented toward selfish rent-seeking behaviour".[297] Given the fact that this study concerns the position of works councils in *private* international corporations, it can be concluded that such rent-seeking behaviour that has the effect of leading to higher wages is less likely to impact on the performance of the undertaking concerned.

Secondly, a lack of know-how amongst works council members can lead to the inefficient participation of the works council in the decision-making process and, in turn,

292 *Ibid.*, p. 677; see also U. Jirjahn, 'Works councils and employment growth in German establishments', 34 *Cambridge Journal of Economics* (2010), p. 480.

293 *Ibid.*

294 A. van den Berg, Y. Grift and A. van Witteloostuijn, 'Works Councils and Organizational Performance: The Role of Top Managers' and Works Councils' Attitudes in Bad Vis-à-vis Good Times', *Journal of Labor Research* (2011), p. 139.

295 A. van den Berg, Y. Grift and A. van Witteloostuijn, 'Managerial Perceptions of Works Councils' Effectiveness in the Netherlands', 50 *Industrial Relations* 3 (2011), p. 499.

296 A. van den Berg, Y. Grift and A. van Witteloostuijn, 'Works Councils and Organizational Performance: The Role of Top Managers' and Works Councils' Attitudes in Bad Vis-à-vis Good Times', *Journal of Labor Research* (2011), p. 155.

297 *Ibid.*

this could have the effect of decreasing the added value of the works council within the undertaking. The access and usage of schooling is very important to remedy such potential shortcomings.

Finally, the works council is perceived to slow down the decision-making process. Particularly with regard to MNCs, this factor can have a significant influence on the perceived added value of the works council due to the fact that the timing and uniform implementation of decisions within international corporations is very important. Due to the delayed implementation of an (intended) decision in case of negative advice rendered by the works council for a period of one month,[298] the works council can significantly delay the decision-making process. The question then arises as to whether the delaying of the decision-making process by the works council *actually* hampers the economic position of the undertaking.

Contrary to the assumed negative impact of a delay in the decision-making process, van den Berg (et al.) found that the opposite effect can be measured.[299] The economic position is negatively affected by 1.8%, if the works council is *not* delaying the decision-making process in good economic times, whereas the economic position is negatively affected by 0.8%, if the works council is delaying the process in times of economic turmoil.[300] In light of these results, it can be concluded that the works council improves the outcome of the consultation process by following a more diligent procedural approach in prosperous times. Therefore, the consultation process serves as a quality assurance mechanism that increases the economic performance of the undertaking. This was also reflected in the most recent survey on the added value of the works council in the Netherlands, which reported that the works council is considered to be an additional quality check for (intended) management decisions by 68% of the respondents.[301]

2.5 *Concluding remarks*

The previous section outlined the added value of works councils in order to highlight the beneficial impact of such a collective voice mechanism on the economic performance of the undertaking.

298 Article 25(6) of the WCA.

299 A. van den Berg, Y. Grift and A. van Witteloostuijn, 'Works Councils and Organizational Performance: The Role of Top Managers' and Works Councils' Attitudes in Bad Vis-à-vis Good Times', p. 151.

300 Van den Berg et al. differentiate between good economic circumstances and bad times, in which reorganisations and/or collective redundancies are effectuated; *ibid.*, p. 137.

301 Regioplan, 'Nalevingsonderzoek van de Wet op de Ondernemingsraden 2011', p. 23.

Whereas a democratic rights approach was chosen in section 1.3 by holding that the right to employee participation is a fundamental right of every employee, an efficiency approach was chosen in this section. While the efficiency of works councils can be questioned given the fact that these are not voluntary established by the liberal market, a number of indicators were brought forward to highlight that the opposite seems to be the case.

Due to the reported decrease in labour fluctuation as well as the increased trust of the workforce in the management (decisions) due to the presence of a works council, the performance of undertakings is positively affected. This in turn is reported to foster incremental product innovation, which is also beneficial for undertakings.

Furthermore, a cooperative approach to consultation between the management and the works council has a positive effect on the undertaking's economic performance.[302] Strikingly, works councils are able to positively affect the economic position when they delay the decision-making process in good times and thus monitor and safeguard the quality of the (intended) decisions that are to be made.

At the same time, the rent-seeking behaviour of works councils negatively affects the economic position of undertakings and must be obviated. Under the Dutch regime, such rent-seeking behaviour is curtailed by the dual mandate of works councils, which includes the duty to act in the interest of the undertaking in addition to representing the interest of employees. The economic position, finally, largely depends on the stance that the management adopts with regard to the works council and whether or not the council is informed at an early stage.[303]

3 Multinational corporations: conceptualisation and analysis of specific characteristics

After having introduced the notion of the Dutch works council in the first part of this study, the second crucial element, namely the multinational corporation in which the works council is established, will be introduced in the following sections.

302 A. van den Berg, Y. Grift and A. van Witteloostuijn, 'Works Councils and Organizational Performance: The Role of Top Managers' and Works Councils' Attitudes in Bad Vis-à-vis Good Times', *Journal of Labor Research* (2011), p. 152.

303 The findings of the Dutch study report a positive impact of 27% on the economic position if the management takes an open-minded stance towards works council involvement and 0.8% improvement once the works council is involved in an early stage; *ibid.*

3.1 *The notion of multinational corporations*

A definition of the notion of MNCs is inevitable due to the existence of a considerable number of definitions of MNCs that are currently present in the literature.[304]

The specific rights of works councils in corporations are codified in articles 25(1)(j), 31(2)(d) and (e) of the WCA as well as article 31(3) of the WCA. What is interesting to note is that no uniform terminology is used in the WCA when it comes to defining what is meant by corporations. While in article 31(3) of the WCA, the term *international group of enterprises* is used, in article 33(3) of the WCA the terminology of *a group of entrepreneurs* is applied. Furthermore, no definition of either of the two terms is provided in the WCA. Even more confusing is the fact that different terminology is used in the WCA in comparison to other laws that are applicable to MNCs. Honée concluded in a similar fashion on this matter by remarking that the terminology is not connected to the civil legislation where a group of undertakings is defined, in particular the structure regime.[305]

Even although no clear definition of the terms group of undertakings or corporation is included in the WCA and has not been added during the subsequent revisions of the Act, a definition can be found elsewhere.[306] Pursuant to article 2:24b of the Dutch Civil Code (DCC),[307] a group is defined as:

> *"A group is an economic unit in which legal persons and commercial partnerships are organizationally interconnected. Group companies are legal persons and commercial partnerships interconnected to each other in one group".*[308]

Honée further points to articles 2:153 and 2:155 of the DCC and the explanatory memorandum to these provisions, in which a group is defined as "a group of undertakings that are separate by virtue of their legal form, but that are connected to one another through shareholdings or otherwise and with the main policy decisions taken at the top management level".[309]

---

304 See for an overview A-W. Harzing, 'An Empirical Analysis and Extension of the Bartlett and Ghoshal Typology of Multinational Companies', 31 *Journal of International Business Studies* 1 (2000).

305 H.J.M.N. Honée, *Concernrecht en medezeggenschapsregelingen*, p. 96.

306 It has to be noted that the Supreme Court in *TNT* adjudicated that the notion of "a group of undertakings" within the meaning of article 33 of the WOR is to be distinguished from the definition given in article2:24b of the DCC. The definition provided here should therefore be seen as guidance and not mutatis mutandis applicable to works councils; HR 14 March 2008, *JOR* 2008/94 m.nt. M. Holtzer (*TNT*).

307 *Burgerlijk Wetboek*, BW.

308 Dutch Civil Law, 'Book 2 Legal Persons – Title 2.1 General provisions', <http://www.dutchcivillaw.com/civilcodebook022.htm> (last accessed 29 September 2017).

309 H.J.M.N. Honée, *Concernrecht en medezeggenschapsregelingen*, p. 51.

It must be noted that a distinction between different types of groups or corporations is made in the literature, but such a distinction will not be made in this study due to the fact that the differences between the different forms of corporations are not a decisive factor for the determination of the position of the works council within such networks. Moreover, the terms *corporation* and *group of undertakings* will be used interchangeably throughout the remainder of this study.[310]

For this analysis, the structure regime is taken as focal point due to the link with the works council's rights pursuant to the regime as well as the link with employee participation rights in the company group (*vennootschapsrechtelijke mede-zeggenschap*).

When examining the definition of a group of undertakings, as is codified in article 2:24b of the DCC, as well as the definition given by Honée, several crucial elements can be identified. Firstly, a group of undertakings is comprised of legal rather than natural persons, which must be either a public limited liability company [*naamloze vennootschap*, N.V.], a private limited liability company [*besloten vennootschap*, B.V.], a cooperative [*coöperatie*] or a mutual insurance society [*onderlinge waarborgmaatschappijen*] in order to fulfil the criteria of the regime applicable to large undertakings, the so-called structure regime [*structuurregime*].[311]

Foundations (*stichtingen*) can also be part of company groups, but are not further examined in this context. In the following sections, both the public limited liability company and the private limited liability company are meant when examining limited liability companies within the meaning of the structure regime.

Secondly, a minimum threshold with regard to the size of limited liability companies is applicable to companies in order to become eligible for the structure regime as laid down in articles 2:153(2)/2:263(2) of the DCC. Pursuant to this provision, at least 100 employees must be working within the Netherlands for the group of undertakings, a works council must have been established and the share capital including all reserves must amount to at least 16.000.000 EUR.[312]

Thirdly, the structure regime is aimed at groups of undertakings that are linked by means of shareholdings or is able to appoint or discharge more than half of the members of the Board of Directors or the Supervisory Board. As was noted by Honée, the legislator assumes the existence of a hierarchical structure within the group of undertakings, in

310 *Ibid.*; Honée argued against a distinction between different forms of groups of undertakings as well; at the same time, a typology of corporations can be found in the economic literature, as was addressed in the landmark publication of C.A. Bartlett and G. Sumantra. *Managing Across Borders: The Transnational Solution* (Harvard Business Press, Boston 1989); see also Y. Hadari, 'The Structure of the Private Multinational Enterprise', 71 *Michigan Law Review* 4 (1973).

311 The structure regime is further discussed in section 3.2.

312 For the threshold amount of share capital see article III of the *Wet van 9 juli 2004*, *Stb.* 2004, 370.

which a topholding with a central management and a number of subsidiaries (dependent on the topholding) as well as possible subholdings exist. A subsidiary is defined in article 2:24a(1) of the DCC as:

> "1. *A subsidiary of a legal person is:*
>   a. *a legal person in which another legal person or one or more of its subsidiaries, whether or not under a contract with other persons entitled to vote, is able to exercise, solely or jointly, more than one half of the voting rights at the General Meeting;*
>   b. *a legal person with regard to which another legal person or one or more of its subsidiaries, whether or not under a contract with other persons entitled to vote, is able to appoint or discharge, solely or jointly, more than one half of the members of the Board of Directors or the Supervisory Board, even if all persons entitled to vote would cast their vote.*
>
> 2. *With a subsidiary is equated a commercial partnership acting in its own name in which the legal person or one or more of its subsidiaries participate as a partner who is fully liable towards the creditors of that commercial partnership for all debts.*
> 3. *For the purpose of paragraph 1, rights attached to shares shall not be linked to a person who holds these shares on behalf of someone else. Rights attached to shares shall be linked to the person on whose behalf these shares are held, if this person has the power to decide how these rights are to be exercised or if he has the power to acquire these shares.*
> 4. *For the purpose of paragraph 1, voting rights attached to pledged shares are linked to the pledgee (holder of the pledge) if he has the power to decide how these rights are to be exercised. If the shares, however, are encumbered with a pledge as security for a loan which the pledgee has provided in the ordinary course of his business, then the voting rights shall only be linked to him if he has exercised them in his own interest.*"[313]

A subsidiary is, therefore, defined as a company, of which half the shares are directly or indirectly via another (holding) company, held by another legal person and which can appoint or discharge the management of the company. These criteria can be further regarded as decisive factors for determining the notion of dependency within a group of undertakings.

313 Dutch Civil Law, 'Book 2 Legal Persons – Title 2.1 General provisions', <http://www.dutchcivillaw.com/civilcodebook022.htm> (last accessed 29 January 2018).

At the European level, particularly in the European Works Council Directive[314] (hereinafter: EWC-Directive) as was transposed into the European Works Council Act [*Wet op de Europese Ondernemingsraden*, WEOR] (hereinafter: EWCA), a similar definition for 'controlling undertakings' in groups of undertakings is applied. As is laid down in article 3 of the EWC-Directive, a controlling undertaking "can exercise a dominant influence over another undertaking (the controlled undertaking) by virtue, for example, of ownership, financial participation or the rules which govern it".[315]

Such dominance can be exercised by either holding or controlling a majority of the share capital or being in a position to appoint more than half of the members of management of the undertaking.[316]

For this study, the definition pursuant to article 2:24a of the DCC is taken as point of departure.

3.2 *The structure regime*

Before turning to the position of the works council in 'large' undertakings under Dutch law, one must briefly introduce the law stipulating the rules applicable to statutory two-tier entities, the so-called structure regime of 1971 [*structuurregeling*] and the recast of the law that took place in 2004.[317]

The Dutch structure regime is unique when compared to the legal system applied to large undertakings in Europe and with regard to the position of shareholders and employees, although board level representation exists in a number of other European jurisdictions.[318] In the following sections, the rationale behind establishing such a regime and the development thereof will be briefly outlined in order to be able to place the role of the Dutch works council into perspective. A detailed analysis of the position of the shareholders as well as of the supervisory and management board will not be made and reference can be made to the large volume of literature that is available on this topic.[319]

314 Directive 2009/38/EC of the European Parliament and of the Council of 6 May 2009 on the establishment of a European Works Council or a procedure in Community-scale undertakings and Community-scale groups of undertakings for the purposes of informing and consulting employees (Recast) [2009] OJ L 122/28.

315 *Ibid.*, article 3(1) of Directive 2009/38/EC.

316 *Ibid.*, article 3(2) of Directive 2009/38/EC.

317 *Wet van 6 mei 1971, Stb.* 1971, 289 (*Structuurwet*); the structure regime also applies to one-tier companies with article 2:164a (1) of the DCC stipulating that "what is provided in Article 2:158 paragraph 2 up to and including 12, 2:159, 2:160, 2:161 and 2:161a on the Supervisory Board, respectively, on the Supervisory Directors shall then apply accordingly to the non-executive Directors of the Open Corporation". The same applies to private limited liability companies (B.V.) pursuant to article 2:274a (1) of the DCC.

318 Cf. R.H. van het Kaar, 'Medezeggenschap en internationale holdings', *Ondernemingsrecht* 33 (2009).

319 See *inter alia* P. van Schilfgaarde, *Van de BV en de NV* (16th edition, Kluwer, Deventer 2013), p. 427 et seq.; see also P. van Schilfgaarde, *Van de BV en de NV* (17th edition, Kluwer, Deventer 2017).

In the early 1970s, a discussion emerged in the Netherlands, *inter alia* at the University of Nijmegen in the person of J.M.M. Maeijer, as to whether the existing system of monitoring and control of the GM shareholders on the management of a particular undertaking was still sufficient.[320] Following the report of the Verdam committee [*Commissie-Verdam*] in 1964,[321] it was found that shareholders did not have the powers to remove the board of management of an undertaking in case of mismanagement and the current system did not allow for a sufficient inclusion of the (plurality of) interests of all the stakeholders in large undertakings.[322] Further, the report recommended that a separation of management and supervisory powers within undertakings should be established in order to maintain a balance of powers, which in turn would improve the position of the shareholders indirectly via the supervisory organ.

Following the Verdam report, consensus was also reached in the Social and Economic Council [*Sociaal-Economische Raad*, SER] in its subsequent advice, which is also referred to as "the wonder of The Hague".[323]

The law stipulating the rules applicable to statutory two-tier entities of 1971 [*structuurwet* 1971], therefore, introduced a separate legal system that would be applicable to 'large' undertakings, through which a statutory supervisory board had to be introduced and rights for shareholders and employees would be introduced with regard to the appointment of such a supervisory organ. The law was therefore based on the advice of the Social and Economic Council on the revision of the company law, which also put forward recommendations regarding the appointment procedure of the supervisory board.[324] This aspect had not been resolved in the earlier report that was published by the Verdam committee.

The law of 1971 was later incorporated into the second book of the Dutch Civil Code and is now laid down in article 2:152-164 of the DCC and articles 2:262-274 of the DCC respectively.[325]

For the application of this separate legal system, the legal status of an undertaking is irrelevant, although the regime is only applicable to Dutch legal forms of undertakings, namely public limited liability companies (N.V.) and private limited liability companies

320 Asser 2-II*, '§1 Geschiedenis en achtergronden van structuurregeling – 517 Wonder van Den Haag', p. 1.

321 See in particular Rapport-Verdam, p. 23 and 25.

322 P.A.M. Witteveen, 'De betekenis van de nieuwe structuurwet voor de positie van de ondernemingsraad', *Onderneming en Financiering* 68 (2005), p. 29.

323 SER Advies 1969/14, *Inzake de Herziening van het Ondernemingsrecht* [MM, on the revision of the company law].

324 *Ibid.*

325 Also articles 2:63a – 63f of the DCC with regard to large cooperative associations and mutual insurance associations.

(B.V.) as well as (to a limited extent) to large cooperative associations and mutual insurance associations.[326] A distinct set of three cumulative criteria are applied to determine whether an undertaking qualifies as a 'structure regime company':[327]

i. The undertaking must have an issued capital of at least 16 million EUR including reserves;
ii. The undertaking is required by law to have a works council either at the level of the central management or at a subsidiary level and
iii. The undertaking must employ at least 100 persons in total within the Netherlands

Once these cumulative criteria have been fulfilled, the undertaking will indicate this to the Chamber of Commerce no later than two months after drawing up its annual accounts by depositing them.[328] Once this indication of fulfilment of the three criteria is made in three consecutive years through the deposit of the annual accounts, the structure regime becomes immediately applicable to the undertaking by operation of law. What is important to note is that without depositing the annual accounts or the presence of a works council in the undertaking, the introduction of the structure regime is not possible due to the fact that the second criterion is not fulfilled. The non-compliance with the depositing of the annual accounts may be one means to circumvent the application of the structure regime. These aspects will be revisited in chapter VI.[329]

At the same time, the presence of a works council pursuant to the minimum requirement of 50 employees, as stipulated in article 2 of the WCA, is not sufficient for the application of the structure regime as such due to the higher minimum requirement of 100 employees as is stipulated in articles 2:153(2)/2:263(2) of the DCC. Temporary staff, *nota bene*, are not counted in the 100 employee threshold.[330] Once the undertaking becomes a 'structure regime company', it must appoint a supervisory board, which is entrusted with the exercise of particular powers pursuant to article 2:164/274 of the DCC. Pursuant to the Management and Supervision Act [*Wet Bestuur en Toezicht*] as applicable since the 1 January 2013,[331] a one-tier structure can also be applied by the structure regime company, resulting in the supervisory board being integrated in the monistic board of the undertaking. The powers and tasks differ depending on the degree

326 SER Advies 2001/02, The Future and Functioning of the Structure Regime, p. 7-8.
327 Article 2:153(2)/2:263(2) of the DCC; Cf. SER advise 2001/02 *The Future and Functioning of the Structure Regime*, p. 8; The threshold amount is adapted regularly, see article III of the *Wet van 9 juli 2004, Stb.* 2004, 370.
328 Cf. B.C.L. Kanen, 'De structuurregeling en adviesrecht', *ArbeidsRecht* 5 (2012), p. 23.
329 See section 3 in chapter VI.
330 R.H. van het Kaar and J.B.A. Hoyink, 'Ondernemingsraad – 3.1.1.2 Structuurvennootschappen', p. 1; see also L.G. Verburg, *Het territoir van de (Nederlandse) ondernemingsraad in het internationale bedrijfsleven*, p. 94.
331 *Wet van 6 juni 2011, Stb.* 2012, 275; see further P. van Schilfgaarde, *Van de BV en de NV* (16th edition, Kluwer, Deventer 2013), p. 165 et seq.

to which the structure regime must be applied within the undertaking as will be subsequently discussed. The law thereby foresees two modes of application, namely a *full* application and a *partial* application of the regime.

3.2.1 Full application of the structure regime

The structure regime is closely linked to the notion of a group of undertakings, as was introduced above in paragraph 3.1, which is characterised by the exercise of dominance by the central management vis-à-vis the subsidiaries.

In this regard, one has to mention the right of a parent company to give instructions to a subsidiary.[332] This aspect was introduced in the context of the notion of the German *Konzern* (which is a distinct concept from a group of undertakings insofar as it encompasses several undertakings that are nevertheless seen as a single economic entity in light of the applicable German law).[333] In such a *Konzern*, the central management can appoint or dismiss the subsidiary's management (the board of directors and the supervisory board, if applicable) and can implement a profit transfer mechanism[334] by which the subsidiary is dominated by the top-holding insofar as the subsidiary cannot determine its own financial policy and thus ultimately its own strategic policy.

Under Dutch law, such a profit transfer mechanism in groups of undertakings is possible pursuant to article 2:105/2:216 of the DCC, because the General Meeting of shareholders (hereinafter: GM) can determine the profit distribution (the so-called *uitkeringstest*) in favour of the parent company (the central management), which is the majority or sole shareholder of the subsidiary.[335] The central management thus has the power to control its subsidiaries.[336]

Because of this close interconnectedness between undertakings within a corporation, the Dutch legislator decided to allow for a distinction to be made between a *full* application of the structure regime and a *partial* application thereof, and even an exemption of some parts of the corporation in case of an application of the regime on another (sub-holding) level. A second factor alongside the interconnectedness of undertakings within a corporation is the often international character of corporations. Due to progressing

---

332 Though there is a discussion in the literature whether or not such a right to give instructions exists; in the *Castleford* case, the Enterprise Chamber ruled that a subsidiary may comply with an instruction as long as it is in line with the subsidiary's own interests; Cf. L. Timmerman, *Over multinationale ondernemingen en medezeggenschap van werknemers* (Kluwer, Deventer 1988), p. 64 et seq.

333 Cf. H.J.M.N. Honée, *Concernrecht en medezeggenschapsregelingen*, p. 51.

334 The so-called *Gewinnabführungsvertrag* or *Beherrschungsvertrag* (MM, profit transfer and controlling agreement) pursuant to § 291(1) German Stock Corporations Act (*Aktiengesetz*, AktG).

335 Cf. L. Timmerman, *Over multinationale ondernemingen en medezeggenschap van werknemers*, p. 71.

336 See also M. Holtzer, *De invloed van werknemers op de strategie van de vennootschap*, p. 40 et seq.; and L. Timmerman, *Over multinationale ondernemingen en medezeggenschap van werknemers*, p. 67.

globalisation and the internationalisation of economic activities, corporations are no longer confined to one country's borders and they now possess a transnational or multinational character.

The structure regime is therefore adapted to the economic environment in which corporations are operating within and even allow for an exemption from the application of the regime for the international top-holding of corporations (the so-called *vrijstelling*) as was discussed in section 3.2.2. Further to this, only a partial application of the regime is necessary at the sub-holding level for corporations, and subsequent subsidiaries of the sub-holding are also exempted from the application thereof (section 3.2.3). The legal prerequisites will be discussed in the following paragraphs.

Once the three cumulative criteria of the structure regime are fulfilled, in principle the regime is fully applied and becomes, therefore, the norm. Derogations from the norm are only possible once specific criteria have been fulfilled. This aspect will be addressed subsequently with regard to the partial application of the regime.

The works council may file an action to obtain interim measures based on the grounds of a failure by the entrepreneur to introduce the structure regime in the undertaking. This can be the case once the undertaking fulfils the cumulative criteria of the structure regime, but the management refuses to introduce the necessary motion to change the undertaking's articles of association. Moreover, the GM of shareholders may refuse to adopt the necessary changes to the articles of association. In such cases, the works council can request the decision of the GM of shareholders to be declared null and void.[337]

Under the full regime, the supervisory board may veto major management decisions such as an (intended) decision of collective redundancy and can appoint or dismiss the board of management of the undertaking. The supervisory board also signs the annual accounts of the undertaking, which are adopted by the GM of shareholders.[338]

Prior to the amendment of the structure regime in 2004, the supervisory board could also appoint its own members (the so-called 'co-option mechanism'). Therefore, the supervisory organ was, to a large extent, independent from the management organ of the undertaking and other stakeholders. After the amendment in 2004, this co-option mechanism was omitted and the right of appointment of the supervisory board now rests with the GM of shareholders under the current regime. This amendment signifies a clear development towards a stronger position of the GM vis-à-vis other stakeholders

337 R.H. van het Kaar and J.B.A. Hoyink, 'Ondernemingsraad – 3.1.1.2 structuurvenootschappen', p. 1.

338 Article 2:101(2)/210(2) of the DCC with regard to the duty of supervisory board members and paragraph 3 concerning the adoption of the accounts by the GM of shareholders.

such as the employees. This is justified by the capital risks that are borne by the shareholders and to adapt the Dutch system to the general developments regarding corporate governance.[339]

Under the regime, the shareholders may appoint the supervisory board (or non-executive board members on a one-tier board),[340] but the works council has an enhanced right of recommendation for one-third of the supervisory board members (or non-executives) and a general right of recommendation for the entire supervisory board (non-executives).[341]

By virtue of this enhanced right of recommendation, the works council can put forward recommendations for one-third of the candidates for the appointment of the supervisory board/one-tier board (but at least one), unless the board "objects to the recommendation on the basis of the expectation that the recommended person is unsuitable to perform the duties of a Supervisory Director or that the Supervisory Board will not be properly constituted if an appointment is made in accordance with the recommendation" (article 2:158(6)/2:268(6) of the DCC).[342] The works council has, pursuant to the structure regime, therefore an important mechanism to influence the appointment of the undertaking's supervisory organ. The supervisory board can serve as an important source of information on the strategic developments within the corporation. The works council can, furthermore, put forward its position on topics under discussion in meetings with the supervisory board, which then serves as second consultation channel alongside the regular consultations with the management board. In addition, the supervisory board members can have a mediating role in consultations between the works council and the management of the corporation. These aspects are further substantiated in the empirical section of this study.

At the same time, the law does not impose an obligation on the works council to make use of its enhanced right of recommendation and it, therefore, remains to be seen in the empirical section of this study whether such an exercise of this right occurs in practice.

339 Cf. B.C.L. Kanen, 'De structuurregeling en adviesrecht', *ArbeidsRecht* 5 (2012), p. 23.

340 The same regime also applies to one-tier boards with non-executive directors; Article 2:164a (1) of the DCC stipulates that "what is provided in Article 2:158 paragraph 2 up to and including 12, 2:159, 2:160, 2:161 and 2:161a on the Supervisory Board, respectively, on the Supervisory Directors shall then apply accordingly to the non-executive Directors of the Open Corporation". The same applies to private limited liability companies (B.V.) pursuant to article 2:274a (1) of the DCC. Where reference is made to the supervisory board members, such reference should be understood to apply *mutatis mutandis* to non-executive board members.

341 Article 2:158/268(6)-(8) of the DCC, as introduced by the Law of 9 July 2004 amending the structure regime, *Stb.* 2004, 370.

342 Dutch Civil Law, 'Book 2 Legal Persons – Section 2.4.6 The Supervisory Board of a large Open Corporation', <http://www.dutchcivillaw.com/civilcodebook022.htm> (last accessed 30 September 2017).

It must be further noted that the recommended candidates for the supervisory board – although being recommended by the works council – does not represent the employees' interests in the supervisory board due to the fact that it is his or her duty to be guided by the interests of the corporation and its affiliated enterprises in their performance thereof.[343]

The candidates that are recommended by the works council must be appointed by the GM of shareholders, unless the recommendation is rejected by the majority of the GM of shareholders, whereby the majority has to hold one-third of the issued share capital.[344]

The supervisory board can also reject the recommendation and must subsequently engage in negotiations with the works council for a period of four weeks if this is the case. The rejection of the recommendation must be justified either on the ground that the recommended person is unsuitable to perform the duties as supervisory board member or on the ground that the supervisory board would otherwise not be properly constituted.[345] If no agreement can be reached within the four-week period, the supervisory board shall request the Enterprise Chamber to pronounce the objection as well-founded. In case the Enterprise Chamber pronounces that the objection of the supervisory board is unfounded, it shall place the recommended person on the list of recommended persons. If, on the contrary, the Enterprise Chamber pronounces that the objection is well-founded, then the works council may recommend a new person to fill the role.[346] The list of candidates is subsequently presented to the GM of shareholders. Once the GM of shareholders rejects a recommended candidate, the procedure must be repeated until the candidate is accepted and appointed by the GM of shareholders.

Due to the fact that this unique system is somewhat alien to foreign investors, the full application of the regime is nuanced by the legislator in light of the investment climate of the Netherlands and the principle of legitimacy.[347] Due to the fact that the Dutch employees could potentially be granted an enhanced right of recommendation for one third of the supervisory board of a multinational corporation, this could lead to a disproportional involvement of Dutch employees compared to other employees in the undertaking. The full structure regime was therefore intended to apply only to those undertakings which are mostly economically active in the Netherlands. This also safeguards the principle of

343 Article 2:140/250(2) of the DCC.

344 Article 2:158/268(9) of the DCC; the second sentence of paragraph 9 has led to much discussion due to the quorum requirement of one-third of the share capital; see for a detailed discussion Asser/Maeijer, Van Solinge and Nieuwe Weme 2-II*, '563 Versterkt aanbevelingsrecht ondernemingsraad'.

345 Article 2:158/268(6) of the DCC.

346 *Ibid.*

347 Cf. R.H. van het Kaar, 'Medezeggenschap en internationale holdings', *Ondernemingsrecht* 33 (2009), p. 3; M. Holtzer, *De invloed van werknemers op de strategie van de vennootschap* (Kluwer, Deventer 2014), p. 74; see further SER advice 2008/01, 'Evenwichtig Ondernemingsbestuur', <https://www.ser.nl/nl/publicaties/adviezen/2000-2009/2008/b26273.aspx> (last accessed 29 September 2017), p. 8 and 24.

territoriality. Consequently, the regime foresees an exemption for 'international' undertakings and for a partial application for Dutch undertakings that form part of a mostly 'international' undertaking. In the following section, these two derogations, exemption and partial application, will be addressed in greater detail.

3.2.2 Exemption from the structure regime

A company can be exempted from the application of the structure regime under certain circumstances. Firstly, a holding company qualifies for an exemption from the regime pursuant to article 2:153(3)(b)/2:263(3)(b) of the DCC, if its activities are "restricted exclusively or almost exclusively to the management and financing of group companies and of its or their participating interests in other legal persons, provided that the employees in service of the [c]orporation and the group companies jointly in majority work outside the Netherlands".[348] What is decisive, therefore, is that the corporation is not confined to economic activities within the Netherlands, but rather the majority of the activities are taking place outside the Netherlands, as well as the fact that the majority of the workforce must be working in a foreign country. Hence, more than half of the corporate activities, both in terms of transactions and workforce, must be located outside of the Netherlands for the top-holding to become exempted from the structure regime.

Once the criteria are fulfilled, the holding company is no longer obliged to maintain a supervisory board – according to Dutch law – and is under no obligation to take the recommendations of the works council with regard to supervisory board members on this holding level into account. This restriction of the structure regime must be welcomed insofar as a transnational application of Dutch law in case of foreign holding companies, namely the structure regime and consequently the WCA, could have unforeseen and undesirable consequences in terms of legitimacy and legal certainty. A transnational application of Dutch law would lead to the extraterritorial application of Dutch law in a foreign country, whose sovereignty would be infringed by such an application and, in turn, it would question the very legitimacy of the regime. Moreover, such an application would lead to legal uncertainty for foreign corporations due to the unforeseeable consequences of such an (unlawful) application of Dutch law and would ultimately result in a negative impact on the investment climate in the Netherlands. Foreign corporations are therefore to be excluded from the application of the regime.

348 Dutch Civil Law, 'Book 2 Legal Persons – Section 2.4.6 The Supervisory Board of a large Open Corporation', <http://www.dutchcivillaw.com/civilcodebook022.htm> (last accessed 29 September 2017); the current wording was introduced by the Law of 8 April 1976, *Stb.* 1976, 228 and 229, on the introduction of Book 2 of the Dutch Civil Code [*Wet van 8 april 1976*]; the term 'group companies' was inserted in the provision pursuant to the Law of 7 December 1983, *Stb.* 1983, 663 [*Wet van 7 december 1983*]; to incorporate the changes pursuant to the Fourth Company Law Directive, Fourth Council Directive 78/660/EEC of 25 July 1978 based on Article 54 (3) (g) of the Treaty on the annual accounts of certain types of companies [1978] OJ L 222.

By way of contrast, however, one can note that the European legislation applicable to the SE and SCE as well as the European works council does not differentiate between the (international) top-holding and the respective subsidiaries.[349] Neither does the legislation in other European countries, which have a similar system of employee participation, such as the German or Swedish model, differentiate between the holdings within corporations.[350]

A second possibility for exemption from the regime (aside from holding companies) applies to undertakings that are only tasked with the exercise of financing activities of a group of undertakings. These holdings hold the shares in the undertakings of the group and finance the group's activities.[351]

Thirdly, all the dependent companies of an undertaking, in which the structure regime is applied, are exempted from the application of the regime pursuant to article 2:153/263(3)(a) of the DCC. The adoption of this exemption stems from the rationale that a uniform corporate strategy can no longer be applied by MNCs once an application of the structure regime at the level of the dependent companies takes places, which would lead to a restriction of the shareholder's rights and thus the top-holdings rights of instruction.[352] Furthermore, an exercise of the employee participation rights is safeguarded on the basis of the rights stemming from the application of the regime on the level of the controlling undertaking, for which the structure regime applies.

The works councils of the dependent undertakings can thereby exercise their enhanced right of recommendation for the appointment of the supervisory board by virtue of article 2:158/268(11) of the DCC. This right of enhanced recommendation for the supervisory board of the controlling undertaking can therefore be regarded as compensation for the exemption from the regime of the undertaking, for which the works council is maintained.[353] The recommendation rights of the works council for the supervisory board are *separately* exercised by each individual works council, which means that the works councils concerned have to agree on a person that they would like to recommend.[354] If, however, a central works council is maintained for the corporation, then the rights are transferred to this central works council and the individual works councils are no longer able to exercise their rights with regard to the adoption of the profile and appointment of the supervisory board member.[355]

349 Cf. R.H. van het Kaar, 'Medezeggenschap en internationale holdings', *Ondernemingsrecht* 33 (2009), p. 9.
350 *Ibid.*
351 Article 2:153/263(3)(b) of the DCC.
352 Asser 2-II*, '545 Volledige vrijstelling voor afhankelijke maatschappij'.
353 *Ibid.*
354 Article 2:158/268(11) of the DCC, second sentence.
355 *Ibid.*, last sentence.

The supervisory board of the controlling undertaking then also consequently fulfils its supervisory role with regard to the subsidiaries.[356]

Finally, a joint venture is exempted from the regime in the event when two or more legal persons represent more than half of the issued capital.[357]

Another possibility to avoid the applicability of the Dutch structure regime is to convert the Dutch undertaking into an SE before fulfilling the cumulative criteria of the regime. Pursuant to the 'before and after' principle,[358] a company can 'freeze' the status quo by converting into an SE, because the regime only foresees a transposition of rights and duties at the moment of conversion and does no longer fall under the national regime after the conversion. This could lead to a situation whereby an undertaking that fulfils the cumulative criteria for the application of the structure regime is nevertheless under no obligation to adopt the structure regime in its articles of association.[359]

3.2.3 Partial application of the structure regime

Once a top-holding is exempted from the application of the regime, the structure regime must be applied at the subsidiary level within a corporation in order to safeguard the rights and obligations for the Dutch activities of the corporation. In most cases, an application of the regime takes place at the level of the Dutch sub-holding, which acts as a coordinating or an umbrella entity for all Dutch subsidiaries.[360] At the sub-holding level, however, only a partial application of the regime is mandatory pursuant to article 2:155/2:265 and article 2:155a/265a of the DCC, once the majority of the corporation's activities take place abroad (i.e., the majority of the workforce is employed abroad).

In order to separate the Dutch activities of the corporation from the international activities, a Dutch sub-holding is then inserted into the corporate group in order to apply the partial structure regime. The top-holding subsequently transfers its shares in the Dutch activities to the Dutch sub-holding, which then assumes a position between the

356 Although article 2:140/250(2) of the DCC does not refer to subsidiaries of the undertakings, the supervisory board controls whether the corporate strategy (and indirectly the strategy applied to the subsidiaries) is in line with the statutes of the undertaking; cf. Asser 2-II*, '545 Volledige vrijstelling voor afhankelijke maatschappij'; see also SER advice 1984/06, 'Advies raden van commissarissen van structuurvennootschappen', p. 72 et seq.

357 Article 2:153/263(3)(d) of the DCC.

358 Article 7(2), Part 3 of the Annex and Recital 18 of the Preamble to Council Directive 2001/86/EC of 8 October 2001 supplementing the Statute for a European company with regard to the involvement of employees [2001] OJ L 294/22.

359 See further R. van het Kaar, 'SEs in the Netherlands', in J. Cremers, M. Stollt and S. Vitols (eds.), *A decade of experience with the European Company* (ETUI, Brussels 2013), p. 147 et seq.

360 Cf. R.H. van het Kaar and E. Smit (eds.), 'Vier scenario's voor de toekomst van de medezeggenschap – Een onderzoek in opdracht van het Ministerie van SZW', p. 147; see paragraph 3.2.4 below for a detailed analysis.

top-holding and the Dutch undertakings of the MNC. In the literature, this insertion of a new management layer is often referred to as the "Netherlands construction" due to the unique system that exists under the structure regime, which allows an exemption of the top-holding as well as a partial application of the structure regime at the level of the sub-holding in combination with the exemption for dependent undertakings.[361]

The central works council is then established at the level of the corporation's Dutch sub-holding pursuant to article 33(3) of the WCA. This construction is frequently applied in multinational corporations, and was confirmed by the 55,6% of the survey respondents.[362] The construction is *nota bene* applied by both multinational corporations of Dutch origin as well as by foreign (i.e., non-Dutch) multinationals.[363]

The construction is applied due to the fact that it is possible to detach the top-holding from the Dutch undertakings and thereby free the top-holding from their obligations under the Dutch employee participation system, such as the obligation to attend consultation meetings[364] and to prevent the Dutch central works council from gaining consultation rights on issues that concern decisions outside of the Netherlands and thus outside the scope of the WCA and the structure regime. Due to the fact that the principle of territoriality is not applicable to the granting of substantial credit to or giving security for substantial debts of another undertaking pursuant to article 25(1)(j) of the WCA, the Netherlands construction further serves as a means of excluding the Dutch employee participation mechanism from such decisions insofar as they concern investments that exist outside the Netherlands.[365]

In the *Douwe Egberts* case, the Enterprise Chamber held that international corporations are permitted to adjust their corporate structure in order to reflect the international character of the corporation.[366]

In cases which concern a multinational corporation of Dutch origin, this is sometimes referred to as the 'push down' or 'degradation'[367] of employee participation.

361 See inter alia L.G. Verburg, *Het territoir van de (Nederlandse) ondernemingsraad in het internationale bedrijfsleven*, p. 305 et seq.; I. Zaal, *De rijkwijdte van medezeggenschap*, p. 181 et seq.; M. Holtzer, *De invloed van werknemers op de strategie van de vennootschap*, p. 136; SER Advies 1992/07, p. 53 – 57;
362 See figure 3.1 in section 3.1 of chapter IV.
363 The sub-holding structure is applied in 46,9% of the responding Dutch MNCs and in 68,2% of the responding foreign MNCs; see figure 3.1 in section 3.1 of chapter IV.
364 Pursuant to article 24(2) of the WCA.
365 Cf. L.G. Verburg, *Het territoir van de (Nederlandse) ondernemingsraad in het internationale bedrijfsleven*, p. 307.
366 OK 16 February 1989, *NJ* 1990/693 (*Douwe Egberts*).
367 Amsterdam Court of Appeal (Preliminary Relief Court) 26 July 2012, *TRA* 2012/100 (*ING*), p. 2.

A further reason for the insertion of a Dutch holding was the limitation of access to information of the Dutch works council, due to the fact that the duty to provide information was limited to the *own* enterprise or entrepreneur respectively.[368] By virtue of the amendment to the WCA, which took effect from 19 July 2013 onwards, a duty to provide information with regard to ownership and control relations within MNCs is now incorporated within the framework of the WCA.[369] This amendment was incorporated after a debate in the Second Chamber after the closure of the research division of Abbott in Weesp was made public.[370] It must be noted, however, that the initial proposal by the Member of the Second Chamber, Hamer, foresaw more extensive rights for works councils in international corporations. The adopted provision does not therefore reflect the objective as formulated by Hamer, namely the attempt to include the works council more intensively in the process of take-overs, mergers, demergers or relocations within international companies.[371]

Under the partial regime, the supervisory board has the same powers as would be the case under the full regime with the exception of the appointment or dismissal of the management board.[372] The right of appointment or dismissal of the board of management rests, under the partial regime, with the GM of shareholders.

Furthermore, all undertakings that are dependent on the sub-holding, to which the regime partially applies, are exempted from the application of the regime pursuant to articles 2:153(3)(a)/2:263(3)(a) of the DCC, due to the fact that it is already applied at a higher level within the corporation. The legislator did not deem it necessary to apply the regime on multiple levels within a corporation. It was deemed sufficient that the appointment of the supervisory board can be influenced by local works councils via the central works council the level of the sub-holding company.

The dependence of an undertaking on the holding is established as soon as more than half of the share capital is held by the sub-holding (2:152/262 of the DCC).

The supervisory board continues, under the partial regime, to be able to veto major management decisions pursuant to article 2:164/274 of the DCC, but it can neither appoint nor

368 Cf. L.G. Verburg, *Het territoir van de (Nederlandse) ondernemingsraad in het internationale bedrijfsleven*, p. 307.

369 *Wet van 26 juni 2013 tot aanpassing van de Wet op de ondernemingsraden in verband met wijziging van de financiering van het scholingssysteem voor leden van de ondernemingsraad en enkele andere wijzigingen van deze wet, Stb.* 2013, 296 [MM, Law of 26 June 2013 amending the WCA on the matter of financing of the training system for members of the works council and some other modifications of this law].

370 Tweede Kamer der Staten-Generaal, 'Onderzoeksafdeling Abbott', <https://zoek.officielebekendmakingen.nl/h-tk-20102011-9-57.html> (last accessed 29 September 2017).

371 Motie van lid Hamer, *Kamerstukken II 2010/11*, 29544, 264.

372 Cf. Asser 2-II*, '542 Uitzonderingen op toepasselijkheid van de structuurregeling'.

dismiss the board of management of the undertaking.[373] The veto, however, only extends to management decisions of the subholding, which is therefore considerably limited since no decisions of the topholding fall under the veto right of the subholding's supervisory board. International corporations with subsidiaries in the Netherlands, therefore, have the freedom to appoint the management of the Dutch holding and thus exert a dominant influence over the strategy of the corporation's Dutch subsidiaries without the involvement of the works council via its recommendation rights for the supervisory board. The position of the works council in international organisations was diminished by virtue of the amendment to the structure regime in 2004.

As a result of the 2004 amendment, the GM of shareholders gained the right to appoint the supervisory board of an undertaking as well as the right to collectively dismiss the supervisory board. In multinational organisations, this has led to a significant change in the power balance with regard to the influence on the composition of the supervisory board. This was the case because under the old regime the supervisory board could appoint its own members (the co-option mechanism) with a right of recommendation for the works council as well as for the GM of shareholders (and thus the parent company in a MNC). This mechanism was omitted from the scope of the new regime. Now, the parent company is able, via the GM of shareholders, to appoint the supervisory board and can, moreover, set aside the recommendations of the works council for two-thirds of the members of the supervisory board without the possibility for the works council to appeal this decision. For the one-third for which the works council has an enhanced right of recommendation, the parent company can reject the recommendations of the works council, but the works council can recommend (an)other candidate(s).[374]

If a parent company wants to exert influence over a subsidiary, the works council is, under the new regime, not in a significant position to influence the appointment of the supervisory organ.

Moreover, the works council has since lost its right of objection [*bezwaarrecht*] against the undertaking's board. The GM of shareholders has equally lost this right of objection. The GM of shareholders may, however, express that it has lost its confidence in the supervisory board,[375] which may result in the immediate removal (dismissal) of all members of the supervisory board.[376] The majority shareholder, which is almost always the parent company in corporate groups, can thus still exercise considerable influence on the management of the subsidiary. It can then be expected that the candidates for the supervisory

373 Articles 2:155/265 and 2:155a/265a of the DCC with regard to the appointment and dismissal of the board of management and article 2:153/263(3) of the DCC with regard to the annual accounts.

374 Cf. P.A.M. Witteveen, 'De betekenis van de nieuwe structuurwet voor de positie van de ondernemingsraad', p. 30.

375 Article 2:161a/171a(1) of the DCC.

376 Article 2:161a/171a(3) of the DCC.

board, following the negative vote of confidence, are appointed in line with the interests of the GM of shareholders and thus the corporation.[377]

In exchange for the loss of this right of objection and in light of the increased powers of the GM, the works councils received the right of enhanced recommendation for one-third of the candidates of the supervisory board.[378]

The supervisory board of a Dutch subsidiary can be further influenced by the parent company by means of a placement of members of the central management in the supervisory organ. While Dutch law precludes employees of an undertaking or of a dependent subsidiary of the undertaking or trade union officials from being appointed as supervisory board members,[379] the law does not preclude the appointment of managers from a parent company.[380]

While it was disputed whether the appointment of a parent company representative is contrary to the notion of independence of the supervisory board, the Enterprise Chamber has ruled that, in principle, such an appointment of a member of the parent company's management is not contrary to the aforementioned independence rule.[381] The independence of the supervisory board thereby derives from article 2:140(2)/250(2) of the DCC, which stipulates "[i]n the performance of their duties the Supervisory Directors (members of the Supervisory Board) shall be guided by the interests of the Corporation and its affiliated enterprise".[382]

A second question in this regard is whether the *majority* of the supervisory board may be comprised of representatives of the parent company.[383] In the *Cyanamid* case, the works council made use of the (then) right of objection due to the fact that two concerned

377 The candidates are temporarily appointed by the Enterprise Chamber upon request of the board of directors pursuant to article 2:161a/171a(3) of the DCC; Cf. J.J.M. van Mierlo, *Medezeggenschap en de spanning tussen WOR en ondernemingsrecht* (Kluwer, Deventer 2013), p. 239.

378 Article 2:158/268(6) of the DCC.

379 Articles 2:140/250(5) concerning the exercise of voting rights in case of a conflict of interests; and the composition of the supervisory board pursuant to article 2:63h (cooperatives or mutual insurance societies) and 2:160/270 of the DCC (public and private limited liability companies).

380 Cf. S.M. Bartman and A.F.M. Dorresteijn, *Van het concern* (8th edition, Kluwer, Deventer 2013), p. 152; see also S.M. Bartman, A.F.M. Dorresteijn and M. Olaerts, *Van het concern* (9th edition, Kluwer, Deventer 2016).

381 OK 11 April 1991, *ROR* 1991/21 (*REGEV*); see also J.M.M. Maeijer, G. van Solinge and M.P. Nieuwe Weme, 'Asser 2-II* De naamloze en besloten vennootschap, 509 Onafhankelijkheid van commissarissen'.

382 Dutch Civil Law, 'Book 2 Legal Persons – Section 2.4.5 The Board of Directors of an Open Corporation and the supervision of the Board of Directors', <http://www.dutchcivillaw.com/civilcodebook022.htm> (last accessed 29 September 2017).

383 See also section 3 in chapter VI in which it is concluded in light of the empirical analysis of this study as well as the recent jurisprudence of the Enterprise Chamber, that such majority representation should not be permitted.

representatives were nominated for two vacancies on the supervisory board of the Dutch subsidiary, notwithstanding the fact that they were not living in the Netherlands, had no proficiency of the Dutch language and possessed no knowledge of the socio-economic environment in the Netherlands.[384] The Social and Economic Council, which was until 1987 competent to adjudicate such cases, declared the nominations as unlawful due to the fact that the composition of the supervisory board would otherwise be considered unreasonable.[385]

In a second case, *Kodak*, the Enterprise Chamber further held that the supervisory board must be "*sufficiently independent from the parent company*".[386] At the same time, the court held that the mere fact that a supervisory board member is also the representative of another undertaking within the MNC does not, as such, constitute an interference with the duty of independence of supervisory board members.[387] As Bartman and Dorrestijn correctly note, international corporations are therefore permitted to apply a uniform corporate strategy and that this does not cause any threat to the independence of the supervisory organs of the Dutch subsidiaries.[388] The recent *TCN* case has shown that a majority of corporate representatives on the board of the Dutch subsidiary are not permitted unless it is sufficiently motivated. The quantitative results in section 4 of chapter IV show that a large corporate representation on the supervisory board of Dutch subsidiaries is present in practice. The implications of the *TCN* case on these practices is also further discussed in section 3 of chapter VI and will therefore not be discussed in any further detail here.

For corporations that are listed on the stock exchange, however, the requirements are somewhat more stringent pursuant to principle 2.1.7 of the CGC 2016, which stipulates that "[t]*he composition of the supervisory board is such that the members are able to operate independently and critically vis-à-vis one another, the management board, and any particular interests involved*".[389] This principle must be applied by listed companies and derogations must be motivated pursuant to the 'comply-or-explain principle'.

It can therefore be concluded that the position of the works council in foreign corporations, through means of institutionalised employee participation, namely through a right of recommendation and right of formal complaint, is significantly weakened due

384 SER 27 September 1983, *ROR* 1971–1984/146 (*Cyanamid*).

385 "*Dit complex van omstandigheden maakt dat de RvC niet naar behoren zal zijn samengesteld*"; SER 27 September 1983, *ROR* 1971–1984/146 (*Cyanamid*); this rule is also laid down in article 2:158/268(6) of the DCC.

386 OK 2 February 1989, *NJ* 1990/86 (*Kodak*).

387 *Ibid.*, para. 3.6 and 3.12.

388 S.M. Bartman and A.F.M. Dorresteijn, *Van het concern* (8th edition, Kluwer, Deventer 2013), p. 153.

389 Monitoring Committee Corporate Governance Code, 'Dutch corporate governance code – Principle 2.1.7 Independence of the supervisory board', <http://www.mccg.nl/?page=4738> (last accessed 30 September 2017).

to the derogations under the structure regime and this difficult position has become even more critical since 2004. It remains to be seen in the empirical section of this study whether the works council is actually making use of its enhanced right of recommendation for one-third of the candidates for the supervisory board and whether or not the parent company is indeed exerting increased influence over its subsidiaries in light of the amendments to the structure regime that took place in 2004.

3.2.4 Voluntary application of the structure regime

While the structure regime must be applied by 'large' undertakings once the undertaking fulfils the three cumulative criteria that are laid down in article 2:153/263(2) of the DCC, article 2:157/267 of the DCC also permits the voluntary application of the regime. The regime can be fully or partially applied, on the one hand, by undertakings that do not fulfil the criteria for the regime or, on the other hand, fully applied by undertakings that are legally bound to apply the partial regime. The voluntary application can also be made in order to reduce the three-year waiting period before the mandatory application of the regime or the application of the regime once the criteria laid down in article 2:153/263(2) of the DCC cease to be fulfilled.

After the introduction of the structure regime in 1971, the voluntary application of the regime was predominantly used as protective measure against take-overs due to the fact that the supervisory board was entrusted with tasks that otherwise rested with the GM of shareholders in non-structure regime companies. Approximately 40% of the listed structure regime companies applied the regime on a voluntary basis, but this percentage has significantly reduced in recent years.[390]

For the application of the structure regime on a voluntary basis, a works council must nevertheless be maintained within the concerned undertaking. The other criteria that must be fulfilled are laid down in the statutes of the undertaking and for a voluntary application of the regime are the presence of (i) the rules applicable to the appointment of the supervisory board[391] and (ii) the rules concerning resolutions that need the approval of the supervisory board.[392]

Furthermore, the (intended) decision to voluntarily apply the structure regime requires the prior consultation of the works council pursuant to article 25(1)(e) of the WCA, due to the fact that a significant change of the organisational structure takes place. Moreover, a change in the undertaking's statutes is necessary, which must be adopted by the GM

390 Asser 2-II*, '534 Vrijwillige toepassing structuurregime; algemeen'.
391 Article 2:158/268 of the DCC.
392 Article 2:164/274 of the DCC.

of shareholders.[393] This question was addressed in the *Heuga* case,[394] which is further examined in section 4.2 with regard to attribution of decisions and co-entrepreneurship. These aspects are left aside here.

In the case at hand, a voluntary application of the structure regime took place at the level of the Dutch sub-holding pursuant to the so-called "Netherlands-construction". The sole shareholder, Heuga Holding, decided to abolish the application of the structure regime. The works council appealed against this (intended) decision before the Enterprise Chamber and subsequently in cassation before the Dutch Supreme Court on the grounds that such an (intended) decision of the GM of shareholders constituted a decision within the meaning of article 25 of the WCA, which requires the prior consultation of the works council.

The structure regime, as it existed in 1971, stipulated that consultation rights arise with regard to the management board decision to recommend a change of the application (or discontinuation of) the structure regime to the GM, the courts in the *Heuga* case explicitly adjudicated that consultation rights arise with regard to the shareholder's decision to alter the undertaking's statutes. Van Schilfgaarde argues that such application of the works council's consultation rights on the shareholder decision to amend the statutes is justifiable insofar as the regime was voluntarily applied.[395]

I agree with Van Schilfgaarde that for *any* voluntary application or discontinuation of the structure regime – either fully or partially – the prior consent of the works council must be obtained due to the change of the organisational structure of the undertaking.[396] Once the regime is voluntarily applied, a significant change in the organisational structure of the undertaking takes place and as such this falls within the scope of article 25(1)(e) of the WCA. Moreover, the *Heuga* judgment shows that a decision by the GM of shareholders can be attributed to the undertaking in question and is therefore also subject to the works councils' consultation rights. Kanen's position, namely that such a decision of the GM of shareholders falls outside the scope of the WCA and is therefore to be excluded from the work councils' consultation, therefore has to be seen critically in light of the *Heuga* judgment.[397] While the point of departure is the independence of shareholder decisions pursuant to article 2:154/264(4) of the DCC, it must be concluded that, on the contrary, the work councils' consultation rights may arise once the shareholders

393 See article 2:154/264(4)-(7) of the DCC, which was introduced by the 2004 amendment of the structure regime; cf. Asser 2-II*, '534 Vrijwillige toepassing structuurregime; algemeen'.

394 HR 26 January 1994, NJ 1994/545 (*Heuga*); see a detailed analysis in L.G. Verburg, *Het territoir van de (Nederlandse) ondernemingsraad in het internationale bedrijfsleven*, p. 163 et seq.

395 P. van Schilfgaarde and J. Winter (eds.), *Van de BV en de NV* (15th edition, Kluwer, Deventer 2009), p. 440.

396 See also G.W. Wesselingh, 'Het afschaffen of beperken van het structuurregime vanwege een (gedeeltelijke) vrijstelling: adviesrecht ondernemingsraad?', *Vennootschap & Onderneming* 6 (2011).

397 B.C.L Kanen, 'De structuurregeling en adviesrecht', *Arbeidsrecht* 5 (2012), p. 25.

adopt decisions, which require prior consultation by the board of management of the undertaking for which the works council is maintained.[398] It is the consensus of the relevant authors that a board of management proposal to the GM of shareholders to apply or discontinue the structure regime is, under all circumstances, subject to the prior consultation of the works council in accordance with article 25(1)(e) WCA.[399]

For a statutory application of the regime, on the contrary, no prior works council consultation is needed due to the fact that the application of the regime is mandatory once the cumulative criteria have been fulfilled.[400]

Another possibility is the discontinuation of the voluntary regime, which is then subsequently replaced by the statutory regime. The question is whether the works council has consultation rights in such a situation. In a similar vein as with the initial application of the statutory regime, the works councils' advice has no impact with regard to situations whereby a voluntarily application of the *partial* structure regime is replaced by a statutory *full* structure regime. The full regime must be applied by the undertaking and the employee participation rights are not infringed under these circumstances.

Once, however, a *full* voluntary regime is to be replaced with a *partial* statutory regime, then a consultation of the works council must be sought due to the loss of influence it will sustain when compared to situation that existed beforehand.

3.2.5 Conclusion

While the works council has considerable consultation rights regarding the application or discontinuation of the structure regime as discussed above, it can nevertheless be concluded that the position of the works council has been weakened following the amendment of the regime in 2004.

While the works council got the enhanced right of recommendation for one-third of the supervisory board members, the GM of shareholders, under the new regime, has the possibility to appoint the other two-thirds of the supervisory board, which prior to the amendment was not the case. In MNCs, therefore, a balance of power is no longer present since the central management is now in a position to effectively influence the appointment of both boards of the subsidiary. As Witteveen correctly noted, the balance

398 See section

399 Cf. See *inter alia* P. van Schilfgaarde, *Van de BV en de NV* (16th edition, Kluwer, Deventer 2013), p. 452; B.C.L Kanen, 'De structuurregeling en adviesrecht', *Arbeidsrecht* 5 (2012), p. 24.

400 *Ibid.*

with regard to the influence of the works council vis-à-vis the shareholders is significantly altered, if not disturbed.[401]

The possibility to place the parent company representatives on the supervisory board of the undertaking further weakens the position of the works council due to the increased influence of the parent company on the subsidiary while, at the same time, no employee participation at the level of the parent-undertaking is exercised (the so-called Netherlands construction in combination with the principle of territoriality precludes an exercise at the level of the top-holding).

Moreover, the loss of the works councils' right of objection against the management board of the undertaking is not compensated in comparison with the position of the GM of shareholders.

It finally remains to be seen whether the works council actually exercises its recommendation rights, that is both the right of enhanced as well as the general right of recommendation, in order to prevent a further weakening of the councils' position. If the remaining rights of the works council are not exercised, this will consequently lead to an absence of corporate employee participation[402] overall and is thus reduced to participation based on case-by-case participation pursuant to the WCA.

4 THE CONCEPTS OF ATTRIBUTION OF AN (INTENDED) DECISION AND CO-ENTREPRENEURSHIP

The employee participation rights stemming from the Dutch legal framework, as were introduced in the previous sections, are relatively extensive and the legal framework is considered to be mature.[403] The application of the employee participation system, however, becomes increasingly difficult within the corporate structure of multinational organisations.[404] Pursuant to the principles of territoriality and legitimacy, an application of the WCA outside the Netherlands is precluded, while *decision-making power* is used within the framework as a connecting factor for the exercise of employee participation rights. Yet, the interactions of the Dutch undertakings belonging to a MNC make the application of the employee participation rights – as far as they are necessary to safeguard the rights of the Dutch employees – in an increasingly international context

401 P.A.M. Witteveen, 'De betekenis van de nieuwe structuurwet voor de positie van de ondernemingsraad', *Onderneming en Financiering* 68 (2005), p. 32.
402 The so-called *vennootschappelijke medezeggenschap.*
403 Social and Economic Council Advice 2008/01, *Evenwichtig ondernemingsbestuur.*
404 See further A.F.M. Dorresteijn, *European Corporate Law* (2nd edition, Kluwer Law International, Deventer 2009), p. 203 – 204.

necessary, while at the same time the actual decision-making power is situated outside of the Netherlands.

Whether or not and under which circumstances a Dutch works council can have consultation rights with regard to (intended) decisions taken at a higher managerial level within a MNC has therefore been the subject of a long-lasting debate in the academic literature[405] and has been addressed in several court proceedings over the last two decades.[406]

The Dutch Supreme Court and the Enterprise Chamber have formulated the concepts of attribution of an (intended) decision and co-entrepreneurship as a response to the legal tension between the exercise of employee participation rights in international corporations and the separate legal entity principle, as well as the principles of territoriality and legitimacy, which altogether preclude an extraterritorial application of the WCA and employee participation rights stemming from the so-called structure regime that was addressed in section 3.2.

In the following sections, a definition of the concepts of attribution of an (intended) decision [*toerekening*] as well as co-entrepreneurship [*medeondernemerschap*] as have been established by the Dutch Supreme Court and the Enterprise Chamber will be introduced and, in light of the existing jurisprudence, an analysis of the concepts will be made in order to establish criteria for the application of the concepts in future disputes between works councils and the corporation. Such criteria open up the possibility for Dutch works councils to potentially (re)gain a consultation right for decisions that are taken on a higher management level within a MNC and thus allows the works councils to exert a greater influence over the decision-making process. In combination with the notion that advice by the works council must be requested "at a time when it can still significantly affect the decision to be taken" (article 25(2) of the WCA), the application of the concept of attribution of an (intended) decision is of significant importance for the position of the works council, especially in multinational corporations and in particular with regard to strategic management decisions.[407]

But before turning to the examination of the criteria for the application of the principles, a definition of the concepts that are to be applied will be given.

405 See *inter alia* L.G. Verburg, *Het territoir van de (Nederlandse) ondernemingsraad in het internationale bedrijfsleven* (Kluwer, Deventer 2007), p. 153 – 190; I. Zaal, *De reikwijdte van medezeggenschap* (Kluwer, Deventer 2013), p. 157 – 159; A.G. van Solinge, *De naamloze vennootschap* (1982), p. 57; L.G. Verburg, 'Toerekening van besluitvorming en medeondernemerschap', *ArbeidsRecht* 9 (2014); P. Ingelse, 'Mede-ondernemen en concernenquête', *Tijdschrift voor Arbeid & Onderneming* 1 (2012).

406 See the case law analysis in the subsequent section.

407 See M. Holtzer, *De invloed van werknemers op de strategie van de vennootschap* (Kluwer, Deventer 2014).

4.1 *The separate legal entity principle*

The fundamental principle of a separate legal entity lies at the heart of company law, which is a universally accepted legal concept.[408] The company is thus to be seen as distinct from its members as was adjudicated in the landmark (English) judgment in *Salomon v. Salomon* in 1897.[409] The entity is thereby regarded as having a corporate veil between the company and third parties.[410] Furthermore, a separation between the company and its shareholders exists as well as a result of the so-called corporate veil.[411]

However, the separate legal entity principle is limited by virtue of the company's statutes and in turn pursuant to the doctrine of *ultra vires* based on these company statutes.[412] Therefore, once the company acts *ultra vires*, the company can no longer rely on the legal protection afforded by the separate legal entity principle and the corporate veil is therefore said to be lifted.[413]

As a starting point, the top-holding of a MNC may not, according to the separate legal entity principle, be regarded as liable for the decisions of its subsidiaries and it is therefore able to independently adopt decisions from other entities within the MNC. By virtue of the separate legal entity principle, the MNC is split up into separate legal entities and, in turn, the risk of failure of a particular activity is shifted to the single entity's creditors while the rest of the enterprise remains unaffected.[414]

Henceforth, a decision rendered by a top-holding that is situated outside of the Netherlands, may not be subject to Dutch law such as the WCA. Yet, under certain circumstances, decisions by the top-holding can be attributed to its (Dutch) subsidiary and the WCA becomes applicable to decisions of the top-holding. These concepts of attribution (*toerekening*) and co-entrepreneurship (*medeondernemerschap*) as well as the criteria necessary for their application will be examined in the following paragraphs.

408 See *inter alia* P. Ireland, I. Grigg-Spall and D. Kelly, 'The Conceptual Foundations of Modern Company Law', 14 *Journal of Law and Society* 1 (1987); M.A. Pickering, 'The Company as a separate legal entity', 31 *Modern Law Review* 5 (1968).

409 (UK) *Salomon v. Salomon & Co.* [1897] A.C. 22 at p. 32.

410 M.A. Pickering, 'The Company as a separate legal entity', 31 *Modern Law Review* 5 (1968), p. 483.

411 *Ibid.*; see also the *Forumbank* judgment in this regard whereby the Dutch Supreme Court held that the shareholders may not take decisions which fall within the competence of the board of directors of the undertaking; HR 21 January 1955, *NJ* 1959/43 (*Forumbank*).

412 Cf. M.A. Pickering, 'The Company as a separate legal entity', 31 *Modern Law Review* 5 (1968), p. 484.

413 This is also sometimes referred to as 'piercing the corporate veil' or *actio pauliana*; Cf. W.J. Slagter, *Enkele rechtsvergelijkende beschouwingen over moeder-dochterverhoudingen* (Kluwer, Deventer 1988), p. 30.

414 A. Cahn and D.C. Donald, *Comparative Company Law* (Cambridge University Press, Cambridge 2010), p. 679.

4.2 *Attribution of an (intended) decision – definition and criteria*

In light of the separate legal entity principle that was introduced above, an (intended) decision is taken by the central management independently from the subsidiary's management without any employee participation rights arising at the level of the subsidiary. Thus, once a decision is taken at a higher organisational level within a MNC, no employee participation by means of the Dutch works council is possible, although such an (intended) decision could potentially qualify for the application of the work councils' consultation rights pursuant to article 25 of the WCA. This discrepancy between (intended) decisions that are taken by the central management without the prior consultation of the works council and the consultation rights of the works council pursuant to article 25 of the WCA has led to the development of the techniques of attribution of (intended) decisions and co-entrepreneurship by the Dutch courts in order to fill this lacuna.[415]

The technique of attribution can thereby be defined as a method whereby an (intended) decision by a third party in relation to an undertaking qualifies as an (intended) decision by the entrepreneur that maintains the undertaking in question. Within groups of undertakings, the top-holding or central management qualifies as such a third party since, from the perspective of the subsidiary and against the background of the separate legal entity principle, such a top-holding maintains an independent position vis-à-vis its subsidiary.

As the Supreme Court established in the *Provincie Zuid-Holland* case,[416] the decision has to be attributed to the entrepreneur when *de facto* the (intended) decision will take its effect.[417] The attribution of an (intended) decision is therefore closely connected to the hierarchical structures that are present in MNCs.

Nonetheless, it was clearly emphasised by the Dutch Supreme Court in *Heuga* that although hierarchical structures are a likely factor for such an attribution, being part of a group of undertakings is *not* in itself grounds for an attribution of the decision made by the central management to the subsidiary's management.[418] Similarly, in *Howson Algraphy*, Advocate General van Soest concluded that neither article 24 nor article 25

415 Co-entrepreneurship will be addressed in the subsequent paragraph 4.3.

416 HR 26 January 2000, *JOR* 2000/3 (*Provincie Zuid-Holland*); the Dutch Supreme Court held that the third party has to be systematically in a position to influence, to a sufficient extent [*stelselmatig een zodanige invloed*], the decision-making of the undertaking for which the works council is maintained; see paragraph 4.3.2 below for an analysis of the case.

417 See also K. Wiersma and R.C. Moed, 'Joint ventures en medezeggenschap: een update', *Onderneming en Financiering* 3 (2013), p. 7.

418 HR 26 January 1994, *NJ* 1994/545 (*Heuga*), p. 4.

of the WCA contains a connecting factor for the automatic attribution of an (intended) decision of management organs of the top-holding to the subsidiary's management.[419]

Thus, it is accepted jurisprudence that a case-by-case assessment must take place in order to determine the influence of the central management vis-à-vis the subsidiary in order to justify an attribution of an (intended) decision to the subsidiary. Yet, a number of criteria, as stipulated by the Dutch Supreme Court and the Enterprise Chamber, can be identified and serve as framework for the establishment of an attribution of decisions within a MNC.

4.2.1 The notion of the wholly-owned subsidiary and overwhelming control

As outlined above, a number of criteria must be fulfilled in order to attribute an (intended) decision by the central management to the local management. The first criterion that can therefore be identified as a precondition is that the subsidiary, to whom the decision is to be attributed, must be wholly owned by the top-holding or any other third party within the group of undertakings, which made the (intended) decision.[420]

The characteristic of a wholly owned subsidiary is that it is at the sole control of a single shareholder, the parent company, over all the shares in the undertaking. While national laws differ with regard to the threshold of share-ownership to be reached in order to qualify for a wholly owned subsidiary, 90% of shares should be owned before it is considered sufficient to establish complete control.[421] It must be noted, however, that EU Member States are allowed to establish a higher threshold of up to a maximum of 95% for overwhelming control.

Within the Dutch legal system, the Enterprise Chamber held in the *PUEM* case that an overwhelming control of the central management is inherent, if (*i*) the province (as it was the case here) holds 99,6% of all shares, (*ii*) 6 of 10 of the members of the supervisory board are appointed by the province and (*iii*) all major management decisions are to be confirmed by the supervisory board and the general meeting of shareholders, which is the province due to the 99,6% share-ownership.[422] In addition to the first aspect of overwhelming share-ownership, the Enterprise Chamber formulated the criterion of decisive influence on the board composition and management decisions as necessary prerequisites for determining the notion of overwhelming control.

419 HR 11 July 1984, *NJ* 1985/212 (*Howson Algraphy*); see also S.M. Bartman and A.F.M. Dorrestijn, *Van het concern* (8th edition, Kluwer, Deventer 2013), p. 188; L.G. Verburg, *Het territoir van de (Nederlandse) ondernemingsraad in het internationale bedrijfsleven*, p. 154.

420 A.G. van Solinge, *De naamloze vennootschap* (1982), p. 57.

421 As is laid down in article 15 of Directive 2004/25/EC of the European Parliament and of the Council of 21 April 2004 on takeover bids [2004], OJ L 142/12.

422 Amsterdam Court of Appeal 27 July 1989, *NJ* 1990/734 (*PUEM*).

The first criterion of decisive influence is therefore fulfilled once almost all the shares of the undertaking are held by a single third-party and this third party is able to determine the decision-making process throughout *all* levels of the undertaking.

4.2.2 The (intended) decision has to be implemented in the subsidiary

The second criterion was formulated by Advocate General van Soest in *Howson Algraphy* and reiterated in the *Heuga* case by holding that an (implementing) decision must be taken by the subsidiary's management which gives effect to the (intended) decision in the subsidiary, provided that such an organ is competent to do so pursuant to the applicable law or the undertaking's statutes.[423] The (intended) decision must, therefore, be effectuated in the subsidiary. Since the (intended) decision was not yet effectuated in the subsidiary in the *Howson Algraphy* case and because only a staff meeting had taken place, the appeal by the works council was regarded as premature.[424]

In the *Heuga* case, Heuga Nederland was a wholly owned subsidiary of the holding company Interface Heuga. The dispute arose when the voluntary application of the structure regime was discontinued by the holding company.[425] The works council of the subsidiary, Heuga Nederland, appealed that decision by holding that pursuant to article 25(1)(e) of the WCA, the prior consultation of the works council was mandatory due to the fact that a major change in the organisational structure took place, which had the effect of significantly reducing the participation rights of the works council. The works council of Heuga Nederland was the only one within the Dutch subsidiaries of Interface Inc. and the Enterprise Chamber, at first instance, held that Heuga Nederland in fact only by chance maintained the works council.[426] The Dutch Supreme Court continued by reaffirming the judgment of the Enterprise Chamber by holding that the decision of the holding to discontinue the voluntary application of the structure regime has to be attributed to the entrepreneur where the (intended) decision will *de facto* take its effect, since the decision significantly affects the consultation rights of the works council at the level of the subsidiary.

The Enterprise Chamber further held in the *PUEM* case that corporate structures, for instance the usage of another holding company between the province and PUEM, do

423 HR 26 January 1994, *NJ* 1994/545 (*Heuga*), para. 2.4; see also the note by J.M.M. Maeijer in HR 11 July 1984, *NJ* 1985/212 (*Howson Algraphy*).

424 HR 11 July 1984, NJ 1985/212 (*Howson Algraphy*), para. 5; Cf. L.G. Verburg, *Het territoir van de (Nederlandse) ondernemingsraad in het internationale bedrijfsleven*, p. 159.

425 See further section 3.2 with regard to the structure regime.

426 HR 26 January 1994, *NJ* 1994/545 (*Heuga*), point III.

not preclude employee participation pursuant to the WCA since the decision can *de facto* make itself felt at the subsidiary level due to the significant impact of the decision.[427]

In other cases whereby the works council successfully invoked the concept of attribution, the (intended) decision of the third party in question had a direct effect on the Dutch undertaking in which the works council was maintained.[428] In a reverse situation, the central works council of the Dutch NS Group successfully invoked an attribution of a decision made at the level of a subsidiary of NS Group, Abellio, upwards to the management of the parent company (NS Groep NV) due to the impact on the strategy of the group as a whole.[429]

In the *Heuga* case an (intended) decision was made to abolish the voluntary application of the regime for large undertakings.[430] In the *Shell Research* case,[431] the research budget was reduced and in the *FNV Ledenservice* cases the third party intended to withdraw from the service agreement and thereby take away an overwhelming amount of the work from FNV Ledenservice.[432] Other measures, which had a considerable effect on the undertaking, were the intended redundancies in the *VNU Publitec* case and the decision not to allow the subsidiary to submit an application for a concession as at stake in the *Novio* case.[433]

4.2.3 The weighing of all interests at stake

A third criterion can be established in light of the *Nering Bögel* judgment of the Enterprise Chamber.[434] The court held that even if an undertaking is part of a corporation, it constitutes an independent legal entity and as such it must weigh the interests of the own undertaking against the corporate strategy when implementing the executory decisions of the central management.[435] The corporate strategy is then one of the factors (although an important one) to be considered by the subsidiary's management when taking a decision, but not the decisive one *per se*. Accordingly, the management of the subsidiary must

427 The Enterprise Chamber is calling such effect '*doorwerken van het besluit*' (the decision "works through"); see also S.M. Bartman and A.F.M. Dorrestijn, *Van het concern* (8th edition, Kluwer, Deventer 2013), p. 198.
428 Cf. L.C.J. Sprengers, 'Toetsing van een adviesprocedure in drie delen', 44 *Sociaal Recht* (2008), p. 6.
429 OK 3 October 2016, *JOR* 2016/333 m.nt. M. Holtzer (*Abellio*).
430 HR 26 January 1994, *NJ* 1994/545 (*Heuga*).
431 OK 02 April 1987, *NJ* 1988/382 (*Shell Research*).
432 OK 13 February 2003, *ARO* 2003/45 (*FNV Ledenservice I*) and OK 28 April 2004, *ARO* 2004/72 (*FNV Ledenservice II*).
433 OK 15 April 2004, *ARO* 2004/63 (*VNU Publitec*) and OK 10 May 2011, *ARO* 2011/92 (*Novio*).
434 OK 10 March 1994, *NJ* 1995/374 (*Nering Bögel*).
435 The Enterprise Chamber held that "*de onderneming dient bij de besluitvorming zelfstandig de betrokken belangen op redelijke wijze af te wegen*"; see also the prior judgement in *Nedlin*, OK 23 October 1997, *JAR* 1997/244 (*Nedlin*).

take into account all interests at stake when in the process of adopting the (intended) decision.

The Enterprise Chamber in *Watts Industries Netherlands* recently reiterated this criterion.[436] The Court held that when taking a decision as a subsidiary within a group of undertakings, such a decision must be taken against the background of not only the corporate strategy but also by weighing all the interests involved, particularly the employee's interests when redundancies or a discontinuation of the undertaking are imminent.

According to the works council, no such weighing of the interests at stake took place, despite the imminent discontinuation of the Dutch subsidiary and the negative effects that that would have on the employees of Watts Industries Netherlands, which were furthermore not offset by the projected returns for the corporation. Further, no research was made into possible alternative solutions to the closure of the Dutch undertaking and proposals by the works council were disregarded with the sole reason being that such proposals would not be feasible within the context of the overall strategy of the corporation. Therefore, no actual effort was made to effectuate the consultation rights of the works council in light of article 25 of the WCA. The Enterprise Chamber came to the same conclusion as the works council and held that the subsidiary's management did not independently take a decision but rather took over, without any criticism or independent consideration, an already taken decision of the central management.[437]

It was thus the top-holding's (intended) decision that was *de facto* directly implemented in the undertaking in question. According to the Enterprise Chamber, such an overwhelming dominance over the corporate strategy was unlawful in light of the employee participation rights. It is further established case law that the management of the subsidiary has a duty to implement decisions only if such an implementing decision is not too detrimental to the economic well-being of the company for which the management is appointed.[438] The subsidiary's management also has the duty to indicate to the works council during the consultation process that is has independently weighed the interests at stake.[439] Even more so, the instructions given by the central management may not endanger the economic continuity of the undertaking, for instance by means of a hive-off of the healthy assets to a newly established enterprise.[440]

436 OK 9 July 2013, *JAR* 2013/223 and *ARO* 2013/141 (*Watts Industries Netherlands*).

437 *Ibid.*, para. 3.1 and 3.8.

438 As established in the *B.A.T.*, *Hyster* and *Nedlin* cases and to which is also referred to as "Hyster-formula"; OK 23 June 1983, *NJ* 1984/571 (*Hyster*); OK 28 November 1991, *NJ* 1992/201 (*BAT*); OK 23 October 1997, *JAR* 1997/244 (*Nedlin*); see also S.M. Bartman and A.F.M. Dorrestijn, *Van het concern* (8th edition, Kluwer, Deventer 2013), p. 202-203.

439 OK 7 July 1988, *NJ* 1989/845 (*Fluke*).

440 The so-called sterfhuisconstructie; Cf. W.J. Slagter, *Enkele rechtsvergelijkende beschouwingen over moeder-dochterverhoudingen* (Kluwer, Deventer 1988), p. 115.

At the same time, the attempt of a corporation to minimise the negative impact of an (intended) decision by increasing the access of the works council to the decision-making process by means of a covenant, can be weighed in favour of the corporation.[441]

4.2.4 The notion of sufficient leeway of the subsidiary and the *effet utile* of employee participation

A fourth criterion was also formulated in the *Nering Bögel* case by the Enterprise Chamber, which held that as long as enough room for manoeuvre is given to the subsidiary, one cannot speak of undermining the consultation rights of the works council in contravention of the WCA. The fact that the management of the subsidiary has a preference to follow the decision of the central management does not thereby preclude a decision-making process at the subsidiary level and to safeguard the *effet utile* of the employee participation rights.[442]

4.2.5 The tangibility of an (intended) decision

The tangibility or concreteness of an (intended) decision can, furthermore, be identified as fifth criterion. As the Enterprise Chamber held in the *Rohm and Haas* case,[443] as long as merely general strategic plans are postulated at the level of the international holding without being able to concretely foresee the impact on the (Dutch) employment situation, then the advice of the Dutch works council does not have to be sought. As long as the management of the subsidiary retains some room for manoeuvre in order to allow the consultation of the works council to have a significant effect on the decision, an attribution of a decision to the local management is not warranted. The Enterprise Chamber found in the case at hand that such room for manoeuvre was still given and therefore did not attribute the decision of the central management to the subsidiary. The decision of the subsidiary's management not to engage in consultation with the works council was thus not regarded as manifestly unreasonable.[444]

The decision of the Enterprise Chamber is to be welcomed insofar as article 25(3) of the WCA stipulates that the "expected consequences for persons working in the enterprise and the measures proposed for dealing with such consequences" have to be submitted to the works council when its prior advice is being sought. Such reasons for an (intended) decision are thereby closely connected to the concreteness of such a decision. By adjudicating in the Rohm and Haas case that general strategic plans at an international level do not qualify for an attribution to the subsidiary's management, the Enterprise Chamber

441 OK 16 February 1989, *NJ* 1990/693 (*Douwe Egberts*).
442 Cf. S.M. Bartman and A.F.M. Dorrestijn, *Van het concern* (8th edition, Kluwer, Deventer 2013), p. 198.
443 OK 12 March 2002, *ARO* 2002/48 (*Rohm and Haas*).
444 The OK held that such a decision was '*niet kennelijk onredelijk*'.

therefore correctly weighed the interests of the works council against the caveat that is laid down in article 25(3) of the WCA.

In the *VNU Publitec* case, by way of contrast, the central management's strategic plan was concrete enough to be put before the works council for consultation.[445] The case concerned a number of successive management decisions, which will be examined separately in the following paragraph. VNU World Directories Inc., which is the US top-holding of the group, maintained a number of undertakings that published the yellow pages. The top-holding held all of the shares in the sub-holding Publimedia B.V., which in turn held all of the shares in VNU Publitec.

VNU Publitec itself was the result of a merger of other subsidiaries among which was Gouden Gids B.V. (hereinafter: GG), for which a works council was established. The first decision concerned the merger which resulted in the creation of VNU Publitec. The works council of GG gave positive advice with regard to the merger in November 2003 and the employees of GG were formally transferred to VNU Publitec on the 1st of February 2004. As a result of the merger, the former GG works council ceased to exist and a new works council for VNU Publitec was established on the 1st of February 2004.

Only shortly after the positive advice was given by GG's works council on the matter of the merger from which VNU Publitec would result, the management of GG presented to the employees the central management's "Operational Improvement Plan" on 16 December 2003. According to this strategic plan, approximately 10% of the employees of VNU Publitec were to be laid off. In the proceedings before the court, the newly established works council of VNU Publitec appealed against this decision and in short argued that the positive advice of (formerly) GG's works council would not have been given if the "Operational Improvement Plan" would have been made available to the GG works council before giving its advice. The appeal, therefore, was directed against the first decision to merge the companies from which VNU Publitec resulted rather than the decision to terminate 10% of the employee contracts.

The Enterprise Chamber, however, found that the appeal was inadmissible given the fact that without the positive advice of GG's works council, neither VNU Publitec nor the VNU Publitec works council would have existed. Due to the fact that VNU Publitec asked for the prior advice of its works council on the matter of redundancies, no manifestly unreasonable decision was made by the undertaking and the appeal was subsequently dismissed.

445 OK 15 April 2004, *JOR* 2004/165 (*VNU Publitec*).

It is further interesting to note that the "Operational Improvement Plan" was concrete enough, according to the Enterprise Chamber, to require the prior advice of the works council, which VNU Publitec accordingly sought. In contrast to the *Rohm and Haas* and *Howson Algraphy* cases, the impact of the strategic plan on the central management on the Dutch subsidiary was concrete enough and therefore the prior consultation of the works council was necessary.[446] In the same judgment, the Enterprise Chamber also held that (the advice of a consultancy firm) on the worldwide IT-strategy was not concrete enough to establish the attribution of such a decision.[447] Advice on an intended change of the worldwide (IT) strategy was therefore not concrete enough, whereas a strategic plan of the central management with intended decisions for the Dutch subsidiary nevertheless fulfilled the concreteness criterion.

Aside from the criterion of concreteness, the Enterprise Chamber clearly noted in the VNU Publitec case that a works councils' appeal to establish the attribution of an (intended) decision can only be admissible if such a decision concerns the undertaking for which the works council is established.[448] As this was the case in VNU Publitec, the first decision concerned a different legal entity, namely GG. It is further established case law that the consultation rights with regard to a particular (intended) decision can be exercised only once.[449]

4.2.6 Personal union of the management(s)

A sixth criterion can be found in the *Shell Research* case.[450] While an (intended) decision must be concrete enough for attribution to the subsidiary with regard to the expected impact on the subsidiary's employees, the judgment in *Shell Research* shows that a direct interference of members of the central management in the decision-making process of the subsidiary's management can qualify as an (intended) decision of the central management for the purposes of attribution. One can speak in such cases of a personal union, since members of the management of the holding company are at the same time members of the management of the subsidiary in question.

In the *Shell Research* case, as was discussed previously in relation to the definition of *significant* in section 1.4.2.3, Shell Internationale Research Maatschappij BV (hereinafter: SIRM) was the sole owner of all of the shares in Shell Nederland BV, which in turn

446 See along the same lines, L.G. Verburg, *Het territoir van de (Nederlandse) ondernemingsraad in het internationale bedrijfsleven*, p. 160.

447 OK 15 April 2004, *JOR* 2004/165 (*VNU Publitec*), para. 3.4.

448 The principle that consultation rights of the works council are only applicable once a decision directly affects the undertaking for which the works council is maintained was established in the *Intergas* case; OK 30 December 2003, *ARO* 2004/18 (*Intergas*).

449 OK 10 May 1990, *NJ* 1992/126 (*Philips/HSA*), para. 3.5.

450 OK 02 April 1987, *NJ* 1988/382 (*Shell Research*).

held all of the shares in Shell Research BV (hereinafter: SR). Two members of SR's management took part in a SIRM meeting that led to the establishment of the 1987 annual budget and acted therefore in personal union both at the level of the holding (SIRM) and the subsidiary (SR). By virtue of such personal union and given the fact that the manager's input had considerable influence on the outcome of the SIRM meeting, an attribution of the decision was, according to the Enterprise Chamber, justified. Therefore, the fact that a personal union was in place, which led to an intervention by the holding in the subsidiary, this was regarded as an important aspect for the attribution of an (intended) decision.

4.2.7 Attribution in the case of share transactions

A seventh issue arises in the context of share transactions, which has been addressed by the Enterprise Chamber in a number of cases. A share transaction is to be distinguished from other transactions such as mergers and acquisitions due to the fact that it is solely the stocks that are transferred, as the assets and liabilities remain within the target undertaking. While such share transactions lead only indirectly to a transaction of a transfer of control within the meaning of article 25(1)(a) of the WCA, it has been argued in the literature and in the jurisprudence that such share transactions nevertheless fall within the scope of the consultation procedure pursuant to article 25 of the WCA.[451] Following the PUEM and later the Brink's cases, it is now established jurisprudence that a transfer of shares constitutes a transfer of control over an undertaking within the meaning of article 25(1)(a) of the WCA.[452] The Enterprise Chamber held in *PUEM* that share transactions are frequently used in practice and adopted a pragmatic approach in its judgment. It held that both share transactions and 'regular' decisions constitute a change to the power-structures within the undertaking [*zeggenschapsstructuren*] and that any distinctions made are artificial. Consequently, the Court held that such a transaction falls within the scope of article 25(1)(a) of the WCA.[453]

In the context of the attribution of an (intended) decision regarding a share transaction, the *Security Services Holding* case (hereinafter: SSH) should also be mentioned.[454] The case concerned the Dutch subsidiaries of the 'Group 4 Securicor PLO', which itself was the result of a merger between two large security service undertakings. The European Commission permitted the merger of the group, however, only under the prerequisite

---

451 L.G. Verburg, *Het territoir van de (Nederlandse) ondernemingsraad in het internationale bedrijfsleven*, p. 169.

452 Amsterdam Court of Appeal 27 July 1989, *NJ* 1990/734 (*PUEM*); OK 24 February 2015, *ARO* 2015/98 (*Brink's*), para. 3.5.

453 Amsterdam Court of Appeal 27 July 1989, *NJ* 1990/734 (*PUEM*), in particular para. 4.7 and 4.8; see also L.G. Verburg, 'Toerekening van besluitvorming en medeondernemerschap', *ArbeidsRecht* 9 (2014), p. 3-5.

454 OK 20 October 2005, *ARO* 2005/191 (*OR Security Services Holding BV*).

that certain activities were sold in order to prevent a concentration within the meaning of EU competition law. As a result of these concessions, the group set up the SSH holding in which the Dutch subsidiaries were placed in order to subsequently sell these off in a so-called controlled auction-process. The transaction itself was construed as a share transaction. The contested issue then concerned the request of the works council to be informed and consulted with regard to the list of potential buyers and ultimately in relation to the proposed sale of SSH to Facilicom by the 'Group 4 Securicor PLO'. While the substantive discussion will not be further addressed in this analysis, it can be noted that the Enterprise Chamber attributed the (intended) decision of the group to sell SSH to Facilicom on the basis that the (intended) decision directly and significantly affected the undertaking for which the works council was maintained.

This case has to be contrasted with a more recent judgement in *DB Schenker Rail* from 2013, which also concerned a share transaction that was contested by the Dutch works council.[455] The case concerned the (intended) decision of the Schenker Rail group, which is a subsidiary of the Deutsche Bahn AG, to move the Dutch subsidiaries of the German Schenker Retail GmbH (the German holding) to a Dutch holding for tax purposes. In order for the said transaction to be effectuated, the 'DB Nederland Holding' was established and the German holding took an (intended) decision to transfer its shares in the Dutch subsidiaries to the 'DB Nederland Holding'. The works council of one of the Dutch subsidiaries, the 'Schenker Rail Nederland' works council, then appealed against this (intended) decision and claimed that the prior consultation of the works council was necessary due to the fact that the (intended) decision could be attributed to the Dutch undertaking.

In its appeal, the works council, however, did not claim that the decision of the German holding had to be attributed to the Dutch undertaking, but that the *cooperation* of the Dutch entrepreneur in the process of the change of the corporate structure should have been subject to prior consultation. What is problematic here is that the German holding, as a shareholder, cannot be barred from exercising its property rights and to transfer its shares to another (Dutch) holding. The works council therefore appealed against the (intended) decision of the management of the Dutch undertaking to cooperate with the German holding in effectuating the share transaction. The Enterprise Chamber in its judgement held, in essence, that such an extension of consultation rights to a change of the corporate structure by means of a share transaction could not be justified. An attribution to the Dutch undertaking would be contrary to the separate legal entity principle. Further, the court held that in light of the fact that the transfer was made solely for fiscal reasons without any significant effects on the Dutch undertaking, the criteria for an attribution of the (intended) decision of the German Schenker Rail holding were

455 OK 20 February 2013, *RO* 2013/43 and *JAR* 2013/120 (*DB Schenker Rail Nederland NV*).

not fulfilled. This case stands out insofar as the works council incorrectly contested the Dutch subsidiary's decision instead of the holding's decision to transfer control over the Dutch subsidiary – the decision that would have fallen within the scope of article 25(1)(a) of the WCA. The recent judgment of the Enterprise Chamber in *SHL Engineering* also confirmed that share transactions could fall under the co-entrepreneurship principle and that prior works council advice must be sought.[456] The case is further discussed below in section 4.3.

4.2.8 Conclusion – the criteria necessary for an application of the technique of attribution of an (intended) decision

Against the background of the jurisprudence discussed above, six (although not necessarily cumulative) criteria for the application of the attribution-technique can be identified. On a general note, however, it must be emphasised that their application depends, to a considerable extent, on the circumstances of each case. The criteria can be further grouped, firstly, as criteria pertaining to the relationship between the undertaking and third parties involved in the case and, secondly, with regard to the nature and substance of the case.[457]

The first group of criteria on the relationship between the undertaking and third parties such as the top-holding in a MNC are important insofar as an (intended) decision of the third party is increasingly decisive for the decision-making of the subsidiary in situations whereby the undertaking is dependent on the third party. In situations whereby the third party has overwhelming control over the undertaking, which in corporate groups is frequently the case once the undertaking becomes a wholly owned subsidiary of the third party, employee participation rights are deprived of their *effet utile* once decisions are taken at a higher management level without obtaining the prior consultation of the works council. Overwhelming control, is thereby not dependent on the ownership of all shares (i.e., 100% of the shares), but rather the actual control over the undertaking for which a share ownership of 75% as well as the right to appoint the majority of the members of the management organs and the right to approve (or veto) all major management decisions can be regarded as sufficient evidence of overwhelming control.

With regard to a possible attribution in situations whereby a third party exercises decisive control over an undertaking, Ingelse argues that the undertaking and its management are under a duty to take *all* the interests of the stakeholders into consideration and may not follow the instructions of the third party, if this were to be contrary to

456 OK 19 October 2016, *JAR* 2016/278 and *TRA* 2017/9 m.nt. I. Zaal (*SHL Engineering*).

457 In a similar vein: L.C.J. Sprengers, 'Toetsing van een adviesprocedure in drie delen', 44 *Sociaal Recht* (2008), p. 6.

the interests of the undertaking.[458] At the same time, the undertaking is economically dependent within a corporate structure and may certainly take the overall corporate interest into consideration when adopting its decision. Yet, as the Enterprise Chamber held in the *Rohm and Haas* case, the corporate strategy may not be the sole determinant in the decision-making process. In light of the *Shell Research* case, the management of the undertaking and the top-holding (or any other third party) is under an enhanced duty to permit the exercise of consultation rights of the works council in situations whereby a personal union between the management of the subsidiary and a holding is present. It can be concluded that an attribution of an (intended) decision is very likely in situations whereby such a personal union of managements is the case due to the fact that the management of the subsidiaries has a significant influence over the decision-making process of the holding without involving the works council. An attribution in such situations rectifies such a circumvention of employee participation rights and precludes the abuse of holding structures.[459]

With regard to the second category of criteria, it must be noted that the courts have repeatedly held that the (intended) decision must be concrete enough to fall within the scope of the WCA.[460] This criterion is to be welcomed in light of article 25(3) of the WCA, which stipulates that the entrepreneur or the third party concerned must supplement the request for advice with a statement of reasons and the consequences to be expected as a consequence of the (intended) decision. Without a concrete plan for the implementation of an (intended) decision, such consequences are hardly foreseeable and the attribution of an (intended) decision at a stage where only global strategic plans are formulated would not be desirable. At the same time, the dilemma that a delayed involvement of the works council precludes effective influence on the decision-making process is becoming visible in the jurisprudence on this matter.[461]

While an earlier involvement of the works council is to be welcomed with regard to an effective and efficient decision-making process within the undertaking, this could rather be achieved by means of the earlier inclusion of the works council in the decision-making process by means of information sharing rather than the attribution of decisions of third parties. The limited application of the principle by the courts is therefore understandable in light of the principle of legal certainty. The criterion that an implementing decision must be made by the subsidiary is thereby closely connected to the

458 P. Ingelse, 'Mede-ondernemen en concernenquête', *Tijdschrift voor Arbeid & Onderneming* 1 (2012), p. 28.

459 The Enterprise Chamber established in the *PUEM* case that an artificial holding structure is not permitted; Amsterdam Court of Appeal 27 July 1989, *NJ* 1990/734 (*PUEM*).

460 OK 12 March 2002, *ARO* 2002/48 (Rohm and Haas); OK 15 April 2004, *ARO* 2004/63 (*VNU Publitec*); HR 11 July 1984, *NJ* 1985/212 (*Howson Algraphy*) and also with regard to co-entrepreneurship in the *Leaf Holland* case; OK 8 June 2006, *ARO* 2006/112 (*Leaf Holland*).

461 See in particular the Novio cases regarding co-entrepreneurship as discussed below; OK 10 May 2011, *ARO* 2011/92 (*Novio*); and OK 29 March 2010, *RO* 2011/19 (*OR Novio*).

aforementioned prerequisite of the concreteness of the (intended) decision. The implementing decision may, however, not be equated with the implementation of an instruction of the top-holding by a subsidiary. The implementing decision is rather to be based upon and must include the prior advice of the works council and cannot be merely an implementation of the top-holding's instructions without taking the rights of all stakeholders into consideration.

Without the implementation of an (intended) decision, any decision within the corporation would potentially fall within the scope of the WCA, which is contrary to the principles of territoriality and legitimacy. The principle of attribution is thus to be limited to situations whereby a foreign undertaking or a third party is *de facto* taking an (intended) decision that directly interferes in the Dutch subsidiary and is to a large extent aimed at this undertaking. The (intended) decision is therefore taken by the top-holding, but this actually falls within the scope of the WCA and is hence subject to the prior consultation duty. This aspect of joint responsibility becomes even more apparent when considering the relationship between the undertakings, as was discussed above.

The weighing of all interests at stake is an important criterion insofar as the controlled subsidiary is *de facto* seldom in a position to deviate from the corporate strategy, a factor which becomes even more apparent with regard to co-entrepreneurship as will subsequently be discussed. Particularly in cases whereby an undertaking is a wholly owned subsidiary, the GM of shareholders, if it deems it to be necessary, can remove the management.

The judgment in *DB Schenker Rail* clearly underlines the limitations of the attribution technique, which cannot be extended to share transactions without a considerable interference of the (intended) decision on the undertaking.[462]

4.3 Co-entrepreneurship – definition and criteria

While the technique of attribution of an (intended) decision is applied by the courts in cases where a specific decision is *de facto* to be attributed to the Dutch undertaking for which the works council is maintained, co-entrepreneurship goes even further and sets aside the separate legal entity principle by considering the third party and the Dutch undertaking to be *de jure* co-entrepreneurs within the meaning of the WCA. It is then

462 Cf. L.G. Verburg, 'De OK, de medezeggenschap en de periode 2007 tot en met 2008', *ArbeidsRecht* 8 (2009); Verburg concluded that an interference must be apparent; see also OK 17 January 2008, *ARO* 2008/36 (*Honeywell*) where such an interference was absent; in the *VNU Publitec* case, by way of contrast, such interference was constituted by the court.

the shared duty of the third party and the entrepreneur of the undertaking for which the works council is maintained to obtain the prior advice of that works council.

The technique can therefore be deemed applicable in situations where *de iure* the (intended) decision will materially and/or factually be taken by a third party and which has *de facto* decision-making powers and can hence be regarded as a co-entrepreneur. The courts, however, do not always make a strict distinction between co-entrepreneurship and the attribution of (intended) decisions.[463]

In the following section, the application of the principle of co-entrepreneurship by the courts will be examined in order to highlight the criteria for the application of the principle.

4.3.1 Direct interference of the third party

The first case, in which the question of (possible) co-entrepreneurship arose, was the *Kamer van Koophandel* case.[464] The case concerned the adoption of the *Wet Kamers van Koophandel 1997* [MM, Chamber of Commerce Law 1997], which changed the division of municipalities that are part of the jurisdiction of the chambers of commerce. Pursuant to the adopted legislation, the jurisdiction for the chamber of commerce of Rotterdam would be reduced by 10%. In order to give some context here, it is the case that the size of the jurisdiction directly affects the amount of income that a chamber would have.

The appeal of the works council of the chamber of commerce of Rotterdam was therefore, in substance, that the decision to reduce the size of the jurisdiction concerned was an (intended) decision within the meaning of articles 25(1)(a),(b) and (d) of the WCA. Further, it was argued that the state of the Netherlands should be regarded as a co-entrepreneur in the case due to the fact that the adoption of the law directly interfered with the activities of the undertakings concerned. The Enterprise Chamber, firstly, established that although a primacy of politics with regard to the legislative powers of the state exists, such decisions could nevertheless be subject to the consultation rights of a works council pursuant to the WCA.[465]

Secondly, the Enterprise Chamber held that the decision of the state directly interfered with the economic activities of the chamber of commerce and it had to be regarded as a co-entrepreneur for the purposes of the applying the WCA and thus declared the appeal

463 The Enterprise Chamber, for instance, applied both concepts in the *Packard Bell* cases alongside each other; OK 9 January 2008, *RO* 2008/22 (*Packard Bell I*); and OK 19 February 2008, *ARO* 2003/73 (*Packard Bell II*); Cf. L.C.J. Sprengers, 'Toetsing van een adviesprocedure in drie delen', 44 *Sociaal Recht* (2008), p. 6.

464 OK 2 April 1998, *NJ* 1998/751 (*Kamer van Koophandel*).

465 OK 2 April 1998, *NJ* 1998/751 (*Kamer van Koophandel*), para. 3.7.

of the works council as admissible. Due to practical reasons, however, the court declared that the decision, as such, would not be declared null and void due to the adverse effects on third parties that would arise (i.e., for undertakings already being struck from the company registry of the chamber of commerce). The court therefore formulated the criterion of *direct interference* for the concept of co-entrepreneurship to be applicable.

4.3.2 The Provincie Zuid-Holland case – systematically in a position to influence the decision-making to a sufficient extent

The second case concerning co-entrepreneurship concerned a legislative measure by the state concerning the modification of the borders of municipalities, which had adverse effects for the employees of several municipalities in the province Zuid-Holland.[466]

The appeal of the works council of the municipalities was very similar to the claim by the works council in the *Kamer van Koophandel* case. The works council argued that the state had to be regarded as a co-entrepreneur within the meaning of the WCA and that the prior advice of the works council had to be sought, due to the fact that the legislative measure directly interfered in the municipalities for which the works council was maintained.

Again, the Enterprise Chamber held, at first instance, that the primacy of politics was not applicable insofar as the exercise of the consultation rights of the works council pursuant to articles 25(1)(d) and (e) of the WCA must be permitted due to the significant impact of the measure on the employees of the municipalities. The Enterprise Chamber thereby referred to the earlier *Kamer van Koophandel* case, in which the criterion of direct interference was established.[467]

The objection in cassation by the province Zuid-Holland allowed the Supreme Court to adjudicate on the concept of co-entrepreneurship for the first time.[468] The Supreme Court held that the criterion of direct interference alone is insufficient to establish the co-entrepreneurship of a third party vis-à-vis the undertaking for which the works council is maintained.[469] Rather, the facts and circumstances of the case must lead to the conclusion that the third party (here, the province) was *systematically* in a position to influence, *to a sufficient extent*, the decision-making of the undertaking for which the works council was maintained.[470] The Supreme Court therefore quashed the earlier

466 HR 26 January 2000, *JOR* 2000/3 (*Provincie Zuid-Holland*); in earlier instance: OK 28 January 1999, *NJ* 1999/185 (*Provincie Zuid-Holland*).

467 OK 28 January 1999, *NJ* 1999/185 (*Provincie Zuid-Holland*), para. 3.6.

468 HR 26 January 2000, *JOR* 2000/3 (*Provincie Zuid-Holland*).

469 HR 26 January 2000, *JOR* 2000/3 (*Provincie Zuid-Holland*), para. 3.4.

470 *Ibid.*; the Supreme Court stipulated: "*Om een ander dan de ondernemer die de ondernemingsraad heeft ingesteld, naast die ondernemer als mede-ondernemer te kunnen aanmerken is nodig dat feiten*

judgment of the Enterprise Chamber and put more emphasis on the criterion of systematic exercise of influence by the third party over the undertaking for which the works council is maintained. The judgment of the Supreme Court also had a political dimension due to the far-reaching implications of a possible influence of a works council of a municipality on the federal legislative process.[471] This discussion, however, falls outside the scope of the current analysis.

While the Supreme Court held in this judgment that the criterion of systematic exercise of influence on the subsidiary was lacking in the relationship between the state and a municipality for which the works council was maintained, this criterion could be fulfilled by means of share-ownership and through the statutory rights of the third party (for instance regarding the appointment of members of the board of the undertaking) vis-à-vis the undertaking for which the works council is maintained. This becomes apparent in the subsequent cases that concerned the private sector.

4.3.3 A high degree of dependency and dominant control of the third party

Three years after the *Provincie Zuid-Holland* judgment, another works council invoked the notion of co-entrepreneurship in an appeal procedure.[472] The case concerned the organisation FNV Ledenservice (hereinafter: FNV LS), which was established in 1998 in order to provide services to the members of the unions that were linked to the organisation, namely the unions FNV Bondgenoten and FNV Bouw. The organisation FNV LS was thereby financed by the unions that were linked to it, whereby FNV Bondgenoten's contributions amounted to 75% of the revenues.

In 2002, the union of FNV Bondgenoten suffered financial difficulties and therefore considered the termination of the service agreement with FNV LS. FNV LS requested the advice of its works council on 21 May 2002.

The works council of FNV LS then appealed to the Enterprise Chamber on the grounds that it considered the notice of the FNV LS's management on 21 May 2002 to constitute an already adopted decision instead of an (intended) decision, for which the advice of the works council could no longer significantly affect the decision within the meaning of article 25 of the WCA.

---

en omstandigheden worden gesteld en, bij betwisting daarvan, aannemelijk gemaakt waaruit volgt dat die ander ten opzichte van de desbetreffende onderneming een positie inneemt die hem stelselmatig een zodanige invloed op de besluitvorming binnen de onderneming verschaft dat gezegd kan worden dat de onderneming mede door die ander in stand wordt gehouden".

471 Cf. L.C.J. Sprengers, 'Haagse grenscorrectie. Provincie kan – gelet op de daaraan te stellen eisen – niet worden aangemerkt als mede-ondernemer ten aanzien van de gemeentelijke organisatie. Betekenis van het "politieke primaat"', 41 *Tijdschrift voor Ambtenarenrecht* (2000).

472 OK 13 February 2003, *ARO* 2003/45 (*FNV Ledenservice I*); and OK 28 April 2004, *ARO* 2004/72 (*FNV Ledenservice II*).

In the *FNV Ledenservice I* judgment, the Enterprise Chamber held that the unions, which were the members of FNV LS, had a *de facto* significant influence over the management of FNV LS. The court held that not only were FNV Bondgenoten and FNV Bouw members of FNV LS, but both unions also had voting rights in the GM of FNV LS as a result of their membership. Further to this, one member of FNV Bondgenoten was the treasurer and one member of FNV Bouw was the secretary of the administrative board of FNV LS. Moreover, FNV Bondgenoten was the main client of FNV LS and FNV LS was not permitted to provide services to persons that were not themselves members of FNV Bondgenoten or FNV Bouw.[473]

However, the Enterprise Chamber held that FNV Bondgenoten was not exerting dominant influence over FNV LS.[474] The court further held that FNV Bondgenoten was not systematically in a position to influence, to a sufficient extent, the decision-making of FNV LS. The claim of co-entrepreneurship was therefore denied by the Enterprise Chamber and it subsequently denied the appeal in its entirety by holding that the request for the advice of the works council of FNV LS was sought in due time. The judgment is understandable insofar as FNV Bondgenoten made an internal strategic decision and did not (yet) exercise its dominant position in order to influence the decision-making process of FNV LS.[475]

Shortly thereafter, however, the works council appealed again before the Enterprise Chamber regarding the same matter.[476] On 19 November 2003, the director of FNV LS proposed during a management meeting to discontinue the undertaking. This (intended) decision was then the subject of a meeting of the works council with the director on 27 November 2003. While the nature and structure of the relationship between FNV LS and the unions remained the same, this time the (intended) decision as such was different from the situation in the first case before the Enterprise Chamber. While in the first case the unions were not considered to have exerted direct influence on FNV LS to fulfil all criteria of co-entrepreneurship, this was fulfilled in this second case according to the court.

Against the background of the correspondence of the parties concerned, the court held that FNV Bouw and FNV Bondgenoten had already decided to discontinue FNV LS and the management of the latter was held to have reconciled itself to the said decision without consulting the works council.[477]

473 OK 13 February 2003, *ARO* 2003/45 (*FNV Ledenservice I*), para. 3.5.

474 *Ibid.*, point 3.6.

475 Cf. L.G. Verburg, 'De Ondernemingskamer, de medezeggenschap en de periode 2009 tot en met 2011', 8 *ArbeidsRecht* (2012), p. 9.

476 OK 28 April 2004, *ARO* 2004/72 (*FNV Ledenservice II*).

477 *Ibid.*, para. 3.3.

Therefore, the management of FNV LS already decided to comply with the decision of the unions in order to discontinue the undertaking without prior consultation of the works council. Moreover, both the criterion of an (intended) decision that directly interferes with the economic activity of the undertaking as well as the criterion that the third party (here the unions FNV Bouw and FNV Bondgenoten) were systematically in a position to influence, to a sufficient extent, the decision-making of the undertaking for which the works council was maintained.

In addition, the Enterprise Chamber held that the relationship between FNV LS and the unions was characterised by a high degree of dependency on the former, which further elevated the need to consider the unions as co-entrepreneurs of FNV LS in order to safeguard the consultation rights of the works council.[478] The unions were, therefore, considered to have exerted dominant control vis-à-vis FNV LS and thus had to be regarded as co-entrepreneurs for the purposes of exercising the consultation rights of FNV LS's works council.[479]

The Enterprise Chamber already ruled in the earlier *NS Reizigers* case that a third party has to be regarded as co-entrepreneur in situations whereby the third party is able to exercise dominant control to such an extent that the undertaking or subsidiary cannot disengage itself from the (intended) decisions taken at the higher management level.[480] Similar to the FNV LS case, NS Reizigers was closely involved in the decision-making process at the subsidiary level and exerted influence to a significant and sufficient extent, which led to the decision of the subsidiary not to apply for the concession.

While the Enterprise Chamber formulated the criteria for co-entrepreneurship in the aforementioned judgments, these cases did not concern situations whereby a foreign third party was involved, which is of particular importance with regard to MNCs.

4.3.4 The Packard Bell cases – co-entrepreneurship possible in the case of a share transaction?

The Packard Bell cases concerned an (intended) decision to sell the undertaking (as well as its subsidiaries) to Gateway by means of a share transaction.[481] The case was significant insofar as the (intended) decision was taken at the level of the topholding and not at the subholding level. The question was, therefore, *inter alia* how far the applicability of the principle of co-entrepreneurship can be extended to third parties that are linked to the

478 *Ibid.*, para. 3.11, 3.13 and 3.15.
479 *Ibid.*, para. 3.17.
480 OK 30 October 2002, *ARO* 2002/171 (*NS Reizigers*); see also S.M. Bartman and A.F.M. Dorrestijn, *Van het concern* (8th edition, Kluwer, Deventer 2013), p. 192.
481 OK 9 January 2008, *RO* 2008/22 (*Packard Bell I*) and OK 19 February 2008, *ARO* 2003/73 (*Packard Bell II*).

undertaking only by means of an intermediary. The Dutch Packard Bell B.V. was held by the Luxembourgian Packard Bell Holding, which is to be regarded as the intermediary for the purposes of this analysis.

In 2006, and prior to the disputed proceedings, the works council of Packard Bell was asked to advise on the transfer of 75% of the shares as well as full control over the Packard Bell holding to Clifford Holding, which was in turn wholly owned by Mr Hui. The works council had given its positive advice to this transaction. Mr Hui was also a member of the supervisory board of Packard Bell and was listed as the managing director of the Packard Bell Holding in Luxembourg.

In 2007, the works council was then initially asked to give its advice on a transfer of the undertaking to the Chinese corporation Lenovo, but this request for advice was later repealed. The reason was that Mr Hui had signed a non-competition agreement with the Taiwanese corporation Gateway, which he would violate by transferring the Packard Bell shares to Lenovo. Therefore, the works council was asked to render its advice on a transfer of Packard Bell to Gateway instead. Gateway then had a right of first refusal on the Packard Bell shares.

The first case before the sub-district court in Arnhem concerned the question of whether the works council had to render its advice on short notice prior to the 30th of November 2007 and whether the external advisor of the works council had to be paid for by the undertaking.[482] The sub-district court, in short, refused the claims of the undertaking by holding that no specific reasons were given as to why the advice had to be rendered on such short notice and the costs for the external advisor had to be paid due to the fact that no explicit confinement of the works councils' advice was stipulated by the entrepreneur beforehand.[483]

The second proceeding before the Enterprise Chamber concerned two separate claims of the works council.[484] Firstly, the works council claimed that because it was not made known to the works council that Gateway was granted a right of first refusal pursuant to the non-competition agreement with Mr Hui, it would have advised differently with regard to the share transaction to Clifford Holding in 2006. Secondly and with regard to co-entrepreneurship, the works council claimed that Clifford Holding as the topholding, had to be regarded as co-entrepreneur and thus had to obtain the prior advice of the works council with regard to the share transaction to Gateway.

482 Cf. L.C.J. Sprengers, 'Toetsing van een adviesprocedure in drie delen', 44 *Sociaal Recht* (2008), p. 1-2.
483 *Ibid.*
484 OK 9 January 2008, *RO* 2008/22 (*Packard Bell I*).

With regard to the first claim of the works council, the Enterprise Chamber dismissed the claim on the grounds that, in short, the works council was unable to present facts that would lead to the conclusion that the advice of the works council on the transfer of shares to Clifford Holding would not have taken place if the works council had knowledge of Gateway's first right of refusal.[485]

On the matter of Hui's (intended) decision to dispose of its shares in Packard Bell and to transfer the said shares to Gateway, the Enterprise Chamber made recourse to the criteria for co-entrepreneurship as had been established in the earlier case law.[486] The court held that neither Hui nor Clifford Holding, with regard to the (intended) decision to dispose of the shares in Packard Bell, were systematically in a position to influence the decision-making of Packard Bell to a sufficient extent.[487] Furthermore, the (intended) decision constituted no direct interference in the decision-making process of Packard Bell according to the court.[488] The fact that Packard Bell was the sole subsidiary of the Clifford Holing, as such, did not constitute sufficient grounds for the fulfilment of the criterion that interference in the decision-making process was inherent. Since neither of the two criteria for co-entrepreneurship were fulfilled in the case at hand, the court dismissed the works council's claim.

The last procedure then concerned the question of how far-reaching the consultation rights of the works council pursuant to article 25(1) of the WCA are.[489]

The works council claimed that Packard Bell and Mr Hui should not have limited themselves to negotiate solely with Gateway, but rather they should have approached the sale of the undertaking on a level playing field. By doing so, the works council proposed to also consider the earlier offer made by Lenovo. The dispute then arose due to the fact that the works council regarded the request for advice on the (intended) decision to transfer the shares in Packard Bell to be interpreted as wider request, which would have included advice on a possible sale to third parties other than Gateway. Packard Bell and Mr Hui, on the contrary, argued that in all the communication after the request for advice, only the single bid of Gateway was on the table and other competitors and the notion of a level playing field were 'out of scope'.[490]

485 *Ibid.*, para. 3.5 – 3.7.

486 See the cases above: OK 2 April 1998, *NJ* 1998/751 (*Kamer van Koophandel*); OK 30 October 2002, *ARO* 2002/171 (*NS Reizigers*); OK 13 February 2003, *ARO* 2003/45 (*FNV Ledenservice I*); and OK 28 April 2004, *ARO* 2004/72 (*FNV Ledenservice II*).

487 OK 9 January 2008, *RO* 2008/22 (*Packard Bell I*), para. 3.10.

488 *Ibid.*, para. 3.12.

489 OK 19 February 2008, *ARO* 2003/73 (*Packard Bell II*).

490 *Ibid.*, para. 3.2.

Given the fact that Mr Hui was not the entrepreneur, who maintained Packard Bell within the meaning of article 1(1)(d) of the WCA, the request of the works council would have led to an extension of the consultation rights to the holding level in the case of a sale of the undertaking for which the works council was maintained. The Enterprise Chamber, however, held that in the case of a share transfer by a top-holding, the works council of the subsidiary (which was linked to the top-holding only indirectly via an intermediary) did not have, at least from the outset, a consultation right within the meaning of article 25(1) of the WCA.[491] Such a right would be permitted, according to the court, only in cases where a purely artificial holding-structure was applied.[492] Against the background of its earlier judgment in the *Packard Bell I* case, the court dismissed the claims of the works council by reiterating that neither Clifford Holding nor Mr Hui could be regarded as the co-entrepreneurs of Packard Bell. Further, Gateway's offer was very reasonable and was adapted in light of the proceedings in favour of Packard Bell's employees. The assumption of the works council that Packard Bell could not have reasonably come to the decision to effectuate the share transfer to Gateway, was dismissed as unfounded by the Enterprise Chamber.[493]

Therefore, it has to be constituted that in cases where a third party holds the shares in an undertaking via an intermediary and where such a construction is not purely artificial (for instance for purely fiscal reasons), such (intended) decisions of topholdings, which are only indirectly linked through another subholding, may not be regarded as decisions of a co-entrepreneur (*medeondernemerschap*) of the undertaking for which the works council is maintained. This judgment is understandable insofar as a third party cannot be expected to take the position of undertakings, which are only indirectly linked to the undertaking, into consideration when taking a decision. In light of the principle of territoriality, any other decision of the court would have brought (intended) decisions within the scope of the WCA, which not even the management of the undertaking for which the works council was maintained could have influenced.

Furthermore, it is questionable whether the change of ownership of Packard Bell on the level of the topholding directly interfered in the undertaking. Therefore, neither one of the three criteria of co-entrepreneurship were fulfilled in the case at hand, according to the court. Neither was the fact that Mr Hui was the sole shareholder of Clifford Holding, managing director of the holding and member of the supervisory board of the Packard Bell Holding sufficient to fulfil the criterion of 'significantly exerting influence to a sufficient extent'. Nor did the share transfers have a considerable (direct) impact on the undertaking. The question of whether the co-entrepreneurship of an indirectly linked

491 *Ibid.*; see also L.C.J. Sprengers, 'Toetsing van een adviesprocedure in drie delen', 44 *Sociaal Recht* (2008), p. 5.

492 See with a similar argumentation S.M. Bartman and A.F.M. Dorrestijn, *Van het concern* (8th edition, Kluwer, Deventer 2013), p. 197.

493 OK 19 February 2008, *ARO* 2003/73 (*Packard Bell II*), para. 3.7 and 3.8.

topholding could be established and whether or not prior consultation of the works council for (intended) decisions of the topholding was necessary, had to be answered in the negative. The case however shows, that once the works council is tasked with rendering its advice on matters concerning higher management levels within a corporation, the territorial limitation of the WCA no longer applies.

The more recent judgement in the *SHL* case confirmed this.[494] The case concerned the request of two shareholders of SHL Holding Cyprus, which is the parent company of the Dutch Seaway Heavy Lifting Engineering (SHL Engineering), to Goldman Sachs regarding a possible sale of their shares in the SHL group. Goldman Sachs acted as experts within the meaning of article 25(1)(n) *junto* article 25(1)(a) of the WCA concerning the possible transfer of power through the sale of the shares. The Enterprise Chamber concluded that the criteria for co-entrepreneurship were fulfilled in the case at hand, because the valuation of the shares directly impacted the (intended) transfer of control following the (expected) positive valuation of the shares by Goldman Sachs.

What is noteworthy here is the fact that two holdings were present between the Dutch SHL Engineering and the shareholders (K&S Cyprus and Acergy). Contrary to the Packard Bell cases, the Enterprise Chamber concluded in this case that a sufficient link between the shareholder's intended decision and the Dutch subsidiary existed.[495] The Cypriot SHL Holding Cyprus (of which K&S Cyprus and Acergy were shareholders) held 100% of the shares in the Dutch SHL Holding, which in turn held all of the shares in SHL Engineering – the latter maintaining a works council which started the proceedings.[496] What is important is the fact that SHL Holding Cyprus and SHL Holding were merely holding-companies with no business activities[497] and that the board of directors was composed of the management members of K&S Cyprus and Acergy.[498] The management representatives were therefore exercising dominant control and the decision directly impacted the Dutch undertaking (SHL Engineering) and the decision to sell the shares therefore fell within the scope of article 25 of the WCA.[499] Consequently, such a decision should have been subject to the prior consultation of the works council of the

494 OK 19 October 2016, *JAR* 2016/278 and *TRA* 2017/9 m.nt. I. Zaal (*SHL Engineering*).

495 *Ibid.*, para. 3.8: "*Naar het oordeel van de Ondernemingskamer is een besluit tot een dergelijke verkoop en overdracht niet alleen een besluit tot overdracht van de zeggenschap in SHL Holding Cyprus, maar, gelet op de verhouding tussen SHL Holding Cyprus en SHL Holding, tevens een besluit tot overdracht van de zeggenschap over de onderneming van SHL Engineering. [...] Een toekomstig houder van de aandelen in SHL Holding Cyprus krijgt derhalve tevens de volledige zeggenschap in SHL Engineering. Op zichzelf is dus voldaan aan de relatie tussen artikel 25 lid 1 onder n en artikel 25 lid 1 onder a van de WOR en is het besluit tot het geven van de betreffende adviesopdracht aan Goldman Sachs een adviesplichtig besluit*".

496 *Ibid.*, para. 2.1 and 2.2.

497 *Ibid.*, para. 2.7.

498 *Ibid.*, para. 3.12.

499 *Ibid.*, para. 3.11.

Dutch subsidiary by the management of both the Cypriot topholding and the management of SHL Engineering in light of these considerations.[500]

4.3.5 The VLM Nederland case – co-entrepreneurship in the case of a change of the articles of association?

The *VLM* case concerned an (intended) decision that was different in nature compared to the previously examined *Packard Bell* cases.[501] VLM Nederland is a subsidiary of the Air France-KLM group and up until 2010, the articles of association of VLM Nederland held that the objective of the undertaking was the transportation of persons and goods by air, which qualified it as an airline or air carrier.

In 2010, the holding VLM België, which was the parent undertaking of VLM Nederland, made a decision to change the subsidiary's articles of association and to change the subsidiary's name. The change of the articles of association was intended to change the objective of VLM Nederland insofar as it is was no longer operating as an air carrier, but rather as staff-management company. Furthermore, VLM België and VLM Nederland subsequently entered a so-called wet lease-agreement with CityJet, another subsidiary of the Air France-KLM group, by virtue of which VLM Nederland would lease its aircrafts as well as personnel to CityJet.

The works council of VLM Nederland appealed against these (intended) decisions and claimed that VLM België had to be regarded as the co-entrepreneur and, therefore, was under the obligation to obtain the prior advice of the works council of VLM Nederland.[502] VLM, on the contrary, claimed that the change to the articles of association did not constitute a significant reduction, expansion or other change in the enterprise's activities pursuant to article 25(1)(d) of the WCA.[503]

Firstly, the Enterprise Chamber constituted that VLM Nederland in fact operated as an independent air carrier and operated flight-routes at its own risk. This was further confirmed by the fact that the majority of revenues stemmed from the sale of tickets and not, as was argued by the management of VLM, from the wet lease of aircrafts and personnel.[504] Therefore, a significant change of the enterprise's activities within the meaning of article 25(1)(d) of the WCA was present and therefore the prior advice of the works council was mandatory.[505]

500 *Ibid.*, para. 3.13 – 3.15 and para. 4 (decision of the court).
501 OK 14 October 2010, *RO* 2011/11 (*VLM Nederland*).
502 *Ibid.*, para. 1.1.
503 *Ibid.*, para. 3.2.
504 *Ibid.*, para. 3.3.
505 *Ibid.*, para. 3.6.

Secondly, the question was whether VLM België could be regarded as co-entrepreneur and therefore was also under the duty to obtain the prior consultation of the works council of VLM Nederland. Given the fact that the changes to the articles of association constituted a significant interference in the activities of VLM Nederland, as was established by the court, the first criterion for co-entrepreneurship was fulfilled.

The court thus further held that VLM België was systematically in a position to influence, to a sufficient extent, the decision-making of VLM Nederland, on the grounds that a committee, which was dominated by VLM België, made all the strategic decisions. Furthermore, VLM België was the sole shareholder of VLM Nederland and the subsidiary was also financially dependent and only performed economic activities on behalf of the group of undertakings.[506]

Given the fact that all the criteria for co-entrepreneurship were fulfilled in the case at hand, the Enterprise Chamber held that the appeal of the works council was well founded and decided that VLM could not have reasonably come to the decision to change the articles of association of VLM Nederland. The case further shows that the nature of the (intended) decision under appeal is of significant importance for the establishment of co-entrepreneurship. Whereas in the *Packard Bell* cases a share transaction was not regarded as considerably influencing the activities of the undertaking concerned, a change in the articles of association nevertheless fulfilled this criterion.

This judgment is understandable insofar as the change of share-ownership in *Packard Bell* did not affect the economic activity of the undertaking, whereas the change of the articles of association in the case at hand would have had a significant impact on the economic activities and, in turn, on the employees of VLM Nederland.

4.3.6 The Novio case – confirmation of the earlier jurisprudence

The most recent case in which co-entrepreneurship was invoked by a works council concerned the public transport undertaking Novio.[507] Novio was, up until 2006, owned by the city of Nijmegen, but was sold to Connexxion that year. In the context of this take-over, a covenant was agreed upon between Connexxion and the works council of Novio, which safeguarded that the rights of the employees of Novio would remain unaltered once Novio became part of the Connexxion group.[508] Important to note is that the employees of Novio were subject to differing break rules compared to employees of

506 The criteria were also applied earlier in case OK 28 April 2004, *ARO* 2004/72 (*FNV Ledenservice II*).
507 OK 10 May 2011, *ARO* 2011/92 (*Novio*).
508 Seven other Novio cases concerned this matter; these are not further discussed here since this falls outside the scope of the co-entrepreneurship analysis.

Connexxion or Hermes, which in essence resulted in longer breaks for Novio employees.[509] Both Novio and Hermes belong to the Connexxion group, which is the parent undertaking of both enterprises.

In the period 2009 – 2012, Novio held the concession for the public transport in the region of Arnhem and Nijmegen (hereinafter: SAN-concession), which was subject to a tendering process for the upcoming period as of 3rd January 2011.

The dispute concerned, in essence, the (intended) decision of Connexxion to instruct Hermes to apply for the upcoming SAN tender procedure instead of Novio due to the fact that a Hermes bid would be more economically viable (i.e., cheaper due to the short breaks of Hermes employees in comparison with Novio employees).[510] Novio, in the following, did not apply for the tender procedure and informed its works council accordingly. The works council then appealed to the Enterprise Chamber on the grounds that Connexxion should be regarded as the co-entrepreneur for the purposes of the (non)-decision to apply for the SAN-concession and that Connexxion was obliged to obtain the prior advice of Novio's works council due to the fact that the co-entrepreneurship criteria were fulfilled.[511]

The works council claimed that the interference of the Connexxion holding on the decision-making process was significant and amounted to co-entrepeneurship. The works council claimed that Connexxion acted as the managing director of Novio (through its chief human resource officer) and that the chief HR officer acted as entrepreneur within the meaning of the WCA vis-à-vis the works council of Novio. Further, Connexxion – the parent company – rather than Novio handled the correspondence with the works council and had issued the request for works council advice on the matter.

The Enterprise Chamber ruled in line with its earlier judgments in *NS Reizigers* and *FNV Ledenservice* by holding that Connexxion was not only the sole shareholder of Novio, but exercised dominant control in the context of the decision under appeal. The court further held that Novio's management only had little autonomy and responsibility with regard to the decision not to apply for the SAN tender. The court therefore concluded that Connexxion was systematically in a position to influence, to a sufficient extent, the decision-making of Novio and thus reiterated the criterion as formulated by the Supreme Court in the *Provincie Zuid-Holland* case.[512]

509 *Ibid.*, para. 2.6.
510 OK 10 May 2011, *ARO* 2011/92 (*Novio*), para. 3.5.
511 OK 29 March 2010, *RO* 2011/19 (*OR Novio*).
512 HR 26 January 2000, *JOR* 2000/3 (*Provincie Zuid-Holland*).

What is interesting to note is the fact that the Enterprise Chamber not only held that Connexxion exercised dominant influence over Novio, but also concluded that the management of Novio only had little autonomy with regard to the (intended) decision and therefore *de facto* no diverging decision, for which the works council's advice could still have been of significant influence, could be made.[513]

While the works council successfully invoked co-entrepreneurship in this case and the court in its judgment declared the decision of Novio (and Connexxion as co-entrepreneur) not to apply for the SAN tender as unlawful, the appeal was ultimately unsuccessful. In the last judgment,[514] the court held that although the decision of Connexxion and Novio was manifestly unreasonable, a judgment which would have had declared the decision null and void could have led to a situation in which none of the public transportation companies would have applied for the SAN-concession in due time. The judgement was thus a rather "Pyrrhic victory" for the works council.

4.3.7 Conclusion – the criteria for co-entrepreneurship

Against the background of the jurisprudence analysed above, it can be constituted that co-entrepreneurship can be successfully invoked in cases where the third party is interfering so substantially in the undertaking that this third party has to be regarded as co-entrepreneur for the purposes of the WCA. The Supreme Court in the landmark judgment in the *Provincie Zuid-Holland* case formulated this substantial interference-criterion by holding that the third party was systematically in a position to influence, to a sufficient extent, the decision-making of the undertaking for which the works council was maintained.[515] Once a third party is systematically in such a position, according to the court, by virtue of a corporate structure or the extraordinary circumstances stemming from the primacy of politics with regard to the legislative powers of the state, such a third party *can* be regarded as co-entrepreneur once this position is used to interfere in the decision-making of the undertaking.

At the same time, the position of the third party, as such, is not sufficient to establish co-entrepreneurship as was emphasised by the Enterprise Chamber in the *Packard Bell* cases.[516] Rather, the third party must exercise influence on the decision-making by means of instructions such as not to apply for a concession, as was the case in *Novio*. Furthermore, the wording of the courts is even more nuanced as not every interference

513 The aspect of marginalised decision-making powers of the affected undertaking was already emphasised by the Enterprise Chamber in the *FNV Ledenservice II* judgement; OK 28 April 2004, *ARO* 2004/72 (*FNV Ledenservice II*).

514 OK 10 May 2011, *ARO* 2011/92 (*Novio*), para. 3.11.

515 HR 26 January 2000, *JOR* 2000/3 (*Provincie Zuid-Holland*).

516 The Enterprise Chamber in its very first judgment established that a 100% shareholding alone is not sufficient grounds for co-entrepreneurship; OK 10 May 1990, *NJ* 1992/126 (*Philips/HSA*).

of a third party leads to a successful application of the co-entrepreneurship principle, but rather influence to a sufficient extent is what is required.[517] Here, the *FNV Ledenservice* and *Novio* cases exemplify the reasoning of the court due to the fact that in both cases the undertaking was in a position whereby it could not withdraw itself from the decisions that were already taken by the top-holding. The criterion of overwhelming control, as was addressed by the court in the *FNV Ledenservice II* case, is to be welcomed as it is closely connected to the actual position of the undertaking vis-à-vis the third party rather than merely the formal position. If therefore the third party "sits on the chair of the managing director of the undertaking", it also has to fulfil the duties of the director with regard to the employee participation rights with respect to the (intended) decision at hand.[518] With regard to the actual exercise of interference in the undertaking, one must also conclude that share transactions on a higher management level within a corporation do not qualify for co-entrepreneurship due to the absence of such interference pursuant to the *Packard Bell* judgments.

The application of the techniques of co-entrepreneurship and attribution are to be regarded as powerful tools for works councils to regain consultation rights in situations where decisions with a significant impact on the Dutch undertaking are made without the prior consultation of the works council. It remains to be seen in the empirical section of this study whether the available juridical tools are actually applied in practice and whether or not the application is indeed beneficial for works councils.

The *Novio* cases, however, show that the successful acknowledgement of co-entrepreneurship or an attribution of an (intended) decision of the third party does not *per se* improve the position of the Dutch works council. The legal proceedings are nonetheless useful as tool for works councils in the negotiations with the management and as a last resort bargaining chip. Still, works councils continue to make seldom recourse to appeal procedures before the Enterprise Chamber, with only 9 (2015) to 18 (2014) cases being adjudicated every year.[519]

---

517 Ingelse argues similarly by holding that incidental interference of the third party is not sufficient for an establishment of co-entrepreneurship; P. Ingelse, 'Mede-ondernemen en concernenquête', *Tijdschrift voor Arbeid & Onderneming* 1 (2012), p. 30.

518 The difference thus being that the third party does not only have "the possibility to exercise its chairmanship", but it must actually "exercises its chairmanship" [*feitelijk op de stoel van de bestuurder plaatsnemen*]; Cf. L.G. Verburg, 'Toerekening van besluitvorming en medeondernemerschap', *Arbeids-Recht* 9 (2014).

519 36 cases were filed with the Enterprise Chamber in 2015 and 45 were filed in 2014. Of these cases around 60% were withdrawn prior to the hearing and only nine cases were adjudicated in 2015 (18 in 2014); Cf. Enterprise Chamber of the Amsterdam Court of Appeal, 'Jaarverslag Ondernemingskamer 2015', <https://www.rechtspraak.nl/SiteCollectionDocuments/jaarverslag-Ondernemingskamer-2015.pdf> (last accessed 1 October 2017), p. 1.

Chapter IV: Quantitative results

1 Introduction

The legal dogmatic analysis that was carried out in chapter III above has led to the identification of a number of potential issues in the application of employee participation rights in practice. The application of these rights, in particular the use and non-use of rights in practice, will constitute the subject matter of this chapter. The research methods applied to obtain the data on Dutch works councils in multinational organisations was outlined in chapter II above. In this chapter the substantive research findings, based on the questionnaire, will be reported in the following sections. In the reporting, a general distinction is made between the overall results based on all responses ('Full sample'), the responses by works councils in Dutch MNCs ('Dutch MNCs') and responses from works councils in foreign MNCs ('Foreign MNCs'). This distinction is made to check whether a difference in the position of works councils in Dutch and foreign multinationals can be observed. It is important to note that due to the small sample size and the even smaller sub-samples of responses from Dutch and foreign MNCs, the results must be treated with a degree of caution. A statistically significant difference could not be determined for most of the topics and no generalisation from these results is possible. The differentiation between Dutch and foreign MNCs is nevertheless reported to examine whether divergent trends between the sub-samples are observable. This hypothesis is based on the findings of Looise and Drucker, who examined the effects of internationalisation on the position of Dutch works councils.[1] They concluded that "*the further away the company is from the national context, from national concern to Dutch MNE and to foreign MNE, the less influence the works council will have and the less serious its role will be*".[2] An effect on the position of works councils in foreign MNCs compared to Dutch MNCs should be visible in this study as well. Therefore, the differences in the responses between the two sub-samples will be reported throughout this chapter.

The chapter will be subdivided in the following sections. Firstly, the general characteristics of the respondent works councils (section 2) and the level at which employee consultation takes place and with whom (section 3) will be examined. Secondly, the role of the works councils within the corporate structure – including the application of the structure regime – and the influence of the parent company (section 4) will be discussed. Thirdly, the substantive rights of Dutch works councils and their (non-)use are examined (section 5), which includes the use of information and consultation rights, but also considers the use of covenants and experts. Lastly, any foreign contact that of Dutch works

---

1 J.K. Looise and M. Drucker, 'Employee participation in multinational enterprises: The effects of globalisation on Dutch works councils', 24 *Employee Relations* 1 (2002).

2 *Ibid.*, p. 37.

councils have (section 6) and the relationship with the EWC (7), if applicable, will be addressed.

2 GENERAL CHARACTERISTICS OF DUTCH WORKS COUNCILS IN MNCS

Against the background of the Dutch legal framework applicable to works councils, as was examined in chapter III of this study, it can be concluded that there exists a broad range of different rules and exceptions relating thereto. This leads to a difference of the setting in which the respective works councils operate as well as differences in the characteristics of the works councils. These characteristics include the sector in which the undertaking operates in, the legal form of the undertaking and the degree of internationalisation in terms of the ratio of employees that are employed outside of the Netherlands and outside of Europe. Further to this, the location of the parent company's headquarters provides a strong indicator of the corporate culture that is present within the MNC.[3] Finally, the legal form combined with the size of the undertaking also determines whether or not a supervisory board must be established.[4]

2.1 Legal form

The participants were asked what legal form the undertaking has adopted, for which the (central) works council is maintained.[5] Unsurprisingly, the vast majority of all respondents indicated that the undertaking was either a private limited liability company (61,1%) or a public limited liability company (33,3%). Moreover, European company forms such as the *Societas Europea* (SE) or *Societas Cooperativa Europea* (SCE) were not reported by the respondents.

Figure 2.1 Legal form of the undertakings (N = 54)

3 *Ibid.*, p. 29-30 and 44.
4 Pursuant to the structure regime as examined in section 3.2 of chapter III and section 3 of chapter VI.
5 Question 7 of the questionnaire; see Annex II.

The majority of undertakings located in the industrial sector are private limited liability companies (B.V.), whereas the respondent transport, construction and installation as well as all water companies were all public limited liability companies (N.V.). The only respondent undertaking that indicated the legal form as being a PLC as well as an N.V. was located in the financial sector. Finally, cooperative associations were only reported as existing in the industrial sector.

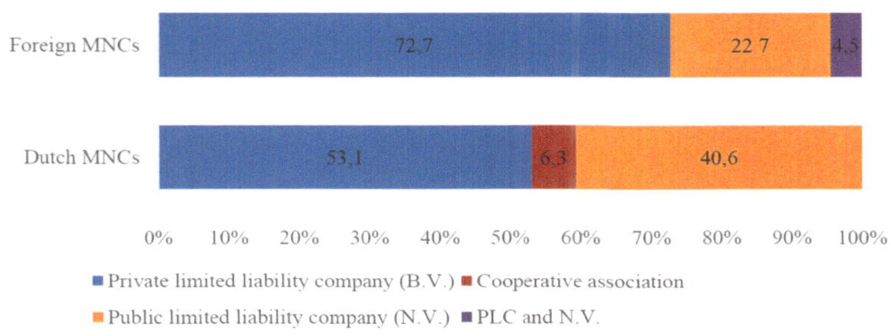

Figure 2.2 *Legal form of undertakings in Dutch (N = 34) and foreign (N = 22) multinational corporations*

When splitting the sample between Dutch and foreign multinational corporations (i.e., those companies having their company seat located outside of the Netherlands), a few additional observations can be made. Dutch multinationals are, in 40,6% of the cases, public limited liability companies, whereas only 22,7% of foreign multinationals (subsidiaries) have adopted this corporate structure. In both Dutch and foreign multinationals, the majority of undertakings were private limited liability companies. The only cooperative association in the sample was a Dutch multinational, whereas the only corporation taking the form of both a PLC as well as an N.V. company form was a foreign multinational. The country of origin also has implications for the corporate culture as will be further examined in the subsequent section.

2.2 *The country of origin of the corporation and corporate culture*

Earlier research on employee participation in multinational corporations indicates that a differentiation has to be made between fully Dutch MNCs, foreign MNCs with Dutch origin and completely foreign MNCs with no Dutch origin, as was discussed in this chapter's introduction.[6]

6 J.C. Looise and M. Drucker, 'Dutch Works Councils in Times of Transition: The Effects of Changes in Society, Organizations and Work on the Position of Works Councils', 24 *Employee Relations* 3 (2003), p. 398-402.

According to the research undertaken by Looise and Drucker, works councils in fully Dutch MNCs scored better in terms of involvement in the decision-making process than works councils in foreign MNCs with a Dutch origin, which in turn score better than the works councils in foreign MNCs.[7] Their conclusion that "*the further away the company is from the national context, from national [corporation] to Dutch [MNC] and to foreign [MNC], the less influence the works council will have and the less serious its role will be*",[8] gives reason to expect a difference in the outcome of the results of this study as well. Therefore, the respondents were asked about the location of the parent company's registered office,[9] as well as the location of the registered office of the division of the MNC, if applicable, in order to determine the corporation's origin and in turn the applicable corporate culture.[10] Not only does the country of origin of the MNC determine, to an overwhelming degree, the applicable corporate culture, but the location of the registered office also has decisive influence on whether or not the structure regime is applicable and to what extent.[11]

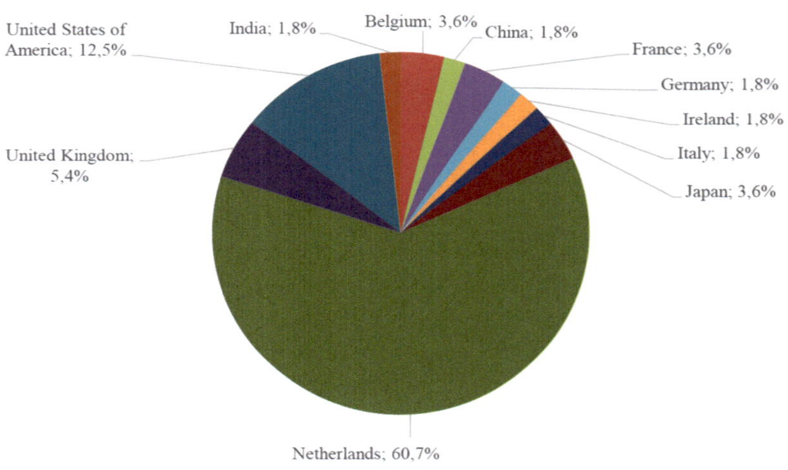

Figure 2.3 Country of the registered office of the topholding (N = 56)

7 *Ibid.*, p. 37.
8 *Ibid.*
9 See also section 1.1 in chapter II for a description of the connecting factor used.
10 Questions 2 and 3 of the questionnaire; see Annex II.
11 See section 3.2 of chapter III and section 3 of chapter VI for a detailed analysis of the structure regime; see section 4 below for the quantitative results.

The responses that were reported by Figure 2.3 show that the majority of respondent undertakings were still of Dutch origin (60,7%), but as 39,3% of companies had a foreign parent company, the high degree of internationalisation of MNCs in the Netherlands becomes salient.[12] The largest group of foreign multinationals are those of US origin (12%), followed by UK-based multinationals (5%) and Japanese, French as well as Belgian MNCs (all 3,6%). These foreign corporations, in turn, overwhelmingly make use of a Dutch (sub)holding-structure (95,8% of the responses) with only two MNCs steering the Dutch subsidiaries from abroad.[13]

2.3 *Employees of the multinationals in the Netherlands and abroad*

Finally, the ratio of employees working in the Netherlands vis-à-vis the number of employees in Europe and worldwide can be utilized to establish how internationally orientated the MNC is. When examining the employee ratio for the Netherlands, it becomes apparent that almost half of the MNCs employ less than 10% of their workforce in the Netherlands (see Table 2.1 below). Furthermore, 82,6% of the MNCs employ only a minority of their workforce in the Netherlands and only a small group (17,4%) employs more than half of its overall workforce in the Netherlands. Moreover, a large group of foreign MNCs employ only a small fraction of their employees in the Netherlands (45,7% of the MNCs have less than 10% of their workforce employed in the Netherlands).

Table 2.1 *Ratio of Dutch employees vis-à-vis the total number of employees of the MNCs (N = 46)*

Q4 The ratio of employees in the Netherlands (in %)

		Frequency	Percent	Valid Percent	Cumulative Percent
Valid	less than 10%	21	37,5	45,7	45,7
	10 - 24%	9	16,1	19,6	65,2
	25 - 49%	8	14,3	17,4	82,6
	50 - 74%	5	8,9	10,9	93,5
	75 - 100%	3	5,4	6,5	100,0
	Total	46	82,1	100,0	
Missing		10	17,9		
Total		56	100,0		

12 See Annex III for an overview of the SPSS data output.

13 One from India and one from Belgium; see also the responses to question 3 in Annex III for an overview of the SPSS data output.

This, however, does not imply that the number of employees is insubstantial. The respondent undertakings employed around 426.084 employees in the Netherlands altogether, which is equivalent to approximately 5,1% of the overall working population of the Netherlands.[14] The impact of a weak works council position or the non-use of rights can therefore be regarded as substantial, irrespective of the fact that a small fraction of the overall MNC's workforce is employed in the Netherlands.

When examining the threshold values for the establishment of a European Works Council (hereinafter: EWC), which is addressed in more detail in section 7 below, it can be remarked that *all* of the MNCs that participated in the survey employ (considerably) more than 150 employees in the Netherlands. Moreover, only three respondents indicated an overall number of employees that was less than 1000. Therefore, the vast majority of all MNCs are obliged to establish and maintain a EWC pursuant to article 4(2) of Directive 2009/38/EC on the European works councils.

Unfortunately, 29 out of 56 respondents (52%) did not reply or answer the sub-question pertaining to the number of employees in Europe, which could have allowed for a definitive answer as to whether or not all threshold values for the establishment of a EWC are fulfilled. Nevertheless, 27 of the respondents to the sub-question regarding the number of employees in Europe indicated a number higher than the threshold value that is necessary for the establishment of a EWC.

3 WHERE DOES EMPLOYEE PARTICIPATION IN THE NETHERLANDS IN MNCS TAKE PLACE AND WITH WHOM?

After having examined the general characteristics of the undertakings, this section addresses the level at which employee participation takes place within the corporation and whom the consultation partner of the works council is.

3.1 At which level within the MNCs does employee participation take place?

A crucial factor for the position of (Dutch) works councils is the level at which the employee participation takes place within a corporation. The analysis of the structure regime (discussed in section 3.2 of chapter III above) and the corresponding case law on attribution and co-entrepreneurship has shown that works councils are sometimes 'degraded' or 'pushed-down' – through the use of holding structures – with regard to

14 According to 'Statistics Netherlands', around 8,3 million persons are working in the Netherlands; CBS, 'Bevolking 15 tot 75 jaar', < https://www.cbs.nl/nl-nl/achtergrond/2016/20/bevolking-15-tot-75-jaar> (last accessed 02 February 2017).

their level of influence on the decision-making process, with adverse effects on employee participation as a result.[15] Moreover, article 25(2) of the WCA stipulates that "*advice shall be requested at a time when it can still significantly affect the decision to be taken*". A core question is therefore whether the timing of consultations within the subholding-structure applied in many MNCs allows for advice that can still significantly affect the decision-making process.

The respondents were asked at which level the (central) works council within their corporation was maintained (Figure 3.1 below).[16] The results are displayed both for the full sample of responses as well as individually for Dutch and foreign MNCs. Subsequently, the participants were also asked whom their dialogue partner was during consultation meetings (Figure 3.2 in the following section).[17]

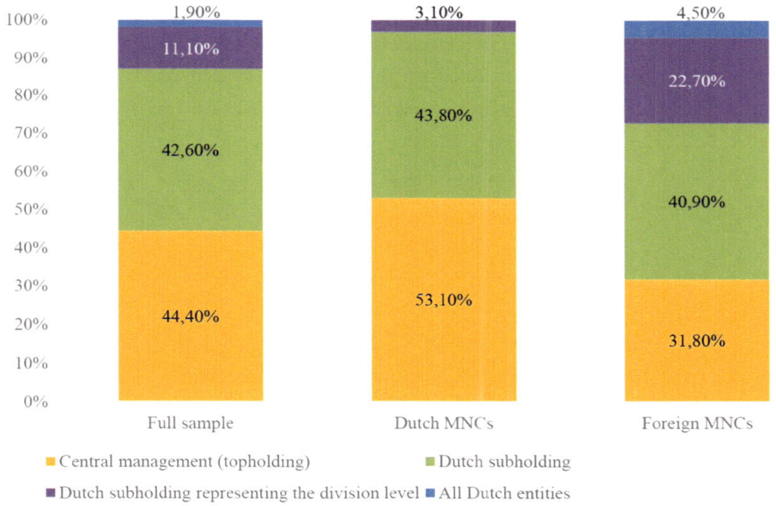

Figure 3.1 *Level of employee participation (N = 54); level of participation in Dutch (N = 32) and foreign MNCs (N = 22)*

According to 44,4% of the respondents, the employee representation body was located at the central management level. This is particularly striking since 60,7% of the respondents also indicated that their corporation had its registered office in the Netherlands (Figure 2.3 above). This negative discrepancy (-16,3%) can be explained by the application of the structure regime by Dutch corporations and the resulting exemption of the

15 See section 4 chapter III for a detailed analysis of the case law on attribution and co-entrepreneurship.
16 Question 8 of the questionnaire; see Annex II.
17 Question 10 of the questionnaire; see Annex II.

topholding in cases whereby the majority of employees work outside the Netherlands. By doing so, a subholding can be set up in order to exempt the topholding from its employee participation obligations.[18] In 53,1% of the Dutch MNCs, a works council was maintained at the central management level. In foreign multinationals, 31,8% of the works councils were maintained at the central management level.[19] The percentage of works councils being maintained at the Dutch subholding-level was very similar in both Dutch (43,8%) and foreign (40,9%) MNCs. In foreign MNCs, works councils were maintained, in 22,7% of the cases, at the Dutch subholding-level which, at the same time, represents the division level (i.e., the works council is located at division rather than top-management level).

As is shown by figure 1.6 below, corporations that apply the structure regime at the highest corporate level are, in the vast majority of cases, also ensuring that employee participation is present at the highest level of the MNC. Corporations with a structure regime in place at subholding level (i.e., the Netherland's construction), accordingly, often have employee participation limited to the subholding level. This also has consequences for the consultation partner of the works council, as will subsequently be addressed.

3.2 *Consultation partner of the Dutch works council*

Alongside the consultation level of the works council, the consultation partner of the works council is also influential for the position of the works council. This is because of the position of the works council's consultation partner, whom can limit access to information and the decision-making process, if the counterpart's position is also limited. (Dutch) country managers are often only acting on behalf of the MNC's central management and may only execute instructions that are given to him by the higher management. Furthermore, access to information is limited in cases when HR managers do not receive information and may not be in the position to elaborate on specific issues. Therefore, the participants were asked whom their dialogue partner(s) was/were (Figure 3.2 below).[20]

18 See sections 3.2 and 4 in chapter III on the so-called "Netherlands construction".

19 In light of the territoriality principle, it is questionable whether indeed 31% of the works councils are located at the level of the central management of a foreign corporation.

20 Question 10 of the questionnaire; see Annex II.

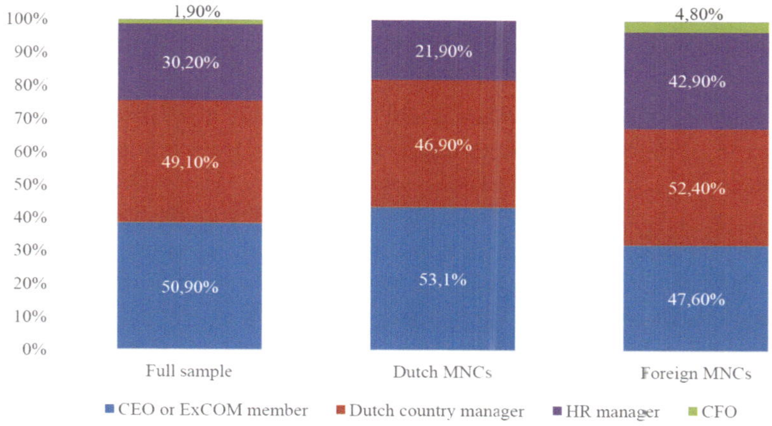

Figure 3.2 *Consultation partner of the (central) works council (N = 53); consultation partner in Dutch (N = 32) and foreign (N = 21) MNCs*

The majority of works councils reported that the CEO or another member of the executive committee[21] of the central management is their consultation partner (50,9%), while almost the same number of works councils stated that the Dutch country manager is their consultation partner (49,1%). Thus, a majority of works councils participate in the decision-making process at the highest level and have reported the CEO as the consultation partner, despite only 44,4% of the works councils being located at the central management level.[22] Therefore, a number of works councils reported their CEO as being the consultation partner *despite* employee participation being located at the subholding level.

In one-third of the consultation meetings, the HR manager was (also) present. Two respondents, however, indicated that *only* the HR manager was present, which could be a potential indicator of a lack of access to all the necessary information as well as additional explanations during consultation meetings. This is because HR managers are not necessarily competent or may not have the mandate to answer all of the work council's questions. Some respondents further reported that the holding director was the first point of contact and was present during consultation meetings, but that the central management was present only on an irregular basis or upon the request of the works council. Finally, one respondent indicated that the CFO was present during the

21 The executive committee or group executive committee is comprised of the chief officers and business heads. In Anglo-Saxon corporations especially, such a board structure is often applied and members of this Executive committee can be important consultation partners for the works councils.

22 See Figure 3.1 above.

consultation meetings and another respondent reported that the managers of divisions were also present during the meetings.

When comparing the responses by employee representatives in Dutch and foreign MNCs, a few differences can be noted. The CEO or another member of the executive committee was, more often than not, the consultation partner (53,1%) of the works council in Dutch MNCs compared to foreign multinationals (47,6%). The Dutch country manager, on the other hand, was more frequently the consultation partner of works councils in foreign MNCs (52,4%) compared to Dutch MNCs (46,9%). A rather significant difference can thus be observed with regard to the presence of HR-managers – in addition to the CEO or country manager as was explained above. Whereas in 21,9% of Dutch MNCs the HR-manager was present during the meetings, the HR-manager as the consultation partner in foreign MNCs was present in 42,9% of the cases.

When comparing the overall responses with the results of the earlier study by van Beurden (et al.), it becomes apparent that the CEO or another member of the central management is the consultation partner of the Dutch works council in the majority of cases.[23] At the same time, the HR manager is often present according to the respondents to this survey. Whereas 44,8% (39 of 87 respondents) indicated that the CEO or member of the central management was the consultation partner in 2009,[24] this was the case in 50,9% of the works councils that participated in this study (an increase of 6,1 percentage points). Further to this, in 2009 43,7% (38 of 87 respondents) stated that the Dutch country manager was the consultation partner, while 49,1% of the respondents to this questionnaire reported as such (an increase of 5,4 percentage points).

A difference in responses can also be discerned with regard to the presence of HR managers. Whereas 9,2% of the respondents in the 2009 survey indicated that the HR manager was the consultation partner, 30,2% of the respondents to this survey indicated that the HR manager was also the consultation partner (+ 21 percentage points). Yet, in only two cases (3,7%) was the HR manager the only consultation partner. In the remaining corporations, the HR manager was present *in addition* to the CEO or the Dutch country manager. Overall, a net decrease of cases where only the HR manager was the consultation partner can be noted (- 5,5 percentage points in comparison to 2009). This can be

23 Cf. R. Goodijk, P. van Beurden and H. van Ees, 'Gebruik, niet-gebruik of onderbenutting? Onderzoek naar de mogelijke onderbenutting van bevoegdheden en mogelijkheden door de (Centrale) Ondernemingsraad in grote Nederlandse ondernemingen', p. 31; in the 1999 study, 82% of the respondents indicated that the CEO was the consultation partner of their works council, but it must be noted that the sample differed considerably due to the fact that it was not exclusively large corporations that participated in this study; Cf. R.H. van het Kaar and J.C. Looise, *De volwassen OR – Groei en grenzen van de Nederlandse ondernemingsraad: Resultaten van het grote OR-onderzoek*, p. 49.

24 R. Goodijk, P. van Beurden and H. van Ees, 'Gebruik, niet-gebruik of onderbenutting? Onderzoek naar de mogelijke onderbenutting van bevoegdheden en mogelijkheden door de (Centrale) Ondernemingsraad in grote Nederlandse ondernemingen', p. 31.

seen as positive indicator of the position of the Dutch works councils in MNCs. Yet, these aspects only address the framework within which the consultation process takes place, and not the content thereof. The latter will be addressed below in section 5.

4 THE ROLE OF THE WORKS COUNCIL WITHIN THE CORPORATE STRUCTURE AND THE INFLUENCE OF THE PARENT COMPANY

It is not only the level at which the works council is maintained and who the consultation partner of the works council is that determines the position of the Dutch works council. Specifically, the structure regime that was introduced in 1971 and the significant recast of this regime that took place in 2004 has effected the position of the Dutch works council in MNCs.

The regime that was discussed in detail in section 3.2 of chapter III, and in particular the detailed rules allowing for an exemption of internationally oriented top-holdings (with the majority of employees working outside the Netherlands), is particularly unique in the EU. The possibility of the Dutch works council to recommend members of the undertaking's supervisory board and especially the enhanced right of recommendation for one-third of the supervisory board members that was identified in chapter III is a very important tool for the works councils to exercise influence over the corporation's decision-making process. Furthermore, the supervisory board was identified as a possible additional source of information as well as channel through which the works councils could convey their position on (intended) decisions.

In order to determine the use of these rights by the works councils in MNCs, the respondents were asked about whether the structure regime applied within their corporation,[25] how long they had applied the regime[26] and whether it was applied on a voluntary basis.[27] Furthermore, the participants were asked about whether their works council had exercised its regular[28] and enhanced[29] right of recommendation at any time over the last four years.

As a second step, the participants were asked about their experiences with regard to the works council's relationship vis-à-vis the supervisory board[30] or – in case the recommendation right was not exercised – what the reasons for the non-use were.[31]

25 Question 11 of the questionnaire; see Annex II.
26 Question 12 of the questionnaire; see Annex II.
27 Question 13 of the questionnaire; see Annex II.
28 Question 19 of the questionnaire; see Annex II.
29 Question 20 of the questionnaire; see Annex II.
30 Questions 21 and 22 of the questionnaire; see Annex II.
31 Question 23 of the questionnaire; see Annex II.

4.1 *Application of the structure regime*

Firstly, the participants were asked whether the structure regime was applied within their corporation. Although the regime must be applied by 'large' undertakings, which is defined by reference to their annual turnover, the number of employees (at least 100) as well as the presence of a works council, this was not always the case (see Figure 4.1 below).

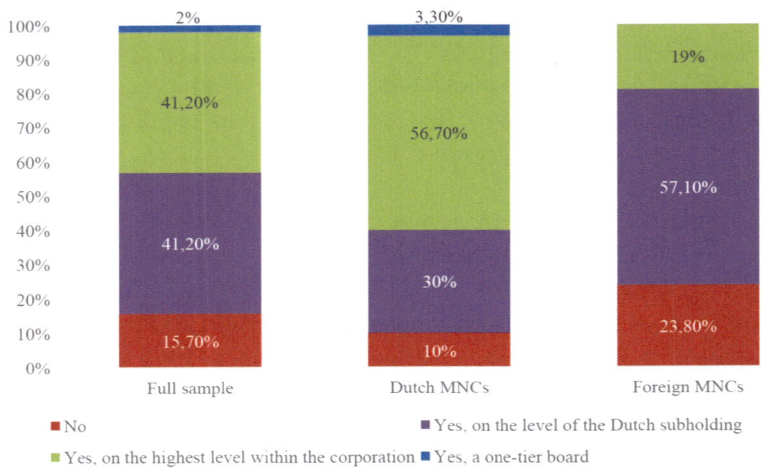

Figure 4.1 *Application of the structure regime within MNCs (N = 51); application of the structure regime within Dutch (N = 30) and foreign (N = 21) MNCs*

The structure regime was applied at top-holding level by 41,2% of the corporations. The same ratio of MNCs applied the regime at Dutch sub-holding level (41,2%). A further 2% of the respondents indicated that a one-tier board structure was applied without specifying at which level within the MNC. It is important to note that throughout this chapter, both the supervisory board and the one-tier board are meant when referring to the supervisory organ in this chapter. The structure regime also applies to one-tier boards with non-executive directors. Pursuant to article 2:164a (1) of the DCC, which stipulates that "*what is provided in Article 2:158 paragraph 2 up to and including 12, 2:159, 2:160, 2:161 and 2:161a on the Supervisory Board, respectively, on the Supervisory Directors shall then apply accordingly to the non-executive Directors of the Open Corporation*". The same applies to private limited liability companies (B.V.) pursuant to article 2:274a (1) of the DCC.

When individually examining the responses by Dutch and foreign MNCs, a number of additional observations should be made. However, the results of this comparison should be treated with a degree of caution. Given the small sample size, a statistical significance cannot be ascertained.

In Dutch MNCs, the structure regime was applied at the highest level of the corporation in the majority of cases (56,7%). The opposite was the case in foreign MNCs, with a majority of corporations applying the structure regime at the Dutch sub-holding level (57,1%). This difference can be explained by the fact that the seat of the foreign corporation was not located in the Netherlands. In light of the principle of territoriality, the Dutch structure regime was not applied at the highest level within the corporation (i.e., outside the Netherlands) but rather at the highest level in the Netherlands. The number of responses in particular, on the application of the structure regime *at the highest level* within foreign corporations is somewhat surprising. The fact that 19% of the respondents indicated that the structure regime was applied at the top-holding level in foreign MNCs, is unexpected in light of the principle of territoriality. If the regime were indeed to be applied at the top-holding level, Dutch employee board level-representation would be applicable to foreign corporations. One explanation for this could be because of incorrect answers supplied by the respondents, because they misunderstood the question, believed to "know" the wrong answer or had forgotten the answer.[32] Due to these uncertainties regarding the validity of the responses, no further analysis of the data is possible.

The data also show that at least one in six MNCs (15,7%) do not apply the structure regime at all, even although it is very likely that these very large corporations fulfil the criteria. All respondent works councils reported employing more than 100 employees for the Dutch entities and a works council was present in all corporations. Furthermore, all corporations are very likely to have more than 16 million EUR in equity capital.[33] It is also noteworthy that the compliance rate is higher in Dutch multinationals (90%) than compared to foreign multinationals (76,2%). Whereas one in ten Dutch multinationals were not applying the regime, almost one in four foreign MNCs did not apply it according to the respondents. The foreign MNCs that were not applying the structure regime had their seat in Belgium (2 MNCs), Canada (1), China (1) and the United States (1).

The enforcement of the application of the structure regime is unclear. As one respondent pointed out, the supervisory board within the MNC concerned was not appointed for two years although the works council regularly tabled the issue. Further to this, it was reported that the corporate management regarded the supervisory board and its role in the decision-making process as superfluous. While such a response may not be representative, these individual cases nevertheless show that corporations apparently can,

32 Cf. O. Sjöström, D. Holst and S.O. Lind, 'Validity of a questionnaire survey: the role of non-response and incorrect answers', 57 *Acta Odontol Scand* 5 (1999), p. 242-243.

33 The survey responses are anonymous, which makes a verification of figures on turnover and capital impossible.

in some cases, neglect their statutory obligations and avoid introducing the structure regime. This therefore constitutes a task for the legislator to adapt the current regime by including an effective enforcement mechanism. The current sanction, i.e., an economic offence (as per articles 1(4) and 6 of the *Wet op de Economische Delicten*) has not had a deterrent effect on some of the corporations. A constant monitoring of the compliance rate by the competent authorities would therefore be desirable. The works councils in such corporations whereby no application of the regime has taken place – despite fulfillment of the criteria – should also endeavor to put more emphasis on this issue. Not only is the supervising organ missing without the application of the structure regime, but the works council also loses the possibility to exercise its (enhanced) recommendation right for one third of the supervisory board. The topic of works councils' recommendation rights for the supervisory board will be revisited below.

As was discussed in section 3.2 of chapter III above, the amendments to the regime in 2004 led to a shift in the balance of interests with regard to the structure regime. Since then, the position of shareholders has been strengthened while the position of the works council has become more limited. Specifically, under these circumstances the works councils in MNCs should demand compliance with the statutory obligations under the regime in order to safeguard its rights thereunder. In concrete terms, the works council may file an action to obtain interim measures based on a failure by the entrepreneur to introduce the structure regime in the undertaking.[34]

Secondly, the participants were asked how long the regime applied within their undertaking. According to the responses, a considerable number of corporations introduced the structure regime only after the amendment of the regime in 2004 (11,3%) or even more recently between 2011-2014 (7,5%) as is shown below (Figure 4.2). However, the majority of respondents were not aware of how long the regime was applicable in their corporation (50,9%).[35]

34 R.H. van het Kaar and J.B.A. Hoyink, *Ondernemingsraad – 3.1.1.2 structuurvenootschappen* (Kluwer online), p. 1; see also section 3.2.1. in Chapter III.

35 The category of 'not applicable' refers to respondents who indicated that the structure regime was not applied in their corporation. Accordingly, no date of introduction can be reported.

Q12 Since when is the structure regime applied within your corporation?

		Frequency	Percent	Valid Percent	Cumulative Percent
Valid	Unknown	27	48,2	50,9	50,9
	1971-2003	8	14,3	15,1	66,0
	2004-2010	6	10,7	11,3	77,4
	2011-2014	4	7,1	7,5	84,9
	Not applicable	8	14,3	15,1	100,0
	Total	53	94,6	100,0	
Missing		3	5,4		
Total		56	100,0		

Figure 4.2 Date of introduction of the structure regime in MNCs (N = 53)

When the respondents were further asked whether the structure regime was applied on a voluntary basis (see Figure 4.3 below), only 62,2% could answer the question definitively with the remainder indicating that they did not know whether the regime was applied on a voluntary basis or not. Such a lack of knowledge on the currently applicable regime also affects the works council's position regarding future changes, such as the question of whether or not a recommendation right is applicable. Consultation rights related to the structure regime, moreover, can only successfully be relied upon once the works council has knowledge of the structure applied as well as the consultation rights attached thereto.[36]

Furthermore, 35,6% of the respondents indicated that the regime was applied on a voluntary basis. As was addressed in section 3.2.4 of chapter III, the voluntary application of the regime was predominantly used as a protective measure against takeovers due to the fact that the supervisory board was entrusted with tasks that otherwise rested with the shareholders in non-structure regime companies. The reported percentage of undertakings applying the regime voluntarily was rather high. The question arises therefore as to whether these responses accurately reflect the situation in practice. Furthermore, a bias can be created as a result of the incorrect answers given by the respondents, because they misunderstood the question, believed to "know" the wrong answer or had forgotten the answer.[37]

36 See section 3.2 in chapter III above for a detailed analysis of the structure regime.

37 Cf. O. Sjöström, D. Holst and S.O. Lind, 'Validity of a questionnaire survey: the role of non-response and incorrect answers', 57 *Acta Odontol Scand* 5 (1999), p. 242-243.

Q13 Is the structure regime applied in your corporation on a voluntary basis?

		Frequency	Percent	Valid Percent	Cumulative Percent
Valid	Yes	16	28,6	35,6	35,6
	No	12	21,4	26,7	62,2
	Unknown	17	30,4	37,8	100,0
	Total	45	80,4	100,0	
Missing		11	19,6		
Total		56	100,0		

Figure 4.3 *Voluntary application of the structure regime (N = 45)*

Thirdly, the participants were asked whether their works council exercised their regular right of recommendation at any time over the last four years.[38] Pursuant to the regular recommendation right, both the works council and the general meeting of shareholders may put forward candidates for election to the supervisory board (or one-tier board), which do not however have to be accepted for the appointment to be successful. The works council can further participate in the drafting the profile of the recommended candidate(s).

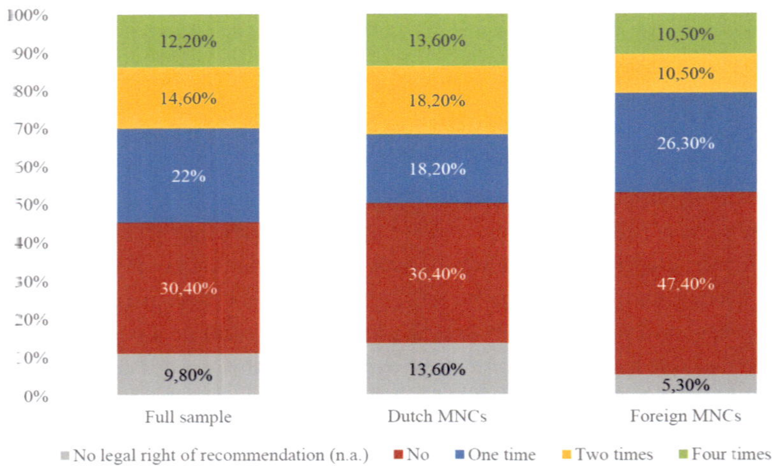

Figure 4.4 *Regular right of recommendation for the supervisory board of the MNCs (N = 41); use of the right in Dutch (N = 22) and foreign (N = 19) MNCs*

38 Question 19 of the questionnaire; see Annex II.

Although 48,8% of the works councils indicated that the regular right of recommendation was exercised at least once, 41,5% indicated that this right was not used at all. The latter group, therefore, does not influence the selection process (by recommending candidates or by participating in the drafting of the profile of the candidate). This certainly leaves room for improvement as the works council can assume an active role and gain a greater insight into the strategic orientation of the corporation. In Dutch MNCs, slightly more respondents indicated that their works councils had used the regular recommendation rights at least once (50%). In foreign MNCs, the respondents indicated that the regular recommendation procedure was used less often.

Finally, the participants were asked whether their works council had made use of the enhanced right of recommendation over the last four years.[39] When comparing the results with regard to the use of the regular vis-à-vis the enhanced right of recommendation, it becomes salient that a larger percentage of works councils make use of the enhanced recommendation right. Thereby, the enhanced recommendation right was predominantly used once, which can be explained by the fact that this right can only be exercised for one-third of the supervisory board whereas the regular recommendation right can be exercised for all appointments and is hence used somewhat more frequently. But although the enhanced recommendation right is used more frequently (64,3%), one-third of the respondents indicated that the right was never made at all (31%). Given the important influence that the works council can have on the composition of (one-third) of the supervisory board as a consequence of this right, it is highly recommendable that this relatively large minority should make more frequent use of it than is presently the case. In the 2009 study conducted by van Beurden (et al.), 36% of the respondents indicated that the right of recommendation was never made.[40]

39 Question 20 of the questionnaire; see Annex II.

40 Cf. R. Goodijk, P. van Beurden and H. van Ees, 'Gebruik, niet-gebruik of onderbenutting? Onderzoek naar de mogelijke onderbenutting van bevoegdheden en mogelijkheden door de (Centrale) Ondernemingsraad in grote Nederlandse ondernemingen', p. 33; it must be noted however that a different sample was used in the 2009 study, which does not allow for a direct comparison of the results.

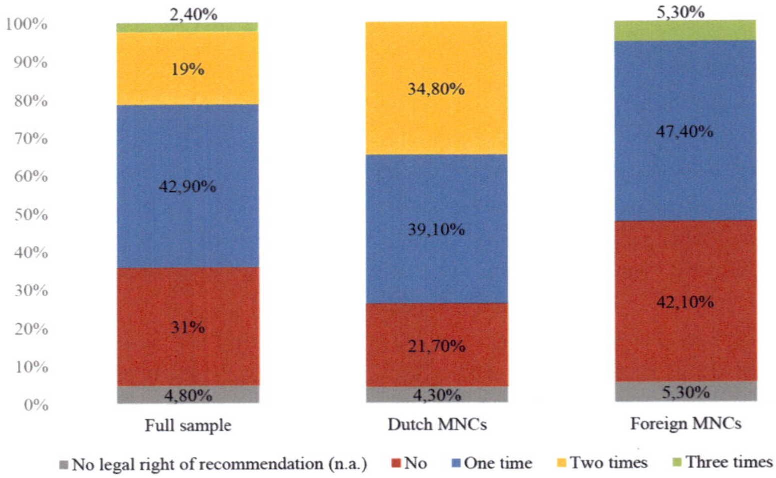

Figure 4.5 *Enhanced right of recommendation for the supervisory board of the MNCs (N = 42)*

It should be noted for the sake of completeness that only a very small minority (4,8%) reported that no statutory right of recommendation was conferred upon their works council. Furthermore, the group of respondents that had indicated that no use of the enhanced recommendation right was made over the last four years were subsequently asked to indicate the reasons why no use of that right was made.[41]

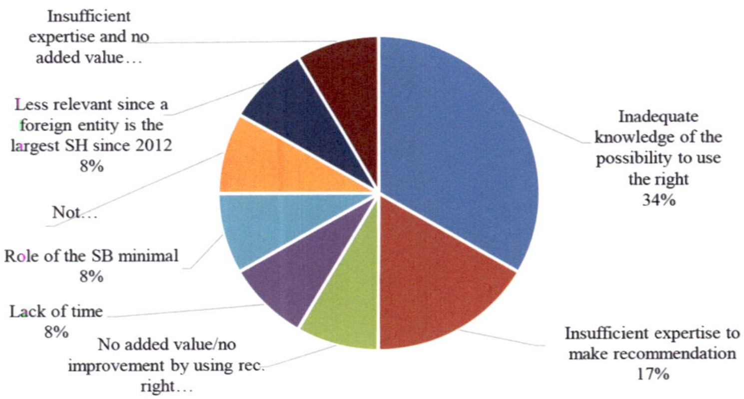

Figure 4.6 *Reasons non-use of the enhanced right of recommendation for the supervisory board of the MNCs (N = 12)*

41 Question 23 of the questionnaire; see Annex II.

Strikingly, 4 out of the 12 works councils (33,3%), that had not exercised their enhanced recommendation right over the last four years, reported having inadequate knowledge of their works council's right to make such recommendations. Thus, even although the enhanced recommendation right is the strongest tool available to the works council under the structure regime, some of these works councils have no knowledge whatsoever of this right. This issue can and should be addressed by informing works councils, in particular those in multinational corporations but also the works councils of smaller undertakings, by means of training and development as well as through the exchange of information via works councils networks. The same holds true for the respondents that indicated that their works council had insufficient expertise to make use of the recommendation right.[42] By means of training as well as information on the recommendation right, the works councils can be put in a position that enables them to make greater use of their recommendation rights.

A third group of respondents indicated either that using the right had no added value, the role of the supervisory board was regarded as minimal or that is was less relevant since a foreign entity became the majority shareholder in 2012. All three types of responses can be understood as indicators of the weak role of the supervisory board or possessing little influence due to the presence of a majority shareholder that influences the supervisory board's composition.

Given the fact that it was the intention of the Dutch legislator to strengthen the position of shareholders – while at the same time failing to adopt similar measures to safeguard the position of works councils in multinational corporations – not much can be done by works councils to improve their position in the current circumstances. Still, works councils can, by adopting an active role during the appointment procedure, establish a proactive role vis-à-vis the majority shareholder (which is very often the parent company within a MNC) to influence the selection process to some extent. In public limited companies (*Naamloze Vennootschap*, NV), use can be made of the works council's speaking right at the general meeting of shareholders (article 2:107a and 2:135 of the DCC) in order to put forward the works council's position.[43]

Lastly, one respondent indicated a lack of time and another indicated that the use of the enhanced recommendation right was not necessary. While it could potentially be the case that the works council's candidate is also recommended at the general meeting of shareholders (with the works council informally exercising influence over the appointment process), not using the right will certainly not improve the position of the works council. This becomes even more salient when one examines whether the works council

42 In total 25% of the respondents indicated that this was the case.

43 See sections 1.4.1.1 and 1.4.5 in chapter III for a detailed analysis of the right to speak at the general meeting of shareholders and the Harrewijn Act.

has more contact with the recommended supervisory board members when compared to the other supervisory board members.[44]

More than two-thirds (65,4%) of the participants reported that greater contact with the recommended supervisory board member(s) exists.[45] Therefore, after approaching the works council candidate, the contacts often continue to exist once the candidate is appointed as a supervisory board member. Although all supervisory board members have to remain independent towards the other organs of the undertaking, this contact can nevertheless be very valuable for the works council in order to gain greater insights into the corporate policy from not only the management's perspective but also from the perspective of the supervising organ. From the supervisory board's perspective, such contact is equally important due to the additional insights that are gained from meetings with the works council, which was pointed out in the interview phase of this study.[46]

4.2 The relationship between the Dutch works council and the supervisory board

After having addressed the application of the structure regime within MNCs in general and the use of the works councils' rights of recommendation, the relationship between the works council and the supervisory board will be examined. The different roles that the supervisory board can perform towards the works council as well as the possible influence that the parent company can exercise over the supervisory board by placing a member of the parent corporation on the supervisory board of the Dutch subsidiary (the so-called *concernfunctionarissen*) will also be addressed.[47]

The participants were, therefore, asked about the composition of the supervisory board within their corporation.[48] The respondents were thereby asked to specify the overall number of supervisory board members as well as the number of corporate representatives and external persons sitting on the supervisory board.[49] Subsequently, they were asked whether he or she thought that any undue influence was being exercised over the

44 Question 21 of the questionnaire; see Annex II.

45 No noteworthy differences are reported by respondents in Dutch MNCs with 68,8% indicating that more contacts exist with the recommended supervisory board members – compared to 60% of the respondents in foreign MNCs.

46 See section 3.4 in chapter V below.

47 See also section 2 in chapter VI for a detailed discussion of possible undue influence of the parent company; such placement is lawful in light of the REGEV judgment of the Enterprise Chamber; OK 11 April 1991, ROR 1991/21 (*REGEV*); Cf. S.M. Bartman and A.F.M. Dorresteijn, *Van het concern* (8th edn., Kluwer, Deventer 2013), p. 152.

48 Question 17 of the questionnaire; see Annex II.

49 'External supervisory board members' are persons neither having a position within the corporate group within the meaning of article 2:158/268(6-8) of the DCC. All supervisory board members should always act independently and guided by the interests of the corporation and its affiliated enterprise (article 2:140/250(2 jo. 5) of the DCC).

supervisory board by the top-management.[50] Further, the participants were asked to indicate how their cooperation with the supervisory board, in terms of access to information and influence on the decision-making process, was perceived and whether the supervisory board had a mediating role between the works council and the management.[51]

Firstly, the composition of the supervisory board was reported by reference to the ratio of corporate members on the supervisory board of the Dutch undertaking by means of a dummy variable (i.e., the number of persons of a higher corporate entity within the MNC in relation to the total number of supervisory board members). A ratio below 50% is, therefore, indicative of fewer corporate members than external supervisory board members. Since more than half of the respondents did not indicate either the total number of supervisory board members or the number of corporate members appointed, the results reported below must be examined with caution with regard to their representativeness. However, the large number of missing responses and especially missing responses pertaining to the number of corporate members on the supervisory board, is in itself an indicator that a considerable number of works councils may not have sufficient enough insight into the composition of the undertaking's supervisory board. Yet, in light of the positive effects that insights into the corporate structure have for works councils in multinational corporations, obtaining such information in order to work more efficiently and effectively and hence to improve their own position within the corporate structure may be useful.

69% of the respondents indicated that the undertaking's supervisory board was comprised of *fewer* corporate than external supervisory board members or an equal number of both, as shown by Figure 4.7 below.[52] However, in about one third of the cases (31%), the supervisory board was comprised of *more* corporate than external members (see Figure 4.7 below for a detailed breakdown).

50 Question 18 of the questionnaire; see Annex II.
51 Question 22 of the questionnaire; see Annex II.
52 No noteworthy differences are reported by respondents between Dutch and foreign MNCs.

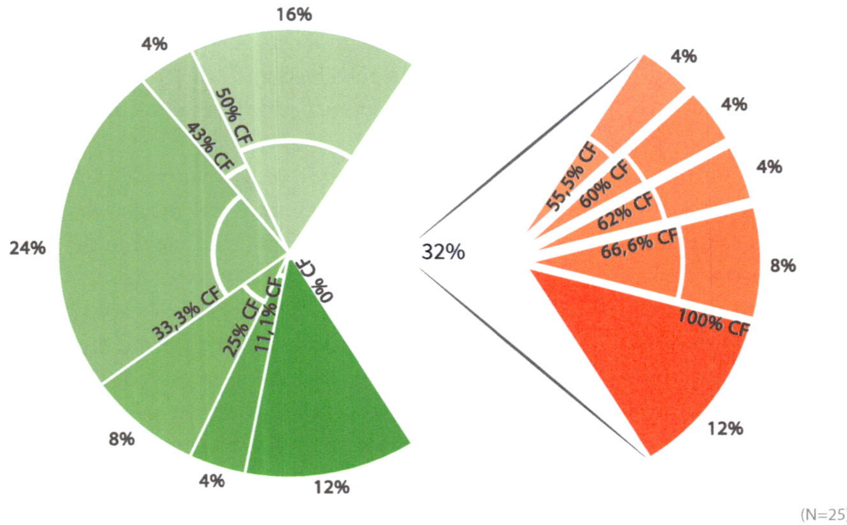

Figure 4.7 *Ratio of corporate representatives (concernfunctionarissen, CF) in the supervisory board of the Dutch subsidiary (N = 25)*

Even although the presence of corporate members on the supervisory board can potentially lead to more informal contact between the works council and members of the parent company, it is certainly doubtful as to whether strict supervision is in place when the members of the parent company's management constitute the majority of the undertaking's supervisory board members.[53]

It can therefore be doubted as to whether the primary duty of the supervisory board members – namely to be guided by the interests of the corporation and the enterprises connected therewith when performing their tasks (article 2:140(2) of the DCC) and thus to be independent from other interests such as those of the parent company – can be sufficiently adhered to.[54] Additionally, the supervisory board ought to be comprised of a majority of external members in order to safeguard the said independence and to ensure the effective application of corporate governance mechanisms.[55] In the questionnaire,

53 See also section 2 in chapter VI below for a detailed discussion.

54 See also R. Hooghiemstra and J. van Manen, 'The Independence Paradox: (im)possibilities facing non-executive directors in The Netherlands', 12 *Corporate Governance: An International Review* 3 (2004), p. 316.

55 The Dutch Corporate Governance Code introduces the principle that all supervisory board members except for one member have to be independent; see also the recast of the Dutch Corporate Governance Code (December 2016), available at: http://www.mccg.nl/download/?id=3364 (last accessed 2 March 2017); Cf. E. Groenewald, 'Corporate Governance in the Netherlands: From the Verdam Report of 1964 to the Tabaksblat Code of 2003', *European Business Organization Law Review* 2 (2005), p. 302.

participants were therefore asked whether it was the works council's perception that undue influence by the top-management was being exercised over the supervisory board of the Dutch undertaking.

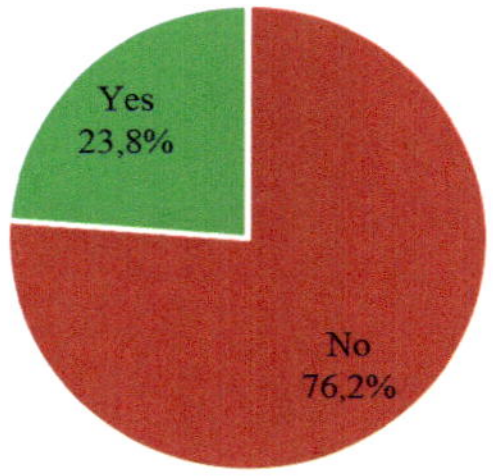

Figure 4.8 *Undue influence by the top-management on the supervisory board in MNCs (N = 42)*

In 32% of the MNCs, a majority of the supervisory board was comprised of corporate representatives and in 50% of the corporations, half of the board was constituted by corporate representatives. Yet, a smaller group of works councils (23,8%) indicated that undue influence was being exercised in their undertaking by the top-management vis-à-vis the supervisory board. Furthermore, for those cases whereby the majority of supervisory board members were members of the top-management, 62,5% of the respondents nevertheless reported that no undue influence was being exercised. This was particularly striking in two cases whereby two-thirds of the supervisory board was comprised of corporate members and the works councils still stated that no undue influence was present. This aspect will be followed up in the interview phase for further clarification.

In a subsequent step, the works councils were asked whether contact with the supervisory board of their corporation led to better access to information. Given the fact that information is the essential prerequisite for the works councils to effectively influence the decision-making process, additional access to information via the supervisory board must be regarded as strengthening the position of the works council. Moreover, ensuring better access to information also highlights the importance of the exercise of the work council's recommendation right in light of the extent of the non-use that was reported by Figure 4.5 above. The use of the recommendation right is thereby an indicator of the active stance of Dutch works councils vis-à-vis the supervisory board of their MNC.

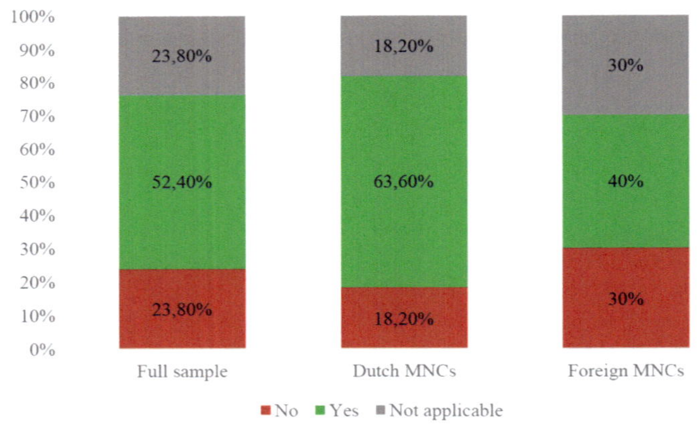

Figure 4.9 *Better access to information by the Dutch works council via the supervisory board of MNCs (N = 42); information access in Dutch (N = 22) and foreign MNCs (N = 20)*

The participants reported, in the majority of cases, that their access to information was improved through contact with the supervisory board (52,4%), while only a minority indicated that contact with the supervisory board did not lead to better access to information (23,8%). In Dutch MNCs in particular, the supervisory board appears to be a source of information, with 63,6% of the respondents answering the question in the affirmative. In foreign MNCs, a large minority (40%) regarded the supervisory board as source of information.

Therefore, the importance of an active works council with regard to the appointment of the supervisory board as well as subsequently maintaining contact is naturally beneficial to the position of the works council. Furthermore, the supervisory board members may have access to information on strategic issues that are specifically valuable for the effective positioning of works councils in multinational corporations. Furthermore, 32,6% of the works councils stated that the access to information had improved, since recommended members were appointed to the supervisory board (see Figure 4.10 below). At the same time, however, the same share of respondents did not experience an improvement in access to information or interference over the decision-making process, after the recommended members were appointed to the supervisory board. The large share of respondents that indicated that the question was "not applicable" can be explained by the fact that a relatively large number of work councils had not exercised their recommendation right over the last four years, as was discussed above. When comparing Dutch and foreign MNCs, it can be noted that access to information has more frequently improved in Dutch MNCs with 39,1% of the respondents answering the question in the affirmative. Only 25% of respondents in foreign MNCs regarded their information access to be improved since their recommendation.

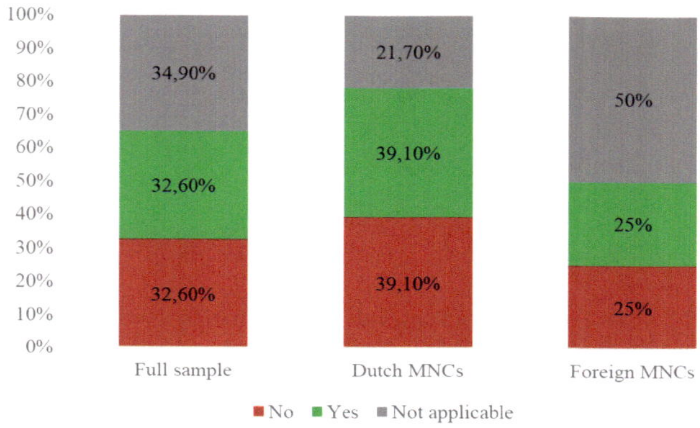

Figure 4.10 *Improvement of access to information and influence on the decision-making process since recommended supervisory board members are present in the MNC (N = 43); access in Dutch (N = 23) and foreign MNCs (N = 20) since the recommendation*

With regard to influence over the decision-making process through contact with the supervisory board, it was reported in the majority of cases that no increased influence was achieved (see below). Yet, 30,2% of the respondents stated that the contact with the supervisory board led to them being more able to influence the decision-making process. Notably, the influence was greater in foreign (35%) compared to Dutch MNCs (26,1%).

While having more influence over the decision-making process via the supervisory board of the corporation certainly strengthens the position of the Dutch works councils, further research during the qualitative phase of this study was necessary to determine the precise impact of the supervisory board in such corporations.

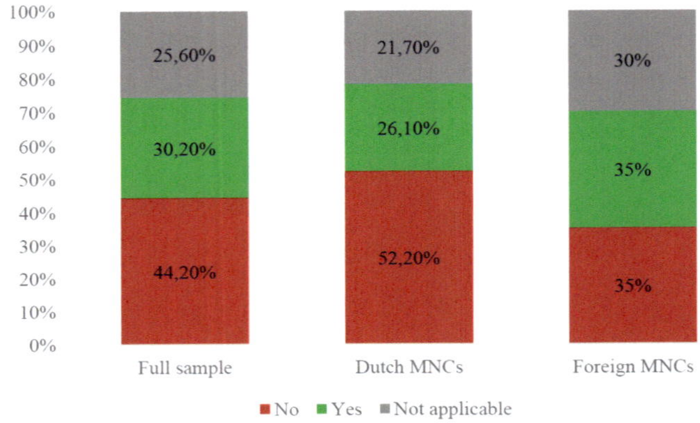

Figure 4.11 *Impact of contacts of the Dutch works council with the supervisory board on the decision-making process (N = 43); in Dutch (N = 23) and foreign MNCs (N = 20)*

Finally, the supervisory board may have a mediating role between the works council and the management due to the supervisory board's monitoring and controlling role.[56] The independence of the supervisory board thereby formally stems from article 2:140(2) of the DCC, which stipulates that the interests of the corporation and the connected enterprises shall guide the supervisory board members.[57] On the basis of this independent position, the supervisory board can then potentially mediate between the conflicting positions that may arise between the management and the employee representatives.

As is shown by Figure 4.12 below, a large group of respondents indeed indicated that the supervisory board fulfils a mediating role (37,2%). Thus, the supervisory board, in more than one-third of the cases, helps to resolve disputes. In Dutch MNCs, the percentage of respondents affirming the mediating role was higher (43,5%) than in foreign MNCs (30%). Hence, increased contact with the supervisory board not only facilitates the work of the work councils by means of an additional information channel and an alternative route to influence the decision-making process, but it may also potentially mediate between the management and the works council if any disputes arise.

56 Cf. A. Demb and F. Neubauer, 'The Corporate Board: Confronting the Paradoxes', 3 *Long Range Planning* 25 (1992), p. 13; R.B. Adams and D. Ferreira, 'A Theory of Friendly Boards', 1 *The Journal of Finance* 62 (2007).

57 This is further emphasised in Principle 2.1 of the 2016 Dutch Corporate Governance Code regarding the profile of supervisory board members and their independence (principles 2.1.7, 2.1.8 and 2.6.4).

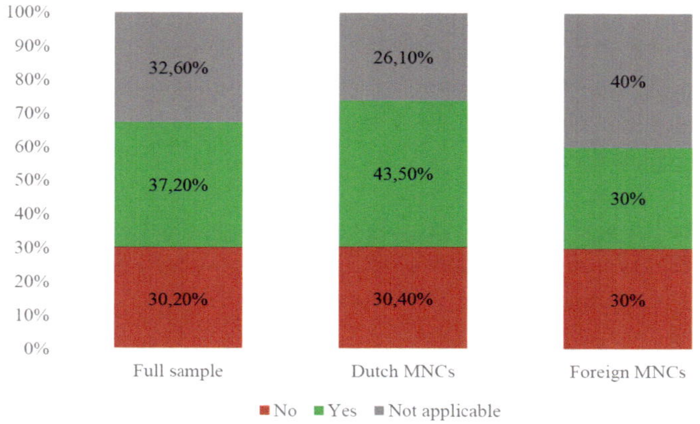

Figure 4.12 Is the supervisory board having a mediating role in MNCs (N = 43); in Dutch (N = 23) and foreign MNCs (N = 20)

Overall the results regarding the relationship between the works council and the supervisory board have shown that, on the one hand, contact between a considerable number of work councils and supervisory boards exists and that they are generally very beneficial to the position of the respective work councils due to better access to information and in particular via the recommended board members. On the other hand, a rather large minority of work councils did not exercise their rights with regard to the supervisory board and therefore eschewed the potential benefits that may flow from a well-established relationship with the supervisory board. Finally, the topic of possible undue influence by the management of the parent company on the supervisory board can be seen in a considerable percentage of cases and should be addressed by work councils due to the potential implications for the (lack of) independence of the corporation's supervisory board.

5 Rights of the Dutch works council in MNCs and their use

The rights of the Dutch works council are not only very extensive in comparison to the rights of employee representatives in other countries, but these rights have been continuously extended over the last few decades.[58]

In the following section, the use and possible non-use of specific rights that were identified in the analytical part of this study as being of particular importance to the position of the Dutch work councils in multinational corporations will be reported.

5.1 Agenda setting of the Dutch works councils

While the rights of Dutch work councils are quite extensive, the restraints in terms of time and resources available to works councils may lead to a choice to focus and be active in specific areas and can result in the underutilisation of the certain rights that are conferred on work councils pursuant to the WCA, the structure regime and other provisions.[59]

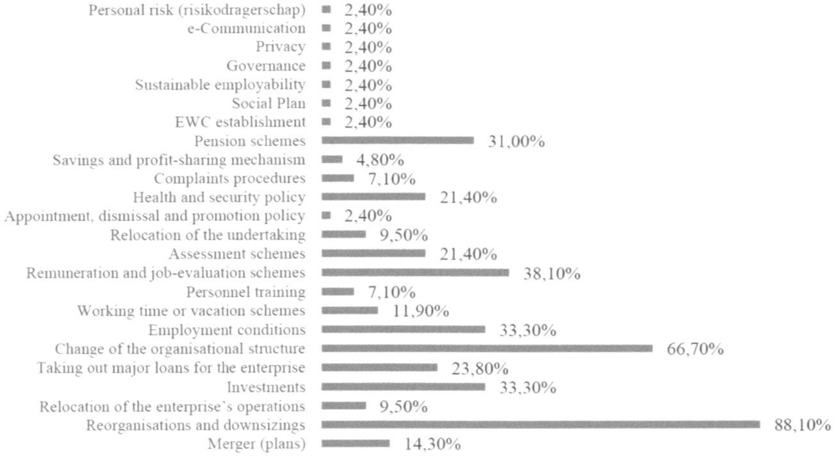

Figure 5.1 Agenda setting of the (central) works councils in MNCs last year (N = 42)

58 See section 1.4 in chapter III above for a detailed examination of these works council rights.

59 The underutilisation was specifically addressed in the earlier study on Dutch works councils in R. Goodijk, P. van Beurden and H. van Ees, 'Gebruik, niet-gebruik of onderbenutting? Onderzoek naar de mogelijke onderbenutting van bevoegdheden en mogelijkheden door de (Centrale) Ondernemingsraad in grote Nederlandse ondernemingen'.

Therefore, the overall agenda setting of Dutch works councils in multinational corporations was determined by asking the respondents which of the listed topics received the most attention of their (central) work council in the previous year, and they were asked to choose from among five topics.[60]

Firstly, the aftermath of the financial crisis and its effects on the Dutch and global economy respectively are clearly still reflected in the agenda setting of the participating works councils with an overwhelming majority of the respondents indicating that reorganisations and downsizings were the highest priority being addressed by their works council (88,1%). For undertakings that were particularly adversely affected, the negotiation of a social plan has taken priority (yet only one works council indicated the existence of such a situation).

Secondly, although Holtzer concluded in his dissertation that Dutch works councils are not dealing sufficiently with (intended) decisions on strategic matters, the empirical data on works councils in large multinational corporations point in the opposite direction.[61] Changes to the organisational structure of the corporation (66,7%), investments (33,3%) as well as to a lesser extent the taking out of major loans (23,8%) and merger (plans) (14,3%) ranked high on the participating works councils' agendas.[62] As was identified in section 1.4 of chapter III, changes to the organisational structure can have especially far-reaching consequences for the Dutch employees and for the position of the Dutch works councils. It is, therefore, a positive indicator that this topic is on the agenda of a large majority of the participating works councils. Moreover, investments can be a strong indicator of the corporation's future strategic orientation, as investments are more likely to be made in those areas of activity that are presumed to be most promising for the MNC. The fact that one-third of the respondents indicated that investments were among the top five priorities of their works council can be regarded as positive indicator of an active role of these works councils on strategic matters. The same holds true for major loans. At the same time, a considerable number of works councils did not regard such topics, i.e., those regarding the strategic positioning of the corporation, to be of high importance. This certainly leaves room for improvement.

60 Question 24 of the questionnaire; see Annex II; significant differences in the responses between Dutch and foreign MNCs cannot be observed.

61 M. Holtzer, *De invloed van werknemers op de strategie van de vennootschap* (Kluwer, Deventer 2014), p. 136, 158–159 and 162 et seq.

62 Such strategic issues are furthermore actually addressed in consultation meetings with the management as further addressed in section 5.2 below.

Thirdly, pension schemes (31%) were also a topic that was high on the works councils' agenda. A recent change in the legislation concerning the works councils' involvement on pension schemes is likely to be a contributing factor to the relatively large percentage of works councils that have put this topic on their agenda.[63]

Finally, "classic" works council topics in the areas of employment conditions (33,3%), remuneration and job-evaluation schemes (38,1%), assessment schemes (21,4%), as well as the health and security policy of the corporation (21,4%) were still regarded as important for the respondent works councils. The same holds true, albeit to a lesser extent, for the working time and vacation schemes (11,9%). Finally, a small group of works councils indicated that new developments in the areas of e-communication, privacy, governance and sustainable employability ranked high on the works councils' agenda.[64]

The priorities of the Dutch works councils have thereby changed with regard to some topics, but have remained stable regarding the main priorities, namely reorganisations and changes to the organisational structure. The ranking is reported by Figure 5.2 below with the ranking of the topics in 1999 displayed in brackets. It must be emphasised that the 1999 study examined the *overall* position of Dutch works councils whereas the current study focuses solely on their position in multinational organisations. Certain topics are therefore more or less likely to be put on the works councils' agenda. It must also be further noted that the relatively high ranking of pension schemes is a result of the current debate on this topic and the related proposed changes to articles 27(1)(a) and 27(7) of the WCA.[65] Moreover, topics such as investments and major loans enjoy much greater attention by the works councils, which is also a result of the greater importance that is attached to such topics in multinational organisations in general. Working time and vacation schemes as well as the health and security policy [*Arbobeleid*], on the contrary, did not receive much attention on the agenda.

63 The new legislation on pensions and company pension-funds is applicable from 1 January 2015 onwards. Undertakings had to align their pension scheme prior to that date, which requires an involvement of the works council pursuant to article 27(7) of the WCA.

64 Indicated by one works council per topic.

65 See in this regard SER advice 2014/05 *Instemmingsrecht OR over arbeidsvoorwaarde pensioen.*

66 Table 4.1 'Onderwerpen naar meeste aandacht', in R.H. van het Kaar and J.C. Looise, *De volwassen OR – Groei en grenzen van de Nederlandse ondernemingsraad: Resultaten van het grote OR-onderzoek*, p. 113.

Topics ranked by priority	2014 (N = 42)	1999 (N = 397)[66]
1. Reorganisations and downsizings (1.)	88,1%	55%
2. Change of the organisational structure [of the corporation] (2.)	66,7%	55%
3. Remuneration and job-evaluation schemes (6.)	38,1%	30%
4. Investments (10.)	33,3%	21%
4. Employment conditions (9.)	33,3%	23%
6. Pension schemes (17.)	31,0%	8%
7. Taking out major loans for the enterprise (18.)	23,8%	2%
8. Assessment schemes (8.)	21,4%	24%
8. Health and security policy (3.)	21,4%	53%
10. Merger (plans) (5.)	14,3%	31%
11. Working time or vacation schemes (4.)	11,9%	47%
12. Change in the location of the enterprise's operations (13.)	9,5%	14%
12. Relocation	9,5%	-
14. Personnel training (7.)	7,1%	24%
14. Complaints procedures (16.)	7,1%	11%
16. Savings and profit-sharing mechanism (15.)	4,8%	13%
17. Appointment, dismissal and promotion policy (14.)	2,4%	14%
17. EWC establishment	2,4%	-
17. Social Plan	2,4%	-
17. Sustainable employability	2,4%	-
17. Governance	2,4%	-
17. Privacy	2,4%	-
17. e-Communication	2,4%	-
17. Personal risk (*risikodragerschap*)	2,4%	-

Figure 5.2 Ranking of topics on the works council agenda by priority in 2014 and 1999

5.2 *Consultation meetings with the management*

Whereas the agenda setting of the Dutch works councils, as addressed in the previous section, gave an indication of the primary objectives of the respondent works councils, the actual consultation of the works councils by the management on (intended) decisions is a decisive factor for evaluating the influence of the works councils over the decision-making process. The consultation rights of the Dutch works council pursuant to article 25 of the WCA are thereby at the heart of the employee participation regime and crucial for the position of the Dutch works council in multinational corporations.

The most important areas, for which prior consultation of the works councils is mandatory were examined in section 1.4 in chapter III above. One issue that was identified was that decision-making on topics, which would fall under one of the rights of the Dutch works council, were frequently decided outside of the Netherlands. It was further concluded that a tension between decision-making at top-holding level and employee participation rights at sub-holding level in the Netherlands became visible especially with regards to the consultation rights pursuant to article 25 of the WCA. Therefore, once the Dutch works council is consulted on (intended) decisions that are inherently international in their nature and are frequently decided at the level of the top-holding, this can be seen as an indicator of the Dutch works council having a strong position within the corporation.

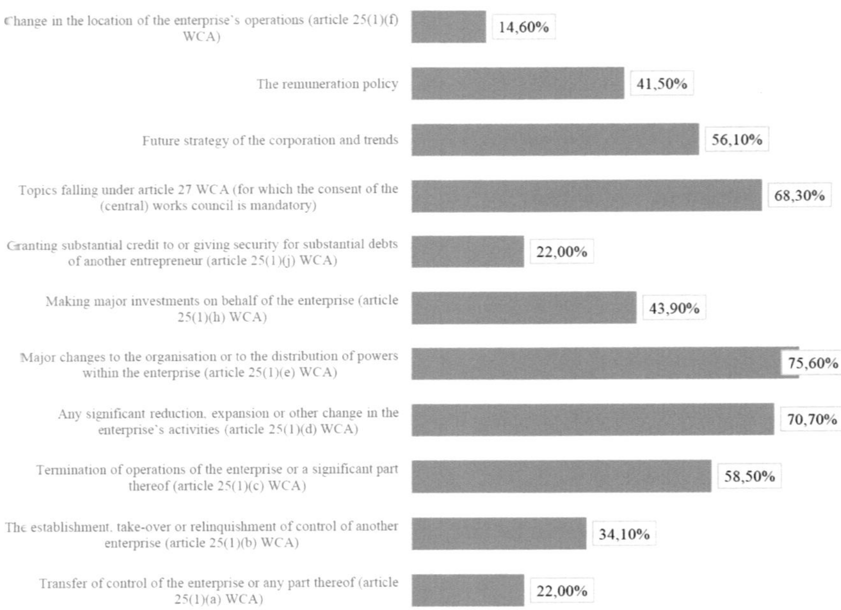

Figure 5.3 Frequencies of agenda points in consultation meetings in the period 2012-2014 in MNCs (N = 41)

Firstly, when examining the responses to the question concerning which topics were discussed in the consultation meetings with the management in the period 2012 – 2014,[67] it becomes visible that the responses to question 24 on the agenda setting of the works council were overall consistent with the topics discussed in the consultation meetings

67 Question 25 of the questionnaire; see Annex II.

with the management. Furthermore, a large majority of consultation meetings between works councils and the management pertained to the termination of certain operations within the corporation (58,5%), as well as significant reductions, expansions or changes in the enterprise activities (70,7%). These responses are very likely to be related to the aftermath of the financial crisis.

A large majority of respondents (75,6%) further indicated that major changes to the organisation or the distribution of powers was subject to the prior consultation of the works council, which must be seen as positive indicator. The consultation of the works council on (intended) decisions regarding changes to the distribution of powers is very important due to the fact that changes to the organisational structure can have significant implications for the future position of the works council. Nevertheless, it remains to be seen in the qualitative analysis whether the consultation of the works council on this matter is indeed of significant influence.

Involving works council on matters concerning the development of the future strategy and trends in the area of economic activity of the respective corporation positively affects the position of the works council due to their involvement in the early stages of the decision-making process. It is safe to assume, therefore, that the earlier the works council is involved in the decision-making process, the higher the impact of the works council's position on the (intended) decision will be. Therefore, the fact that a majority of respondents (56,1%) indicated that their works council was consulted on the future strategy of their corporation and possible trends can be seen as indicative of a relatively strong position of the Dutch works councils in MNCs.

Furthermore, a relatively large number of respondents (43,9%) reported that their works council was consulted on (intended) decisions concerning the adoption of major investments. Relatively few works councils, however, were consulted on (intended) decisions to grant substantial credit to or giving security for substantial debts of another entrepreneur (22%), notwithstanding the fact that such credits within the corporation or securities for substantial debts can have considerable future implications for the MNC.

"Classical" topics such as matters falling within the scope of article 27 of the WCA were unsurprisingly addressed in the majority of consultation meetings (68,3%), but only an (albeit large) minority of works councils were consulted on the remuneration policy within their corporation (41,5%). This could be caused by the centralised adoption of the remuneration policy for the entire MNC. The implementation of such a policy should be, nevertheless, subject to prior works council consultation – insofar as it also concerns the remuneration policy on the Dutch level – in light of the legal framework.

However, when comparing the responses by works councils maintained in Dutch MNCs (i.e., corporations having their headquarters within the Netherlands) with the responses by works councils that are maintained in foreign MNCs (i.e., having their headquarters outside of the Netherlands), a number of differences can be identified.

In order to ascertain whether these differences between the two groups of works councils regarding the areas of consultation are significant, a two-proportion z-test was applied. The procedure for a two-proportion z-test can be validly employed only if both samples satisfy the standard binomial requirement that $n \times p$ *and* $n(1 - p) \geq 5$, where n are the sample sizes and p is the percentage.[68] The response percentages are rounded to full digit numbers in order to obtain the z-scores.

Sub-question	Dutch MNCs		Foreign MNCs	
	$n \times p$	$n(1 - p)$	$n \times p$	$n(1 - p)$
Q25.1 Transfer of control	5,04	15,96	4	16
Q25.2 Take-over of control	10,08	10,92	4	16
Q25.3 Termination of operations	10,08	10,92	14	6
Q25.4 Significant reduction or other change in the enterprise's activities	14,07	6,72	15	5
Q25.5 Major changes to the organisation or distribution of powers	14,07	6,72	17	3
Q25.6 Making major investments	9,03	11,97	9	11
Q25.7 Granting substantial credit to or giving security for substantial debts of another entrepreneur	5,04	15,96	4	16
Q25.8 Topics falling under art. 27 WCA	13,02	7,98	15	5
Q25.9 Future strategy of the corporation and trends	15,96	5,04	7	13
Q25.10 The remuneration policy	7,98	13,02	9	11
Q25.11 Change in the location of the enterprise's operations	2,94	18,06	3	17

Figure 5.4 Standard binomial requirements for the sub-samples of works councils in Dutch MNCs (N = 20) and foreign MNCs (N = 21)

Due to the fact that the scores must be greater or equal to 5, the two-proportion z-test cannot be validly employed for those sub-questions where the scores shown by Figure 5.4 (above) are below five. Therefore, the differences in percentages for sub-questions 25.1, 25.2, 25.5, 25.7 and 25.11 cannot be validly be compared by means of a two-proportion z-test. Although the statistical significance for these sub-questions cannot be tested, it can be reported that the establishment, take-over or relinquishment of control of another

68 Stat Trek, 'Hypothesis Test: Difference Between Proportions', <http://stattrek.com/hypothesis-test/difference-in-proportions.aspx> (last accessed 25 October 2017).

enterprise (Q25.2) is discussed in the consultation meetings of Dutch MNCs in 47,6% of the cases whereas this issue is addressed only in 20% of the consultation meetings in foreign MNCs. Furthermore, major changes to the organisation or to the distribution of powers within the enterprise (Q25.5) is less frequently discussed in the consultation meetings of Dutch MNCs (66,7%) compared to consultation meetings in foreign MNCs (85%). No large differences can therefore be reported for the responses on the topics pertaining to the transfer of control of the enterprise or any part thereof (Q25.1), granting substantial credit to or giving security for substantial debts of another entrepreneur (Q25.7) as well as change in the location of the enterprises operations (Q25.11).

For the remaining sub-questions, for which the two-proportion z-test can be validly applied, the pooled sample proportion as well as the standard error (SE) must be computed in order to determine whether a statistical significance between Dutch MNCs and foreign MNCs exists.[69] The results of the two-proportion z-tests for sub-questions Q25.3, Q25.4, Q25.6, Q25.8, Q25.9 and Q25.10 are shown in Figure 5.5 below. The z-score is subsequently compared to its corresponding p-value by means of the normal distribution calculator, which "*is the probability of observing a sample statistic as extreme as the test statistic*".[70] The difference between the two samples is significant once the p-value is smaller than the significance level of 95% with $p < 0{,}05$.[71]

Sub-question	Pooled sample proportion	Standard Error (SE)	Z-score	P-value
Q25.3 Termination of operations	0,6	0,0234	-1.454	0.07353
Q25.4 Significant reduction or other change in the enterprise's activities	0,71	0,0201	-0.5862	0.2776
Q25.6 Making major investments	0,44	0,0241	-0.1382	0.44433
Q25.8 Topics falling under art. 27 WCA	0,68	0,0212	-0.9007	0.18406
Q25.9 Future strategy of the corporation and trends	0,56	0,0241	2.6565	0.00391
Q25.10 The remuneration policy	0,41	0,0236	-0.4486	0.32636

Figure 5.5 *Test of statistically significant differences between Dutch and foreign MNCs' consultation meetings (two-proportion z-test)*

69 First, the pooled sample proportion is computed as follows: $p = \frac{(p_1 \times n_1 + p_2 \times n_2)}{n_1 + n_2}$
Second, the standard error is computed as follows: $SE = \sqrt{p \times (1 - p) \times \left[\frac{1}{n_1} + \frac{1}{n_2}\right]}$
Subsequently, the z-score can be calculated by: $z = \frac{(p_1 - p_2)}{SE}$

70 Stat Trek, 'Hypothesis Test: Difference Between Proportions', <http://stattrek.com/hypothesis-test/difference-in-proportions.aspx> (last accessed 25 October 2017).

71 The p-values are computed using the online z-test calculator for two population proportions; Social Science Statistics, 'Z Test Calculator for 2 Population Proportions', <http://www.socscistatistics.com/tests/ztest/> (last accessed 25 October 2017).

When examining the p-values for the differences in probability of the topics being discussed in Dutch and foreign MNCs, it can be concluded that no statistically significant difference between consultation meetings in Dutch and foreign MNCs exists for almost all of the topics reported by Figure 5.5 above. However, a statistically significant difference *can* be reported for the future strategy of the corporation and the trends being discussed in consultation meetings (p = 0.00391 with a confidence interval of 95%). Whereas works councils in Dutch MNCs were consulted on future strategies in 76,2% of the cases, this topic was only addressed in 35% of the cases in consultation meetings of foreign MNCs. Therefore, Dutch works councils are significantly more often consulted on the future strategy of the corporation and can influence the decision-making process at an early stage, while works councils in foreign MNCs are significantly less often consulted on such matters. Such differences of involvement on such strategic issues can certainly be a determinant of the position of Dutch works councils. Therefore, particular attention will be given to the (lack of) consultation of the works councils on future strategic developments within the corporation in the interview-phase in order to identify possible reasons for the absence or presence of the works councils' involvement in these issues. A complete overview of the responses in Dutch and foreign MNCs is displayed below in Figure 5.6.

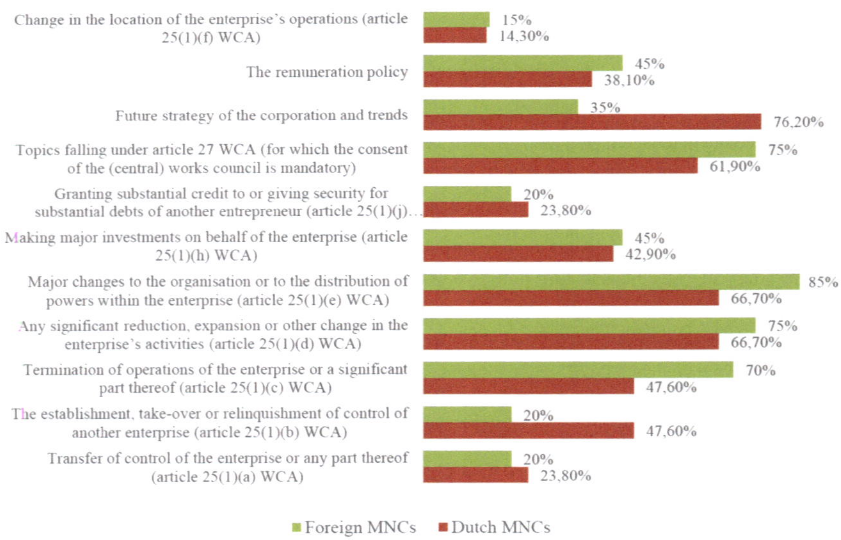

Figure 5.6 *Overview of all responses on consultation frequencies in Dutch (N = 21) and foreign MNCs (N = 20)*

Lastly, when comparing the responses with the results of the 1999 survey by van het Kaar and Looise, a number of differences can be identified (see Figure 5.7 below). Not only are some topics higher on the consultation agenda, but it is also the case that the frequency of topics being discussed at the consultation meetings is higher. The Dutch works councils in multinational organisations are, therefore, overall more frequently consulted than the general population of Dutch works councils when compared to the 1999 results. However, due to the differences in the general characteristics of the two samples, a direct comparison of the scores is not possible.

Consultation topic	2014 (N = 41)	1999 (N = 866)[72]
1. Major changes to the organization (art. 25(1)(e) WCA) [1.]	75,6%	26%
2. Any significant reduction, expansion or other change in the enterprise's activities (article 25(1)(d) WCA) [3.]	70,7%	12%
3. Article 27 WCA topics	68,3%	4%
4. Termination of operations of the enterprise or a significant part thereof (article 25(1)(c) WCA) [10.]	58,5%	3%
5. Future strategy of the corporation and trends	56,1%	-
6. Making major investments on behalf of the enterprise (article 25(1)(h) WCA) [5.]	43,9%	10%
7. The remuneration policy	41,5%	-
8. The establishment, take-over or relinquishment of control of another enterprise (article 25(1)(b) WCA) [2.]	34,1%	12%
9. Transfer of control of the enterprise or any part thereof (article 25(1)(a) WCA) [6.]	22,0%	6%
9. Granting substantial credit to or giving security for substantial debts of another entrepreneur (article 25(1)(j) WCA)	22,0%	-
11. Change in the location of the enterprise's operations (article 25(1)(f) WCA) [9.]	14,6%	3%

Figure 5.7 *Ranking of agenda points in consultation meetings by priority in 2014 and 1999*[72]

5.2.1 Frequency of consultation meetings

Another indicator of influence on the decision-making by the works council is the frequency of consultation meetings. Not only are a minimum of two consultation meetings on the general operation of the enterprise mandatory pursuant to articles 24 and 31a of the WCA, but the frequency of such consultations is also an indicator of the overall involvement of the works council in the decision-making process.

72 Table 3.2 *Onderwerpen adviesrecht* in R.H. van het Kaar and J.C. Looise, *De volwassen OR – Groei en grenzen van de Nederlandse ondernemingsraad: Resultaten van het grote OR-onderzoek*, p. 77.

Therefore, the participants were asked how often such consultation meetings took place within the organisation.[73]

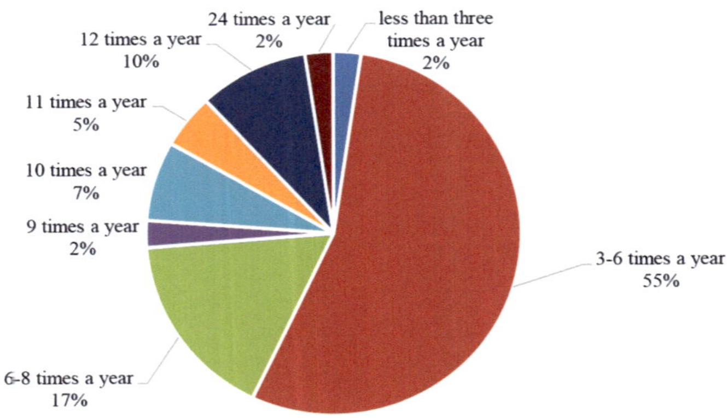

Figure 5.8 Frequency of consultation meetings in MNCs (N = 42)

As the results in Figure 5.8 show, the consultation meetings took place three to six times a year in the majority of undertakings (54,8%), whereas only one works council reported fewer consultation meetings. It can be further noted that in about 43% of the corporations, more than six meetings took place with 11,9% of the respondents indicating that consultation meetings took place on a monthly or even bi-weekly basis. Based on the sample population, three to six consultation meetings (median) took place on average per year.[74]

The frequency of consultation meetings, therefore, can be seen as an indicator that (overall) the works councils is sufficiently involved in the decision-making process given the fact that the management has a statutory obligation to explain the "*expected consequences for persons working in the enterprise and the measures proposed for dealing with such consequences*" as stipulated by article 25(3) of the WCA. At the same time, the management must be able to first formulate (intended) decisions as well as to determine the expected consequences before the works council is consulted. A higher frequency of more than (on average) six to eight consultation meetings, consequently, cannot be regarded as decisive factor for improving the position of Dutch works councils. Rather, the quality of the consultation as well as the question of whether the works council's advice is sufficiently influential over the decision-making process must be determined. As the analysis in section 5.2 above on the topics for which the works councils are consulted has shown,

73 Question 34 of the questionnaire; see Annex II.

74 With a mean of 3,21 and a standard deviation of 1,881 based on the categorical distribution of the sample; no significant differences can be observed between Dutch and foreign MNCs.

consultation on topics such as future strategies of the corporation are not always sought. This holds especially true for foreign MNCs. Moreover, prior works council advice regarding the granting of substantial credits is also not frequently obtained.

Therefore, while the frequency of meetings can be regarded as sufficient, more attention should be paid to the topics addressed in consultation meetings by Dutch works councils.

5.2.2 Presence of supervisory board members in consultation meetings

The exercise of the recommendation rights and particularly the resulting access to information via the supervisory board was identified as another important factor for the position of the Dutch works council in section 4.2 above. At the same time, a large number of Dutch works councils do not exercise their recommendation rights.

Another aspect concerning the overall relationship between the works council and supervisory board is the presence of supervisory board members at consultation meetings. Due to the independent position of the supervisory board and the role of the supervisory board as a decision-control organ within the undertaking, the presence of members of the supervisory board at consultation meetings can certainly have added value. Article 24(2) of the WCA stipulates that supervisory board members must be present at the meetings on the general operation of the enterprise at least twice per year. Therefore, the respondents were asked how often supervisory board members attended consultation meetings pursuant to article 24 of the WCA in their undertaking.[75]

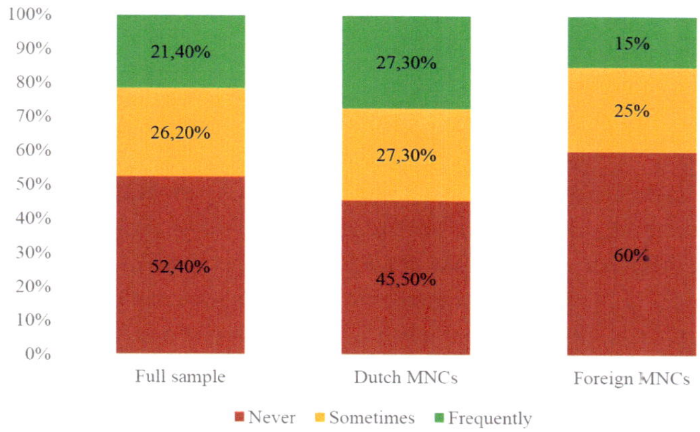

Figure 5.9 *Presence of supervisory board members in consultation meetings in MNCs (N = 42); in Dutch (N = 22) and foreign MNCs (N = 20)*

75 Question 36 of the questionnaire; see Annex II.

The results show that in the majority of multinationals, the supervisory board members are 'never' present during consultation meetings of the works council and the management (52,4%). The ratio is even higher in foreign multinationals with 60% of the respondents indicating that supervisory board members were never present. In Dutch MNCs, 45,5% of the respondents indicated that supervisory board members were 'never' present. Furthermore, only in 26,2% of the undertakings were supervisory board members 'sometimes' present during consultation meetings and in only a small minority of MNCs (21,4%) were supervisory board members 'frequently' present (15% in foreign multinationals). In Dutch multinationals, the supervisory board members were somewhat more often present during consultation meetings. In light of duty pursuant to article 24(2) of the WCA to attend at least two consultation meetings, the survey results show non-compliance of this requirement by a majority of supervisory board (members).

Yet, especially in corporations whereby the CEO of the MNC or other members of the top-management are also supervisory board members of the Dutch sub-holding, the presence of these individuals at consultation meetings could be beneficial for the consultation process. However, the responses show that, so far, little use is made of this possibility, which is in line with the responses on the use of the regular and enhanced recommendation rights (Figure 4.4 and Figure 4.5 above) as well as the results of the 2009 survey.[76] Consequently, a greater use of the possibility to include supervisory board members in consultation meetings is recommendable, especially in cases whereby members of the higher management are also appointed as supervisory board members of the Dutch sub-holding. Such presence could also be beneficial if a particular supervisory board member has a specific expertise on the topic concerned in the consultation meeting at hand (such as financial experts or legal professionals in a specific area of law).

5.2.3 Time available for advices of the works council

Aside from the overall setting in which consultation meetings take place (i.e., the number of meetings as well as the presence of supervisory board members), the time available to works councils for formulating advice on an (intended) decision is of central importance for determining the influence of the works council on the decision-making process. Specifically, article 25(2) of the WCA stipulates that the management shall request the "*advice [...] [of the works council] at a time when it can still significantly affect the decision to be taken*".

76 In 2009 a frequency of use of 2,5 on a 5-point scale was reported; see R. Goodijk, P. van Beurden and H. van Ees, 'Gebruik, niet-gebruik of onderbenutting? Onderzoek naar de mogelijke onderbenutting van bevoegdheden en mogelijkheden door de (Centrale) Ondernemingsraad in grote Nederlandse ondernemingen', p. 34.

Nevertheless, the question remains as to whether the time available to works councils is indeed sufficient in practice for formulating such advice. Therefore, the participants were asked to indicate whether this was the case within their corporation.[77]

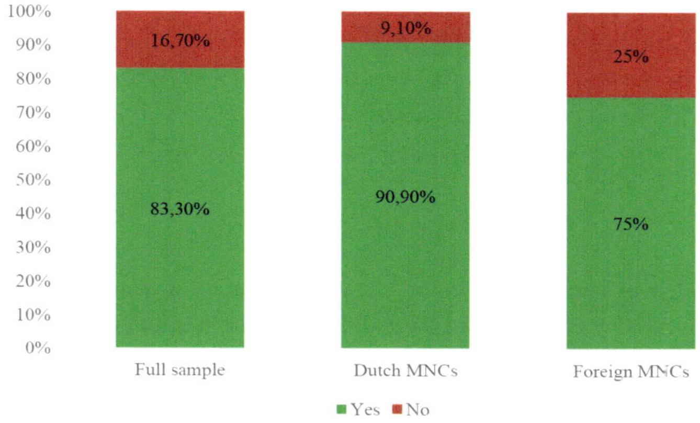

Figure 5.10 *Sufficiency of the time available for works council advices in MNCs (N = 42); in Dutch (N = 22) and foreign MNCs (N = 20)*

Clearly the majority of Dutch works councils in MNCs are given sufficient time to formulate its advice on an (intended) decision, as was indicated by 83,3% of the respondents. Thus, no disproportionate time pressure was inherent for the vast majority of works councils when formulating their advice. That being said, when comparing the responses for Dutch and foreign MNCs, some differences can be observed. In Dutch MNCs, 9 out of 10 respondents reported to have sufficient time to formulate their advice. In foreign MNCs, on the other hand, 1 out of 4 respondents (25%) reported that their works council was not given sufficient time to formulate its advice. Especially in foreign corporations whereby strategic decisions are made at the international level and only subsequently implemented at country level, the lack of time for the involvement of works council involvement is inherent in some cases.

77 Question 39 of the questionnaire; see Annex II.

This can be a source for potential disputes. As was discussed in the section on the attribution of (intended) decisions and co-entrepreneurship in section 4 of chapter III above, foreign MNCs are, in some cases, violating the consultation rights of Dutch works councils by failing to obtain prior advice on (intended) decisions that significantly affect their Dutch workforce. The lack of sufficient time for works council to formulate advice on key issues can be linked to this and gives cause for concern due to the late involvement of the Dutch works councils in the decision-making process in these cases. Works councils should, therefore, demand sufficient time for preparing their advice, which is also beneficial to the undertaking due to the enhanced quality of the advice once sufficient time has been given for deliberation thereon.

5.2.4 Disputes whether prior consultation of the works council is necessary

A further indicator of an effective works council consultation is the number of disputes relating to whether an (intended) decision of the management is to be subjected to prior works council consultation or not. Pursuant to the exhaustive list found in article 25(1) of the WCA, all (intended) decisions falling under one of the categories of that article must be subjected to prior works council advice.[78] Nevertheless, it is not always clear whether a topic falls under one of the provisions located in article 25 of the WCA. Therefore, the participants were asked whether there was a difference of opinion between the management and their works council on the necessity of prior works council advice on an (intended) decision.[79]

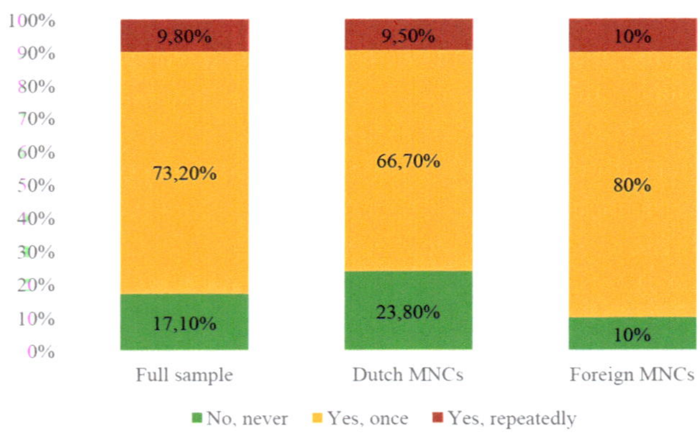

Figure 5.11 Frequency of disputes whether prior consultation of the Dutch works council was necessary (N = 41); in Dutch (N = 21) and foreign MNCs (N = 20)

78 See also section 1.4.2 in chapter III above for a detailed analysis.
79 Question 38 of the questionnaire; see Annex II.

The overwhelming majority of respondents indicated that their works council 'once' had a dispute with the management over the question of whether an (intended) decision had to be subject to prior consultation (73,2%). Only a small minority had 'repeatedly' disputes on this matter (9,8%). At the same time, only 17,1% of the respondents indicated that their works council 'never' had disputes with the management over the necessity of prior works council consultation. No significant difference can therefore be reported between Dutch and foreign MNCs regarding the frequency of disputes. A small difference can be observed between the sub-samples regarding the occurrence of a dispute either 'once' or 'never'.[80]

When comparing the results with the responses to the 1999 study carried out by van het Kaar and Looise, one must conclude that an increasing number of disputes are arising within the undertakings concerned. Whereas 31% of the respondents in 1999 reported that no disputes had arisen, this was only in 17,1% of the cases indicated in this study (+13,9%).[81] Furthermore, 55% of the respondents indicated in 1999 that such a dispute occurred once, compared to 73,2% in 2014 (+18,2%).[82] Finally, the number of repeated disputes *decreased* since 1999. While 14% of the respondents of the 1999 survey stated that disputes were occurring repeatedly, only 9,8% of the participants of this survey indicated such repeated disputes (-4,2%). Overall, however, the number of disputes appears to have increased overall with 82,9% of the respondents indicating one or more disputes in their undertaking in 2014 compared to 69% in 1999 (+ 13,9%).[83]

Despite 82,9% of all participants having indicated that their works council had at least one dispute with their management, only very few works councils submitted an appeal to the Enterprise Chamber (*Ondernemingskamer*) since 1 January 2011 as is shown by Figure 5.12 below.[84] It should be noted that the number of appeals to the Enterprise Chamber is traditionally very low with only very few appeals per year.[85]

80 Due to the small sample sizes, differences between the sub-samples should not be overestimated here. Indeed, a small difference can be observed regarding the occurrence of a dispute 'once' (80% in foreign vs. 66,7% in Dutch MNCs).

81 Table 3.10 *Geschillen adviesplichtigheid* in R.H. van het Kaar and J.C. Looise, *De volwassen OR – Groei en grenzen van de Nederlandse ondernemingsraad: Resultaten van het grote OR-onderzoek*, p. 86.

82 *Ibid.*

83 *Ibid.*

84 Pursuant to article 26 of the WCA; see also section 1.4.4 in chapter III above for an analysis of the right of appeal.

85 Cf. R.H. van het Kaar and J.C. Looise, *De volwassen OR – Groei en grenzen van de Nederlandse ondernemingsraad: Resultaten van het grote OR-onderzoek*, p. 85.

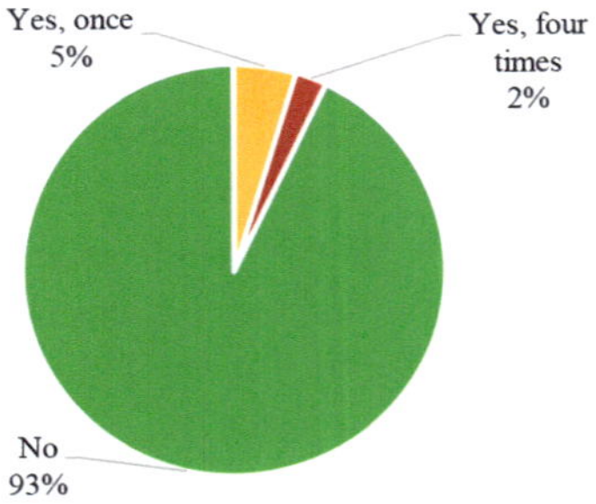

Figure 5.12 Appeals to the Enterprise Chamber of the Amsterdam Court of Appeal (N = 42)

In total, only three works councils lodged an appeal whereby two works councils did so only once. One works council appealed four times to the Enterprise Chamber. Interestingly all appeals were made by works councils that were maintained in Anglo-Saxon multinational corporations.

Overall, a discrepancy can be observed between, on the one hand, disputes arising between management and the works council on matters such as the necessity of prior works council consultation, and on the other hand the absence of litigation by works councils through the appeal procedures. This phenomenon can be explained by the fact that litigation should be used as a last resort due to fact that the relationship between the management and the works council is often irreconcilably affected by such events. The case law analysis that was carried out in section 4 of chapter III above shows that both the Enterprise Chamber as well as the Supreme Court have repeatedly declared (intended) decisions null and void once the undertaking, for which the works council is maintained, is significantly affected by the (intended) decision.

Further research on the resolution of disputes within undertakings has to be made in the qualitative part of this study in order to identify reasons for the discrepancy of repeated disputes on the necessity of consultation and at the same time the absence of appeals by works councils.

5.2.5 Who takes the initiative for ad-hoc consultation meetings?

Finally, the participants were asked, on the topic of works council consultations, whether ad hoc consultation meetings took place between the management and their works council pursuant to article 23 of the WCA, and if so, whom was taking the initiative to convene such ad hoc consultation meetings.[86]

86 Question 35 of the questionnaire; see Annex II.

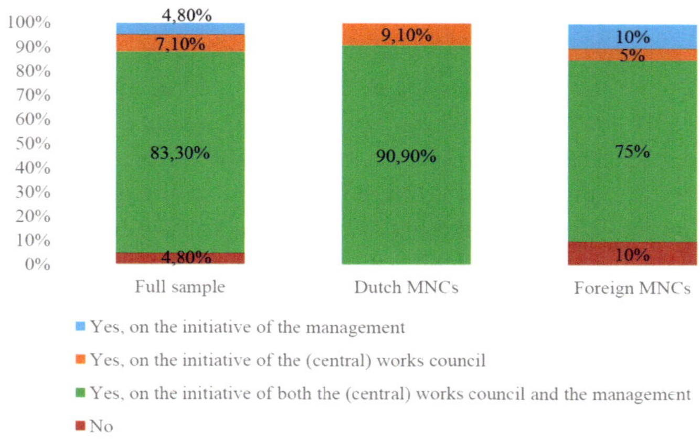

Figure 5.13 *Possibility of ad-hoc consultation meetings between the management and the works council in MNCs (N = 42); in Dutch (N = 22) and foreign MNCs (N = 20)*

Firstly, it can be noted that only two works councils indicated that no such ad-hoc consultation meetings took place. Both responses were given by works councils that are maintained in foreign MNCs (10%), although the small number of total responses does not permit a test on the statistical significance of the difference in responses given by works councils in Dutch and foreign MNCs respectively.

Secondly, a large majority of respondents indicated that ad hoc consultations took place on both the initiative of the works council as well as on the management's initiative (83,3%). These results correspond with the so-called Dutch 'polder model'. Pursuant to the 'polder model', a stakeholder approach is historically chosen by Dutch undertakings whereby all stakeholders including employee representatives participate in the decision-making process in order to achieve an outcome that is in the best interests of the undertaking as a whole. The Dutch stakeholder approach is based on the concept that "*the needs of shareholders cannot be met without satisfying to some degree the needs of other stakeholders*".[87] The outcome is a cooperative stance towards consultation procedures between the management as well as the employee representatives, which also becomes visible from the results of this questionnaire. Due to the possibility and willingness of both the management and the works council towards addressing issues at ad hoc consultation meetings according to almost all respondents, a cooperative approach towards issues in the undertaking concerned is possible whenever the need arises.

87 D. Jimali, 'A Stakeholder Approach to Corporate Social Responsibility: A Fresh Perspective into Theory and Practice', 82 *Journal of Business Ethics* 1 (2008), p. 217; see also R.E. Freeman, *Strategic Management: A Stakeholder Approach* (Pitman, Boston 1984).

5.3 Additional rights under a covenant

Another very important tool for the works councils in MNCs is the possibility to agree upon a covenant in addition to the existing consultation rights pursuant to article 25 of the WCA as well as the co-determination rights that are present under article 27 of the WCA. Following the territoriality principle, the rights of the Dutch works council in MNCs are inherently limited to the undertaking's activities in The Netherlands. As was shown in section 3 of chapter III above, multinational organisations can use their corporate structure (e.g., by using a sub-holding structure) to limit, to a large extent, the access to information as well as to the decision-making process once activities are located outside of the Netherlands. Specifically, the application of the structure regime, including the exemption of international top-holdings, (as was discussed in section 3.2 of chapter III above) contributes to this phenomenon.

By virtue of a covenant, however, additional rights alongside those stemming from the WCA or the structure regime can be agreed upon between the undertaking and the works council on a contractual basis to better link the employee participation mechanisms to the decision-making structure. Therefore, the rights of the works council can be extended despite the scope of the existing rights being limited from the outset to the Netherlands due to the applicability of the territoriality principle.

The respondents were asked whether a covenant was concluded in their undertaking and which additional rights were agreed upon pursuant to article 32 of the WCA.[88]

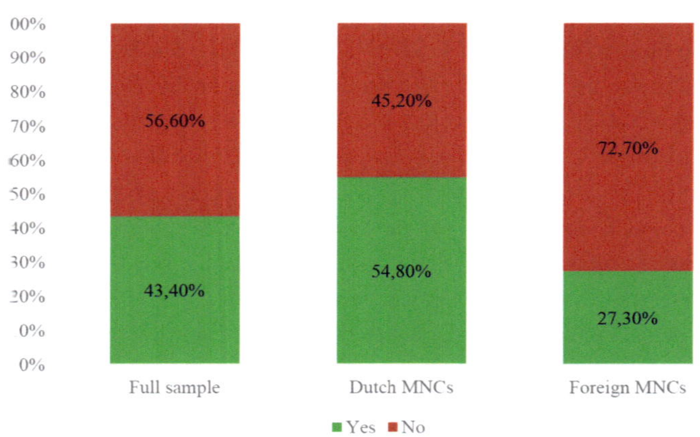

Figure 5.14 Frequency of covenants concluded under art. 32 WCA (N = 53); in Dutch (N = 31) and foreign MNCs (N = 22)

88 Questions 14 and 15 of the questionnaire; see Annex II.

Overall, a minority of works councils (43,4%) had concluded a covenant with their respective undertaking, as the results in Figure 5.14 show.[89] This certainly leaves room for improvement, especially since covenants are a very important tool to address the discrepancies between the legal framework under the WCA, on the one hand, and the actual decision-making structure applied in multinational corporations on the other. Nevertheless, a considerable number of works councils have already concluded covenants and in particular have been granted additional information rights on international matters as shown by Figure 5.15 below.

In 54,5% of the covenants agreed upon, information on international matters as well as additional consultation rights were included. This in turn allows works councils to gain not only a better overview of the overall strategy of the multinational organisation, but also the ability to influence the decision-making process at a time when the works council's input can still be of significant influence. Though the presence of such rights in the covenant does not equate to greater influence of works councils *per se*, the mere presence nevertheless shows that the Dutch works councils in these corporations are better integrated in the corporate structure compared to other works councils without such rights. The degree of actual influence pursuant to such information rights-clauses is addressed in the subsequent follow-up interviews.[90]

A further important right conferred by the covenants – according to the responses – is the right to conduct consultation meetings with the executive director of the MNC (in cases where this was not available beforehand). As was discussed in section 3.2 of chapter III on the structure regime and in light of the provisions of the WCA, the entrepreneur is deemed to be the executive director of the undertaking that maintains the works council. Under the structure regime, therefore, the Dutch country manager is most often the entrepreneur within the meaning of the WCA and hence the entrepreneur present during consultation meetings.

45,5% of the respondents that said they had a covenant indicated that instead of the designated consultation partner, the executive director of the MNC was present at these meetings. This factor, especially in combination with increased information rights on international matters as well as extended consultation rights, leads to an improved position of the Dutch works council in multinational organisations. At the same time, the 56,6% of the works councils that indicated that no covenant was agreed upon lacked such a tailor-made agreement. Such a covenant, however, could allow the employee

89 The results are also lower than the results of the 2009 survey, in which 45% of the respondents indicated that no use of a covenant was ever made; R. Goodijk, P. van Beurden and H. van Ees, 'Gebruik, niet-gebruik of onderbenutting? Onderzoek naar de mogelijke onderbenutting van bevoegdheden en mogelijkheden door de (Centrale) Ondernemingsraad in grote Nederlandse ondernemingen', p. 34.

90 See section 3.2.2 in chapter V below.

participation mechanism in these undertakings to be better linked to the decision-making and corporate structures.

Strikingly, when selecting only those responses that indicated that the parent company's registered office was situated outside of the Netherlands (i.e., foreign MNCs), only 27,3% of the respondents indicated that a covenant had been concluded. Compared to 54,8% of works councils in Dutch MNCs having indicated the presence of a covenant, a considerably smaller number of works councils of foreign MNCs had evidently concluded a covenant with the corporation even although (especially) decision-making structures in foreign MNCs are likely to fall outside the scope of the Dutch employee participation regime due to the operation of the territoriality principle. The difference between Dutch and foreign MNCs having concluded a covenant is thereby statistically significant with a p-value of 0.02275, whereby a 95% confidence interval was applied for a two-proportion z-test ($p < 0.05$).[91]

Therefore, a paradoxical situation can be observed: while in foreign MNCs it is the case that corporate decisions typically fall outside the scope of the Dutch employee participation law and hence the number of areas whereby the Dutch regime is insufficiently linked to the decision-making structures is *greater*, which might necessitate a covenant unless such (intended) decisions do not directly and significantly affect the Dutch subsidiaries, the number of individual solutions by means of covenants is *lower* in foreign MNCs than for Dutch multinationals.

This difference can be explained with reference to several explanations. Firstly, in Dutch MNCs whereby the majority of the MNC's economic activities fall outside the Netherlands, they have the option of applying the mitigated structure regime that has the effect of exempting the central management from the Dutch employee participation regime.[92] By means of a covenant, Dutch works councils in Dutch MNCs can nevertheless (re)-gain participation rights. This can explain, to a certain extent, the relatively high number of covenants that are operational in Dutch MNCs. Secondly, foreign MNCs are (with the exception of German MNCs) not subjected to a similar employee board level participation mechanisms in their home country and come from a different corporate culture background (such as the Anglo-Saxon (enlightened) shareholder model).[93] Due to the different corporate culture backgrounds of such foreign MNCs, the idea of granting even more rights to works councils is rather unlikely compared to Dutch MNCs.[94] The lower number of covenants in foreign MNCs can therefore be explained by

91 See section 5.2 for a detailed explanation of the application of a two-proportion z-test.
92 See section 3.2 in chapter III above for a detailed analysis of the structure regime.
93 Cf. J.C. Looise and M. Drucker, 'Dutch Works Councils in Times of Transition: The Effects of Changes in Society, Organizations and Work on the Position of Works Councils', 24 *Employee Relations* 3 (2003), p. 399.
94 *Ibid.*, p. 401.

the absence of such far-reaching employee participation rights in foreign corporate cultures and a resulting reluctance of the (central) management to grant additional rights to Dutch works councils.

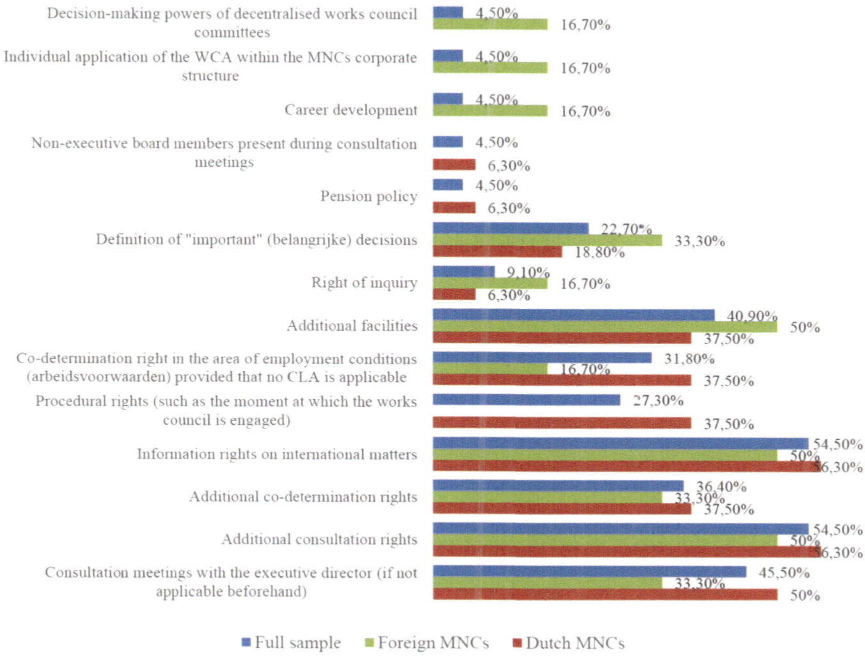

Figure 5.15 *Additional rights of the Dutch works councils in MNCs by means of a covenant pursuant to art. 32 WCA (N = 22); in Dutch (N = 16) and foreign MNCs (N = 6)*

When examining the responses concerning the additional rights conferred by covenants as shown by Figure 5.15 above, it can be concluded that in the majority of covenants, additional consultation rights and information rights on international matters are conferred upon the works councils (both 54,5%). To a somewhat smaller extent, works councils are granted additional facilities (40,9%) and have consultation meetings with the executive director instead of the Dutch country manager (45,5%), if this was not applicable beforehand.

Moreover, about one-third of the respondents indicated that additional procedural rights as well as additional co-determination rights were granted to their works council. Additional procedural rights, such as the moment at which the works council is involved in the decision-making process, are potentially very beneficial. Given the fact that the moment at which the works council has to be involved is difficult to determine in a multinational corporate setting, provisions that are contained in such a covenant can clarify this.[95]

Furthermore, it is noteworthy that two works councils have a right of inquiry conferred upon them by means of a covenant. As was discussed in section 1.4.6 of chapter III above, such a right of inquiry is very desirable for works councils in order to address possible mismanagement within the undertaking by means of this fast and efficient dispute resolution mechanism. The adoption of legislation regarding such a statutory right to Dutch works councils lacks political feasibility. That notwithstanding, many authors have argued in favour of such a right.[96] In the absence of a legislative basis, such a right of inquiry could be conferred upon the works council by means of a covenant as was reported by two respondents. From the responses it can, however, not be determined whether the right was conferred upon the works council by the management of the Dutch subsidiary in order to allow the works council to appeal decisions by the parent company or by the central management directly. In both cases, Dutch or formerly Dutch multinational corporations were concerned.

A comparison of the responses by employee representatives in Dutch and foreign MNCs has to be treated with caution due to the very low sub-sample sizes.[97] The responses show that in foreign MNCs, the definition of 'important' decisions is often included in a covenant. Consultation meetings with the executive director are less frequently included and procedural matters (such as the timing of when the works council will be consulted) are fully absent in covenants that are concluded with foreign MNCs. The latter aspect of procedural agreements is especially noteworthy, because such issues pertaining to the timely involvement of Dutch works councils in foreign MNCs are a main point of concern in both the literature and jurisprudence.

Overall, the responses on the rights conferred under a covenant show that a broad variety of matters are covered, which highlights the tailor-made nature of such agreements on the basis of the contractual freedom of the parties involved.

5.4 Access to financial information

Access to information is an important prerequisite for the effective functioning of works councils as was previously discussed in section 1.4.1 in chapter III of this study. Therefore, the entrepreneur is under a duty to provide general information concerning the activities

95 See also sections 1.4.3 and 1.4.5 in chapter III above.
96 See section 1.4.6 in chapter III above on a (potential) right of inquiry.
97 16 responses from Dutch MNCs and six responses from foreign MNCs.

and financial results of the enterprise relating to the preceding period at least twice a year pursuant to article 31a of the WCA. In particular article 31a (6) of the WCA stipulates that financial information must also be provided twice a year either orally or in writing by the entrepreneur within the meaning of the WCA.

Due to the importance of access to information for works councils, the respondents were asked how frequently financial and economic information was communicated to them.[98] Furthermore, they were asked to indicate whether the information provided by the undertaking was limited to the Dutch entities of the MNC and in which language such information was provided.[99] The results are reported below.

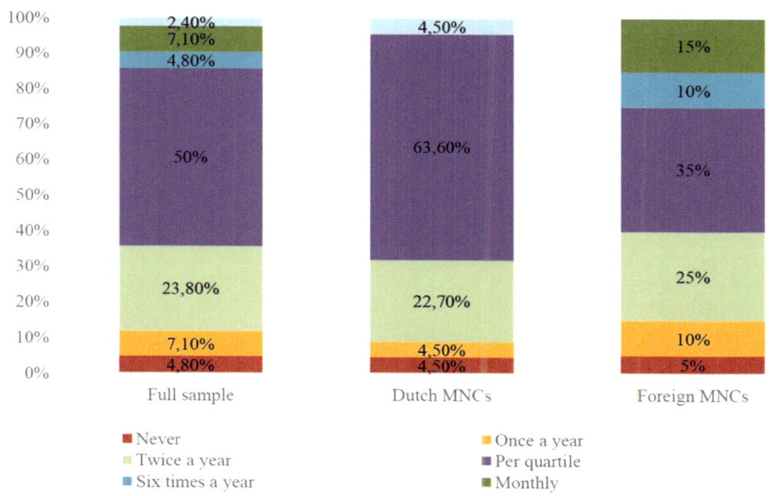

Figure 5.16 *Frequency of communication of financial and economic information to Dutch works councils in MNCs (N = 42)*

When examining the frequency with which works councils are provided with financial and economic information, it can be reported that 11,9% of the works councils 'never' received such information or only did so 'once a year', notwithstanding the fact that article 31a of the WCA clearly stipulates that such information must be provided at least two times per year. In the two cases in which no information was provided to the works council, this concerned a Dutch and a foreign works council. Therefore, no difference between Dutch and foreign MNCs can be observed in this regard. Two out of three cases where information was only given once a year pertained to foreign MNCs.

98 Question 27 of the questionnaire; see Annex II.

99 Questions 28 and 29 of the questionnaire; see Annex II.

A majority of works councils, furthermore, received information on a quarterly basis (50%). Especially in Dutch MNCs, information was provided on a quarterly basis (63,6%). Since large multinational corporations are, in almost all cases, also listed on a stock exchange, the reporting of corporate benchmarks is already done on a quarterly basis. The data are then provided to the Dutch works councils in the same intervals. A small minority of MNCs even provide such information even more often than on a bi-monthly (4,8%) or for some even on a monthly basis (7,1%). It is also noteworthy that in foreign MNCs, information was provided on a monthly or bi-monthly basis in 25% of the cases. One respondent indicated that information was provided in every consultation meeting whereby a frequency of three to six consultation meetings was indicated in their response to question 34. Finally, 23,8% of the respondents indicated that information was provided twice a year, which is the statutory minimum laid down by article 31a of the WCA (with no significant difference being reported between Dutch and foreign MNCs).

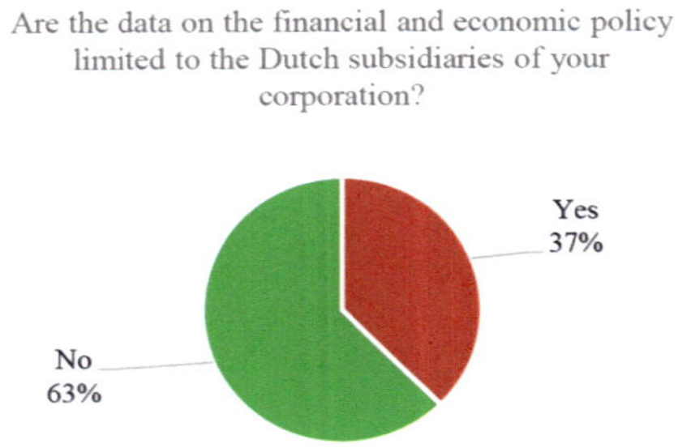

Figure 5.17 Scope of the financial information provided in MNCs (N = 40)

When turning to the scope of the information provided, one can conclude that such information was in two-thirds of the cases *not* limited to the Dutch subsidiaries of the corporation (see Figure 5.17 above).[100]

Arguably, a large majority of works councils (62,5%) therefore have access to information that goes beyond the Dutch part of the MNC and can thus provide insight into the overall corporate performance and (to some extent) into the strategy of the MNC. The remainder of works councils that have no access to information that goes beyond the Dutch entities of the group can nevertheless be compared to the data that is made publicly available and that are reported by the parent corporation on a regular basis, owing to its disclosure duties vis-à-vis the stock exchange authorities and its shareholders.

100 No significant differences can be reported regarding the responses from Dutch and foreign MNCs.

Overall, the works councils have access to a large amount of information concerning the MNC. The question remains, however, whether works councils are utilising the information available due to the technical nature of the information. The availability of the information should therefore ideally be combined with an explanation of these data in the meetings relating to the general operation of the enterprise by the management (article 24 of the WCA) in order to provide the works council with additional context of the information. Another difficulty could be the language of the supplied information, as will subsequently be discussed.

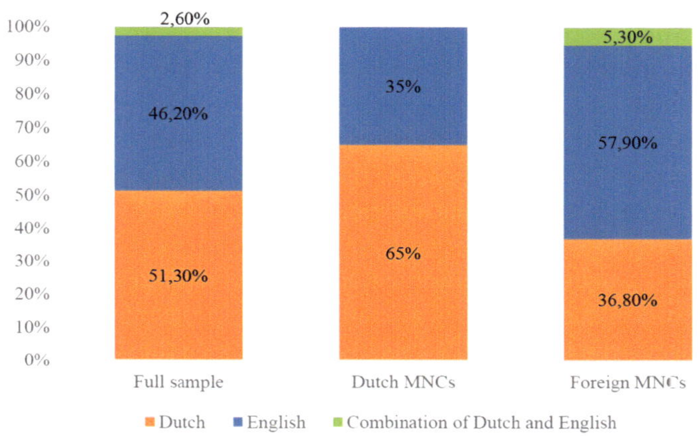

Figure 5.18 *Language of the financial and economic information provided to Dutch works councils in MNCs (N = 39); in Dutch (N = 20) and foreign MNCs (N = 19)*

As the responses reported by Figure 5.18 above show, information on the financial and economic policy of the MNC was provided to the Dutch works council in either Dutch (51,3%) or English (46,2%).

No respondents indicated that the documents were submitted in another language with the exception of one respondent stating that the documents were provided in both English and Dutch. A possible language barrier therefore exists for works council members that do not understand English well enough to comprehend the content of documents that are supplied in English. Hereby, the use of translation services can be highly beneficial for understanding the specific meaning of the documents submitted. The language aspects will be revisited when addressing the European works council, due to the fact that language as well as cultural barriers can play a role in that context as well.[101]

101 See section 7 below.

5.5 *Access to information on the holding structure of the corporation*

While the Dutch works councils already possess extensive information rights regarding the undertaking in which the works council is maintained, additional information rights were conferred upon Dutch works councils by virtue of the Act of 26 June 2013.[102] Pursuant to the Act, which is incorporated into article 31(2)(d) and (e) of the WCA, information regarding the power structures [*zeggenschapsverhoudingen*] and linkages within a network of companies must be provided to Dutch works councils. The Act came into effect on 19 July 2013 and such information should have been submitted to all of the works councils in MNCs whom responded to this questionnaire. All the works councils in this sample are maintained within a group of undertakings within the meaning of the WCA. And given the very high relevance of such power structures within multinational corporations and the resulting difficulties for Dutch works councils to determine "who *de facto* is the person in charge?" for the purposes of the decision-making process, this aspect was addressed in questions 30 – 33 of the questionnaire.

The respondents were asked whether such information was provided to their works council and whether the works council took any initiative to obtain the information.[103] Subsequently, the respondents who indicated that such information on the power structures was provided to their works council, were asked whether the information was useful for the operation of the works council.[104] Respondents who indicated that such information was *not* submitted were asked what the reasons were for such an absence of access to information.[105]

It can be noted that the majority of works councils (59,5%) indeed received information on the holding structures within their corporation in accordance with the recent legislative amendment. This majority therefore has insight into the corporate structure of the entire corporation since the scope of the provision includes *all* entities within the group of undertakings and even includes the duty to provide information on the long-term relations that are of fundamental importance to the continuation of the enterprise. This topic will subsequently be revisited in the context relating to the questions of whether the information was useful.

102 See section 1.4.1 in chapter III above for a detailed analysis.
103 Questions 30 and 31 of the questionnaire; see Annex II.
104 Question 32 of the questionnaire; see Annex II.
105 Question 33 of the questionnaire; see Annex II.

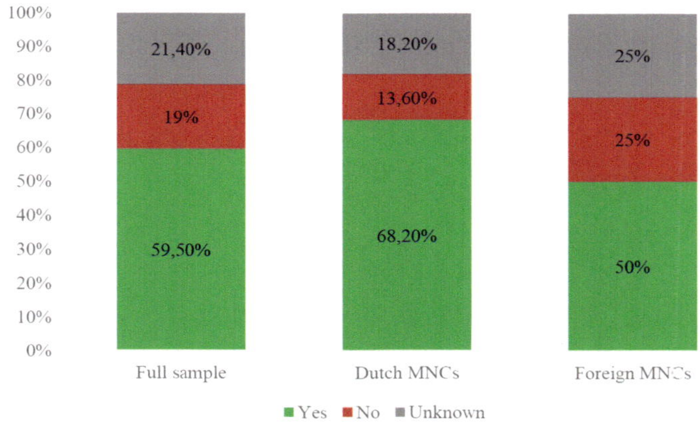

Figure 5.19 Access to information on the holding structures in MNCs by Dutch works councils (N = 42); in Dutch (N = 22) and foreign MNCs (N = 20)

At the same time, 19% of the works councils did not receive such information. In foreign MNCs, one in four (25%) of the works councils did not receive such information, whereas 13,6% of respondents from Dutch MNCs reported having not received such information.

While in one case the respondent indicated in the follow-up question, on the reasons pertaining to the lack of access to the information, that such information was already available via the corporation's intranet; a majority of the respondents reported a lack of knowledge as constituting the reason as to why the information was not given. Thereby, it was indicated in one case that a lack of knowledge from both the management and the works council existed and in one case the works council did not know that such a right existed. In yet another case, it was reported that the management was not aware of what information had to be provided. Finally, in the case of two foreign MNCs, the executive committee refused to provide the information and only provided information after a specific request of the works council concerned was formulated. The information provided was thus limited as a consequence of the works council's request.

In the majority of cases (51,2%), the management itself provided the information without the prior initiative of the works council (see Figure 5.20 below).

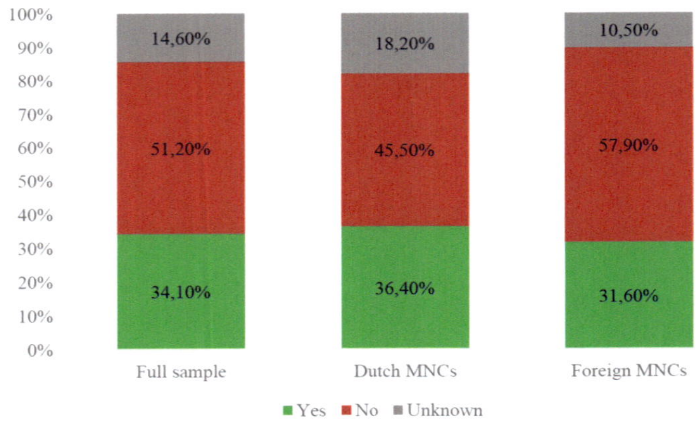

Figure 5.20 Has your (central) works council itself requested the information on the holding structure in the entire corporation? (N=41); in Dutch (N=22) and foreign MNCs (N=19)

A third group of respondents indicated that it is was not known whether the works council received such information (21,4%). The fact that one in five works councils (for foreign MNCs, one in four) did not know whether such information was available, means that works councils have to determine whether information on the holding structure within their corporation already exists and whether or not they have access to such information. Otherwise the information should be requested due to the significant insights into the power structures within the corporation that can be gained through accessing such information, as is discussed below.

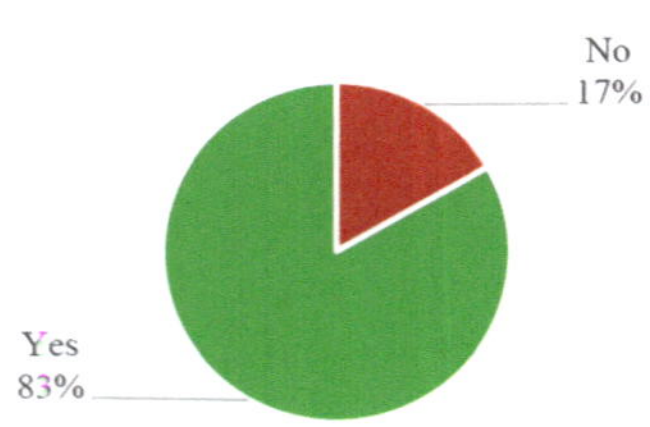

Figure 5.21 Are the submitted data on the holding structure containing useful information for the work of your (central) works council? (N = 24)

When examining the responses on the question of whether the information proved to be useful for the works councils concerned (see Figure 5.21 above), it must be concluded that an overwhelming majority of the respondents did indeed find this information to be useful (83%).[106]

A better insight into the relationship between the location of the actual decision-making power vis-à-vis the management of the undertaking for which the works council is maintained was indicated as an important factor by one respondent. Another respondent also indicated that the information was useful for his or her works council due to the insights into the actual decision-making structures, and added that the information also gave an indication of how these individuals (i.e., the decision-makers) could be contacted by the works council. Hence, the availability of such information can be very important for the (in)formal contact of a (central) works council in a large multinational corporation in order for it to become involved in the decision-making process at the earliest possible moment.

In concluding, the majority of works councils have access to information on the holding structures within their corporation, which proves to be useful in the overwhelming majority of cases. Therefore, the access to this information can be regarded as improving the position of those Dutch works councils. Nevertheless, a large minority, 41%, of the works councils do not know whether such information is available to them or they do not receive the information by the management. Due to the infringement of article 31(2) of the WCA and the rights of the Dutch works councils concerned, an improvement of the position of these works councils regarding their access to information would naturally be desirable.

5.6 *The use of experts by Dutch works councils*

The analysis of the legal framework applicable to Dutch works councils, as was examined in chapter III of this study, has shown that not only do the rights stem from the WCA, the structure regime and other legislative acts, but the framework has also become increasingly complex and multifaceted (e.g., with exemptions for international corporations under the structure regime). Specifically, works councils in multinational corporations are confronted with increasingly complex holding structures within the MNC, which consequently results in a more difficult decision-making structure. Furthermore, the impact of (intended) decisions on the Dutch subsidiaries for which the works council is maintained is not always clear. Therefore, the access to and use of experts pursuant to article 16 of the WCA is of crucial importance in order for works councils to effectively

106 No significant difference between Dutch (85,7%) and foreign MNCs (80%) can be observed.

and efficiently exercise their consultation and co-determination rights.[107] The possibility to obtain expert information prior to the works councils' advice or consent on an (intended) decision is closely linked to the position of the works council within the corporation and its potential to influence the decision-making process.

In order to determine the use of experts by works councils in MNCs, the participants of the survey were asked whether their works council had made use of internal as well as external experts over the last three years.[108] The participants were further asked to indicate their response on a three-level Likert scale (never – sometimes – frequently).[109]

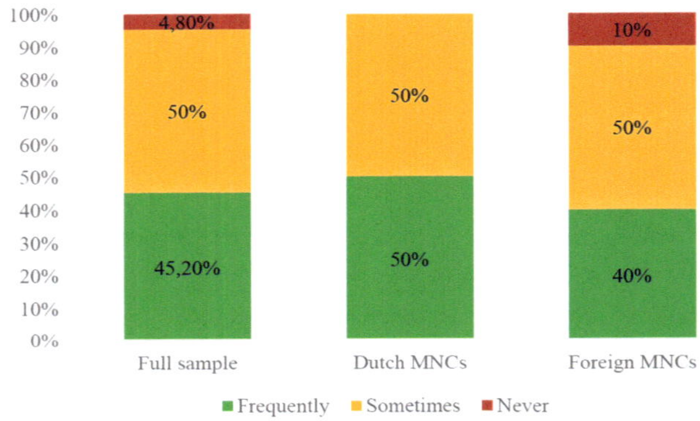

Figure 5.22 *The use of internal experts by Dutch works councils in MNCs (N = 42); in Dutch (N = 22) and foreign MNCs (N = 20)*

The overwhelming majority of works councils had used both internal and external experts with only two respondents indicating that no use of internal experts was made (see Figure 5.22 above) and one respondent stating that no use of external experts was made (Figure 5.23 below). Notably, both respondents that indicated that their works council never made use of internal experts over the last three years were members of works councils in foreign MNCs. The respondent that indicated that no use of external experts was made was also a member of a works council in a foreign MNC. But due to the small sub-sample sizes, no statistically significant conclusions can be derived from these observations. In Dutch MNCs, internal experts are used slightly more often when compared to foreign MNCs. Whereas works councils in Dutch MNCs made 'frequent' use of internal experts in 50% of the cases, this was the case in 40% of the cases for the foreign MNCs, according to the responses.

107 See also section 1.4.7.2 in chapter III for a detailed analysis.
108 Questions 26.1 and 26.2 of the questionnaire; see Annex II.
109 See section 1.2.1 in chapter II for a description of the methodology applied in the survey and for the use of Likert scales.

Turning to the use of external experts, slightly more respondents (50%) reported that they 'frequently' made use of external experts when compared to those who 'sometimes' made use of external experts (47,5%). What is also important to point out here is that works councils in Dutch MNCs made slightly more use of external experts compared to works councils in foreign MNCs (52,4% compared to 47,4%).

When comparing the use of internal versus external experts by works councils, one can note that external experts are more frequently used – in both Dutch and foreign MNCs. The tendency to use internal experts less frequently can be explained by the reservations of certain works councils towards internal experts, on account of the fear that the information and expert opinions provided are formulated incorrectly in order to intentionally mislead the works council. External experts might be regarded as a more independent source, therefore, compared to internal experts.

When comparing these results with the results of the 2009 study conducted by van Beurden (et al.), it becomes apparent that considerably less works councils indicated that they 'never' made use of external experts. Whereas the 2009 study results showed that 28,7% 'never' or 'almost never' made use of external experts (25 out of 87 respondents), for the purposes of this study, only one such case (2,5%) indicated that they 'never' or 'almost never' made use of external experts.[110] The responses pertaining to the 'frequent' use of external experts was, overall, congruent with the results of the earlier research, albeit being somewhat lower. A total of 39,1% of the respondents indicated that they 'always' or 'almost always' made use of external experts in 2009, compared to the 50% of respondents to this survey (an increase of 10,9%).[111] Unfortunately, no data on the use of internal experts were reported in the 2009 study that was carried out by van Beurden (et al.).

110 R. Goodijk, P. van Beurden and H. van Ees, 'Gebruik, niet-gebruik of onderbenutting? Onderzoek naar de mogelijke onderbenutting van bevoegdheden en mogelijkheden door de (Centrale) Ondernemingsraad in grote Nederlandse ondernemingen', p. 33.

111 *Ibid.*

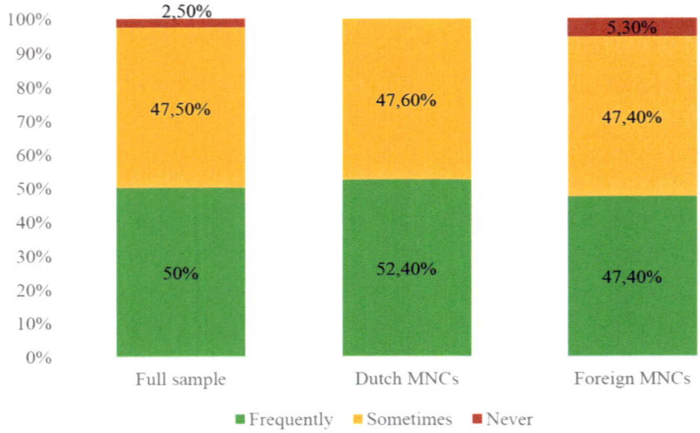

Figure 5.23 The use of external experts by Dutch works councils in MNCs (N = 40); in Dutch (N = 21) and foreign MNCs (N = 19)

5.7 Access to training and personal development

Due to the recent abolishment of the levy on training that had to be paid by undertakings for half of the costs of training and development of their works councils (the so-called *scholingsheffing*), training and development were aspects that were also addressed in this survey. In the advice given by the Social and Economic Council in 2011, the Council concluded that the old training and development regime no longer enjoyed the social partner's support[112] due to the increasing emphasis on decentralised and individual solutions within undertakings rather than a "one size fits all approach" by virtue of the *Gemeenschappelijk Begeleidingsinstituut Ondernemingsraden* [MM, common coaching institute for works councils] (hereinafter: GBIO).[113]

112 The Social and Economic Council's social partners are trade unions (Federation of Netherlands Trade Unions (FNV), National Federation of Christian Trade Unions in the Netherlands (CNV) and Trade union federation for Professionals (VCP)) and industry organisations (Confederation of Netherlands Industry and Employers (Vereniging VNO/NCW), Association of Small and Medium-sized Enterprises (MKB Nederland) and Dutch Organisation for Agriculture and Horticulture (LTO)); the SER also has Crown appointed members, who are independent experts, to complete the tripartite council.

113 SER advice 11/04, 'Toekomst scholing en vorming leden ondernemingsraad', <http://www.ser.nl/ nl/~/media/db_adviezen/2010_2019/2011/b29643.ashx> (last accessed 4 March 2017), p. 13.

Under the old regime, the levy paid by the undertakings was used by the Social and Economic Council to subsidise, in essence, the courses and certified coaches of the GBIO, which then subsequently provided the necessary training to works councils. The emphasis on increased flexibility then led to the unanimous advice of the Social and Economic Council in favour of the abolishment of the old regime on the basis of a levy, which ceased to be applicable as of 19 July 2013 after the Act was adopted by the Dutch Parliament on 26 June 2013.[114]

Therefore, since July 2013 the entrepreneur is no longer obliged to pay the annual levy for training and development and at the same time training courses for works councils are no longer subsidised via the GBIO. The Social and Economic Council emphasised in this regard that works councils must nevertheless make sure that access to training and development, both qualitatively and quantitatively, is available.[115] The wording of article 18 of the WCA has therefore been amended and now stipulates that training and development must be *of sufficient quality*. Moreover, training and development is considered to be beneficial for the degree of professionalism of the works councils and can therefore directly contribute to increasing the quality of the Dutch works councils because of the improved expertise of its members.

5.7.1 Training and courses for Dutch works councils

Since the abolishment of the levy on training for undertakings, approximately one year has passed since the adoption of the new regime and the carrying out of this survey. In the meantime, negotiations between the management and works councils by the respondent MNCs should have been carried out in order to safeguard the works councils' rights to training and development of sufficient quality pursuant to article 18(2) of the WCA. The costs for training thereby have to be borne by the entrepreneur pursuant to articles 22(1) and (3) of the WCA, which stipulates that any costs that are necessary for the fulfilment of the tasks of the works council must be borne by the entrepreneur pursuant to paragraph one.[116] The respondents were therefore asked whether they were satisfied with the arrangements on training and development within their corporation.[117]

114 *Wet van 26 juni 2013 tot aanpassing van de Wet op de ondernemingsraden in verband met wijziging van de financiering van het scholingssysteem voor leden van de ondernemingsraad en enkele andere wijzigingen van deze wet, Stb.* 2013, 296.

115 SER advice 11/04, 'Toekomst scholing en vorming leden ondernemingsraad', p. 22.

116 Training and development falls within the scope according to article 22(3) of the WCA.

117 Question 42 of the questionnaire; see Annex II.

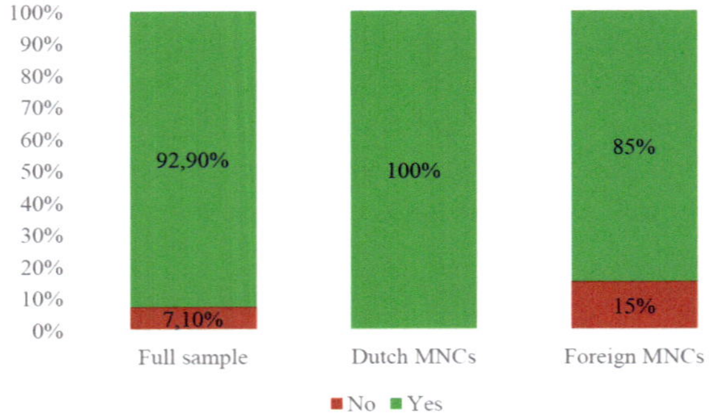

Figure 5.24 Satisfaction of Dutch works councils regarding training and development in MNCs (N = 42); in Dutch (N = 22) and foreign MNCs (N = 20)

When examining the responses (Figure 5.24 above), one has to conclude that an overwhelming majority of works councils were satisfied with access to training and development (92,9%). The respondents were then asked to specify further in a sub-question. The respondents stated that the necessity of training for their works council was recognised by the management within their corporation. While in some cases agreements had to be made for each individual training course or prior approval had to be obtained, generally speaking, works councils have a free hand in determining what training is useful for the performance of their duties. Some respondents, further to this, indicated that a budget for the works council or a budget per works council member was determined for each calendar year, but the works council was able to determine how this budget was spent. Another respondent stated that an annual plan for training and coaching was agreed upon between the management and the works council.

Therefore, the objective of the advice of the Social and Economic Council prior to the abolishment of the levy, namely the decentralisation and individualisation of training and developing works councils,[118] can be seen as being fulfilled for the group of works councils in large multinational organisations given the fact that an overwhelming majority of works councils regarded the agreements that were concluded as being satisfactory. The results were thereby in line with a very recent survey carried out by the Social and Economic Council's *Commissie Bevordering Medezeggenschap* (CBM).[119]

Yet, three works councils indicated that the agreements on training were not satisfactory for their works council (7,1% of the overall responses). Notably, all three works councils

118 SER advice 11/04, 'Toekomst scholing en vorming leden ondernemingsraad', <http://www.ser.nl/ nl/~/media/db_adviezen/2010_2019/2011/b29643.ashx> (last accessed 4 March 2017), p. 13.

119 SER Commissie Bevordering Medezeggenschap, 'Ontwikkelingen gebruik OR-scholingsfaciliteiten', <http://tinyurl.com/kn45e7y> (last accessed 25 October 2017).

were maintained in subsidiaries of foreign MNCs (15% of the responses in foreign MNCs).[120] All three works councils further reported that the costs of training and coaching were insufficiently borne by the entrepreneur due to the fact that the management did not recognise the added value of such training being carried out. One respondent further stated that the corporation also tried to impose their views on the content of such training and coaching courses.

In conclusion, the framework on training and coaching that has been applicable since July 2013 is, in overall terms, satisfactory for works councils in large corporations. Nevertheless, a small number of works councils have had their right to training of sufficient quality denied because of the entrepreneur's refusal to bear the necessary costs, which in practice renders the exercise of the works councils' right impossible. Since this significantly weakens the position of these works councils, sufficient monitoring by the relevant government authorities is necessary in order to ensure compliance with the *training of sufficient quality* criterion.[121]

5.7.2 Personal development of the members of Dutch works councils

Notwithstanding the recent changes to the training and development facilities for works councils and the concomitant financial arrangements, the individual situation of works council members also affects their performance and in turn the overall position of their works council. Therefore, the participants of the survey were asked questions on topics that could affect their performance as works council members. The questions concerned the time available for their works council tasks vis-à-vis their regular tasks, whether they had negative experiences with their superiors, whether the works council membership hampered their career and whether they felt being unqualified for performing their tasks as works council member.[122]

The respondents were asked to indicate on a five-point Likert scale their responses to the questions with the following possible answers: 'completely disagree', 'disagree', 'undecided', 'agree' and 'completely agree'. The responses are subsequently reported.

120 Due to the absence of a sufficient number of respondents to both sub-samples (Dutch MNCs and foreign MNCs), no test on the possible statistical significant difference of training in Dutch and foreign MNCs can be applied.

121 Such as *Stichting Certificering Opleiding Ondernemingsraden* (SCOOR); see further, H. van den Tillaart and J. Warmerdam, *Ontwikkelingen in scholing van ondernemingsraden: Terugblik op de afgelopen jaren en verwachtingen voor de toekomst* (ITS, Nijmegen 2016); the study by van den Tillaart and Warmerdam concluded that works councils (and especially in large corporations) are overwhelmingly satisfied with their training and development opportunities.

122 Questions 41.1 – 41.4 of the questionnaire; see Annex II.

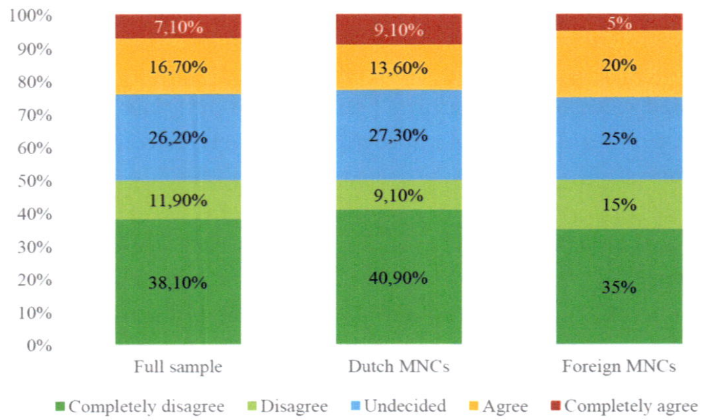

Figure 5.25 *I am not having enough time for my work as employee representative due to a high workload and other duties (N = 42); in Dutch (N = 22) and foreign MNCs (N = 20)*

Firstly, time constraints were identified as a possible (negative) factor for the performance of works council members. The lack of time was, furthermore, identified as a possible factor for the underutilisation of works council rights in earlier studies.[123]

Therefore, the participants were asked whether their workload as employees of the undertaking as well as other duties might result in a lack of time available for their work as employee representatives. Yet, the results displayed by Figure 5.25 above show that the majority of respondents (50%) either 'disagree' or 'completely disagree' that they had a lack of time for their work as employee representatives. Further, while a relatively large group of respondents were 'undecided' as to the question of whether enough time was available to them to perform their work as employee representatives (26,2%), only a minority selected 'agrees' or 'completely agrees' that a lack of time was indeed applicable to their circumstances (23,8%). No noteworthy differences can be observed when comparing the sub-sample of responses from Dutch and foreign MNCs.

Given the fact that corporations with a large workforce are less affected by the absence of a small number of personnel due to their function as works council members, the problem of balancing the workload with the tasks as an employee representative is, in light of the responses received, rather small in multinational corporations. The use of exemptions from work duties (*vrijstelling*) for members of the works council may further

123 R. Goodijk, P. van Beurden and H. van Ees, 'Gebruik, niet-gebruik of onderbenutting? Onderzoek naar de mogelijke onderbenutting van bevoegdheden en mogelijkheden door de (Centrale) Ondernemingsraad in grote Nederlandse ondernemingen', p. 7; R.H. van het Kaar and E. Smit, 'Vier scenario's voor de toekomst van de medezeggenschap – Een onderzoek in opdracht van het Ministerie van SZW', (Ministerie van SZW, The Hague 2006), p. 76.

lessen the impact of a lack of time for the performance of works council tasks. The use of such exemptions can therefore explain the lower percentage of works council members indicating a lack of time for their duties in the works council, whereas a majority of works councils had reported such time constraints in earlier research.[124]

At the same time, the exemption of employee representatives from work can have the effect of increasing the distance between the works council and its constituents (i.e., the corporation's Dutch workforce). Work exemptions will be further addressed in section 3.3.3 of chapter V which pertains to the qualitative results of this study.

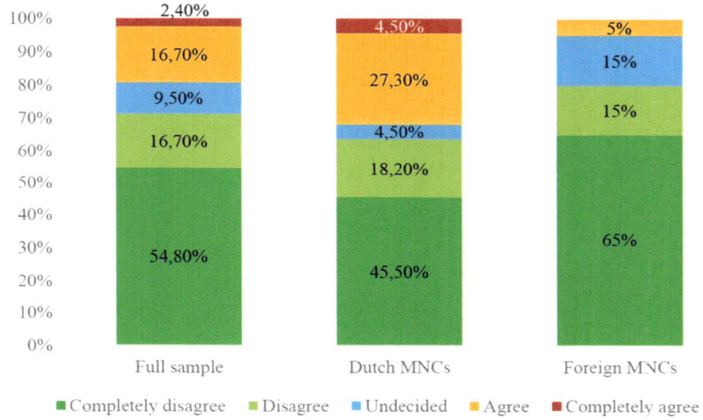

Figure 5.26 Due to my work as employee representative, I have had negative experiences with my immediate supervisors (N = 42); in Dutch (N = 22) and foreign MNCs (N = 20)

Secondly, works council members could potentially have negative experiences with their superiors due to their dual role as employee representatives, on the one hand, and by virtue of being an employee of the undertaking on the other. Furthermore, in the study published by van het Kaar and Smit, it was argued that negative experiences with direct superiors could be inherent in those cases whereby the work as an employee representative was not taken into account in the calculation of their workload, which consequently leads to overburdening the employee concerned.[125]

124 M. van Ewijk and M. van Engelen, 'De faciliteiten, bevoegdheden en informatievoorziening van OR-en en het effect van het netwerk op het functioneren van de OR', report for the *Ministerie van SZW* (Elsevier, Den Haag 2002), p. 22.

125 R.H. van het Kaar and E. Smit (eds.), 'Vier scenario's voor de toekomst van de medezeggenschap – Een onderzoek in opdracht van het Ministerie van SZW', p. 77.

According to the responses, however, the large majority of participants (71,4%) either 'disagree' or 'completely disagree' with the statement that their work as an employee representative created tension with their superiors. In the sample, most multinational corporations take their employees' duties as employee representatives into consideration in their management approach, which in turn prevents tensions from arising in the first place. Yet, eight respondents (19,1%) indicated that they did indeed have negative experiences with their immediate superiors. These cases of negative experiences were mostly reported in Dutch MNCs with 31,8% of the respondents indicating to 'agree' or 'fully agree' with the statement. In foreign MNCs, 5% of the respondents indicated to 'agree' with the statement of having had negative experiences. Overall, one-fifth of employee representatives (19,1%) were negatively affected in their relationship within their team due to their membership in a works council despite the fact that works councils in MNCs can be overall characterised as more professional bodies compared to works councils in small undertakings. This was also reflected in the responses to the statement concerning the (possible) negative impact of their work as an employee representative on their future career (Figure 5.27 below).

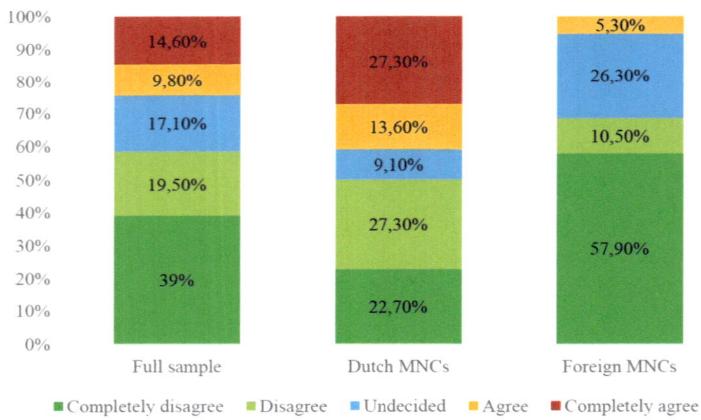

Figure 5.27 The work as employee representative hampers my career (N = 41); in Dutch (N = 22) and foreign MNCs (N = 19)

While a majority of respondents (58,5%) still indicated that the work as an employee representative did not adversely affect their career, 24,4% of the participants stated that they either 'agree' or 'completely agree' that their works council membership hampers their career. When comparing the responses between Dutch and foreign MNCs, one can note that respondents from primarily Dutch MNCs perceived a negative impact on their career (40,9% compared to 5,3% in foreign MNCs).

The percentage of participants that reported a negative impact on their career was lower than the figures produced in earlier studies, but the responses can be regarded as unrepresentative of the overall population of works council members given the fact that it was predominantly the chairmen or official secretaries of the works councils that filled in the questionnaire.[126] It must be noted, however, that a quarter of respondents still felt that the prohibition of placing works council members in a disadvantageous position (article 21 of the WCA) was not sufficient to alleviate any negative ramifications for their career prospects.

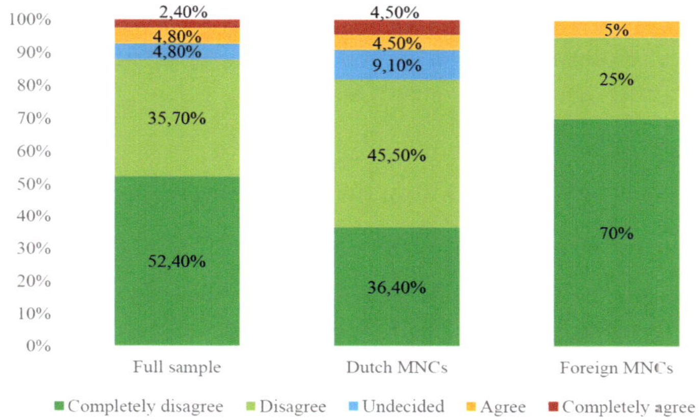

*Figure 5.28 I am **not** sufficiently qualified for my work as employee representative (N = 42); in Dutch (N = 22) and foreign MNCs (N = 20)*

Finally, a lack of sufficient qualification and expertise of employee representatives can be identified as a possible (negative) factor for the position of Dutch works councils. Earlier studies identified, as a point of concern, the lack of expertise and thereby particularly a lack of expertise on strategic issues.[127] However, a differentiation must be made between works councils in general and the relatively small group of works councils in large corporations, as was concluded in the study by van het Kaar and Looise.[128] Indeed, an overwhelming majority of respondents (88,1%) either 'disagree' or 'completely disagree' with the statement that they were not sufficiently qualified for their work as an employee representative. Furthermore, only three respondents (7,2%) 'agree' or 'completely agree' with the statement that they lacked the necessary expertise for their work as an employee

126 *Ibid.*, p. 74-75.

127 R.H. van het Kaar and J.C. Looise, *De volwassen OR – Groei en grenzen van de Nederlandse ondernemingsraad: Resultaten van het grote OR-onderzoek*, p. 87 and 113; see also R.H. van het Kaar and E. Smit (eds.), 'Vier scenario's voor de toekomst van de medezeggenschap – Een onderzoek in opdracht van het Ministerie van SZW', p. 82.

128 R.H. van het Kaar and J.C. Looise, *De volwassen OR – Groei en grenzen van de Nederlandse ondernemingsraad: Resultaten van het grote OR-onderzoek*, p. 115.

representative (two respondents from Dutch MNCs and one respondent from a foreign MNC).

Therefore, the opposite trend compared to earlier studies on works council performance in the Netherlands can be observed with a majority rather than a minority indicating that they believe to have the necessary expertise for their work as an employee representative. At the same time, it must be noted that works councils in the largest corporations can be characterised, according to the indications of the respondents, by a significantly higher degree of professionalism as well as the fact that access to training and development is, in overall terms, highly satisfactory (see Figure 5.24 above). The question of whether the management also perceives the works council as being professional will be addressed in the follow-up interviews as subsequently addressed.

6 Foreign contacts of Dutch works councils and involvement in transnational issues

The Dutch works council rights are limited to the Dutch territory pursuant to the principle of territoriality that was discussed *inter alia* in sections 1.4 and 3.2 of chapter III above. Nevertheless, the works council members can establish contacts with employee representatives within the MNC in other countries and employee representatives outside the Netherlands through existing networks such as GoodCorp,[129] SEEurope[130] and other (European) works council and trade union networks. Moreover, Dutch works councils can be consulted by management on transnational issues once these directly affect the Dutch subsidiaries and fall within the scope of article 25 of the WCA, on the basis of a covenant (article 32 of the WCA) or on a voluntary basis.

The participants were therefore asked whether they had contact with employee representatives within their corporation that were located outside of the Netherlands.[131] Furthermore, the participants were asked whether their works council was involved in issues that concerned the Netherlands and at least one other country and were consequently regarded as being transnational issues.[132]

129 GoodCorp is a network of researchers and trade unionists by European Trade Union Institute (https://www.etui.org/Networks/GoodCorp-the-research-network-on-Corporate-Governance).

130 WP Europe (formerly SEEurope) is a network of the European Trade Union Institute involving legal, economic and industrial relations experts (https://www.etui.org/Networks/SEEurope-the-research-network-on-the-European-Company-SE).

131 Question 43 of the questionnaire; see Annex II.

132 Question 45 of the questionnaire; see Annex II.

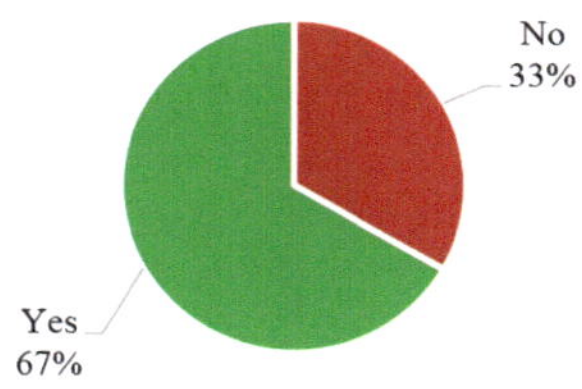

Figure 6.1 *Are you maintaining contacts with employee representatives within your corporation outside the Netherlands? (N = 42)*

As is shown by Figure 6.1 above, the majority of works council members established contact with the employee representatives of foreign subsidiaries of their corporation (66,7%).[133] Some of the respondents thereby referred to the European works council through which their Dutch works council maintained contact with employee representatives (and potentially also with management representatives in the EWC) abroad. Others, however, also indicated that they participated in a European network of works councils or even had an international employee participation mechanism, in addition to their EWC, in place. Another respondent stated that *instead* of a EWC, a worldwide employee participation structure was maintained within the corporation as well as contact through an international trade union association.[134]

At the same time, one third of the participants (33,3%) indicated that no contact with employee representatives within their corporation outside the Netherlands existed. Although such contact may not be the highest priority for the performance of works councils, these contacts nevertheless allow employee representatives to gain broader insights into the activities of the corporation for which their works council is maintained. Furthermore, such contact could prove helpful if transnational reorganisations or other (intended) decisions of transnational scope are effectuated within the corporation.

133 No significant difference can be observed when comparing the responses between Dutch (68,2%) and foreign MNCs (65%).

134 See section 3.6 in chapter V below for further examples of good practice.

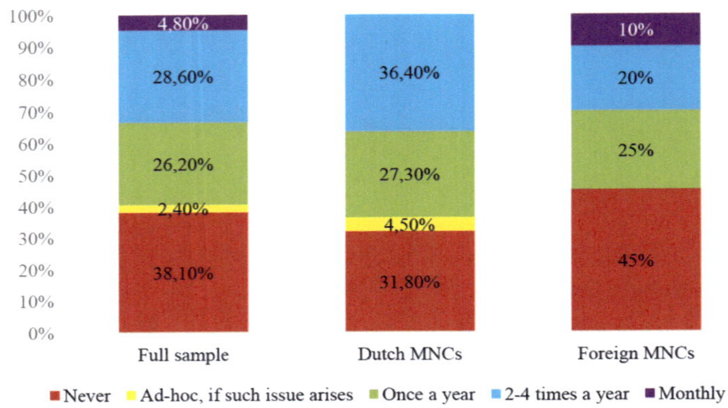

Figure 6.2 *Involvement of Dutch works council in transnational issues within MNCs (N = 42); in Dutch (N = 22) and foreign MNCs (N = 20)*

Surprisingly, only a minority of respondents indicated that their Dutch works council was never involved in consultations over transnational issues (38,1%), as was shown above. Furthermore, a large group (54,7% of the respondents) stated that their works council was involved in consultation on transnational issues a few times per year. A very small minority was involved on a regular basis (4,8%) or on an ad hoc basis, if that was deemed necessary (2,4%).

Although these responses are an indication of the frequency of consultation of Dutch works councils on transnational issues, the timing and the quality of the consultations were not addressed by this questionnaire. Therefore, it remains to be seen at which stage of the decision-making process that the Dutch works councils will be involved and to what extent works councils are able to effectively participate in the decision-making process when it comes to transnational issues. This aspect will be addressed in the follow-up interviews, which are reported in the following chapter of this study.

7 THE RELATIONSHIP WITH THE EUROPEAN WORKS COUNCIL

The position of the Dutch (central) works council was the focal point of the quantitative analysis on the basis of the questionnaire in the previous sections. However, the relationship between the Dutch works council and the European works council is also of great importance for the effective functioning of employee participation in multinational corporations. The European legislative framework that is applicable to multinational corporations, such as Directive 2005/56/EC on cross-border mergers, the SE Regulation (EC) 2157/2001 and SE Directive 2001/86/EC on the European company, Directive 2001/23/EC on transfer of undertakings and especially Directive 2009/38/EC on European works councils will henceforth be analysed. In light of the applicable European framework, the relationship between the Dutch (central) works council and the EWC is very important, as the EWC is supranational in nature whereas the Dutch works council rights are inherently limited to the Netherlands. At the same time, EWC rights are, in the majority of cases, limited to the so-called subsidiary requirements of the Directive, which are more limited when compared to the rights that are enjoyed by Dutch works councils. The EWC rights are limited to information and consultation, whereas Dutch works councils enjoy significantly greater and more extensive rights such as co-determination and recommendation rights under the so-called structure regime. The information and consultation rights of Dutch works councils are also more clearly formulated and more extensive than the rights that are currently present under the EWC-Directive.

At the same time, however, EWCs are maintained at a different and often higher level within MNCs, as is shown below. The relationship between the EWC and the Dutch works council may therefore strengthen the position of Dutch works councils. The relationship with the EWC allows for possible access to information on other European subsidiaries of the MNC, an increased employee representative's network as well as formal or informal meetings with members of a higher management tier within the corporation or even the central management via the EWC. In order to assess the relationship between the Dutch works councils and the EWC, as well as the position of the EWC within the MNC in general, the participants were asked to indicate, firstly, whether a EWC was maintained within their corporation.[135] Subsequently, only the respondents that indicated that a EWC was indeed maintained within their MNC were then asked to answer the questions on the relationship between their works council and the EWC. Not all of the respondent MNCs maintained a EWC. As a result of this, the total number of respondents for this part of the questionnaire was lower than the overall number of responses to the questionnaire (with an N = 29). The smaller number of responses could thereby potentially lead to differences in the results occurring by chance due to the small sample size rather than being statistically significant.[136] However, the homogeneity of the sample does not threaten the validity of the sample. Nevertheless, the results must be treated with some degree of caution.

135 Question 44 of the questionnaire; see Annex II.

136 Cf. R.P. Carver, 'The Case Against Statistical Significance Testing', 48 *Harvard Educational Review* 3 (1978), p. 9.

Firstly, the respondents were asked whether a European works council was maintained in their corporation (see Figure 7.1 below).

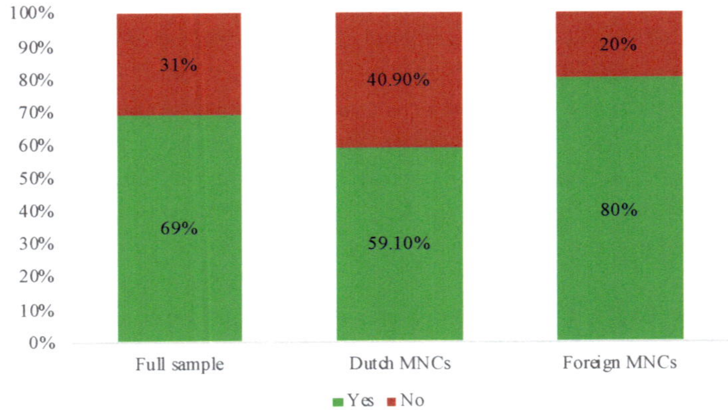

Figure 7.1 *Frequency of European works councils in MNCs (N = 42)*

A number of observations can be made from the data. Firstly, the results show that the majority of corporations maintained a EWC (69%). Secondly, it should be noted that the compliance rate in foreign MNCs, with 80% having a EWC, was considerably higher than in Dutch MNCs (59,1%).

Thirdly, when examining the threshold values that are found in Directive 2009/38/EC, that are applicable to all of the corporations that were included in this survey, one must most certainly conclude that[137] all MNCs examined should maintain a EWC according to the criteria set forth in the EWC Directive for 'Community-scale undertakings'.[138] The relatively large number of multinational corporations *without* a EWC (31%) must therefore be considered as an infringement of the applicable EU legislative framework. At the same time, the compliance rate reported in this survey is consistent with and even substantially higher than the one reported in earlier research produced by the European Trade Union Institute (hereinafter: ETUI), which reported an overall compliance rate of 44% in 2015 for a total number of approximately 2400 MNCs with a minimal increase of 15-30 EWCs per year.[139] The EWC-regime is, therefore, so far not as widely applied in

137 Not all respondents indicated the number of employees situated within the EU. But all of the respondents stated that their MNC employs more than 1000 employees and more than 150 in the Netherlands. Therefore, it is very likely that the criteria set forth in article 2(1)(a) of the EWC Directive are fulfilled.

138 Namely an overall number of 1000 employees within the EU as well as at least 150 employees in at least two EU Member States (article 2(1)(a) of the EWC Directive); the provisions equally apply to any 'Community-scale group of undertakings' pursuant to article 2(1)(c) of the EWC Directive.

139 S. De Spiegelaere and R. Jagodzinski, *European Works Councils and SE works councils in 2015: Facts and figures* (ETUI, Brussels 2015); R. Jagodzinski and I. Pas, 'The EWC landscape on the eve of the transposition deadline of the recast directive 2009/38/EC – Evidence from the ETUI database of European

multinationals as the Dutch works council regime. The Dutch regime, under the provisions of the WCA, has a substantially higher compliance rate of 94% in MNCs.[140] It will therefore take several decades to achieve a comparable compliance rate for the EWC considering the current growth rate.[141]

In order to assess the interplay between the Dutch works councils and the EWCs, the participants were subsequently asked whether they were – aside from their membership in a Dutch (central) works council – also a member of the EWC within their corporation.[142] This is because personal contact with employee representatives and an informal exchange of information between the EWC and the Dutch works council can improve the overall position of the employee representation bodies within MNCs. This, in turn, is therefore beneficial for the position of the Dutch works council due to the (informal) access to information and the consultation process that exists under the auspices of the EWC via these individuals with a dual mandate. Furthermore, Dutch employee representatives may have contact with members of the central management in EWC consultation meetings whereas such access is often not the case for Dutch works councils due to the application, under the structure regime, of the so-called 'Netherlands-construction'.

According to the responses, a majority of the respondents were both members of the EWC and the Dutch (central) works council within their corporation (58,6%).[143] Since mostly the chairmen of Dutch works councils filled in the questionnaire, this ratio does *not* correspond with the overall degree of overlap between the two works councils (since central works councils are comprised of up to 25 members pursuant to article 6 of the WCA). The responses show that an overlap between the two works councils indeed exists, that in turn allows for an exchange of information between the two employee representation bodies. Moreover, the responses of the participants to the subsequent questions on the relationship between their Dutch works council and the EWC can be considered as being very reliable due to the first-hand insights of the respondents and their EWC-membership.

Works Councils', <Evidence-from-the-ETUI-database-of-European-Works-Councils> (last accessed 8 March 2017), p. 8; the survey by van het Kaar and Looise also reported a lower compliance rate for the Netherlands with 40% of the respondents stating that a EWC was maintained (19 of 47 respondents) in 1999; Cf. R.H. van het Kaar and J.C. Looise, *De volwassen OR – Groei en grenzen van de Nederlandse ondernemingsraad: Resultaten van het grote OR-onderzoek*, p. 234.

140 A compliance rate of 94% was reported for Dutch works councils in large undertakings having more than 200 employees; see Regioplan, 'Nalevingsonderzoek van de Wet op Ondernemingsraden 2011', <http://tinyurl.com/n58duhc> (last accessed 8 March 2017), p. 7.

141 R. Jagodzinski and I. Pas, 'The EWC landscape on the eve of the transposition deadline of the recast directive 2009/38/EC – Evidence from the ETUI database of European Works Councils', <http://tinyurl.com/ltvg8kd> (last accessed 25 October 2017), p. 8.

142 Question 46 of the questionnaire; see Annex II.

143 See the responses to question 46 in Annex II.

A crucial aspect for the access to information and effective influence on the decision-making process, is the level at which a works council is maintained within a given corporation. Whereas the Dutch works council regime is inherently limited to the Netherlands due to the application of the 'Netherlands-construction' and in light of the principle of territoriality, the EWC is confined to the European Union and thus enjoys much wider scope. Therefore, the participants were asked to indicate at which level the EWC was maintained within their MNC.[144]

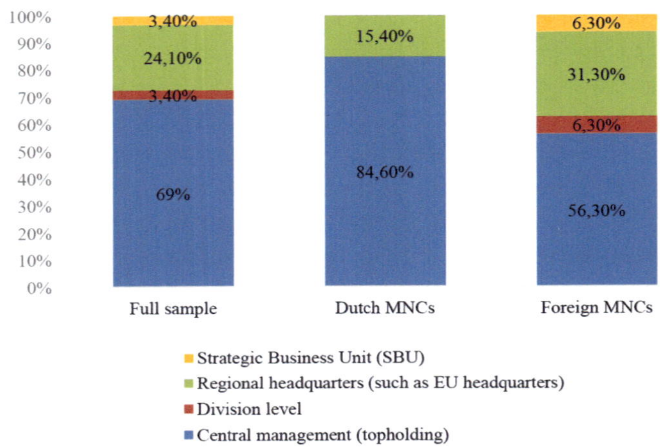

Figure 7.2 *Position of the EWC within the corporate structure in MNCs (N = 29); in Dutch (N = 13) and foreign MNCs (N = 16)*

A majority of EWCs were maintained at the level of the central management of the MNC (69%), as the results in the figure above show. In Dutch MNCs especially, the EWC was maintained at the central management level (84,6%). In foreign MNCs also, a majority of EWCs were maintained at the highest level in the corporation (56,3%). A further 24,1% of the EWCs were maintained at the level of the regional headquarters for the EU, while only one EWC was maintained at division level and another EWC at the level of a strategic business unit (SBU).[145] In foreign MNCs, the percentage of EWCs at regional level (often EU-headquarters level) was relatively high (31,3%). This means that in these cases, the EWCs are maintained at the highest possible level within the EU, if the top-holding is situated outside the EU.

144 Question 47 of the questionnaire; see Annex II.

145 These results are thereby consistent with the earlier survey conducted in 1999; Cf. R.H. van het Kaar and J.C. Looise, *De volwassen OR – Groei en grenzen van de Nederlandse ondernemingsraad: Resultaten van het grote OR-onderzoek*, p. 238.

Overall, two-thirds of the EWCs are located at the highest level within the respective corporation and can potentially participate in the strategic decision-making process for the entire MNC pursuant to the information and consultation rights laid down in the EWC-Directive. In addition, it can be noted that when selecting only foreign MNCs, the majority of EWCs are still maintained at the level of the central management (56,3%).

The actual influence of the EWC, however, is largely dependent on the rights conferred upon the council in the negotiations of the special negotiating body (hereinafter: SNB) with the management. So-called 'article 13 EWCs' are largely limited to the status of information forums without consultation rights or even co-determination rights.[146] The actual rights of the EWC and their resulting influence on the decision-making process are addressed below (see Figure 7.5) and will be further addressed in the sections containing the follow-up interviews.

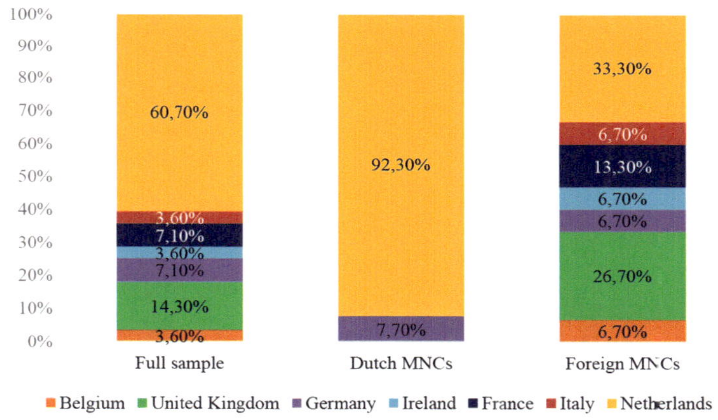

Figure 7.3 *Location of the EWC in MNCs (N = 28); in Dutch (N = 13) and foreign MNCs (N = 15)*

Furthermore, the participants were asked to indicate where their EWC was located.[147] The results show that the majority of European works councils are located in the Netherlands (60,7%). In this regard, it can be noted that a large correlation exists between the country of origin of the corporation and the location of the EWC. This becomes particularly visible when examining the responses from Dutch MNCs in comparison to foreign MNCs.

146 See P. Marginson (et al.), *Negotiating European Works Councils: An Analysis of Agreements under Article 13*, report for the European Foundation for the Improvement of Living and Working Conditions (1998).

147 Question 48 of the questionnaire; see Annex II.

When combining the responses to the question on the registered office of the corporation (question 2 of the questionnaire) and the responses on the location of the EWC, it becomes apparent that both the registered office of the corporation and the location of the EWC are identical (see Figure 7.4 below). Notably, the EWCs of Japanese and Indian MNCs were located in the UK. Some EWCs of European MNCs were based in another EU Member State, which leads to the question of whether the location of some EWCs in a country other than the country of origin of the MNC can be explained by the presence of a large ratio of the workforce in another EU Member State. Unfortunately, the absence of any information on the EU Member State with the largest workforce of the respective MNCs prohibits further analysis of this aspect.

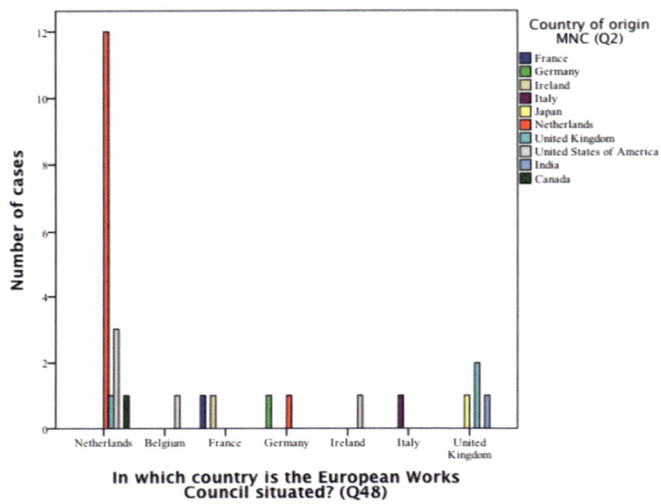

Figure 7.4 *EWC location in relation to the registered office of the respective MNC (N = 28)*

After having examined the location and level at which EWCs are maintained in multinational corporations, the substantial rights of EWCs as well as the exchange of information with the Dutch works council will be addressed in the remainder of this section.

Whereas Dutch works councils enjoy wide-ranging statutory rights pertaining to information, consultation and codetermination pursuant to the provisions of the WCA, EWCs are subject to a regime based on the contractual freedom of the parties (i.e., the management of the MNC and the employee representatives). After establishing an SNB pursuant to article 5 of the EWC Directive, the contracting parties may agree on additional participation rights in light of the principle of contractual freedom. At the same time, however, the subsidiary requirements laid down in Annex I to the EWC Directive and the employee participation rights stipulated therein must not be undermined. The participants were therefore asked to indicate whether their EWC enjoys additional rights compared to the statutory fallback rules.[148]

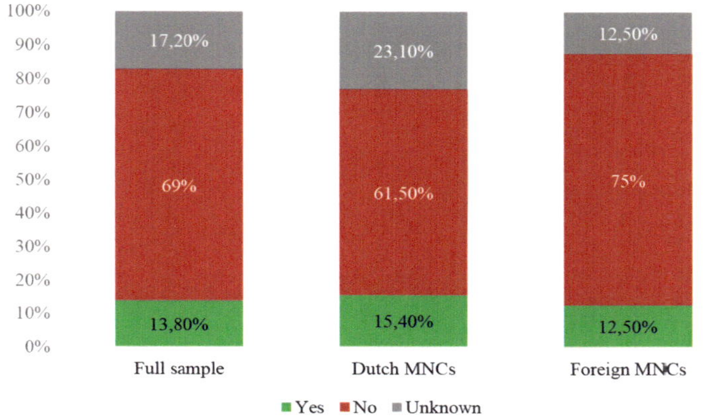

Figure 7.5 *Conferral of additional rights to the EWC in MNCs (N = 29); in Dutch (N = 13) and foreign MNCs (N = 16)*

The responses in Figure 7.5 above show that an overwhelming majority of EWCs do not enjoy more rights than those codified in the subsidiary requirements of Annex I to the EWC Directive (69%). Moreover, 17,2% of the respondents indicated that they had no knowledge of the existence of additional rights for their EWC. No notable differences between the responses from Dutch and foreign MNCs can be reported. The number of EWCs enjoying additional rights was slightly higher in Dutch (15,4%) compared to foreign MNCs (12,5%). Due to the very small sample size, such comparisons should, however, be treated with caution.

Overall, only a small minority of EWCs (13,8%) enjoy more than the minimum requirements stipulated by the Directive. When comparing the rights of the EWC and the Dutch legal framework on employee participation, it must be concluded that the overwhelming majority of EWCs do not have equally strong employee participation rights and are thus in a weaker position than Dutch (central) works councils.

Nevertheless, in several cases, EWCs are located at the central management level within the corporation (see Figure 7.2 above). Although the rights of the EWC are, in most cases, limited to information and consultation rights, such information can nevertheless be helpful for the functioning of Dutch (central) works councils. In order to test for

148 Question 49 of the questionnaire; see Annex II.

the exchange of information between the EWC and Dutch works councils, the survey participants were subsequently asked whether they were satisfied with this information exchange.[149]

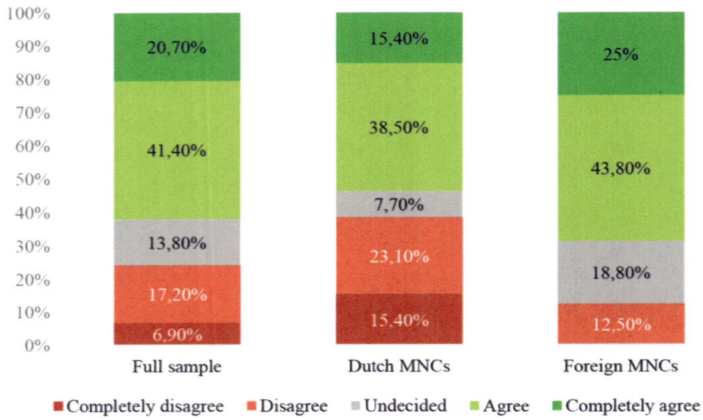

Figure 7.6 *I am satisfied with the exchange of information between the EWC and my (central) works council (N = 29); in Dutch (N = 13) and foreign MNCs (N = 16)*

When examining the responses above, it must be concluded that such information exchange is adequately taking place according to a majority of the respondents. About two-thirds of the participants (62,1%) reported that they either 'agree' or 'strongly agree' with the statement that they were satisfied with the information exchange between the two employee representation bodies. Only a quarter of the respondents (24,1%) 'disagreed' or 'completely disagreed' that the information exchange was adequate.

When comparing the responses from Dutch and foreign MNCs respectively, some differences are noteworthy. In Dutch MNCs, 38,5% of the respondents indicated that they were 'not satisfied' or 'completely dissatisfied' with the information exchange between their works council and the EWC. In foreign MNCs, on the other hand, only 12,5% of the respondents were 'dissatisfied' with the information exchange.

This means that a considerable number of Dutch works councils are not exposed to adequate information channels with their EWC colleagues. Such an exchange of information could constitute vital information for the Dutch works councils and hence improve the position of these works councils in multinational organisations. Moreover, EWCs can benefit from the information provided by Dutch employee representatives, which

149 Question 50.1 of the questionnaire; see Annex II.

could, overall, improve the position of the employee representation bodies within the MNC concerned. Moreover, the question arises as to whether the EWC performs a supporting role for Dutch employee representatives in terms of ensuring that the latter are fulfilling their role.[150]

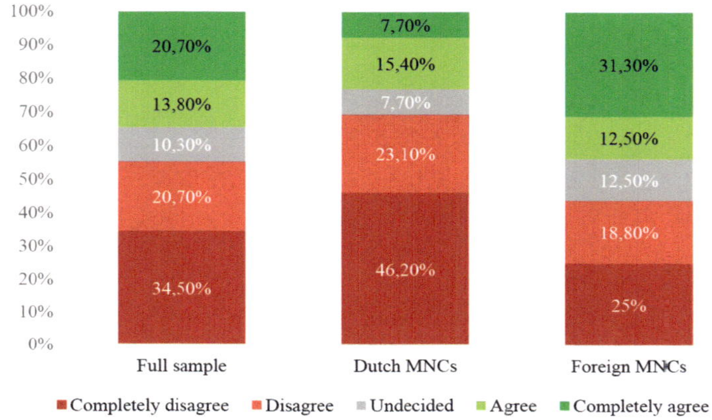

Figure 7.7 *The European Works Council supports me with regard to my duties as (central) works council member (N = 29); in Dutch (N = 13) and foreign MNCs (N = 16)*

Although the majority of respondents indicated that they were satisfied with the information exchange between their works council and the EWC (Figure 7.6 above), a majority of them (55,2%) did *not* regard the EWC as being supportive vis-a-vis the fulfillment of their duties as member of the Dutch works council (Figure 7.7 above). In Dutch MNCs, 69,3% of the respondents indicated that the EWCs were not supportive in ensuring that the works council fulfilled their duties. In foreign MNCs, 43,8% of the respondents did not regard the EWC as being supportive.

The question is, consequently, whether the lack of support stems from the limited rights of EWCs or the lack of cooperation between the two respective bodies. One-third of the respondents, however, stated that they 'agree' or 'completely agree' that the EWC was supporting their work as a member of the Dutch works council (34,5%). The percentage of respondents that perceived the EWC as being helpful was higher in foreign (43,8%) compared to Dutch MNCs (23,1%). The question, therefore, arises as to whether in Dutch MNCs especially, the European works council is regarded as a hindrance rather than a help. One possible scenario could be a hypothetical approval of a measure by the EWC, which may be consulted much earlier than the Dutch works council. The Dutch works

150 Question 50.3 of the questionnaire; see Annex II.

council may not support such an approval, but could be overruled by the EWC. Another aspect, which may explain the lower ratio of positive responses in Dutch MNCs, could be the (lack of) sufficient confidentiality within the EWC. These aspects could be the source of future research and additional empirical research regarding the relationship between national works councils and EWCs.

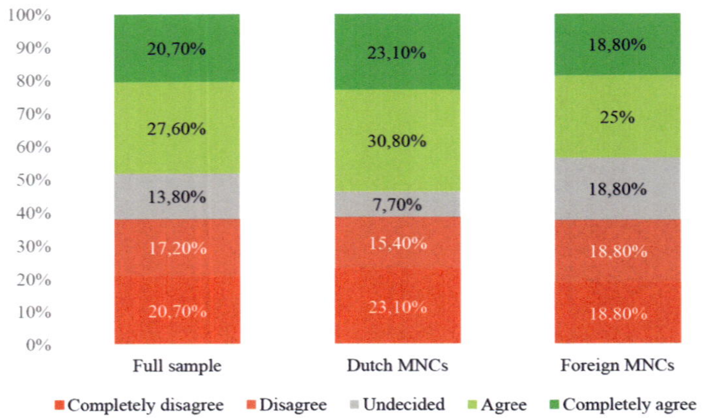

Figure 7.8 *The atmosphere is open and informal during meetings of the European Works Council (N = 29); in Dutch (N = 13) and foreign MNCs (N = 16)*

Subsequently, the participants were asked to indicate whether they regarded the atmosphere during EWC consultation meetings as being open and informal.[151] Due to the cultural differences and the differences between the various European employee participation regimes, the question subsequently arises as to whether the employee representatives that are participating in the meetings can convene in an open and informal manner. This in turn can be regarded as being beneficial for the outcome of the consultation process.

The results displayed in Figure 7.8 above show that the responses are somewhat divergent. While 37,9% of the respondents indicated that the atmosphere during EWC meetings was neither not open nor informal, 48,3% stated that they 'agree' or 'completely agree' that the atmosphere during consultation was both open and informal. It must therefore be concluded that in some EWCs, the various national employee representatives are able to overcome cultural differences as well as differences regarding the nature of the employee representation regimes and convene in an open and informal manner, whereas this is not the case for the other group of EWCs. Notably, no differences can be

151 Question 50.2 of the questionnaire; see Annex II.

observed in this regard between responses by employee representatives in Dutch vis-à-vis representatives of foreign MNCs.

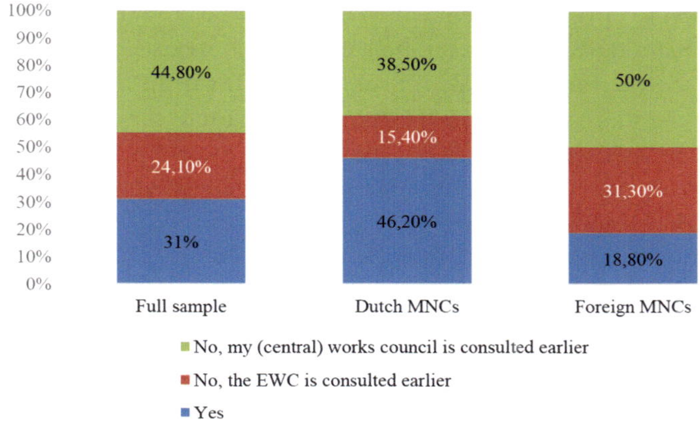

Figure 7.9 *Timing of consultation of both the Dutch works council and the EWC in MNCs (N = 29)*

Finally, the participants were asked whether their Dutch works council and the EWC maintained in their MNC were consulted at the same time on (intended) management decisions.[152] EWCs should "*receive information earlier or at the same time as the national employee representation bodies*", but "*must not reduce the general level of protection of employees*" as recital 37 of the Preamble of the EWC Directive stipulates.

Interestingly, the opposite practice is applied in a large number of corporations as was shown by the answers supplied by the respondents (44,8%), due to the fact that their (central) works council was consulted earlier than the EWC was. Furthermore, in only one-third of the cases the two employee representation bodies were consulted at the same time (31%) and one-fourth of the participants stated that the EWC was consulted earlier than their Dutch (central) works council. It is thereby of high importance for Dutch works councils to obtain the relevant information from the EWC in order to fulfil their own duties in cases where the EWC is consulted *earlier*, in order to safeguard the notion that their Dutch works council can effectively influence the decision-making process. This would certainly have the effect of benefiting the position of the Dutch works councils in multinational corporations.

152 Question 51 of the questionnaire; see Annex II.

8 Summary and conclusion – the *status quo* of Dutch works councils in MNCs anno 2014/2015

In this chapter, the position of Dutch works councils in multinational corporations was examined by means of a quantitative analysis on the basis of a questionnaire that was distributed among Dutch central works councils. The objective of the quantitative analysis was to obtain data on the *status quo* anno 2014/2015 with regard to the position of the Dutch works councils in MNCs and to identify trends among the sample obtained. The last large-scale surveys on Dutch works councils were conducted in 1999 and 2009, which naturally warrants an update of the quantitative data on Dutch works councils.

The legal analysis of the framework applicable to Dutch works councils in chapter III was used as starting point for formulating the survey questions. Moreover, the previous surveys conducted in 1999 and 2009 were taken into account, as much as possible, in order to make the results comparable.

For the survey, a large sample of 185 Dutch central works councils was drawn from the Mezzo-database of the Social and Economic Council as well as from the MNO Foundation's list of members according to the pre-defined criteria of size, turnover, transnationality and position of the works council within the undertaking. In total, 56 questionnaires were returned, which constitutes a percentage return rate of 30,3%.[153]

8.1 *Responses are divided on the overall position of Dutch works councils in MNCs*

On the basis of the results of the questionnaire, it can be concluded that the majority of Dutch works councils in multinational corporations are in a strong position, but exceptions are nevertheless apparent. Dutch works councils are, in the overwhelming majority of cases, in receipt of sufficient information and are regularly consulted on crucial topics that fall within the scope of article 25 of the WCA, as was illustrated in this chapter as well as in chapter V below. Moreover, key rights are used by most works councils and the access to training and development is considered as satisfactory by almost all of the respondents, although some exceptions can be observed here as well.

This divide in the results is also reflected in the answers to the question on the general perception of the works council's position. When asked how the members of the works council perceived the position of their works council in times of increasing internationalisation,[154] a slight majority (54,5%) indicated that their position did not deteriorate or

153 See Annex IV for the non-response rates per questionnaire item.

154 Question 40 of the questionnaire; see Annex II.

were undecided as to whether increasing internationalisation had a negative influence on the position of their works council; whereas 45,4% agreed or strongly agreed that the position had deteriorated (see Figure 8.1 below).[155] That being said, this does not hold true for all works councils.

In foreign MNCs, 60% of the respondents indicated that their position had deteriorated compared to 45,4% of the respondents in Dutch MNCs. In foreign MNCs, 5% of the respondents reported that they were very positive about the position of their works council, especially in light of increasing internationalisation (i.e., that they 'strongly disagreed' with the statement) and 15% were positive about their position (20% in total). In Dutch MNCs, 13,6% of the MNCs regarded their position as being very positive and 18,2% were positive about their position (31,8% in total).

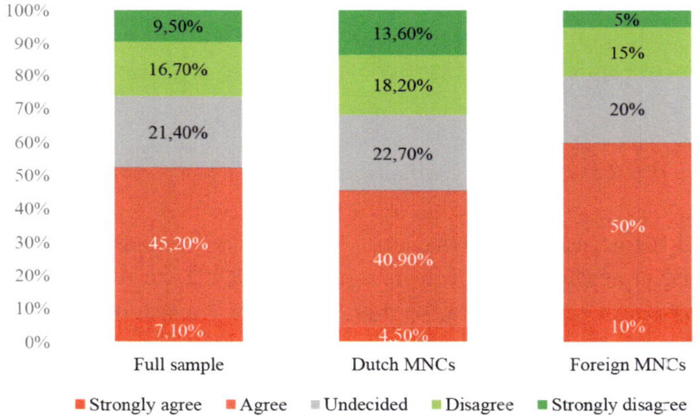

Figure 8.1 *The position of my (central) works council has deteriorated as a result of increasing internationalisation (N = 42); in Dutch (N = 22) and foreign MNCs (N = 20)*

8.2 *Information rights of Dutch works councils in MNCs*

Timely access to information, at least twice a year pursuant to article 31a of the WCA, is the foundation for the effective participation of works councils in the decision-making process. Access to financial information is, according to the responses, overall considered

155 The responding members of works councils in Dutch MNCs indicated a slightly more positive perception of their position with 54,5% disagreeing that the position had worsened or were undecided. No statistical significant difference, however, can be reported between works councils in Dutch and works councils in foreign MNCs.

as being sufficient, given the fact that 88,1% received the necessary information at least twice a year.[156] It can be further noted that such information was, in two-thirds of the cases, not limited to the Dutch subsidiaries of the corporation, which allows the works councils to gain insights into the overall performance of the MNC. About one in ten works councils, however, did not receive such information or only received insufficient information in light of the statutory minimum codified in article 31a of the WCA. Works councils that do not have access to the information are thus placed in a difficult position.

In addition to financial information, Dutch works councils have a right to access information on the holding-structure and the linkages between the undertakings [*zeggenschapsverhoudingen*] within their entire corporation pursuant to the recent Act of 26 June 2013.[157] From the received survey responses, it appears that such information is provided to works councils in the majority of cases (59,5%). However, one fifth of works councils did not receive such information and indicated, in most cases, that possessing a lack of knowledge about this right was the reason as to why this was the case. In two cases, the central management explicitly refused access to the necessary information.

8.3 *Consultation rights of Dutch works councils in MNCs*

Similar to the requirement for access to information, Dutch works councils were frequently consulted on crucial topics falling within the scope of article 25 of the WCA.[158] The topics on which consultation took place were thereby largely consistent with the agenda of the works councils and are hence commensurate with their own priorities. Moreover, consultations meetings took place three to six times a year in the majority of undertakings, with an even higher average of meetings for the overall population with six to eight meetings per year.[159] Therefore, the overall frequency of consultation meetings can be considered as being satisfactory in light of the statutory requirements under the WCA. Furthermore, a relatively large number of respondents indicated that their consultation partner was the CEO of the corporation or another member of the central management (50,9%). This finding is rather striking since more Dutch works councils are maintained at the subsidiary level within the corporation, but the CEO is nevertheless the works councils' consultation partner.[160] Moreover, the HR manager was the only consultation partner of the Dutch works council in two of the cases reported, whereas

156 Section 5.4 above.
157 Section 5.5 above.
158 See sections 3.2 and 5.2.
159 43% of the corporations have more than six meetings per year and 11,9% of the respondents indicated that consultation meetings take place on a monthly or even bi-weekly basis, which results in a higher frequency of consultations on average.
160 See section 3.2.

in one-third of the cases, the HR manager was present *in addition* to a member of the management.

When examining the relationship with supervisory boards, a different conclusion must be made. Supervisory board members are, in the majority of cases, never present at the consultation meetings (52,4%) and are only sometimes present in one fourth of the respondent corporations. This attendance ratio is too low in light of the legal obligation to attend meetings that is codified in article 24(2) of the WCA. Furthermore, in light of the principle of good corporate governance and with regard to the potential benefits of the presence of supervisory board members, this non-attendance should be regarded as a point of attention.[161]

When turning to the substance of the consultation meetings, one can conclude that the aftermath of the financial crisis has also affected the consultations in MNCs, with a majority of the respondents indicating that reorganisations were the subject of most consultation meetings. A statistically significant difference between works councils in Dutch vis-à-vis foreign MNCs could be observed regarding consultation on the topic of the future strategy of the corporation and future trends. Whereas works councils in Dutch MNCs were consulted on this topic in 76,2% of the cases, this topic was only addressed in 35% of the respondent foreign MNCs. This can, therefore, have adverse effects for the position of works councils in foreign MNCs compared to their counterparts in Dutch MNCs. Furthermore, works councils in foreign MNCs are also considerably less frequently consulted on abroad transactions (i.e., takeovers, mergers and acquisitions).[162] Such abroad transactions can have a considerable influence on the position of the Dutch undertaking(s) in the medium and long-term and hence the position of the Dutch works council as well. Yet, the greater involvement of works councils on strategic matters might prove difficult to achieve, especially in foreign MNCs due to the differences in corporate culture and the resulting absence of similarly strong employee participation regimes in the MNC's country of origin.

8.4 *The use of covenants*

The rights of Dutch works councils in MNCs are inherently limited to the Netherlands due to the principle of territoriality. The decision-making structures applied in multinational corporations include the Dutch subsidiaries, but are certainly not limited to

161 See best practice provision 2.3.6 of the Dutch Corporate Governance Code 2016, which holds that "[t]he chairman of the supervisory board should in any ensure that [...] i. the supervisory board has proper contact with the management board, the employee participation body (if any) and the general meeting".

162 Although this result is not statistically significant on a 95% confidence interval; see section 5.2 for further details.

them. Rather, the decision-making structures applied reflect the multinational scope of the corporations' operations. Employee participation does, therefore, not follow control under all circumstances anymore.[163] Covenants, pursuant to article 32 of the WCA, can be regarded as a tool to develop a regime of employee participation that fits within the decision-making structures of multinational corporations. The results of the survey also show that a considerable number of additional rights are conferred upon Dutch works councils.[164] Yet, only a minority of undertakings have concluded a covenant with their works councils (43,4%), which certainly leaves room for improvement (if the management cooperates).

An important observation of the analysis is that when comparing the use of covenants in foreign corporations with Dutch MNCs, a considerably smaller number of foreign MNCs have concluded a covenant with their Dutch works council. This difference is statistically significant.[165] Therefore, a paradoxical situation can be observed: while in foreign MNCs corporate decisions fall, more often, outside the scope of the Dutch legal framework on employee participation (and hence the number of areas whereby the Dutch regime is insufficiently linked to the decision-making structures is *greater*), the number of individual solutions to improve the linkage by means of covenants is *lower* in foreign MNCs than for Dutch multinationals. This significant difference could be caused by a number of different factors. The relatively high ratio of Dutch MNCs having a covenant in place can be explained by the fact that after the implementation of the structure regime, by which employee participation is limited under the 'Netherlands construction', the works council can (re)-gain participation rights at the highest level within the MNC if a covenant has been concluded. Moreover, Dutch undertakings are more likely accept employee participation in the decision-making process due to the application of the stakeholder model within Dutch society (i.e., the 'Polder model').[166] Foreign MNCs, on the contrary, are – with the exception of German corporations – not subjected to a similar employee participation mechanism in their home country and often come from a different corporate culture background such as the Anglo Saxon (enlightened) shareholder model.[167] Given the difference in corporate culture between foreign MNCs compared to Dutch MNCs, the idea of granting even more rights to works councils is rather unlikely despite being highly desirable for the position of the Dutch works council within the MNCs concerned.[168]

163 Referred to as the *medezeggenschap volgt zeggenschap* principle; see *inter alia* I. Zaal, *De reikwijdte van medezeggenschap* (Kluwer, Deventer 2014), p. 1.

164 See Figure 5.15 in section 5.3 above.

165 See section 5.3 above.

166 Cf. J.K. Looise and M. Drucker, 'Employee participation in multinational enterprises: The effects of globalisation on Dutch works councils', 24 *Employee Relations* 1 (2002), p. 32.

167 Cf. J.C. Looise and M. Drucker, 'Dutch Works Councils in Times of Transition: The Effects of Changes in Society, Organizations and Work on the Position of Works Councils', 24 *Employee Relations* 3 (2003), p. 399.

168 *Ibid.*, p. 401.

8.5 *Other key rights of Dutch works councils*

In addition to the information and consultation rights of Dutch works councils in MNCs, as well as the extension thereof by means of covenants, a number of additional rights were identified as being crucial for the functioning of Dutch works councils.

Firstly, the structure regime and the significant recast of this regime in 2004 has affected the position of the Dutch works council in MNCs.[169] The quantitative results show that the structure regime is, at least in one in six corporations, not applied at all, even although the likelihood of these very large corporations fulfilling the necessary criteria is very high.[170] The enforcement of the application of the structure regime, however, is unclear and gives cause for concern. Here lies a task for the legislator to adapt the current regime by including an enforcement mechanism; monitoring the compliance rate by the competent authorities would also be desirable. In addition, the works councils in corporations which do not comply with the regime – despite fulfillment of the necessary criteria – should put more emphasis on this issue. Moreover, 37,8% of the respondent works councils could not indicate whether the regime was applied in their undertaking on a voluntary basis. Given the fact that the recommendation rights of works councils are linked to certain changes in the application of the regime, the works councils concerned should investigate the current status of the regime's application in their MNC.[171] Aside from the application of the structure regime as such, Dutch works councils exercised their regular right of recommendation at least once, in 48,8% of the cases, and their enhanced recommendation right in 64,3% of the cases within the last four years. Given that almost half of the works councils did not exercise their regular right of recommendation and one-third of works councils did not exercise their enhanced right of recommendation for the supervisory board, a more frequent exercise of these rights would be highly recommendable. The majority of works councils indicated a lack of knowledge as the main reason for not making use of these rights. By exercising their recommendation rights, works councils can not only improve their own position, but can also assume an active role vis-à-vis the management and the shareholders of the corporation. Furthermore, the establishment and maintenance of good relationships with the supervisory board leads, in the majority of cases, to better access to information.[172]

Secondly, Dutch works councils in multinational corporations are facing increasingly complex holding structures within the MNC and an increasing number of topic areas, which results in a more cumbersome decision-making procedure. It can be positively

169 Sections 4.1 and 4.2 above.

170 All respondents reported more than 100 employees for the Dutch entities. It is also very likely that 16 million EUR in equity capital is achieved by all MNCs.

171 See section 3.2 in chapter III above for a detailed analysis of the structure regime.

172 See in detail section 4.2.

noted that the overwhelming majority of works councils use both internal and external experts in order to effectively exercise their rights. Only two responding works councils indicated that no use of internal experts was made and one works council stated that they did not make use of external experts within the last three years.[173] Considering that experts are, according to half of the respondents, currently only 'sometimes' involved, it would be recommendable to increase the use of experts to further improve the quality of the advice given by the works councils.

Thirdly, it can be concluded that the overwhelming majority of Dutch works councils are satisfied with the training and development opportunities within their undertaking (92,9%).[174] The recent amendment of article 18(2) of the WCA regarding the requirement of training and development *of sufficient quality* is, therefore, fulfilled in multinational corporations according to almost all of the respondents.[175]

In three cases, however, the respondents indicated that their entrepreneur offered training and development that was insufficient for their works council, which deserves further attention in light of the *sufficient quality* criterion. Furthermore, only a small minority (23,8%) reported that they did not have enough time for their work as employee representative due to a high workload and other duties.[176] The facilities for the work of employee representatives in multinational corporations can thus be considered as being overall sufficient, although a considerable number of employee representatives (one in five) had negative experiences with superiors and slightly more (about one in four) experienced time pressures.

8.6 The relationship between the Dutch works councils and the EWC

Ensuring that Dutch works councils are able to have foreign contact and the relationship with the EWC were the final topic areas covered by the survey. The results showed that the majority of Dutch works councils maintained foreign contact (66,7%), but this was often exclusively through the EWC and thus not outside their own corporate network.[177]

Furthermore, about one third of the works councils did not have foreign contact despite the multinational business-structure of their undertaking. This certainly leaves room for improvement, since an exchange of ideas with employee representatives within the MNC in other countries as well as the exchange of best practices with representatives

173 See section 5.6 above.
174 See section 5.7.1 above.
175 See section 5.7.2 for further details.
176 *Ibid.*
177 See section 6 above.

outside the Netherlands would be highly beneficial. This can also be done through existing networks to improve the position of the works councils.[178] At the same time, it can be positively noted that the majority of Dutch works councils are involved in the decision-making process when it concerns transnational issues (61,9%).

When turning to the relationship of the responding Dutch works councils with the EWC, it can be concluded that a EWC is maintained in the majority of MNCs (69%).[179] But virtually all of the MNCs that were included in this survey fulfilled the criteria for 'Community scale undertakings' for which the EWC Directive and hence the establishment of a EWC are both applicable and mandatory. Therefore, the non-compliance rate of 31% is far too high. Of the EWCs currently maintained in multinational corporations, the majority (69%) did not having more rights other than those stipulated in the statutory fallback rules of Annex I to the EWC Directive.[180] Despite most EWCs having limited participation rights, the majority were maintained at the level of the central management (69%) or at the level of the regional EU headquarters (24,1%). Therefore, the EWC can certainly serve as important information channel for the Dutch works councils given the often-higher level at which the EWC is maintained within the MNC. The supportive role of the EWC was also acknowledged by the majority of respondents.

In conclusion, Dutch works councils are overall characterised by a high degree of professionalism and the position of the majority thereof can be regarded as being satisfactory in light of the applicable legal framework. Yet, several areas were identified whereby an improvement of the status quo would be highly desirable. The position of Dutch works councils in foreign MNCs is thus worthy of being highlighted. Given the significantly lower degree to which such works councils are involved in the decision-making process on international matters and future development, their position is certainly more difficult compared to their counterparts in Dutch MNCs.

178 Such as GoodCorp and SEEurope; see section 7 above for further details.

179 See section 7 above.

180 A total of 17,2% of the respondents indicated that they had no knowledge of the existence of additional rights for their EWC.

Chapter V: Qualitative results

1 Introduction

The quantitative analysis of the works councils' position in The Netherlands that was carried out in the previous chapter showed that a number of issues regarding the application and compliance with the Dutch employee participation legislation exists in practice. Even although Dutch works councils in large corporations are, overall, characterized by a high degree of professionalism, a number of areas could be identified whereby an improvement in the status quo would be highly desirable. Shortcomings could mainly be identified in the areas of (i) information rights (i.e., timely access to financial information and information on the corporate structure), (ii) consultation rights (i.e., discrepancy between Dutch and foreign corporations regarding the scope of the consultation and the use of covenants) and (iii) corporate governance (i.e., presence of a supervisory board, use of recommendation rights and the presence of supervisory board members at consultation meetings). Moreover, the facilities provided by the corporation to the works council (such as the training of works council members, secretarial support, coordination of the participation process by the management and access to experts) can also play a role in this regard. In order to answer why these shortcomings exist and, more importantly, how these shortcomings can be overcome in practice, can only be done by means of explorative, qualitative research due to the close-ended nature of the quantitative research.

This chapter first provides a short overview of the employee participation process *de lege lata* (section 2). The current legal framework was taken as a point of departure and the interview topics corresponded with the participation rights laid down in the WCA. Subsequently, the individual aspects of the employee participation process will be discussed in greater detail. The focus thereby lies in the examples of good practice developed by the corporations that participated in this study, which will be used as the basis for positing the recommendations on how to improve employee participation in international corporations (chapter VI). In section 3, the examples of good practice that are applied by multinational corporations will be mapped out. On the basis of the 58 semi-structured interviews conducted,[1] a total of 143 examples of good practice were ascertained (see Figure 1.1 below). An index of all examples of good practice can be found in Annex I of this study.

1 See chapter II for the methodological approach and the structure of the semi-structured interviews.

In this study, reference is made to good practices instead of best practices. The term good practice is preferred because of the fact that the identified practices are not the only solution to the problem, nor can they be regarded as more suitable than others. Future research may indeed produce other good practices that are indeed better suited for improving the position of works councils in multinational corporations.

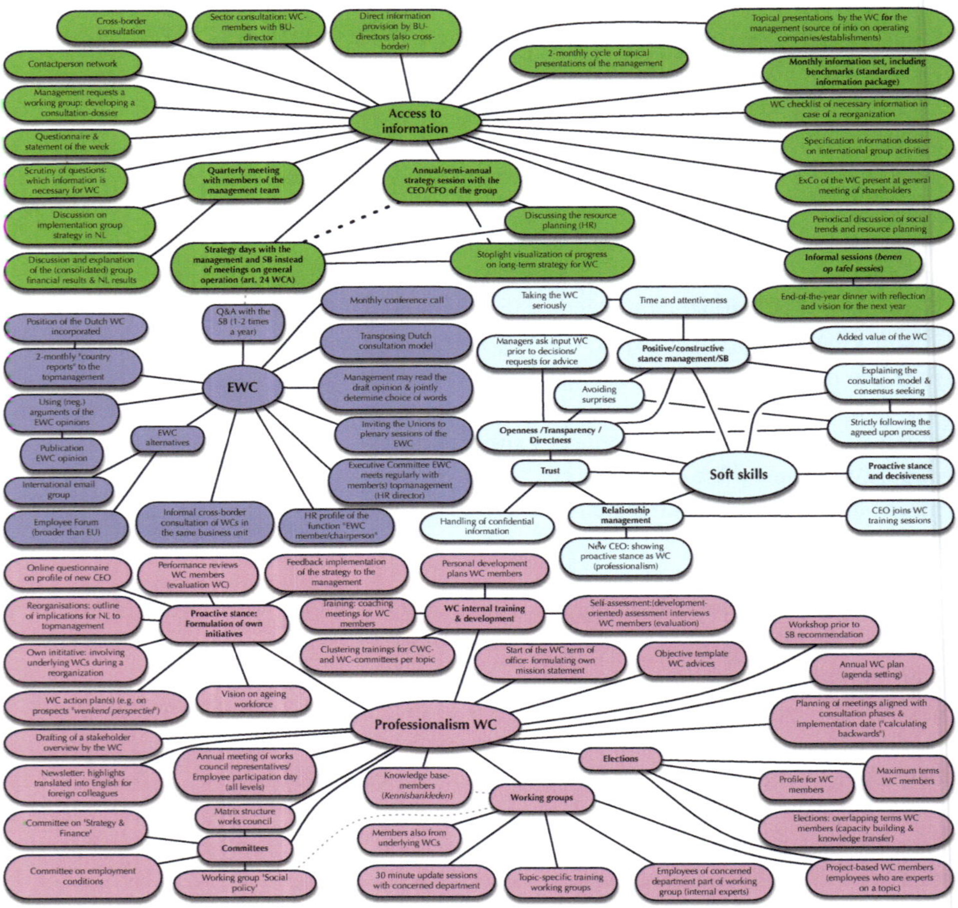

Figure 1.1 Examples of good practice identified on the basis of 58 interviews with stakeholders in MNCs (2015).

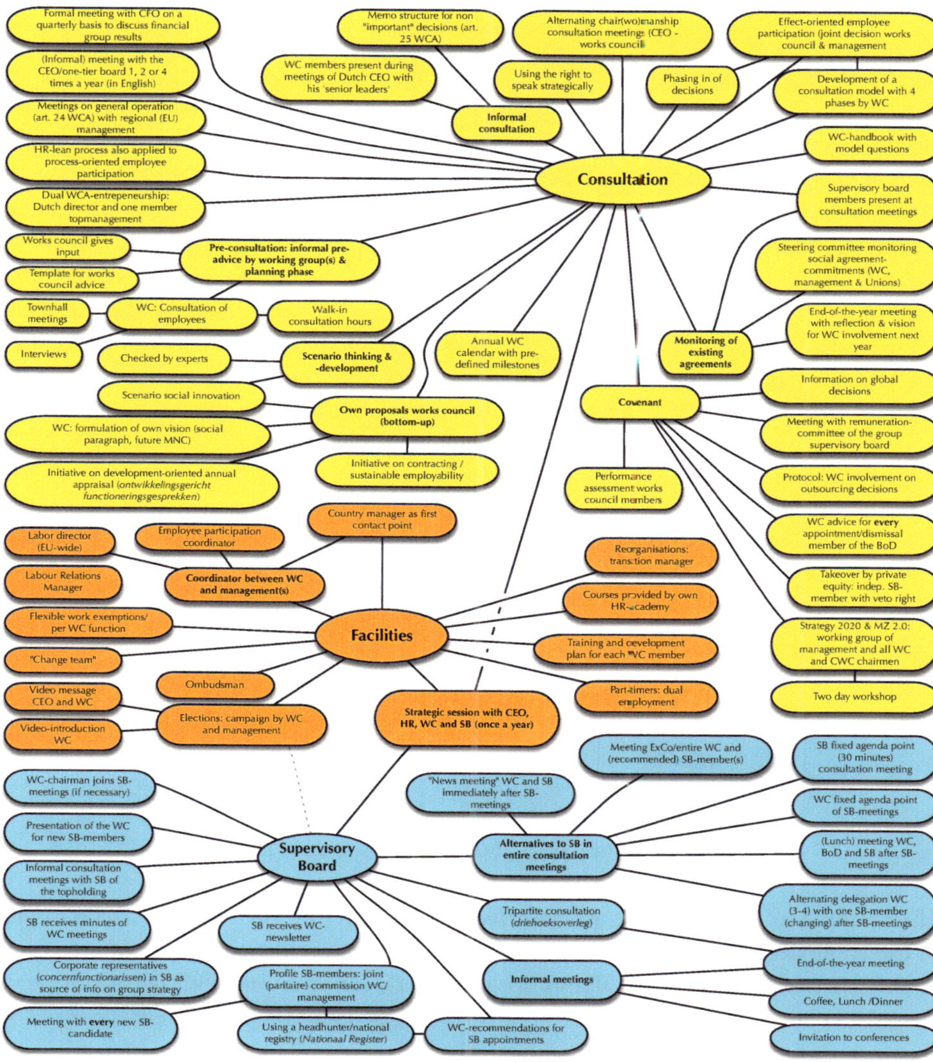
Formal meeting with CFO on a quarterly basis to discuss financial group results
Memo structure for non "important" decisions (art. 25 WCA)
Alternating chair(wo)manship consultation meetings (CEO - works council)
Effect-oriented employee participation (joint decision works council & management
(Informal) meeting with the CEO/one-tier board 1, 2 or 4 times a year (in English)
WC members present during meetings of Dutch CEO with his 'senior leaders'
Using the right to speak strategically
Phasing in of decisions
Development of a consultation model with 4 phases by WC
Meetings on general operation (art. 24 WCA) with regional (EU) management
Informal consultation
WC-handbook with model questions
HR-lean process also applied to process-oriented employee participation
Consultation
Supervisory board members present at consultation meetings
Dual WCA-entrepeneurship: Dutch director and one member topmanagement
Works council gives input
Pre-consultation: informal pre-advice by working group(s) & planning phase
Steering committee monitoring social agreement-commitments (WC, management & Unions)
Template for works council advice
Townhall meetings
WC: Consultation of employees
Walk-in consultation hours
End-of-the-year meeting with reflection & vision for WC involvement next year
Interviews
Checked by experts
Scenario thinking & -development
Annual WC calendar with pre-defined milestones
Monitoring of existing agreements
Information on global decisions
Scenario social innovation
Own proposals works council (bottom-up)
Covenant
WC: formulation of own vision (social paragraph, future MNC)
Meeting with remuneration-committee of the group supervisory board
Initiative on contracting / sustainable employability
Initiative on development-oriented annual appraisal (ontwikkelingsgericht functioneringsgesprekken)
Performance assessment works council members
Protocol: WC involvement on outsourcing decisions
Country manager as first contact point
WC advice for every appointment/dismissal member of the BoD
Labor director (EU-wide)
Employee participation coordinator
Reorganisations: transition manager
Coordinator between WC and management(s)
Labour Relations Manager
Takeover by private equity: indep. SB-member with veto right
Courses provided by own HR-academy
Flexible work exemptions/ per WC function
Facilities
Strategy 2020 & MZ 2.0: working group of management and all WC and CWC chairmen
"Change team"
Training and development plan for each WC member
Ombudsman
Part-timers: dual employment
Two day workshop
Video message CEO and WC
Elections: campaign by WC and management
Strategic session with CEO, HR, WC and SB (once a year)
Video-introduction WC
Meeting ExCo/entire WC and (recommended) SB-member(s)
SB fixed agenda point (30 minutes) consultation meeting
WC-chairman joins SB-meetings (if necessary)
"News meeting" WC and SB immediately after SB-meetings
WC fixed agenda point of SB-meetings
Presentation of the WC for new SB-members
Supervisory Board
Alternatives to SB in entire consultation meetings
(Lunch) meeting WC, BoD and SB after SB-meetings
Informal consultation meetings with SB of the topholding
Alternating delegation WC (3-4) with one SB-member (changing) after SB-meetings
SB receives minutes of WC meetings
SB receives WC-newsletter
Tripartite consultation (driehoeksoverleg)
End-of-the-year meeting
Corporate representatives (concernfunctionarissen) in SB as source of info on group strategy
Profile SB-members: joint (paritaire) commission WC/ management
Informal meetings
Coffee, Lunch /Dinner
Meeting with every new SB-candidate
Using a headhunter/national registry (Nationaal Register)
WC-recommendations for SB appointments
Invitation to conferences

The interviews were conducted with 24 MNCs with representatives of Dutch central works councils (25 interviews) and the respective management (19 interviews) as well as supervisory board members (14 interviews). The interviews took place between January and October 2015 and lasted roughly between 60 to 90 minutes each. The audio-recordings were subsequently transcribed and coded by means of ATLAS.ti.[2] The responses and the results thereof will be discussed in the remainder of this chapter.

These examples of good practice, however, do not constitute an exhaustive list of practices, but are rather a collection of possible solutions to the problems of effective employee participation in MNCs. Moreover, similar practices reported in some of the interviews were combined into one "good practice-term", which covers the spirit of the measures used in order to avoid overlap. These examples of good practice could then be clustered. This was done according to the different phases of the employee participation process – the information and consultation phases as well as the monitoring of the impact of the decisions made – and according to the different stakeholders involved, which are the works council, the supervisory board, the (facilities provided by) the management and the European works council. Lastly, the interaction between the individuals involved and the necessary soft skills were identified as being an important factor in the effective participation process and is consequently treated as another 'good practice-cluster'.[3]

Figure 1.2 Clusters of good practices identified in the qualitative phase

The examples of good practice are reported according to the identified clusters of topics of the employee participation process. The clusters that are deemed relevant are access to information (3.1), the consultation process (3.2), facilities provided by the corporation (3.2.1), the relationship between the works council and the supervisory board (3.4), the degree of professionalism of the (central) works council (3.5), the relationship with the European works council (3.6) and the soft skills necessary for effective employee

2 See Annex VI for the codebook used in this analysis.
3 See also Figure 1.2 below.

participation (3.7). These clusters will be used to structure the identified examples of good practice.

The individual examples of good practice are, however, highly interrelated. This means that it is very often the case that one practice is a prerequisite for the effective application of another good practice. For instance, the introduction of a monthly information dossier provided by the management to the works council allows for the implementation of an informal pre-advice phase in which the works council can give input on the basis of the information provided in the dossier. Therefore, it is important to note that all aspects of the employee participation process, as grouped in the clusters above, are necessary for an effective and efficient employee participation process. These links will be pointed out in the subsequent sections, if applicable. At the same time, certain aspects such as the access to information and the application of (formal) consultations are more important than others, as will be explained below in more detail.

2 Preliminary remarks

The Dutch Works Council Act clearly delineates the duties of the entrepreneur to give the works council an opportunity to render advice on any proposed decision that falls within the scope of article 25 of the WCA. The most relevant topics and possible issues that could arise in the context of multinational corporations were discussed in chapter III above. Important in this context is, however, that the management only has a duty to inform the works council of its intended decision and does not have to engage in earlier (informal) consultations with the works council. According to the relevant legislation, it is only *after* the management has made an (intended) decision within the meaning of article 25 of the WCA that the works council is given the opportunity to render its advice on the topic (see Figure 2.1 below). Although the works council's advice must be *requested at a time when it can still significantly affect the decision to be taken* (article 25(2) of the WCA), the question arises as to whether this is the case in practice. In large MNCs especially, the timing of access to information and participation in the decision-making process is crucial. This becomes visible when one analyses the case law of the Enterprise Chamber of the Amsterdam Court of Appeal in proceedings based on the attribution of decisions of the parent company (*toerekening*) and co-entrepreneurship (*medeondernemerschap*).[4]

4 See section 4 in chapter III above.

Figure 2.1 *Process of employee participation under the Dutch Works Council Act (de lege lata)*

Therefore, one could argue that the employee participation process pursuant to the WCA cannot be applied effectively and efficiently in MNCs.[5] The shortcomings of the WCA have the effect of hampering effective and efficient employee participation in light of the often speedy decision-making process that is present in MNCs, and in light of the transnationality of management structures within these corporations. It is sometimes stated that "decisions are taken on a higher level within the corporation and we are being confronted with the consequences of such a decision for the Dutch undertakings".[6] While it is was not foreseen by the Dutch legislator that Dutch works councils would have a say in the global strategy of the corporation in light of the principle of territoriality, the question arises as to whether effective employee participation is possible *despite* the lack of formal rights at the highest management level of a corporation. The subsequent analysis of the applied examples of good practice will show that very often the management grants the (central) works council extra-legal rights once they see an added value of it in terms of time and cost-effectiveness, as well as the achievement of better deliberated decisions. Moreover, some corporations have applied practical solutions to the implementation of rights pursuant to the WCA in the context of the above-mentioned multilevel decision-making structure that is present in many MNCs. These solutions and additional, extra-legal rights of central works councils are to be regarded as examples of good practice due to their positive impact on the employee participation process in the respective corporations. How they impact the decision-making process and why they are to be regarded as examples of good practice will be addressed, in greater detail, in the subsequent analysis of the clusters.

5 Other authors that are critical on this aspect are *inter alia* I. Zaal, *De reikwijdte van medezeggenschap* (Kluwer, Deventer 2014), p. 2-3 and 35-36; R.H. van het Kaar, 'GS Rechtspersonen, artikel 25 WOR, aant. 5', <http://deeplinking.kluwer.nl/?param=00AA3EDE&cpid=WKNL-LTR-Nav2> (last accessed 23.10.2017).

6 Interviews 10:29, 15:8 and 31:12.

3 MAPPING OF EXAMPLES OF GOOD PRACTICE APPLIED IN MULTINATIONAL CORPORATIONS

After having given a general overview as starting point, we now turn to the mapping of the examples of good practice that were reported during the interview phase of this study.

3.1 *Access to information*

The first 'good practice-cluster' to be discussed is that of 'access to information'.[7] This cluster was chosen as the starting point due to the fact that timely access to information is the crucial prerequisite to effective employee participation and therefore it is of the utmost importance for the application of the overwhelming majority of the other examples of good practice that subsequently follow. This is also reflected in the applicable legislation. Articles 24, 25(3), 27(2) and 31-31d of the WCA stipulate a number of obligations on the employer to provide information, with article 31 of the WCA being the core provision by stating that "*if requested to do so, the entrepreneur shall in a timely fashion provide the Works Council and its committees with all the information and data such as they may reasonably be deemed to require in order to perform their duties*".[8] As was stated above, this obligation may be at odds with the multilevel management structure that is present in many MNCs. The entrepreneur, whom has the obligation to provide all the necessary information according to article 31 of the WCA, may not actually possess this information due to the fact that, for instance, the respective decision may be taken by a business unit director, whom is based in another country.

At the same time, it can be positively noted that good practices relating to the access to information were often reported in the interview phase (23 good practices and 144 interview quotations). This shows that the importance of access to information is also reflected in practice and exhibits that the management is willing to apply practical solutions to facilitate this aspect of effective employee participation.

---

7 See Annex I for an overview of all examples of good practice related to this cluster.

8 Article 21(a) of the EU Social Charter similarly mandates that employee representatives are "*to be informed regularly or at the appropriate time and in a comprehensible way about the economic and financial situation* [...]"; see also, article 27 of the EU Charter of Fundamental rights holds that works councils must "*be guaranteed information and consultation in good time in the cases and under the conditions provided for by Community law and national laws and practices*".

3.1.1 Access to (reoccurring) information on a continuous basis

One problem faced by works councils is the lack of timely access to information that is necessary for their work. The works council may receive information either too late or may only receive incomplete information. At the same time, a lot of the information that is necessary for the work councils' work is reoccurring (i.e., business processes are often repeated and information is gathered by the corporation on these processes in a standardised manner). A number of good practices were developed to facilitate the CWC's access to such reoccurring information (for instance access to financial benchmarks, employee numbers, sick-leave, etc.) on a continuous basis. In two corporations, a '*monthly digital information dossier*' was agreed upon between the management and the works council.[9] The works council and the entrepreneur agreed upon a number of indicators such as production numbers, the ratio of permanent to flexible employment relationships and sick-leave of employees. The digital information dossier is updated on a monthly basis by the management and it is accessible to the CWC at all times. Given the extra-legal nature of such a dossier, the entrepreneur and the works council made use of a covenant pursuant to article 32 of the WCA to put their agreement on a more formal footing. It is worth noting that this agreement was signed after a confrontational situation whereby the works council noted that the necessary information was being provided too late or being provided as incomplete. In order to avoid such confrontations in the future, the digital information dossier was agreed upon.[10] In the second corporation, the dossier primarily contains the consolidated figures of the Dutch undertaking that are submitted to the parent company on a regular basis and is referred to as a '*standardized information package*'.[11] Such access to an information package can also be specified for the corporate group's international activities. This can, for instance, take the form of a quarterly update on the financial results of the group in comparison with the results of the Dutch subsidiary[12] or on a case-by-case basis whenever a financial transaction takes place.[13]

9 Interview 1:18: "*door onze bestuurder krijgen we elke maand een dataset, een boekje, met kengetallen. Ook niet financieel maar wel ziektepercentages, productieaantallen, aantal vaste/flexibele medewerkers, leeftijdsopbouw van het personeel. Die data die wij gezamenlijk hebben gedefinieerd als benodigd om ons werk te kunnen doen, is een aantal jaren geleden gezamenlijk gezegd: "hier willen wij inzage in". Dat krijgen wij als een digitaal info-set van [het concern] elke maand*"; this is also called the 'standardized information package' (interview 47).

10 Interview 1:19: "*Wel helaas naar een conflictsituatie. Wij hebben wel gezegd van we hadden juist de indruk dat wij informatie vaak te laat kregen, onvolledig of niet; en dan moet je het afdwingen. Dus hebben wij gezegd: wij willen maandelijks een vaste set; die kun je ook volgen en bijhouden. Dan is het ook gedefinieerd: dit moet er instaan. En toen is dan in een paritaire werkgroep tussen OR en [concern] directie afgestemd welke data we dan krijgen elke maand. Toen is dat boekje in het leven geroepen*".

11 Interview 47:11.

12 Interviews 16, 39 and 47.

13 Interview 42:8: the financial committee of the CWC is informed about all major loans.

The advantage of such an information dossier lies in the predefinition of necessary information for the day-to-day working of the works council. The management can also be sure that it provides the information that is deemed necessary for the CWC and hence conflicts can be avoided about whether or not certain information has been provided. Another advantage lies in the fact that such a dossier can be based upon the standardised, internal reports drawn up by the corporation on a continuous basis, which is thus more resource efficient (such as in the case of the consolidated results that are compiled for the parent company).

This good practice has therefore increased the foreseeability and transparency of the decision-making process for the works council and makes access to information much more (time) efficient for both parties. While such an information dossier is useful for reoccurring, standardised data, it should not replace the need to provide additional information in cases of *inter alia* reorganisations and other extraordinary decisions.

In another corporation, the works council has developed a '*checklist of necessary information in case of a reorganisation*'.[14] By doing so, the works council is prepared for future reorganisations or, like in the case of this corporation, reducing its own workload due to the fact that intended decisions to reorganise frequently take place.

A third noteworthy good practice does not pertain to the scope of the information to be provided, but rather concerns the source of the information. Aside from the uncertainty as to what information is necessary for the works council, it is often difficult for the entrepreneur within the meaning of the WCA (very often the Dutch statutory director) to provide the information. The main reason, according to the interviewed respondents, is the fact that the organisation structure of corporations is based on business units (hereinafter: BU) or divisions that span several countries.[15] It is therefore only for legal and fiscal reasons that a structure with a Dutch (sub)-holding and separate legal entities for the business activities is maintained.[16] The works council is maintained and the (designated) entrepreneur within the meaning of the WCA is specified according to the legal structure of the corporation and not the organisational structure. This results in a situation whereby in multinational corporations, the (designated) entrepreneur is not necessarily the most desirable consultation partner for the works council. One solution to this information gap that is applied is to '*designate business unit or division directors as information source*' and to sometimes also include consultation partners for topics

14 Interview 4:15.

15 This was indicated, for instance, in interviews 3, 14, 16, 24 and 34.

16 The same legal structure is applied in other countries as well and is not country-specific to the Netherlands; see for instance an interview (38:26) with a member of the management: "*En dat is in alle landen trouwens. Dat hebben we gewoon in elk land. Dus we hebben eigenlijk een hele simpele structuur. Er is een holding. We hebben een tussenholding even vanwege de financiering die we hebben. En nog verder gewoon in ieder land één BV*".

concerning that specific business unit or division.[17] For instance, the business unit director responsible for IT may be based in Germany, but will provide the Dutch central works council with information regarding his IT-business unit. In light of the digitalisation of organisational processes, such information can be provided without any onerous time constraints on the respective business unit or division director. The advantage of such a system clearly lies in the fact that the source of the information is based on the availability of the necessary information, rather than the formal, legal designation of the entrepreneur within the meaning of the WCA.

Such information and consultation structures with business unit directors can also be structured into so-called '*sector consultations*'. In the corporation in question, formal meetings between CWC-members, who are delegates of one business-unit works council,[18] and the respective business unit director are planned on a regular basis. These meetings take place in addition to the formal consultation meetings of the CWC with the entrepreneur within the meaning of the WCA. The delegation of CWC-members has no mandate to formally give advice to the BU director, but rather exchanges information with the director on the state of affairs in the BU concerned.[19] The delegation in turn reports this information at the CWC meetings, which not only improves the CWC's level of information, but it also enhances the level of consultation meetings with the entrepreneur, whom is often unaware of all the developments taking place at BU-level. This is particularly the case if cross-border BU structures are present with reporting taking place outside the Dutch statutory director's sphere of influence. For the BU directors, these sector consultations provide a source of information on the shop-level developments in his or her BU and is therefore regarded as being of added value and worthy of investing in.

In addition, one works council reported to periodically receive information by the business unit directors by means of monthly presentations on a rotating basis. In the corporation in question, not only did the designated entrepreneur give presentations relating to the current state of the business, but the directors for research and development, IT, sales and so forth also gave presentations on their business field in the other consultation meetings.[20]

---

17 Interviews 1 and 22.

18 Which can be an individual works council on the level of an establishment or a group works council within the meaning of article 33 (2) of the WCA.

19 Interview 39:12: "*Maar die OR-leden hebben ook, wij noemen dat sectoroverleg met hun sectordirecteur. Wij hebben daarin geen verantwoordelijkheden gemandateerd aan hun. Dus dat is veelal elkaar informeren over wat er speelt op dat niveau*".

20 Interview 1:35: "*Wij hebben nu gezegd voor 2015 we willen niet zes keer per jaar een presentatie van de bestuurder alleen maar over marktaandeel, productieaantallen. Wij willen in een soort cyclus alle processen een keer specifiek behandeld zien. Dus de directeur van IT die komt de komende overlegvergadering [vertellen] wat zijn visie en zijn plannen zijn en welke investeringen zijn goedgekeurd. Welke systemen gaan we ontwikkelen […]. Volgende [overlegvergadering] komt misschien de directeur ontwikkeling,*

3.1.2 Access to information on the (group) strategy

One of the main issues regarding the position of Dutch works councils is the lack of access to and influence on the corporation's strategy.[21] Indeed, several interview respondents stated that no information on the corporate strategy or major business decisions that influence the strategy of the group was shared.[22] This could either be caused by a lack of access to information by the consultation partner of the CWC,[23] whom does not know the strategy either – a point which is in itself a cause for concern – or due to the fact that only *early* access to such information is not possible due to the share-price sensitivity that is inherent in major business decisions.[24]

Possible good practices regarding access to information on the group's strategy or crucial business decisions that affect the strategy are therefore reported in this section. Access to such information is predominantly informal. This is caused by the extra-legal nature of such information on the group's (international) strategy in light of the principle of territoriality, which limits the information rights that are available to Dutch works councils.[25]

Despite the lack of formal information rights on that matter, several works councils succeeded in convincing the management of the added value of informing the CWC on the topic and receiving feedback (e.g., on the implementation in the Netherlands) in return. Information on the strategy of the MNC is either provided in '*quarterly meetings with members of the management*', during '*(semi-)annual strategy sessions with the CEO and/or CFO of the group*' or so-called '*strategy days with the management and supervisory board*'.[26] On a smaller scale is information on the Dutch strategy and the impact of the corporate strategy on the Dutch subsidiary that is shared and discussed by the Dutch management, albeit on a more frequent basis.[27]

During the '*quarterly meetings with members of the management*', the works council can receive insights into the performance of the group as a whole.[28] This meeting can be combined with the sector consultations of the BUs that was discussed above. Due to the often practiced quarterly reporting cycle of listed corporations, no additional documentation has to be compiled by the management. The meeting is furthermore used for a

directeur verkoop en dan willen we meer thematisch werken. Het betreffende directielid komt dan ook zelf presenteren en ons bestuurder is dan altijd aanwezig".

21 See sections 5.2 – 5.4 in chapter IV above.

22 Interviews 21, 29, 31, 38 and 41.

23 Interviews 21 and 41; the manager (interview 41:8) indicated, however, that it is possible to anticipate, to a certain extent, the likely changes to the strategy based on the development of the corporation in the past. This is then also shared with the works council.

24 Interview 38:12.

25 See sections 1.4, 3.2 and 4.2.8 of chapter III.

26 Interviews 23, 24, 27, 32, 34 and 45.

27 Interviews 3, 5, 6, 10, 14, 15, 17, 20, 22, 26 and 42.

28 Interview 23:22.

discussion on the implementation of the group strategy in the Netherlands. The works council can signal issues related to the implementation and ideally provide solutions for these obstacles. In addition to that, this meeting can be used for the discussion of the (consolidated) quarterly financial results of the Dutch activities of the group and the group financial results overall.[29]

A second good practice, which goes a bit further than the quarterly meetings with the (Dutch) management, are '*(semi-)annual strategy sessions with the CEO and/or CFO of the group*'.[30] During these sessions, the CEO or the CFO of the group discusses the strategy of the group as a whole and also provides the works council with explanations of the strategy's effect on the Dutch establishments. While the works councils in these corporations do not have formal consultation rights on this matter, they nevertheless receive all the information on the future strategy of the group and can adapt their strategy (ideally) accordingly. Based on information about the group strategy, the works council in one corporation also discusses with the HR-department the effects on the 'future resource planning', which may affect the Dutch workforce.[31] The resource planning (i.e., which skills do employees need in the future and which training facilities must be provided) is closely linked with the long-term strategy of the corporation. Therefore, not only a discussion of the overall corporate strategy, but also of the underlying human resource plans is important for the works council's position in the decision-making process. Such a discussion of the resource planning is sometimes also combined with a discussion on the broader social trends that may impact the MNC's resource planning.

The management may, however, be reluctant or unable to provide precise (financial) figures and progress indicators on strategic targets to the works council. In one corporation, the management alternatively informs the CWC on the basis of a 'stoplight visualisation of the progress on the long-term strategy'.[32] Not only does the works council receive information on the various targets of the long-term strategy (in the case of this MNC, until 2020), but they also receive updates on the progress that has been made so far in the regular consultation meetings. The management signals the progress in red, yellow and green instead of using precise figures. This nevertheless enables the works council to follow the progress that has been made so far and to make an assessment of the current strategic developments. The management, on the other hand, does not need to provide exact figures (yet) concerning the corporation's global strategy.

29 See section 3.1.1 above.
30 Interviews 26, 32, 36 and 45.
31 Interview 22:6.
32 Interview 42:26.

The examples of good practice that were discussed above, however, do not include the supervisory board. The amount of contact between the works council and the supervisory board is rather low, as was pointed out in the quantitative chapter of this study.[33] In light of ensuring good corporate governance, good practices such as '*strategy days with the management and supervisory board*' are particularly noteworthy.[34] Not only does the CWC in question value these strategy days due to the explanations provided by the managers present, but the supervisory board also value these sessions. The interviewee pointed out that the works council received information on the strategy and – on the basis of the questions posed by the supervisory board members during the meeting – what the position of the supervisory board is likely to be.[35] The supervisory board members value the meetings as well, because of the additional explanations provided by the managers and for the CWC's reaction to the strategic plans. The strategy days have replaced the meetings on the general operation of the undertaking (article 24 of the WCA) and therefore do not impose an additional time constraint on the persons involved therein. The tripartite meetings on the strategy are therefore a time-efficient means of discussing the strategy with all of the corporation's internal stakeholders, while at the same time avoiding any information asymmetries on or miscommunication of (parts of) the corporate strategy.

Finally, the general meeting of shareholders can also be a source of information for the works council. The works council's chairperson has a right to speak at the shareholders meeting as was discussed in chapter III.[36] In one corporation, the entire executive committee [*dagelijks bestuur*] of the CWC was allowed to be present during the shareholders meeting.[37] According to the interviewed manager and CWC-member, this creates valuable contacts between the shareholders and the employee representatives, whereby the breaks during the general shareholders meeting are used to make informal contacts. Despite the lack of a formal role of the employee representatives, such contact should nevertheless not be underestimated for the mutual understanding of the stakeholders.[38]

---

33 See chapter IV above.

34 Interview 39:26.

35 Interview 39:26: "[...] *elk jaar hebben we wat we noemen strategische dagen. En dan komen de directeuren bij ons hun strategisch plan voor de komende drie jaar toelichten. Je zou dat kunnen zien als een vergadering over de algemene gang van zaken in het bedrijf. Dat zijn vaak voor ons zijn dat 2-3 dagen en bij die dagen nodigen wij ook de commissarissen uit om in de vergadering aanwezig te zijn. En de commissarissen waarderen dat ook – geven ze aan – omdat ze op die manier niet alleen de plannen nog eens extra toegelicht krijgen door de directeuren individueel. Maar ook de reacties van de OR zien op die plannen. En zij zelf stellen ook geregeld vragen in die vergadering dan aan een directeur. En zo zien wij als OR hoe de raad van commissarissen tegen dingen aankijkt. En de raad van commissarissen merkt aan ons hoe wij tegen dingen aankijken*".

36 Section 1.4.5 of chapter III.

37 Interviews 32 and 42.

38 Interview 32:13 and 42:15.

3.1.3 Informal access to information

Almost all interview respondents emphasised the importance of informal contacts outside of the formal information channels that were discussed above. Aside from the day-to-day or ad-hoc informal contacts, which were often also existing in practice, several good practices will be discussed in this section. 'Regular informal sessions' (*benen-op-tafel sessies*) with members of the management and the works council are particularly noteworthy in this context.[39] These meetings are primarily used as a pre-discussion prior to the formal consultation meetings or as informal "heads-up meetings", during which the CEO of the MNC[40] or the Dutch management team provides information to the (executive committee of the) CWC about current developments.[41] Both interview respondents from the management and works council valued such meetings due to the possibility it presented to exchange information at an early stage. Given the sensitive nature of the topics discussed, participation in these meetings was often limited to the executive committee of the CWC and the Dutch CEO and/or HR-director. Such meetings, however, were only used in corporations where both sides stressed the openness and transparency of their relationship as well as a high level of mutual trust.[42]

The use of such regular informal meetings also improved the formal consultation meetings, because both sides were not surprised by the topics that were tabled and because arguments were exchanged on the matter at an early stage. The management, for instance, can include arguments made by the CWC-members during the informal meetings in its (draft) request for advice (hereinafter: RfA).[43]

In some corporations, an '*end-of-the-year dinner with management, CWC and supervisory board*' was organised as well. The reflection of the progress made in the last year as well as a vision for the next year, particularly the corporate strategy and the role and impact on the workforce, stand central in this meeting. Not only is the meeting used for informal contact, but the CEO of the corporation in question gives a presentation over the previous year and his vision for the upcoming year.[44] In yet another corporation, working groups consisting of members of the management, the CWC and the

39 Interviews 5, 14, 18, 21, 22 and 29.

40 Interview 21.

41 See *inter alia* interview 22:9: *"De directeur personeelszaken en ikzelf hebben altijd enige weken voorafgaande aan de formele overlegvergadering een informeel "4 Augen Gespräch". Wat inmiddels een "10 Augen Gespräch" is geworden over wat er in de lucht hangt. En dat is op basis van vertrouwelijkheid en dat is nooit geschonden. Waarin we eigenlijk al aangegeven aan de voorzitter en de secretaris en een derde lid van de ondernemingsraad wat er in de lucht hangt. Wat er zou kunnen gaan gebeuren en hoe we ons daarop voorbereiden. En dat geeft de OR ook de gelegenheid om daarop te reageren. Om daarover te praten en dan is het – wanneer we het in de overlegvergadering brengen – voor de drie nummers 1 tot en met 3 van de OR geen verrassing meer. En we hebben daardoor dus een hele open gedachtewisseling".*

42 See section 3.7 below for a detailed discussion of these "enabling" good practice examples.

43 The use of draft RfAs in a process-oriented employee participation model is discussed in detail in section 3.2 below.

44 Interview 28:5.

supervisory board get together to discuss topics of importance (for instance productivity and work perception by the employees).[45] Such a meeting with all three stakeholders also allows for a monitoring of the agreements made, an aspect which is seldom taken into account.[46]

3.1.4 The works council and employees as source of information

The interview respondents highlighted the fact that not only it is important for the works council to receive all the necessary information. But it is also important for the works council and the employees to become an important source of information, both for the CWC and the management, as well as for the supervisory board.

Turning first to the employees as source of information, a '*contact person-network among the workforce*' is a good practice that was named by four respondents.[47] In corporations with many establishments especially, such a contact person-network is important for feedback on the implementation of decisions at the Dutch sub- or top-holding level. As one respondent pointed out, many management layers exist between the central management, which consults the central works council, and the shop floor level. As to how far the decisions have the desired effect, is assessed by the CWC through its contact person-network.[48] The contact persons are reimbursed for their time spent and are contacted by the CWC on an ad-hoc basis. The contact person-network is also a means for employees to gain first hand insights into the employee participation mechanisms, which increases interest in works council candidacies of those network members.[49]

A second good practice for gaining the input of employees is through the use of '*questionnaires and statements of the week*' by the works council on topics that are currently on the agenda. In times of inexpensive digital corporate information networks, such questionnaires can provide the works council with first-hand arguments on a topic and

45 Interview 19:16.

46 Only 6 out of 58 interview respondents indicated that monitoring agreements were included in the decision-making process.

47 Interviews 2, 3, 5 and 21.

48 Interview 3:45: "*Maar die kunnen zich aanmelden, en die krijgen ook bepaalde faciliteiten in termen van tijd en die hebben ook als rol-, er worden uitvragen gedaan richting die mensen als er iets speelt. Dus ze hebben ook een rol in de controle van de afspraken die je centraal maakt. [...] Soms maak je hier in goede harmonie afspraken met elkaar en zie je op de werkvloer, dat het niet uitgevoerd wordt. Dat kan zijn omdat de afspraken niet goed zijn, maar ook vaak dat er andere motieven [een] rol spelen, met name bij leidinggevenden. Maar goed, daar is dat contactpersonen netwerk dus belangrijk voor. Om te zorgen dat centraal gemaakte afspraken ook decentraal nagekomen worden*".

49 Interview 2:10.

significantly improve its position in the consultation process.[50] Statements of the week are used to determine the current position of the employees on a given topic. By doing so, the works council receives opinions on a topic, which in turn improves the position of the works council vis-à-vis the management due to it being able to gain improved insights on the matter.[51]

The good practices on employee input are certainly not exhaustive and different means to gain first-hand input by employees naturally exist. What is important to note is that such input from the shop-floor level significantly increases the validity of the position of the works council on an (intended) decision. The works council can therefore increase the '*scrutiny of its questions towards the management*' by involving employees in the pre-advice phase.[52]

The works council can also be a source of information prior to the start of a consultation phase on an (intended) decision for the management.[53] One possibility is the requesting of a smaller working group of the works council that develops a consultation dossier together with the management.[54] The working group informs the management on the matter at hand and can also indicate the likely position of the works council on the (intended) decision.[55] The works council is thereby an important source of information on the establishments within the corporate group.[56]

Another good practice is the planning of '*topical presentations by the works council for the management*'.[57] The works council can inform (in this case) the CEO or other members of the management and also show a proactive stance on topics that are important for one or more establishments. This is also important as the (Dutch) central management only indirectly receives information through its information channels. When receiving

---

50 Interview 29:12: "[...] *als ondernemingsraad heb je gewoon een hele stevige zaak dan. Je hebt gewoon munitie. Je kan aantonen dat er van de 1000 mensen in Nederland er zo'n 400 respons geven. Wat best hoog is. En allemaal toch wel van dezelfde toon. [...] Toen zijn we gaan reduceren dat 66% toch wel een hele leuke duidelijke uitgesproken mening hierover had. En dan heb je wel munitie. Dan kun je zeggen het is niet zomaar, het betreft niet een paar individuen. Het speelt wel echt iets binnen de organisatie*".

51 Interview 4:33.

52 Two respondents in interviews 7 (a works council member) and 10 (management) emphasised the importance of a high level of scrutiny that is necessary for works council questions in the consultation process.

53 Interviews 9 and 16.

54 See interviews 8, 18, 23, 25, 34 and 40 (works councils); interviews 15, 22, 36, 38, 40 and 45 (management) and interview 19 (supervisory board); the use of working groups is discussed in section 3.5.3 below.

55 The use of working groups within a process-oriented consultation model is discussed in greater detail in section 3.2 below.

56 Interview 42:5.

57 Interview 20:30: "*We hebben ook tijdens onze jaarlijkse training een soort presentatie gegeven waar ook onze CEO dan bij was. En dat komt dan weer terug in het bedrijf. Dus dan zie je toch wel dat dat wat effect heeft*".

information directly from the representatives of a certain establishment, such less filtered information is embraced and regarded as necessary for informed decision-making, according to one management interviewee.[58]

Finally, other works councils of the MNC in other countries can be a source of information as well. By means of '*cross-border consultation*' with German, Belgian, French or American companies, employee representatives can provide the Dutch works council with insights into the implementation of corporate initiatives in other countries.[59] Reorganisations or changes to corporate policies (for instance the assessment of employees) are often simultaneously enacted throughout establishments in several countries, as was pointed out by several works councils. While the EWC is an important platform for exchanging information on transnational issues (as per article 1(4) of the EWC-Directive),[60] additional, more frequent and topic-specific alternatives are noteworthy. The exchange between the works councils allows the Dutch CWC and their counterparts to keep each other informed and to avoid surprises or to be played off against each other by the management.[61] This issue is of particular relevance for MNCs with a business unit-structure that spans across several countries.[62]

3.2 *Consultation*

Once the works council has sufficient and timely access to information, it should advise the management on the (intended) decision at hand in an efficient and effective manner.[63] When being consulted, the works council can influence the decision-making process either formally by means of advice (article 25 of the WCA) as well as informally. Both examples of good practice regarding formal and informal means of consultation will be discussed in the following section.[64]

58 Interview 9:14: "*En je moet altijd beseffen – ik bedoel dat is een bekend spelletje – ga een stuk informatie doorgeven aan een kring van mensen. Hoe eindigt dat? Eenieder percipieert op zijn eigen manier en ik vind je moet op begeven moment begrijpen dat bepaalde argumenten; kijk een manager zit soms met hele andere problemen dan iemand die in een [...]afdeling werkt – mag ik dat dan ook even horen graag*".

59 Interviews 2, 15, 21 and 39.

60 Directive 2009/38/EC of the European Parliament and of the Council of 6 May 2009 on the establishment of a European Works Council or a procedure in Community-scale undertakings and Community-scale groups of undertakings for the purposes of informing and consulting employees [2009] OJ L 122/28.

61 Interview 39:33: "*Dus als er ontwikkelingen spelen op meerdere sites dan heb ik vaak telefonisch contact met de werknemersvertegenwoordiging, de Betriebsrat in Duitsland. En dan wisselen we met elkaar uit waar we staan, wat we ervan vinden. Ook daar met de gedachte wij moeten elkaar niet verrassen*".

62 Interview 15:53.

63 And assuming that the topic falls under one of the topics for which the works council has a right of consultation pursuant to article 25 of the WCA or the works council is being consulted informally. Another possibility is the works council's right of initiative (*initiatiefrecht*) pursuant to article 23(3) of the WCA that is discussed further in section 3.2.4 below.

64 See Annex I for an overview of all examples of good practice related to this cluster.

Once the works council is involved at an early stage in the decision-making process, the position of the CWC will naturally improve. The works council can give input, for instance, in the form of pre-advice that is incorporated in the management's intended decision and this is done so at a stage when more and alternative solutions are being considered.

3.2.1 Formal consultation and effective structuring of consultation meetings

The formal consultation procedure pursuant to article 25 of the WCA is well-known and is applied in the decision-making procedures that are used by the corporations included in this study. It is worth reiterating, however, that on topics such as the future strategy of the MNC or mergers and acquisitions, a significant difference exists between Dutch and foreign MNCs.[65]

While formal consultation procedures are applied in all corporations, it is nevertheless useful to make an inventory of the good practices that are being applied. These examples of good practice may lead to a more efficient application of formal consultation procedures and may help to improve the position of works councils that are not consulted or only are only consulted at a late stage in the decision-making procedure.[66] At the same time, these examples of good practice are not a replacement, but rather an addition to existing consultation and co-determination rights pursuant to articles 25 and 27 of the WCA.[67]

The first example of good practice concerns the frequency of consultation meetings. The quantitative analysis that was discussed in section 5.2.1 of chapter IV above showed that consultation meetings take place very frequently with an average of six to eight meetings per year. The interview phase showed that works councils, whom meet even more frequently with the management both formally and informally, can influence the decision-making process at an early stage due to their frequent moments of contact with the management. In addition to these frequent meetings, some works councils have negotiated additional moments of contact with representatives of the top-holding's management.

65 Dutch multinational corporations consult their (central) works council significantly more often on these topics. See section 5.2 in chapter IV above regarding the quantitative findings of this study. The main differences between Dutch and foreign MNCs are further discussed in section 2 of chapter VI below.

66 See also section 4 in chapter IV above on the concepts of attribution of (intended) decisions and co-entrepreneurship regarding the issue of non-consultation.

67 As well as other rights derived from the WCA (information rights) and the DCC (*inter alia* the right to speak at the general meeting of shareholders).

One works council even managed to have the 'article 24 WCA meetings on the general operation of the enterprise (*algemene gang van zaken bespreking*) with the regional (EU) management' instead of their own entrepreneur within the meaning of article 1(1)(e) of the WCA. The works council requested these meetings with the regional management, because their own management did not have the decision-making power and could not sufficiently provide the works council with the necessary information pursuant to article 24 of the WCA.[68] In corporations with employee participation at the top-holding level and with the CEO as the consultation partner, such additional meetings may not be necessary. However, for works councils whose formal consultation partner is the CEO, additional contact moments with the business unit or regional management are certainly useful. The format of so-called sector consultations, as were discussed in section 3.1.1 above, is also relevant here. In these sector consultations, a delegation of the (central) works council meets with a business unit director to discuss the current state of affairs. While such sector consultations were primarily used as a source of information by the interviewed works councils, these meetings could also extend to a consultation on the general operation of the business unit in question.

Another example of good practice is the scheduling of meetings with the CEO, CFO or another member of the board of the corporation on a quarterly or six-monthly basis.[69] The meetings are particularly useful for discussing the current and future strategy of the corporation, and are sometimes convened upon the request of the CEO in order to gain additional input from the CWC.[70] The meetings with the CFO allow primarily for a comparison of the financial results of the Dutch subsidiary with the group as a whole.[71] A number of works councils argued that, prior to the establishment of such periodical meetings with members of the top-management, employees of the corporation, who are

68 Interview 21:5: "*En sinds kort, omdat het toch vrij nieuw is, hebben wij al aangegeven: wij zitten met de verkeerde mensen om tafel. En wij willen graag om tafel zitten, zeker van tijd tot tijd, met de mensen die op regionaal niveau zitten. En voorlopig hebben [we] als ondernemingsraad, niet als cor, [...] ingekleed dat de regionale vertegenwoordiging, de artikel 24 vergaderingen doet. [...] Om in ieder geval wel informatie te krijgen rechtstreeks en niet via via*".

69 Meetings with the CEO were mentioned in interviews 7, 9, 16, 23, 28 and 48. Meetings with the CFO, in which the financial results were discussed, are reported in interviews 20 and 27. Meetings with other members of the (one-tier) board were mentioned in interview 25.

70 Interview 23:12: "*Ja, de centrale ondernemingsraad spreekt ook met de CEO van [de concern] holding. Mede op verzoek van die CEO. Omdat ze heel veel beslissingen op global niveau nemen. Als centrale ondernemingsraad hebben we gezegd, willen we invloed uitoefenen en we doen dat alleen binnen de Benelux. Dan krijgen we een voorgekauwd verhaaltje waar we in principe een ja of nee op kunnen zeggen. Maar er is volstrekt geen rekening gehouden met de uitwerking op de Benelux. Dus we hebben gezegd we willen op global niveau veel meer aangesloten bij de ontwikkelingen van de ideeën. En dat heeft de bestuurder ook toegezegd. En een keer in de drie maanden zitten we met de CEO. En we kunnen vragen stellen en hij gaat ons helemaal toelichten waar ze mee bezig zijn. Financieel toelichting geven*".

71 Interview 27:6: "*O: op het niveau van het virtueel hoofdkantoor, is er geen medezeggenschap? I: nee. Want die zit virtueel in Londen, dus daar hebben wij geen medezeggenschap. Maar wij zitten wel met de CFO aan tafel eens in de vier maanden. Die komt naar Nederland toe en gaat dan de Group cijfers met ons doorspreken. En dat komt omdat dat soort dingen relevant zijn voor de Group [...] medewerkers.*"

employed in the Netherlands, but whom perform so-called "group shared services" (for instance IT or human resource activities), fell outside of the Dutch employee participation model. The Dutch works councils argued that their involvement only allowed for participation within the Netherlands. These shared services employees, however, fell under the control of a (business unit) manager in another country, whom could potentially initiate a reorganisation that would affect the Dutch shared services employees.[72] The argument of the works councils, therefore, was that they would have to have consultation meetings with the manager in question in order to be able to effectively perform their role as employee representatives.

In one corporation, this even led to the establishment of a dual WCA-entrepreneurship within the meaning of article 1(1)(e) of the WCA.[73] Both the Dutch statutory director as well as a member of the executive committee of the corporation were designated as consultation partners of the works council. The Dutch director remained the consultation partner for all of the affairs concerning the Dutch undertaking. In addition, one executive member (in this case the general counsel of the MNC) informs and consults the works council on matters concerning the employees of the "group's shared services".[74] The HR-director of the Dutch subsidiary served as linking pin in order to avoid issues regarding the coordination between the two WCA-entrepreneurs.[75] This agreement was concluded by means of a covenant pursuant to article 32 of the WCA. The works council met three times a year with the general counsel regarding matters concerning the shared services employees. The works council received, through this dual WCA-entrepreneurship, information on group-related matters, including information about the group financial results and (intended) acquisitions.[76] In order to be able to provide adequate advice, the works council reserved two of the nine seats for representatives

72 Interview 27:17: "*En dan komt de CIO die dus niet in de top board maar wel in de ExCo zit; die besluit dat hij zijn IT-organisatie anders gaat indelen. En dan zitten we opeens met 60 medewerkers die in een herstructurering zitten. Die niet via de head of legal of de CFO bij ons terechtkomen omdat die er niet eens wat van afweten. Omdat die man gewoon denkt: als ik mijn organisatie anders wil invullen dan doe ik het dan toch. Dus dan zijn wij achteraf bezig met aan iedereen te vertellen van wacht even dat kan niet*".

73 Interviews 27 and 45.

74 Interview 27:10.

75 Interview 45:10.

76 Interview 27:13: "*Drie keer per jaar zitten wij met die dame, head of legal, aan tafel. En zij nodigt over het algemeen de CFO ook uit om te komen. Omdat die alles weet over de acquisities die plaatsvinden. Cijfers en hoe Group het doet. Dus wij krijgen ook gewoon meteen te horen hoe het bedrijf ervoor staat. En dan kunnen wij naar voren brengen wat voor dingen wij tegenkomen voor specifiek die Group mensen. Zo is de OR dus ook georganiseerd. We hebben negen zetels, zeven zijn Nederlands – onderverdeeld over kiesgroepen – twee zijn gereserveerd en kunnen nooit ingevuld worden door Nederlandse werknemers. Die zijn van Group. En die twee mensen. Ik zorg ervoor dat zij de vergaderingen voorzitten. Dus ik ga in die vergaderingen, zit ik er gewoon naast, ik bereid hen redelijk voor maar zij moeten voorzitten. Zij moeten nadenken over onderwerpen. Zij moeten alert zijn. Zij moeten in gesprekken met die WOR-bestuurder als er iets voor valt*".

of the shared services employees. These employees also took the lead in the consultation meetings three times a year.[77]

This example of good practice exemplifies a pragmatic and effective application of the Dutch employee participation regime within a multinational corporation. For employees working for group-related services that are not limited to the Netherlands especially, such dual WCA-entrepreneurship allows for employee participation on matters that affect these employees. Therefore, this example of good practice may be suitable for other MNCs with group-related activities in the Netherlands.

Another example of good practice concerns the presence of supervisory board members at consultation meetings. The quantitative analysis that was discussed in section 5.2.2 of chapter IV above, showed that in 53% of the cases, the supervisory board members were 'never' present and only present 'sometimes' in 26% of the cases. While article 24(2) of the WCA stipulates a duty for supervisory board members to be present at consultation meetings at least twice a year; this rule is evidently not followed in practice in most of the cases. Some interviewees reported that this absenteeism may be caused by the lengthiness of the consultation meetings and the fact that most of the topics discussed during the meeting were already known to the supervisory board members.[78] On the contrary, some MNCs resolved this time constraint by supplying supervisory board members on a rotating basis, which meant that each individual supervisory board member only had to attend a few meetings per year.[79] Another argument raised was that directors, whom are very open during consultation meetings and inform the works council extensively on an informal basis, may not be willing to share information extensively if supervisory board members are present more often.[80] Some multinationals have therefore developed a practical application of article 24(2) of the WCA in relation to supervisory board members. Firstly, one works council sends an alternating delegation of three to four representatives to a meeting with one supervisory board member.[81] The meeting takes place after the

77 *Ibid.*

78 Interview 11:9: "[...] *Hoe gaan we dat zodanig invullen dat je daar over en weer daar maximaal profijt van hebt. In plaats van dat je een soort automatisme van structuren gaat want dat is natuurlijk niet optimaal. Een overlegvergadering is een overlegvergadering met het bestuur. Want anders dan zal men een beetje proberen bij te houden maar een groot deel gaat langs één dus dat is niet efficiënt. Er zijn genoeg andere onderwerpen waar we met elkaar wel over kunnen spreken. [...] Het moet wel efficiënt zijn – en dan is het voor jou efficiënt en voor mij efficiënt*".

79 Interviews 17:12, 26:12 and 32:9.

80 Interview 39:35: "*We hebben dus niet de commissarissen in de vergadering. De reden waarom we dat niet doen is omdat hier de directie aangaf [...] of de bestuurder toen zei: ja let wel op want de verwachting is dat je dan een stuk minder informatie gaat krijgen van de directeuren. Als de directeuren best open zijn met de ondernemingsraad; ook geregeld zeggen ik ga jullie nu iets vertellen maar mag niet in de notulen. Want ik wil dat wel jullie vertellen zodat jullie het weten. Maar het kan niet in de notulen terechtkomen. Dat soort momenten verlies je, was de mening van de bestuurder als je de commissarissen vaker gaat uitnodigen. Dan ga je dat niet meer krijgen, dan ga je meer de formelere kant uit. Dat is de reden dat wij ervoor gekozen hebben om de commissarissen weer niet bij die vergadering aanwezig te hebben*".

81 Interview 39:23.

supervisory board meetings and each time with another supervisory board member. The interviewee indicated that by means of these informal contact moments, each supervisory board member meets all the members of the central works council (due to the repetitiveness of the meetings with different delegations) and minimises the time constraints on the persons involved. It must be noted, however, that such informal meetings should not replace the formal article 24(2) WCA meetings whereby all three stakeholders (management, supervisory board and works council) should be present.

A second example of good practice brings together all three stakeholders while increasing the efficiency of the meeting. In two MNCs, the article 24 WCA meeting on the general operation of the undertaking was scheduled as part of the quarterly supervisory board meetings.[82] The works council is a fixed agenda point (30 minutes) during the meeting. An interviewed supervisory board member emphasised that not only does the works council have more moments of contact with the supervisory board, but the supervisory board can also observe the interaction between works council and management.[83] In addition, another interviewee in the same MNC noted that the supervisory board can follow the developments in the corporation much more closely and the supervisory board was able to ask critical questions at the tripartite meetings.[84] These meetings are also important for the works council because it can give input to stakeholders and influence the decision-making process. Another added value of the meetings is the increased frequency of tripartite meetings (*driehoeksoverleg*) from two to four times a year or more. In another MNC, such additional meetings are carried out more informally, for example as a lunch meeting following the supervisory board meetings (this occurred 3-4 times a year).[85]

A third example of good practice goes further than the tripartite meetings and is therefore noteworthy. In some MNCs, a "strategy session" with the CEO, HR-director, (central) works council and supervisory board is held, during which the corporate strategy as a whole is discussed as well as the (implementing) strategy for the Dutch subsidiaries.[86] The session is also an opportunity for the works council to become acquainted with (new) supervisory board members and to gain first-hand access to the vision of members

82 Interviews 19 and 35.

83 Interview 19:14: "[...] *in het begin was het zo dat ik afstemde met de OR, en formeel moet de OR één keer aan tafel komen per jaar met de RvC. Ik weet niet precies hoe het gegaan is, maar hebben we niet samen voorgesteld van: kunnen we niet zorgen dat de OR elke RvC vergadering aanwezig is, en dat doen we dus nu ook. Dus we hebben elk jaar, elke bijeenkomst dat, we komen vier keer per jaar bij elkaar – uitgezonderd even extra vergaderingen, want dit is standaard. [...] En dan hebben we dus een agenda, een standaard agendapunt is steeds OR. [...]toevallig had ik het daar met [een andere commissaris] over: goh, dat is een goed model want daardoor zit je als RvC veel dichter op de bal. Je ziet ook een beetje hoe het gaat met de board en de OR. En de OR brengt daar ook zelf punten in*".

84 Interview 35:5.

85 Interviews 36:14 and 46:11.

86 Interview 36:22 and 22:14.

of the top-management and supervisory board on the strategy.[87] The supervisory board members also gain better insights into the current state of affairs and can better monitor the management's decision-making. Improving the relationship with the supervisory board is therefore beneficial for the position of the (central) works council as well.

Access to information on the strategy also facilitates the agenda-setting of the works council, which is further discussed in section 3.5 below.

Another example of good practice that was mentioned in the interview phase is an alternating chair(wo)manship of consultation meetings by the entrepreneur and the works council's chairperson. In three corporations,[88] the chairperson of the (central) works council and the entrepreneur (whom is most often the Dutch statutory director or the CEO of the MNC) chairs the consultation meetings on an alternating basis. According to one interviewee, this creates a less formal and accessible atmosphere during the meetings.[89] The alternating chairperson-approach also allows the works council chairperson to steer the meetings that he is chairing and to determine, to a certain extent, the meeting's agenda.[90]

A final example of good practice concerns an alternative use of the works council's right to speak at the general meeting of shareholders. In section 1.4.5 of chapter III, the limited scope of the right to speak was already elaborated upon. Having concluded that it is questionable as to whether this creates a genuine influence,[91] it is noteworthy that some works councils are using the right as bargaining tool vis-à-vis the management.[92] One works council chairperson pointed out that instead of actually using the right to speak at the general meeting, the works council discussed the issues on the general meeting's agenda with the management. The management and supervisory board preferred no statements to be made by the works council during the general meeting, according to the interviewee, and therefore they discussed the issues with the works council at an

87 Interview 22:14: "*Verder heeft de OR ook met enige regelmaat, ook strategische dagen, dat ze, zoals dat in Nederland noemen, een hijssessie. En dan zijn vaak ook de leden van de raad van bestuur, de directeur van de HR en/of zijn de nieuwe medewerkers van de [RvC] daar geweest. Dan kun je aan elkaar ruiken en proeven en kijken wat je aan mekaar hebt. [...] [Een nieuw RvC-lid] is langs geweest voor een dagdeel. En ja die wil natuurlijk veel weten van de OR, hoe zijn jullie erin. En de OR wil weten, hoe zit jij erin? Wat ga jij voor ons doen. Je bent onze commissaris met een versterkt adviesrecht, wat kun jij voor ons betekenen? Dus wordt dan goed afgestemd. Dus dan is er geen verrassing. [..] Ze is erg sterk op het gebied van diversity. Nou ja dan heb je al een stukje agenda bepaalt. En OR zal vertellen van wij houden ons bezig met die vraagstukken en die vraagstukken. En dat levert voor haar weer mogelijkheid op om in de raad van bestuur en in de raad van commissarissenvergadering mij vragen te stellen van let je daarop. Want vanuit de OR begrijpen we dat in dit en dit concerns zijn*".

88 Interviews 5, 22 and 26.

89 Interview 22:21.

90 Most interview respondents indicated that the agenda was jointly determined by the management and works council in a meeting prior to the consultation meetings (*agendaoverleg*).

91 See the concluding remarks in section 1.4.5 of chapter III.

92 Interview 3.

earlier stage.[93] The fact that the management and the supervisory board wanted to avoid negative publicity at the general meeting, therefore, allowed the works council to influence the remuneration policy or major business decisions that required approval at the general meeting of shareholders.[94] The right to speak also extends to the appointment and dismissal of statutory directors and can be helpful in conjunction with the article 30 WCA consultation right of the works council.[95] The interviewee further pointed out that through such an alternative use of the right to speak, the works council succeeded in having a non-financial target included in the variable remuneration package of the board of directors.

3.2.2 Use of covenants to extend formal consultation rights and procedures

In addition to the existing (formal) consultation rights of works councils, article 32 of the WCA allows for the conclusion of a covenant between the works council and the management. In the previous chapter on the quantitative results, it was already argued that covenants are a very useful tool of works councils in MNCs for the adaptation of the employee participation mechanisms to the (often) cross-border decision-making structures.[96] In addition to the inventory of rights conferred by means of covenants in the quantitative chapter, a number of other examples of good practice were mentioned in the interview phase. The use of such additional rights and their effect on the works councils' position in practice will also be highlighted below. Covenants can be used in many different ways. One possibility is the extension of existing rights to cover additional areas (for instance international topics). Another possibility is the agreement on new and additional works-council rights. A third possibility is the clarification of existing rights. All three forms of covenant use are reported to be applied in practice and will be discussed hereafter.

The first example of good practice concerns the extended scope of the right of access to information to include a half-yearly reports on the global state of affairs within the MNC.[97] This specific covenant was concluded after a takeover by a private equity firm and the resulting transition from a Dutch to a foreign multinational. The works council was

93 Interview 3:56: "*Dus je [ ] probeert het spreekrecht veel meer te gebruiken door te zeggen van "ja, als we hier niet uitkomen met elkaar, in het voortraject, dan ga ik wel gebruiken maken van mijn spreekrecht en dan vind ik er ook wat van". En de Raad van Bestuur, de Raad van Commissarissen vindt het niet prettig als ik daar als centraal ondernemingsraad voorzitter zeg, tegen de aandeelhouders "dit is niet goed, dat is niet goed, dat klopt niet". Dus wat wij bijvoorbeeld gerealiseerd hebben is dat er in het variabele beloningscomponent van de Raad van Bestuur ook niet-financiële targets zitten*".

94 Article 2:107a of the DCC requires the approval of major business decisions "leading to changes in the identity or character of the Corporation"; the works council's right to speak is laid down in paragraph 3 of article 2:107a of the DCC; the right to speak on the remuneration policy is stipulated in article 2:135(2) of the DCC.

95 Interview 3:58.

96 Sections 5.3 and 8.4 of chapter IV.

97 Interview 23:20-21; see also section 3.1.2 above.

not consulted on abroad investments,[98] but was merely informed about such intended decisions. In addition to access to information on (intended) decisions at the global level, the works council was also informed about the current state of affairs of a joint venture that the MNC had recently concluded.[99] The advantage of having this broad access to information lies in the fact that the works council can better anticipate which strategic or organisational changes will occur and can subsequently engage in discussions with the Dutch management regarding the potential impact on the Dutch subsidiaries of the MNC.

In addition to this information right, it is worth noting that an independent supervisory board member with veto rights was appointed in this MNC, after a takeover by the private equity firm.[100] The independent member was able to use his veto right to block decisions that ran contrary to the takeover agreement and was able to monitor the implementation of the agreements that were made. This independent supervisory board member was present during the consultation meetings between the management and works council and gave his input on the implementation of the takeover agreement. He could also be contacted by the works council for a meeting without the management being present, if this was necessary.[101] Both the presence of the independent supervisory board member during the consultation meetings as well as the possibility of meetings without the management being present were stipulated in the covenant signed between the works council and the management.[102] The conclusion of the covenant and the appointment of the independent supervisory board member were only possible due to the time-sensitive nature of the takeover negotiations, according to the interviewee. The position of the works council was relatively strong given the fact that its (positive) advice in light of article 25(1)(e) of the WCA was necessary for a speedy conclusion of the negotiations. By making use of its right to consult a (legal) expert,[103] the works council successfully managed to have these rights contained in a covenant.[104] The timing of the conclusion of such a covenant is therefore important.

Additional rights can also pertain to strategic issues. In one MNC, the management and works council convened a two-day workshop in order to discuss the strategy 2020 for the MNC and to formulate a corresponding employee participation vision for 2020.[105] The works council was then informed on the progress made by means of the stoplight visualisation that was discussed above in section 3.1.2. This example of good practice is

98 A matter that falls outside the scope of article 25 of the WCA.
99 Interview 23:24.
100 Interview 23:37 and 39.
101 Interview 23:45.
102 *Ibid.*
103 Article 16 of the WCA.
104 The interviewed management representative of the MNC did not regard the works council's additional information rights on global issues as useful; interview 25:17.
105 Interviews 40:13 and 42:27.

noteworthy, as the works council did not have to be reactive. Instead, the works council formulated – together and through consultation with the management – a vision for 2020 that was linked with the overall long-term corporate strategy. Subsequently, the targets were monitored through a stoplight visualisation mechanism, which allowed the works council to influence the decision-making process at an early stage. If successful, the position of the works council will be significantly improved.

Aside from the overall strategy, outsourcing decisions as well as other reorganisation decisions often have a significant impact on a Dutch (subsidiary of a) MNC. One works council has therefore formulated a proposal on how to become involved in outsourcing issues.[106] This has resulted in a covenant on outsourcing decisions. The works council is consulted on such outsourcing decisions based on this agreement, even if the designated country for the outsourcing is located outside of the EU.[107] The interviewee stated that, primarily, the social consequences of such an outsourcing project, both for the employees in the Netherlands and for the employment conditions in the designated country, were important issues to the CWC. This was also important in light of the corporate social responsibility (CSR) mechanisms that were implemented in the MNC.[108]

Another important aspect concerned the cash-flow policy of the corporate group. Due to the fact that the parent company holds all the shares of the Dutch sub-holding and its right of instruction,[109] it is able to apply a corporate cash-flow policy that also applies to the Dutch subsidiary.[110] By doing so, profits made by the Dutch subsidiary may be transferred to the parent company. Such a cash transfer, however, falls within the scope of the works council's consultation right pursuant to article 25(1)(j) of the WCA.[111] Despite the works council's right of consultation, it may occur that the cash-flow policy is altered without having sought the CWC's prior consultation. Such intended changes to the cash policy led to conflicts at companies such as KLM[112] and Tata Steel.[113] In order to avoid a

106 Interview 3:39.

107 And therefore outside the scope of the EWC that is established in the MNC in question.

108 See for instance A. Beckers, Taking Corporate Codes Seriously: Towards Private Law Enforcement of Voluntary Corporate Social Responsibility Codes (Maastricht University, Maastricht 2014); R. Jenkins, R. Pearson and G. Seyfang, Corporate Responsibility and Labour Rights: Codes of Conduct in the Global Economy (Earthscan Publications, London 2002).

109 Article 2:239 (4) of the DCC.

110 The *Forumbank* case and the second sentence of article 2:239 (4) of the DCC limits the right of instruction in light of the autonomy of the Dutch management and the interest of the Dutch undertaking vis-à-vis the corporate interest; see also R.G.M. Dahmen, 'De aanwijzingsbevoegdheid van het gewijzigde artikel 2:239 lid 4 BW: toepassing, toetsing, afdwingbaarheid en aspecten van aansprakelijkheid in concernperspectief', 2 *Tijdschrift voor vennootschaps- en rechtspersonenrecht* (2014), p. 62.

111 See section 1.4.2 in chapter III.

112 Financieel Daagblad, 'Parijs aast op meer macht bij KLM', <https://fd.nl/ondernemen/1172470/parijs-aast-op-meer-macht-bij-klm> (last accessed 24.10.2016).

113 Financieel Daagblad, 'Doorsluizen van kasmiddelen naar holding stuit op verzet van ondernemingsraad Tata Steel', <https://fd.nl/ondernemen/1090639/doorsluizen-van-kasmiddelen-naar-holding-stuit-op-verzet-van-ondernemingsraad-tata-steel> (last accessed 24.10.2016).

repeat of similar issues, one works council concluded a covenant whereby the council's as well as the supervisory board's role in cash transfer-situations was stipulated.[114] Through the works council's involvement, a balance between the financial stability of the Dutch subsidiary and the parent company is sought, according to the interviewee.

Another aspect of the financial policy of a corporation is the management's remuneration. In order to be able to voice the works council's position on the corporate remuneration policy, one works council negotiated a meeting with the remuneration committee of the group's supervisory board. In the MNC in question, the works council was maintained at the sub-holding level and therefore had no formal right to render an opinion in relation to the remuneration policy.[115] The works council therefore concluded a covenant to have this right granted and also to ensure communication with the CEO of the entire group twice per year on the basis of this agreement.[116] While the works council has no direct influence on the decision-making through these additional rights, it nevertheless allows it to gain access to important decision-makers within the MNC and to receive important information on the MNC's financial policy. Another works council acquired the right of prior consultation on *every* appointment or dismissal of members of the management board. While article 30 of the WCA stipulates that the works council must be consulted on appointments or dismissals of the statutory director,[117] the works council in question was being consulted prior to every decision in this regard.[118] This example of good practice is useful to note, as the statutory director is not always the consultation partner of the works council, or rather is not exclusively the consultation partner of the works council.[119] By having a right of consultation regarding every appointment, the works council and the prospective manager can get acquainted with each other and establish an (in)formal working relationship as early as possible. The works council can also influence, to a certain extent, the appointment decision by stressing certain qualities that the prospective manager should have.

Finally, covenants are also used to clarify works council rights and the employee participation process in a MNC. Four interviewees said that a so-called "employee participation statute" or "charted employee participation" covenant was concluded in their MNC.[120] In this document, management and works council laid down the way in which the central works council is organised, which facilities were available, as well as the amount of work exemption that every representative received. The interviewee added that, unfortunately,

114 Interview 44:9.

115 Article 2:135(2) of the DCC stipulates that the works council only has such a right to speak if the council is maintained in the undertaking. This is not the case once a holding-structure is being applied pursuant to the so-called "Netherlands construction"; see also section 3.2 in chapter III above.

116 Interview 48:8.

117 Article 1(1)(e) of the WCA.

118 Interview 44:15.

119 See section 3.2 in chapter III above for the quantitative results on this point.

120 Interviews 1:20, 2:20, 5:66 and 29:7.

this employee participation charter was currently only applied in the CWC and not at the level of the underlying (business unit) works councils. In another corporation, the annual appraisal of employee representatives is based on the persons' performance in the works council. The manner in which the appraisal of the employee representative's performance is conducted, is laid down in a separate covenant.[121] The works council members are thereby assessed on the basis of their work exemption.[122] At the same time, this agreement stipulated the development goals for works council representatives and possible training arrangements. Agreeing on a common standpoint regarding the way in which employee participation is organised and facilitated, is certainly beneficial for both the management and the works council. Moreover, the clarification of unclear terms in the WCA (such as a definition of *important* decisions) can be included in such an agreement.[123]

3.2.3 Informal consultation

Aside from formal consultation rights, informal consultation rights are regarded as being of high importance for the day-to-day operation of works councils. Informal consultation allows the works council to influence the decision-making process on issues that do not necessarily fall within the scope of its formal consultation remit. It is based on a good relationship with the management as well as on the basis of pragmatic concerns (i.e., the works council's input is beneficial to the decision-making process) and not simply a *de jure* right to be consulted prior to the decision being made. Therefore, informal consultation rights are an important means for works councils to improve their position within MNCs. Based on these preliminary observations, it is not surprising that in the majority of interviews one or more informal consultation practices were mentioned.[124]

It is often the case that such informal meetings take place between (members of) the works council and members of the Dutch management,[125] but they also take place with members of the top-management (for instance the CEO or CFO).[126] The informal meetings can also include supervisory board members (for instance in the form of an end-of the year dinner that was examined in section 3.1.3 above).[127] Such informal consultations

121 Interview 48:30.

122 For instance, one works council member has a 30% exemption from his regular work and his assessment is carried out for this one-third of his working time.

123 Which is already the case in 22,7% of the agreements by means of a covenant; see figure 1.32 in section 5.3 of chapter IV above.

124 In 35 out of 58 interviews (17 out of 25 corporations) informal consultation practices were mentioned; interviews 1, 2, 4-9, 14-22, 25, 27, 28, 32-34, 37-39, 42, 43, 45, 48-50 and 52-54.

125 23 out of 35 respondents (on the topic of informal consultations) reported to have informal consultation meetings between the works council and Dutch management; interviews 1:13, 2:15, 4:12, 5:28, 7:45, 8:11, 9:36, 14:9, 16:14, 17:9, 18:4, 20:16, 22:13, 25:20, 34:16, 37:17, 43:10, 45:11, 48:9, 49:1, 52:1, 53:1 and 54:1.

126 Interviews 6:3, 9:36, 15:10, 21:9, 42:14 and 50:1.

127 Interviews 22:13, 28:10 and 32:6.

are sometimes also initiated by the management itself in order to receive input form the works council at an earlier stage.[128] Being able to present an undecided issue to the works council for discussion is helpful for better decision-making, as was pointed out by one Dutch statutory director.[129] In order to make certain topics debatable, the management and works council in two MNCs agreed to remove the label "*important* decision" [*belangrijk besluit*] within the meaning of article 25 of the WCA and rather decided that they would have a consultation on every topic of importance.[130] For topics falling within the scope of one of the categories that are found in article 25(1)(a-n) of the WCA, the regular consultation procedure is followed. For all other topics, which are important but that do not fall within the scope of one of the categories contained in article 25 of the WCA, a memo-structure is used instead. The works council's advice is therefore sought prior to decisions that fall outside the scope of *important* decisions pursuant to article 25 of the WCA and the works council's input is incorporated in the subsequent management decision.[131] Such a pragmatic approach to *important* and unimportant decisions within the meaning of article 25 of the WCA is useful insofar as it allows for the works council's input to be incorporated into the management's decision. This improves, on the one hand, the position of the works council insofar as it can exert its influence. On the other hand, such a memo-structure should be treated with some degree of caution. The works council does not have a right to appeal pursuant to article 26 of the WCA under such an informal consultation mechanism. By agreeing to use the memo-structure for some topics, therefore, may lead to an exclusion of some topics that would normally fall within the scope of article 25 of the WCA, but are nevertheless excluded. Works councils should scrutinise every decision for which the memo structure is applicable in order to avoid any erosion to their article 25 consultation rights. But despite this caveat, such an alternative, informal mechanism to incorporate works councils' advices is certainly to be welcomed. The interviewed respondents pointed out that such a memo-structure was proving to be successful in their MNC and was also very time-efficient due to the absence of a discussion on whether or not a topic is to be regarded as *important*. An important

128 Interview 25:20; see also section 3.2.6 below for further examples of good practice on the early involvement of works councils through (informal) pre-advice.

129 Interview 43:10.

130 Interviews 36 and 37.

131 Interview 36:12: "*De wet zegt als het belangrijk is dan is het adviesplichtig. Wat is belangrijk. [...] En we hebben dus best wel een keer met de koppen tegen elkaar geslagen van wat moeten we hier nou mee. [...] En toen hebben gezegd van weet je wat we doen. We parkeren even discussie van wat belangrijk is en we spreken af: we nemen jullie mee in de grote en de kleine wijzigingen of het belangrijk is of niet dat label halen we even ervan af. Dat kan alleen en dat is ook een beetje risico nemen, dat kan alleen als we vanuit kunnen uitgaan dat wij elkaar vertrouwen. En dat we op tafel leggen wat jullie moeten weten, wat jullie op tafel leggen wat jullie willen weten. En dat jullie eerlijk en oprecht zijn in de behandeling daarvan. [...] En dat is denk ik heel erg goed gegaan. Waardoor je inderdaad dat label – is iets adviesplichtig of niet – voorkomt. En we hebben gewoon afgesproken dan zetten we dat in een memo. En of het nou een adviesaanvraag is of een memo. [...] Dan nemen wij jullie aanbevelingen mee en dan nemen we jullie redenatie mee en dan zorgen we dat we het zo goed zo mogelijk doen dat ook in lijn is met wat jullie als OR belangrijk vinden*".

prerequisite, however, is a good and transparent relationship between the management and the works council, and one that is based on trust.[132]

Another noteworthy – albeit less far-reaching – example of a good practice is the presence of works council members during periodical meetings of the Dutch management team and senior leaders within the undertaking.[133] While the works council's advice is not an integral part of these meetings, it can nevertheless give its input during such meetings and receive information on topics that may develop into a formal consultation dossier at a later stage.

Perhaps the most important finding on informal consultation practices is the fact that such informal consultations often take place at an early stage in the decision-making process. Several managers stated that in a phase when the deadline for a definitive decision is still far away and hence where time-pressure is less of an issue, input from the works council can be much better incorporated through informal (pre-)consultations.[134] The works council, according to the management respondents, then also has the necessary time to prepare for the formal consultation procedure, which also improves the time efficiency of the participation process. In the following section 3.2.6, such a pre-consultation phase as well as a process-oriented application of the participation process will be examined in greater detail.

Overall, this analysis of good practice examples regarding the application of covenants has shown that article 32 WCA agreements can be applied in a multitude of different ways. All examples of good practice thereby help to clarify or extend the rights of the works council and to reinforce the works councils' position in the MNC at hand. In order to conclude such a covenant, the timing of the start of the negotiations is also important. Some works councils have been particularly successful in using a major reorganisation (for instance a takeover by a competitor or private equity firm) to leverage better information and consultation rights.

---

132 See section 3.7 below for an examination of soft skills reported in the interview phase.

133 Interview 41:9: *"Communicatie kan je gewoon niet genoeg doen namelijk, punt. Kan niet. Dus wat wij nu doen is dat ook in verschillende bijeenkomsten met senior leaders, vragen we ook mensen van de ondernemingsraad om erbij te komen en daar praat ik met mijn senior leaders wat er aan de hand is. En dan horen zij dat ook".*

134 Interview 14:16: *"Kijk, je moet mensen de tijd geven om dingen te verwerken en om vragen te stellen. En om te discussiëren. En dat werkt gewoon veel beter als je op dat moment nog niet hoeft te besluiten, als er op dit moment nog geen spanning op staat. Dus je kunt beter zo vroeg mogelijk het gesprek aangaan en heb je alle tijd. Kun je nog eens discussiëren als er nog ergens een pijnpunt is, kun je het daar ook nog eens over hebben. Of kun je kijken hoe je dat doet en staat er geen druk op. En tegen die tijd heb je het onderwerp eigenlijk al afgehandeld."*; also interviews 25:20, 33:5, 38:5 and 45:4.

3.2.4 Scenario development and own initiatives by the works council

It is also the case that the works council, on its own initiative or on the invitation of the management,[135] can put forward proposals and consult employees and external experts on these proposals.[136] In this section, works council initiatives are discussed which are related to consultation, while examples of good practice on the improvement of the works councils' professionalism will be discussed in section 3.5 below. Such initiatives are also valued by the management and supervisory board respondents, who emphasised the value of bottom-up input through such works council proposals, insofar as they were constructive.[137]

In light of the works council's right of initiative, several examples of good practice are worth highlighting. The first example concerns an initiative on contracting and sustainable employability.[138] The works council formulated an initiative on contracting with regard to the hiring of groups of external personnel through temporary work agencies. The respondent indicated that the CWC saw an issue in the corporation regarding the status of temporary workers in light of sustainable employability. In order to tackle the issue, the CWC hired external experts and built a case, which was subsequently presented to the management. By bringing the issue of temporary agency work to the attention of the management, the works council created a discussion on the broader topic of sustainable employability within the corporation and showed a proactive stance by building a case. While the proposal may ultimately not be (fully) acted upon by the management, the works council nevertheless initiated a discussion on an issue that was not on the management's agenda before. Such an initiative of the works council can also take the form of their own vision on the future of the MNC and the role of the works council based on scenarios.[139] By formulating such scenarios, the works council prepares itself for future developments within the MNC and uses these scenarios as starting point for a discussion with the management. The respondent indicated that these scenarios have subsequently led to a joint scenario development by the CEO and the central works council. The works council, therefore, succeeded in influencing the future strategy of the corporation to some extent.

---

135 Interview 26:17: "*Dus dat hebben we keer op keer aan de orde gebracht. Op een gegeven moment is er een vraag gesteld wat zou dan, vanuit jullie optiek, een goed bedrijfsmodel zijn? [...] Daar hebben wij een notitie voor gemaakt. Kort in twee A4'tjes. En daar kwam dus al dat functionele model kwam daarin tot uiting*".

136 Article 23 of the WCA in conjunction with the article 16 WCA right of the works council to hear experts.

137 Interview 5:35: "*Dat is best goed hoe ze dat doen. Ook al bij die cultuurprogramma zeggen ze mij: dit is wat wij horen; let daarop; hoe kun je dat meer bottom-up; hoe kun je dat sneller bottom-up gaan doen. Er is een hele goeie input die ik krijg*"; interview 10:39: "*Maar ik vind wel dat in zo'n situatie belang vanuit een OR-perspectief heel helder aangegeven moet zijn en dat het niet iets moet zijn waarbij ze hun mandaat enorm oprekken. Dat vind ik ook niet nodig. Dus het mag wel een beetje over de rand als dat praktisch nuttig is* [...]".

138 Interview 3:53.

139 Interview 3:51.

Another works council respondent indicated that based on an assessment of the works council's position in the MNC,[140] the works council identified social innovation as an area whereby it could make a difference.[141] On the basis of this assessment, the works council also determined that an expert in social innovation should be appointed as a supervisory board member for the Dutch subsidiary of the group through the works council's enhanced recommendation right.[142]

An interesting example of good practice is the initiative that was reported by one works council on development-oriented annual appraisal meetings [*ontwikkelingsgericht functioneringsgesprekken*].[143] The works council observed that appraisal meetings within the corporation were only focused on the person's performance during the preceding year. The respondent pointed out, however, that in the corporation much more attention should have been paid to the development of the employee in the upcoming five to ten years in light of the ongoing digitalisation of the workplace. Having identified this omission from the personal development of employees in the appraisal, the works council formulated a proposal to that effect. The proposal was subsequently presented to the HR-department and jointly implemented by the works council and the HR-department throughout all the Dutch entities.[144] The proposal was also valued very highly by the CEO of the multinational and it was to be implemented throughout the entire corporation.

In addition, the works council also applies these so-called development-oriented appraisal meetings for the evaluation of the works council's work, which will be further discussed in section 3.5.4 below. This example of good practice clearly shows that a works council can put forward its own proposals by means of a bottom-up approach, which are then subsequently taken over by the management and implemented. Not only does the works council achieve the implementation of their own agenda point, namely the inclusion of a development aspect for all employees in their annual assessment, but it also shows the management that the works council is proactive and is able to formulate

140 In this case a Dutch MNC with a private-equity background and employee participation limited to the Dutch sub-holding level.

141 Interview 7:17: "[...] *waar kunnen wij dus invloed op uitoefenen? Voor mij is dat op het HR-deel, op het sociale, naar het mensdeel. Daar kun je invloed op uitoefenen. En op basis daarvan hebben we dus ook gekozen voor sociale innovatie. Waar kunnen het verschil maken. En dat is op dat aspect, en daar moet je dan ook de commissaris bij kiezen*".

142 See section 3.2 in chapter III and section 4.1 in chapter IV for a detailed analysis of the works council's (enhanced) right of recommendation.

143 Interview 42.

144 Interview 42:21: "*Wij hebben als cor hebben wij een initiatief genomen voor ontwikkelingsgericht functioneringsgesprekken. We hadden overal wel functioneringsgespreken maar dat was meer van hoe liep het de afgelopen jaar, ben je tevreden en gaan we zo door. En we hebben gezegd je ziet toch heel veel ontwikkeling binnen het bedrijf. Het wordt steeds hightech meer. Dus onze mensen moeten mee en het vaart der volkeren. Dus we hebben gezegd natuurlijk moet je kijken naar het afgelopen jaar. Maar je moet ook nog kijken waar staat deze fabriek over vijf jaar of over 10 jaar. En wat voor medewerker heb ik dan nodig. Dus wij hebben een initiatiefvoorstel geschreven. En dat heet ontwikkelingsgericht functioneringsgesprek. En dat hebben samen met HR helemaal uitgewerkt en dat is sinds dit jaar loopt dat*".

pragmatic solutions. Consequently, the proposal was received positively by the management and will subsequently be implemented throughout the whole MNC.[145]

In order to achieve such proposals that are of sufficient quality and can be utilised, some works councils make use of experts to check the proposals first.[146] But the employees can also be an important source of information for the development of such proposals as well as a source of feedback on the final version. This input can be done through walk-in consultation hours,[147] town hall-meetings[148] or interviews with affected employees or departments.[149] The added value of such bottom-up input was also noted by the management respondents, who stressed the importance of the works council as "sounding board" [*klankbord*] and an important source of feedback on the (un)successful implementation of strategies.[150]

3.2.5 Monitoring of decisions

After having examined various examples of good practice that improve the works councils' influence on the decision-making process, one must also examine the phase that comes *after* a decision has been made. Strikingly, very few corporations (and their works councils) have practices in place to monitor the implementation of decisions that have been made.[151] Works councils and management engage in consultations in a repetitive manner and subsequent decisions are often based on prior consultations on (intended) decisions. The monitoring of previous decisions is therefore crucial for an improvement of future decision-making in the long-term interest of the corporation. Moreover, works councils often formulate conditions that are attached to their positive advice. A monitoring of the implementation of those conditions as well as the final decision itself is

---

145 Interview 42:22: "*[De CEO] stond meteen achter. Prima initiatief zei hij. Dit gaan we uitrollen binnen [het hele concern] in Nederland. En we doen het nu als cor zelf ook. Dus met onze cor leden hebben we ook OGF-gesprekken [ontwikkelingsgericht functioneringsgesprekken]*".

146 Interview 8:10.

147 Interviews 7:31, 8:16 and 8:32.

148 Interviews 8, 9, 10, 18, 25, 38 and 41.

149 Interviews 8:14 and 37:10.

150 Interviews 22:23 ("*En als je alleen met de divisiedirectie praat [...] dan heb je een beperkt zicht. Maar als je met de ondernemingsraad praat, dan is het veel breder. En ik krijg je iets wat een dan ook wel heet tegenwoordig: wisdom of the crowd. [...] Dus voor mij is een heel machtige vorm van sounding. Dus als ik merk dat er bij ideeën van ons absoluut geen gevoel is bij de ondernemingsraad dan is het voor mij een teken van moeten we het dus niet doen. Of althans niet zo. Er zijn altijd meer wegen die naar Rome leiden*".) and 32:16 ("*wat ik de cor nog weleens adviseer is zeggen jongens jullie zijn de ogen en oren in de organisatie. Je weet wat er speelt. Je weet ook of de strategie die jullie rechtstreeks gehoord hebben van het bestuur, of die goed is overgebracht in jullie onderdelen. En als je nou het gevoel hebt dat deze strategie die jullie rechtstreeks gehoord hebben, dat die niet goed is overgebracht. Omdat er allemaal lagen tussen zitten, managementlagen. Dan moet je eigenlijk het bestuur daarop aanspreken*").

151 Interviews 5, 18, 22, 25, 40 and 48; interestingly, only one CWC-respondent mentioned monitoring practices compared to five management representatives (with all respondents coming from different MNCs).

therefore of crucial importance. On a more general level, it is of course also important for the corporation as a whole to monitor the development and implementation of corporate strategies.

One of the few examples of good practice used in this regard is the end-of-the year meeting, which was already discussed above in section 3.1.3. During the meeting, a reflection on the previous year as well as the (employee-participation related) issues that were on the agenda can be undertaken.[152] The advantage is that, in the MNC in question, all three stakeholders – i.e., management, supervisory board and works council – are present. This certainly facilitates a good reflection on the previous year from all perspectives. One, however, can note that this meeting only takes place once a year. The meeting is therefore primarily useful for a reflection on major developments, but it cannot be used to assess the multitude of decisions that are subject to consultation or co-determination by the works council every year.

In another multinational, a steering committee composed of management, works council and union representatives is used to monitor social agreement commitments.[153] The works council is given a position at the negotiating table between the management and unions, and facilitates the monitoring of the implementation of the social plan. The advantage of such a steering committee, therefore, lies in the constant monitoring of the agreements that have been made, rather than an assessment only once a year by means of an end-of-the-year meeting. Such a steering committee is certainly useful for the monitoring of agreements made in the area of social plans and reorganisations, which also includes dismissals.

The monitoring is, however, limited to social plans in the example described above. Very few works councils have succeeded in concluding agreements with the management on the monitoring of all consultation and co-determination dossiers. In two Dutch multinationals, the works council is involved at a very early stage in the consultation process and during which constant evaluation takes place. If the final decision has been made, the works council and the management also agree on the form and temporal dimensions of the decision monitoring period.[154] In yet another MNC, monitoring is only applied for major reorganisations by way of multiple consultation dossiers (referred to as waves by the interviewee) throughout a six-week interval.[155]

152 Interview 19:16.

153 Interview 40:34.

154 Interviews 5:21 and 48:27: "*Vaak spreken we in het advies ook een aantal afspraken af. En daar zitten monitoringafspraken in. Zeker met deze grote adviestrajecten die er lopen. Ik heb nu een advies uitgebracht, zoveel afspraken heb ik nog nooit gehad. 26 afspraken gemaakt. En waarbij afspraken – zeven – uit een aantal monitoringafspraken bestaat die weer van a tot en met o geloof ik lopen qua deelgebieden*".

155 Interview 25:24: "*Wat we bijvoorbeeld met de transitie doen is dat we 1 keer per 6 weken leveren we ook een soort van status aan van hoe staat het met alle waves zoals dat dan heet. Hoeveel hebben we nou gehad, hoeveel mensen zijn weg gegaan? Vrijwillig, hoeveel forced*".

A final and practical example of a good practice is to maintain working groups, which are used in some MNCs for preparing a consultation dossier,[156] which becomes active after the finalisation of the process. The working group can then monitor the implementation of the decision made, as well as any agreements made between the management and the works council (for instance, any conditions included in the works council's advice).[157] This example of good practice is also welcomed by the management, because of the additional check as to whether or not the decision is having the intended effect.[158]

Despite the usefulness and necessity of effectively monitoring the decisions that have been made, which includes the works council advice, very few practices were reported at this stage. This is striking insofar as both management and works councils have an interest in determining whether or not the decisions made are having the intended effect and are implemented as agreed. Works councils should therefore pay more attention to this aspect, also because of the positive effect it has on the influence of the works council on the decision-making process.

3.2.6 Process-oriented employee participation schemes

The majority of examples of good practice that were discussed above are standalone practices that are not applied within a broader employee participation scheme. Yet, some works councils have agreed upon a comprehensive participation scheme with the management, which covers the entire decision-making process. In addition to the formal consultation process pursuant to article 25 of the WCA, additional steps are incorporated to ensure a more effective and time-efficient participation process, as is shown by figure 3.1 below. The formal consultation process is illustrated in blue, whereas the steps in green are those which are additionally applied in practice.

In formal terms, works councils are involved at the moment of the intended management decision, which is submitted to the works council together with a request for advice. According to article 25(4) of the WCA, at least one consultation meeting must take place prior to the works council's advice on the matter. Subsequently, the management takes a decision thereon and must (potentially) respect the standstill period of one month (article 25(6) of the WCA), if the decision derogates from the works councils advice. In MNCs, however, this process can be problematic once a decision is taken at a higher level or across business units and multiple jurisdictions. As was argued in section 1.4.2

156 See section 3.2.6 below for a detailed discussion of process-oriented consultation practices, including the use of working groups.

157 Interview 40:25: "*En we hebben in veel gevallen de afspraak dat bepaalde projectgroepen ook na implementeren van het besluit ook nog even intact blijft waarin we zeggen van dit zijn dan een aantal punten die we naar zes maanden ook even evalueren van: dit hebben we aan elkaar beloofd; dit is wat wij dachten dat eruit zou komen, zien we dat ook gebeuren? Zo hou je mekaar denk ik ook wel scherp*".

158 *Ibid.*

of chapter III, it is doubtful as to whether the works council's advice can still be regarded as being of significant influence, if it is only requested after the top-holding has given its instruction to the Dutch (sub-holding) management.[159] Moreover, the formal consultation process is less efficient, according to some of the interviewees, due to the fact that the works council can only give positive or negative advice on the (intended) decision that was submitted by the management. The works council cannot give its input on the (intended) decision, which can subsequently be incorporated by the management *prior* to formally requesting the works council's advice. Thus, the management would have to formally submit a new request for advice every time it changes its (intended) decision in accordance with the feedback given by the works council.

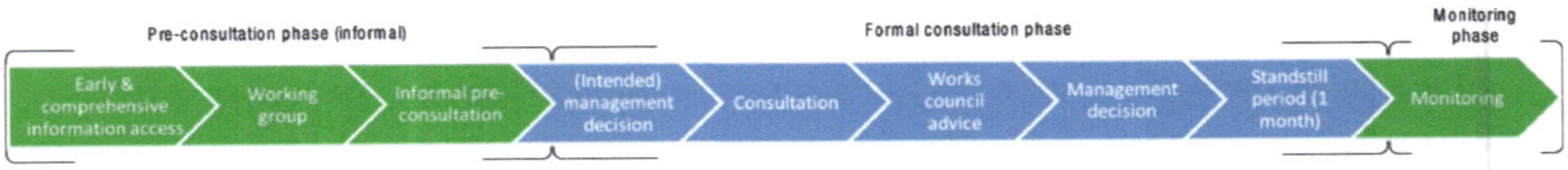

Figure 3.1 *Process-oriented employee participation model on the basis of the interview responses (blue: formal consultation (art. 25 WCA), green: additional practices applied by MNCs)*

Therefore, some works councils have established a pre-consultation phase, which takes place before the formal consultation phase. An indispensable prerequisite of such a pre-consultation phase is the timely and comprehensive access to information.[160] A range of examples of good practice aimed at access to information were discussed in section 3.1 above. *Inter alia* the use of digital information dossiers as well as informal meetings (*benen-op-tafel sessies*) and sector consultations are conducive to timely and comprehensive information access.

Making use of a pre-consultation phase is also more resource -intensive for works councils. The management may communicate ideas to the works council, which ultimately may not result in a formal request for advice. Or the management may present the works council with several alternatives instead of one (intended) management decision. This increased workload can best be compensated – according to the interviewees – by making use of committees, working groups or project-based works council positions or

159 See also section 4 of chapter III on the attribution of (intended decisions) and co-entrepreneurship.

160 Interview 14:17: *"Als dat nuttig is, moet je dat doen. [...] Hoe groter de verandering is, zeker conceptueel, hoe belangrijker het is om de tijd te nemen. Want vaak, wat je merkt, is dat als je vanuit ons perspectief kijkt, dan zie je andere dingen als potentieel probleem als dat je het uit het perspectief van de ondernemingsraad ziet. En vaak wel, maar soms komen er dingen uit waaraan je helemaal niet aan hebt gedacht; waarom vragen ze dat nou. Het is vreemd. Maar dan moet je wel de tijd hebben om te snappen van waarom vraag je dat nu eigenlijk. [...] En soms heeft dat te maken met dat je het niet goed hebt uitgelegd wat het precies inhoudt. Soms zijn het natuurlijk ook terechte zaken waar je ziet van ja, daar heb ik niet aan gedacht".*

so-called "knowledge-base members" (*kennisbankleden*). These examples of good practice will be discussed in greater detail in section 3.5.3 below.

The input from the working groups is subsequently incorporated by the management in the final (intended) decision, which is then submitted to the works council with the formal request for advice. The working group, therefore, has no mandate to decide on behalf of the works council, but rather it provides input to the management in the conceptual phase. The working group also communicates with the other members of the works council on the current state of affairs of the issue at hand.

The formal consultation process then only takes a very short period of time to conclude and is even sometimes concluded within the same day.[161] Therefore, by involving the works council at an early stage does not necessarily mean that this will slow things down, but may actually be faster as was pointed out by several management interviewees from the MNCs that apply such a model.[162] A positive effect is also the increased certainty with which the management receives a positive response to its formal request for advice. Because the works council gives its input in the informal pre-consultation phase, the management can incorporate these issues in its request. This in turn, means that the standstill-period of one month can, in almost all cases, be avoided.[163] The management can, moreover, clear up any misunderstandings and provide an explanation at an early stage, which accordingly prevents delays in the decision-making process.[164] Overall, such a process is therefore more time-efficient in practice, despite the higher time investment that is required in the pre-consultation phase.

Another positive aspect is that this process is very predictable for both the management and works council. Instead of determining the consultation procedure on an ad-hoc basis for each new request for advice, such an employee participation model need only be established once and applied to all consultation procedures. This saves time for both

161 Interview 32:8: "*We hebben toen eenmaal de contouren goed zichtbaar waren, zijn er adviesaanvragen geschreven. Maar die kende ze eigenlijk al qua inhoud doordat ze in de voorbereiding betrokken waren. Op het moment dat het adviesaanvraag wordt ingediend, dus hij is klaar en wordt ingediend. En dezelfde dag nog komt het advies. Omdat ze eigenlijk al in de voorbereiding van de adviesaanvraag hun inbreng hebben gehad. Dat betekent een enorme versnelling van het proces omdat je op één dag hebt men vorige week én de adviesaanvraag, het advies, het sociaal plan en het besluit van de directie naar aanleiding van het advies; op één dag! En dat kwam omdat inderdaad in de hele voorfase gewoon de ondernemingsraad meegenomen is*".

162 Interviews 14:28, 38:7 and 45:22.

163 The works council, of course, can still make use of the possibility to give negative advice pursuant to article 25(6) of the WCA.

164 Interview 14:28: "*Naar mijn idee: als je vroeg begint, minimaliseer je ook de hoeveelheid werk en allemaal de verstoring op de normale processen. Want als je gewoon te laat begint en je probeert dan heel snel iets daar doorheen te drukken, dan leidt dat tot een gigantische piek, tot frustratie en ook tot formele vragen, die je eigenlijk met een beetje uitleg drie maanden eerder gewoon had kunnen voorkomen. Die gewoon formeel beantwoord moeten worden*".

parties. By applying the process on a frequent basis, the consultation partners gain experience with the model, which is in turn beneficial for the decision-making process as a whole. This is also particularly helpful for complex consultation dossiers, as one works council interviewee pointed out. Only where managers refuse to apply the agreed-upon process, did problems occur.[165]

In some cases, a timeframe is established in which the pre-consultation and consultation phases must be completed. This allows the management to pinpoint the date at which it will receive the advice from the works council and subsequently implement the decision. By calculating backwards from the intended date of implementation, the management can plan the consultation and pre-consultation meetings in such a way that the intended timeframe of the project at hand can be (in most cases) adhered to. The works council and management have agreed upon an annual consultation agenda for this purpose (see also section 3.5.2 below).[166]

Finally, a monitoring phase is added after the implementation of a decision. The decisions made are reviewed by the management and the works council at an agreed upon date to ensure that the implemented decision has the intended effect.[167] For this purpose, working groups are sometimes retained, which then monitor whether the intended effect of the decisions is visible in practice.[168]

---

165 Interview 8:36: "*Wat je nog wel steeds ziet is dat het altijd dezelfde lijnmanagers zijn die er altijd weer vanaf willen wijken, die het dan ineens weer anders willen doen, omdat zij dat dan denken dat het makkelijker is, in hun hoofd, terwijl, daar waar de processen altijd goed gaan, die volgen dit traject heel keurig dit traject. Gaan niet langzamer, die gaan niet sneller. Volgen heel solide eigenlijk dit proces. En dat zijn over het algemeen ook adviestrajecten die heel soepel – hoe complex zij ook zijn – maar eigenlijk vanuit het consultatieproces heel soepel verlopen*".

166 Interview 8:17: "*wij hebben teruggerekend: wij hebben altijd een consultatie, een consultation meeting hè, [ ] die hebben we maandelijks ingepland met het bestuur. Dus elke maand hebben we, het hele jaar door hebben we die gepland. Hoe hebben we die gepland? Die hebben we in het midden van de maand gepland, en altijd een week ervoor en een week erna hebben we nog een plenaire ondernemingsraadvergadering, die hebben we ook al ingepland voor het hele jaar. Dat faciliteert ons het volgende: dat wij altijd een advies of een consultatietraject kunnen hebben waarin wij de adviesaanvraag en het advies kunnen bespreken met de ondernemer. Mochten we daar niet uitkomen dan hebben we nog, dan moeten we weer terug, dan hebben we ook nog een fallback dat we een week erna met de ondernemingsraad bij elkaar zitten, zodat we nog wel voor het einde van die maand advies kunnen geven. Al dan niet negatief of positief, maar dat is eigenlijk de gedachte erachter. [ ] Dat gaat erg goed*".

167 Interviews 5:21, 18:19, 25:24, 40:25 and 48:27.

168 Interview 40:25: "*En we hebben in veel gevallen de afspraak dat bepaalde projectgroepen ook na implementeren van het besluit ook nog even intact blijft waarin we zeggen van dit zijn dan een aantal punten die we naar zes maanden ook even evalueren van: dit hebben we aan elkaar beloofd; dit is wat wij dachten dat eruit zou komen, zien we dat ook gebeuren? Zo hou je mekaar denk ik ook wel scherp*".

3.3 *Facilities*

In order to ensure effective employee participation, the provision of sufficient facilities by the enterprise are a necessary prerequisite. To this end, the Dutch Works Councils Act stipulates that the entrepreneur has the duty to allow the works council to "*use any facilities that he may have at his disposal in his capacity as entrepreneur and which the Works Council and its committees may reasonably be deemed to require in order to perform their duties*" (article 17 of the WCA). The works council may also set up committees (article 15 of the WCA), may consult experts (article 16 of the WCA) and any costs incurred by the works council must be borne by the entrepreneur (article 22 of the WCA). Finally, article 18 of the WCA stipulates the minimum threshold of works exemptions for works council and committee members. The works councils act therefore grants works councils a number of rights and stipulates a number of duties for undertakings in order to achieve effective employee participation. However, times constraints have been especially identified as an ongoing issue for employee representatives in previous studies. The quantitative results of this study showed that 23,8% of the respondents experienced time-constraints at some point in time (see section 5.7.2 in chapter IV).

The interview respondents were therefore asked to what extent they experienced issues related to the topic of facilities. But more importantly, they were asked what examples of good practice existed in order to overcome issues (for instance work exemption-related problems) and to improve employee participation. These practices will be reported in the following sections below.

3.3.1 Elections

The first set of good practice examples concerns elections of employee representatives. In this paragraph, the facilities supplied by the corporation and the management specifically will be highlighted. The internal strategies of the works councils concerning elections will be subsequently be addressed in section 3.5.5 below.

One issue that is often raised in the literature and also raised by the interview respondents is the lack of interest among (especially young) employees in taking part in employee participation, often caused by the incompatibility between regular work and works council tasks.[169] In times of the increased 'flexibilisation' of work and a higher percentage

169 See for instance interview 43:11: "*Maar de feiten zijn dat het zo is en wij struggelen echt; het fenomeen medezeggenschap, hoe krijg ik nou de jonge ambitieuze meneer of mevrouw die hier werkt zo gek of zo goed dat hij zegt daar ga ik mijn tijd eens insteken. En dan roep ik echt wel van een podium: het is goed voor je carrière. En je leert er veel van en het is goed voor je ontwikkeling. Ik bedoel ik zeg echt de goede dingen wel. Je mag ook een keer bij me komen lunchen ook. Maar toch doen ze het niet*"; see also *inter alia* A. Nauta (et al.), 'Expedities in sociale innovatie: Hoe ondernemingsraadsleden hun rol beleven en uitoefenen', NCSI working paper (2008), <http://dare.uva.nl/document/2/61737> (last accessed

of flexible employment relationships,[170] participation in a works council is often not of high interest for many individuals. This may be caused by a decreased sense loyalty of employees vis-à-vis the company. However, the provisions of the WCA also makes the participation of flexible employees more difficult. Article 6(3) of the WCA stipulates that employees must have been working for at least one year in the undertaking in order to become eligible for a works council candidacy.[171] Due to the shortening of employment relationships, the interest in joining a works council is further decreased. Another issue concerns part-time employees, which is another form of flexible employment.

One interview respondent noted that part-time employees, in their undertaking, were unable to become an employee representative due to their small appointment of circa 10-12 hours per week. In order to overcome this, a dual employment model was created within the corporation. The employees received – alongside their regular part-time employment contract – an appointment for the (central) works council for a certain number of hours in a separate contract.[172] This has led to two works council delegates in the central works council, whom are part-time employees of the MNC. By creating such a dual employment model within the corporation, the management facilitates a better reflection of the workforce within the works council. This subsequently improves the employee participation process and is therefore beneficial to both the management and the works council respectively.

Other examples of good practice are aimed at stimulating candidacies for (central) works councils.[173] Some works councils campaign together with the management in order to highlight the importance of the works council as well as the advantages of becoming an employee representative. In one corporation, the CEO and the chairperson of the CWC recorded a joint video message highlighting the role of the CWC, the influence of the council and the skills that representatives gain during their term as a member.[174] One CEO noted that he is using the membership in the works council as a sales pitch during the elections by highlighting the skills – gaining a broad view of the company, working together, leading a company and insights into the annual accounts – that can be gained through a "mini-MBA".[175]

---

24 October 2017), p. 17; R.H. van het Kaar en E. Smit (eds.), 'Vier scenario's voor de toekomst van de medezeggenschap – Een onderzoek in opdracht van het Ministerie van SZW', (2006), p. 10.

170 See for instance the explanatory memorandum of the new Dutch labour and dismissal law (*Wet Werk en Zekerheid*), *Kamerstukken II* 2013/14, 33818, no. 3, p. 4 et seq.

171 See section 1.5.1 in chapter III.

172 Interview 3:46: "*Ja die hebben 10, 12 uur een contract als [reguliere werknemer]. Maar die hebben dan ook, ik neem een voorbeeld, een contract van 10 uur voor medezeggenschap. Dus die zitten in de ondernemingsraad van productie, en die zijn afgevaardigd. Zij doen dat in een duobaan. Dus wij hebben ook een duobaan gecreëerd binnen de COR, waar twee [deeltijd werknemers] op zitten*".

173 Interviews 10, 16, 17, 22, 38, 42 and 43.

174 Interview 42:25.

175 Interviews 22:12, 43:11 and 38:18: "*Hebben [we] ook gebruikt als sales pitch bij de verkiezingen om, het is toch lastig om kandidaten te krijgen. Je zou ze het kunnen zien als een soort mini-MBA. Want je leert*

While these examples of good practice are useful for other MNCs as well, it should be noted that very few managers actively campaign among their workforce for the works council, despite a much larger group stressing their positive stance towards the works council (16 out of 19 interviewed managers expressly stated that the CWC was of added value to them).

3.3.2 Training and development

After a works council is elected, the training and development of the members is important. Works councils themselves have developed internal examples of good practice in this regard, which will be discussed in section 3.5 below.

In some MNCs, the management discusses the training and development plan with the works council and even strives to develop a coherent training programme, which is also in line with the changes that the MNC faces.[176] But as one manager pointed out, a coherent training programme has not currently been established, which combines internal and external training possibilities.[177] Yet, such a training programme could be beneficial for works councils due to the increased synergies that could be gained from a combination of internal and external training opportunities. Several MNCs, for instance, have an internal training programme that is offered through their human resources department. In 9 out of 10 cases, as one interviewee reported, this internal academy may be able to offer the same training as an external party.[178] Not only can the person benefit from the training, but it will also be less costly for the MNC. The likelihood that access to certain training is granted by the management to works council members is therefore higher, according to the interviewed management representative.[179] In yet another case, the human resources department and the works council together selected an external party for supplying specific training, which is necessary for both CWC-members and

samenwerken, je leert met vertrouwelijke dingen omgaan. Je leert jaarrekening te snappen. Je krijgt een blik in de keuken van de bedrijfsleiding mee en dergelijke. Dus je leert ongelofelijk veel".

176 Interviews 10:13 and 40:35.

177 Interview 40:35: *"Een van de dingen die op mijn lijstje staat is inderdaad een gestructureerd opleidingsplan. Het is nu, vind ik het tenminste, redelijk adhoc. [...] Het is wel een centrale ondernemingsraad of commissies gaan gewoon 1-2 dagen regelmatig de hei op, zeg ik altijd maar. Dat is hun opleidingstraject. Maar er ligt geen plan aan ten grondslag. Geen echt plan. Er zijn ondernemingsraden waar het wel gebeurt. Dus ik zeg niet dat het niet gebeurt. Maar daar zouden we veel meer synergie uit kunnen halen".*

178 Interview 5:70: *"We hebben onze eigen HR-academie waarin we dus interne opleiding hebben. [ ] Bij de scholing daar heb je een stukje financiële scholing, die plaats vindt bij COR leden. Maar bijvoorbeeld een van de secretaresses die wilde meer de communicatie kant op, en aan kwam [een COR-lid] eens, die zij: dit is een goeie meid die presteert uitstekend, wat vind jij daarvan. Ben jij het daarmee eens? Dan zeg ik nee dat is een goed verhaal gaan de communicatie doen, maar dat is een externe training, we gaan eerst kijken binnen onze eigen Academy of we een passende training hebben. En die hadden wij ook een dat doet ze nu. En op die manier vindt dat plaats".*

179 Interview 5:71.

members of the HR-department.[180] Also in this example, a joint approach was chosen in order to avoid the overlap of training programmes and to create synergy effects.

Overall, works council representatives indicated that they were satisfied with the training opportunities, which is also reflected in the results of the quantitative part of this study with 92,9% of respondents stating that they were satisfied in this regard.[181]

3.3.3 Work exemptions of works council members and temporary (working group) members

Aside from qualified employee representatives through elections and training and development, work exemptions are an important determinant for the participation in the works council. If employee representatives have enough time for their works council-related tasks, then they can effectively influence the decision-making process. To this end, article 18(3) of the WCA stipulates a minimum of 60 hours a year and additional work exemptions for those representatives, whom are either member of a committee or the central works council. The exact amount of work exemptions must be agreed upon by the entrepreneur and the works council. As stated above, 23,8% of the questionnaire respondents experienced issues regarding the amount of time they had for their tasks as representatives. Therefore, the issue of sufficient work exemptions for representatives is still a point of concern and was hence raised in the interview phase of this study.

The interview responses on the topic of work exemptions are compiled in Table 1 below. The responses are not a comprehensive overview of all the agreements that exist in multinational corporations between management and works council. Inferences based on these responses should therefore be treated with some caution and a generalisation on the basis of these results is not possible. The responses nevertheless highlight some of the issues as well as the solutions adopted by MNCs on this issue.

180 Interview 15:27.

181 See section 5.7.1 in chapter IV above.

Table 1 *Overview of work exemptions in multinational corporations according to interview responses (24 out of 58 interviews) [WC = Works Council; CWC = Central Works Council; ExCo = Executive Committee of the Works Council (dagelijks bestuur)]*

#	No exemptions	10% (0,5 days)	20% (1 day)	30% (1,5 days)	35% (1,75 days)	50%	100%	Other
1:21			WC			Chair-person		Additional exemptions during peak periods
4:7							ExCo	CWC: table with exemptions per task
5:33							Entire CWC	
7:58						Chair		Other WC-members: partial exemptions; use of project-based WC members (*kennisbankleden*)
9:44								Flexible exemptions, never 100%
8:5 & 10:12							Chair	Own full-time function of EWC and CWC chairperson & flexible exemptions CWC members
14:22 & 15:54							ExCo	Exemptions WC-members unknown
21:25	Chairperson “takes” 25-30% but no formal agreement							
23:33 & 25:33	No formal agreement and neg. influence on performance reviews (interviewed manager regards issues as not as grave)							

#	No exemptions	10% (0,5 days)	20% (1 day)	30% (1,5 days)	35% (1,75 days)	50%	100%	Other
27:24 & 45:19	No formal agreement and neg. performance reviews WC-members that do not meet targets (interviewed manager: I rather have complaining WC-members than ones who get detached from their workplace)							
29:5			WC		CWC			
31:3						Chair		No formal agreement other WC-members
37:14		WC	WC +CWC	ExCo	CWC+EWC			
39:3				25-30% WC				
40:36 & 42:3							Chair	<50% exemption other WC-members
47:18		WC	ExCo					
48:28								Chair: 65% exemption, but ad-hoc for remaining WC
50:2			WC		CWC (40%)	CWC+ Chair/EWC (60%)		CWC: table with exemptions per task
51:1			Chair					Exemptions WC-members unknown

A first observation to be made is the diversity of agreements adopted in the various MNCs. Whereas some multinationals have adopted a clear scheme applicable to exemptions based on the functions fulfilled by a representative, other MNCs have no policy in place. Moreover, several respondents stated that agreements only exist for the chairperson of the CWC and not for the other employee representatives.[182] The absence of agreements in several MNCs is commensurate with the questionnaire results, whereby a considerable minority reported issues regarding (the absence of) policies on work exemptions. The absence of agreements on this matter should be treated as a point of concern, because article 18(3) of the WCA expressly states that an agreement on the specific exemptions should be concluded between the management and the works council. The absence of said agreement naturally has negative consequences for employee representatives, as several interviewees reported. Two interviewees[183] stated that not only was there no policy in their MNC, but their membership in the works council was also having a negative influence on their performance reviews.[184] What is also worrying is in this context, was the response from the two interviewed managers in the concerned MNCs. One of the two managers did not regard the issue of a lack of time and negative performance reviews as being as grave as claimed by the CWC-respondent.[185] The other manager went further and stated that complaining employee representatives – due to a lack of work exemptions – is preferable to representatives, whom become detached from their regular work.[186]

182 Interviews 14:22, 15:54, 31:3 and 48:28.

183 Both a chairperson of a works council in a foreign MNC.

184 Interview 23:33: "*Omdat ik niet aan mijn targets kon voldoen omdat ik dan niet op de afdeling was maar voor de centrale ondernemingsraad werkte. Ik vond dat belachelijk. Dat is uiteindelijk [...] stilgevallen. Is nooit echt hersteld. Het enige wat [zij] wel gedaan hebben is de verwijzing naar de ondernemingsraad uit het dossier gehaald. Omdat dat wettelijk niet toegestaan is. Dat je zegt: hij zit in de cor, dus hij functioneert niet. Daarop heb ik een maandje geleden toen [een OR-lid] weg viel of dat duidelijk werd, speelde het nog steeds. Ik was zo druk ik kwam niet meer aan mijn normale werkzaamheden toe. Ik vond het toch wel heel belangrijk omdat je ziet zo'n bedrijf in transitie dat moet goed begeleid worden door de cor. Heb ik ervoor gekozen om gewoon voor de cor dingen te blijven doen. Mijn managers ondersteunen dat, alleen daarboven niet. Dus op een gegeven moment krijg je dan dat alle pijlers krijgen weer een andere bestuurder. De bestuurders krijgen weer een ander manager. En de manager zegt van: goh jij staat op dat budget en jij doet niks; dus daar word ik op afgerekend. Jij moet dat werk gaan doen. Daar hebben we gewoon discussie over*". See also interview 27:24: "*Dus we hebben ook meerdere OR leden die slechte beoordeling hebben omdat er zogenaamde targets niet zijn gehaald. Maar het zijn tijdschrijven voor de organisatie. En moeten wij ook weer discussie aan met het MT die zegt van: maar het is logisch dat dat weg wordt gehaald. Nee maar wij zitten in beoordelingsgesprekken die gewoon ronduit vervelend zijn. Dus doe daar wat aan*".

185 Interview 25:33: "*[W]at ik zie is dat ze het als heel, een aantal het als heel zwaar ervaart en vind[en] dat ze soms ook volledig vrijgesteld moeten worden, of het liefst 2-3 dagen hieraan willen besteden. Dat snap ik aan de ene kant, aan de andere kant zie ik een hele grote inefficiëntie qua vergaderingen*".

186 Interview 45:19: "*ja, dus ik heb liever ondernemingsraadleden die klagen bij mij over het feit dat ze in een spagaat zitten en moeten medezeggen en ook nog hun werk moeten doen, en chargable zijn en daar gedoe over hebben met de baas zeg maar. Dat heb ik liever dan mensen die in alle vrijheid zich aan de medezeggenschap kunnen wijden, wat voor hunzelf misschien heel prettig is, maar die in no time, losgezongen kunnen raken van hun dagelijkse praktijk en daarin dus minder doelmatig worden*".

A few MNCs have concluded a formal agreement on flexible work exemptions.[187] Such flexible exemptions, which are then also communicated to line-managers, allow works council members to invest more time in works council-related matters during peak periods without negative repercussions for their regular employment relationship. It is crucial, according to the respondents, that the management communicates the importance of the exemptions to the line-managers concerned in order to avoid negative performance reviews, which are often conducted by the line-managers. In one case, the works council respondent indicated that instead of a negative review due to his works council engagement, he received an additional review for his chairmanship of the CWC from the Dutch statutory director.[188]

The examples of schemes for exemptions based on roles as well as flexible work exemptions show that flexible and customised solutions are being employed. The negative impact on performance reviews – despite many managers expressing their appreciation for their works council's performance – remains, however, a point that deserves further attention.

3.3.4 A single point of contact between works council and management

A quite important aspect relating to the effective employee participation in multinationals is the timely and effective inclusion of the CWC in the decision-making process. The main issue here is the presence of multiple decision-making lines within multinationals (in the form of business units, country structures), which often do not match the legal structure of the MNC.[189] Another issue, which was pointed out in the interviews, is the fact that foreign managers may not be familiar with the Dutch so-called 'Poldermodel'. The stakeholder approach followed in the Netherlands is often not applied within the corporation as a whole. Several interviewees pointed out that especially in Anglo-Saxon MNCs, this issue was apparent.[190]

In order to overcome these issues of multiple communication lines (including employee participation procedures to be followed) as well as different corporate cultures, several MNCs have created a position that serves as linking pin. The employee participation coordinator is a single point of contact and helps to facilitate an information exchange from the management to the central works council and vice versa. In one MNC, the employee participation coordinator is the contact point for both the central management and the central works council, but also for the European works council.[191] The

187 Interviews 9:44 and 1:21.

188 Interview 7:60.

189 See also section 8.4 in chapter IV as well as section 1.5 in chapter III.

190 Interviews 1:11 (and 1:25), 10:18, 12:10, 19:24, 23:55 and 34:4.

191 Interviews 3:55 and 5:4.

coordinator is employed by the human resources department and is in regular, often daily, contact with both the CWC and the board of the MNC. The coordinator pointed out that not only is his role to distribute information to and from the works council and the management, but also to ensure that all processes are followed correctly.[192] In light of the above discussed process-oriented employee participation model, such a coordinating person is noteworthy. By having a single point of contact, a timely and correct application of the agreed-upon process can be guaranteed. Moreover, the coordinator can assist managers and employee representatives (also plant-level works councils) in applying the devised participation process.

In two other multinationals – both Anglo-Saxon – the coordinator's role is even broader. In one of the two MNCs, the so-called labour director is the linking pin between the top-management and all works council and labour unions. According to the interviewee, this labour director and his small team received reports on all works council-related issues and subsequently advises the top-management thereof.[193] Given the expertise of this labour director and his formal role within the MNC, the parent company accepts employee participation-related decisions based on the director's judgement, according to the interviewee. In the second MNC, the coordinator is referred to as the labour relations manager. This person is also the linking pin between the management and works councils, but their remit is focused on communication rather than with a formal decision-making role. According to the interviewed manager, this increased and better-structured form of communication is crucial for the prevention of disputes.[194] It is noteworthy that this relations manager, as well as an internal HR-manager, were introduced after a series of legal proceedings between the MNC and the works council in order to improve the relationship and communication between them. This person is, according to the interviewee of the works council, often an informal as well as a formal point of contact.[195]

Both the labour director and labour relations manager are examples of good practice, because they may be able to bridge the lack of mutual understanding between an (often) Anglo-Saxon parent company and the Dutch (central) works council. Dutch works councils relatively often struggle with the difference between the overall corporate

192 Interview 56.

193 Interview 36:16: "*En ik denk wat [het concern] daarin ook goed doet, we hebben een, zoals dat heet, ex-US labour director. Dat is een [...] Engelsman. Die heeft een heel klein team van drie man aan zich rapporteren en alles wat met labour, dus Unions, works counsels, wijzigingen, sites sell, whatever; dat komt ook bij hem terecht. Dus hij is ook de goeroe, de expert op het gebied van labour. Hij snapt ook hoe dat werkt. En heeft ook formeel die rol dat als hij zegt het klopt wat dat rare Nederland doet want dit en dat en dat is de achtergrond. Dan is het ook volkomen acceptabel voor de Amerikanen*".

194 Interview 41:10: "*ja het is misschien iets te simpel, tijd en aandacht. Maar het is wel voor 80% is het wel mijn antwoord. Tijd en aandacht. En dan eens wat verder aangevuld met het feit dat we nu met [de labour relation manager] hebben we echt iemand die echt dedicated op de ondernemingsraad-achtige zaken [is], heel belangrijk*".

195 Interview 4:36.

culture and the stakeholder approach ('Poldermodel') applied in the Netherlands, as was pointed out at the beginning of this section. By creating the role of a coordinator between the top-management and the works council, the MNC not only better structures the employee participation processes, but also facilitates a better mutual understanding. The coordinator can "translate" issues for the top-managers and assess the necessary steps to be taken. For the example of the labour director especially, who is apparently a labour law expert,[196] shows that while top-managers may not have the necessary expertise regarding Dutch and EU employee participation law, they can rely on an expert advisor. The works council also has a contact point for issues that cannot be resolved (entirely) by the Dutch management. Finally, this coordinator can structure employee participation processes in all of the EU Member States to ensure that timely consultation, in light of the applicable legislation, duly takes place.

Another example of good practice is the so-called "change team" (*veranderteam*), which was introduced in one Dutch multinational. In the MNC in question, several reorganisations took place simultaneously and it was often the case that the decisions (and the advice of the works council) were not implemented correctly. According to the interviewee, ad-hoc solutions to unforeseen problems in the implementation phase for some decisions were applied. In addition, false incentives led to suboptimal decisions, according to the interviewee.[197] The works council, therefore, proposed the creation of a change team, which is mostly comprised of external experts on change management and one HR-representative. The interviewee further stated that the discussions were now better focused on the necessary changes and were more constructive due to the change team's professional input.[198]

In yet another MNC, a coordinator was appointed for the course of a large scale reorganisation after the takeover by a private equity firm. The transition manager primarily oversaw the implementation of the takeover, but was also the point of contact for the works council during the reorganisation phase and regularly gave presentations on the current status of the various processes. The works council representative noted in the interview that the regular updates on the large scale transition through a single point

196 According to the interviewee; interview 36:16.

197 Interview 26:24: "*wij veranderen heel veel in het bedrijf. En in het verleden heeft bijna iedere verandering nog niet tot een verbetering geleid. Omdat ze gedreven zijn door, wat ik net al zij, false incentives. Je moet personeel afbouwen, terwijl er geen bedrijfsmatige argumentatie voor is. Anders dan je moet in de kosten naar beneden. Je zag ook heel vaak dat als er dan een [...] advies en een besluit was genomen. Dat in de uitvoering dat daar heel snel afgeweken werd van wat je eigenlijk afgesproken had. Door allerlei toeredenaties en gelegenheidsoplossingen. We hebben ook in het traject gezegd er moet nu een professionele verandercapaciteit in het bedrijf komen. Nu moet elke manager dat er maar bij doen. Alsof operationeel personeel sturen hetzelfde is als het veranderen van bedrijfsprocessen. Wij hebben gezegd dat zijn verschillende specialiteiten. Dus we hebben nu een professioneel veranderteam. Dus door de raad van bestuur is ingesteld die direct de dialoog met de medezeggenschap voert*".

198 Interview 26:31.

of contact was very useful.[199] In larger reorganisations especially, the appointment of a single coordinator – either on an ad-hoc basis such as a transition manager or on a more permanent basis – could somewhat assuage the issue of timely and comprehensive access to information for works councils.

3.4 *Relationship with the supervisory board and corporate governance*

The relationship between the works council and the supervisory board is one of the cornerstones for the effective supervision of corporate decision-making.[200] Such supervision is an integral part of corporate governance, which is illustrated by the absence of such supervision in the public housing-corporation scandals that have beset the Netherlands in recent years.[201]

Scandals such as the *Vestia*-case have shown that supervisory board members were unable (or unwilling) to intervene in cases of mismanagement. One obstacle to the effective supervision by the supervisory board is the one-sided access to information that is granted to supervisory board members by the management that it is tasked with monitoring. The quantitative results of this study also showed that in multinational corporations, the supervisory board at the Dutch sub-holding-level is often comprised of corporate representatives (*concernfunctionarissen*).[202] In half of the supervisory boards, 50% of the board members were corporate representatives and in 32% of the cases, even a majority of the supervisory board came from within the corporation. It was concluded in the quantitative chapter above that, especially in the latter group of corporations with a majority of corporate representatives, an undue corporate influence may be exercised. The Enterprise Chamber of the Amsterdam Court of Appeals came to a similar conclusion in the recent *Thomas Cook* judgment of 1 July 2016.[203]

One solution to counter such a lack of supervision could be an increased emphasis on the relationship between the works council and the supervisory board. The works council can serve as alternative source of information for the supervisory board and vice versa. For the works councils in multinational corporations especially, regular contact with the

199 Interview 23:30.

200 See for an overview R.V. Aguilera and G. Jackson, 'The Cross-National Diversity of Corporate Governance: Dimensions and Determinants', 3 *The Academy of Management Review* 28 (2003).

201 See for instance *Kamerstukken II* 2011/12, 29 435, no. 227 and 253 on the Vestia scandal, in which the public housing corporation almost had to file for bankruptcy after having bought derivatives worth 22 billion Euros, which lost their value during the financial crisis with a net worth of 9,9 billion Euros in 2012. The lack of governance mechanisms in this semi-public sector, which is exemplified by the Vestia case that led to a loss of more than 2 billion Euros for the taxpayer, led to several legislative initiatives being enacted.

202 See figure 4.7 in section 4.2 of chapter IV above; see also section 3 in chapter VI below.

203 OK 1 July 2016, JAR 2016/12 (*OR Thomas Cook*), para. 3.8.

supervisory board can be beneficial for the improvement of the works council's position in the decision-making process. It was reported by interview respondents, whom were also works council members, that they had access to information on strategic decisions via the supervisory board. The supervisory board can also serve as a medium to voice concerns on issues that the management does not agree with (i.e., the supervisory board can have a mediating role).[204]

In this section, examples of good practice that are aimed at improving the relationship between the works council and supervisory board will be discussed.

3.4.1 (Alternative forms of) formal consultation meetings

The quantitative results of this study showed that supervisory board members attend formal consultation meetings 'frequently' only in 21% of the cases according to the respondents.[205] Even more strikingly, 53% of the survey-respondents indicated that the supervisory board members 'never' attended consultation meetings despite the duty to attend consultation meetings on the general operation of the enterprise at least twice per year (article 24(2) of the WCA). One reason could be the exemption in article 24(3) of the WCA, which exempts an entrepreneur to attend the meetings if the undertaking or group of undertakings has jointly established at least five works councils pursuant to the WCA.[206]

When asked about this during the interview phase, some supervisory board members indicated that being present during an entire consultation meeting on the general operation of the enterprise was inefficient and very time-consuming.[207] While supervisory board members have the duty to attend such meetings, the respondents indicated that alternative forms of such tripartite meetings (*driehoeksoverleg*) were more beneficial.

In one MNC, the meeting on the general operation of the undertaking is not scheduled as a separate consultation meeting, but rather this is done after the quarterly meeting of the supervisory board. The advantage here is a very practical one: the entire supervisory

204 See *inter alia* P.D. Olden and G.T.M.J. Raaijmakers, 'De president-commissaris als mediator?', 5 *Ondernemingsrecht* (2016), p. 22 et. seq.; at the same time, the supervisory board has no duty to mediate: HR 9 July 2010, RO 2010/55 (*ASMI*), paras. 3.5.1. - 3.5.19.

205 See section 5.2.2 of chapter IV above.

206 Article 24(3) of the WCA stipulates that "*Het in het vorige lid bepaalde geldt niet ten aanzien van een onderneming die in stand wordt gehouden door een ondernemer die ten minste vijf ondernemingen in stand houdt waarvoor een ondernemingsraad is ingesteld waarop de bepalingen van deze wet van toepassing zijn, dan wel door een ondernemer die deel uitmaakt van in een groep verbonden ondernemers die te zamen ten minste vijf ondernemingsraden hebben ingesteld waarop de bepalingen van deze wet van toepassing zijn.*"

207 Interview 11:8: "*Het is niet professioneel [...], maar ik geeft ook toe dat je daar vier uur zit en je hebt niks te doen. Daar wordt je niks gevraagd. Een heel groot deel van de informatie kan ik niks mee, het voegt niks toe aan datgene wat wij al hebben. Dus laten we op een andere manier hier invulling aan geven*".

board as well as the managers are present for the quarterly board meeting. In addition, the interviewee indicated that one of the international managers of the parent company is often also present on that day as well.[208] By having the meeting with the works council immediately thereafter, the works council can communicate with both the management and the supervisory board, as well as international managers. The interviewed manager also indicated that the works councils right to information on international developments (article 31(3) of the WCA) is tackled at such a meeting.

In two corporations, the works council and any related topics are a fixed agenda point during the meetings of the supervisory board.[209] For this agenda point, the works council then joins the meeting of the management and supervisory board, which takes place four to five times a year. Similar to the previous one, this example of good practice is a practical application of the article 24 meetings on the general operation of the enterprise. The interview respondent further pointed out that through this practice, supervisory board members could more readily follow the developments in the decision-making process.[210] For the works council, such regular meetings allow for better insights into the overall decision-making structure and they consequently receive more information on an issue at hand. The works council also witnesses the interaction between the management and the supervisory board on current issues and gives its input during the meeting.[211] Alternatively, the discussion between management, works council and supervisory board can be a fixed agenda point for one of the regular consultation meetings of the management and works council (i.e. 30 or 60 minutes). This would also enhance the time-effectiveness of the tripartite meetings that pertain to the general operation of the undertaking.

---

208 Interview 36:14: "*Dus wij combineren de raad van commissarissen meetings met de ondernemingsraad. [...] De raad van commissarissen is er niet bij in de ov-vergaderingen. Zij krijgen wel de notulen. Maar ze zitten daar niet, schuiven daar niet aan. [...] O: en dat is dan echt een driehoeksgesprek? I: ja daar zitten ze allemaal bij. Dus raad van commissarissen, bestuurder en de bestuurder kan dan ook bijvoorbeeld de internationale manager zijn om het concernperspectief mee te nemen in het kader van de informatievoorzieningsrecht wat een OR heeft. En is inderdaad dus OR, bestuurder en de RVC zit dan bij elkaar*".

209 Interviews 19:30 and 38:17: "*Die zitten gewoon aan dezelfde tafel. En geven zeker input en die commissarissen vragen dat ook aan ze. Dus ik denk dat ik er letterlijk kan zeggen elke commissarisvergadering zijn zij. En de OR is er ook aanwezig in de commissarisvergadering om de commissarissen op de hoogte brengen van voortgang op een aantal thema's die de OR heeft opgepakt. Bijvoorbeeld [...] de ouder wordende populatie in de fabrieken*".

210 Interview 19:30: "*Ik weet niet precies hoe het gegaan is, maar hebben we samen voorgesteld van: kunnen we niet zorgen dat de OR, elke RvC vergadering aanwezig is, en dat doen we dus nu ook. Dus we hebben elk jaar, elke bijeenkomst dat, we komen vier keer per jaar bij elkaar – uitgezonderd even extra vergaderingen [...] En dan hebben we dus een agenda, een standaard agendapunt is steeds OR. [...] toevallig had ik het daar met [een commissaris] over: goh, dat is een goed model want daardoor zit je als RvC veel dichter op de bal. Je ziet ook een beetje hoe het gaat met de board en de OR. En de OR brengt daar ook zelf punten in*".

211 *Ibid.*

In addition to meetings on the general operation, formal meetings between (a delegation of) the works council and supervisory board members are important. The supervisory board receives information primarily from the management that it is tasked with monitoring. By receiving information from the works council on a regular basis in periodical meetings, the information asymmetry between supervisory board and management can be reduced.[212] For the works council, such periodical meetings are a means for improving its position in the decision-making process. Moreover, the works council can receive additional information from the board members that it did not receive from the management.

At the same time, such meetings are time-consuming. Therefore, one works council implemented a mechanism through which an alternating delegation of the works council meets with one of the supervisory board members.[213] The meeting is planned after the quarterly supervisory board meetings for practical reasons and is similar to the other two practices that were discussed above. Through this mechanism, the works council members meet a different supervisory board member four times a year. The supervisory board members meet different employee representatives, which consequently improves the relationship between the two organs. Instead of only a select committee of the works council (for instance the chairperson and secretary), all employee representatives meet with the supervisory board.

Finally, in another multinational, the works council meets with their recommended supervisory board member (*voordrachtscommissaris*) after the supervisory board meetings have taken place.[214]

All these examples of good practice show that the duty of the supervisory board to attend consultation meetings can be implemented in a practical manner. Not only are the above-mentioned practices less time-consuming, but they also create additional means of influence for the works council. The works council is able to meet, in one case, not only the supervisory board members, but they are also present during the presentations that are given by international managers for the benefit of the supervisory board. The interaction between the parties and the possibility for the works council to give its input are noteworthy for the improvement of the works council's position in the decision-making process.

212 See for instance R.B. Adams and B. Ferreira, 'A theory of friendly boards', 1 *Journal of Finance* 62, p.220: "[...] both monitoring and advising by the board are more effective when the board is better informed. Finally, in both roles, the board depends crucially on the CEO for firm-specific information.

213 Interview 39:23.

214 Interview 15:45.

3.4.2 Informal meetings between works council and supervisory board members

In addition to formal meetings, informal meetings were mentioned by several interview respondents as important means of communication.[215] The above-mentioned information asymmetry was mentioned here as well. One interviewee pointed out that it was important for the supervisory board to inquire about topics that the management did not mention.[216]

Informal meetings allow for an (ad-hoc) communication of often sensitive issues that are currently on the corporation's agenda. Several interviewees reported that they valued such informal meetings as it constituted a means to inquire about the works councils or supervisory board's opinion on a given topic. For instance, prior to the general meeting of shareholders, the works council and their recommended supervisory board member exchange information informally.[217] In light of the works council's right to speak at the general meeting (articles 2:107a, 2:134a, 2:135, 2:144a and 2:158 of the DCC),[218] such an informal exchange of information prior to the meeting can be very useful for the works council. An informal exchange of information also sometimes takes place before the supervisory board meetings.[219] For supervisory board members, such meetings are a means of receiving updates on the current state of affairs within the various departments directly from the employees rather than via the management.[220] Another interviewee pointed out that he checks in such meetings to determine whether the relationship between the management and the works council is positive, constructive and results in a dialogue.[221] A much-valued informal setting is the end-of-the-year meeting, at which all three stakeholders (management, works council and supervisory board) are present.[222] The meeting often takes place in an informal setting and concerns either a specific topic[223] or the general situation within the MNC.[224]

Informal meetings can also take place with the (supervisory) board of the top-holding or the corporate representatives (*concernfunctionarissen*) in the supervisory board of the Dutch undertaking. Such meetings give the works council additional insights into

215 Interviews 3, 4, 5, 6, 11, 12, 13, 15, 19, 21, 23, 30, 31, 42, 44 and 54.

216 Interview 6:13: "*Mijn collega [...] heeft regelmatig dat contact om te horen wat er speelt. Wat zijn dingen, die er spelen, wat de directie niet alles verteld heeft. Je hebt op die manier een directe ingang in het bedrijf, want je kunt als commissarissen een dubbele check doen. Nagaan of alles loopt zoals het hoort te lopen*".

217 Interview 26:13.

218 See also section 1.4.5 in chapter III above.

219 Interviews 12:3 and 19:21.

220 Interview 35:9.

221 Interview 6:12.

222 Other forms are invitations to conferences or simply coffee or lunch meetings; see also section 3.1.3 above.

223 Interview 19:16: "*Dan zitten we als OR, RvC en board ook bij elkaar en toen hebben we met werkgroepjes ook nagedacht van: hé, hoe kunnen we productiviteit verbeteren maar ook arbeidsbeleving*".

224 Interview 28:5: "*En we hebben in december [...] een vergadering met de directie, raad van commissarissen, centrale ondernemingsraad waarbij [de CEO] een uitgebreide presentatie houdt*".

the broader corporate strategy and the works council can potentially influence decision-making at the top-holding-level as a result of this. One works council interviewee stated that they meet twice a year with the CEO, as well as the supervisory board of the group on the topic of the remuneration policy.[225] In another MNC, it was decided that there should always be two corporate representatives that sit on the supervisory board of the Dutch subsidiary.[226] The central works council is in favour of this ratio, according to the interviewee, because it enables the CWC to address the top-management on the basis of their responsibility as supervisory board members.[227] The corporate representatives can certainly be an important contact point for Dutch works councils and can help improve their position in the decision-making process. It should be warranted, however, that the supervisory board can still fulfil its role without any undue influence from the parent company, once such corporate representatives are present.

3.4.3 Exchange of information between the works council and supervisory board

The formal and informal consultation meetings that were discussed above are the main sources of information for the works council (and for the supervisory board). A few additional examples of good practice are noteworthy due to their practical usefulness in fostering the exchange of information between the works council and supervisory board.

Firstly, the works council in one MNC gives a presentation on the employee participation structure, the agenda (priorities) and on the last major reorganisation to the new supervisory board members.[228] By doing so, the works council provides the new supervisory members with vital information on the status quo and specifically the past track record of employee participation in the MNC. The works council does this proactively, which is an important trait that managers want to see in a works council, according to the interviewees.[229] Such a presentation also allows for contact with all supervisory board members at an early stage in their term of appointment.[230] By presenting the works council's

225 Interview 48:7; the topic of the remuneration policy notably corresponds with the works council's right to speak at the general meeting of shareholders (article 2:135 of the DCC).

226 The supervisory board is comprised of two external and two internal board members (corporate representatives); see section 4 in chapter IV as well as section 3 in chapter VI on the issue of supervisory board composition in Dutch subsidiaries of MNCs.

227 Interview 15:43: "*Nou we willen altijd zorgen, dat als er besluiten worden genomen door de top van [het concern], dat we ook via de RvC-lijn aan zouden kunnen spreken. [...]Je hebt ook als RvC-lid een verantwoordelijkheid om iets te zeggen over hetzelfde besluit wat daar genomen is. Je kunt niet zeggen, ik hier alleen maar een RvC-pet op en ik heb niks te maken met het besluit wat ik daarachter heb genomen*".

228 Interview 13:7.

229 Interviews 33:6, 34:5 and 40:18.

230 The CWC gives the presentation to all new board members and not only those who are appointed after an (enhanced) recommendation by the works council.

agenda,[231] the council also (potentially) improves its position in the decision-making process by bringing these topics to the attention of the supervisory board.

A second example of good practice is the submission of the minutes of *all* consultation meetings as well as the works council's preparatory meetings to the supervisory board.[232] While this should be standard practice, it is worth reiterating the importance of the supervisory board having this additional source of information. The supervisory board can see in the minutes the stance of the works council on a given topic and this is importance because not all supervisory board members (or none at all)[233] are always present during consultation meetings.

Thirdly, one interviewee reported that as the CWC chairperson, he could join the supervisory board meetings when they discuss certain topics in order to exchange information and opinions on the matter.[234] The interviewee pointed out that this is extraordinary and only done when it concerns major issues. The request was granted by the CEO of the MNC based on the merits of the argument and the input by the CWC chairperson rather than a formal right. Moreover, this example shows that a proactive stance of the (chairperson of) the CWC can provide the council with an opportunity to participate in the decision-making process more effectively.

Lastly, the supervisory board should also receive the works council's newsletter or any other means of communication by the CWC. While only two interviewees mentioned this example of good practice, one supervisory board member pointed out that this newsletter is another source of information on the issues that the works council is currently dealing with.[235]

3.4.4 Election of supervisory board members

This last section concerns the election of supervisory board members and examples of good practice that works councils apply in relation thereto. The quantitative results showed that in one in six multinationals, no supervisory board is maintained at the

231 See also section 3.5.2 below on the topic of works council agenda-setting.

232 Interview 35:10.

233 See section 3.2.1 above.

234 Interview 11:16: "*Toen heb ik wel het initiatief genomen en ik om te zeggen: [CEO van het concern], ik wil ook graag deelnemen aan die vergadering. Maar dat, en dat vind ik dan het mooie wel van het contact wat binnen [het concern] dan toch is. Daar wordt de ruimte ook gecreëerd. Formeel hebben [we] natuurlijk geen enkel recht om in die vergadering deel te nemen. Geen enkel. Maar toch gaat het op basis van de inhoud en de kwaliteit van de argumenten en wat is het issue at stake*".

235 Interview 19:22: "*Nou ik heb ook gezegd in de OR: je moet niet alleen zorgen dat je mij goed informeert, maar ook het andere commissaris lid. En dat doen ze ook. Dus, ja wij krijgen ook altijd het OR-blaadje, dan weten we een beetje [met] welke dingen [ze] er bezig zijn*"; interview 35:11.

Dutch (sub-holding) level.[236] In addition, works council do not always make use of their regular and enhanced right of recommendation for vacancies on the board.[237] The first point to be made is not an example of good practice but rather a plea to use the existing recommendation right by works councils for every supervisory board appointment.[238] Several works councils indicated that they are not using their rights due to a lack of time and experience,[239] a general passiveness by the employee representatives[240] or because of measures by the management that are designed to curtail the works council's enhanced recommendation right.[241]

Secondly, works councils should become involved in the creation or updating of the profiles for supervisory board members, rather than being active only at the point of appointment itself. The supervisory board must prepare its profile pursuant to article 2:158 of the DCC and "*when this profile is made, and afterwards each time when it is changed, it will be discussed by the Supervisory Board at the General Meeting and with the Works Council*".[242]

The first set of good practice examples therefore concern the profile for supervisory board members. A number of works councils participate in the development of the supervisory board's profile together with the board and the management.[243] The works council in one MNC, for instance, raised the point of increasing the number of female members on the board. Whereas in another MNC, the works council and the board were looking for a candidate that fits the corporation and whom would be beneficial to the current development. The work council's input can be particularly beneficial in sustaining a link between the board and the shop floor-level. Several works councils have, furthermore,

236 See section 5.2.2 in chapter IV.

237 *Ibid.*

238 See earlier research on the non-use of works council rights *inter alia* P. van Beurden, H. van Ees and R. Goodijk, 'Gebruik, niet-gebruik of onderbenutting? – Onderzoek naar de mogelijke onderbenutting van bevoegdheden en mogelijkheden door de (Centrale) Ondernemingsraad in grote Nederlandse ondernemingen'.

239 Interview 23:41: "*Ik denk vanwege de snelheid van de overname. En misschien dat we dat als ondernemingsraad dat eerder had moeten zien en daar initiatief voor hadden moeten nemen. Echt onervarenheid vanuit de cor denk ik dat wel meespeelt*".

240 Interview 21:29 on a question why no influence was exercised on the appointment oft wo new supervisory board members: "*Die ken ik niet want we hebben heel wat wisselingen gehad de laatste tijd. Dus ja, de cor heeft er zich voor uitgesproken om het niet te doen. Geen gebruik te maken van het aanbevelingsrecht. En gewoon gebruik te maken van de situatie zoals die nu is. Dat werkt voor ons het beste*".

241 Interview 33:9: "*Maar ze houden zich wel het recht voor, eventueel als het zich op negatieve manier zou ontwikkelen binnen [het concern], om dan alsnog een commissaris aan te wijzen vanuit de ondernemingsraad. Nou goed dat proberen wij natuurlijk een beetje te voorkomen. Door mensen te zoeken in die commissarisrollen die acceptabel zijn voor de ondernemingsraad. Zodat we dat circus, zeg maar, tot een redelijk proportie kunnen beperken*"; and interview 21:28: "*Dat wordt eigenlijk afgekapt. We hebben het ter sprake gebracht, dat wij eventueel van ons aanbevelingsrecht gebruik willen maken. Maar goed, dat werd eerst een paar keer werd dat lacherig ontvangen. Je doet maar, maar dat wordt toch niks. Maar in de loop, als je blijft herhalen, dan wordt het wat toegankelijker*".

242 Article 2:158 (3), last sentence, of the DCC.

243 Interviews 3:60, 4:23, 5:53, 9:23, 13:3, 15:42, 18:31, 28:11, 42:18 and 46:6.

developed their *own* profile prior to making use of their enhanced right of recommendation (*profielschets*).[244] After having developed a profile, some works councils make use of 'headhunters' to find a suitable candidate.[245] Other works councils use the repository of candidates in the "*Nationaal Register*".[246] The works councils in two MNCs did not expressly use a 'headhunter', but rather searched for a suitable candidate in their own stakeholder network.[247] The CEO in one of the two corporations reported that the proposed works council candidate was unknown to him, but was actually very beneficial to the undertaking after his appointment.[248] This example shows that the works council can succeed in recommending a suitable candidate, which in turn constitutes an asset for the MNC. In addition, such recommended candidates have closer relationships with the works council (due to the contact prior to the recommendation and their profile), which in turn benefits the works council. Not only do works councils gain more information through (in)formal contact with the recommended supervisory board members, but these board members are also more likely to have "an open ear" for the concerns of the works council.[249]

After a profile for the board is developed, a suitable candidate must be found. In one MNC, the works council proposed installing a joint committee of two works council and two management representatives.[250] In the MNC in question, no supervisory board was present beforehand, because the criteria of the structure regime were not met earlier. The works council also organised an internal workshop prior to the establishment of the joint committee to develop their own position on the profile.[251] This committee formulated advice for a supervisory board candidate, which was supported by both the management and the works council. Both the interviewed works council's chairperson as well as the manager were pleased with this procedure.[252]

Finally, once a potential candidate has been pre-selected, the works council should meet with them in order to become acquainted with each other. In three MNCs, the works council meets with every new candidate.[253] This gives the works council the possibility to give feedback to the management on the potential candidate and to influence the selection, if necessary. The works council should also stay informed of the selection process, if

244 Interviews 26:15, 38:14, 39:25, 46:5 and 48:2.
245 Interview 15:39.
246 Interview 46:4.
247 Interviews 26:15 and 38:14; see also section 3.5 below on the development of a stakeholder overview.
248 Interview 38:14: "*[De commissaris] is aangedragen door de ondernemingsraad. En ik moet zeggen toen kende ik hem niet. Toen was ik ook niet zo Nederland gefocust. Maar als je de naam een keer kent, kom je die ook overal tegen en achteraf gezien hebben we daar ook wel onwaarschijnlijk sterke commissarissen*".
249 See sections 3.4.1 and 3.4.2 above.
250 Interview 7:10.
251 Interview 7:11; see also section 3.5 below regarding internal procedures by works councils to improve their professionalism.
252 Interviews 7:13 and 38:17.
253 Interview 15:42, 32:7 and 42:18.

possible. In yet another three corporations, the works council is given updates about the selection process.[254] It must be noted, though, that this is not standard practice in many of the multinationals included in the qualitative phase of this study.

3.5 *Professionalism of the works council*

The examples of good practice that were discussed above also require a large degree of professionalism by (central) works councils in multinational corporations. Being able to participate in the decision-making process at an early stage requires expertise but also the ability to discuss potential decisions with the management. The Dutch works councils act includes additional rights, such as the right to information on international developments (article 31(3) of the WCA) which has existed since 2013, and additional (consultation) rights are currently being discussed by the Dutch legislator.[255] An extension of works council rights also requires an efficiently organised council, which is capable of coping with the increased workload. In multinational corporations especially, the works council members must also take into account both the position of the Dutch undertaking as well as the corporation's overall strategy in their work. In short, central works councils in MNCs should show a high degree of professionalism, if they are to succeed in having an effective position in the decision-making process.

In the interview phase of this study, a number of good practice examples aimed at improving the efficiency of the works council were mentioned. For the sake of clarity, these practices have been grouped in the following sections below.

3.5.1 Proactive stance of the works council

Firstly, the works council should show a proactive stance and implement measures on its own initiative. By formulating its own initiatives, the works council not only advances issues on its agenda, but such proposals are also often welcomed by the management (or rather, the lack of such proposals is criticised).[256] Initiatives by works councils can extend to all aspects of the company's (business) activities. The examples of good practice discussed hereafter are therefore only examples, but they are certainly not exclusively representative of initiatives that can be taken up by works councils.

254 Interview 9:23, 13:3 and 42:18.

255 Currently a consultation right regarding the remuneration of top-managers is being pending in the Second Chamber (*Tweede Kamer*) but the item has not been placed on the agenda since late 2016; *Kamerstukken II* 2015-2016, 34 494, no. 2.

256 Interviewees 33:6, 34:5, 40:19 and 42:22 value works council proposals, whereas interviewees 18:24 and 34:5-11 (also) criticised the lack of a proactive CWC; see also section 3.2.4 above.

Some works councils have developed initiatives on topics that currently affect their corporation, the sector in which the undertaking is operating in or society in general.[257] Whereas one of these initiatives concerns the ageing workforce,[258] another concerns the adaptation of workplaces as well as the training of employees to meet the changing demands of their profession (such as digitalisation and robotisation effects).[259] Yet another initiative that was recorded was the creation of a so-called 'social paragraph' whereby the works council – in light of market forces and the current position of the MNC – formulates a vision on working in the company and to improve employability in the undertaking.[260] Together with the management and after much discussion, this vision was then implemented throughout the corporation by subsequent projects such as sustainable employability, according to the interviewee.

Aside from a vision on the future of the undertaking, works councils can also formulate a stance on current reorganisations. It is often the case that reorganisations and changes to the corporate strategy are developed at the top-holding-level. The implications of such a reorganisation are potentially different for the Dutch undertaking, especially if the Dutch subsidiary is not located in the home market of the multinational (i.e., the corporation is foreign and has *inter alia* a Dutch subsidiary). One works council therefore formulated a memo on the implications of the intended reorganisation for the Netherlands for the top-management of the MNC.[261] While such a letter is not likely to change the overall strategy – which is a prerogative of the management – the CEO of the corporation listened to the Dutch central works council's arguments and consultations were initiated. A works council can also provide feedback on the implementation of a strategy to the management, a point which was raised by one management interviewee.[262]

257 Interviews 3:38, 7:13, 12:11, 22:5, 35:8 and 35:17,

258 Interview 38:17.

259 Interview 22:6.

260 Interview 3:38: "*Dat is eigenlijk een visie vanuit het medezeggenschap [...] op de menselijke factor binnen het bedrijf. Waarbij we uiteraard wel rekening houden met een aantal marktontwikkelingen. We plaatsen het wel in een kader, maar we hebben ook bepaalde ideeën over hoe je de werkgemeenschap vorm moet geven binnen de onderneming. Maar goed, we zijn vorig jaar uiteindelijk na heel veel discussie gekomen tot een gezamenlijke visie op werkgeverschap, goed werkgeverschap. En dat werken we nu uit in allerlei deeltrajecten. Duurzame inzetbaarheid is daar een deeltraject van*".

261 Interview 15:18.

262 Interview 32:16: "*Je weet ook of de strategie die jullie rechtstreeks gehoord hebben van het bestuur, of die goed is overgebracht in jullie onderdelen. En als je nou het gevoel hebt dat deze strategie die jullie rechtstreeks gehoord hebben, dat die niet goed is overgebracht. Omdat er allemaal lagen tussen zitten, managementlagen. [...] Kijk, ze hebben nooit zo'n inhoudelijke, afgezien van misschien in detail, inhoudelijke opvatting over de strategie. Ze kunnen veel meer beoordelen van wordt die strategie, wordt hij nou goed gecommuniceerd. Wordt hij goed overgebracht, is het begrijpelijk, hebben mensen het begrepen, wordt er iets mee gedaan, wordt er actie op genomen. En daarin hebben ze een uiterst nuttige functie. In het zijn van die ogen en oren in de organisatie. Dat is ook vaak voor een bestuur heel belangrijk, voor een bestuurder heel belangrijk; ik heb het altijd zo gebruikt ook*".

Another example of good practice is the involvement of underlying works councils by the central works council during a reorganisation in the form of a meeting of works councils (*medezeggenschapsdag*).[263] During the meeting, input from the employee representatives within the corporation is collected and compiled in a position paper. Gaining input from underlying works councils should certainly be done not only for large scale reorganisations such as in the case at hand, but for such major restructuring especially, the input from all sites within the country through their employee representatives is important for the adoption of a common stance on the matter at hand.

The works council can also take a proactive stance on topics other than reorganisations or strategic decisions. In one case, the works council distributed a questionnaire among the employees to gather input from the workforce on the profile for a new CEO of the MNC.[264] The CWC also engaged in a discussion, based on the questionnaire results, with the supervisory board as well as other stakeholders.[265] This example shows that the CWC can have an influence on important corporate decisions by engaging in a dialogue with the management and the supervisory board that is based on arguments from the workforce. This example of good practice is, therefore, also an example of the works council's role as the company's "sounding board" (*klankboord*).

3.5.2 Agenda setting

Secondly, it is important to determine the works council agenda. The setting of an agenda also goes hand in hand with developing a proactive stance that was discussed above. The works councils can formulate, one the one hand, a mission statement, policy goals or action points, which can be the result of initiatives such as the social paragraph that was discussed above. On the other hand, varying stakeholders are also important for the implementation of said goals.

At the start of its term of office, one works council, for example, formulated its own mission statement.[266] In such a mission statement, the main topics of importance for the works council's upcoming legislative term could be formulated. By going through

263 Interview 15:17.

264 Interview 26:9; in the MNC in question, a new CEO had to be appointed. The works council took the initiative to develop a profile for this new envisaged CEO (*profielschets*).

265 Interview 26:9: "*Wij hebben destijds al bij de benoeming van [de CEO], nee bij het feit dat er een nieuwe CEO al zou komen een initiatief genomen richting raad van commissarissen. We hebben gezegd van: goh, jullie gaan met nieuwe bestuursvoorzitter kiezen, wij willen daar graag invloed op hebben. En die invloed bestaat uit dat wij een profielschets jou aanleveren over de nieuwe bestuursvoorzitter. Dat hebben we toen gedaan met een enquête onder alle personeelsleden. Een elektronische enquête. Heb ik gesprekken gevoerd met leden van de raad van commissarissen en de raad van bestuur en ook nog klanten. En dat heeft geleid tot een profielschets wat voor ons een toekomstige bestuursvoorzitter zou moeten zijn*".

266 Interview 26:18.

such a process of formulating its mission statement, the works council could also create a clearer vision on topics of importance for the undertaking in the upcoming years. The mission statement can, moreover, facilitate the subsequent agenda setting with the management.

Another example of good practice is an annual employee participation agenda, which closely corresponds with the previous good practice.[267] The interviewee reported that the works council ranks topics on an annual basis and puts them on the agenda for the consultation meetings with the management. Such topics included, for instance, leadership, quality of working and the assessment procedure for employees. The works council thereby becomes result-orientated and works with a view to ensuring that the measures have their intended effect, according to the interviewee. The works council is supported in this agenda-setting process by an external consultant.

The internal agenda setting by the works council can, in a second step, also be aligned with the management's consultation agenda. The planning of meetings can then be done as such that the consultation phase and the intended implementation date of an (intended) decision are aligned. The intended implementation date is used as starting point and the time necessary for the consultation phase and meetings (both internally by the works council as well as with the management) can be calculated backwards.[268] By aligning the meeting agenda of the works council with the consultation agenda, a time-efficient process can therefore be implemented.

3.5.3 Committees and working groups

Once a works council has formulated its mission statement and scheduled its agenda, the working method must also be determined. Specifically, the internal structuring of the works council is important. Several interview respondents indicated that decision-making within their MNC is determined via a matrix-structure. The decision-making powers lie with several persons according to business areas (portfolios) across formal business units. The Works Council Act, allows for the structuring of employee participation in accordance with the organisational structure of the undertaking. Yet, quite often the (central) works council only has a consultation partner from the central (Dutch) management (see section 3.2 in chapter IV). Having consultation meetings with the central

267 Interview 26:29: "*Wij werken ook vanuit een jaarplan. [...] Dus wij hebben het meer over wat is nou het effect voor het bedrijf. En [...] hoe kunnen wij waarnemen dat dat ook gerealiseerd wordt. Wij noemen dat resultaatgericht medezeggenschap, dat is ook de methode die van mijn adviseur afkomt. Die hebben een organisatiebureau die op resultaatgerichtheid is gebaseerd. En daar hordt ook bij dat wij een jaarplan hebben. Dus wij hebben eigen initiatieven. Wij hebben een keer het leiderschap van [het concern] op de agenda gezet. Wij hebben het beoordelingssysteem van [het concern] op de agenda gezet. Wij hebben de kwaliteit van werken op de agenda gezet. Dat zijn allemaal strategische onderwerpen*".

268 See also section 3.2.6 above on the application of a process-oriented consultation model.

(Dutch) management is an important determinant for effective employee participation. But at the same time it is important that the works council has contact with other managers (for instance business unit directors) as well. To this end, one central works council has applied a matrix structure to itself, which mirrors the MNCs matrix organisation.[269] Alongside the regular consultation meetings with the management, members of the CWC also have sector consultation-meetings with the respective business unit directors. The CWC members, whom are representatives from a certain business unit (e.g., R&D), have periodical meetings with their respective business unit director.[270] In these meetings, business unit specific issues are discussed and the works council delegate reports back on these issues in the CWC. The added value for the works council lies in the additional access to information and consultation at the business unit level. The added value for the unit directors lies in the access to information on issues at the shop floor-level. Moreover, business unit directors are less often invited to the general consultation meetings. Therein lies the added value of such sector consultations for both management and works council, according to the interviewee.[271]

Other examples of good practice that were reported concerned the use of committees and working groups in general. The use of committees (article 15 of the WCA) in important areas such as strategy and finance, social policy and employment conditions were reported by some works councils.[272] Other works councils additionally make use of working groups to divide the council's workload more efficiently. In one MNC, for example, members of the underlying works councils participate in the working groups of the central works council.[273] In another case, the CWC delegates two to three of its members to a working group, which is supplemented by employees from the department concerned in the request for advice.[274] The latter contributes to the content-related input on the matter at hand to the working group, while the works council representatives safeguard the correct application of the consultation process. This allows the works council to deal with several topics simultaneously and it increases the quality of its advice due to the input from the affected unit within the undertaking. Yet another example of good practice aimed at incorporating feedback from the affected unit(s) in the request for advice, is the planning of interview sessions (*hoorzittingen*) with the concerned employees.[275]

269 Interview 39:13.

270 *Ibid.*: "*Dus wij hebben eigenlijk een matrix gemaakt in onze ondernemingsraad. Waarbij we overleg hebben van OR-leden die vanuit productie komen met de productiedirecteur. OR leden die van R&D komen met de R&D-directeur. Dat zijn de sector-overleggen die ze hebben. En we hebben daar ook nog naast hebben wij commissies en dat zijn vaak inhoudelijke commissies*".

271 Interview 39:14.

272 Interviews 21:27 and 24:18.

273 Interview 26:23.

274 Interview 37:10: "*Dan gaat nooit de hele cor daarover praten, gaan twee of drie mensen inzitten. Meestal de voorzitter en ik. Ik moet de brieven schrijven. Dan halen wat expertise erbij en dat is meestal van de desbetreffende afdeling. Want wij hebben verstand van het proces maar de inhoud, dat moet van de afdeling zelf komen*".

275 Interview 8:16.

Valid arguments by the employees are then incorporated in the works council's advice. The meetings between (members of) the works council and the impacted staff can also be used for an update for the staff on the current state of the reorganisation at hand, for example in 30-minute update sessions.[276]

Another example of good practice is the creation of project-based works council positions.[277] For consultation dossiers on a specific topic (e.g., financial services or a new R&D project), sufficient expertise may not be available among the works council members. To overcome this knowledge-gap, project-based representatives join the works council in the working group. The temporary members enjoy the same rights and duties during the consultation period and contribute to the works council's advice. This leads to better advice and a decision of the management based on the expertise of the temporary members, as one interviewee pointed out.[278] Another positive aspect of such project-based works council members lies in the potentially greater willingness of employees to become involved in employee participation. One respondent noted that employees are often not willing to stand for election and become a representative for three years (or more). Yet, project-based representatives may be easier to find due to the shorter term and topical approach of the assignment, which is of greater interest to experts in one of the corporation's fields of activity.[279] Such project-based memberships could, therefore, resolve the lack of willing candidates and at the same time enhance the quality of the works councils' advice.

An alternative solution to the issue of the lack of works council expertise on a specific topic are so-called "knowledge-base members" (*kennisbank-leden*). Instead of joining a committee or working group on an ad-hoc basis, the persons in the knowledge-base can be called upon by the works council, if a lack of expertise or manpower in the works council occurs.[280] In the MNC concerned, between 20 and 30 persons are at the disposal of the works council. The "knowledge-base members" indicate the topics to which they are able to contribute to, which is noted down in the registry of the works council. Once a person is invited to participate in a project, the same rights and duties (such as

276 Interview 39:34; and with due observance of the works council's confidentiality requirements (article 20 of the WCA).

277 Interviews 42:6, 47:15 and 48:22; see also section 3.5.4 below regarding examples of good practice concerning the election of works councils.

278 Interview 47:15: "*Nu hebben wij ook een aantal pensioendeskundige die werkzaam zijn bij [het concern] en die onze klanten eigenlijk voorzien van vergelijkbare adviezen. Dus we hebben aan de bestuurder gevraagd of we die deel uit mochten laten maken van de ad hoc commissie. En daar heeft hij in toegestemd en dat heeft eigenlijk geleid tot een heel goed en heel gedegen verhaal. En dan ook [...] vanuit het medewerkersperspectief. Een heel gedegen verhaal over waar we met pensioenen naartoe moeten*".

279 Interview 40:22.

280 Interview 7:54: "*Maar we hebben ook kennisbank-leden. Dus wij doen altijd een oproep, en dat doen we via een town-meeting, maar ook via onze OR actueel blad, [...] aan wie wil meewerken aan de medezeggenschap. En dat noemen we kennisbank-leden. En dan zijn er mensen die zeggen: ik wil wel meedoen voor een project, of ik wil wel meedoen voor die vier jaar*".

confidentiality requirements) apply to the "knowledge-base members". In addition to the expertise of the temporary members of the working group, such a knowledge-base also strengthens the involvement of the employees with their representatives and also enhances the visibility of the works council.[281]

Finally, one works council reported that their working groups are trained specifically on the topic at hand.[282] In the MNC in question, a working group was established in the context of a consultation on a new job valuation system (*functiewaarderingssysteem*). In order to be able to provide the works council with well-formulated pre-advice, the working group members participated in training on the new, intended job valuation system. This example of good practice shows that the division of tasks within a works council through committees and working groups can be further improved by means of topic-specific trainings. The training and development of employee representatives will be further discussed in section 3.5.4 below.

3.5.4 Internal training and development

The training and development of works council members is an important pre-requisite for effective employee participation. To achieve this, the Dutch legislator has laid down in article 18(2) of the WCA that "*the entrepreneur shall give members of the Works Council and its standing committees [...] any training and development of sufficient quality which they deem necessary to enable them to perform their duties*".[283]

However, aside from the employer's duty to provide training of sufficient quality, the works council can apply internal measures as well. To improve the council's own functioning and the effectiveness of employee participation, a number of works councils apply additional training and development tools. These are supplementary to the company's duty and do not replace the traditional training obligations.

The first example of good practice is a very practical one and concerns the clustering of trainings for the central and underlying works councils in the MNC. In one MNC, several works councils and/or committees, who are interested in training on a specific topic, are grouped together.[284] The advantage of such clustering is not only financial, according to the interviewee, but the works councils (and committees) also exchange ideas and best practices on that specific topic during the training. Especially in large MNCs, such an exchange can be particularly useful to improve the exchange of practices between

281 Interview 7:59.
282 Interview 15:27.
283 See also section 1.4.7.4 in chapter III regarding recent developments as well as section 5.7 in chapter IV for the quantitative results of this study on this topic.
284 Interview 42:7.

works councils.[285] It is furthermore noteworthy that works councils can also make use of courses offered internally by the MNC. In one MNC, for instance, the HR-academy offers training courses which contained very similar training to the ones that were sought by the works council.[286]

A second example of good practice is individual coaching meetings with each works council member.[287] The executive committee of the works council conducts these coaching meetings once a year. It is typically the case that more than one member has a similar issue that arises out of the meeting and a training course is subsequently scheduled on that specific issue for the entire works council. These meetings are therefore useful for identifying problems or knowledge gaps among the works council members. The coaching meetings can also be used for moments of reflection with the employee representative on his or her performance in the council in the previous year. A similar example of good practice goes even further and concerns self-assessment and internal performance reviews of the works council and its members. In three corporations, works councils have concluded agreements with the management about a (self-)assessment of the work of the works council.[288] In two cases, the works councils have introduced a personal development plan for their members, which is subsequently reviewed every year.[289] The development plan contains targets and competences that were identified by the works council as important milestones. Whether these milestones are reached and what can further be improved in the future is then subject to review. In one of the MNCs, the works councils' initiative on the assessment of the company's employees was subsequently also internally applied by that works council. The works council from thereon made use of the so-called development-oriented annual appraisal meetings so as to assess the progress of the individual employee representative.[290] Subsequently, the works council also applied the same practice to its own work and made use of the same format.[291] The executive committee of the works council conducts the interviews with the works council members once a

285 See also section 3.5.6 below on the annual employee representation day.

286 Interview 5:70.

287 Interview 2:29: "*We doen elk jaar ook nog coaching gesprekken waarbij we aangeven aan OR leden van waar heb je nog behoefte aan, wat zou je nog willen leren. [...] Dat plannen we daar wel in en vaak zien we dat een aantal mensen met hetzelfde probleem worstelen en dan doen we gewoon na een OR vergadering of naar een commissievergadering zeggen we oké: wij halen een externe deskundigen erbij en dan gaan we nog eens een keer een training doen op dat gebied*".

288 Interviews 5:69, 42:22 and 48:29.

289 Interviews 5:69 and 42:22.

290 See section 3.2.4 above on the works council's initiative.

291 Interview 42:22: "*En we doen het nu als cor zelf ook. Dus met onze cor leden hebben we ook OGF-gesprekken [ontwikkelingsgericht functioneringsgesprekken]. Verleden jaar zijn we daarmee begonnen in september/oktober. En we hebben de vier DB-leden die hebben ieder 3-4 mensen, daar hebben ze OGF-gesprek mee. Want nou hoe zit je nu in de cor. We gebruiken hetzelfde ontwikkelingsgericht formulier. Dus daar gaan we doorheen van wat vind je veilig, wat vind je niet veilig, waar zitten die ontwikkelpunten, wat vind je leuk, waar krijg je energie van, waar niet*".

year with a view to identifying points for improvement and the development of that representative.

In another case, the assessment is not purely internal, but is part of the representative's annual appraisal.[292] If a person is exempted from their regular work for 30% of his or her works council engagement, then 30% of the assessment is based on their performance as an employee representative. That assessment is done separately from the regular appraisal and is not directly accessible for the person's line manager. The assessment is (similar to the ones previously discussed) focused on personal development and training agreements for the employee representatives.[293] All these examples of good practice show that despite the entrepreneur's duty to provide training, additional (personal) development plans by works councils can improve the level of professionalism of its members. One of the interviewed managers noted thereto that such measures are welcomed by the management and facilitated to help improve the professionalism of their works council.[294]

3.5.5 Works council elections

An important prerequisite for professional works councils are elections with enough candidates, whom ideally represent the entire workforce and have the necessary expertise necessary to effectively participate in the decision-making process. This ideal situation, however, is often not the case with many works councils, whom face difficulties in finding suitable candidates.[295] Linked to this problem is a situation whereby representatives do not resign and remain in the works council for decades – sometimes without working any longer due to full work exemptions.[296] Another issue is the knowledge transfer from resigning works council members to newly elected representatives.

292 Interview 48:29.

293 Interview 48:30: *"Het is niet altijd even zichtbaar voor je direct leidinggevenden. En we doen dat volgens het model van succesvol functioneren, dat is een intern model hoe dat wordt vastgelegd. Proberen ook voor iedereen afspraken te maken. Dat zijn ontwikkelafspraken en eventuele scholingsafspraken. Wat willen we bereiken met elkaar. En we kennen [een] beoordelingscode van één tot en met vijf en zeggen van als je 30% vrijgesteld bent met de ondernemingsraad. Dan wordt 30% van jouw beoordeling wordt bepaald door de bijdrage vanuit de medezeggenschap"*.

294 Interview 5:69: *"Op het OR werk dat vond ik heel goed. En dat alle ook beoordeeld worden op de gedragscompetenties. En dan zie je dus dat ze daarin meegaan en dat ze dus ook zelf willen beleven en dat vind ik uitstekend. En dat gaan we dit jaar ook doen"*.

295 See SER Commissie Bevordering Medezeggenschap, 'Vacatures en samenstelling OR', *Sociaal-Economische Raad* (2014), p. 2.

296 See for example interview 34:8 in which an interviewee noted that a large part of their works council is "disconnected" from their constituencies; *"ze zien ook wel dat ze disconnected raken van de achterban. Het is een groep die relatief lange bedrijfservaring heeft. In heel veel gevallen ook niet goed inzetbaar is in werk. De ondernemingsraad [is] ook een beetje een vlucht"*. Another interviewee emphasised the importance of diversity – among genders, business entities and positions within the MNC (interview 40:21): *"[...] rondom de verkiezingen [...], twee jaar geleden, hebben we ook heel bewust ingezet op meer diversiteit. En dat niet alleen op basis van man-vrouw maar ook puur op hebben wij wel de juiste groepen aan boord, met name binnen de centrale ondernemingsraad. [...] Ons innovation center, R&D, die was niet vertegenwoordigd in de medezeggenschap. Daar werken toch een aantal mensen. Belangrijk speerpunt*

Before discussing the few examples of good practice reported in the interviews, one can note that a proactive and transparent works council is conducive to improving the interest of employees in its work. Moreover, communicating the works councils' influence on the decision-making process can benefit the interest of the workforce in their representation. This is being done by some of the works councils that were interviewed in this study through newsletters, walk-in hours, update sessions with the concerned department, townhall-meetings and notably by explaining the applied employee participation process.[297] Therefore, by applying the examples of good practice that were discussed in this chapter, the issue of the lack of interest in the works council and a lack of available candidates can be (partially) alleviated.

Turning to the examples of good practice, it is worth repeating that by using committees and working groups with project-based or "knowledge-base members", a shortage of capacity can be overcome.[298] Becoming involved on a project basis also helps to spike interest in becoming a full-time employee representative in the future, as one interviewee noted.[299]

Another example of good practice is the formulation of a profile for future works council members.[300] The profile can include important aspects of the work of the works council as well as expertise that is particularly sought after in the council. While the number of suitable candidates is decreasing, the overall quality of the works council can be improved. Shortages in candidates can furthermore be substituted by the above-mentioned project-based members. Such a profile could also be used for the creation of a balanced works council in terms of gender, age and years of service as well as business unit affiliation.

Moreover, a maximum term for works council members can be adopted in the works council's rules of procedure pursuant to article 12(2) of the WCA. By limiting the number of terms per council member, the practice whereby a small group of persons is continuously reappointed can be avoided, especially where the members are no longer

---

binnen onze hele visie/strategie. Zo waren nog een aantal onderdelen niet in vertegenwoordigd. [...] Plus dat wij ook meer diversiteit in mensen hebben gekregen, in die zin: tot daarvoor was het allemaal mensen, wij noemen dat even de blue collar. [...] En nu echt meer een balans ook met mensen die wij het hoger personeel noemen. En dat is ook een juiste afspiegeling van onze organisatie. Ik bedoel, je moet weten dat in Nederland een derde hoger personeel [en] twee derde werkzaam [is] in de fabrieken, even grofweg. Die balans zien we nu ook terug in de medezeggenschap".

297 Interviews 7:31 (interviews and walk-in hours), 8:16 (update sessions with concerned department), 8:30 (explaining the employee participation process to employees), 31:21 (newsletter with highlights translated into English), 47:17 (works council meetings open to all employees).

298 See section 3.5.3 above.

299 Interview 2:10: "*Het is ook een beetje een kweekvijver voor het OR lidmaatschap. [...] Het is een beetje geproefd, en dat lijkt dan leuk*".

300 Interview 40:22.

representative of the workforce.[301] Younger employees can also be stimulated to serve a short term in the works council and to gain experience by participating in the decision-making process. At the same time, it is important to ensure a knowledge transfer from the former to the newly elected employee representatives. It is often the case that the entire works council is re-elected after three years (or two or four years pursuant to article 12(2) of the WCA) and the (thus far) achieved professionalism of the works council is (partially) lost. To ensure continuous capacity building, overlapping terms of works council members and re-election of only half or one-third of the council is therefore another noteworthy example of good practice.[302] In the CWC in question, only one-third of the representatives are replaced. This leads to a situation whereby one-third is very experienced, one-third is somewhat experienced and one-third is comprised of new employee representatives. The experienced members can then transfer their knowledge and practices to the newer members. The new members, at the same time, contribute fresh ideas to the council. Again, such a practice depends on the availability of enough candidates. The management can facilitate this by emphasising the importance of a representative works council and facilitating the work of the council in general (work exemptions, training and support).[303]

3.5.6 Annual employee representation day

Lastly, some works councils organise an annual employee representation day (*medezeggenschapsdag*). On that day, all employee representatives within the MNC in the Netherlands meet with members of the management. The annual day is primarily useful for the information exchange between the various works councils, committees, working groups and the central works council as well as with the management. The day can, furthermore, be used to discuss current developments of general importance (e.g., a new corporate strategy or sectorial developments). The day can also be used by the CEO or chairperson of the supervisory board to address all employee representatives.

It is worth noting that such an annual employee representation day is obligatory under German law pursuant to article 53 *Betriebsverfassungsgesetz* (BetrVG).[304] The

301 Another argument raised is also that managers and supervisory board members also have limited terms and re-election possibilities; see interview 9:42.

302 Interview 32:20: "*Probleem bij elk ondernemingsraad is natuurlijk dat er door de wisseling, de verkiezingen, dat je elke keer weer met nieuwe mensen te maken krijgt die het allemaal een beetje opnieuw moeten leren. En dat is dus wel een belangrijke. En dat proberen ze wel maar het lukt natuurlijk niet altijd. Dat je een soort dakpansgewijze opbouw krijgt met de mensen met ervaring en een beetje ervaring en geen ervaring. Dat je zorgt dat die cor samenstelling zodanig is dat er voldoende mensen zijn die weten hoe het gaat en die weten hoe ze het moeten doen en die het andere weer kunnen leren. Als die weer opgeleid zijn dat ze dan enzovoort. Die overdracht van kennis, overdracht van ervaring dat ze die goed geregeld krijgen*".

303 See section 3.3 above.

304 *Betriebsverfassungsgesetz in der Fassung der Bekanntmachung vom 25. September 2001 (BGBl. I S. 2518), das zuletzt durch Artikel 6 des Gesetzes vom 17. Juli 2017 (BGBl. I S. 2509) geändert worden ist.*

Betriebsräteversammlung under German law must be held at least once a year. The central works council must present an activity report for the previous year and the entrepreneur must present a report on a number of topics, including personnel and social affairs, the current economic position of the undertaking and the future development. Such an annual employee participation day is certainly useful for MNCs operating in the Netherlands as well. In fact, a few MNCs have already organised such a day or have recently introduced it.[305] Such an annual day can also be used to formulate a common agenda for the upcoming year and to reflect on the previous year, similar to the strategic session of works council, management and supervisory board (see sections 3.1.3 and 3.2.5 above).

3.6 Relationship with the European works council

Alongside employee representation at the national (Dutch) level, multinational corporations also have to apply European legislation on employee representation if they meet certain threshold criteria. Since 1994, and most recently pursuant to the recast Directive 2009/38/EC,[306] European works councils must be established in Community-scale undertakings or groups of undertakings (as per article 2(1)(a) and (c) of the Directive). In light of the Directive's threshold criteria,[307] all of the multinationals included in this study are assumed to fulfill the criteria for the establishment of a European works council (hereinafter: EWC). In the quantitative part of this study, 69% of the respondents indicated that a EWC was indeed maintained in their MNC.[308] Therefore, not only can Dutch (central) works councils influence the decision-making process in their MNC, but EWCs (if established) can also fulfil this role.

In the analysis of the quantitative results above, it was furthermore concluded that an exchange of information with the EWC is beneficial to the position of the Dutch works council. This is caused by the broader scope of the EWC and the fact that a large percentage of EWCs are maintained at the central management level. Therefore, Dutch works

305 Interviews 15:17 and 42:17: "*Wij organiseren zelf ook een medezeggenschapsdag ieder jaar. Voor alle medezeggenschapers in Nederland. [...] Dan zijn er 200 medezeggenschappers denk ik. Daar is [de CEO] altijd, die doet een presentatie. [...] Zo vaak zie je het hoofdbestuur niet natuurlijk. En weleens goed van hoe denkt [de CEO] nu over veiligheid en hoe denkt die nou over kwaliteit. Wat is daarvoor nodig. Je roept vaak wel: "maar [de CEO] die vindt het belangrijk"; ja zeggen ze: het zal wel. Maar dan horen ze het zelf en dan kunnen ze het meenemen naar hun bedrijf: onze grote baas staat er ook achter. Dat is wel goed om dat eens een paar keer of een keer per jaar te doen*".

306 Directive 2009/38/EC of the European Parliament and of the Council of 6 May 2009 on the establishment of a European Works Council or a procedure in Community-scale undertakings and Community-scale groups of undertakings for the purposes of informing and consulting employees (Recast) [2009], OJ L 122/28.

307 Article 2(1)(a) of Directive 2009/38/EC states, "*1 000 employees within the Member States and at least 150 employees in each of at least two Member States*".

308 See figure 7.1 in section 7 of chapter IV above.

councils often have access to a higher management level via their EWC.[309] Based on these findings, interview respondents were asked how they utilised the EWC for their work as employee representatives.

3.6.1 Consultation and pre-consultation meetings

At the EU-level as well, some Dutch works councils established a similar process-oriented consultation model like the one that was established in the Netherlands, which was discussed in section 3.2.6 above. For example, one works council established a system with working groups and pre-consultation in the EWC.[310] The interviewee further pointed out that at the EU level especially, the application of an informal pre-consultation is useful to get a grasp of the context of an (intended) decision.[311] In return, the management receives the draft opinion of the EWC in the pre-consultation phase. The management may also suggest changes to the wording of the draft opinion without altering the content thereof.[312] This example shows that – despite the difference in formal information and consultation rights between the Dutch and EU level – a very similar and constructive employee participation system can be established. The example also shows the added value of the early involvement of the EWC in the decision-making process. At the same time, it must be noted that such a far-reaching participation mechanism is the exception rather than the rule.[313]

Another example of good practice is an informal consultation with the top-management (*benen op tafel gesprekken*), for instance with the CEO and CFO.[314] Informal cross-border information exchange is also possible between works councils (as well as managers). In one MNC, works councils within the same business unit have regular contact with their counterpart in other countries (e.g., the *Betriebsrat* in Germany) as well as the managers in that respective unit.[315] Such an exchange between works councils is particularly important for units that are working for shared services within the MNC and that are situated in multiple countries.

---

309 See section 7 in chapter IV above.

310 Interview 8:39: "*Een soortgelijk model werkt ook heel goed op Europees niveau, alleen zijn het dan opinies in plaats van adviezen. Maar, het is wat minder dwingend dan de Nederlandse wet*".

311 Interview 8:44: "*juist door die conceptfase en die planningsfase krijg je veel meer context van waarom iets moet gebeuren. Niet alles kan op papier, dat snap ik ook wel, maar als je dan wel de volledige context met mekaar kan delen omdat je in die informele fase zit, dat helpt enorm om dingen goed te begrijpen*".

312 Interview 8:46: "*Wat ik wel doe, als ik bijvoorbeeld de opinie heb geschreven, dan mogen ze wel de woordkeuze aanpassen zonder dat ze de inhoud mogen aanpassen. [...] Ik check dat altijd bij een aantal Engelse leden in de raad van "is de content gewijzigd met dit voorstel?". Dan vind ik het prima. Daar heb ik niet zoveel moeite mee. Dat is een beetje de zachte kant van de relatie. Ze hebben ook het gevoel; mijn intentie is niet om hun onderuit de zak te geven. Maar feitelijk te zeggen of ik iets goed vond of niet. Dat is de intentie*".

313 This example notably concerned an Anglo-Saxon multinational.

314 Interview 31:9.

315 Interview 15:53.

Turning to formal consultations, a few examples of good practice are also noteworthy. Firstly, in one MNC, the executive committee of the EWC regularly meets with members of the top-management. This is particularly important in this case, because the MNC is German and all of the major decisions are decided in Germany. Therefore, it is very important from the Dutch works council's perspective to meet with the German top-management via the EWC. This is also in line with the quantitative findings, according to which the EWC meets with members of the top-management more often compared to the Dutch CWC. Another example is a meeting with the chairman of the supervisory board, during which questions by the EWC can be asked and subsequently answered.[316]

Secondly, in some countries, management personnel are the assigned EWC-representatives for that country and sometimes no works council is established (yet). In such cases in particular, it may be useful to invite trade union representatives to the EWC plenary meetings.[317] By inviting trade union representatives, as one interviewee pointed out, the EWC can provide the necessary context on issues such as reorganisations and social plans (for which the unions are only involved at a later stage). Given the sensitiveness of the strategic information, the union representatives had to sign a confidentiality agreement in that particular case.

Finally, monthly conference calls by the entire EWC (or other forms of communication such as video-conferences or SharePoint applications) are useful practical solutions to the logistical problems that are inherent in EWCs.[318] In the majority of cases, EWC-members only meet once or twice a year for a plenary session.[319] However, the speed of decision-making and reorganisations warrants timelier employee involvement. By using such tools – in addition to the more frequent informal meetings that were discussed above – works councils can act more effectively on current developments.

3.6.2 Country reports as feedback mechanism for the top-management

One example of good practice that was reported in the interview phase in this study, must be pointed out because it utilises the EWC specifically for Dutch works councils. Whereas the aforementioned practices are primarily aimed at influencing decision-making at the European level, this practice is mainly aimed at communicating topics of concern to the Dutch business entities.

316 Interview 8:57.
317 Interview 8:43.
318 Interview 8:56.
319 70% of EWCs meet once a year in a plenary meeting and 23% meet twice a year; see S. De Spiegelaere and R. Jagodzinski, *European Works Councils and SE Works Councils in 2015: Facts & figures* (ETUI aisbl, Brussels 2015), p. 30.

This is noteworthy, because quite often the Dutch works councils do not have a member of the top-management as a consultation partner.[320] However, communicating to the management the possible consequences of an intended decision from an employee perspective is an important function of the works council. Some works councils have, for this reasoned, developed a memo on the implications of the intended reorganisation for the Netherlands for the top-management of the MNC (discussed in section 3.5.1 above). A works council in an Anglo-Saxon multinational has chosen a different approach and implemented a country-report system via the EWC.[321] The national works councils write a country report, which the country representatives in the EWC then submit to the chairperson of the one-tier board of the MNC. The country feedback is submitted every two months and is – according to the interviewee – as objectively formulated as possible. From a Dutch perspective, the advantage of such a country report lies in the possibility to submit unfiltered feedback on the Dutch situation to the top-management. The interviewee further pointed out that the middle management is not particularly in favour of such a process, because of its loss of control on what is reported to the top-management. From a works council perspective, however, such a reporting mechanism improves its position precisely because of this unfiltered feedback. In addition, the middle management became more transparent about intended decisions, because of the direct communication channel between works councils and the top-management.[322]

The country feedback does not only include feedback from the central Dutch works council, but can also include feedback from site-works councils. For such grassroots operations in particular, information is valued by the senior management, according to the interviewee. The feedback mechanism therefore allows for input from all Dutch works councils via the central works council and the EWC.

To conclude, the EWC may not often provide Dutch employee representatives with more information or additional consultation rights. This is due to the fact that Dutch (central) works councils are often involved in the decision-making process earlier than EWCs,

320 See section 3.2 in chapter IV.

321 Interview 8:58: "*wij hebben als Europese raad hebben wij ook een country feedback elke twee maanden. En die gaat naar de voorzitter van de one-tier board, de chairman [...]. Daar sturen wij een keer per twee maanden ons feedback per land toe en dat is echt behulpzaam*".

322 Interview 8:60: "*En dat is niet dat wij dan zeggen van dit is een oordeel, want dit is wat wij zien, dat is de emotie die er leeft, maar objectief. En dat werkt erg goed en daarmee ga je een stukje beïnvloeden in het breedste zin los van adviesaanvragen; dan ben je toch een beetje een thermometer en maak je gebruik van je medewerkers in de positieve zin. Dat middenmanagement vindt het wat minder dat proces, dat vind ik ook wel grappig om te zien. Maar het is niet zo dat wij het publiceren, maar meer dat wij tegen het senior management zeggen: deel maar met wie je denkt dat het goed is om te delen. Als jij dat je lijnen wil ingroeien, dan mag dat met ons toestemming. [...] En dat werkt erg goed, dan krijg je ook van het middenmanagement het juiste verhaal te horen, want ze weten dat het er toch terecht gaat komen. Dat werkt goed*".

according to the quantitative results of this study.[323] But this example of good practice shows that Dutch works councils can use this platform to communicate their position to the higher management by means of such country reports.

3.6.3 Incorporating the EWC position in the standpoint of the Dutch (central) works council

Dutch works councils can also use the EWC's position on a given matter to their advantage. The EWC must be involved in matters pertaining to the intended management decisions with a transnational scope (i.e., those which have an impact on two or more EU Member States, such as strategic plans or large scale reorganisations).[324] In light of the jurisprudence of the European Court of Justice[325] and the Tribunal de Grande Instance Nanterre and Versailles (in the Renault Vilvoorde case),[326] transnational reorganisations must be discussed at European level in good time to ensure that the *effet utile* of the Directive is applied. This means that in some cases, issues are discussed at the European level earlier than they would be communicated at the national level.[327]

Once the management has informed and consulted the EWC, the rationale of the intended decision is motivated by the management. This provides, in turn, the Dutch works council with context regarding subsequent implementing decisions at the national level. Once such implementing decisions are subject to the Dutch consultation procedure, works councils can therefore use the arguments – both positive and negative – that were raised by the EWC in their own advice. Thus, making use of the EWCs position on the matter can be beneficial for the position of the Dutch works council in its consultations. In this context, it is worth noting that one EWC publishes its opinion (the equivalent of an advice at Dutch level) so that local works councils can make use of their arguments.[328]

---

323 Only a small minority of EWCs (13,8%) enjoy more rights than the minimum requirements set forth in the Directive under the fallback rules (see figure 1.52 in section 7 of chapter IV); CWCs are also more often consulted earlier than EWCs with 44,8% of CWCs being consulted earlier than the EWC (see figure 1.56 in section 7 of chapter IV).

324 See article 1(a) of the Annex of Directive 2009/38/EC regarding the subsidiary requirements referred to in article 7 of the Directive.

325 Case C-349/01 *Betriebsrat der Firma ADS Anker GmbH v. ADS Anker GmbH*, EU:C:2004:440; Case C-151/09 *Federación de Servicios Públicos de la UGT v Ayuntamiento de La Línea de la Concepción, María del Rosario Vecino Uribe, Ministerio Fiscal* (UGT-FSP), EU:C:2010:452.

326 Tribunal de Grande Instance Nanterre, *Renault Vilvoorde* [4 April 1997] *Sociaalrechtelijke Kronieken* 1997, 339-340; and Tribunal de Grande Instance Versailles, *Renault Vilvoorde* [7 May 1997] *Sociaalrechtelijke Kronieken* 1997, 336-339.

327 Article 25 of the WCA stipulates that advice on an intended decision shall be requested at a time when it can still significantly affect the decision to be taken; it is the prevailing view in the jurisprudence on the attribution of intended decisions and co-entrepreneurship (discussed in section 4 of chapter III) that such an advice must be requested only if the (intended) decision directly impacts the Dutch undertaking(s) ("*rechtstreeks ingrijpt*").

328 Interview 8:41.

One can therefore conclude that Dutch works councils can make use of EWCs, both as platform to communicate their position as well as an additional source of information. By using EWCs, the position of Dutch works councils can be improved despite the shortcomings of the EWC framework, compared to the Dutch regime.[329]

3.7 *Soft skills necessary for effective employee participation*

The final section of this chapter discusses the criteria, which are not examples of good practice like the ones discussed above, but are rather linking pins. In fact, no successful application of the examples of good practice described in this chapter would be possible without these linking pins, which are hereinafter referred to as 'soft skills'.

35 out of 58 respondents indicated that openness and transparency are the most important linking pin for them in this regard (section 3.7.1). Transparency thereby often goes hand in hand with trust in the consultation partner and the possibility to safely share confidential information (15 out of 58; section 3.7.2). Seeing the added value in the works council (27 out of 33) and taking it seriously (11 out of 33) were also frequently mentioned by interviewed management and supervisory board members (section 3.7.2). Other often-mentioned soft skills are a constructive attitude (15 out of 58; section 3.7.4) and an active relationship with the management and the so-called "*polderen*" (consensus-based decision-making).

3.7.1 **Openness and transparency at the core**

The most important linking pin for the successful application of an effective employee participation mechanism is transparency and openness, according to the interviewees. Transparency thereby relates to both the transparency surrounding the (intended) decisions to be made as well as transparency surrounding the intended decision-making process.

Transparency about (intended) decisions relates to the timely informing of works councils by the management, albeit in light of confidentiality restrictions such as share price-sensitive information.[330] Ideally, the works council is timely updated on all

329 See *inter alia* European Commission, 'Report of the Group of Experts on the implementation of Recast Directive 2009/38/EC on European Works Councils – December2010', Ares(2011)22826, <www.ec.europa.eu/social/BlobServlet?docId=6436&langId=en>.

330 Interview 18:19: "*Dus ik zeg transparantie is het belangrijke wat er is. Op het moment dat je dingen gaat verbergen, gaan mensen het overdenken: waarom gaan ze dingen verbergen en wat betekent dat precies. En als je heel transparant bent, dan weet iedereen waar we het over hebben. Staan we allemaal op dezelfde datapunten. Eigenlijk is het heel belangrijk door het hele traject heen wat je met de mensen doet en door het jaar heen; dat iedereen zo snel mogelijk op het juiste datapunt zit. Zodra je een datapunt hebt waar jij al hier bent en de rest staat nog hier [ver achter], heel frustrerend de mensen bij te halen. Voor*

developments in the undertaking that have an impact that warrants an involvement of the CWC. It is worth noting that some managers pointed out that transparency also includes instances whereby the manager does not know the answer to the works council's question. Especially in the case of share price-sensitive issues such as mergers and acquisitions, managers indicated that they tell their works council that they currently cannot inform them but will do so at a later stage.[331] Being transparent is also important from a works council perspective. Some interviewees pointed out that is also important to inform the management about meetings with supervisory board members[332] and to bring issues to the attention of the management in a timely manner as well.[333] Another important aspect of transparency and openness is the possibility to regain agility and competitiveness as corporation. One manager pointed out that by sharing information early and in an informal manner, the decision-making process could be accelerated and decisions could be adopted quicker.[334] This saves the MNC resources and may give it a competitive advantage due to a quicker response to developments in the market.

The advantage of such a transparent approach lies mainly in the fact that all stakeholders are not surprised by (intended) decisions and are involved in the decision-making process as soon as is possible. At the same time, such a high degree of transparency and openness requires trust in the consultation partner and constructive dialogue. These factors will be discussed in greater detail below.

---

die mensen ook, die voelen zich steeds achter gesteld. Dus probeer ik steeds zo veel mogelijk en zo kort mogelijk cyclisch met die mensen te spreken zodat ze bij jou, in jouw referentiekader zitten hoe de wereld hier voorstaat in [het concern]".

331 See *inter alia* interview 10:22: "*Ik zit er heel simpel in. Er zijn helemaal geen lastige onderwerpen, want wij hebben in principe niks te verbergen. Wij nemen onze beslissingen transparant en op basis van feiten – hopelijk. En wij hoeven het ook niet overal over eens te zijn, dat mag. Maar ik vind wel dat als je de OR serieus neemt, dan moet je ze ook gewoon goed informeren. En goed informeren kan dus ook betekenen: "ik weet het niet". Er wordt vaak verondersteld dat wij alles weten, maar dat is ook niet zo. Of ik weet het wel, maar ik mag het je nog niet zeggen. Maar dat schept dan wel te verplichting dat zodra ik het wel mag zeggen, dat ook communiceer*"; and interview 5:36: "[...] *wat we doen is dat we dan op zondag hebben we [de] eerste sessie met de cor, waarbij we ze dus zeggen van dit is wat we gaan presenteren morgen. Dit is koersgevoelig dus mondje dicht en vanaf 7:30 uur wordt het bekendgemaakt en dat doen we ook met de bestuurders van de vakorganisaties, dus we hebben twee sessies. Zo gaan we daarmee om. Ze weten het van tevoren*".

332 Interviews 19:20, 22:10 and 40:32.

333 Interview 39:10.

334 Interview 18:21: "*Dus uiteindelijk is een Wet op de ondernemingsraden is toch gewoon een bureaucratisch ding, die in de huidige – als je eenmaal zo groot bent dat je zo'n COR moet hebben – dan heb je eigenlijk een rem gekregen. Je kan niet meer agile zijn als een klein bedrijf wat wel; die daar geen last van heeft. Die op deelgebieden jou zo uit kan manoeuvreren. Je zit hier nog zes weken te praten, nog twee weken, nog vier weken te schrijven [...]. En het probleem is niet opgelost en het heeft wel 2 tot 3, 4 of 5 maanden geld gekost. En je bent je opportuniteit misschien kwijt. Dus die tijd van beslissing nemen, die inkorten door met name zo veel mogelijk informatie te delen [...] die is enorm belangrijk. Als je dat niet doet, dan heb je echt een probleem in je besluitvorming naar voren toe*".

3.7.2 Trust and ensuring confidentiality

An important pre-requisite to transparency and openness is trust and the handling of confidential information with integrity. Given the repetitiveness of consultation procedures, trust between the stakeholders should be created over time and on the basis of fruitful negotiations. Fruitful negotiations do not necessarily mean that both management and the works council must be in agreement on the course of action to be taken. But the negotiations are, rather, to be conducted in mutual respect and with useful input from the works council.[335] Starting such fruitful negotiations for the first time can be problematic due to the lack of previous positive consultation experiences, as one management[336] and one works council interviewee[337] pointed out. Once the established employee participation process has been repeatedly applied in practice, both management and works council representatives reported that in times of significant disagreement on an issue, this did not cause the relationship to become adversely affected.[338]

Maintaining mutual trust is therefore of paramount importance, especially with regard to confidential information. One management interviewee noted that recently confidential information had been leaked by a member of the works council. The management then subsequently decided not to inform the works council as extensively as before and to limit the involvement to the legal minimum stipulated in the WCA.[339] In the overwhelming majority of responses on this issue, however, managers indicated that confidential information was not leaked by their works council.[340] The label 'confidential information' should, on the other hand, not be misused by the management to prevent the works council from effectively participating in the decision-making process. Some

335 See for instance interview 9:22: "*dat was ook mij eerste punt: ik wil dat het wederzijds respectvol is, naar beide kanten. Onzinverhalen krijg je ook net zo hard terug en we moeten wel serieus met elkaar omgaan. [...] Respect bouw je niet op door te zeggen: "ik ben de baas." [...] Respect bouw je op doordat het wederzijds respect is, maar dat ook men respect voor je heeft vanwege je kennis, ervaring, maar ook je handelen*".

336 Interview 36:12: "*toen we op een gegeven moment ook veel discussies kregen over, want daar is de wet natuurlijk helemaal niet duidelijk over, wat is belangrijk. [...] Daar dachten ze [in een vestiging] heel anders over dan hoe wij daarover dachten als bestuurders. En we hebben dus best wel een keer met de koppen tegen elkaar geslagen van wat moeten we hier nou mee. [...]En toen hebben gezegd [...] [w]e parkeren even discussie van wat belangrijk is en we spreken af: we nemen jullie mee in de grote en de kleine wijzigingen of het belangrijk is of niet dat label halen we even ervan af. Dat kan alleen en dat is ook een beetje risico nemen, dat kan alleen als we vanuit kunnen uitgaan dat wij elkaar vertrouwen. [...] En dat jullie eerlijk en oprecht zijn in de behandeling daarvan. [...] En dan moet je zeggen ik vertrouw jou en ik weet helemaal niet of jij wel te vertrouwen ben. [...] En dat is denk ik heel erg goed gegaan. Waardoor je inderdaad dat label – is iets adviesplichtig of niet – voorkomt. En we hebben gewoon afgesproken dan zetten we dat in een memo*".

337 Interview 8:34: "*Dat vertrouwen moet groeien, en hoe constructiever je als beide partijen erin zit, en hoe meer ervaring je krijgt binnen het proces, hoe makkelijker dat ook gaat. Moet ik eerlijk bekennen*".

338 Interview 22:27.

339 Interview 25:37: "*Het vertrouwen is wel een paar keer geschaad wat mij betreft. Daar hebben we ze ook op aangesproken. En dan spreken we niet een persoon aan maar we spreken iedereen aan. En dat [...] heeft ons ook doen besluiten om bepaalde informatie niet meer te geven. Heel bewust vanuit de bestuurder*".

340 Interviews 32:14, 38:9, 39:31, 40:28, 42:12, 43:7, 45:7

works councils indicated in the interviews that an embargo is placed on all information that they receive from the management. Such practices hinder effective employee involvement, because works council members may not speak to employees of units concerned about the issue at hand.[341] Such non-disclosure agreements can also create tensions within the works council, if some members receive information while others do not.[342]

Another aspect is that mutual trust should also not be misinterpreted by making decisions behind closed doors between, for instance, the chairperson of the works council and the CEO.[343] Also in this regard, transparency should prevail and all (intended) decisions should be communicated to at least two or more works council members. One practical solution is to always have informal meetings between the executive committee of the works council and the manager in question.

3.7.3 Taking the works council seriously and valuing its input

Aside from trust and the handling of confidential information, taking the consultation partner seriously is another important pre-requisite for effective participation. Being taken seriously and whether the input given is valued, are factors that are not measurable or quantifiable, but are nevertheless important for successful employee involvement. And irrespective of the level of training – some works councils predominantly consist of blue-collar workers whereas other are primarily comprised of white-collar representatives – can the person concerned sense whether he or she is being taken seriously.[344] When implementing a process-oriented consultation process whereby the works council is involved at an early stage, its input is regarded as valuable by the management. This in turn shows that valuing the input of the works council and considering it as being of

341 Interview 21:12: "*Het verdedigingsmiddel is altijd van dit is gevoelige informatie omdat we beursgenoteerd zijn. En in negen van de 10 gevallen betwijfel ik het. [...]. Men gaat er tegenwoordig wat soepeler mee om. Als dat echt heel gevoelige informatie is, net als met fusies en overnames, dan word ik er wel bij betrokken als voorzitter. Maar dan moet ik dus onder embargo tekenen onder geheimhouding tot een bepaalde periode*".

342 Interview 48:12: "*[...] we hebben toen een NDA, een nondisclosure agreement moeten tekenen. Er hebben een aantal mensen heeft daar moeite mee gehad. Een aantal mensen was verrast, verbaast dat een aantal medezeggenschappers, waaronder ik dus meer informatie had dan de rest. Maar ik had wel de NDA getekend dus ik heb het ook op dat moment niet verder gedeeld. En dat heeft ook intern wel tot een stuk discussie geleid van hoe kan het dat jij het wel weet en wij niet*".

343 Interview 9:19: "*als je een-tweetjes gebruikt – weet je wat ik doe met jou: ik moet iets met jouw hebben en daarna mag je iets van mij hebben. Zo bedoel ik het niet en dat zie ik ook. En dat vind ik dodelijk, want op het moment waardoor een MZ op de zeggenschapsstoel gaat zitten – je kan mekaar bijna blackmailen. En dat is de dood in de pot*".

344 See for instance interview 10:33: "*het gaat om authenticiteit. Neem je ze nou echt serieus of zit je daarbij en denk je: dat moet, maar liever niet. En ik denk dat voelen mensen haarscherp aan, daar hoef je geen hoge opleiding voor te hebben. Je weet precies wanneer je serieus genomen wordt en wanneer niet, dat voel je. Maar dat geldt met alles. Als iemand zich niet serieus genomen voelt, dan wordt het altijd een stuk minder productief. Dus ik denk dat dat altijd wel, tenminste vanuit mijn kant, gelukt is*".

added value are the foundations for an efficient decision-making process. The results of this qualitative analysis are not quantifiable nor representative of employee participation in multinationals in general. But a trend between many soft skills and the examples of good practice discussed in this chapter can nevertheless be observed. The use of informal meetings and the application of consultation practices that go beyond the statutory minimum were frequently reported in interviews in which also transparency, openness, trust, correct handling confidential of information and a positive stance of the management vis-à-vis the works council were present.[345] While one cannot infer from these trends that a presence of these soft skills is necessary in all cases, one can nevertheless assume that without a certain level of transparency and trust, the implementation of the examples of good practice discussed in this chapter would be impossible.

3.7.4 Relationship management and constructivism of the management and works council

Alongside taking works councils seriously, several respondents indicated that a consensus-seeking attitude and striving towards a constructive working relationship were also important factors.[346]

Given the culture of the Rhineland-model whereby the stakeholders in the undertaking are working together in the best interest of the undertaking, many interviewees reported that a constructive attitude was important. The Dutch polder model often leads to a less formalistic and consensus-seeking attitude of the consultation partners.[347] An approach based on facts is, according to the interviewees, more successful from a works council's perspective than a formalistic approach solely based on statutory rights. Because of the works council's role as sounding board for the shop floor-level, an approach based on factual knowledge improves its position in the decision-making process due to the added value of its input for the management.[348] Such a less formalistic approach also avoids a

345 The code co-occurrence (i.e., both the example of good practice and the soft skills are in some way associated with each other and coded by the author in the analysis of the interview transcripts) was analysed in ATLAS.ti; see chapter II for a detailed overview of the methodology that was applied in this study.

346 Interviews 10:10, 11:17, 12:14, 14:21, 22:22, 23:4, 24:11, 27:20 and 32:20.

347 See for instance interview 23:4: "*ik kies niet een oppositiemodel, maar proberen om er samen met de bestuurder uit te komen. Dus laagdrempelig alles te houden ondanks dat je misschien heftig het niet met elkaar eens bent. Moet je toch op een prettige manier met elkaar kunnen blijven communiceren. [...] En in die situatie kun je op zich veel meer betekenen, [dan] dat je de harde lijn kiest en dat je met allerlei advocaten en procedures in aanraking komt. Dat is eigenlijk een beetje die insteek zoals ik die de laatste jaren gevolgd heb. En ik denk ook dat dat het meest succesvol mee bereikt hebben, dan dat we de harde lijn gevolgd hebben*".

348 Interview 27:20: "*Dus we proberen niet in die valkuil te stappen waarin we het heel formalistisch aanpakken. Dat hebben we namelijk in het verleden gedaan. Voordat je het weet sta je inderdaad bij de rechter. We hebben nooit letterlijk bij de rechter gestaan maar wij hebben wel twee verzoekschriften ingediend. Tijdens de fusie. En dan is het heel moeilijk om weer terug te komen. Dus wat je probeert te doen is juist omdat die kennis heel goed is. Dus juist omdat we weten wat onze rechten zijn. Is het heel makkelijk*

discussion of whether or not an issue falls within the scope of the works councils' consultation right. Instead of a discussion on whether or not the consultation right is applicable, works councils in some multinationals give their advice regardless of the applicable legal framework. As was discussed above in section 3.2.3, a memo structure instead of formal advice can be used for such situations. It is important however, that an agreement on such a less formalistic consultation procedure is laid down beforehand – for instance by means of a covenant (article 32 of the WCA) – to avoid discussions on the applicable consultation procedure.

4 *Concluding remarks: Towards process-oriented employee participation*

A multitude of examples of good practice were discussed in this chapter. The structure of this chapter may suggest that the seven sections on information, consultation, facilities, supervisory board relations, professionalism of the works council, EWC relations and soft skills are distinct from each other; but while the seven clusters were discussed independently of each other for the sake of clarity, these clusters should be regarded as one network of good practice examples. Many of the practices are applied together in practice and some – such as the philosophy of early access to information and informal consultations at an early stage – are pre-requisites for other examples of good practice. At the same time, these practices are not mutually exclusive and the list of good practices discussed in this study should not be regarded as being exhaustive. The interviews have shown that it is crucial that the stakeholders involved in the decision-making process operate in a spirit of mutual trust and by applying a transparent employee participation mechanism. Such a mechanism is, in some multinationals, far-developed and has resulted in the implementation of a participation scheme that is based on several consultation phases instead of one (see section 3.2.6).[349]

The use of process-oriented consultation models especially – which are agreed upon in advance between management and works council – are noteworthy examples of good practice. Both management and works council decide on a time-efficient and effective participation process, which is subsequently applied in the consultation procedures that follow.[350] The timely and comprehensive involvement of works councils is often a major issue in multinational corporations. The issues of timely works council involvement in

om tegenover [de CEO] te zitten. Dat is natuurlijk een man. En als hij iets wil en hij wil dat het per se op die manier, dat je gewoon inderdaad gewoon oprecht… eigenlijk gewoon blijft zitten. Laten hem uitrazen. En uiteindelijk leg je dan heel rustig uit waarom je denkt dat het niet op die manier kan. En dat is dan niet omdat je vindt omdat de WOR dat zegt. Maar omdat je merkt dat in de praktijk, dus naar de medewerkers toe, dat wat op die manier gedaan wil worden niet op de manier kan. Maar daar staan ze dan voor open".

349 According to article 25 of the WCA.

350 See also section 4 in chapter VI.

particular – while swift decision-making and flexibility are crucial from a management perspective – have led to the adoption of process-oriented consultation models. In the pre-consultation phase, information is shared informally and can the works council can establish a working group and give input on the matter at hand, which can then be incorporated in the management's formal request for advice. These examples of good practice are described by interviewees from both management and works council as being very beneficial for the decision-making process due to quicker decision-making and better substantiated decisions. One manager noted that by involving the works council very early in the decision-making process, the formal consultation procedure was completed much quicker. And even more importantly, he noted that while the management often prepares decisions for the month, it is unrealistic to assume that the works council can deliver its advice in a fraction of that time after being informed and consulted on the matter.[351] Therefore, by involving the works council at the earliest possible moment, this speeds up rather than slows down the decision-making process.[352]

Such early participation of the works councils requires a large degree of professionalism and the provision of the necessary facilities that were discussed in sections 3.3 and 3.5 above. If the works council wants to give input on a range of topics, the use of working groups or project-based employee representatives has proven to be a successful practice in several multinationals.

351 Interview 45:5: "*Zodanig dat als je uiteindelijk komt tot de uiteindelijke request for advice, of voor consent, dat je eigenlijk al het hele traject met elkaar doorlopen hebt. Ik heb geleerd dat mensen die ergens over mee moeten denken en zich een beeld ergens van moeten vormen, die hebben tijd nodig om, zoals het als ik het altijd maar zeg, alle zijpaden die je inslaat met betrekking tot het testen van een bepaalde richting, en daar hoort bij dat je ook kan meanderen over ja maar, waarom hebben we niet dat gekozen. Je loopt vaak in een valkuil dat je als bestuurder met je team die hele gedachte piste al hebt doorlopen en dat vervolgens bij de medezeggenschap of for that matter bij medewerkers of bij andere stakeholders neerlegt. En verwacht dat, ze hebben dat al even in 1/10 van de tijd ook kunnen doen, en dat werkt natuurlijk niet altijd zo. Dus hoe eerder je mensen betrekt bij het nadenken over dingen en ze de gelegenheid geeft om dezelfde gedachtepistes te maken en te zeggen nou dan zullen we dan weggetje eens inslaan, dat loopt toch dood, terug naar de hoofdweg, andere weggetje inslaan, hé, dit lijkt wel zinvol, zullen wij dat een nieuwe hoofdweg maken*".

352 Interview 45:22: "*Nee, ik vind dat de ondernemingsraad het niet vertraagd. Maar dat doen ze ook alleen maar omdat ze in een redelijk vroegtijdig stadium, denk ik althans, worden geïnformeerd over wat we willen. Als je dat niet doet, tenminste zo zou ik als OR lid ook zijn, ja hallo, je legt me nu zo'n pakket met informatie neer en je moet binnen een week een antwoord hebben. [...] Dus dan loop je het risico dat je daar bedacht had dat je binnen drie of zes weken uit zou zijn en dat gaat in een keer drie maanden duren. Dan vind ik niet dat je daar de OR al teveel de schuld van moet geven, dat ligt dan ook bij jezelf vind ik*".

Chapter VI: A bird's eye view on Dutch works councils in MNCs

Main findings based on the qualitative and quantitative results of this study

1 Introduction

This aim of this study was to examine the position of Dutch works councils in multinational corporations. The foregoing chapters addressed the position of Dutch works councils in MNCs from a legal dogmatic, quantitative and qualitative perspective. Based on the findings in these chapters, this chapter focuses on the main findings of this analysis. By taking a bird's eye view, the chapter will address three main aspects.

Firstly, the main differences between Dutch and foreign MNCs, based on the foregoing analysis, will be discussed (section 2 below). These findings are noteworthy in themselves, given the fact that such differences are but one explanatory factor for the potential differences of positions of works councils in Dutch and foreign MNCs. These differences are also relevant for the second and third main findings that will be discussed in this chapter.

The second main aspect discussed thereafter concerns the position of Dutch works councils within the corporate governance structure of the respective MNC (section 3 below). This includes the presence of a supervisory board as a prerequisite, the composition of the supervisory board (including the works council's recommendation rights) and the presence of supervisory board members at consultation meetings. An important link lies here with the Dutch Corporate Governance Code of 2016 (hereinafter CGC 2016). Based on both the quantitative as well as the qualitative findings, it will be analysed what the role of the works council regarding the corporate governance structure of the MNC is. It will be further analysed whether and how the influence of the works council can be improved based on the examples of good practice that were collected in this study as well as in light of the recent jurisprudence of the Enterprise Chamber of the Amsterdam Court of Appeals (*Ondernemingskamer*).

Thirdly, the concept of a process-oriented employee participation will be discussed in the final section of this chapter (section 4 below). Based on the empirical and legal dogmatic analysis that was carried out in the previous chapters, it will be examined how far a process of employee participation can be shaped within MNCs. Based on the examples of good practice, this section will address the importance of not only using works council rights individually, but also the importance of agreeing with the management on an employee participation process that is applied consistently throughout the corporation.

2 MAIN DIFFERENCES BETWEEN DUTCH AND FOREIGN MNCs BASED ON THE QUANTITATIVE ANALYSIS

The first part of this chapter will discuss the main differences between the position of Dutch works councils in Dutch and foreign MNCs, based on the quantitative analysis that was carried out in chapter IV.[1] The aim of the quantitative analysis was, on the one hand, to examine the application of the legislative framework in practice. One the other hand, it was examined whether divergent trends between the sub-samples of Dutch and foreign MNCs could be observed. Thereby, the findings of Looise and Drucker, who examined the effects of internationalisation on the position of Dutch works councils, were taken as starting point.[2] They concluded that "*the further away the company is from the national context, from national concern to Dutch MNE and to foreign MNE, the less influence the works council will have and the less serious its role will be*".[3] An effect on the position of works councils in foreign MNCs compared to Dutch MNCs should also be visible in this study. Indeed, a number of differences between Dutch and foreign MNCs could be observed in this study, which will be discussed in this section. A distinction is made between Dutch and foreign MNCs, as was outlined in chapter II.

2.1 Level of employee participation and the position of the consultation partner

From the outset, it must be noted that top-holdings (i.e., the general controlling undertaking of the company group) of foreign MNCs are further away from Dutch employee participation. This is unsurprising insofar as foreign MNCs do not fall within the scope of the Dutch employee participation regime, which includes *inter alia* the Works Council Act and the structure regime. In light of the territoriality principle, Dutch employee participation is not located at the highest level in foreign MNCs. This is also reflected in the results of this study. In Dutch MNCs, works councils are more often located at the level of the central management when compared to foreign MNCs (53,1% in Dutch compared to 31,8% in foreign MNCs, see figure 3.1 in section 3.1 of chapter IV). The level at which the works council is maintained subsequently influences the (choice of) the consultation partner. Dutch works councils have, slightly more often, the CEO of the corporation as their consultation partner (53,1% in Dutch compared to 47,6% in foreign MNCs see

1 The quantitative results were collected according to the methodology that was laid out in chapter II.

2 J.K. Looise and M. Drucker, 'Employee participation in multinational enterprises: The effects of globalisation on Dutch works councils', 24 *Employee Relations* 1 (2002).

3 *Ibid.*, p. 37.

figure 3.2 in section 3.2 of chapter IV). But the difference between Dutch and foreign MNCs is less apparent when it comes to the consultation partner of the works council. Two factors may be contributing to this. First, Dutch multinationals are to a large extent 'internationalised' and do not employ (in most cases) the majority of their workforce within the Netherlands. These multinationals have "outgrown" their home market and are multinational corporations based in the Netherlands rather than Dutch MNCs. Due to the fact that it is possible to detach their international activities from the activities in the Netherlands under the structure regime and in the context of the territoriality principle, employee participation is often limited to the activities of the corporate group in the Netherlands.[4]

When comparing the results regarding the consultation partner of works councils in Dutch and foreign MNCs, one can conclude that in nearly half of the corporations, the CEO is one of the consultation partners of the works council. These results are especially positive for works councils in foreign MNCs. Despite the greater distance between the foreign top-holding and the Dutch subsidiaries of the corporation, these works councils are consulted by the central management. At the same time, these results show that in the other half of cases, employee participation is largely limited to the Dutch activities of the corporate group. Also noteworthy is the fact that in foreign MNCs, 42,9% of the works councils also have a HR-manager as their consultation partner compared to 21,9% of works councils in Dutch MNCs. While it is sometimes argued that Dutch works councils are too often having only HR-managers as their consultation partners, no empirical evidence could be found that supports this argument. It was only in 3,7% of the cases that a HR-manager was the sole consultation partner of the works councils and furthermore, the qualitative results based on the semi-structured interviews did not provide results that could substantiate this claim. These results, however, do not show on which topics works councils are being consulted and whether the works council is consulted by the central management on crucial decisions that fall within the scope of the consultation right (article 25 of the WCA).

A greater difference can be observed when comparing the responses regarding the overall position of the works councils in Dutch and foreign MNCs respectively. In Dutch MNCs, a small majority of works councils (54,5%) reported that their position had not deteriorated as a result of increasing internationalisation or noted that they were undecided on this matter. In foreign MNCs, on the other hand, increasing internationalisation had a greater impact on the position of the works council, according to the responses (60% indicated that their position had deteriorated, see figure 8.1 in section 8.1 of chapter IV). Therefore, works councils in foreign MNCs perceive that their position has deteriorated to a greater extent when compared to respondents from Dutch MNCs. The reasons

4 See section 3.2 in chapter III for an analysis of the structure regime and the possibility to apply the mitigated structure regime.

why works councils in foreign MNCs perceive a greater deterioration of their position is partly due to several factors. A number of these contributing factors will be discussed in the remainder of this section 2.

2.2 *Access to information in Dutch MNCs compared to foreign MNCs*

One crucial aspect for the position of Dutch works councils is that of access to information. Timely access to information in a comprehensive manner was identified as being a crucial prerequisite for effective employee participation.[5] Differences regarding the access to information in general (i.e., does access exist), the timeliness of the access to information and the quality of the information provided could be factors that explain the differences in the position of works councils in Dutch and foreign MNCs respectively.

Works councils have to receive financial and economic information at least twice a year (article 31a of the WCA). No significant differences can be observed between Dutch and foreign MNCs in this regard (see figure 5.16 in section 5.4 of chapter IV). However, two out of three cases where information was only provided once a year were intimated by respondents from foreign MNCs. When examining the responses concerning the access to information on the holding structures in MNCs (*zeggenschapsverhoudingen*), the differences are more salient (see figure 5.19 in section 5.5 of chapter IV). 68,2% of works councils in Dutch MNCs responded that they receive such information and 13,6% indicated that they do not receive such information (18,2% unknown). In foreign MNCs, 50% of works council representatives responded that they received the relevant information (25% unknown). But 25% of works councils in foreign MNCs indicated that they do not have access to information on the holding structure within their corporate group. While these results are not statistically significant, works councils in foreign MNCs reported twice as often that they do not receive such information in comparison to their counterparts in Dutch MNCs.

Access to information on the holding structure in corporate groups, however, is an important prerequisite for the works councils to effectively participate in the decision-making process. Such information is also a necessary prerequisite for the identification of participation rights, such as the question of whether or not an undertaking, for which the works council is maintained, is the subsidiary of a Dutch or foreign company. If an undertaking is the subsidiary of a Dutch (sub-) holding, the structure regime may be applicable on the level of the (sub-) holding rather than the undertaking for which the works council is maintained. In the case of foreign undertakings (for instance, a UK Limited or German GmbH) whereby a Dutch works council is maintained for the

5 See sections 5.4 and 5.5 in chapter IV and section 3.1 in chapter V.

Dutch establishment, the question arises as to whether the structure regime is applicable. In light of the limitative list of company forms to which the structure regime is applicable (*naamloze vennootschap, besloten vennootschap* or *coöperatieve verenigingen*), it must be concluded that the regime would not be applicable to foreign company forms. Information on the corporation's holding structure are therefore vital for works councils in MNCs to determine their rights and to effectively participate in the decision-making process. The enforcement of the information right[6] (that was introduced in 2013) of works councils is therefore a point of concern, because only half of the works councils in foreign MNCs have access to such information and one in four indicated that such information is not provided. Thus, for works councils in foreign MNCs, but certainly also for works councils in Dutch MNCs that do not receive this information (13,6%), they would certainly benefit from greater enforcement of the right enshrined in article 31(2)(d-e) of the WCA.

In light of the foregoing analysis, it can be concluded that access to information is, in the majority of cases, satisfactory in light of the applicable legal framework. The access is slightly better for works councils in Dutch MNCs compared to foreign MNCs, especially regarding information on the holding structures (*zeggenschapsverhoudingen*) of the corporate group. But no significant differences regarding the general access to economic and financial information (at least twice a year) can be observed. In 11,9% of the cases, however, access to information is less frequent than the statutory minimum of twice a year, which in itself is a point of concern.

The qualitative analysis that was carried out on the basis of the semi-structured interviews has furthermore shown that a large number of examples of good practice (23 in total on information access with 144 interview quotations) have been developed on this matter (see section 3.1 in chapter V). But the qualitative analysis has also shown that especially for information on the group strategy and major business decisions are, in some MNCs, not shared with the works council.[7] While such business decisions may not immediately impact the Dutch undertaking and therefore may not fall within the scope of the works councils' information and consultation rights,[8] such information is nevertheless of great importance in order for the works council to participate in the decision-making process.

6 *Wet van 26 juni 2013 tot aanpassing van de Wet op de ondernemingsraden in verband met wijziging van de financiering van het scholingssysteem voor leden van de ondernemingsraad en enkele andere wijzigingen van deze wet, Stb.* 2013, 296.

7 Interviews 21, 29, 31, 38 and 41; see section 3.1.2 in chapter V.

8 See, for instance, the VLM case in which the Enterprise Chamber held that the worldwide strategy does not fall within the scope of article 25 of the WCA and is therefore not included in the ambit of 'attribution of an intended decision'; see also section 4 in chapter III.

2.3 *Access to and use of consultation rights in Dutch MNCs compared to foreign MNCs*

Consultation rights are also at the core of the employee participation framework, alongside information rights. An inherent tension between a Dutch works councils' consultation rights and the corporate holding-structure exists in MNCs, as was concluded in chapter III above.[9] This tension arises in light of the territoriality principle and given the fact that decisions are taken at a higher level within corporate groups, while consultation rights only apply for (intended) decisions that have an impact on the Dutch undertaking. Differences between Dutch and foreign MNCs can therefore be observed with regard to the access to and use of consultation rights at the level of the Dutch subsidiary of the MNCs for the period 2012-2014.[10]

Differences concerning the frequency of consultations can be observed on four main topics, which fall within the scope of the article 25 WCA consultation right (see figure 5.6 in section 5.2 of chapter IV). Firstly, major organisational changes (article 25(1)(e) of the WCA) are more frequently the subject of consultation in foreign MNCs (85%) compared to Dutch MNCs (66,7%). Secondly, the termination of operations of the enterprise or a significant part thereof (article 25(1)(c) of the WCA) is more often on the agenda in consultation meetings in foreign MNCs (70%) compared to Dutch MNCs (47,6%). The opposite can be observed for consultations on mergers and acquisitions of another undertaking (article 25(1)(b) of the WCA). Works councils in Dutch MNCs are more often consulted on these intended transactions (47,6%) compared to foreign MNCs (20%). Finally, works councils in Dutch MNCs are more often consulted on the future strategy of the corporation and trends (76,2%) compared to works councils in foreign MNCs (35%). It is noteworthy that the results on the topic 'future strategy of the corporation and trends' are statistically significant.[11] While the results for the other three categories are not statistically significant, the responses nevertheless give an indication of the differences between Dutch and foreign MNCs regarding the consultation of their works council.

Two observations can be made with regard to these results. Firstly, the fact that works councils in foreign MNCs are more frequently consulted on organisational changes and terminations of (parts of) the undertaking, can be an indication of reorganizations and downsizings in the MNCs. One possible explanation could be that foreign MNCs could have been more severely affected after the financial crisis of 2007 and the subsequent

9 See section 1.4.2 in chapter III.

10 See section 5.2 in chapter IV for a detailed overview.

11 See a detailed analysis of the statistical significance of the results in section 5.2 in chapter IV.

recession that occurred in the EU[12] that took place during the execution of the quantitative analysis (2012-2014), including the Netherlands.[13] Another potential explanation could be that foreign MNCs undertook more organisational changes than their Dutch counterparts without any apparent reasons. A third possible explanation could indeed be that foreign MNCs consulted their works council more often on such reorganizations and downsizings, although this possibility is less likely. Secondly, works councils in Dutch MNCs are significantly more often consulted on the future strategy of the corporation and trends compared to their counterparts in foreign MNCs. Foreign MNCs may take decisions on the corporate strategy abroad and – due to the lack of a direct impact of such a decision, albeit being of great importance for the Dutch subsidiary – without the legal obligation to consult the Dutch works council. But also 'international' Dutch MNCs do not necessarily have to consult their Dutch works council on such strategy changes. In international corporate groups that employ more than half of their workforce outside of the Netherlands, the so-called mitigated structure regime (*verlicht structuurregime*) can be applied.[14] Under this mitigated regime, the Dutch parent company (i.e., the international holding company of the group) can be exempted from applying the regime, but instead the duty to comply with the structure regime applies to the Dutch sub-holding of the company group. This splitting of the international activities of the group from the obligation to apply the structure regime is referred to as 'Netherlands construction' (*Nederland-constructie*).[15] Therefore, Dutch MNCs can also – if the mitigated regime is applied – take decisions on the worldwide corporate strategy without having to consult their works council. Nevertheless, an overwhelming majority of works councils in Dutch MNCs are consulted on this topic (76,2%), which positively contributes towards the position of these works councils in the decision-making process.

---

12 See *inter alia* European Commission Directorate-General for Economic and Financial Affairs, 'European Economic Forecast – Autumn 2011', <http://ec.europa.eu/economy_finance/publications/european_economy/2011/pdf/ee-2011-6_en.pdf> (last accessed 11 July 2017), p. 1-5; European Commission Directorate-General for Economic and Financial Affairs, 'European Economic Forecast – Autumn 2012', <http://ec.europa.eu/economy_finance/publications/european_economy/2012/pdf/ee-2012-7_en.pdf> (last accessed 11 July 2017), p. 1-5; European Commission Directorate-General for Economic and Financial Affairs, 'European Economic Forecast – Autumn 2013', <http://ec.europa.eu/economy_finance/publications/european_economy/2013/pdf/ee7_en.pdf> (last accessed 11 July 2017), p. 1-5.

13 Centraal Bureau voor de Statistiek (CBS), *De Nederlandse economie 2011* (Den Haag/Heerlen, 2012), p. 3; Centraal Bureau voor de Statistiek (CBS), *De Nederlandse economie 2012* (Den Haag/Heerlen, 2013), p. 3 and 8 et seq.; Centraal Bureau voor de Statistiek (CBS), *De Nederlandse economie 2013* (Den Haag/Heerlen, 2014), p. 3 and 8 et seq.; Centraal Bureau voor de Statistiek (CBS), *Nederland in 2014: Een economisch overzicht* (Den Haag/Heerlen, 2015), p. 3.

14 Article 2:153(3)(b)/2:263(3)(b) of the DCC: if the activities of the top-holding are "restricted exclusively or almost exclusively to the management and financing of group companies and of its or their participating interests in other legal persons, provided that the employees in service of the [c]orporation and the group companies jointly in majority work outside the Netherlands".

15 See *inter alia* M. Holtzer, *De invloed van werknemers op de strategie van de vennootschap* (Kluwer, Deventer 2014).

One explanation lies in the corporate culture of Dutch MNCs, which may be more consensus-oriented in light of the so-called "Polder-model" in comparison to the Anglo-Saxon enlightened shareholder-model.[16] Another explanation lies in the use of covenants (article 32 of the WCA), which can be used to confer additional (consultation) rights on works councils. A strong difference between Dutch and foreign MNCs can be observed concerning the use of covenants. Covenants are used in 54,8% of the Dutch MNCs compared to 27,3% in foreign MNCs (see also 5.14 in section 5.3 of chapter IV).[17] In the majority of covenants (54,4%), additional information rights on international matters and consultation rights have been agreed upon. Therefore, a paradoxical situation can be observed: while in foreign MNCs decisions are more often taken at a higher level in the group and fall outside the scope of Dutch employee participation rights, covenants are used less-often in these foreign MNCs.[18] This, in turn, could be one explanation for the difference of positions of works councils in Dutch and foreign MNCs. Dutch works councils may have more influence on the decision-making process due to the additional rights conferred upon them by means of a covenant.

The significant difference between Dutch and foreign MNCs concerning the use of covenants can be explained with recourse to various explanations. Dutch MNCs often apply the mitigated structure-regime, which splits the international and Dutch activities, and, in essence, limits the structure regime to the Dutch activities of the group. By means of a covenant, some of the rights of Dutch works councils in Dutch MNCs are regained following the application of the mitigated regime, as was indicated by the responses on the rights conferred by covenants. In 50% of the covenants, consultation meetings with the CEO are agreed upon (see also figure 5.15 in section 5.3 of chapter IV). Foreign MNCs, on the other hand, often do not have a similar system of employee participation (with the exception of German MNCs). Due to the lack of familiarity with employee participation in the home country of the MNCs (for instance Anglo-Saxon MNCs), granting additional rights through covenants is even less likely to occur. These factors could contribute to the reluctance of foreign MNCs to conclude covenants with their Dutch works council, which may explain the difference in results.

Another factor could be the time available for the works councils' advice. Article 25 of the WCA expressly stipulates that the advice of the works council must be sought at a time when it can still significantly affect the decision that is to be taken (article 25(2) of the WCA).[19] The timing of the consultation and the time available for the works councils' advice is therefore an important factor in this regard. The responses to the questionnaire

16 Many of the foreign MNCs included in the quantitative sample are from an Anglo-Saxon background; see figure 2.3 in section 2.2 of chapter IV.

17 With the difference of results being statistically significant; see section 5.3 in chapter IV for a detailed analysis.

18 See also section 5.3 in chapter IV.

19 See also section 5.2.3 in chapter IV.

show that sufficient time for the councils' advice is available in the large majority of cases (83,3%, see also figure 5.10 in section 5.2.3 of chapter IV). But some difference can also be observed in this regard when comparing the results for Dutch and foreign MNCs. In Dutch MNCs, one in ten works councils (9,1%) reported to not have sufficient time available for preparing and giving its advice. In foreign MNCs, on the other hand, one in four respondents (25%) indicated that their works councils does not have sufficient time to render its advice. While these results are not statistically significant, they nevertheless show that a greater tension between decisions taken at an international level and timely works council advice exist in foreign compared to Dutch MNCs. The development of the concepts of attribution of decisions (*toerekening*) and co-entrepreneurship (*medeondernemerschap*) by the Enterprise Chamber of the Amsterdam Court of Appeals (*Ondernemingskamer*) must be mentioned in this context. The cases on attribution and co-entrepreneurship highlight the tension between the application of employee participation rights under Dutch law in an increasingly international context, while at the same time the actual decision-making power is situated outside of the Netherlands.[20] It can be positively noted that a large number of examples of good practice on informal consultation, which often takes place prior to the formal consultation procedure, are developed in foreign MNCs.[21] Whether these examples of good practice have been developed in response to the lack of time for the advice of works councils, cannot be determined due to the anonymous nature of the questionnaire responses. Here, future research is necessary in order to determine whether these practices are effective in overcoming the reported issues.

Finally, the presence of and coordination with a European works council (EWC) can be an influential factor for the position of Dutch works councils in the context of the consultation process. The percentage of MNCs maintaining a EWCs is considerably higher in foreign (80%) compared to Dutch MNCs (59,1%).[22] The EWC is often maintained at the highest possible level within the MNC or at the level of the EU regional headquarters, with two-thirds of EWCs being maintained at the highest possible level in the EU (see figure 7.2 in section 7 of chapter IV). In Dutch MNCs, the EWC is maintained at the central management level in 84,6% of the cases compared to 56,3% in foreign MNCs. But an additional 31,3% of EWC are maintained at the level of the regional (EU) headquarters of the foreign MNC. Due to the fact that these EWCs are often maintained at a higher level within the MNC than compared to the Dutch (central) works council, it is important that there is a good communication channel between both works councils. This exchange of information was more positively assessed by respondents in foreign MNCs

20 See section 4 in chapter III for a detailed analysis.

21 15 out of the 19 MNCs where examples of good practice on informal consultation were reported, are foreign MNCs; see section 3.2.3 in chapter V for a detailed overview of the reported examples of good practice.

22 See figure 7.1 in section 7 of chapter IV.

(see figure 7.6 in section 7 of chapter IV). 68,8% of the respondents in foreign MNCs held positive views regarding the exchange of information between their works council and the EWC. In Dutch MNCs, on the other hand, 53,9% assessed the information exchange as being positive. Furthermore, 38,5% of the respondents in Dutch MNCs were either 'dissatisfied' or 'completely dissatisfied' with the information exchange mechanism. In foreign MNCs, 12,5% were 'dissatisfied' with no respondents being 'completely dissatisfied'. These results show that in Dutch MNCs especially, the information exchange is not regarded as being satisfactory, which should be a point of attention in light of the additional information channels that a EWC could provide. The results are consistent with the responses to the added value that the EWC has for works council members (see figure 7.7 in section 7 of chapter IV). Employee representatives in Dutch MNCs overwhelmingly do not see the EWC as being supportive of their work (69,3%) and only 23,1% regarded the EWC as being supportive (7,7% undecided). In foreign MNCs, responses were divided with 43,8% of the respondents regarding the EWC as supportive and 43,8% regarding it as not-supportive (12,5% undecided).

When comparing the responses on the EWC as an information channel and its supportive role, one can conclude that EWCs are overall regarded as more beneficial to works councils in foreign MNCs. The lack of an effective information exchange between Dutch works councils and the EWC, as well as the lack of a supportive role, could therefore be aspects that potentially weaken the position of works councils in Dutch MNCs. But given the limitations of this study's scope, future research on the relationship between national (Dutch) and European works councils is necessary in order to investigate and further understand these aspects, as was concluded in section 7 of chapter IV.

2.4 *Presence of supervisory board members in consultation meetings*

Another determinant for the position of Dutch works councils is the presence of supervisory board members at consultation meetings. In this paragraph, a number of differences between Dutch and foreign MNCs will be discussed that are of specific relevance to the works councils' position in the consultation process. The position of works councils within the corporate governance structure of MNCs will be discussed in more detail in section 3 below.

Members of the Dutch supervisory board must be present at consultation meetings on the general operation of the undertaking (article 24(2) of the WCA), which must take place at least twice a year.[23] In addition, one or more members of the supervisory board

23 In this section, the supervisory board of the Dutch undertaking, for which the works council is maintained, is meant. The supervisory board of (foreign) topholdings outside the Netherlands is not subject to Dutch law in light of the territoriality principle and therefore also falls outside the scope of this study.

should be present for the discussion of a proposed decision at the consultation meeting pursuant to article 25(4) of the WCA. Therefore, a clear obligation exists for supervisory board members to be present during consultation meetings on the general operation of the Dutch undertaking and formal consultation meetings on matters falling within the scope of article 25(1) of the WCA. It is therefore striking that in the majority of cases, supervisory board members are 'never' present at consultation meetings (see Figure 2.1 below).[24]

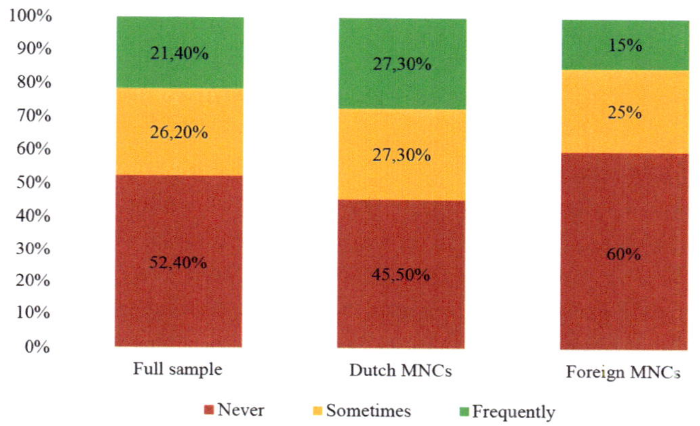

Figure 2.1 *Presence of supervisory board members in consultation meetings in MNCs (N = 42); in Dutch (N = 22) and foreign MNCs (N = 20)*

When comparing the responses from Dutch and foreign MNCs, some additional observations can be made. In Dutch MNCs, a large minority of respondents indicated that supervisory board members were 'never' present (45,5%). In foreign MNCs, on the other hand, board members were 'never' present in 60% of the cases. Furthermore, one in four respondents in Dutch MNCs indicated that board members were 'frequently' present. In foreign MNCs, one in six respondents (15%) indicated that board members were 'frequently' present. It can therefore be concluded that board members are considerably more often present in Dutch MNCs when compared to their foreign counterparts. But also in Dutch MNCs, in 45,5% of the cases the lack of compliance with the obligation to participate in the consultation meetings was noted.

The presence of supervisory board members at consultations can have a positive influence on the position of the works council in the decision-making process. Yet, only a minority of respondents indicated that contacts with the supervisory board improved the position of their works council (see 4.11 in section 4.2 of chapter IV). It is noteworthy

24 See also section 5.2.2 in chapter IV.

that respondents in foreign MNCs indicated more often that contacts with supervisory board members improved their position. 35% of the respondents in foreign MNCs answered the question in the affirmative and 35% did not see an improvement of their position through contacts with the supervisory board. In Dutch MNCs, only 26,1% indicated that the contacts were beneficial to their position, whereas 52,2% did not see an improvement of their position through the additional contact.

The access to information through the supervisory board, on the contrary, was better in Dutch MNCs (see figure 4.9 in section 4.2 of chapter IV). A majority of 63,6% of respondents in Dutch MNCs reported that better access to information existed via the supervisory board of their corporation. In foreign MNCs, a minority of 40% reported receiving better access to information via the supervisory board with 30% indicating that this was not the case. Moreover, the information access via recommended supervisory board members pursuant to the works councils' enhanced recommendation right was better in Dutch MNCs, although the responses were more divided (see 4.10 in section 4.2 of chapter IV). 39,1% of respondents in Dutch MNCs indicated that information access improved and an equal percentage of respondents indicated that no improvement of access occurred. In foreign MNCs, 25% regarded access to information as being improved and 25% did not regard information access to have improved since the enhanced recommendation.

Therefore, a mixed conclusion can be drawn from the responses. Access to information from the supervisory board as well as an improvement of access to information through the use of the enhanced recommendation right can be observed on the basis of the responses in Dutch MNCs. In foreign MNCs, on the other hand, respondents indicated a greater impact of their contacts with the board on the decision-making process despite the lower ratio of respondents indicating access to information via the supervisory board. One explanation could be that respondents in Dutch and foreign MNCs perceive the impact of the supervisory board on their position in the decision-making process differently. The perception of the supervisory board's role could be a related factor in this regard. Respondents in Dutch MNCs indicated in 43,5% of the cases that the supervisory board has a mediating role in their corporation (see figure 4.12 in section 4.2 of chapter IV). In foreign MNCs, on the other hand, 30% of the respondents perceived the supervisory board as having a mediating role. 30% did not regard it as having a mediating role in both Dutch and foreign MNCs. Therefore, respondents in Dutch MNCs regard the supervisory board, more often than not, as having a mediating role.

Overall, one can conclude that access to information via the supervisory board is greater in Dutch MNCs when compared to foreign MNCs. In Dutch MNCs, supervisory board members are also more frequently present at consultation meetings. It can therefore be concluded that, overall, the position of the works council vis-à-vis the supervisory board is better in Dutch MNCs compared to its foreign counterparts in light of these findings. Another aspect concerns the use of the enhanced recommendation right in Dutch and foreign MNCs. In Dutch MNCs, an overwhelming majority of works councils made use of this right (73,9%) over the last four years,[25] whereas works councils in foreign MNCs made use of this right in only 52,7% of the cases.[26] This difference can, to some extent, explain the differences in responses between works councils in Dutch and foreign MNCs.

Next to and in light of these findings on the differences between Dutch and foreign MNCs, other factors have also been identified as main aspects that may influence the position of Dutch works councils. Corporate governance aspects, such as the composition of supervisory boards of Dutch subsidiaries of MNCs, as well as the role of the works council within the governance regime are determinants of the position of the works council. These aspects will be further discussed in the following section 3.

3 THE POSITION OF DUTCH WORKS COUNCILS WITHIN THE CORPORATE GOVERNANCE STRUCTURE OF MNCs[27]

The second main finding of this study concerns the position of the works council within the corporate governance structure of its MNC. Based on both the quantitative – as was discussed in the previous section and in chapter IV in greater detail – as well as the qualitative findings, it will be analysed what the role of the works council regarding the corporate governance structure of the MNC is. This section further addresses whether and how the works councils' influence can be improved based on the examples of good practice collected in this study as well as in light of the recent jurisprudence of the Enterprise Chamber of the Amsterdam Court of Appeals.

3.1 General remarks

The corporate governance regime in multinational corporations is an important factor for the position of Dutch works councils.[28] The role of the works council in this corporate

25 In the period 2011-2014, prior to the data collection by means of the questionnaire; see also chapter II for a detailed overview of the methodology used.

26 See also figure 4.5 in section 4.1 of chapter IV.

27 Parts of the analysis in this section have already been published; see M. Meyer, 'Employee Participation in Multinational Corporations: Corporate Governance and the Role of Works Councils', 14 *Tijdschrift voor Ondernemingsbestuur* 4 (2017).

28 Corporate governance can be defined by reference to the UK Corporate Governance Code (2016), which served as role-model for the Dutch CGC 2016: "*Corporate governance is the system by which companies are directed and controlled. Boards of directors are responsible for the governance of their companies. [...] The responsibilities of the board include setting the company's strategic aims, providing the leadership to put them into effect, supervising the management of the business and reporting to shareholders on their*

governance framework and particularly its influence over the composition of the supervisory board under the structure regime is an important factor for the position of Dutch works councils. The independence of supervisory board members – and the influence of the parent company on the supervisory board – as well as the work councils' influence over the composition of the supervisory board through its (enhanced) recommendation right are at the core of this topic. In light of the foregoing analysis of the differences between Dutch and foreign MNCs, the presence of supervisory board members in consultation meetings will be revisited in this section as well.

Before turning to the substantial findings, one must revisit the development of the current regime which was discussed in chapter III above.[29] The recast of the structure regime in 2004 brought about major changes to the corporate governance framework by abandoning the co-optation mechanism and transferring the right of appointment of the supervisory board to the general meeting of shareholders. At the same time, the works council received the enhanced recommendation right for one third of the supervisory board, but it also lost its right of objection [*bezwaarrecht*] against appointments to the supervisory board. The prevailing view in the literature is that the general meeting of shareholders has gained influence whereas the works council has lost influence as a result of the 2004 recast.[30]

The position of the works council after the recast of the structure regime was therefore an important point of attention in this study and specifically in the context of the quantitative and qualitative analysis. Questions in the online survey concerned the presence of a supervisory board, the use of the (enhanced) recommendation right, the composition of the supervisory board and the presence of supervisory board members at consultation meetings. These elements have been selected for the analysis in thus study due to the importance of them on the position of Dutch works councils in light of the corporate governance in their MNC. The applicable corporate governance framework was not applied by all of the corporations that were included in the quantitative sample, as will be further explained below. But at the same time, examples of good practice have been developed by works councils, in most cases, together with the management and supervisory board. These examples of good practice aim to overcome some of the issues that arise due to the tension between corporate decision-making at an international level outside the scope of Dutch law and employee participation within the Dutch subsidiary.

stewardship. The board's actions are subject to laws, regulations and the shareholders in general meeting"; Financial Reporting Council, *The UK Corporate Governance Code* (The Financial Reporting Council Limited, London 2016).

29 See in particular section 3.2 of chapter III on the structure regime.

30 See *inter alia* P.A.M. Witteveen, 'De betekenis van de nieuwe structuurwet voor de positie van de ondernemingsraad', 6 *Onderneming en Financiering* 68 (2005), p. 30 et seq.; M. Holtzer, *De invloed van werknemers op de strategie van de vennootschap* (Deventer, Kluwer 2014), p. 75 et seq.; H.H. Kersten, 'De onafhankelijke toezichthouder', *Ondernemingsrecht* 2004/43 (2004), p. 9; L.C.J. Sprengers, 'De ondernemingsraad en de raad van commissarissen: een vorm van vennootschapsrechtelijke medezeggenschap', 10 *Tijdschrift Arbeidsrechtpraktijk* 1 (2017).

3.2 *Application of the structure regime (revisited)*

The structure regime was examined in section 3.2 of chapter III. One has to reiterate that the Dutch structure regime, as introduced in 1971, is unique in Europe *inter alia* due to the applicability of employee participation on the level of the corporation (*vennootschaps-rechtelijke medezeggenschap*) rather than relying solely on employee participation in the undertaking (*ondernemingsrechtelijke medezeggenschap*).[31]

Once the cumulative criteria for the applicability of the structure regime are fulfilled (undertakings having an issued capital (including reserves) of at least 16 million Euro, 100 employees within the Netherlands and maintaining a works council),[32] the annual accounts must be lodged with the company registry (*handelsregister* of the *Kamer van Koophandel*). If the substantive criteria are fulfilled in three consecutive years and if the annual accounts have been lodged with the company registry, the structure regime automatically (*van rechtswege*) becomes applicable to Dutch and also foreign corporations and these corporations must establish a supervisory board.[33]

3.2.1 Non-compliance with the structure regime

In MNCs, the (almost always, sole) shareholder of the Dutch sub-holding is the parent company. Pursuant to the structure regime (article 2:158/268 of the DCC) the general meeting of shareholders (i.e., the parent company) should appoint two-thirds of the supervisory board and the (central) works council recommends one-third of the supervisory board, which needs to be approved by the shareholder.

The analysis of the quantitative data, however, has shown that a considerable number of MNCs that were included in the empirical analysis – that fulfil the three cumulative criteria described in section 3.2 above – do not fulfil their obligations and do not maintain a supervisory/one-tier board at the level of its Dutch subsidiaries. 15,7% of the total number of MNCs included in the quantitative sample do not maintain a supervisory/one-tier board for its Dutch subsidiaries, even although the likelihood of these very large

31 Employee board level representation (hereinafter: EBLR) is also applied in 17 other EU Member States (18 out of 28 in total), but the structure regime's (enhanced) recommendation mechanism as well as the opt-out for international holdings makes it unique; see further L.C.J. Sprengers, 'De ondernemingsraad en de raad van commissarissen: een vorm van vennootschapsrechtelijke medezeggenschap', 1 *Tijdschrift Arbeidsrechtpraktijk* 10 (2017).

32 Article 2:153(2)/2:263(2) of the DCC.

33 The same regime also applies to one-tier boards with non-executive directors; Article 2:164a (1) of the DCC stipulates that "what is provided in Article 2:158 paragraph 2 up to and including 12, 2:159, 2:160, 2:161 and 2:161a on the Supervisory Board, respectively, on the Supervisory Directors shall then apply accordingly to the non-executive Directors of the Open Corporation". The same applies to private limited liability companies (B.V.) pursuant to article 2:274a (1) of the DCC.

corporations fulfilling the three cumulative criteria is very high.[34] In foreign MNCs, the percentage is higher, with 23,8% of MNCs not applying the regime. Overall, one in six MNCs do not have a supervisory/one-tier board on the level of its Dutch subsidiaries.[35] The applicable article 2:153/2:263 of the DCC does not contain a sanction for non-compliance, despite the fact that it is a mandatory provision.

But such absence of a supervisory board or non-executives in a one-tier board – despite fulfilment of the article 2:153-criteria – is, firstly, an economic offence pursuant to article 1(4) and article 6 of the *Wet op de Economische Delicten* [MM: Economic Offences Act] and the works council can initiate a procedure at the sub-district court (*Kantonrechter*) to demand compliance with the regime.[36] The non-existence of the supervisory board is furthermore problematic in light of the (revised) Dutch Corporate Governance Code.[37] The CGC 2016 does not create legal obligations, but it must be followed by listed companies on the basis of the comply-or-explain principle.[38] The CGC 2016 does not contain a provision mandating the establishment of a supervisory board or the presence of non-executive directors in a one-tier board. The Code, however, does contain multiple provisions outlining the crucial role of the supervisory board in monitoring the continuity and long-term value creation of the company.[39] In the absence of a supervisory board or non-executive directors, this role cannot be fulfilled and there is consequently a monitoring component missing in the undertaking concerned.

It is the author's opinion, the lack of a sanctioning mechanism in article 2:153/2:263 of DCC lies at the core of this issue. The absence of compliance monitoring also contributes to the non-compliance with the regime. A sanctioning mechanism would be desirable in the case of non-compliance with the duty to lodge the annual accounts at the company registry or (if the accounts have been filed) the failure to establish a supervisory board *despite* lodging the annual accounts at the registry (for instance by not amending the statutes accordingly). It should be noted that such non-compliance is not limited to MNCs, which were the subject of the empirical research, but is also an issue in smaller companies.

34 A verification is not possible due to the anonymous nature of the questionnaire responses, which do not include company names.

35 One corporation included in the sample has a one-tier board and therefore fulfils its duties under the structure regime and is not included in the 15.7% of cases that do not maintain a supervisory/one-tier board.

36 See also W.J. Slagter, *Compendium Ondernemingsrecht* (8th edition, Kluwer, Deventer 2005), p. 363-364.

37 Revised Dutch Corporate Governance Code 2016, www.mccg.nl/?page=4738 (last accessed 22 May 2017).

38 The CGC 2016 also has considerable spill-over effects (*reflexwerking*) on non-listed companies because sectors or individual companies voluntarily apply the principles or have (sectoral) codes in place that are modelled on the CGC 2016.

39 *Inter alia* principles 1.1. and 1.5 of the CGC 2016.

Aside from the possibility to lodge an appeal with the sub-district court, which should be an *ultimum remedium*, the works council should use its right of access to information to inquire about the current governance structure and whether the criteria of the structure regime are fulfilled by the undertaking.[40]

3.2.2 The works councils' recommendation right and presence of supervisory board members in consultation meetings

The non-compliance with the structure regime by MNCs is also problematic for works councils, because of the dependency of their recommendation rights on the existence of a supervisory board.[41] If no supervisory board is maintained at the level of the Dutch sub-holding (or lower tier within the Dutch corporate structure), the works councils' (enhanced) right of recommendation cannot be used. This weakens its influence in the decision-making process within the MNC because the council can no longer use its regular recommendation right (*gewoon aanbevelingsrecht*)[42] and its enhanced recommendation right for one third of the supervisory board (*versterkt aanbevelingsrecht*).[43]

To obtain information on whether a duty to establish a supervisory board exists is therefore inherent in the interests of works councils.[44] The WCA contains several relevant provisions in this regard.[45] Central to this is the consultation on the company's general operation (article 24 of the WCA), which must be organised at least twice a year. During this consultation, the management provides the works council with information on the general status quo of the undertaking and '*with general information concerning the activities and financial results of the company relating to the preceding period and in particular regarding the matters mentioned in Article 25*' (article 31a of the WCA).[46]

40 See sections 1.4.4 and 1.4.5 in chapter IV as well as section 3.1 in chapter V for a detailed overview on the use of information rights and examples of good practice applied in MNCs included in this study.

41 The same requirements apply to one-tier boards as well.

42 Article 2:158(5)/2:268(5) of the DCC.

43 Article 2:158(6)/2:268(6) of the DCC; based on the questionnaire responses (N = 42), 64% of the (central) works councils are using their enhanced right of recommendation whereas 31% are not using that right. This is a point of concern which I addressed previously in M. Meyer, 'De positie van Nederlandse ondernemingsraden in internationale concerns: een pleidooi voor procesgerichte medezeggenschap', *Tijdschrift Recht en Arbeid* 2016/45, p. 16.

44 And should be done prior to any significant decisions, which may affect the corporate governance of the corporation as was exemplified in the *Smurfit Kappa/Solidus Solutions* case concerning a division and subsequent merger of a Dutch subsidiary of the group; Rb. Noord-Nederland 25 May 2016, *JOR* 2016/230 m. nt. M. Holtzer (*OR Solidus Solutions*).

45 See also section 1.4 of chapter III for a detailed overview of relevant works council rights under the Dutch framework.

46 Such information is also relevant in the context of possible private equity (majority) shareholders due to the implications for the composition of the supervisory board. Especially in the case of a majority private equity shareholder, one or more representatives of that private equity investor are often members of the supervisory board of the undertaking; see also J.E. Ligterink (et al.), 'Private equity in Nederland: een stakeholder-perspectief', *Kamerstukken II* 2016/17, 34267, 10, p. 36; in this report, the case of Action

The presence or absence of a supervisory board as well as possible (re-)elections of supervisory board members should also be discussed at these meetings.[47] It is also important to note that supervisory board members have a duty to attend these article 24-meetings on the general operation of the undertaking (article 24(2) of the WCA). However, a majority of supervisory board members in MNCs do not fulfil their obligation to attend such meetings (see Figure 2.1 above).[48] This is particularly rife in foreign MNCs[49] as respondents indicated that supervisory board members 'never' attend such consultation meetings in 60% of the cases (45.5% in Dutch MNCs).[50] The qualitative analysis further shows that the presence of supervisory board members during consultation meetings is especially valued by the works council representatives according to those whom were interviewed.[51] The examples of good practice discussed in section 3.4 of chapter V also showed that a number of alternative solutions for works councils to formally and informally consult with the supervisory board. Establishing employee participation processes, which include information and consultation procedures with the supervisory board are, therefore, viable options that could be used to improve the position of works councils in MNCs. The importance of process-oriented employee participation mechanisms is further addressed below in section 4.

3.3 *Composition of the supervisory board and possible undue influence*

The composition of the supervisory board is a crucial factor in the effective corporate governance. From the works councils' perspective, this is therefore an important aspect, also in light of the exercise of the councils' recommendation rights. The independence of the individual supervisory board members is also important for works councils in light of its objective, namely employee representation and acting in the interest of the proper functioning of the undertaking ('*in het belang van het goed functioneren van de onderneming in al haar doelstellingen*').[52]

The supervisory board, on the other hand, must have the interests of the undertaking as its core objective (article 2:140/2:250 of the DCC) and should remain independent of any

is examined in which 60% of the supervisory board is comprised of representatives of the private equity investor (page 124).

47 Article 31d of the WCA on the compensation of supervisory board members is another relevant topic which should be discussed in such a meeting.

48 One reason could be the exemption in article 24(3) of the WCA, which exempts an entrepreneur to attend the meetings if the undertaking or group of undertakings has jointly established at least five works councils pursuant to the WCA (see section 3.4.1 of chapter V above).

49 Foreign MNCs are defined as having their registered office located outside of the Netherlands; see also chapter II above for a detailed overview of the methodology applied in this study.

50 See also section 2.4 above.

51 See section 3.4 of chapter V.

52 C.f. A. van den Berg, 'Ondernemingsraad en Goed Bestuur: een Institutioneel-Economisch Benadering', 20 *Tijdschrift voor Arbeidsvraagstukken* 4 (2004), p. 414.

partial interest ('*zonder last of ruggespraak*') and each individual member must have sufficient expertise.[53] A supervisory board with a composition based on expertise and a high level of independence of its members is therefore at the core of the works councils' interest, which aligns with the objectives of the supervisory board to a considerable degree.

A number of provisions in the CGC 2016 specifically discuss the role of the supervisory board and principle 2.1 stipulates that '*[t]he management board and the supervisory board should be composed such that the requisite expertise, background, competencies and – as regards the supervisory board – independence are present for them to carry out their duties properly*'. In light of article 2:140/2:250 of the DCC and the CGC 2016, Koelemeijer[54] correctly observed in a recent article that independence and impartiality must be the primary goals for supervisory board members when fulfilling their tasks. To ensure their independence and impartiality, supervisory board members should neither be employees of the corporation or a dependent company nor a labour union representative involved in collective agreement negotiations in the undertaking.[55] These restrictions, however, do not apply to corporate representatives, whom are employees of the parent company and at the same time supervisory board members of the Dutch sub-holding. Furthermore, the CGC 2016 – despite the emphasis on the independence of supervisory board members – exempts corporate supervisory board representatives by including an exception to Principle 2.1.8. of the Code:

> '*A supervisory board member is not independent if [he] (...):*
> *(vii). is a member of the management board or supervisory board – or is a representative in some other way – of a legal entity which holds at least ten percent of the shares in the company,* ***unless the entity is a group company.***' [emphasis added]

According to the CGC 2016, corporate representatives are therefore regarded as being independent. It is however questionable whether the supervisory board can act independently and fulfil its role in the best interest of the undertaking for which it is maintained, once the majority of the supervisory board are, at the same time, members of the management of the parent company.[56]

---

53 '[W]ettelijk uitgangspunt is en blijft dat de raad van commissarissen als orgaan van de vennootschap handelt en zich bij de vervulling van zijn toezichthoudende taak richt naar het belang van de vennootschap en de daarmee verbonden onderneming. Dat belang vergt dat commissarissen zonder last of ruggespraak en volstrekt onafhankelijk opereren'; Kamerstukken II 2003/2004 28179, 5, p. 43 en Kamerstukken II 2003/2004, 28179, 3, p. 33.

54 M. Koelemeijer, 'De herziene Corporate Governance Code: (nieuwe) accenten in effectief toezicht', 14 *Tijdschrift voor Ondernemingsbestuur* 2 (2017), p. 58.

55 Article 2:160/2:270 of the DCC.

56 And this is also the prevailing view in the literature and my standpoint; see A. van den Berg, 'Ondernemingsraad en Goed Bestuur: een Institutioneel-Economisch Benadering', 20 *Tijdschrift voor Arbeidsvraagstukken* 4 (2004), p. 414; L. Sprengers, 'De ondernemingsraad en de raad van commissarissen: een vorm van vennootschapsrechtelijke medezeggenschap', 1 *Tijdschrift Arbeidsrechtpraktijk* 10

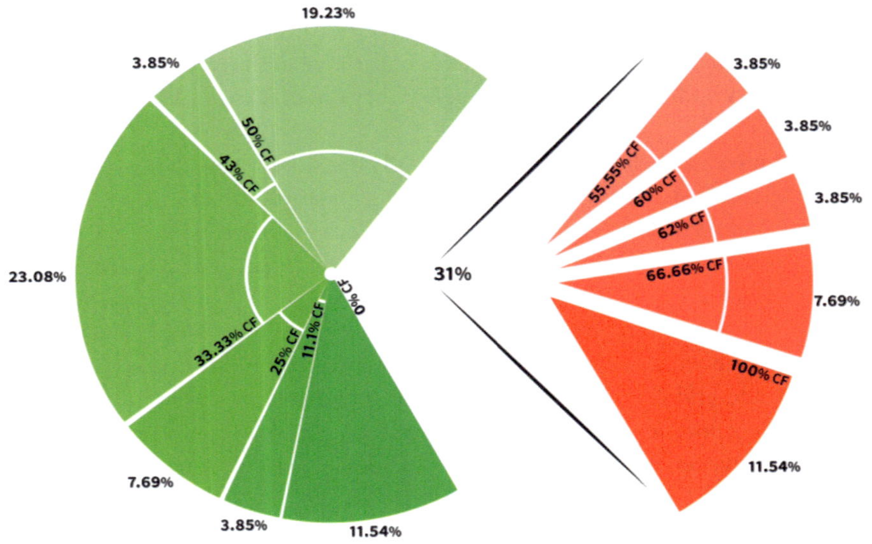

Figure 3.1 *Ratio of Corporate Representatives (concernfunctionarissen, CF) in the Supervisory Board of MNCs (N = 25)*

In 50% of the MNCs examined, at least half of the supervisory board was comprised of corporate representatives (see Figure 3.1 above).[57] In its *Kodak* and *Cyanamid* judgments, the Enterprise Chamber held that once the supervisory board is comprised of a majority of corporate representatives, then the board is not properly constituted ("*niet naar behoren is samengesteld*"). The Enterprise Chamber more recently confirmed its position on this matter insofar as it held that the supervisory board must be composed in such a way that it can exercise its tasks independently, which was not the case in the situation at hand.[58]

In the *Thomas Cook* case, all three supervisory board seats were intended to be filled by corporate representatives (i.e., members of the management of the parent company, the so-called *concernfunctionarissen*) and the works councils enhanced recommendation right was not respected. The case concerned the Thomas Cook group, a multinational corporation with Thomas Cook Plc. (UK) as a parent company and a holding company – Thomas Cook Investment Limited – above the Dutch subsidiary, Thomas Cook

(2017); see also M. Meyer, 'De positie van Nederlandse ondernemingsraden in internationale concerns: een pleidooi voor procesgerichte medezeggenschap', *Tijdschrift Recht en Arbeid* 2016/45 (2016), p. 15.

57 See also section 4.1 in chapter IV for a detailed analysis of the quantitative results regarding the application of the structure regime in the MNCs included in this study.

58 Hof Amsterdam (OK) 1 July 2016, *JOR* 2016/273 and *JAR* 2016/210 m.nt. I. Zaal (*Thomas Cook Nederland*), para. 3.8.

Nederland (hereinafter: TCN). TCN was obliged by law to apply the (mitigated) structure regime from the 8th of March 2016 onwards after fulfilling the criteria in three consecutive years.[59] The works council of TCN was informed of this on 25 January 2016 and a consultation procedure was initiated, in which the works council specifically addressed the importance of having independent supervisory board members and *inter alia* asked that, in the case of the application of the mitigated structure regime, the chairperson of the supervisory board should be an 'independent' (i.e., external) person.[60] The works council adopted a proactive stance, which was in line with the examples of good practice that were discussed in chapter V above.

The management, however, indicated that due to TCN being part of the Thomas Cook group, it wished to "make sure that its interests are presented" by also having internal board members on the board of the Dutch subsidiary, TCN.[61] Following the consultation procedure, the management of TCN informed the works council on 3 March 2016 – five days prior to the deadline for the statutory application of the (mitigated) structure regime – that it would appoint three internal, corporate supervisory board members. The appointment was made on 4 March 2016.[62] The works council, not having been consulted on the appointment of the three board members (because the consultation procedure concerned the application of the structure regime after 8 March) and not having been able to exercise its enhanced recommendation right, lodged an appeal before the Enterprise Chamber.

The Enterprise Chamber, firstly, held that the appointment on 4 March 2016 constituted a topic that falls within the scope of the works councils' right of advice pursuant to article 25(1)(e) of the WCA.[63] It furthermore held that the choice of appointing three internal supervisory board members was insufficiently motivated vis-a-vis the works council, especially in light of the works councils' condition of having sufficiently independent supervisory board members. The composition of the supervisory board therefore had to be as such that it could exercise its tasks independently,[64] which could not be the case if all board members were internal (corporate) representatives.[65] The supervisory board

59 *Ibid.*, para. 2.3.

60 *Ibid.*

61 *Ibid.*, para. 2.8 and 3.7.

62 *Ibid.*, para. 2.10.

63 *Ibid.*, para. 3.4.

64 See also the Enterprise Chamber's *Corus* judgment on the importance of the weighing of interests – both of the group and of the Dutch subsidiary – in the case of a mitigated structure regime; Hof Amsterdam (OK) 13 March 2003, *Ondernemingsrecht* 2003/16, *JAR* 2003/88 and *JOR* 2003/85.

65 Hof Amsterdam (OK) 1 July 2016, *JOR* 2016/273 and *JAR* 2016/210, para. 3.8: "*Zonder nadere toelichting is niet aannemelijk dat daaraan wordt voldaan indien de raad van commissarissen enkel bestaat uit personen in dienst van TC Group. De door TCN gegeven toelichting komt erop neer dat het belang van TCN steeds samenvalt met het belang van TC Group. Die opvatting is in zijn algemeenheid niet juist. De raad van commissarissen zal telkens moeten beoordelen in hoeverre de belangen van TCN parallel lopen met*

may, therefore, not be fully comprised of corporate representatives, unless this is further motivated, according to the Enterprise Chamber in paragraph 3.8 of the judgment.

Koelemeijer disagreed in her assessment[66] of this aspect of the judgment with Sprengers[67] by holding that under a mitigated structure regime, the supervisory board can be comprised of 100% of corporate representatives. Indeed, it is true that the Enterprise Chamber added that, while from the outset a supervisory board with 100% of corporate representatives is unduly constituted, such a composition can be motivated by the undertaking.[68] While one can agree with Koelemeijer that the election of a supervisory board that is fully comprised of corporate representatives is possible in light of this judgment (if motivated),[69] it can be argued that the supervisory board would nevertheless be unduly composed for its decision-making in a situation such as in the TCN-case. Article 2:140/2:250 of the DCC stipulates not only that a supervisory board member has to act in the best interest of the company (i.e., the subsidiary).[70] Paragraph 5 specifies that:

> *'A Supervisory Director does not participate in the deliberations and decision-making if he has a direct or indirect personal interest therein that is contrary to the interests meant in paragraph 2. If, as a result, no resolution of the Supervisory Board can be passed, the resolution shall be passed by the by the General Meeting, unless the articles of incorporation provide otherwise'.*[71]

Therefore, it can be argued that a supervisory board member whom has another interest that is contrary to the interests of the subsidiary for which the supervisory board is maintained, may not participate in deliberations and decision-making if that person

de belangen van Group/het concern en dient de vrijheid te hebben die afweging zelfstandig te maken, ook al wordt het belang van TCN vanzelfsprekend mede bepaald door het concernbelang".

66 M. Koelemeijer, 'De herziene Corporate Governance Code: (nieuwe) accenten in effectief toezicht', 14 *Tijdschrift voor Ondernemingsbestuur* 2 (2017), p. 61.

67 L. Sprengers, 'De ondernemingsraad en de raad van commissarissen: een vorm van vennootschapsrechtelijke medezeggenschap', 1 *Tijdschrift Arbeidsrechtpraktijk* 10 (2017).

68 Hof Amsterdam (OK) 1 July 2016, JOR 2016/273 and *JAR* 2016/210, para. 3.8: "Zonder nadere toelichting is niet aannemelijk dat daaraan wordt voldaan indien de raad van commissarissen enkel bestaat uit personen in dienst van TC Group". [MM, emphasis added]

69 The Enterprise Chamber also held in para. 3.8 that solely citing the interest of the corporate group is insufficient.

70 It is true that the interest of the corporate group may be weighed in the decision-making of the supervisory board members, but it is doubtful whether the board member can act independently and in the best interest of the undertaking when they possess other interests, namely that of the group as a whole, as their primary objective.

71 'Een commissaris neemt niet deel aan de beraadslaging en besluitvorming indien hij daarbij een direct of indirect persoonlijk belang heeft dat tegenstrijdig is met het belang bedoeld in lid 2. Wanneer de raad van commissarissen hierdoor geen besluit kan nemen, wordt het besluit genomen door de algemene vergadering, tenzij de statuten anders bepalen'; unofficial English translation from Dutch Civil Law <http://www.dutchcivillaw.com/civilcodebook022.htm> (last accessed 29 May 2017).

is a corporate representative.[72] This may particularly be the case in situations such as in the TCN case where all supervisory board members were corporate representatives. The works council should therefore scrutinise every supervisory board appointment and exercise its right to be consulted on the profile of supervisory board members. The works council should also exercise its (enhanced) recommendation right so as to increase the number of independent board members.[73]

In addition to the legal issues linked with the presence of corporate representatives on supervisory boards, it is doubtful whether the long-term interest of the undertaking is best achieved when there is a supervisory board that is comprised of a majority of corporate representatives.[74] The supervisory board largely depends on the management for its access to information. This one-sided information access can be lessened by increased contacts with the works council, which can be a valuable source of 'shop-floor level' information. And for works councils in multinational corporations, regular contact with the supervisory board can be beneficial for the improvement of the works councils' position in the decision-making process, as was elaborated upon in the qualitative chapter V (section 3.4).

The Enterprise Chamber consequently held that by only appointing three internal supervisory board members on 4 March was unlawful, also because such a decision would significantly limit the works councils' right of recommendation pursuant to article 2:268(5-6) of the DCC.[75] The Enterprise Chamber continued by holding that it was "unconvincing" (*ongeloofwaardig*) that a decision to appoint three supervisory board members – four days prior to the statutory deadline to apply the structure regime – is an unrelated matter and that the timing was coincidental.[76] The Enterprise Chamber ordered TCN to withdraw its decision to appoint the three internal supervisory board members and to consult the works council on this matter, with due respect of the issue of board composition and the matter of board member independence.

The case exemplifies the importance of board composition and the crucial role that the works council can play in highlighting matters such as the independence of board

72 The interest of the corporation may be a factor in the deliberations, but may not be the decisive one *per se*; see inter alia S.M. Bartman, 'Hoge Raad weet zich niet goed raad met het concern', *Ondernemingsrecht* 2016/77, p. 366 and 370; he writes (p. 366): '*Zonder kenbare en begrijpelijke afweging met het belang van de eigen onderneming kan een besluit van de (dochter-)ondernemer dan ook niet de toets van art. 26 lid 5 WOR doorstaan*'.

73 Several works councils in MNCs have developed their own profile (*profielschets*) prior to making use of their enhanced right of recommendation; interviews 26:15, 38:14, 39:25, 46:5 and 48:2.

74 And in light of the fact that the supervisory board is one of the main cornerstones of corporate governance; see also R.V. Aguilera and G. Jackson, 'The Cross-National Diversity of Corporate Governance: Dimensions and Determinants', 3 *The Academy of Management Review* 28 (2003).

75 Hof Amsterdam (OK) 1 July 2016, JOR 2016/273 and *JAR* 2016/210, para. 3.9.

76 *Ibid.*, para. 3.10.

members, but also the relationship between corporate governance, corporate strategy and the position of the Dutch subsidiary (or subsidiaries) in this regard.

4 PROCESS-ORIENTED EMPLOYEE PARTICIPATION IN MNCs

The first section of this chapter highlighted the main differences between Dutch and foreign MNCs based on the quantitative findings of this study. The second section concerned the role of works councils within the corporate governance framework, which can be identified as one of the issues that influences the position of Dutch works councils. The final section of this chapter has a different focus, namely the use of mechanisms to organise the employee participation process to improve the works councils' position in MNCs. The interview responses showed that Dutch works councils have developed a multitude of examples of good practice aimed at improving employee participation within their MNC (see chapter V above). The qualitative analysis conducted also revealed that some works councils have developed process-oriented employee participation schemes,[77] which have several objectives.

Firstly, management and works council members may agree upon a comprehensive participation regime covering (parts or the complete) decision-making process. By doing so, both the works council and the management know when and in what manner the works council is involved in the decision-making process on an intended measure. Secondly, both parties can decide whether or not the works council is involved informally in the process in addition to the formal consultation process. This aspect increases flexibility for the negotiations as will be further outlined below. Thirdly, such an agreement on the process can help to concretise the topics that are to be covered by the employee participation regime. The legal dogmatic analysis has shown that, in particular, the timing of the works councils' involvement can be problematic in MNCs rather than the question of whether or not the council is being consulted on the (intended) decision.[78] By agreeing on topics that are to be covered by the participation process and the timing of the councils' involvement, some of the tensions between swift decision-making and ensuring a timely works council involvement can be assuaged. Fourthly, works councils reported to have a more effective influence on the decision-making process through the use of such a process-oriented approach. Having a mechanism in place that allows for a more efficient consultation process is described as a win-win for both the management and the works council, which has the effect of benefitting the works councils' position in the decision-making process and therefore serves the overall objective of an effective

77 See also section 3.2.6 in chapter V on the reporting of examples of good practice.

78 See in particular section 4 of chapter III on the concepts of attribution and co-entrepreneurship, which highlight the tension between timely consultation of works councils pursuant to article 25(2) of the WCA and transnational decision-making processes in MNCs.

involvement of the works council. Finally, the use of a monitoring phase aims at ensuring that the measures have their intended effect. The monitoring covers the implementation phase and continues in some cases for a longer period of time to follow-up on large-scale decisions (such as reorganisations or merger transactions).

In the following section 4.1, the process-oriented practices applied in the MNCs covered in this study will be introduced. In the following section 4.2, the various aspects of this model will be discussed in more detail.

4.1 *Elements of process-oriented employee participation applied in practice*

The employee participation process *de lege lata* was discussed in detail in the legal dogmatic analysis (chapter III) and sections 2 and 3.2.6 of the qualitative analysis (chapter V).

The figure below shows the formal employee participation process in blue. One has to note that the formal consultation phase also includes access to information on the intended decision pursuant to article 25(3) of the WCA, which is submitted to the works council alongside the intended management decision. Such information, however, is limited to the summary of the reasons for the decision, its expected consequences for persons working in the enterprise and the measures proposed for dealing with such consequences. The works council may request additional information that is necessary for the fulfilment of its duties (article 31 of the WCA).[79] In the context of this analysis, it is important to note that the timing of such information and consultation is at the moment of an intended management decision. This is important insofar as the works councils' involvement is at a relatively late stage in the decision-making process. One exception is the provision found in article 25(1)(n) of the WCA, which stipulates that the works council must also be consulted in cases where the management is "commissioning an expert from outside the enterprise to advise on any of the matters" falling under article 25(1) of the WCA.[80]

The case law on attribution of (intended) decisions by parent companies of Dutch undertakings and co-entrepreneurship have shown that involvement is at times too late.[81] The quantitative analysis in chapter IV has further shown that one in four works councils

79 See also section 1.4.1 in chapter III.

80 Such consultation right also extends to the right of consultation on potential share transactions that may be done following up on the expert's advice; see OK 19 October 2016, *JAR* 2016/278 and *TRA* 2017/9 m.nt. I. Zaal (*SHL Engineering*); see section 4 in chapter III for a more detailed analysis of the *SHL Engineering* case.

81 Article 25(2) of the WCA: "[the works council's] advice shall be requested at a time when it can still significantly affect the decision to be taken".

in foreign and one in ten works councils in Dutch MNCs regards the time available for rendering its advice insufficient.[82]

The interview phase has additionally shown that the formal consultation phase is relatively inflexible, leaving only limited room for flexibility on both the side of the works council and management, if no informal measures are taken. According to article 25 of the WCA, the works council is consulted at least once before its advice on the decision is to be rendered.[83] But the works council may be able to give valuable input in the preliminary phase prior to the management's intended decision and the start of the formal consultation procedure, as will subsequently be discussed.

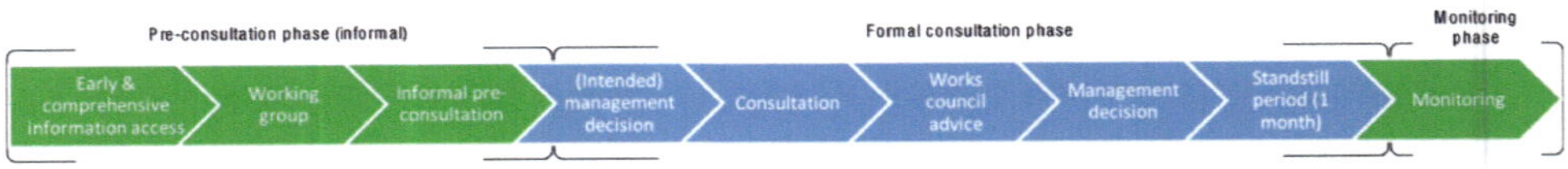

Figure 4.1 *Process-oriented employee participation model on the basis of the interview responses (blue: formal consultation (art. 25 WCA), green: additional practices applied by MNCs)*

It is also worth noting that in all MNCs included in the empirical analysis, the formal consultation procedure has been applied in accordance with the legislative framework. The pre-consultation and monitoring elements are rather adopted in addition to the existing framework in order to improve the employee involvement in the decision-making process and to make it more time-efficient. The statutory consultation process is not replaced in the surveyed corporations.

4.2 *Pre-consultation of works councils in the process-oriented participation model*

The early and comprehensive access to information for the consultation is one of the main issues faced by works councils in MNCs. Not only was it reported by a number of works councils that the time available for their advice was insufficient, as was discussed in the previous section. An overwhelming majority of works councils also reported that disputes arise, at least sometimes, as to whether prior consultation of works councils is necessary.[84] A range of good practice examples applied in MNCs are aimed at dealing with this issue. Aside from the provision of information in (digital) information dossiers, which are updated regularly by the management and accessible to the works council on

82 See figure 5.10 in section 5.2.3 chapter IV.
83 Article 25(4) of the WCA.
84 See figure 5.11 in section 5.2.4 of chapter IV.

a continuous basis,[85] access to information also exists through informal meetings prior to the start of the statutory consultation procedure. The involvement of the works council in the preliminary phase is especially important in cases pertaining to large-scale projects, as one (management) interviewee pointed out.[86] The planning of a large project starts usually one month before the adoption of an intended decision that falls within the scope of article 25 of the WCA. In the past, according to this former CEO, the works council was not involved prior to the request for advice and had no prior information access. The management, after submitting the initial request for advice, was flooding the works council with follow-up requests for advice for the related aspects of the (intended) decision. While such a timing is in in accordance with the formal requirements under article 25 of the WCA, its application in practice is problematic for both the works council and the management. The management would like to receive the advice of the works council as soon as possible, within four to eight weeks according to the interviewee, but the works council has to investigate the topic at hand, address the multitude of requests for advice and adopt its position on the matter. A CEO of another MNC mentioned a similar issue. He further noted that the management, albeit thoroughly planning and considering the impact on its workforce, frequently consults the works council in the preliminary phase to gain their input.[87]

In another case, the works council questioned the assumptions that were made by the management in the process of a major reorganisation of the corporation. By providing input from a shop-floor perspective, the works council could give valuable input prior to the start of the formal consultation procedure and could at the same time effectively influence the decision-making process.[88] The provision of information in the preliminary phase is, therefore, not a one-way communication channel. The input from the works council can benefit the management's decision making by providing information from within the organisation and by challenging the assumptions made.

Such involvement in the preliminary phase can significantly improve the works councils' position. By having insights into the alternative solutions rather than receiving the final (intended) decision, the works council can influence the decision-making process

85 See section 3.1.1 in chapter V for a detailed overview.

86 Interview 9:26.

87 Interview 14:17: "*Het hangt van het onderwerp af. Hoe groter de verandering is, zeker conceptueel, hoe belangrijker het is om de tijd te nemen. Want vaak, wat je merkt, is dat als je vanuit ons perspectief kijkt, dan zie je andere dingen als potentieel probleem als dat je het uit het perspectief van de ondernemingsraad ziet. En vaak wel, maar soms komen er dingen uit waaraan je helemaal niet aan hebt gedacht [...]. Dat is het voordeel van geen druk daarop hebben. Als je geen druk daarop hebt staan, en je wil die termijnen van zes weken en zoverre, die wil je allemaal aanhouden en je schiet dan wat in*".

88 Interview 15:23: "*De laatste grote reorganisatie, commerciële transformatie waarbij alle commerciële onderdelen van [het concern] op zijn kop zijn gegroeid. Dan ben je ook aan het meepraten over als of alles nog niet eens een concept is. En dan probeer je zoveel mogelijk je invloed uit te oefenen en input mee te geven van dit vinden wij belangrijk. Vanuit de kennis die wij hebben, vanuit de business, vanuit de werkvloer eigenlijk stel je soms ook vraagtekens bij aannames die gedaan worden. En dan probeer je zo inderdaad al vooraf bij te sturen*".

much more effectively. The works council also has considerably more time available to adopt a position on the matter due to its earlier involvement. The works council has to invest more resources to participate in such a preliminary phase due to the increased number of consultation meetings. The works council may also be involved in projects that may ultimately not be pursued by the management and therefore no (intended) decision is taken. This increased workload can be alleviated to a certain extent by making use of working groups.[89] Instead of the entire works council, smaller working groups are involved in the pre-consultation phase and report back to the works council on a regular basis. The working group is not taking the decision (i.e., issuing advice) on behalf of the works council, but it participates in the preliminary phase on behalf of the council and reports back regularly. The use of working groups helps to alleviate the workload for the works council members, establishes timelines for the consultation dossier and gives input to the management regarding potential issues at an early stage.[90] In some cases, employees with specific knowledge of the topic at hand are involved in the working groups as well. The employees have the status of temporary (works council) working group members and have the same rights and duties as regular employee representatives.[91] The use of such temporary members and working groups in general is supported by both the management and the works council in the MNCs that make use of them and that were included in this study. The management representatives highlighted that the intended measures receive greater support if employees of the department(s) concerned are involved and the employees gain experiences as well. The works council representatives further noted that the input from the department concerned also increases the support from the councils' side and gives the works council the opportunity to maintain closer cooperation with the workforce on the issue at hand. The use of such 'ad-hoc' members also allows the works council to tackle multiple projects simultaneously and to internalise the necessary expertise for some of the more specialised dossiers such as pensions.[92]

89 See also section 3.5.3 in chapter V for an overview of examples of good practice concerning the use of committees and working groups.

90 *Inter alia* interview 8:11: "*Die werkgroep heeft geen mandaat, die adviseert het management.* [...] [Voor] *een ondernemingsraad van 15 personen, hebben wij zeg maar vijftien personen beschikbaar, dan doen we vier mensen als afvaardiging vanuit de ondernemingsraad, om de workload een beetje te* [verdelen] [...]. *Die spreken in de planningsfase af wat het tijdspad wordt: dus wat worden de tijdslijnen, wanneer verwacht je advies, wanneer moet het selectieproces gaan starten, die hele fase. Die duurt altijd minimaal twee weken, maar mag ook drie maanden duren. Minimaal twee weken. En dat is allemaal nog in, alles kan daar wijzigen en veranderen, en uiteindelijk is management verantwoordelijk om het definitieve besluit over de adviezen. Daar gaan wij niet over. De werkgroep adviseert onder voorbehoud, met een disclaimer op, dat de hele OR dat anders mag zien, maar dit is gewoon van die individuen het advies aan management. Dan komt daar een soort draft* [adviesaanvraag] *fase in. Die draft* [adviesaanvraag] *gaat dan naar de volledige ondernemingsraad*".

91 These temporary members are referred to as "task group members", "project-based employee representatives" or "ad-hoc members": see section 3.5.3 in chapter V for an overview of examples of good practice concerning the use of committees and working groups.

92 Due to a change of legislation, the topic of pensions was often on the agenda of the MNCs that participated in the study; see also sections 5.1 and 5.2 in chapter IV for an overview of the works council and the consultation agenda in MNCs.

An important aspect of the informal pre-consultation phase is the establishment of a time plan for the dossier. In some cases, the management and works council develop a time plan for the individual dossier at the start of the pre-consultation phase, which can also be in the form of an annual employee participation plan.[93] Such planning includes the setting of milestones, agreement on deadlines and the agreement of minimum-timeframes for the informal consultation phase or the formulation of (pre)-advices. In some cases, use of a template is made for reoccurring consultation dossiers with pre-defined phases and timelines.[94]

4.3 *Monitoring during and after the implementation phase*

The timely and comprehensive pre-consultation facilitates a swift completion of the formal consultation phase pursuant to article 25 of the WCA, with complex dossiers in some cases being completed in a few weeks, according to several interview responses. A handful of MNCs reported the use of process-oriented employee participation mechanisms, focusing on the pre-consultation and (formal) consultation phase. However, even fewer interview participants reported that mechanisms were in place for the period during and after the implementation phase.

After the completion of the formal consultation procedure (including a possible standstill period[95]), it is often the case that complex decisions have to be implemented. But the correct implementation of decisions in accordance with the negotiation result in the consultation phase is also important for the works council in light of its dual mandate, namely safeguarding employees' rights and acting in the best interests of the company. Aside from the proper implementation of the decision at hand, it is also important for work councils in light of future consultation rounds on other (related) topics.

The works council in one MNC indicated that they monitor, together with the management, whether the decision and the implementation thereof is having the intended effect in practice.[96] In the MNC concerned, the working group of the works council, which participated in the pre-consultation phase, remained intact throughout the implementation phase to monitor the actual outcomes of the decision(s) made. In two cases, the management and works council agreed upon a date at which the decision taken would be revisited and evaluated as to whether the implementation had been successful and had its desired effect.[97] In yet another case, an interviewee stated that for very large

93 Interviews 18, 26, 36, 38, 39, 45.

94 Interviews 8:9, 18:35 and 26:29.

95 It is noteworthy that no use of the standstill-period had to be made in the MNCs where process-oriented participation mechanisms are used.

96 Interview 40:28; see also section 3.2.6 of chapter V above.

97 Interviews 5:21 and 48:27; see also section 3.2.6 of chapter V above.

(reorganisation) dossiers, the monitoring takes place in intervals to constantly monitor the implementation of requests for advice that are part of the larger dossier.[98] These four examples of good practice show that monitoring is an important aspect of the consultation process, especially in more complex dossiers. It should therefore be an integral part of the participation process and agreements on the monitoring should be made explicit. Monitoring of decisions and the use of performance indicators is certainly a core aspect of management and crucial for evidence-based decision making.[99] Therefore, it may be very well possible that implicitly monitoring decisions takes place as part of the employee participation process. But to ensure an effective and efficient participation process, including monitoring, agreements on the monitoring during the implementation phase should be enacted. By doing so, both the management and works council can benefit from the appraisal of decisions made for future dossiers and in turn improve the overall decision-making process.

4.4 *Final remarks*

The process-oriented employee participation approach discussed above is not meant to solve all the issues related to the difficult position of Dutch works councils in MNCs, especially in light of the differences between Dutch and foreign MNCs that were discussed in the first section of this chapter. But this approach aims at overcoming one of the main issued faced by Dutch works councils and the Dutch management: the timing of (intended) decisions and the involvement of the Dutch works council in light of international decision-making structures. The examples of good practice have shown that by agreeing on a process for the involvement of the works council, issues relating to the structure of employee involvement can be overcome – despite possible disagreement on the content of an intended decision. The use of such a process-oriented approach also ensures flexibility, an aspect that was emphasised especially by management interviewees, while also allowing for an early and comprehensive involvement of the works council. The interview responses have also shown that such an early involvement in a structured manner can increase the efficiency of the consultation process and be more time-effective than a traditional approach that relies on the statutory framework (article 25 of the WCA). Such an approach can therefore potentially create win-win situations for

98 Interview 25:24: "*ja heel soms. Wat we bijvoorbeeld met de transitie doen is dat we 1 keer per 6 weken leveren we ook een soort van status aan van hoe staat het met alle waves zoals dat dan heet. Hoeveel hebben we nou gehad, hoeveel mensen zijn weg gegaan, vrijwillig hoeveel forced. Dus er is wel een vorm van monitoring hoe het proces verloopt*".

99 Evidence-based decision making can be defined as "*evidence-based practice is about making decisions through the conscientious, explicit and judicious use of the best available evidence from multiple sources by (1) asking, (2) acquiring, (3) appraising, (4) aggregating, (5) applying and (6) assessing to increase the likelihood of a favourable outcome*"; see E. Barends, D.M. Rousseau and R.B. Briner, *Evidence-Based Management: The Basic Principles*, Center for Evidence-Based Management (CEBMa, Amsterdam 2014), p. 2.

both an improved position of Dutch works councils in MNCs as well as a higher quality of works councils' advice, while simultaneously ensuring flexibility of the decision-making process. Such a comprehensive employee participation model, however, requires the willingness of the management to involve the works council at an early stage and also a high level of professionalism by the works council.[100] This in turn requires a high level of trust, transparency and constructivism by the management, the works council as well as the supervisory board. Without these soft skills as linking pins, the application of these examples of good practice would be impossible, according to the interview respondents.[101]

100 See section 3.5 of chapter V for an overview of examples of good practice related to the professionalism of Dutch works councils in MNCs.

101 See section 3.7 of chapter V for an analysis of the soft skills necessary for the application of the examples of good practice discussed throughout this study.

Chapter VII: Conclusion

1 Introduction

This study has examined the position of Dutch works councils in multinational corporations from a legal dogmatic as well as from an empirical perspective. The research has set out to explore the following main research question: 'what is the status quo of the position of Dutch works councils in multinational corporations?'. In relation to this question, the study also aimed to answer the following question: 'and how can the position of Dutch works councils in MNCs be improved within an increasingly globalised economy?'.

The study's approach was twofold and focused, in the first part, on analysing the current legal framework that is applicable to Dutch works councils with a specific focus on multinational corporations. The rights and duties pursuant to the Works Councils Act as well as the structure regime and the related case law were examined in chapter III of this study. The case law on the attribution of decisions (*toerekening*) and co-entrepreneurship (*medeondernemerschap*) were two of the main aspects that were examined in that section, due to the significant relevance and impact that these decisions have on the position of the Dutch works council. This case law shows the underlying tensions that exist between corporate decision making on a globalised scale and the timely involvement of the works council in light of the impact of such decisions on the Dutch subsidiaries of MNCs. The legal dogmatic analysis further showed that a range of rights exist for Dutch works councils, ranging from information and consultation rights on intended decisions to rights such as the right to recommend one third of the supervisory board of the undertaking.[1] The chapter also addressed a number of rights that have been recently introduced, especially those concerning employee participation on the level of the corporation (*vennootschapsrechtelijke medezeggenschap*), such as the right to speak at the general meeting of shareholders or on the remuneration of top-managers within the corporation.[2]

The analysis in chapter III served as an inventory of the rights available to Dutch works councils in MNCs. The extent to which the legal framework on employee participation is also applied in practice was the focus of the following empirical analysis that formed the basis of the second part of this study. The answer to the sub-question 'to what extent the employee participation rights are applied in practice?' is a mixed one. The analysis of the results in chapter IV has shown that many of the rights are frequently used in practice.

1 The so-called employee board-level representation (EBLR).
2 Employee participation is traditionally linked to the undertaking and the individual establishments (known as the so-called *ondernemingsrechtelijke medezeggenschap*).

Works councils often have, in the majority of cases, the CEO or another member of the MNC's executive committee as their consultation partner. And works councils are consulted, in almost all cases, more frequently than the statutory minimum that is stipulated in the WCA. The structure regime is also applied, in the large majority of cases, in line with the mandatory nature of the regime. Furthermore, works councils also typically have additional rights pursuant to covenants that have been concluded in accordance with article 32 of the WCA. One must also note that appeals to the Enterprise Chamber pursuant to article 26 of the WCA or appeals to the sub-district court (*Kantonrechter*) pursuant to article 36 of the WCA are scarcely utilised. However, the analysis of the quantitative results highlighted several issues concerning compliance, by some of the MNCs included in this study, with the legal framework and the non-use of some of the works councils' rights. The quantitative results on the use and non-use of participation rights was discussed, at length in chapter IV of this study as well as in chapter VI, which discussed the main differences between Dutch and foreign MNCs. In the following section 2, the main quantitative findings will be summarised briefly.

2 SUMMARY OF THE MAIN QUANTITATIVE FINDINGS

The main quantitative findings concern the topics of consultation, the presence of supervisory board members, the application of the structure regime and the under-utilisation of the works council's rights. These findings will be briefly summarised in the subsequent sections.[3]

2.1 Information and consultation of Dutch works councils

An important main finding is, firstly, that management representatives of MNCs frequently inform and consult their (central) works council, and an overwhelming majority of works councils indicated that they had sufficient time in which to deliver their advice.[4] But while a majority of works councils are consulted in a timeous and sufficient manner, some works councils indicated that they do not have enough time to render their advice, with 16,7% of works councils in the overall sample reporting that this was indeed the case (25 % in foreign MNCs).[5] Works councils in foreign MNCs are, furthermore, significantly less frequently consulted on the future strategy of the MNC and trends when compared to their counterparts in Dutch MNCs (35% compared to

3 See chapter IV for a detailed report of the topics as well as section 2 of chapter VI for a detailed examination of the main differences between Dutch and foreign MNCs with respect to the quantitative results.

4 See section 5.2 of chapter IV concerning the responses relating to the consultation processes in MNCs.

5 See figure 5.10 in section 5.2.3 of chapter IV.

76,2%).[6] And works councils in foreign MNCs are also considerably less often consulted on merger and takeover decisions in comparison to their counterparts in Dutch MNCs (20% compared to 47,6%). Such differences can be seen as one potential determinant for the position of Dutch works councils in MNCs, due to the importance of these topics for the future wellbeing of the corporation and the Dutch subsidiary.

The subsequent qualitative analysis and the inventory of examples of good practice has shown that such topics can be addressed in a constructive manner with due respect to the sensitivity of such matters, which will be elaborated upon in greater detail below. The use of covenants also proved to be a useful tool for Dutch works councils, as they permitted involvement in the consultation process. Works councils in foreign MNCs, however, indicated that covenants were concluded less often, preferring instead the adoption of a negotiated consultation model that is tailored to the individual MNC.[7]

2.2 *Presence of supervisory board members*

Secondly, and in the context of consultation meetings, one of the main issues that was identified concerns the presence of supervisory board members at consultation meetings.[8] Supervisory board members are 'never' present at consultation meetings in the majority of MNCs that were included in this study.[9] That ratio is even higher in foreign MNCs, with 60% of works council respondents indicating that supervisory board members were 'never' present at such meetings. In light of the duty of supervisory board members to attend consultation meetings in accordance with article 24 of the WCA and the duty to attend consultation meetings in accordance with article 25of the WCA,[10] such non-compliance engenders cause for concern. The frequent absence of one of the three internal stakeholders of the undertaking during the consultation meetings must therefore be regarded as another factor that can adversely affect the position of works councils in MNCs. The interview phase of this study showed that the frequent exchange of information and arguments between the stakeholders, including the relationship between the works council and the supervisory board, can improve the decision-making

6 See figure 5.6 in section 5.2 of chapter IV as well as the analysis of the results in the corresponding section.

7 See section 5.3 in chapter IV for a detailed overview thereof.

8 See also sections 5.2.2 in chapter IV and 3.2.2 in chapter VI for a detailed discussion of this issue.

9 And 'sometimes' in 26,2% of the cases. A further 21,4% of respondents indicated that supervisory board members are 'frequently' present.

10 Article 25(4) WCA: "The Works Council shall not render advice on a proposed decision as mentioned in paragraph (1) until the matter in question has been considered at least once in a consultation meeting. **Article 24, paragraph (2), shall apply mutatis mutandis to the discussion of the proposed decision at the consultation meeting**". [MM, emphasis added]; at least one representative of the supervisory board must attend the consultation meetings.

process and benefit the corporation in the longer term.[11] Such non-compliance with the statutory obligations of supervisory board members should also be a point of attention for the legislator and other concerned stakeholders.

2.3 *Application of the structure regime*

Thirdly, it must be noted that not all multinationals fulfil their legal obligations regarding the application of the structure regime and maintain a supervisory board at the Dutch level. Article 2:153/2:263 of the DCC clearly stipulates that the structure regime must be applied once the three cumulative criteria are fulfilled over three consecutive years. This study has shown that in 15,7% of the multinationals that were included in the quantitative part of this study, this was not the case (23,8% in foreign MNCs).[12] It was argued in the analysis in chapter VI above[13] that the absence of a sanction mechanism in article 2:153/2:263 of the DCC, as well as a lack of compliance-monitoring, contributes to the observed non-compliance with the structure regime. This in turn negatively affects the position of Dutch works councils due to the absence of a supervisory board that controls managerial decision-making. The works council, as a result, can no longer use their enhanced recommendation right for one third of the supervisory board (*versterkt aanbevelingsrecht*), if the structure regime is not applied, notwithstanding the fact that the criteria have been fulfilled. Works councils should therefore play a signalling role by indicating the duty to apply the structure regime once the criteria are fulfilled, with the *ultimum remedium* being an appeal to the sub-district court (*Kantonrechter*). A verification of whether or not the criteria are fulfilled could be done with relatively small effort given the works councils' access to information and the right of access to information on the holding structures within the MNC.[14]

2.4 *(Non)-use of the works councils' recommendation rights*

Fourthly, and in relation to the previous point, one has to note that works councils do not always make use of their regular and enhanced recommendation right for supervisory board members.[15] About one-third of works councils indicated that no use of the regular (30,4%) or the enhanced recommendation right (31%) was made; there therefore exists room for improvement in this regard. From a governance perspective, these rights – alongside the works councils' influence on the profile of supervisory board

11 See section 3.4 in chapter V for a detailed overview of the qualitative results on this topic.
12 See also section 4.1 in chapter IV and section 3 in chapter VI for a detailed analysis.
13 See section 3.2.1 in chapter VI.
14 See also section 1.4.1 in chapter III.
15 See figures 4.4 and 4.5 in section 4.1 of chapter IV.

members – are the strongest rights that works councils have in order to influence the (supervision of) corporate decision-making. While it is true that supervisory board members should be independent from any partial interest ('*zonder last of ruggespraak*') and should have the interest of the undertaking as their core objective (article 2:140/2:250 of the DCC), influencing the profile for future supervisory board members (for instance by including references to the importance of social or societal aspects or by reference to the new principle 2.5 of the CGC 2016 on culture) can be beneficial for the position of the works council in the long run.[16] By using its own enhanced recommendation right for one-third of the supervisory board, the works council can significantly impact social aspects through its selection. Works councils can furthermore select a potential candidate that has a background that is suitable in light of the works councils' agenda.[17]

Finally, one has to emphasise that works council are still under-utilising several rights alongside the non-use of the recommendation rights for members of the supervisory board.[18] The quantitative analysis has also shown that works councils do not frequently use their right to call in experts[19] (internal or external), do not know whether access to information on the holding structure of their MNC exists[20] and one-third of respondents (33%) indicated that they do not maintain contact with employee representatives within their MNC in other countries.[21] There is certainly room for improvement in this regard, and this can be done by relying upon existing tools. Through training and raising awareness of these rights, as well as existing networks and platforms on employee participation in the Netherlands and in Europe, the position of (Dutch) works councils could be further improved.

When answering the question 'to what extent are the rights identified in the legal dogmatic analysis applied in practice and can differences between Dutch and foreign MNCs be observed?' one can conclude that particularly the differences between Dutch and foreign MNCs with regard to consultation topics can be seen as one potential determinant for the position of Dutch works councils in MNCs, due to the importance of these topics for the future wellbeing of the corporation and the Dutch subsidiary.

16 Which is to some extent confirmed by the questionnaire responses; see figures 4.9 – 4.12 in section 4.2 of chapter IV.

17 See also section 3.4.4 in chapter V.

18 A finding that was already made in 2009; R. Goodijk, P. van Beurden and H. van Ees, 'Gebruik, niet-gebruik of onderbenutting? Onderzoek naar de mogelijke onderbenutting van bevoegdheden en mogelijkheden door de (Centrale) Ondernemingsraad in grote Nederlandse ondernemingen', report: *Ministerie van Sociale Zaken en Werkgelegenheid* (2009).

19 See figures 5.22 and 5.23 in section 5.6 of chapter IV.

20 See figures 5.19 and 5.20 in section 5.5 of chapter IV.

21 See figure 6.1 in section 6 of chapter IV.

Also the absence of supervisory board members[22] and the compliance with the structure regime and the related use of recommendation rights by works councils could be identified as determinant for the position of Dutch works councils in MNCs. A greater emphasis by Dutch works councils as well as other stakeholders (i.e. both legislators and experts in the field) on the topics discussed in this section could help improving the position of works councils in MNCs.

3 SUMMARY OF THE MAIN QUALITATIVE FINDINGS

The final research question posed was: 'to what extent exist examples of good practice that are aimed at facilitating the employee participation process in MNCs?'. To answer this question, the qualitative analysis was based on 58 semi-structured interviews and revealed a multitude of practical solutions and a total of 143 examples of good practice (see chapter V above). The results that were clustered according to the different phases of the employee participation process and the stakeholders involved, are multifaceted and reflective of the participation culture that is present in the respective MNC.

The clusters used are:

1. Access to information
2. Consultation
3. Facilities by the management
4. Relationship between works council and supervisory board
5. Professionalism of works councils
6. Relationship with the European works council
7. Soft skills

3.1 *Tailor-made approaches to employee participation*

The examples of good practice show that through negotiation and long-term experiences with participation mechanisms, tailor-made employee participation processes can be achieved. The management, supervisory board and works council respondents overwhelmingly emphasised the benefits of such tailor-made approaches due to the increased flexibility and time-effectiveness of several good practices. The development of comprehensive process-oriented participation frameworks is especially noteworthy. Due to the integral approach taken by the management, works council and supervisory board together, they have improved the statutory participation process in order to ensure

22 Or non-executive directors in one-tier boards.

the timely involvement of works councils and better decision-making, according to the respondents.[23] Examples such as these show that works council involvement, which is a fundamental right enshrined in the Dutch Constitution and provided for in the EU legal framework, is not only necessary but it can also be beneficial to companies by harnessing the expertise of the works council members and the input from their constituencies. The use of a pre-consultation phase whereby (a working group of) the works council informally participates in the decision-making process can be particularly beneficial in order to accelerate the subsequent formal consultation phase and improve the works council position by enabling it to give input at an early stage.

3.2 *Monitoring of decisions*

Another important finding of the qualitative analysis is the existence of an (often-lacking) monitoring phase. Only few interview respondents indicated that, by default, the decisions being made were monitored in the implementation phase and subject to appraisal by the management and works council after a certain period of time (for instance six or twelve months). While it is very well possible that monitoring is carried out implicitly, responses from the interviewees show that by formulating an explicit monitoring plan, both the management and the works council (and also the supervisory board) benefit from obtaining better insights into the progress made and gain valuable knowledge for upcoming consultation topics.[24]

3.3 *(Digital) information packages*

Further noteworthy examples of good practice include *inter alia* the use of standardised information packages or digital information dossiers, which are regularly updated.[25] The efficient access to reoccurring information reduces the administrative burden for the management and ensures timely access to information for works councils, which makes these good practice examples beneficial for both stakeholders. The use of annual or semi-annual strategy meetings as a platform to exchange information between management, works council and supervisory board are also noteworthy in this context.[26] These meetings can serve as monitoring instance of previously completed consultation dossiers. And more importantly, these meetings can be taken a good moment to discuss

23 See also section 3.2.6 in chapter V and section 4 in chapter VI for a detailed overview.

24 In accordance with the rational-decision making theory, given the fact that consultation processes are repetitive and knowledge from previous consultation rounds benefits all stakeholders involved and should lead to better decision-making in the long run; see J. Von Neumann and O. Morgenstern, *Theory of Games and Economic Behavior* (60th anniversary ed., Princeton University Press, Princeton 2007).

25 See section 3.1.1 in chapter V.

26 See section 3.1.2 in chapter V.

the outlook for the upcoming business year and highlight potential upcoming issues that deserve the attention of all three internal stakeholders (i.e., the management, supervisory board and works council).

3.4 *Professionalised employee participation structures*

Finally, one must conclude that many of the interviewed works council representatives pay particular attention to the need for professional employee participation structures. A total of 32 examples of best practice were identified in the interview phase of this study that concern the professionalism of works councils. These range from internal training and development plans, the use of working groups and to the formulation of own initiatives.[27] Many of these examples of good practice could be beneficial to the work of other works councils and could be transferable to other MNCs. Platforms on the national[28] and European level[29] aimed at the exchange of information and employee participation practices could also play a role in disseminating such good practices so as to improve the position of works councils in other corporations. Other initiatives aimed at the relationship between works councils and supervisory boards in light of good corporate governance can also play a role in communicating examples of good practice and to inform the stakeholders involved.[30]

4 OUTLOOK AND FUTURE CHALLENGES FOR THE POSITION OF (DUTCH) WORKS COUNCILS IN MULTINATIONAL CORPORATIONS

Based on the analysis of the legal framework, the quantitative and the qualitative analysis and coming back to the main research question ('what is the status quo of the position of Dutch works councils in multinational corporations?'), one can conclude that the position of the majority of the examined Dutch works councils is solid. Several aspects, however, do need to be worked on by works councils, other stakeholders and the legislator in order to improve the position of works councils and to safeguard their statutory rights – a theme that was emphasised throughout this study. The qualitative analysis and the inventory of examples of good practice in particular has shown that many solutions to timely and efficient employee participation already exist in practice. The most

27 See section 3.5 in chapter V for a detailed overview of all examples of best practice related to works council professionalism.

28 Such as the Dutch MNO Foundation, which is already facilitating an exchange of good practices within its network.

29 Such as the GoodCorp and WPEurope (formerly SEEurope) Networks and similar initiatives; see further ETUI, <http://www.worker-participation.eu> (last accessed 27 September 2017).

30 Such as the *Alliantie voor medezeggenschap en governance* that was initiated in 2015 by the Social and Economic Council of the Netherlands, <http://www.or-en-commissaris.nl/> (last accessed 27 September 2017).

far-reaching solutions are those comprehensive and process-oriented employee participation schemes.

Yet one must also point out that the empirical part of this study only included a relatively small sample, and was concluded within a period of two years. This study was based on the responses by Dutch central works councils[31] in multinational corporations to the questionnaire that was circulated in 2014, at the end of the financial and economic crisis. The study was furthermore based on semi-structured interviews with works council representatives, managers and supervisory board members from 24 multinational corporations. While this study provided insights into the application of employee participation rights in practice (quantitative phase), and while it has revealed a multitude of good practice examples (qualitative phase), the results are nevertheless limited in scope. The data collection took place in a relatively short period of only one year and took place shortly after the economic crisis. The data were collected during the timeframe 2014 to 2015 and within the specific sample of multinational corporations and more specifically their Dutch subsidiaries. While the results of the qualitative phase may be certainly transferable to other undertakings, further research should nevertheless be conducted on this topic. One possibility would be to repeat the data collection among works councils in MNCs. The results of the quantitative phase may have been affected by the aftermath of the financial crisis or other factors. A future benchmarking of the results could therefore prove useful to scrutinise whether similar results could be observed. And by repeating the study, a comparison could be made and further trends concerning the development of employee participation mechanisms may become identifiable.

The qualitative phase was explorative in nature and was aimed at collecting as many examples of good practice as possible. The sample of 24 multinationals and a total of 58 interviews is nevertheless relatively small and more research on topics such as the impact of the new Dutch CGC 2016[32] would be desirable in this regard.

Finally, other factors that may impact the position of (Dutch) works councils in MNCs should be subject to further research. One important recent development is company mobility within the European Union. At the time of writing, the European Commission is in the process of preparing a new legislative package on corporate mobility, which includes a draft Directive on cross-border conversion of companies and cross-border divisions. It is expected that the legislative package will be unveiled in late 2017.[33] This new Commission package may impact the position of works councils in MNCs. Recent

31 Or the works council exercising employee participation rights at the highest possible level within the Netherlands.

32 Which was adopted in December 2016 after the completion of the qualitative phase of this study.

33 European Commission DG Justice and Consumers, 'EU Company law upgraded: Rules on digital solutions and efficient cross-border operations', <http://ec.europa.eu/newsroom/just/item-detail.cfm?item_id=58190> (last accessed 28 September 2017).

research[34] on company mobility in the EU shows that company groups in particular (i.e., MNCs), have made use of cross-border company mobility tools that are already available under the current framework, such as the cross-border mergers Directive[35] and the European company (Societas Europaea).[36] The proposed Directive on cross-border conversions of companies may have an impact on the position of (Dutch) works councils. A study on this topic by the Hans Böckler Foundation examined the use of foreign company forms in Germany with the aim of circumventing German employee board-level participation rules.[37] The study found that 94 companies with more than 500 employees (which would make the *Drittelbeteiligungsgesetz*[38] applicable) are already using foreign company forms that no longer fall within the scope of the German employee board-level representation regime. Through EU legislation, such as the proposed cross-border company conversion Directive, this phenomenon could be amplified and could also affect the position of Dutch works councils. It remains to be seen whether the Commission company mobility package will enter into force and what its practical effect will be. In addition, company mobility within Europe with recourse to the already existing legal instruments may impact the position of works councils as well. That being said, such cross-border company mobility also necessitates further research in this field.[39]

34 T. Biermeyer and M. Meyer, Identification of cross-border mergers where the issue of employee participation has arisen (2008-2012) (external report), Brussels: European Trade Union Institute (Etui).

35 Directive 2005/56/EC of the European Parliament and of the Council of 26 October 2005 on cross-border mergers of limited liability companies, [2005] OJ L 310/1.

36 Council Regulation (EC) No 2157/2001 of 8 October 2001 on the Statute for a European company (SE), [2001] OJ L 294/1.

37 S. Sick, *Mitbestimmungsfeindlicheres Klima*, Mitbestimmungsförderung Report Nr.13, <https://www.boeckler.de/pdf/p_mbf_report_2015_13.pdf> (last accessed 28 September 2017).

38 *Drittelbeteiligungsgesetz vom 18. Mai 2004 (BGBl. I S. 974), das zuletzt durch Artikel 8 des Gesetzes vom 24. April 2015 (BGBl. I S. 642) geändert worden ist.*

39 See the recently launched cross-border company mobility project that was commissioned by the European Trade Union Institute and the European Commission (http://www.maastrichtuniversity.nl/corporate-mobility-project).

Bibliography

Journal articles

R.B. Adams and B. Ferreira, 'A theory of friendly boards', 1 *Journal of Finance* 62 (2007)

J.T. Addison and P. Teixeira, 'The Effect of Works Councils on Employment Change', 45 *Industrial Relations* 1 (2006)

J.T. Addison, C. Schnabel and J. Wagner, 'Works councils in Germany: their effects on establishment performance', *Oxford Economic Papers* 53 (2001)

R.V. Aguilera and G. Jackson, 'The Cross-National Diversity of Corporate Governance: Dimensions and Determinants', 3 *The Academy of Management Review* 28 (2003)

J. Armour and W.G. Ringe, 'European Company Law 1999–2010: Renaissance and crisis', 48 *Common Market Law Review* 1 (2011)

K.L. Barriball and A. While, 'Collecting data using a semi-structured interview: a discussion paper', *Journal of Advanced Nursing* 19 (1994)

S.M. Bartman, 'Hoge Raad weet zich niet goed raad met het concern', *Ondernemingsrecht* 2016/77 (2016)

S.M. Bartman and M. Holtzer, 'Enquêterecht voorzichtig onder het mes', *Ondernemingsrecht* 14 (2010)

R. Beltzer, 'Vakbonden en collectieve arbeidsvoorwaardenvorming: de juridische legitimatie erodeert', *Nederlands Juristenblad* (2010)

A. van den Berg, 'Ondernemingsraad en Goed Bestuur: een Institutioneel-Economisch Benadering', 20 *Tijdschrift voor Arbeidsvraagstukken* 4 (2004)

A. van den Berg, Y. Grift and A. van Witteloostuijn, 'Works Councils and Organizational Performance: The Role of Top Managers' and Works Councils' Attitudes in Bad Vis-à-vis Good Times', *Journal of Labor Research* (2011)

A. van den Berg, Y. Grift and A. van Witteloostuijn, 'Managerial Perceptions of Works Councils' Effectiveness in the Netherlands', 50 *Industrial Relations* 3 (2011)

M.C.T. Burgers, 'Wet Harrewijn; (hoe) werkt het in de praktijk?', 20 *ArbeidsRecht* (2008)

R.P. Carver, 'The Case Against Statistical Significance Testing', 48 *Harvard Educational Review* 3 (1978)

C. Coglianese, 'Empirical analysis and administrative law', *University of Illinois Law Review* (2002)

J.A.M. Cornelissens, 'Enkele beschouwingen bij het 10-jarig bestaan van de Wet op de ondernemingsraden', 14 *Katholiek Staatkundig Maandschrift* 2 (1960)

J.L. Cotton et al., 'Employee Participation: Diverse Forms and Different Outcomes', 13 *The Academy of Management Review* 1 (1988)

R. Czaja, 'Questionnaire Pretesting Comes of Age', 9 *Marketing Bulletin* (1998)

R.G.M. Dahmen, 'De aanwijzingsbevoegdheid van het gewijzigde artikel 2:239 lid 4 BW: toepassing, toetsing, afdwingbaarheid en aspecten van aansprakelijkheid in concernperspectief', 2 *Tijdschrift voor vennootschaps- en rechtspersonenrecht* (2014)

A. Demb and F. Neubauer, 'The Corporate Board: Confronting the Paradoxes', 3 *Long Range Planning* 25 (1992)

E. Deutskens et al., 'Response rate and response quality of internet-based surveys', 15 *Marketing Letters* 1 (2004)

P.J. Dortmond, 'Toegang tot de algemene vergadering en besluiten buiten vergadering', *Ondernemingsrecht* 45 (2010)

P.J. Dortmond, M.J. Kroeze and R.G.J. Nowak, 'De aangenomen amendementen bij de wetsvoorstellen bestuur en toezicht, flexibilisering bv-recht, spreekrecht OR, uitvoeringswet aandeelhoudersrichtlijn en invoeringswet titel 7.13 BW', *Ondernemingsrecht* 9 (2010)

B. van Duren-Kloppert, 'Enquêterecht en medezeggenschap: tijd voor Doornroosje om te ontwaken?', *ArbeidsRecht* 36 (2004)

F.B.J. Grapperhaus, 'Over legitimatie en rol van de vakbond', *Ondernemingsrecht* 83 (2011)

E. Groenewald, 'Corporate Governance in the Netherlands: From the Verdam Report of 1964 to the Tabaksblat Code of 2003', *European Business Organization Law Review* 2 (2005)

Y. Hadari, 'The Structure of the Private Multinational Enterprise', 71 *Michigan Law Review* 4 (1973)

A-W. Harzing, 'An Empirical Analysis and Extension of the Bartlett and Ghoshal Typology of Multinational Companies', 31 *Journal of International Business Studies* 1 (2000)

P.F. van der Heijden, 'Harrewijn revisited', *OR Informatie* 4 (2014)

M. Holtzer, 'Het spreekrecht van de ondernemingsraad van de naamloze vennootschap bij belangrijke besluiten', *Ondernemingsrecht* 114 (2010)

R. Hooghiemstra and J. van Manen, 'The Independence Paradox: (im)possibilities facing non-executive directors in The Netherlands', 12 *Corporate Governance: An International Review* 3 (2004)

H. Hsieh and S.E. Shannon, 'Three Approaches to Qualitative Content Analysis', 15 *Qualitative Health Research* 9 (2005)

P. Ingelse, 'Mede-ondernemen en concernenquête', *Tijdschrift voor Arbeid & Onderneming* 1 (2012)

P. Ireland, I. Grigg-Spall and D. Kelly, 'The Conceptual Foundations of Modern Company Law', 14 *Journal of Law and Society* 1 (1987)

D. Jimali, 'A Stakeholder Approach to Corporate Social Responsibility: A Fresh Perspective into Theory and Practice', 82 *Journal of Business Ethics* 1 (2008)

U. Jirjahn, 'Ökonomische Wirkungen des novellierten Betriebsverfassungsgesetzes – Was können wir vor dem Hintergrund zunehmender Globalisierung und veränderter arbeitsorganisatorischer Bedingungen erwarten?', *ZAF* 2 and 3 (2005)

U. Jirjahn, 'Works councils and employment growth in German establishments', 34 *Cambridge Journal of Economics* (2010)

U. Jirjahn and K. Kraft, 'Do Spillovers Stimulate Incremental or Drastic Product Innovations? Evidence from German Establishment Data', 73 *Oxford Bulletin of Economics and Statistics* 4 (2011)

R.B. Johnson et al., 'Toward a Definition of Mixed Methods Research', 1 *Journal of Mixed Methods Research* 2 (2007)

B.C.L. Kanen, 'De structuurregeling en adviesrecht', *ArbeidsRecht* 5 (2012)

H.H. Kersten, 'De onafhankelijke toezichthouder', *Ondernemingsrecht* 2004/43 (2004)

M. Koelemeijer, 'De herziene Corporate Governance Code: (nieuwe) accenten in effectief toezicht', 14 *Tijdschrift voor Ondernemingsbestuur* 2 (2017)

J.K. Looise and M. Drucker, 'Employee participation in multinational enterprises: The effects of globalisation on Dutch works councils', 24 *Employee Relations* 1 (2002)

J.K. Looise and M. Drucker, 'Dutch Works Councils in Times of Transition: The Effects of Changes in Society, Organizations and Work on the Position of Works Councils', 24 *Employee Relations* 3 (2003)

M. Meyer, 'De positie van Nederlandse ondernemingsraden in internationale concerns: een pleidooi voor procesgerichte medezeggenschap', *Tijdschrift Recht en Arbeid* 2016/45 (2016)

M. Meyer, 'Employee Participation in Multinational Corporations: Corporate Governance and the Role of Works Councils', 14 *Tijdschrift voor Ondernemingsbestuur* 4 (2017)

R.G.J. Nowak, 'Het wetsvoorstel spreekrecht OR bij belangrijke ava-besluiten', *Ondernemingsrecht* 59 (2009)

C.W.P. Ommeren and D.J.W.M. Kemperink, 'Het spreekrecht van de ondernemingsraad', *ArbeidsRecht* 5 (2011)

M.A. Pickering, 'The Company as a separate legal entity', 31 *Modern Law Review* 5 (1968)

O. Sjöström, D. Holst and S.O. Lind, 'Validity of a questionnaire survey: the role of non-response and incorrect answers', 57 *Acta Odontol Scand* 5 (1999)

L.C.J. Sprengers, 'Toetsing van een adviesprocedure in drie delen', 44 *Sociaal Recht* (2008)

L.C.J. Sprengers, 'Haagse grenscorrectie. Provincie kan – gelet op de daaraan te stellen eisen – niet worden aangemerkt als mede-ondernemer ten aanzien van de gemeentelijke organisatie. Betekenis van het "politieke primaat"', 41 *Tijdschrift voor Ambtenarenrecht* (2000)

L.C.J. Sprengers, 'De ondernemingsraad en de raad van commissarissen: een vorm van vennootschapsrechtelijke medezeggenschap', 1 *Tijdschrift Arbeidsrechtpraktijk* 10 (2017)

L.G. Verburg, 'De OK, de medezeggenschap en de periode 2007 tot en met 2008', *ArbeidsRecht* 8 (2009)

L.G. Verburg, 'Toerekening van besluitvorming en medeondernemerschap', *ArbeidsRecht* 9 (2014)

J. Waddington, 'What do Representatives Think of the Practices of European Works Councils? Views from Six Countries', 9 *European Journal of Industrial Relations* 3 (2003)

G.W. Wesselingh, 'Het afschaffen of beperken van het structuurregime vanwege een (gedeeltelijke) vrijstelling: adviesrecht ondernemingsraad?', *Vennootschap & Onderneming* 6 (2011)

K. Wiersma and R.C. Moed, 'Joint ventures en medezeggenschap: een update', *Onderneming en Financiering* 3 (2013)

P.A.M. Witteveen, 'De betekenis van de nieuwe structuurwet voor de positie van de ondernemingsraad', *Onderneming en Financiering* 68 (2005)

I. Zaal, 'Spreekrecht voor de ondernemingsraad', *Tijdschrift Recht en Arbeid* 17 (2009)

I. Zaal, 'De rol van de OR ten aanzien van aandeelhoudersbesluiten', 10 *ArbeidsRecht* 2 (2015)

BOOKS

E. Babbie, *The Practice of Social Research* (12th edn., Wadsworth, Belmont 2010)

C.A. Bartlett and G. Sumantra, *Managing Across Borders: The Transnational Solution* (Harvard Business Press, Boston 1989)

S.M. Bartman and A.F.M. Dorresteijn, *Van het concern* (8th edition, Kluwer, Deventer 2013)

S.M. Bartman, A.F.M. Dorresteijn and M. Olaerts, *Van het concern* (9th edition, Kluwer, Deventer 2016)

A. Beckers, *Taking Corporate Codes Seriously: Towards Private Law Enforcement of Voluntary Corporate Social Responsibility Codes* (Maastricht University, Maastricht 2014)

A. Cahn and D.C. Donald, *Comparative Company Law* (Cambridge University Press, Cambridge 2010)

K. Cools et al., *Het recht van enquête: Een empirisch onderzoek* (Kluwer, Deventer 2009)

J.W. Creswell and V.L. Plano Clark (eds.), *Designing and Conducting Mixed Methods Research* (2nd edition, SAGE, London 2011)

J.W. Creswell, *Research Design: Qualitative, Quantitative and Mixed Methods Approaches* (3rd edition, SAGE, London 2009)

S. De Spiegelaere and R. Jagodzinski, *European Works Councils and SE Works Councils in 2015: Facts & figures* (ETUI aisbl, Brussels 2015)

A.F.M. Dorresteijn, *European Corporate Law* (2nd edition, Kluwer Law International, Deventer 2009)

J. van Drongelen and S.F.H. Jellinghaus, *Collectief Arbeidsrecht – Deel 1: Wet op de ondernemingsraden* (2nd edn., Uitgeverij Paris, Zutphen 2010)

U. Flick, *An Introduction to Qualitative Research*, (SAGE, London 2009)

U. Flick, E. von Kardorff and I. Steinke (eds.), *A Companion to Qualitative Research* (SAGE, London 2004)

R.E. Freeman, *Strategic Management: A Stakeholder Approach* (Pitman, Boston 1984)

P.F. van der Heijden, *Rood's Wet op de Ondernemingsraden* (Kluwer, Deventer 2004)

M. Holtzer, *De invloed van werknemers op de strategie van de vennootschap* (Kluwer, Deventer 2014)

H.J.M.N. Honée, *Concernrecht en medezeggenschapsregelingen* (Kluwer, Deventer 1981)

R. Jenkins, R. Pearson and G. Seyfang, *Corporate Responsibility and Labour Rights: Codes of Conduct in the Global Economy* (Earthscan Publications, London 2002)

R.H. van het Kaar and J.C. Looise, *De volwassen OR – Groei en grenzen van de Nederlandse ondernemingsraad: Resultaten van het grote OR-onderzoek* (Samsom, Alphen aan den Rijn 1999)

R.H. van het Kaar and E. Smit (eds.), *Vier scenario's voor de toekomst van de medezeggenschap – Een onderzoek in opdracht van het Ministerie van SZW* (Amsterdam/Utrecht 2006)

C.J. Lammers, *Organiseren van bovenaf en van onderop. Een beknopte inleiding in de organisatiesociologie* (Het Spectrum, Utrecht 1993)

J.J.M. van Mierlo, *Medezeggenschap en de spanning tussen WOR en ondernemingsrecht* (Kluwer, Deventer 2013)

J. Von Neumann and O. Morgenstern, *Theory of Games and Economic Behavior* (60th anniversary ed., Princeton University Press, Princeton 2007)

P.P. van Schaik, *De adviesplichtige intentieverklaring: Het adviesrecht van de ondernemingsraad bij een overname* (Celsus juridische uitgeverij, Tilburg 2010)

P. van Schilfgaarde and J. Winter (eds.), *Van de BV en de NV* (15th edition, Kluwer, Deventer 2009)

P. van Schilfgaarde, *Van de BV en de NV* (16th edition, Kluwer, Deventer 2013)

P. van Schilfgaarde, *Van de BV en de NV* (17th edition, Kluwer, Deventer 2017)

C. Seale, *The Quality of Qualitative Research*, (SAGE, London 1999)

W.J. Slagter, *Enkele rechtsvergelijkende beschouwingen over moeder-dochterverhoudingen* (Kluwer, Deventer 1988)

W.J. Slagter, *Compendium Ondernemingsrecht* (8th edition, Kluwer, Deventer 2005)

L. Sprengers, *De wet op de Ondernemingsraden bij de overheid. Op weg naar een arbeidsrecht voor ambtenaren en werknemers* (Kluwer, Deventer 1998)

Statistics Netherlands, *Internationalisation Monitor 2013* (Statistics Netherlands, The Hague 2013)

H. van den Tillaart and J. Warmerdam, *Ontwikkelingen in scholing van ondernemingsraden: Terugblik op de afgelopen jaren en verwachtingen voor de toekomst* (ITS, Nijmegen 2016)

L. Timmerman, *Over multinationale ondernemingen en medezeggenschap van werknemers* (Kluwer, Deventer 1988)

L.G. Verburg, *Het territoir van de (Nederlandse) ondernemingsraad in het internationale bedrijfs-leven* (Kluwer, Deventer 2007)

L.G. Verburg, *Rood's Wet op de ondernemingsraden* (2nd edition, Kluwer, Deventer 2013)

P.J. Verdam et al., *Rapport herziening van het ondernemingsrecht* (Staatsuitgeverij, 's-Gravenhage 1965)

E. Verhulp, *Vrijheid van meningsuiting van werknemers en ambtenaren* (Sdu, The Hague 1997)

I. Zaal, *De reikwijdte van medezeggenschap* (Kluwer, Deventer 2013)

Chapters of books

P. Boxall and J. Purcell, 'An HRM Perspective on Employee Participation', in A. Wilkinson et al. (eds.), *The Oxford Handbook of Participation in Organizations* (Oxford University Press, Oxford 2010)

M.B. Brewer, 'Research design and issues of validity', in H.T. Reis and C.M. Judd (eds.), *Handbook of research methods in social and personality psychology*, (Cambridge University Press, Cambridge 2000)

W.F. De Nijs, 'Medezeggenschap', in W.H.J. Reynaerts (eds.), *Arbeidsverhoudingen: Theorie en Praktijk* (Stenfert Kroese, Leiden and Antwerp 1987)

R.B. Freeman and E.P. Lazear, 'An Economic Analysis of Works Councils', in J. Rogers and W. Streeck, *Works Councils: Consultation, Representation, and Cooperation in Industrial Relations* (University of Chicago Press, Chicago 1995)

R.H. van het Kaar, 'SEs in the Netherlands', in J. Cremers, M. Stollt and S. Vitols (eds.), *A decade of experience with the European Company* (ETUI, Brussels 2013)

U. Kelle and C. Erzberger, 'Qualitative and Quantitative Methods: Not in Opposition', in U. Flick, E. von Kardorff and I. Steinke (eds.), *A Companion to Qualitative Research* (SAGE, London 2004)

J. Lamers (*red.*), M. van Kempen, M. Meyer, K. Wiersma and P. Witteveen, 'De OR en aandelenoverdracht in internationale concerns', in R. Houweling and L. Sprengers (eds.), *70 jaar VvA: einde van het begin (lustrumbundel VvA)* (Wolters Kluwer, Deventer 2016)

C. Schmidt, 'The Analysis of Semi-structured Interviews', in U. Flick, E. von Kardorff and I. Steinke (eds.), *A Companion to Qualitative Research* (SAGE, London 2004)

E. Schmieman, 'De bevoegdheden van de advocaat-generaal bij het Gerechtshof Amsterdam in het enquêterecht (art. 2:345 lid 2 en 2:355 lid 1 BW)', in G. van Solinge and M. Holtzer (eds.), *Geschriften vanwege de Vereniging Corporate Litigation 2003-2004, Serie vanwege het Van der Heijden Instituut, deel 75* (Kluwer, Deventer 2004)

W. Streeck, 'Works Councils in Western Europe: From Consultation to Participation', in J. Rogers and W. Streeck, *Works Councils: Consultation, Representation, and Cooperation in Industrial Relations* (University of Chicago Press, Chicago 1995)

J. Visser, 'The Netherlands: From Paternalism to Representation', in J. Rogers and W. Streeck, *Works Councils: Consultation, Representation, and Cooperation in Industrial Relations* (University of Chicago Press, Chicago 1995)

P.A.M. Witteveen et al., '9 Ondernemingsraad en enquêterecht', in L.C.J. Sprengers and G.W. van der Voet (eds.), *De toekomst van de medezeggenschap: Aanbevelingen aan de wetgever* (Kluwer, Deventer 2009)

Working papers and reports

E. Barends, D.M. Rousseau and R.B. Briner, *Evidence-Based Management: The Basic Principles*, Center for Evidence-Based Management (CEBMa, Amsterdam 2014)

P. van Beurden, H. van Ees and R. Goodijk, 'Gebruik, niet-gebruik of onderbenutting? – Onderzoek naar de mogelijke onderbenutting van bevoegdheden en mogelijkheden door de (Centrale) Ondernemingsraad in grote Nederlandse ondernemingen', Report for *Ministerie van Sociale Zaken en Werkgelegenheid* (GITP, Groningen 2009)

T. Biermeyer and M. Meyer, Identification of cross-border mergers where the issue of employee participation has arisen (2008-2012) (external report), Brussels: European Trade Union Institute (Etui)

Centraal Bureau voor de Statistiek (CBS), *De Nederlandse economie 2011* (Den Haag/Heerlen, 2012)

Centraal Bureau voor de Statistiek (CBS), *De Nederlandse economie 2012* (Den Haag/Heerlen, 2013)

Centraal Bureau voor de Statistiek (CBS), *De Nederlandse economie 2013* (Den Haag/Heerlen, 2014)

Centraal Bureau voor de Statistiek (CBS), *Internationaliseringsmonitor 2015 – Derde kwartaal* (CBS, Den Haag 2015)

Centraal Bureau voor de Statistiek (CBS), *Nederland in 2014: Een economisch overzicht* (Den Haag/Heerlen, 2015)

European Commission, 'Report of the Group of Experts on the implementation of Recast Directive 2009/38/EC on European Works Councils – December 2010', Ares(2011)22826, <www.ec.europa.eu/social/BlobServlet?docId=6436&langId=en>

Financial Reporting Council, *The UK Corporate Governance Code* (The Financial Reporting Council Limited, London 2016)

M. Jaarsma and F. van Berkel, 'Trends in Dutch international trade' (Internationalisation Monitor, Statistics Netherlands, The Hague 2013)

A. Nauta (et al.), 'Expedities in sociale innovatie: Hoe ondernemingsraadsleden hun rol beleven en uitoefenen', NCSI working paper (2008), <http://dare.uva.nl/document/2/61737>

S. Sick, *Mitbestimmungsfeindlicheres Klima*, Mitbestimmungsförderung Report Nr.13, <https://www.boeckler.de/pdf/p_mbf_report_2015_13.pdf>

J. Waddington et al., 'Managers, BusinessEurope and the development of European Works Councils', *ETUI Research Paper* 6 (2016), <https://ssrn.com/abstract=2792020>

Electronic sources

Alliantie voor medezeggenschap en governance, 'Medezeggenschap en toezicht: een starke combinatie', <http://www.or-en-commissaris.nl/> (last accessed 27 September 2017)

Bedrijfscommissie voor de Overheid, 'Gevolgen WOR-wijzigingen 19 juli 2013', <https://www.bedrijfscommissieoverheid.nl/actueel/2013/gevolgen-wor-wijzigingen-19-juli-2013/> (last accessed 29 September 2017)

Centraal Bureau voor de Statistiek (CBS), 'Bedrijven; bedrijfsgrootte en rechtsvorm', <CBS data catalogue> (last accessed 24 October 2017)

Centraal Bureau voor de Statistiek (CBS), 'Bevolking 15 tot 75 jaar', <https://www.cbs.nl/nl-nl/achtergrond/2016/20/bevolking-15-tot-75-jaar> (last accessed 02 February 2017).

Centraal Bureau voor de Statistiek (CBS), 'Werkzame en totale beroepsbevolking', <https://www.cbs.nl/NR/rdonlyres/9278A94C-243D-4FEA-B61F-57BF68E6F479/0/pb14n041.pdf> (last accessed 23 August 2017)

Dutch Civil Law, 'Book 2 Legal Persons – Title 2.1 General provisions', <http://www.dutchcivillaw.com/civilcodebook022.htm> (last accessed 29 September 2017).

Dutch Civil Law, 'Book 2 Legal Persons – Section 2.4.5 The Board of Directors of an Open Corporation and the supervision of the Board of Directors', <http://www.dutchcivillaw.com/civilcodebook022.htm> (last accessed 29 September 2017).

Dutch Civil Law, 'Book 2 Legal Persons – Section 2.4.6 The Supervisory Board of a large Open Corporation', <http://www.dutchcivillaw.com/civilcodebook022.htm> (last accessed 30 September 2017).

Dutch Civil Law, 'Section 2.8.1 Rules for resolving disputes between shareholders', <http://www.dutchcivillaw.com/civilcodebook022.htm> (last accessed 29 September 2017).

Eerste Kamer der Staten-Generaal, '29.818 Wet medezeggenschap werknemers', <http://www.eerstekamer.nl/wetsvoorstel/29818_wet_medezeggenschap> (last accessed 29 September 2017)

Enterprise Chamber of the Amsterdam Court of Appeal, 'Jaarverslag Ondernemingskamer 2015', <https://www.rechtspraak.nl/SiteCollectionDocuments/jaarverslag-Ondernemingskamer-2015.pdf> (last accessed 1 October 2017)

Enterprise Chamber of the Amsterdam Court of Appeal, 'Jaarverslag Ondernemingskamer 2016', <https://www.rechtspraak.nl/SiteCollectionDocuments/Jaarverslag-ondernemingskamer-2016.pdf> (last accessed 29 January 2018)

European Commission DG Justice and Consumers, 'EU Company law upgraded: Rules on digital solutions and efficient cross-border operations', <http://ec.europa.eu/newsroom/just/item-detail.cfm?item_id=58190> (last accessed 28 September 2017).

European Commission Directorate-General for Economic and Financial Affairs, 'European Economic Forecast – Autumn 2011', <http://ec.europa.eu/economy_finance/publications/european_economy/2011/pdf/ee-2011-6_en.pdf> (last accessed 11 July 2017)

European Commission Directorate-General for Economic and Financial Affairs, 'European Economic Forecast – Autumn 2012', <http://ec.europa.eu/economy_finance/publications/european_economy/2012/pdf/ee-2012-7_en.pdf> (last accessed 11 July 2017)

European Commission Directorate-General for Economic and Financial Affairs, 'European Economic Forecast – Autumn 2013', <http://ec.europa.eu/economy_finance/publications/european_economy/2013/pdf/ee7_en.pdf> (last accessed 11 July 2017)

ETUI, <http://www.worker-participation.eu> (last accessed 27 September 2017)

M. van Ewijk and M. Engelen, 'De faciliteiten, bevoegdheden en informatievoorziening van OR-en en het effect van het netwerk op het functioneren van de OR', <https://docs.szw.nl/pdf/35/2003/35_2003_3_3371.pdf> (last accessed 2 November 2017)

Financieel Daagblad, 'Parijs aast op meer macht bij KLM', <https://fd.nl/ondernemen/1172470/parijs-aast-op-meer-macht-bij-klm> (last accessed 24 October 2016)

Financieel Daagblad, 'Doorsluizen van kasmiddelen naar holding stuit op verzet van ondernemingsraad Tata Steel', <https://fd.nl/ondernemen/1090639/doorsluizen-van-kasmiddelen-naar-holding-stuit-op-verzet-van-ondernemingsraad-tata-steel> (last accessed 24 October 2016)

J.B. Huizink, 'Arbeidsovereenkomst, artikel 30 WOR, aant. 5', <http://deeplinking.kluwer.nl/?param=00BF59DE&cpid=WKNL-LTR-Navigator> (last accessed 29 September 2017)

R. Jagodzinski and I. Pas, 'The EWC landscape on the eve of the transposition deadline of the recast directive 2009/38/EC – Evidence from the ETUI database of European Works Councils', <Evidence-from-the-ETUI-database-of-European-Works-Councils> (last accessed 8 March 2017)

R.H. van het Kaar, 'GS Rechtspersonen, commentaar op artikel 25 WOR', <http://deeplinking.kluwer.nl/?param=00BFDF2A&cpid=WKNL-LTR-Navigator> (last accessed 29 September 2017)

R.H. van het Kaar, 'GS Rechtspersonen, artikel 25 WOR, aant. 3A', <http://deeplinking.kluwer.nl/?param=00BFDF2C&cpid=WKNL-LTR-Navigator> (last accessed 29 September 2017)

R.H. van het Kaar, 'GS Rechtspersonen, artikel 25 WOR, aant. 4', <http://deeplinking.kluwer.nl/?param=00BFDF2F&cpid=WKNL-LTR-Navigator> (last accessed 29 September 2017)

R.H. van het Kaar, 'GS Rechtspersonen, artikel 25 WOR, aant. 14', <http://deeplinking.kluwer.nl/?param=00BFDF3A&cpid=WKNL-LTR-Navigator> (last accessed 29 September 2017).

R.H. van het Kaar, 'GS Rechtspersonen, artikel 31 WOR, aant. 1', <http://deeplinking.kluwer.nl/?param=00C4AF50&cpid=WKNL-LTR-Nav2> (last accessed 30 September 2017)

R.H. van het Kaar and J.B.A. Hoyinck, 'Ondernemingsraad – 3.1.1.2 Structuurvennootschappen', <http://deeplinking.kluwer.nl/?param=00B225AF&cpid=WKNL-LTR-Nav2> (last accessed 2 November 2017)

Maastricht University, 'Cross-border Company Mobility project', <http://www.maastricht-university.nl/corporate-mobility-project> (last accessed 2 November 2017)

J.M.M. Maeijer, G. van Solinge and M.P. Nieuwe Weme, '509 Onafhankelijkheid van commissarissen', in J.M.M. Maeijer, G. van Solinge and M.P. Nieuwe Weme, Asser 2-II, *De naamloze en besloten vennootschap* (Kluwer, 2009) <http://deeplinking.kluwer.nl/?param=00C511FA&cpid=WKNL-LTR-Nav2> (last accessed 2 November 2017)

J.M.M. Maeijer, G. van Solinge and M.P. Nieuwe Weme, '534 Vrijwillige toepassing structuurregime; algemeen', in J.M.M. Maeijer, G. van Solinge and M.P. Nieuwe Weme, Asser 2-II, *De naamloze en besloten vennootschap* (Kluwer, 2009) <http://deeplinking.kluwer.nl/?param=00C511FA&cpid=WKNL-LTR-Nav2> (last accessed 2 November 2017)

J.M.M. Maeijer, G. van Solinge and M.P. Nieuwe Weme, '542 Uitzonderingen op toepasselijkheid van de structuurregeling', in J.M.M. Maeijer, G. van Solinge and M.P. Nieuwe Weme, Asser 2-II, *De naamloze en besloten vennootschap* (Kluwer, 2009) <http://deeplinking.kluwer.nl/?param=00C511FA&cpid=WKNL-LTR-Nav2> (last accessed 2 November 2017)

J.M.M. Maeijer, G. van Solinge and M.P. Nieuwe Weme, '545 Volledige vrijstelling voor afhankelijke maatschappij', in J.M.M. Maeijer, G. van Solinge and M.P. Nieuwe Weme, Asser 2-II, *De naamloze en besloten vennootschap* (Kluwer, 2009) <http://deeplinking.kluwer.nl/?param=00C511FA&cpid=WKNL-LTR-Nav2> (last accessed 2 November 2017)

J.M.M. Maeijer, G. van Solinge and M.P. Nieuwe Weme, '563 Versterkt aanbevelingsrecht ondernemingsraad', in J.M.M. Maeijer, G. van Solinge and M.P. Nieuwe Weme, Asser 2-II, *De naamloze en besloten vennootschap* (Kluwer, 2009) <http://deeplinking.kluwer.nl/?param=00C511FA&cpid=WKNL-LTR-Nav2> (last accessed 2 November 2017)

J.M.M. Maeijer, G. van Solinge and M.P. Nieuwe Weme, '742 Enquêtebevoegdheid vereniging van werknemers in concernverhoudingen', in J.M.M. Maeijer, G. van Solinge and M.P. Nieuwe Weme, Asser 2-II, *De naamloze en besloten vennootschap* (Kluwer, 2009) <http://deeplinking.kluwer.nl/?param=00C511FA&cpid=WKNL-LTR-Nav2> (last accessed 2 November 2017)

J.M.M. Maeijer, G. van Solinge and M.P. Nieuwe Weme, '§1 Geschiedenis en achtergronden van structuurregeling – 517 Wonder van Den Haag', in J.M.M. Maeijer, G. van Solinge and M.P. Nieuwe Weme, Asser 2-II, *De naamloze en besloten vennootschap* (Kluwer, 2009) <http://deeplinking.kluwer.nl/?param=00C511FA&cpid=WKNL-LTR-Nav2> (last accessed 2 November 2017)

Minister van Soziale Zaken en Werkgelegenheid, 'Brief van 5 oktober 2005', <http://tinyurl.com/pym5u9g> (last accessed 29 September 2017).

Monitoring Committee Corporate Governance Code, 'Dutch corporate governance code – Principle 2.1.7 Independence of the supervisory board', <http://www.mccg.nl/?page=4738> (last accessed 30 September 2017)

Österreichische Nationalbibliothek – ALEX Historische Rechts- und Gesetzestexte Online, 'Deutsches Reichsgesetzblatt Jahrgang 1920', <http://tinyurl.com/p9jh7n8> (last accessed 30 September 2017)

Regioplan, 'Nalevingsonderzoek van de Wet op Ondernemingsraden 2011', <http://tinyurl.com/n58duhc> (last accessed 31 October 2017)

SER Commissie Bevordering Medezeggenschap, 'Vacatures en samenstelling OR', *Sociaal-Economische Raad* (2014) <https://www.ser.nl/nl/themas/or-en-medezeggenschap/vacatures-samenstelling-or.aspx> (last accessed 2 November 2017)

SER Commissie Bevordering Medezeggenschap, 'Ontwikkelingen gebruik OR-scholingsfaciliteiten', *Sociaal-Economische Raad* (2014) <https://www.ser.nl/~/media/files/internet/publicaties/overige/2010_2019/2014/cbm-ontwikkeling-gebruik-or-scholingsfaciliteiten.ashx> (last accessed 2 November 2017)

Social and Economic Council, 'English translation of the Dutch Works Councils Act', <http://tinyurl.com/lzhw4uz> (last accessed 2 November 2017)

Social and Economic Council, 'SER Resolution concerning the merger code 2000', <https://www.ser.nl/~/media/files/internet/talen/engels/2000/20000317.ashx> (last accessed 2 November 2017)

Social Science Statistics, 'Z Test Calculator for 2 Population Proportions', <http://www.socscistatistics.com/tests/ztest/> (last accessed 25 October 2017)

Stat Trek, 'Hypothesis Test: Difference Between Proportions', <http://stattrek.com/hypothesis-test/difference-in-proportions.aspx> (last accessed 25 October 2017)

Tweede Kamer der Staten-Generaal, 'Onderzoeksafdeling Abbott', <https://zoek.officielebekendmakingen.nl/h-tk-20102011-9-57.html> (last accessed 29 September 2017)

I. Wajon, P. Vlug and E. Enneking, 'Naleving van de Wet op de Ondernemingsraden: Stand van zaken begin 2017', <https://www.rijksoverheid.nl/binaries/rijksoverheid/documenten/rapporten/2017/10/17/onderzoeksrapport-naleving-wor/Eindrapport+Onderzoek+Naleving+WOR+juni+2017.pdf> (last accessed 15 January 2018)

Judgements (Court of Justice of the European Union)

Case C-212/97 *Centros Limited v. Erhvervs- og Selskabsstyrelse*, EU:C:1999:126

Case C-208/00 *Überseering BV v. Nordic Construction Company Baumanagement GmbH (NCC)*, EU:C:2002:632

Case C-167/01 *Kamer van Koophandel en Fabrieken voor Amsterdam v. Inspire Art Ltd*, EU:C:2003:512

Case C-349/01 *Betriebsrat der Frima ADS Anker GmbH v. ADS Ankler GmbH*, EU:C:2004:440

Case C-44/08 *Akavan Erityisalojen Keskusliitto AEK ry e.a. v. Fujitsu Siemens Computers Oy*, EU:C:2009:533

Case C-151/09 *Federación de Servicios Públicos de la UGT v. Ayuntamiento de La Línea de la Concepción, María del Rosario Vecino Uribe, Ministerio Fiscal* (UGT-FSP), EU:C:2010:452

Case C-429/16 *Ms Ciupa and Others v. Łódź Hospital*, EU:C:2017:711

Judgements (the Netherlands)

Supreme Court (*Hoge Raad*)

HR 21 January 1955, *NJ* 1959/43 (*Forumbank*)

HR 11 July 1984, *NJ* 1985/212 (*Howson Algraphy*)

HR 17 March 1993, *ROR* 1993/16 (*Smit Vlootbeheer*)

HR 26 January 1994, *NJ* 1994/545 (*Heuga*)

HR 7 October 1998, *NJ* 1999/778 (*NS Reizigers*)

HR 26 January 2000, *JOR* 2000/3 (*Provincie Zuid-Holland*)

HR 6 June 2003, *NJ* 2003/486 (*Pich/Scheipar*)

HR 4 February 2005, *NJ* 2005/127 (*Landis*)

HR 13 July 2007, *JOR* 2007/178 and *ARO* 2007/80 (*ABN AMRO*)

HR 14 March 2008, *JOR* 2008/94 m.nt. M. Holtzer (*TNT*)

HR 2 June 2017, *RO* 2017/59 (*OR/DA Retailgroep B.V.*)

Enterprise Chamber of the Amsterdam Court of Appeal (*Ondernemingskamer*)

OK 13 November 1980, *NJ* 1981/258 (*Batco*)

OK 1 May 1980, *NJ* 1981/272 (*Linge Ziekenhuis*)

OK 10 December 1981, *NJ* 1983/24 (*Ford*)

OK 23 June 1983, *NJ* 1984/571 (*Hyster*)

OK 2 April 1987, *NJ* 1988/382 (*Shell Research*)

OK 16 April 1987, *NJ* 1988/183 (*Stolk*)

OK 7 July 1988, *NJ* 1989/845 (*Fluke*)

OK 2 February 1989, *NJ* 1990/86 (*Kodak*)

OK 16 February 1989, *NJ* 1990/693 (*Douwe Egberts*)

OK 10 May 1990, *NJ* 1992/126 (*Philips/HSA*)

OK 11 April 1991, *ROR* 1991/21 (*REGEV*)

OK 10 March 1994, *NJ* 1995/374 (*Nering Bögel*)

OK 17 March 1994, *NJ* 1995/408 (*Janssen Pers*)

OK 10 July 1997, *JAR* 1997/164 (*NS Reizigers*)

OK 23 October 1997, *JAR* 1997/244 (*Nedlin*)

OK 2 April 1998, *NJ* 1998/751 (*Kamer van Koophandel*)

OK 28 January 1999, *NJ* 1999/185 (*Provincie Zuid-Holland*)

OK 10 September 1999, *Ondernemingsrecht* 1999/83 (*IJsselwerf*)

OK 12 March 2002, *ARO* 2002/48 (*Rohm and Haas*)

OK 30 October 2002, *ARO* 2002/171 (*NS Reizigers*)

OK 13 February 2003, *ARO* 2003/45 (*FNV Ledenservice I*)

OK 13 March 2003, *Ondernemingsrecht* 2003/16, *JAR* 2003/88 and *JOR* 2003/85 (*Corus*)

OK 29 September 2003, *ROR* 2003/33 (*Top Craft*)

OK 10 December 2003, *ARO* 2003/186 (*ERU Beheer*)

OK 30 December 2003, *JOR* 2004/102 and *JAR* 2004/45 (*Intergas*)

OK 28 April 2004, *ARO* 2004/72 (*FNV Ledenservice II*)

OK 15 April 2004, *ARO* 2004/63 and *JOR* 2004/165 (*VNU Publitec*)

OK 18 May 2004, *ARO* 2004/74 (*Esteves*)

OK 5 October 2005, *ARO* 2005/186 (*Smit Transformatoren*)

OK 20 October 2005, *ARO* 2005/191 (*OR Security Services Holding B.V.*)

OK 8 June 2006, *ARO* 2006/112 (*Leaf Holland*)

OK 03 May 2007, *JOR* 2007/143 and *ARO* 2007/80 (*ABN AMRO*)

OK 9 January 2008, *RO* 2008/22 (*Packard Bell I*)

OK 17 January 2008, *ARO* 2008/36 (*Honeywell*)

OK 19 February 2008, *ARO* 2003/73 (*Packard Bell II*)

OK 24 November 2008, *JOR* 2009/9 (*Fortis*)

OK 10 December 2008, *ARO* 2009/1 (*AHAM*)

OK 29 March 2010, *RO* 2011/19 (*OR Novio*)

OK 27 May 2010, *JOR* 2010/189 (*PCM*)

OK 14 October 2010, *RO* 2011/11 (*VLM Nederland*)

OK 25 February 2011, *NJ* 2011/335 (*Marigot c.s./IA groep en Rapar*)

OK 10 May 2011, *ARO* 2011/92 (*Novio*)

OK 30 May 2012, *ARO* 2012/94 and *JAR* 2012/181 (*Stichting Het Brabants Orkest*)

OK 20 February 2013, *RO* 2013/43 and *JAR* 2013/120 (*DB Schenker Rail Nederland NV*)

OK 9 July 2013, *JAR* 2013/223 and *ARO* 2013/141 (*Watts Industries Netherlands*)

OK 1 July 2016, *JOR* 2016/273 and *JAR* 2016/210 m.nt. I. Zaal (*Thomas Cook Nederland*)

OK 3 October 2016, *JOR* 2016/333 m.nt. M. Holtzer (*Abellio*)

OK 19 October 2016, *JAR* 2016/278, *TRA* 2017/9 m.nt. I. Zaal (*OR SHL Cyprus Holding*)

Other courts

Amsterdam Court of Appeal 27 July 1989, *NJ* 1990/734 (*PUEM*)

Amsterdam Court of Appeal 20 May 1999, *JAR* 1999/146 (*Verzinkerij Johan Vis*)

Amsterdam Court of Appeal (Preliminary Relief Court) 26 July 2012, *TRA* 2012/100 (*ING*)

Bedrijfscommissie voor de Overheid 20 June 1997, *JAR* 1997/155 and *ROR* 1997/28 (*Politieregio Rotterdam-Rijnmond*)

Hof Arnhem, *JAR* 2008/314 and *ROR* 2009/15 (*Vion Retail Groenlo BV en De Groene Weg BV*)

Ktg. Rotterdam 24 November 1995, *JAR* 1996/4

President of the District Court of Arnhem 4 May 1995, *KG* 1995/247 (*Stichting Accon*)

Rb. Noord-Nederland 25 May 2016, *JOR* 2016/230 m. nt. M. Holtzer (*OR Solidus Solutions*)

SER 27 September 1983, *ROR* 1971–1984/146 (*Cyanamid*)

JUDGEMENTS (OTHER JURISDICTIONS)

France

Tribunal de Grande Instance Nanterre, *Renault Vilvoorde* [4 April 1997] *Sociaalrechtelijke Kronieken* 1997, 339-340

Tribunal de Grande Instance Versailles, *Renault Vilvoorde* [7 May 1997] *Sociaalrechtelijke Kronieken* 1997, 336-339

United Kingdom

Salomon v. Salomon & Co. [1897] A.C. 22

LEGISLATION (EU)

Council Directive 78/660/EC of 25 July 1978 based on Article 54(3)(g) of the Treaty on the annual accounts of certain types of companies [1978] OJ L 222/11

Council Directive 98/59/EC of 20 July 1998 on the approximation of the laws of the Member States relating to collective redundancies [1998] OJ L 225/16

Council Regulation (EC) No. 2157/2001 of 8 October 2001 on the Statute for a European Company (SE) [2001] OJ L 294/1

Council Directive 2001/86/EC of 8 October 2001 supplementing the Statute for a European Company with regard to the involvement of employees [2001] OJ L 294/22

Directive 2002/14/EC of the European Parliament and of the Council of 11 March 2002 establishing a general framework for informing and consulting employees in the European Community – Joint declaration of the European Parliament, the Council and the Commission on employee representation [2002] OJ L 80/29

Directive 2004/25/EC of the European Parliament and of the Council of 21 April 2004 on takeover bids [2004] OJ L 142/12

Directive 2005/56/EC of the European Parliament and of the Council of 26 October 2005 on cross-border mergers of limited liability companies [2005] OJ L 310/1

Directive 2007/36/EC of the European Parliament and of the Council of 11 July 2007 on the exercise of certain rights of shareholders in listed companies [2007] OJ L 184/17

Directive 2009/38/EC of the European Parliament and of the Council of 6 May 2009 on the establishment of a European Works Council or a procedure in Community-scale undertakings and Community-scale groups of undertakings for the purposes of informing and consulting employees [2009] OJ L 122/28

Legislation (the Netherlands)

Primary legislation

Wet van 10 September 1970, Stb. 1970, 414

Wet op de ondernemingsraden 1971, Stb. 1971, 54

Wet op de ondernemingsraden 1976, Stb. 1976, 225

Wet op de ondernemingsraden 1979, Stb. 1979, 448

Wet van 6 mei 1971 (Structuurwet), *Stb.* 1971, 289

Wet van 8 april 1976, Stb. 1976, 228 and 229

Wet van 7 december 1983, Stb. 1983, 663

Wet van 18 april 2002 tot wijziging van boek 2 van het Burgerlijk Wetboek alsmede enige andere wetten in verband met de openbaarmaking van de bezoldiging en het aandelenbezit van bestuurders en commissarissen, Stb. 2002, 225

Wet van 9 juli 2004, Stb. 2004, 370

Wet van 14 juni 2006 tot wijziging van de Wet op de ondernemingsraden in verband met het verschaffen van informatie over de hoogte van inkomens van topkader, bestuurders en toezichthouders van ondernemingen aan de ondernemingsraad (Wet Harrewijn), *Stb.* 2006, 286

Wet openbaarmaking uit publieke middelen gefinancierde topinkomens, Stb. 2006, 95

Wet van 30 juni 2010 tot wijziging van Boek 2 van het Burgerlijk Wetboek in verband met de invoering van een recht voor de ondernemingsraad van naamloze vennootschappen om een standpunt kenbaar te maken ten aanzien van belangrijke bestuursbesluiten en besluiten tot benoeming, schorsing en ontslag van bestuurders en commissarissen alsmede ten aanzien van het bezoldigingsbeleid, Stb. 2010, 257

Wet van 6 juni 2011 tot wijziging van boek 2 van het Burgerlijk Wetboek in verband met de aanpassing van regels over bestuur en toezicht in naamloze en besloten vennootschappen, Stb. 2012, 275

Wet van 26 juni 2013 tot aanpassing van de Wet op de ondernemingsraden in verband met wijziging van de financiering van het scholingssysteem voor leden van de ondernemingsraad en enkele andere wijzigingen van deze wet, Stb. 2013, 296

Wet van 14 juni 2014 tot wijziging van verschillende wetten in verband met de hervorming van het ontslagrecht, wijziging van de rechtspositie van flexwerkers en wijziging van verschillende wetten in verband met het aanpassen van de Werkloosheidswet, het verruimen van de openstelling van de Wet inkomensvoorziening oudere werklozen en de beperking van de toegang tot de Wet inkomensvoorziening oudere en gedeeltelijk arbeidsongeschikte werkloze werknemers (Wet werk en zekerheid), *Stb.* 2014, 216

Wet van 22 juni 2016 tot wijziging van de Wet op de ondernemingsraden en de Pensioenwet in verband met de bevoegdheden van de ondernemingsraad inzake de arbeidsvoorwaarde pensioen, Stb. 2016, 249

Besluit van 29 augustus 2017 tot wijziging van het Besluit van 23 december 2004 tot vaststelling van nadere voorschriften omtrent de inhoud van het jaarverslag (Stb. 747), *Stb.* 2017, 332

Parliamentary documents (*Kamerstukken*)

Brief van minister Asscher (SZW) aan de Tweede Kamer over de stand van zaken van de medezeggenschap in Nederland van 7 maart 2013, Kamerstukken II 2012/13, 29818, no. 36, p. 6

Kamerstukken I 2009/10, 31877, E

Kamerstukken II 2016/17, 34267, 10

Kamerstukken II 2013/14, 33818, no. 3 (*Wet Werk en Zekerheid*)

Kamerstukken II 2010/11, 29544, 264

Kamerstukken II 2010/11, 32887, No. 3

Kamerstukken II 2008/09, 31877, nr. 3

Kamerstukken II 2003/2004, 28179, 3

Kamerstukken II 2001/02, 28163, no. 5

Advices of the Social and Economic Council (SER)

SER Advies 1969/14 *Inzake de Herziening van het Ondernemingsrecht*

SER Advies 1973/14 *Inzake wijziging van de WOR tot de instelling van groeps-ondernemingsraden*

SER Advies 1976/20 *Verstrekking door de ondernemer van informatie aan de ondernemingsraad*

SER Advies 1992/07 *Knelpunten Wet op de ondernemingsraden*

SER Advies 2001/02 *Het functioneren en de toekomst van de structuurregeling*

SER Advies 2003/12 *Aanpassing van de Wet op de ondernemingsraden*

SER Advies 2008/01 *Evenwichtig Ondernemingsbestuur*

SER Advies 2011/04 *Toekomst scholing en vorming leden ondernemingsraad*

SER Advies 2014/05 *Instemmingsrecht OR over de arbeidsvoorwaarde pensioen*

Legislation (other jurisdictions)

Germany

Drittelbeteiligungsgesetz vom 18. Mai 2004 (BGBl. I S. 974), *das zuletzt durch Artikel 8 des Gesetzes vom 24. April 2015* (BGBl. I S. 642) *geändert worden ist*

Miscellaneous

N. Jansen, *Legitimiteit van de vakbond als (mede)ontwerpers van collectieve arbeidsvoorwaarden* (diss.), forthcoming

Executive summary

This book sets out to answer two main questions, namely, what is the status quo of the position of Dutch works councils in multinational corporations? And which tools within the Dutch legal framework can be utilised in order to secure the successful involvement of the works council in the decision-making process in light of the increasingly globalised economy?

Much research has been carried out on Dutch works councils in general, mostly by means of an analysis of the appropriate legal framework. Little research, however, has hitherto been conducted on the position of works councils in multinational corporations (MNCs), and, so far, no empirical data has been collected for the Netherlands.

The aim of this study is to examine the position of Dutch works councils in multinational corporations in the context of the tension between globalised decision-making by MNCs, on the one hand, and employee participation at the local level in the Netherlands, on the other. This examination enhances the body of knowledge on the position of Dutch works councils within MNCs, both through the examination of the applicable legal framework and the collection of empirical data. This analysis presented is based on quantitative data through an online questionnaire among (central) works councils and qualitative data through interviews with works council members and management and supervisory board members. Based on the data, an inventory of issues in practice is made and examples of good practice aimed at overcoming these issues are collected.

The study's findings show that many participation rights are frequently used in practice, but not under all circumstances. Particularly, differences between Dutch and foreign MNCs regarding information and consultation rights are noteworthy; as well as certain corporate governance aspects, such as the application of the structure regime, the presence of supervisory board members in consultation meetings, and the non-use of a number of rights by works councils.

The inventory of examples of good practices further revealed that a multitude of potential solutions are applied in practice. The good practices show that, through negotiation and long-term experiences with participation mechanisms, tailor-made employee participation processes can be achieved. The management, supervisory board and works council respondents overwhelmingly emphasised the benefits of such tailor-made approaches due to their increased flexibility and time-effectiveness.

Overall, the position of the examined Dutch works councils is solid. However, works councils, management and supervisory boards as well as other stakeholders and the legislator need to continue working on several aspects in order to improve the position of works councils and to safeguard their statutory rights – a theme that is emphasised throughout this study.

Annex I: Good practices overview

Q

R

S

T

W

Annex II: Questionnaire | Quantitative results

Maastricht University *Leading in Learning!*

De positie van de Nederlandse ondernemingsraad in internationale concerns

Pagina 1

Dit onderzoek maakt deel uit van een dissertatieonderzoek dat in opdracht van Stichting MNO onder leiding van professor Ferdinand Grapperhaus aan de Universiteit Maastricht wordt uitgevoerd.
Uw antwoorden zijn van groot belang om de representativiteit van de onderzoeksresultaten te borgen en daardoor uiteindelijk aanbevelingen te kunnen doen om de positie van de Nederlandse ondernemingsraad in internationale concerns te bevorderen. De kernvraag is hoe de positie van de ondernemingsraad in een globaliserende economie verbeterd kan worden. Het invullen van de enquête kost u ongeveer 30 minuten.
In een tweede fase van het promotieonderzoek worden interviews met ondernemingsraadsleden afgenomen. Indien u bereid bent mee te werken aan deze tweede stap, zou ik u willen verzoeken dat aan mij aan het einde van de enquête kenbaar te maken. Uw contactgegevens voor een deelname aan de interviews worden niet in het onderzoeksrapport opgenomen en de anonimiteit van uw antwoorden blijft gewaarborgd. Alle antwoorden worden op een algemene wijze en niet herleidbaar tot individuele deelnemers weergegeven. Mocht u vragen hebben dan kunt u mij hierover te allen tijde benaderen op onderstaand telefoonnummer of e-mailadres.

Bij voorbaat dank voor de moeite en de tijd die u aan het invullen van de enquête besteedt,

Marcus Meyer

Promovendus | Universiteit Maastricht
marcus.meyer@maastrichtuniversity.nl
T: 043 38 83 567

Pagina 2

1. **In welke sector is uw onderneming actief?** *

- ◯ Industrie
- ◯ Bouw- en installatiebedrijven
- ◯ Transport
- ◯ Handel en zakelijke dienstverlening
- ◯ Financiële instellingen en verzekeringswezen
- ◯ Gezondheidszorg en welzijn
- ◯ Overheidssector
- ◯ Detailhandel
- ◯ Landbouw, bosbouw en visserij
- ◯ Energievoorziening
- ◯ Andere, namelijk: [ ]

2. **In welk land bevind zich de hoofdzetel van de hoogste concernmoeder (in welk land bevindt zich het hoofdkantoor van het concern)?** *

[ ]

3. **Indien uw concern divisies, een matrixorganisatie of een geographische organisatiestructuur kent: in welk land is de zetel van dit onderdeel van het concern gevestigd waarin uw (C)OR is ingesteld?**

Er is sprake van een matrixorganisatie indien een concern is opgedeeld naar verschillende gezichtspunten, bijvoorbeeld naar productgroep en naar geografische regio. Van een geografische organisatiestructuur is sprake indien een concern is opgedeeld op basis van geographische regio's.

[ ]

4. **Aantal werknemers van uw bedrijf in 2014.**

Indien onbekend, graag het antwoordveld open laten.

In Nederland: [ ]

In Europa: [ ]

Wereldwijd: [ ]

5. **Bent u naast lid van de ondernemingsraad tevens lid van de centrale ondernemingsraad (dan wel van een OR, die medezeggenschap uitoefent bij de hoogste Nederlandse vennootschap in het concern)?** *

De (centrale) ondernemingsraad is de hoogste medezeggenschap uitoefenende ondernemingsraad in Nederland.

- ◯ Nee
- ◯ Ja

6. **Welke positie binnen uw (C)OR neemt u in?** *

- ◯ Voorzitter (C)OR
- ◯ Ambtelijk secretaris (C)OR
- ◯ Lid Dagelijks Bestuur (DB) van de (C)OR
- ◯ Overig lid van de (C)OR

7. **Welke rechtsvorm heeft de onderneming waarin de (C)OR is ingesteld?** *

- ◯ Besloten vennootschap (B.V.)
- ◯ Naamloze vennootschap (N.V.)
- ◯ Coöperatieve vereniging
- ◯ Europese vennootschap (Societas Europea, SE)
- ◯ Europese coöperatieve vereniging (Societas Cooperativa Europea, SCE)
- ◯ Andere (buitenlandse) rechtsvorm, namelijk: [ ]

8. **Op welk niveau is de (centrale) ondernemingsraad binnen uw concern ingesteld?** *

- ◯ Centraal bestuur (concernniveau)
- ◯ Nederlandse subholding
- ◯ Divisieniveau
- ◯ Regionaal hoofdkantoor
- ◯ Nederlandse subholding die het divisieniveau vertegenwoordigt
- ◯ Andere, namelijk: [ ]

9. **Voor hoeveel vestigingen is de (centrale) ondernemingsraad ingesteld?**

[ ]

10. Wie is de overlegpartner van uw (C)OR (meerdere antwoorden mogelijk)? *

- [ ] Directeur/lid van het centraal bestuur
- [ ] Nederland directeur
- [ ] HR-directeur
- [ ] Andere, namelijk: ______

11. Wordt de structuurregeling binnen uw concern toegepast en zo ja, op welk niveau?

Het structuurregime betekent dat er een verplichting bestaat tot instelling van een Raad van Commissarissen (RvC) bij grote vennootschappen. Deze RvC heeft naast de toezichthoudende functie, belangrijke goedkeuringsbevoegdheden. Nota bene: als de meerderheid van de werknemers van het concern buiten Nederland werkzaam is, kan de topholding voor een vrijstelling van het structuurregime in aanmerking komen. Het structuurregime moet dan wel op een lager niveau binnen het concern worden toegepast. Men noemt dit het "verzwakt structuurregime".

- ○ Nee
- ○ Ja, op het hoogste niveau binnen het concern
- ○ Ja, op het niveau van de Nederlandse subholding
- ○ Ja, op divisieniveau
- ○ Ja, namelijk op het niveau van: ______

Pagina 3

12. Sinds wanneer wordt de structuurregeling binnen uw concern toegepast?

- [ ] Onbekend
- [ ] Toepassing sinds: ______

13. Vindt een vrijwillige toepassing van het structuurregime binnen uw concern plaats?

Op voet van artikel 2:157 BW kan een vennootschap die niet verplicht is het structuurregime (volledig of verzwakt) toe te passen, dat op basis van vrijwilligheid doen.

- ○ Ja
- ○ Nee
- ○ Onbekend

14. Is een ondernemingsovereenkomst (convenant) met uw (C)OR afgesproken waarin aanvullende bevoegdheden aan de (C)OR worden toegekend (volgens artikel 32 WOR)?

Artikel 32 WOR houdt in dat aan de (C)OR bij een overeenkomst verdere bevoegdheden, dan deze die in de WOR genoemd worden, kunnen worden toegekend.

- ◯ Ja
- ◯ Nee

Pagina 4

15. Welke aanvullende bevoegdheden zijn door de ondernemingsovereenkomst (convenant) aan uw (C)OR toegekend?

- ☐ Overleg met het centraal bestuur (indien vooraf niet van toepassing)
- ☐ Op het gebied van het adviesrecht
- ☐ Op het gebied van het instemmingsrecht
- ☐ Recht op informatie over internationale aangelegenheden
- ☐ Procedurele rechten (bijvoorbeeld tijdstip van inschakeling)
- ☐ Instemmingsrecht op het gebied van de arbeidsvoorwaarden (indien geen CAO van toepassing is)
- ☐ Aanvullende faciliteiten
- ☐ Op het gebied van het enquêterecht
- ☐ Definitie van 'belangrijke' besluiten
- ☐ Andere, namelijk: ________

16. Bij hoeveel besluiten van het concern was de (C)OR betrokken?

In 2011: ☐

Alleen met betrekking tot Nederland: ☐

In 2012: ☐

Alleen met betrekking tot Nederland: ☐

In 2013: ☐

Alleen met betrekking tot Nederland: ☐

Pagina 5

17. Hoe is de Raad van Commissarissen binnen uw concern samengesteld?

Een concernfunctionaris is een functionaris die afkomstig is van een hoger onderdeel van het concern.

Totaal aantal commissarissen: [ ]

Concernfunctionarissen: [ ]

Externe leden: [ ]

18. Meent u dat er sprake is van te grote invloed op de Raad van Commissarissen door de concernleiding?

- ◯ Ja
- ◯ Nee

19. Heeft uw (C)OR in de afgelopen vier jaar van het gewone aanbevelingsrecht voor leden van de Raad van Commissarissen gebruik gemaakt?

De algemene vergadering en de OR kunnen aan de RvC personen aanbevelen om als commissaris te worden voorgedragen. Dit is het 'gewone' aanbevelingsrecht. De RvC is niet verplicht deze aanbeveling over te nemen.

- ◯ Geen aanbevelingsrecht wettelijk toegestaan (niet van toepassing)
- ◯ Nee
- ◯ Ja (graag aantal invullen): [ ]

20. Heeft uw (C)OR in de afgelopen vier jaar van het versterkt aanbevelingsrecht voor leden van de Raad van Commissarissen gebruik gemaakt?

Volgens artikel 2:158(5)(6)/268(5)(6) BW bestaat in een structuurvennootschap een versterkt aanbevelingsrecht voor één derde van de RvC leden door de ondernemingsraad. Als de vennootschap niet aan de voorwaarden voor het structuurregime voldoet, wordt geen aanbevelingsrecht toegekend.

- ◯ Geen aanbevelingsrecht wettelijk toegestaan (niet van toepassing)
- ◯ Nee
- ◯ Ja (graag aantal invullen): [ ]

Pagina 6

21. Is er sprake van meer contact met de voordrachtscommissaris(sen) in vergelijking met andere leden van de Raad van Commissarissen?

- ◯ Ja
- ◯ Nee

22. Welke ervaringen heeft uw (C)OR gehad met betrekking tot de samenwerking met de Raad van Commissarissen?

	Ja	Nee	Niet van toepassing
Door contacten met de Raad van Commissarissen bestaat een goede toegang tot informatie.	☐	☐	☐
Door contacten met de Raad van Commissarissen bestaat een adequate invloed op de besluitvorming.	☐	☐	☐
Is de toegang tot informatie en invloed op de besluitvorming verbeterd sinds voordrachtscommissaris(sen) deel uitmaken van de RvC?	☐	☐	☐
Heeft de Raad van Commissarissen ook een bemiddelende rol?	☐	☐	☐

23. Waarom maakt uw (C)OR geen gebruik van zijn versterkt aanbevelingsrecht voor leden van de Raad van Commissarissen?

(U mag maximaal 3 antwoordmogelijkheden kiezen)

- ☐ Onvoldoende op de hoogte van de mogelijkheid
- ☐ Onvoldoende deskundigheid (C)OR om aanbevelingen te doen
- ☐ Het levert niets op/geen verbetering door aanbeveling
- ☐ Gebrek aan tijd
- ☐ Andere, namelijk: ____________

Pagina 7

24. Welke van de volgende onderwerpen hebben in het afgelopen jaar de meeste aandacht van uw (C)OR gehad?

(U mag maximaal 5 onderwerpen kiezen)

- ☐ Fusie(plannen)
- ☐ Reorganisaties en inkrimpingen
- ☐ Bedrijfsverplaatsing
- ☐ Investeringen
- ☐ Aangaan van nieuwe kredieten
- ☐ Wijziging organisatiestructuur
- ☐ Arbeidsvoorwaarden
- ☐ Werktijd- of vakantieregeling
- ☐ Werkoverleg
- ☐ Opleiding personeel
- ☐ Belonings- en functiewaarderingssystemen
- ☐ Beoordelingssystemen
- ☐ Verhuizing bedrijf
- ☐ Aanstellings-, ontslag- en bevorderingsbeleid
- ☐ Arbobeleid
- ☐ Klachtenbehandeling
- ☐ Spaar- en winstdelingsregelingen
- ☐ Pensioenverzekeringen
- ☐ Andere onderwerpen, namelijk: ______

25. Welke onderwerpen zijn tijdens het overleg met het bestuur in de periode 2012 - 2014 besproken (meerdere antwoorden mogelijk)?

- ☐ Overdracht van de zeggenschap over de onderneming (art. 25 lid 1 sub a WOR)
- ☐ Vestigen, overnemen of afstoten van zeggenschap (art. 25 lid 1 sub b WOR)
- ☐ Beëindiging van werkzaamheden of een belangrijk onderdeel daarvan (art. 25 lid 1 sub c WOR)
- ☐ Belangrijke inkrimping of uitbreiding van de werkzaamheden (art. 25 lid 1 sub d WOR)
- ☐ Belangrijke wijziging in de organisatie (art. 25 lid 1 sub e WOR)
- ☐ Het doen van een belangrijke investering ten behoeve van de onderneming (art. 25 lid 1 sub h WOR)
- ☐ Belangrijk krediet en het stellen van zekerheid voor een andere ondernemer [binnen het concern] (art. 25 lid 1 sub j WOR)
- ☐ Onderwerpen volgens artikel 27 WOR (waarvoor instemming van de (C)OR is vereist)
- ☐ Toekomstige strategie van het concern en trends
- ☐ Het beloningsbeleid
- ☐ Relocatie
- ☐ Andere, namelijk: ________

26. Maakt uw (C)OR gebruik van deskundigen?

	Nooit	Soms	Regelmatig
Heeft uw (C)OR in de afgelopen drie jaar interne deskundige ingeschakeld?	○	○	○
Heeft uw (C)OR in de afgelopen drie jaar externe deskundige ingeschakeld?	○	○	○

27. Hoe vaak worden gegevens over het financieel en economisch beleid aan uw (C)OR verstrekt (volgens artikel 31a WOR)?

- ○ Onbekend
- ○ Nooit
- ○ Een keer per jaar
- ○ Twee keer per jaar
- ○ Meer dan twee keer per jaar, namelijk: ________

Pagina 8

28. In welke taal worden de gegevens over het financieel en economisch beleid verstrekt?

- ◯ Nederlands
- ◯ Engels
- ◯ Andere, namelijk: [ ]

29. Zijn de verstrekte gegevens over financieel en economisch beleid beperkt tot de Nederlandse vestigingen van uw concern?

- ◯ Ja
- ◯ Nee

30. Vindt een verstrekking van informatie over de zeggenschapsverhoudingen in het gehele concern plaats (volgens artikel 31 lid 2 WOR met inwerkingtreding van de wetswijziging van 19 juli 2013)?

- ◯ Ja
- ◯ Nee
- ◯ Onbekend

31. Heeft uw (C)OR zelf om die informatie omtrent de zeggenschapsverhoudingen in het gehele concern gevraagd?

- ◯ Ja
- ◯ Nee
- ◯ Onbekend

Pagina 9

32. Leveren de verstrekte gegevens omtrent de zeggenschapsverhoudingen nuttige informatie op voor het functioneren van uw (C)OR?

- ☐ Ja
- ☐ Nee
- ☐ Nadere toelichting: [ ]

33. **Waarom worden deze gegevens niet aan uw (C)OR verstrekt?**

Pagina 10

34. **Hoe vaak vinden overlegvergaderingen met uw overlegpartner plaats (volgens artikel 24 en 31a WOR)?**

- ◯ Minder dan drie keer per jaar
- ◯ Drie tot zes keer per jaar
- ◯ Meer dan zes keer per jaar, namelijk:

35. **Vinden er tussentijdse overlegvergaderingen plaats (volgens artikel 23 WOR)? Zo ja, wie neemt daartoe het initiatief? Uw (C)OR of de bestuurder van de onderneming?**

- ◯ Nee
- ◯ Ja, zowel op initiatief van de (C)OR als ook op initiatief van de bestuurder
- ◯ Ja, op initiatief van de (C)OR
- ◯ Ja, op initiatief van de bestuurder

36. **Hoe vaak zijn leden van de Raad van Commissarissen aanwezig tijdens overlegvergaderingen (volgens artikel 24 WOR)?**

	Nooit	Soms	Regelmatig
Antwoord:	◯	◯	◯

37. **Heeft uw (C)OR sinds 1 januari 2011 een of meer keren beroep ingesteld bij de ondernemingskamer van het Amsterdamse Gerechtshof?**

- ◯ Nee
- ◯ Ja, te weten (aantal invullen):

38. Is er tussen ondernemer en uw (C)OR wel eens verschil van mening opgetreden of een voorgenomen besluit adviesplichtig was?

- ◯ Nee, nog nooit
- ◯ Ja, een enkele keer
- ◯ Ja, herhaaldelijk

39. Is de tijd die besteed kan worden aan het uitbrengen van (C)OR adviezen in overwegende mate toereikend?

- ◯ Ja
- ◯ Nee

40. Geef aan in hoeverre u eens bent met de volgende stelling: "mijn (C)OR ervaart zijn positie als verslechterd in gevolg van toenemende internationalisering."

	Geheel oneens	Grotendeels oneens	Neutraal	Grotendeels eens	Geheel eens
Antwoord:	◯	◯	◯	◯	◯

41. Geef aan in hoeverre de volgende stellingen op u van toepassing zijn.

	Niet van toepassing				Helemaal van toepassing
Er is te weinig tijd voor mijn OR werk door werkdruk en verplichtingen	◯	◯	◯	◯	◯
Ten gevolge van mijn OR werk heb ik negatieve ervaringen met directe leidinggevenden gehad	◯	◯	◯	◯	◯
Het OR werk remt mijn eigen carrière	◯	◯	◯	◯	◯
Ik ben niet deskundig genoeg om mijn OR-werk te doen	◯	◯	◯	◯	◯

42. Bent u tevreden met uw scholingsmogelijkheden en met de afspraken voor scholing in uw concern?

- ☐ Ja
- ☐ Nee
- ☐ Nadere toelichting: __________

Pagina 11

43. Heeft u contacten met werknemersvertegenwoordigers binnen het concern in andere landen?

☐ Ja

☐ Nee

Nadere toelichting:

☐

44. Is een EOR in uw concern ingesteld? *

○ ja

○ nee

45. Wordt uw (C)OR in het overleg betrokken bij aangelegenheden die in Nederland en minstens één ander land spelen (transnationale aangelegenheden)?

Er is sprake van een Europese (of transnationale) dimensie als aangelegenheden voor de gehele internationale onderneming van belang zijn, of voor tenminste twee ondernemingen of vestigingen van een internationale onderneming of een internationale groep in twee verschillende betrokken staten.

○ Nooit

○ Een keer per jaar

○ 2-4 keer per jaar

○ Meer dan vier keer, namelijk:

Pagina 12

46. Bent u lid van de EOR? *

○ Ja

○ Nee

47. Op welk niveau binnen het concern is de EOR ingesteld? *

○ Centraal bestuur (concernniveau)

○ Divisieniveau

○ Regionaal hoofdkantoor (bijvoorbeeld Europees hoofdkantoor)

○ Andere, namelijk:

48. Is de EOR in Nederland gevestigd? *

- ○ Ja
- ○ Nee, namelijk in: ____

49. Zijn aan de EOR binnen uw concern extra bevoegdheden toegekend ten opzichte van de wettelijke verplichting?

Op het moment dat de bijzondere onderhandelingsgroep en het hoofdbestuur van de onderneming geen overeenkomst hebben gesloten treden de referentievoorschriften in werking (volgens artikel 15 e.v. WEOR)

- ○ Ja
- ○ Nee
- ○ Onbekend

50. Geef aan in hoeverre de volgende stellingen op u van toepassing zijn.

	Niet van toepassing				Helemaal van toepassing
Ik ben tevreden met de uitwisseling van informatie tussen de EOR en mijn (C)OR	○	○	○	○	○
Er is sprake van een open en informeel sfeer tijdens EOR bijeenkomsten	○	○	○	○	○
De EOR ondersteunt mij in mijn (C)OR werkzaamheden	○	○	○	○	○

51. Wordt de EOR en uw (C)OR gelijktijdig over belangrijke onderwerpen geraadpleegd?

- ○ Ja
- ○ Nee, de EOR wordt vroeger geraadpleegd
- ○ Nee, mijn (C)OR wordt vroeger geraadpleegd

Pagina 13

52. **Heeft u nog feedback op de vragenlijst?**
Zijn naar uw mening belangrijke onderwerpen niet ter sprake gekomen en indien van toepassing, welke?

53. **Mag ik u nog eens benaderen voor vervolgonderzoek? Zo ja, wilt u uw contactgegevens hier achterlaten?**

De anonimiteit van uw bovenstaande antwoorden blijft gewaarborgd.

Naam:

Telefoonnummer:

E-mailadres:

» **Redirection to final page of Enquêtes Maken** (wijzigen)

ANNEX III: SPSS OUTPUTS | QUANTITATIVE RESULTS

Q1 In which sector is your undertaking operating?

		Frequency	Percent	Valid Percent	Cumulative Percent
Valid	Agriculture, forestry and fisheries	1	1,8	1,8	1,8
	Catering	1	1,8	1,8	3,6
	Construction and installation companies	2	3,6	3,6	7,1
	Financial institutions and insurance	2	3,6	3,6	10,7
	Healthcare and welfare	2	3,6	3,6	14,3
	HR service provider	1	1,8	1,8	16,1
	Industry	22	39,3	39,3	55,4
	Information and communication	3	5,4	5,4	60,7
	Retail	5	8,9	8,9	69,6
	Mineral extraction	1	1,8	1,8	71,4
	Trade-related and other business services	9	16,1	16,1	87,5
	Transport	6	10,7	10,7	98,2
	Water and waste management	1	1,8	1,8	100,0
	Total	56	100,0	100,0	

Q2 In which country is the real seat of the topholding situated?

		Frequency	Percent	Valid Percent	Cumulative Percent
Valid	Belgium	2	3,6	3,6	3,6
	China	1	1,8	1,8	5,4
	France	2	3,6	3,6	8,9
	Germany	1	1,8	1,8	10,7
	Ireland	1	1,8	1,8	12,5
	Italy	1	1,8	1,8	14,3
	Japan	2	3,6	3,6	17,9
	Netherlands	34	60,7	60,7	78,6
	United Kingdom	3	5,4	5,4	83,9
	United States of America	7	12,5	12,5	96,4
	India	1	1,8	1,8	98,2
	Canada	1	1,8	1,8	100,0
	Total	56	100,0	100,0	

Q3 In which country is the real seat of the part of the business of the corporation located for which your (central) works council is maintained (if your corporation is organised by divisions, matrix or geographical structure)?

		Frequency	Percent	Valid Percent	Cumulative Percent
Valid	Belgium	1	1,8	2,1	2,1
	Netherlands	46	82,1	95,8	97,9
	India	1	1,8	2,1	100,0
	Total	48	85,7	100,0	
Missing		8	14,3		
Total		56	100,0		

Q4 Employee numbers in the Netherlands, EU and total number of employees

#	# employees NL	# employees EU	# employees Total
1	-	-	-
2	600		6.000
3	1.800	40.000	120.000
4	-	-	-
5	1.200	2.000	3.500
6	15.000	20.000	21.000
7	100.000	10.000	120.000
8	9.900	19.000	22.000
9	-	-	-
10	6.000	10.850	10.850
11	12.000	40.000	110.000
12	11.000	-	-
13	4.000	5.000	15.000
14	5.000	-	15.100
15	1.600	-	40.000
16	17.000	-	64.000
17	1.300	-	20.000
18	4.500	-	32.000
19	1.800	6.500	23.000
20	7.000	11.000	22.000
21	7.500	-	24.000
22	4.500	19.400	23.000

#	# employees NL	# employees EU	# employees Total
23	33.000	33.200	34.000
24	3.500	-	-
25	20.000	35.000	35.000
26	4.900	-	50.000
27	940	87.258	138.000
28	5.000	2.000	7.617
29	20.000	-	23.000
30	2.700	-	370.000
31	2.500	-	-
32	1.000	-	30.000
33	3.200	21.000	76.000
34	3.200	100.000	350.000
35	2.000	-	22.000
36	17.000	-	100.000
37	1.100	-	15.000
38	2.200	25.000	140.000
39	500	-	33.000
40	1.000	4.500	12.600
41	2.150	-	-
42	10.000	-	85.000
43	10.000	12.500	-
44	20.000	35.000	35.000
45	-	-	1.750
46	17.800	10.800	-
47	3.500	4.500	12.000
48	2.000	-	22.000
49	3.000	8.000	25.000
50	4.310	17.160	27.850
51	2.200	40.000	65.000
52	3.500	-	63.000
53	3.200	8.000	16.000
54	3.000	-	60.000
55	3.184	-	174.000
56	2.800	-	80.000

Q5 Are you, aside from your membership in a works council, also member of the central works council (or the equivalent works council exercising employee participation on the highest Dutch undertaking within the corporation)?

		Frequency	Percent	Valid Percent	Cumulative Percent
Valid	No	7	12,5	12,7	12,7
	Yes	48	85,7	87,3	100,0
	Total	55	98,2	100,0	
Missing		1	1,8		
Total		56	100,0		

Q6 Which position within the (central) works council are you occupying?

		Frequency	Percent	Valid Percent	Cumulative Percent
Valid	Official secretary of the CWC	9	16,1	16,7	16,7
	Member of the executive committee of the CWC	13	23,2	24,1	40,7
	Regular member of the CWC	8	14,3	14,8	55,6
	Chairman of the CWC	24	42,9	44,4	100,0
	Total	54	96,4	100,0	
Missing		2	3,6		
Total		56	100,0		

Q7 What is the legal form of the undertaking for which the (central) works council is maintained?

		Frequency	Percent	Valid Percent	Cumulative Percent
Valid	Private limited liability company (B.V.)	33	58,9	61,1	61,1
	Cooperative association	2	3,6	3,7	64,8
	Public limited liability company (N.V.)	18	32,1	33,3	98,1
	PLC and N.V.	1	1,8	1,9	100,0
	Total	54	96,4	100,0	
Missing		2	3,6		
Total		56	100,0		

Q8 At which level is the (central) works council within your corporation maintained?

		Frequency	Percent	Valid Percent	Cumulative Percent
Valid	All Dutch entities	1	1,8	1,9	1,9
	Central management (topholding)	24	42,9	44,4	46,3
	Dutch subholding	23	41,1	42,6	88,9
	Dutch subholding representing the division level	6	10,7	11,1	100,0
	Total	54	96,4	100,0	
Missing		2	3,6		
Total		56	100,0		

Q9 For how many establishments is the (central) works council maintained?

		Frequency	Percent	Valid Percent	Cumulative Percent
Valid	1	3	5,4	5,9	5,9
	2	4	7,1	7,8	13,7
	3	5	8,9	9,8	23,5
	4	7	12,5	13,7	37,3
	5	6	10,7	11,8	49,0
	6	6	10,7	11,8	60,8
	7	4	7,1	7,8	68,6
	9	6	10,7	11,8	80,4
	10	1	1,8	2,0	82,4
	11	1	1,8	2,0	84,3
	13	2	3,6	3,9	88,2
	15	1	1,8	2,0	90,2
	32	1	1,8	2,0	92,2
	35	1	1,8	2,0	94,1
	360	1	1,8	2,0	96,1
	450	1	1,8	2,0	98,0
	500	1	1,8	2,0	100,0
	Total	51	91,1	100,0	
Missing		5	8,9		
Total		56	100,0		

Q10 Who is the dialogue partner of your (central) works council in consultation meetings (multiple answers possible)?

		Responses		Percent of Cases
		N	Percent	
Dialogue partner of the central works council[a]	CEO or ExCOM member	27	38,6%	50,9%
	Dutch country manager	26	37,1%	49,1%
	CFO	1	1,4%	1,9%
	HR manager	16	22,9%	30,2%
Total		70	100,0%	132,1%

a. Dichotomy group tabulated at value 1.

Q11 Is the structure regime applied in your corporation and if so, at which level?

		Frequency	Percent	Valid Percent	Cumulative Percent
Valid	No	8	14,3	15,7	15,7
	One-tier board	1	1,8	2,0	17,6
	Yes, on the highest level within the corporation	21	37,5	41,2	58,8
	Yes, on the level of the Dutch subholding	21	37,5	41,2	100,0
	Total	51	91,1	100,0	
Missing		5	8,9		
Total		56	100,0		

Q12 Since when is the structure regime applied within your corporation?

		Frequency	Percent	Valid Percent	Cumulative Percent
Valid	Unknown	27	48.2	50.9	50.9
	1971-2003	8	14.3	15.1	66.0
	2004-2010	6	10.7	11.3	77.4
	2011-2014	4	7.1	7.5	84.9
	Not applicable	8	14.3	15.1	100.0
	Total	53	94.6	100.0	
Missing		3	5.4		
Total		56	100.0		

Q13 Is the structure regime applied in your corporation on a voluntary basis?

		Frequency	Percent	Valid Percent	Cumulative Percent
Valid	Yes	16	28.6	35.6	35.6
	No	12	21.4	26.7	62.2
	Unknown	17	30.4	37.8	100.0
	Total	45	80.4	100.0	
Missing		11	19.6		
Total		56	100.0		

Q14 Is a covenant agreed upon with additional rights being given to your (central) works council (ex. article 32 WCA)?

		Frequency	Percent	Valid Percent	Cumulative Percent
Valid	Yes	23	41,1	43,4	43,4
	No	30	53,6	56,6	100,0
	Total	53	94,6	100,0	
Missing		3	5,4		
Total		56	100,0		

Q15 Which additional rights are conferred to your (central) works council by virtue of this covenant?

		Responses		Percent of Cases
		N	Percent	
Additional rights through a covenant[a]	Consultation meetings with the executive director (if not applicable beforehand)	10	13,2%	45,5%
	Additional consultation rights	12	15,8%	54,5%
	Additional co-determination rights	8	10,5%	36,4%
	Information rights on international matters	12	15,8%	54,5%
	Procedural rights (such as the moment at which the works council is engaged)	6	7,9%	27,3%
	Co-determination right in the area of employment conditions (*arbeidsvoorwaarden*) provided that no CLA is applicable	7	9,2%	31,8%
	Additional facilities	9	11,8%	40,9%
	Right of inquiry	2	2,6%	9,1%
	Definition of "important" (*belangrijke*) decisions	5	6,6%	22,7%
	Pension policy	1	1,3%	4,5%
	Non-executive board members present during consultation meetings	1	1,3%	4,5%
	Career development	1	1,3%	4,5%
	Individual application of the WCA within the MNCs corporate structure	1	1,3%	4,5%
	Decision-making powers of decentralised works council committees	1	1,3%	4,5%
Total		76	100,0%	345,5%

a. Dichotomy group tabulated at value 1.

Q16 In how many (intended) decisions was your (C)WC involved in 2011-2013; decisions limited to NL and total number of decisions per year

#	2011	2011 NL	2012	2012 NL	2013	2013 NL
1						
2		4		4		3
3		5		4		5
4	2	2	2	2	2	2
5	6	6	5	5	6	5
6						
7						
8	6	6	7	7	6	5
9						
10	8	7	10	8	9	6
11	15	15	14	14	15	15
12						
13	7	6	11	10	9	7
14	0	0	0	0	0	0
15		25		30		28
16						
17	10	9	10	8	10	8
18						
19	7	4	5	2	8	5
20	22	22	26	26	39	39
21	22		25		23	
22	25	20	25	20	25	20
23	50	50	50	50	100	50
24						
25	10		11		13	
26						
27	40	40	58	58	18	18
28	6	6	8	8	10	10
29	12	12	11	11	10	9
30	10	10	14	14	12	12
31	2	25	2	35	2	40
32						
33	0	0	0	0	0	0
34	0	5	0	5	0	5
35	0	10	0	10	0	15
36		6		12		9

#	2011	2011 NL	2012	2012 NL	2013	2013 NL
37		3		2		2
38		12		10		8
39		2		2		1
40	5	4	4	3	4	4
41						
42	20	20	20	20	20	20
43		3		2	1	1
44		4		4		4
45						
46						
47	10	6	8	6	12	7
48						
49	12	8	17	12	17	14
50		5		5		10
51						
52	1		2		1	3
53	13		14		18	
54	10	10	11	11	6	6
55	14	14	13	13	7	7
56						

Q17 Ratio of the supervisory board being comprised of members of a higher entity within the MNC

		Frequency	Percent	Valid Percent	Cumulative Percent
Valid	0%	3	5,4	12,0	12,0
	11,1%	1	1,8	4,0	16,0
	25%	2	3,6	8,0	24,0
	33,3%	6	10,7	24,0	48,0
	43%	1	1,8	4,0	52,0
	50%	4	7,1	16,0	68,0
	55,5%	1	1,8	4,0	72,0
	60%	1	1,8	4,0	76,0
	62%	1	1,8	4,0	80,0
	66,6%	2	3,6	8,0	88,0
	100%	3	5,4	12,0	100,0
	Total	25	44,6	100,0	
Missing		31	55,4		
Total		56	100,0		

Q18 Do you think that undue influence is exercised by the top-management on the supervisory board?

		Frequency	Percent	Valid Percent	Cumulative Percent
Valid	No	32	57.1	76.2	76.2
	Yes	10	17.9	23.8	100.0
	Total	42	75.0	100.0	
Missing		14	25.0		
Total		56	100.0		

Q19 Has in the last four years your (central) works council exercised its regular right of recommendation for members of the supervisory board?

		Frequency	Percent	Valid Percent	Cumulative Percent
Valid	One time	9	16,1	22,0	22,0
	Two times	6	10,7	14,6	36,6
	Four times	5	8,9	12,2	48,8
	No	17	30,4	41,5	100,0
	No legal right of recommendation (not applicable)	4	7,1	9,8	58,5
	Total	41	73,2	100,0	
Missing		15	26,8		
Total		56	100,0		

Q20 Has in the last four years your (central) works council exercised its enhanced right of recommendation for members of the supervisory board?

		Frequency	Percent	Valid Percent	Cumulative Percent
Valid	One time	18	32,1	42,9	42,9
	Two times	8	14,3	19,0	61,9
	Three times	1	1,8	2,4	64,3
	No	13	23,2	31,0	95,2
	No legal right of recommendation (not applicable)	2	3,6	4,8	100,0
	Total	42	75,0	100,0	
Missing		14	25,0		
Total		56	100,0		

Q21 Are you having more contact with the recommended supervisory board members in comparison with the other members of the supervisory board?

		Frequency	Percent	Valid Percent	Cumulative Percent
Valid	No	9	33,3	34,6	34,6
	Yes	17	63,0	65,4	100,0
	Total	26	96,3	100,0	
Missing		1	3,7		
Total		27	100,0		

Q22.1 Better access to information exists through contacts with the supervisory board

		Frequency	Percent	Valid Percent	Cumulative Percent
Valid	No	10	17,9	23,8	23,8
	Yes	22	39,3	52,4	76,2
	Not applicable	10	17,9	23,8	100,0
	Total	42	75,0	100,0	
Missing		14	25,0		
Total		56	100,0		

Q22.2 Better influence on the decision-making process exists through contacts with the supervisory board

		Frequency	Percent	Valid Percent	Cumulative Percent
Valid	No	19	33,9	44,2	44,2
	Yes	13	23,2	30,2	74,4
	Not applicable	11	19,6	25,6	100,0
	Total	43	76,8	100,0	
Missing		13	23,2		
Total		56	100,0		

Q22.3 Is the access to information and influence on the decision-making process improved since recommended supervisory board member(s) are appointed?

		Frequency	Percent	Valid Percent	Cumulative Percent
Valid	No	14	25,0	32,6	32,6
	Yes	14	25,0	32,6	65,1
	Not applicable	15	26,8	34,9	100,0
	Total	43	76,8	100,0	
Missing		13	23,2		
Total		56	100,0		

Q22.4 Is the supervisory board having a mediating role?

		Frequency	Percent	Valid Percent	Cumulative Percent
Valid	No	13	23,2	30,2	30,2
	Yes	16	28,6	37,2	67,4
	Not applicable	14	25,0	32,6	100,0
	Total	43	76,8	100,0	
Missing		13	23,2		
Total		56	100,0		

Q23 Why does your (central) works council make no use of its enhanced right of recommendation for members of the supervisory board?

		Frequency	Percent	Valid Percent	Cumulative Percent
Valid	Inadequate knowledge of the possibility to use the right	4	30,8	33,3	33,3
	Insufficient expertise of the (central) works council to make recommendations	2	15,4	16,7	50,0
	No added value/no improvement by using recommendation right	1	7,7	8,3	58,3
	Lack of time	1	7,7	8,3	66,7
	Role of the SB minimal	1	7,7	8,3	75,0
	Not necessary	1	7,7	8,3	83,3
	Less relevant since a foreign entity is the largest SH since 2012	1	7,7	8,3	91,7
	Insufficient expertise of the (central) works council to make recommendations and no added value	1	7,7	8,3	100,0
	Total	12	92,3	100,0	
Missing		1	7,7		
Total		13	100,0		

Q24 Which of the following topics has received the most attention of your (central) works council last year (you may select a maximum of 5 topics)?

		Responses		Percent of Cases
		N	Percent	
Agenda of the (central) works council last year[a]	Q24.1 Merger (plans)	6	3,2%	14,3%
	Q24.2 Reorganisations and downsizings	37	20,0%	88,1%
	Q24.3 Change in the location of the enterprise's operations	4	2,2%	9,5%
	Q24.4 Investments	14	7,6%	33,3%
	Q24.5 Taking out major loans for the enterprise	10	5,4%	23,8%
	Q24.6 Change of the organisational structure of the corporation	28	15,1%	66,7%
	Q24.7 Employment conditions	14	7,6%	33,3%
	Q24.8 Working time or vacation schemes	5	2,7%	11,9%
	Q24.10 Personnel training	3	1,6%	7,1%
	Q24.11 Remuneration and job-evaluation schemes	16	8,6%	38,1%
	Q24.12 Assessment schemes	9	4,9%	21,4%
	Q24.13 Relocation	4	2,2%	9,5%
	Q24.14 Appointment, dismissal and promotion policy	1	0,5%	2,4%
	Q24.15 Health and security policy	9	4,9%	21,4%
	Q24.16 Complaints procedures	3	1,6%	7,1%
	Q24.17 Savings and profit-sharing mechanism	2	1,1%	4,8%
	Q24.18 Pension schemes	13	7,0%	31,0%
	Q24.19 EWC establishment	1	0,5%	2,4%
	Q24.20 Social Plan	1	0,5%	2,4%
	Q24.21 Sustainable employability	1	0,5%	2,4%
	Q24.22 Governance	1	0,5%	2,4%
	Q24.23 Privacy	1	0,5%	2,4%
	Q24.24 e-Communication	1	0,5%	2,4%
	Q24.25 Personal risk (*risicodragerschap*)	1	0,5%	2,4%
Total		185	100,0%	440,5%

a. Dichotomy group tabulated at value 1.

Q25 Which topics have been discussed in the consultation meetings with the management in the period of 2012 – 2014 (multiple answers possible)?

		Responses		Percent of Cases
		N	Percent	
Agenda consultation meetings[a]	Q25.1 Transfer of control of the enterprise or any part thereof (article 25(1)(a) WCA)	9	4,3%	22,0%
	Q25.2 The establishment, take-over or relinquishment of control of another enterprise (article 25(1)(b) WCA)	14	6,7%	34,1%
	Q25.3 Termination of operations of the enterprise or a significant part thereof (article 25(1)(c) WCA)	24	11,5%	58,5%
	Q25.4 Any significant reduction, expansion or other change in the enterprise's activities (article 25(1)(d) WCA)	29	13,9%	70,7%
	Q25.5 Major changes to the organisation or to the distribution of powers within the enterprise (article 25(1)(e) WCA)	31	14,9%	75,6%
	Q25.6 Making major investments on behalf of the enterprise (article 25(1)(h) WCA)	18	8,7%	43,9%
	Q25.7 Granting substantial credit to or giving security for substantial debts of another entrepreneur (article 25(1)(j) WCA)	9	4,3%	22,0%
	Q25.8 Topics falling under article 27 WCA (for which the consent of the (central) works council is mandatory)	28	13,5%	68,3%
	Q25.9 Future strategy of the corporation and trends	23	11,1%	56,1%
	Q25.10 The remuneration policy	17	8,2%	41,5%
	Q25.11 Change in the location of the enterprise's operations (article 25(1)(f) WCA)	6	2,9%	14,6%
Total		208	100,0%	507,3%

a. Dichotomy group tabulated at value 1.

Q26.1 Has your (central) works council brought in an internal expert in the last three years?

		Frequency	Percent	Valid Percent	Cumulative Percent
Valid	Never	2	3,6	4,8	4,8
	Sometimes	21	37,5	50,0	54,8
	Frequently	19	33,9	45,2	100,0
	Total	42	75,0	100,0	
Missing		14	25,0		
Total		56	100,0		

Q26.2 Has your (central) works council brought in an external expert in the last three years?

		Frequency	Percent	Valid Percent	Cumulative Percent
Valid	Never	1	1,8	2,5	2,5
	Sometimes	19	33,9	47,5	50,0
	Frequently	20	35,7	50,0	100,0
	Total	40	71,4	100,0	
Missing		16	28,6		
Total		56	100,0		

Q27 How often are the financial and economic information communicated to your (central) works council (ex. article 31a WCA)?

		Frequency	Percent	Valid Percent	Cumulative Percent
Valid	Never	2	3,6	4,8	4,8
	Once a year	3	5,4	7,1	11,9
	Twice a year	10	17,9	23,8	35,7
	Per quartile	21	37,5	50,0	85,7
	Six times a year	2	3,6	4,8	90,5
	Monthly	3	5,4	7,1	97,6
	In every consultation meeting	1	1,8	2,4	100,0
	Total	42	75,0	100,0	
Missing		14	25,0		
Total		56	100,0		

Q28 In what language are the data on the financial and economic policy provided?

		Frequency	Percent	Valid Percent	Cumulative Percent
Valid	Combination of Dutch and English	1	2,5	2,6	2,6
	Dutch	20	50,0	51,3	53,8
	English	18	45,0	46,2	100,0
	Total	39	97,5	100,0	
Missing		1	2,5		
Total		40	100,0		

Q29 Are the data on the financial and economic policy limited to the Dutch subsidiaries of your corporation?

		Frequency	Percent	Valid Percent	Cumulative Percent
Valid	Yes	15	37,5	37,5	37,5
	No	25	62,5	62,5	100,0
	Total	40	100,0	100,0	

Q30 Are information on the holding structure (the power structures linking the entities) within the entire corporation provided to your (central) works council (ex. article 31(2) WCA)?

		Frequency	Percent	Valid Percent	Cumulative Percent
Valid	Yes	25	44,6	59,5	59,5
	No	8	14,3	19,0	78,6
	Unknown	9	16,1	21,4	100,0
	Total	42	75,0	100,0	
Missing		14	25,0		
Total		56	100,0		

Q31 Has your (central) works council itself requested the information on the holding structure in the entire corporation?

		Frequency	Percent	Valid Percent	Cumulative Percent
Valid	Yes	14	25,0	34,1	34,1
	No	21	37,5	51,2	85,4
	Unknown	6	10,7	14,6	100,0
	Total	41	73,2	100,0	
Missing		15	26,8		
Total		56	100,0		

Q32 Are the submitted data on the holding structure containing useful information for the work of your (central) works council?

		Frequency	Percent	Valid Percent	Cumulative Percent
Valid	No	4	16,0	16,7	16,7
	Yes	20	80,0	83,3	100,0
	Total	24	96,0	100,0	
Missing		1	4,0		
Total		25	100,0		

Q33 Why is the information on the holding structure not provided to your (central) works council?

		Frequency	Percent	Valid Percent	Cumulative Percent
Valid		49	87.5	87.5	87.5
	De meeste gegevens zijn via de interne website voor iedereen toegankelijk	1	1.8	1.8	89.3
	Geen idee	1	1.8	1.8	91.1
	Milaan, geeft alleen informatie als dat gevraagd wordt. De EOR wordt ook niet veel verteld.	1	1.8	1.8	92.9
	Onkunde van het management, mogelijk niet duidelijk wat de bedoe-ling is. En het heeft geen prioriteit.	1	1.8	1.8	94.6
	Onwetendheid bij beide partijen	1	1.8	1.8	96.4
	Sinds 2013 geen verandering in zeggenschapsverhoudingen	1	1.8	1.8	98.2
	Wordt nooit verstrekt door de directie. Om getallen/cijfers moet altijd om gevraagd worden.	1	1.8	1.8	100.0
	Total	56	100.0	100.0	
Missing					
Total					

Q34 How often are consultation meetings with the designated management taking place (ex. article 24 and 31a WCA)?

		Frequency	Percent	Valid Percent	Cumulative Percent
Valid	less than three times a year	1	1,8	2,4	2,4
	3-6 times a year	23	41,1	54,8	57,1
	6-8 times a year	7	12,5	16,7	73,8
	9 times a year	1	1,8	2,4	76,2
	10 times a year	3	5,4	7,1	83,3
	11 times a year	2	3,6	4,8	88,1
	12 times a year	4	7,1	9,5	97,6
	24 times a year	1	1,8	2,4	100,0
	Total	42	75,0	100,0	
Missing		14	25,0		
Total		56	100,0		

Q35 Are ad-hoc consultation meetings taking place (ex. article 23 WCA)? If so, who is taking the initiative? Your (central) works council or the management of the undertaking?

		Frequency	Percent	Valid Percent	Cumulative Percent
Valid	Yes, on the initiative of the (central) works council	3	5,4	7,1	7,1
	Yes, on the initiative of the management	2	3,6	4,8	11,9
	Yes, on the initiative of both the (central) works council and the management	35	62,5	83,3	95,2
	No	2	3,6	4,8	100,0
	Total	42	75,0	100,0	
Missing		14	25,0		
Total		56	100,0		

Q36 How often are members of the supervisory board present in consultation meetings (ex. article 24 WCA)?

		Frequency	Percent	Valid Percent	Cumulative Percent
Valid	Never	22	39,3	52,4	52,4
	Sometimes	11	19,6	26,2	78,6
	Frequently	9	16,1	21,4	100,0
	Total	42	75,0	100,0	
Missing		14	25,0		
Total		56	100,0		

Q37 Has your (central) works council one or more times made an appeal at the Enterprise Chamber of the Amsterdam Court of Appeal since 1 January 2011?

		Frequency	Percent	Valid Percent	Cumulative Percent
Valid	Yes, once	2	3,6	4,8	4,8
	Yes, four times	1	1,8	2,4	7,1
	No	39	69,6	92,9	100,0
	Total	42	75,0	100,0	
Missing		14	25,0		
Total		56	100,0		

Q38 Has there been at times a difference of opinions between your (central) works council and the management whether prior consultation for an (intended) decision was required?

		Frequency	Percent	Valid Percent	Cumulative Percent
Valid	Yes, once	30	53,6	73,2	73,2
	Yes, repeatedly	4	7,1	9,8	82,9
	No, never	7	12,5	17,1	100,0
	Total	41	73,2	100,0	
Missing		15	26,8		
Total		56	100,0		

Q39 Is the time available to your (central) works council for formulating an advice overall sufficient?

		Frequency	Percent	Valid Percent	Cumulative Percent
Valid	Yes	35	62,5	83,3	83,3
	No	7	12,5	16,7	100,0
	Total	42	75,0	100,0	
Missing		14	25,0		
Total		56	100,0		

Q40 Please indicate in how far you agree with the following statement: "The position of my (central) works council has deteriorated as a result of increasing internationalisation"

		Frequency	Percent	Valid Percent	Cumulative Percent
Valid	Strongly disagree	4	7,1	9,5	9,5
	Disagree	7	12,5	16,7	26,2
	Undecided	9	16,1	21,4	47,6
	Agree	19	33,9	45,2	92,9
	Strongly agree	3	5,4	7,1	100,0
	Total	42	75,0	100,0	
Missing		14	25,0		
Total		56	100,0		

Q41.1 I am not having enough time for my work as employee representative due to a high workload and other duties

		Frequency	Percent	Valid Percent	Cumulative Percent
Valid	Completely disagree	16	28,6	38,1	38,1
	Disagree	5	8,9	11,9	50,0
	Undecided	11	19,6	26,2	76,2
	Agree	7	12,5	16,7	92,9
	Completely agree	3	5,4	7,1	100,0
	Total	42	75,0	100,0	
Missing		14	25,0		
Total		56	100,0		

Q41.2 Due to my work as employee representative, I have had negative experiences with my immediate supervisors

		Frequency	Percent	Valid Percent	Cumulative Percent
Valid	Completely disagree	23	41,1	54,8	54,8
	Disagree	7	12,5	16,7	71,4
	Undecided	4	7,1	9,5	81,0
	Agree	7	12,5	16,7	97,6
	Completely agree	1	1,8	2,4	100,0
	Total	42	75,0	100,0	
Missing		14	25,0		
Total		56	100,0		

Q41.3 The work as employee representative hampers my career

		Frequency	Percent	Valid Percent	Cumulative Percent
Valid	Completely disagree	16	28,6	39,0	39,0
	Disagree	8	14,3	19,5	58,5
	Undecided	7	12,5	17,1	75,6
	Agree	4	7,1	9,8	85,4
	Completely agree	6	10,7	14,6	100,0
	Total	41	73,2	100,0	
Missing		15	26,8		
Total		56	100,0		

Q41.4 I am not sufficiently qualified for my work as employee representative

		Frequency	Percent	Valid Percent	Cumulative Percent
Valid	Completely disagree	22	39,3	52,4	52,4
	Disagree	15	26,8	35,7	88,1
	Undecided	2	3,6	4,8	92,9
	Agree	2	3,6	4,8	97,6
	Completely agree	1	1,8	2,4	100,0
	Total	42	75,0	100,0	
Missing		14	25,0		
Total		56	100,0		

Q42 Are you satisfied with the training opportunities and the respective arrangements in your corporation?

		Frequency	Percent	Valid Percent	Cumulative Percent
Valid	No	3	5,4	7,1	7,1
	Yes	39	69,6	92,9	100,0
	Total	42	75,0	100,0	
Missing		14	25,0		
Total		56	100,0		

Q43 Are you maintaining contacts with employee representatives within your corporation outside the Netherlands?

		Frequency	Percent	Valid Percent	Cumulative Percent
Valid	No	14	25,0	33,3	33,3
	Yes	28	50,0	66,7	100,0
	Total	42	75,0	100,0	
Missing		14	25,0		
Total		56	100,0		

Q44 Is a European Works Council maintained in your corporation?

		Frequency	Percent	Valid Percent	Cumulative Percent
Valid	Yes	29	51,8	69,0	69,0
	No	13	23,2	31,0	100,0
	Total	42	75,0	100,0	
Missing		14	25,0		
Total		56	100,0		

Q45 Is your (central) works council involved in issues that concern the Netherlands and at least one other country (transnational issues)?

		Frequency	Percent	Valid Percent	Cumulative Percent
Valid	12 times a year	2	3,6	4,8	4,8
	2-4 times a year	12	21,4	28,6	33,3
	Once a year	11	19,6	26,2	59,5
	Ad-hoc, if such issue arises	1	1,8	2,4	61,9
	Never	16	28,6	38,1	100,0
	Total	42	75,0	100,0	
Missing		14	25,0		
Total		56	100,0		

Q46 Are you a member of the European Works Council?

		Frequency	Percent	Valid Percent	Cumulative Percent
Valid	Yes	17	58,6	58,6	58,6
	No	12	41,4	41,4	100,0
	Total	29	100,0	100,0	

Q47 At which level within your corporation is the European Works Council maintained?

		Frequency	Percent	Valid Percent	Cumulative Percent
Valid	Central management (topholding)	20	69,0	69,0	69,0
	Division level	1	3,4	3,4	72,4
	Regional headquarters (such as EU headquarters)	7	24,1	24,1	96,6
	Strategic Business Unit (SBU)	1	3,4	3,4	100,0
	Total	29	100,0	100,0	

Q48 Is the European Works Council situated in the Netherlands

		Frequency	Percent	Valid Percent	Cumulative Percent
Valid	Netherlands	17	58,6	60,7	60,7
	Belgium	1	3,4	3,6	64,3
	France	2	6,9	7,1	71,4
	Germany	2	6,9	7,1	78,6
	Ireland	1	3,4	3,6	82,1
	Italy	1	3,4	3,6	85,7
	United Kingdom	4	13,8	14,3	100,0
	Total	28	96,6	100,0	
Missing		1	3,4		
Total		29	100,0		

Q49 Are additional rights conferred to the European Works Council within your corporation compared to the subsidiary requirements (i.e. the statutory fallback rules)?

		Frequency	Percent	Valid Percent	Cumulative Percent
Valid	Yes	4	13,8	13,8	13,8
	No	20	69,0	69,0	82,8
	Unknown	5	17,2	17,2	100,0
	Total	29	100,0	100,0	

Q50.1 I am satisfied with the exchange of information between the EWC and my (central) works council

		Frequency	Percent	Valid Percent	Cumulative Percent
Valid	Completely disagree	2	6,9	6,9	6,9
	Disagree	5	17,2	17,2	24,1
	Undecided	4	13,8	13,8	37,9
	Agree	12	41,4	41,4	79,3
	Completely agree	6	20,7	20,7	100,0
	Total	29	100,0	100,0	

Q50.2 The atmosphere is open and informal during meetings of the European Works Council

		Frequency	Percent	Valid Percent	Cumulative Percent
Valid	Completely disagree	6	20,7	20,7	20,7
	Disagree	5	17,2	17,2	37,9
	Undecided	4	13,8	13,8	51,7
	Agree	8	27,6	27,6	79,3
	Completely agree	6	20,7	20,7	100,0
	Total	29	100,0	100,0	

Q50.3 The European Works Council supports me with regard to my duties as (central) works council member

		Frequency	Percent	Valid Percent	Cumulative Percent
Valid	Completely disagree	10	34,5	34,5	34,5
	Disagree	6	20,7	20,7	55,2
	Undecided	3	10,3	10,3	65,5
	Agree	4	13,8	13,8	79,3
	Completely agree	6	20,7	20,7	100,0
	Total	29	100,0	100,0	

Q51 Are both the European Works Council and your (central) works council consulted at the same time on important issues?

		Frequency	Percent	Valid Percent	Cumulative Percent
Valid	Yes	9	31,0	31,0	31,0
	No, the EWC is consulted earlier	7	24,1	24,1	55,2
	No, my (central) works council is consulted earlier	13	44,8	44,8	100,0
	Total	29	100,0	100,0	

Annex IV: Overview of missing answers | Quantitative analysis

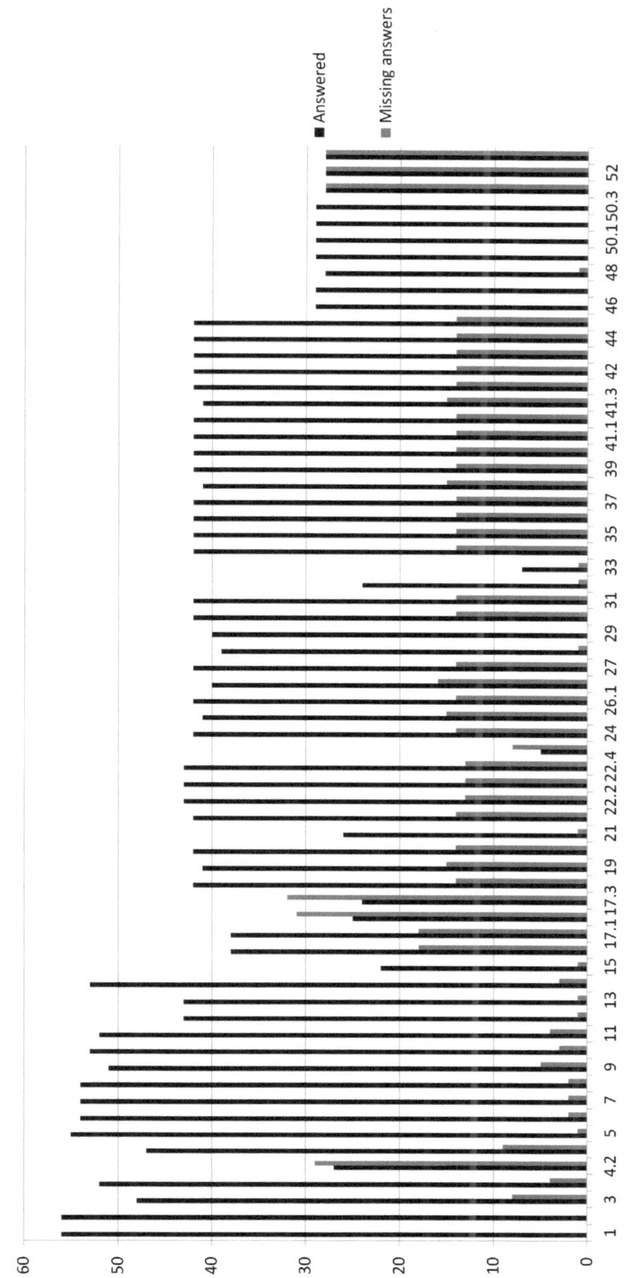

Overview of missing answers (red) for each of the questions posed in the quantitative part of this study (chapter IV).

Annex V: Sector data CBS | Quantitative analysis

Table 1 Establishments by sector and number of employees (CBS, 2014)

Sector	150 - 200	200 - 250	250 - 500	500 - 1000	1000 - 2000	> 2000	Total	%
A Agriculture, forestry and fisheries	5	10	5	5	0	0	25	0,52%
B Mineral extraction	5	5	5	0	0	0	15	0,31%
C Industry	230	115	220	110	50	20	745	15,54%
D Energy	5	5	5	0	5	5	25	0,52%
E Water and waste management	10	10	10	5	5	0	40	0,83%
F Construction and installation companies	55	30	50	25	25	5	190	3,96%
G Retail	170	105	185	85	30	25	600	12,51%
H Transport and storage	65	40	75	30	15	15	240	5,01%
I Catering	20	10	20	10	10	5	75	1,56%
J Information and communication	25	30	45	20	5	15	140	2,92%
K Financial services	20	10	25	15	10	10	90	1,88%
L Leasing and real estate	20	10	20	5	0	0	55	1,15%
M Specialised traderelated services	55	50	95	40	20	10	270	5,63%
N Leasing and other traderelated services	135	70	145	65	30	25	470	9,80%
O Public administration and public services	80	50	95	65	40	25	355	7,40%
P Education	145	115	175	85	35	25	580	12,10%
Q Healthcare and social welfare	110	80	195	185	140	85	795	16,58%
R Culture, sport and recreation	15	10	15	5	0	0	45	0,94%
S Other services	15	5	15	5	5	0	45	0,94%
T Households	0	0	0	0	0	0	0	0,00%
U Extraterritorial organisations	0	0	0	0	0	0	0	0,00%
A-U All economic activities	1180	755	1395	765	430	270	4795	100,00%

Annex VI: Interview protocol | Qualitative results[1]

1 Introduction

This protocol was used for the interviews conducted with the management representatives, the supervisory board and the central works council of the multinational corporations included in this study.

29 central works councils had indicated their willingness to participate in the follow-up interviews. In total, a maximum of 87 interviews could have been conducted with works council representatives, members of the management and the supervisory board. The actual number of interviews, however, depended on the willingness and availability of the management and the supervisory board to participate in the study. 58 interviews were conducted and the results are reported in chapter V of this study.

Each interview lasted 60 to 90 minutes. The audio recordings of the interviews were transcribed and subsequently coded with ATLAS.ti (see annex VI for the codebook). Core issues identified in the quantitative part of this study were addressed in the follow-up interviews, namely:

(i) Who actually conducts the consultations on behalf of the management.
(ii) The perception of the Dutch works council from the management's and supervisory board's view.
(iii) The discrepancy between Dutch and foreign MNCs regarding the consultation of the works council on the future strategy of the MNC and trends.
(iv) The dispute resolution mechanisms used once a disagreement between the management and the works council arises on the question whether or not a topic falls under article 25 WCA.
(v) The presence (or absence) of supervisory board members in consultation meetings between the management and the works council.
(vi) The independence of supervisory board members vis-à-vis the presence of corporate executives on the board of the Dutch subholding.
(vii) The use of experts, in particular internal experts by the works councils.
(viii) The relationship between the Dutch works council and the EWC as well as foreign employee representatives.
(ix) Other forms of employee participation used alongside the more formal works council structure.

1 Translated from Dutch.

1.1 Interview questions for (central) works council members

1.1.1 Structure of the interview

1. Introduction of the researcher and the study, structure and purpose of the interviews.
2. What is your position within the MNC?
3. What is your position within the works council?
4. How is the consultation of the (central) works council by the management taking place?
5. What is the relationship with the supervisory board?
6. What is the relationship with the European works council, if maintained, and how are contacts with foreign employee representatives maintained?
7. Are other forms of employee participation used within the undertaking?

1.1.2 Interview questions

1. General
    - 1.1. What is your position within the MNC?
        - 1.1.1. Since when are you working for the MNC?
    - 1.2. What is your position within the works council?
        - 1.2.1. Since when are you a member of the works council?
    - 1.3. Have important reorganisations taken place within the last 5 years?

2. Consultation between the works council and the management
    - 2.1. [Questionnaire results] You indicated in the questionnaire that [topic] is high on the works council agenda. Does that correlate with the developments within the MNC?
        - 2.1.1. With other words, are topics high on the agenda of your works council, which are currently not urgent?
    - 2.2. [Questionnaire results] How frequently is your works council consulted by the management
    - 2.3. At which stage in the consultation process is your works council becoming involved?
    - 2.4. Is your works council consulted on international issues that are having a (potential) impact on the Dutch employees of the MNC?
    - 2.5. What is the role of your works council in the decision-making process?
        - 2.5.1. Does the works council actively propose solutions on issues arising in the decision-making process?
    - 2.6. What is the management's attitude towards the works council?
        - 2.6.1. Is information provided and consultation requests sufficiently explained and reasons given (for advices)?

2.6.2. [Where information is withheld]: which steps have been taken by the works council to get the information?

2.7. [Questionnaire results] The majority of works councils indicated that disputes whether an issue must be subject to prior works council consultation are sometimes or even frequently arising. Yet, very few cases of litigation are occurring. How are these tensions resolved in your MNC?

2.8. How are information communicated to the other employees?

2.8.1. How are *zzp'ers*, flex-workers, *uitzendkrachten* and *gedetacheerden* involved in your MNC?

3. Use of experts

3.1. [Questionnaire results] You have indicated to [frequency] use external experts. When are you using external experts and is this facilitated by the MNC?

3.2. [Questionnaire results] You have indicated to make [frequency] use of internal experts

3.2.1. [Why are internal experts *not* used by your works council]

3.2.2. When are such internal experts used?

3.2.3. Is this helpful for the decision-making process?

3.2.4. Does the management facilitate this?

4. Structure regime

4.1. If applicable: You indicated in the questionnaire that the structure regime is applied in your MNC

4.1.1. How is the relationship between your works council and the supervisory board?

4.1.1.1. How is the relationship with the *voordrachtscommissaris*?

4.1.2. [Questionnaire results] undue influence of the parent company → paradox between the number of corporate SB members and the responses by works councils

4.1.3. The supervisory board members are, according to the questionnaire, present/not present in consultation meetings?

4.1.3.1. What is the role of the supervisory board members in such consultations?

5. EWC and foreign contacts

5.1. [Questionnaire results] An EWC is present/not present in your MNC.

5.1.1. Why is no EWC present despite your MNC fulfilling the criteria for this?

5.1.2. How are information shared between the EWC and your works council?

5.1.3. Is your Dutch works council actively engaging in communication with the EWC (meetings, phone, email, ...)?

5.2. [Questionnaire results] You have indicated that you are (not) having foreign contacts with employee representatives.

5.2.1. Why are you not having contacts with your foreign colleagues?

5.2.2. What information is shared with your foreign counterparts?

6. Other forms of employee participation within your MNC

6.1. Are other forms of employee participation, aside from the works council structure, applied within your MNC?

6.2. How is the exchange of information between such other forums and your works council organised?

1.2 Interview questions for the board of management

1.2.1 Structure of the interview

1. Introduction of the researcher and the study, structure and purpose of the interviews.
2. What is your position within the undertaking?
3. What is the relationship between the Dutch subsidiary and the central management of the MNC?
4. How is consultation of the management with the central works council taking place?
5. What is the role of the central works council from the management's perspective?
6. Are other forms of employee participation used within the undertaking?

1.2.2 Interview questions

1. General

1.1. What is your formal position within the MNC?

1.2. Is the MNC listed at a stock exchange?

1.3. What is the general economic position of the MNC anno 2014/2015 and in how far is the level of competition increased or decreased?

1.4. How important is the location in the Netherlands for the MNC (in terms of ratio of employees in NL and abroad; the general importance of the Netherlands)?

1.5. Have important reorganisations taken place within the last 5 years? [Follow-up: and how was the cooperation with the works council in this regard?]

2. Consultation of the (central) works council
   2.1. Are you participating in the consultation meetings with the CWC or is another member of the management fulfilling this role?
   2.2. Is the participation of the (central) works council in the decision-making process important for the commitment of the workforce within your MNC?
   2.3. When is the (central) works council being involved in the decision-making process?
   2.4. Do you and the management perceive the central works council as professional and efficient? [OR] What is the management's perception of the (central) works council?
   2.5. Are you consulting the works council on strategic issues?
      2.5.1. At which stage in the decision-making process?
      2.5.2. Is the works council's input valued for the implementation of such a strategy?
   2.6. What is your opinion on the presence of supervisory board members in consultation meetings of the management and the works council?
   2.7. Has there been a disagreement between the management and the works council whether an issue has to be subject to prior works council advice (*adviesplichtig onderwerp*)?
      2.7.1. How was such a dispute resolved? [Recourse to litigation is rarely made albeit indications that tensions between management and works councils are occurring much more frequently]
   2.8. Dutch works councils may use internal and external experts to assist them in formulating their advices (art. 16 WCA).
      2.8.1. Do you see an added value of the expert assistance for the works council advices?
      2.8.2. Is the use of internal experts facilitated, and if so, how?

3. Use of covenants [→ implementation of additional works council rights on a contractual basis to better link the employee participation mechanisms to the decision-making process]
   3.1. Is a covenant agreed upon between the management and the works council?
      3.1.1. Could you elaborate on the additional rights laid down in the agreement?
      3.1.2. Why not?
   3.2. What was the motivation of the management to grant additional rights to the central works council? [if applicable]

3.3. The questionnaire results indicated that significantly less often covenants are used in foreign corporations compared to Dutch MNCs. Do you see a reason for such a difference, keeping in mind that foreign corporations are not subject to Dutch law except for their Dutch subsidiaries?

4. Structure regime (if applicable)
   4.1. Is the structure regime applied in your MNC?
   4.2. Is a member of the central management (or higher management tier) sitting on the supervisory board of the Dutch subholding → *concernfunctionarissen*?
   4.3. How do you perceive such presence of a member of the central/higher management on the supervisory board of your undertaking?

1.3 Interview questions for the supervisory board

1.3.1 Structure of the interview

1. Introduction of the researcher and the study, structure and purpose of the interviews.
2. What is your position towards the undertaking (external or corporate supervisory board member)?
3. What is the relationship between the supervisory board and the (central) works council?
4. Consultation of the management with the (central) works council.
5. Role of the (central) works council from the supervisory board's perspective.

1.3.2 Interview questions

1. What is your position within the supervisory board and towards the MNC?
   1.1. What is your function within the supervisory board (tasks, rights and duties)?
   1.2. Are you appointed as external supervisory board member, member of a higher entity within the MNC?
   1.3. What is the primary objective of your supervisory board?
   1.4. Have you been appointed on the recommendation of the works council?
      1.4.1. If so, are you having a closer relationship with the works council compared to your fellow supervisory board members?
   1.5. How is the profile for candidates of the supervisory board determined?
      1.5.1. Is the works council involved in this process?
      1.5.2. What is the ratio between foreign and Dutch supervisory board members?

1.5.2.1. Is a diversity of (corporate) culture backgrounds beneficial for the MNC and the work of the supervisory board?

1.6. How is your supervisory board obtaining information?

1.6.1. And is the relationship with the works council helpful in this regard?

2. Are you (and/or other supervisory board members) present during consultation meetings of the management and the (central) works council?

2.1. If yes:

2.1.1. What is your role in such consultation meetings?

2.1.1.1. Are you seeing your role as being an observer?

2.1.1.2. Having a mediating role?

2.1.2. Is your presence during consultation meetings helpful in fulfilling your role as supervisory organ?

2.2. If no:

2.2.1. What are the reasons for your non-presence?

2.2.2. Do other means of communication exist between you and the works council?

2.3. Are you consulting the works council on strategic issues?

2.4. Do you perceive the central works council as professional and efficient? [OR] What is the supervisory board's perception of the central works council?

3. How do you perceive your relationship with the management?

3.1. Do you perceive your role as impartial from the other bodies (works council and management, shareholders) → undue influence on the supervisory board?

Annex VII: Code Book | Qualitative results

ATLAS.ti Report

Coding interviews -complete-
Code groups (selection)
Report created by Marcus Meyer on 31 Jan 2018

◈ 1 Organisation MNC

33 Members:

! 1 Business unit structure: issues re legal and economic reality

! 1 General: cooperative

! 1 General: Corporate culture

! 1 General: Corporate structure

! 1 General: Country chair (system)

! 1 General: Development of the undertaking

! 1 General: Economic position

! 1 General: Family undertaking

! 1 General: General facts

! 1 General: History of the MNE

! 1 General: Impact financial crisis

! 1 General: Importance of the Dutch establishments

! 1 General: Importance R&D

! 1 General: Other

! 1 General: Performance of the Dutch establishments

! 1 General: Position Dutch establishments: being a frontrunner in the MNC

! 1 General: Position Dutch establishments: importance link Dutch CEO and Global board

! 1 General: Position Dutch establishments: influence private equity

! 1 General: Position of the Dutch establishments

! 1 General: Role of the government authorities

! 1 General: Union influence

! 1 MNC classification: Chinese Parent
Linked Codes:
– is a → ! 1 MNC classification: Foreign MNE

! 1 MNC classification: Dutch MNE
Linked Codes:
← is part of – ! 1 MNC classification: Dutch MNE with foreign bachground (private equity)

! 1 MNC classification: Dutch MNE with foreign bachground (private equity)
Linked Codes:
– is part of → ! 1 MNC classification: Dutch MNE

! 1 MNC classification: Foreign MNE
Linked Codes:
← is a – ! 1 MNC classification: Chinese Parent

! 1 MNC classification: Foreign MNE with Dutch origin
Linked Codes:
← is part of – ! 1 MNC classification: Japanese parent
← is a – ! 1 MNC classification: US parent

! 1 MNC classification: German parent

! 1 MNC classification: Indian parent

! 1 MNC classification: Japanese parent
Linked Codes:
– is part of → ! 1 MNC classification: Foreign MNE with Dutch origin

! 1 MNC classification: Private Equity parent company

! 1 MNC classification: US parent
Linked Codes:
– is a → ! 1 MNC classification: Foreign MNE with Dutch origin

! 1E Reorganisation/change in employment conditions

! 1J From lifetime employment to employability

◈ 2 Organisation CWC

16 Members:

! 2 CORstructure

! 2 CORstructure: (Absence of) contacts with the parent company

! 2 CORstructure: committees for each business unit with rights (covenant)

! 2 CORstructure: Elections and representativeness

! 2 CORstructure: EP structure and EP level in the MNE

! 2 CORstructure: GOR (group works council)

! 2 CORstructure: matrix structure in WC - committees for each business unit and for specific topics

! 2 CORstructure: Other information

! 2 ESOP: foundation holds shares in the MNC on behalf of the employees

! 2 ESOP: Foundation receives newsletter CWC

! 2 ESOP: informal contacts foundation and CWC on an irregular basis

! 2 ESOP: informal contacts foundation and SB on an irregular basis

! 2 GORstructure: maintained for NL employees and employees working for shared service employees

! 2 Vaste landelijke commissie (VLC)

! 2D Relationship with Labour Unions

! 2H Role of the works council during a reorganisation

3 INFORMATION RIGHTS

60 Members:

! 3 "cross-border consultation"

! 3 Access to information
Linked Codes:
← is associated with – ! 3 Financial information: quarterly update financial results parent company (in comparison to fin. results NL subsidiary)

! 3 Access to information: (external) experts of the management give presentations to CWC

! 3 Access to information: (neg.) CWC is not receiving adequate information

! 3 Access to information: (neg.) CWC is not receiving information regarding financial matters and/or the strategy

! 3 Access to information: (neg.) info on strategic decisions are not shared by the management

! 3 Access to information: (neg.) management labels projects as pilot to exclude CWC

! 3 Access to information: (neg.) management uses piecemeal approach

! 3 Access to information: Checklist on necessary information for reorganisations

! 3 Access to information: Continuous exchange COR-RvB
Linked Codes:
← is associated with – ! 3 Limitations access to info: Only available information can be shared (limitations management)
← is associated with – ! 3 Limitations access to info: Window of opportunity

! 3 Access to information: CWC is being involved at an early stage

! 3 Access to information: heads-up for the CWC chairman (shareprice sensitive)

! 3 Access to information: management provides CWC with explanations

! 3 Access to information: Monthly digital info-set by the management with pre-defined benchmarks

! 3 Access to information: Network of contact persons within the organisation

! 3 Access to information: only limited for information on individual redundancies of employees

! 3 Access to information: overall sufficient provision of information by the management

! 3 Access to information: provided by division heads directly to works council (also cross-border)

! 3 Access to information: provided informally at the earliest possible moment

! 3 Access to information: sector-consultations

! 3 Access to information: standardised information package (compiled for top-holding but also provided to CWC)

! 3 Financial information: added value big picture financial situation, also for RfAs

! 3 Financial information: all info financial transactions are shared with CWC

! 3 Financial information: group results given to CWC alongside site- results

! 3 Financial information: meeting on a quarterly basis --> explanation of NL and corporate fin results

! 3 Financial information: quarterly update financial results parent company (in comparison to fin. results NL subsidiary)
Linked Codes:
– is associated with → ! 3 Access to information

! 3 General meeting of shareholder: added value presence CWC

! 3 General meeting of shareholders: DB of the CWC present

! 3 Informal info: Benen op tafel-sessies (informal meetings between management and DB of the COR)

! 3 Informal info: quarterly meeting with MT members on implementation of strategy in NL

! 3 Informal info: scheduling informal meetings with managers in case of reorganisations

! 3 Informal info: Short lines of communication

! 3 Informal info: strategy discussed in a broader context than NL

! 3 Information by CWC: giving a presentation for the CEO/MT

! 3 Information by CWC: Statement of the week & response by the employees

! 3 Information by CWC: Works council as source of information

! 3 Limitations access to info: no information and consultation of the CWC on large investments change of corporate structure

! 3 Limitations access to info: Only available information can be shared (limitations management)
Linked Codes:
– is associated with → ! 3 Access to information: Continuous exchange COR-RvB

! 3 Limitations access to info: Scrutiny of questions (don't lose your credit)

! 3 Limitations access to info: Window of opportunity
Linked Codes:
– is associated with → ! 3 Access to information: Continuous exchange COR-RvB

! 3 Limitations access to information: share-price sensitive information cannot be shared early

! 3 Management – Access to information: CWC as valuable source of information on operating companies for CEO/management

! 3 Management – Access to information: questionnaire among employees in NL – strong case vis-a-vis management

! 3 Monitoring: (neg.) management does not provide information for monitoring of agreements

! 3 Strategy – Access to information: bimonthly cyclus of presentations by the heads of business units

! 3 Strategy – Access to information: CEO of the MNC discusses the strategy with the CWC

! 3 Strategy – Access to information: CEO of the MNC discusses the strategy with the CWC once a year

! 3 Strategy – Access to information: CFO of the MNC discusses the strategy with the CWC once a year

! 3 Strategy – Access to information: global information shared on a quarterly basis

! 3 Strategy – Access to information: info on current state of the MNC and the impact on the Dutch entities is provided by the management

! 3 Strategy – Access to information: info on strategic decisions are shared by the management

! 3 Strategy – Access to information: strategy days during which the directors present their plans, SB present (AGVZ)

! 3 Strategy – Access to information: strategy meeting CEO: added value for management and CWC

! 3 Strategy – Access to information: strategy of the MNC "proactively informed"/ discussed with the CWC

! 3 Strategy: CWC informed on progress on long-term strategy via stop-light visualisation

! 3+4 House in order (lean proces-oriented employee participation mechanism)

! 3+4 House in order: more efficiency, but not as reorganisation tool (e.g. less CWC members)

! 3+4 House in order: reasons for application

! 3+4 House in order_ calculating backwards from the moment of implementation

! 3E5 Representativeness_Part-timers represented in the COR

3.1 INFO - CONTINUOUS ACCESS

5 Members:

! 3 Access to information
Linked Codes:
← is associated with – ! 3 Financial information: quarterly update financial results parent company (in comparison to fin. results NL subsidiary)

! 3 Access to information: Checklist on necessary information for reorganisations

! 3 Access to information: Monthly digital info-set by the management with pre-defined benchmarks

! 3 Access to information: provided by division heads directly to works council (also cross-border)

! 3 Strategy – Access to information: bimonthly cyclus of presentations by the heads of business units

4 CONSULTATION RIGHTS

178 Members:

! 4 Adde value: works council as sounding board

! 4 Added value: Explaining the necessary steps to the works council
Linked Codes:
– is associated with → ! 4 Process-oriented consultation: + RB: process with planning phase/draft phase - working group + management & short consultation phase

! 4 Added value: Explaining the strategy to the works council & employees (must be able to explain it to be succesful)
Linked Codes:
– is associated with → ! 4 Process-oriented consultation: + RB: process with planning phase/draft phase - working group + management & short consultation phase

! 4 Added value: I&C improved after successful first test-case on WC participation

! 4 Agenda – Consultation: planning days on which the CWC-members can come forward with questions for a specific consultation dossier

! 4 Consultation CWC internal: pre-advice (preadvies) subjacent works councils within the formal consultation traject (bottom-up into for the CWC).

! 4 Consultation other: steering committee monitoring social agreement- commitments (management, CWC, unions)

! 4 Consultation partner: CEO and CFO present as well as business unit manager concerned

! 4 Consultation partner: formal meetings with CFO on a quarterly basis to discuss fin. results

! 4 consultation partner: formal meetings with the CEO on a quarterly basis

! 4 consultation partner: formal meetings with the CEO twice a year
Linked Codes:
– is part of → ! 4 Formal consultation: meetings

! 4 consultation partner: meetings with the CEO possible, if necessary.

! 4 consultation partner: meetings with the one-tier board twice a year

! 4 Covenant: "Charted Medezeggenschap"

! 4 Covenant: Application covenant
Linked Codes:
← is associated with – ! 4 Covenant: clarifying organisational changes on the level of the topholding (by-laws)
← is associated with – ! 4 Covenant: Reasons no covenant

! 4 Covenant: assessment of CWC work

! 4 Covenant: clarifying organisational changes on the level of the topholding (by-laws)
Linked Codes:
– is associated with → ! 4 Covenant: Application covenant

! 4 Covenant: CWC advises on every election/dismissal of a new director, not only the "bestuurder i.d.z.v. de WOR"

! 4 Covenant: CWC and SB as gatekeepers for the cashflow of the NL undertaking --> for the continuity of the business

! 4 Covenant: Handbook personnel rules - all agreements with CWC in one folder; changes subject to consent of CWC

! 4 Covenant: independent supervisory board member with veto rights

! 4 Covenant: joint venture - decisions/information shared with CWC

! 4 Covenant: meeting on the remuneration policy of the whole group with the SB remuneration committee

! 4 Covenant: neg. cons consultation right at topholding-level

! 4 Covenant: Reasons no covenant
Linked Codes:
– is associated with → ! 4 Covenant: Application covenant

! 4 Covenant: recommendation rights for RvT

! 4 Covenant: specifying information rights of the CWC (int. scope)

! 4 Covenant: Strategy 2020 + MZ 2.0: working group of all WC chairman, CWC chairman and management

! 4 Dual WOR-entrepeneurship: access to information: practical issues

! 4 Dual WOR-entrepeneurship: consultation meetings

! 4 Dual WOR-entrepeneurship: ExCo entrepeneur

! 4 Dual WOR-entrepeneurship: frequency of consultation

! 4 Dual WOR-entrepeneurship: HR director as linking pin

! 4 Dual WOR-entrepeneurship: reasons application

! 4 Dual WOR-entrepeneurship: works council division of tasks (NL - shared services)

! 4 Dual WOR-entrpeneurship (bestuurderschap): one ExCo member and NL director

! 4 Formal consultation: (neg.) assessment procedure changed without consulting CWC: annulment of decision as a signal to corporate

! 4 Formal consultation: (neg.) Cash-policy: management of the parent decides over investments with Dutch reserves without EP involved

! 4 Formal consultation: (neg.) CWC does not adequately question maangement decisions (manager!)

! 4 Formal consultation: (neg.) Decisions declared share price-sensitive (koersgevoelig)

! 4 Formal consultation: (neg.) every RfA is under embargo and with confidentiality

! 4 Formal consultation: (neg.) limitations - only operational issues, no strategic ones

! 4 Formal consultation: (neg.) no consultation of the CWC on decisions affecting NL after change of corporate structure

! 4 Formal consultation: (neg.) Strategy: works council not consulted on the changes to the strategy

! 4 Formal consultation: advice of the works council as yellow card --> constructive criticism

! 4 Formal consultation: Appointment CEO: precondition that WC consultations are chaired by him

! 4 Formal consultation: art. 24 (AGVZ) meetings with regional management

! 4 Formal consultation: consensus driven (Rhineland model)

! 4 Formal consultation: Inviting CEO of the parent-company and consultation meeting in English

! 4 Formal consultation: meeting with the CEO of the MNC once a year

! 4 Formal consultation: meetings
Linked Codes:
← is part of – ! 4 consultation partner: formal meetings with the CEO twice a year

! 4 Formal consultation: on the Dutch level satisfactorily

! 4 Formal consultation: Rotating chair(wo)manship between CEO and COR chairman

! 4 Formal consultation: secured loans --> consultation CWC applicable

! 4 Frequency of consultation meetings

! 4 General Consultation: as early as possible, but only once an issue is relatively certain

! 4 General Consultation: CEO not always suitable dialogue partner on employee issues

! 4 General Consultation: CEO of the MNC the consultation partner of the CWC

! 4 General Consultation: CFO as statutory consultation partner accompanied by the HR-director Europe

! 4 General Consultation: Evolutionary model (niet hierarchische poldercultuur)

! 4 General Consultation: Global HR-director as consultation partner

! 4 General Consultation: management asks more advice, but sometimes less elaborate on extra-legal issues --> practical approach

! 4 General Consultation: Management Dutch subsidiary needs room for maneuvre to implement decisions of the parent

! 4 General Consultation: Other: de bestuurder is geen tegenstander maar een medestander.

! 4 General Consultation: pragmatic arguments for added value WC consultation instead of formal legal basis

! 4 General Consultation: Timing of consultation

! 4 General: Cross-border spill-over effects

! 4 Informal consultation meetings

! 4 Informal consultation meetings: management can share undecided issues with CWC for discussion

! 4 Informal consultation: (neg.) CWC proposes to meet only every 6 weeks (manager!)

! 4 Informal consultation: added value informal contacts CWC and topmanagement via corporate SB member

! 4 Informal consultation: added value informal contacts CWC- management and SB

! 4 Informal consultation: added value meetings

! 4 Informal consultation: added value removing label "important" decision

! 4 Informal consultation: CEO: Probing whether WC finds manager suitable

! 4 Informal consultation: country chair on stakeholder relations

! 4 Informal consultation: end of the year dinner with reflection and vision for EP next year

! 4 Informal consultation: in Germany and the Netherlands: beginning early to overcome differences in legislation

! 4 Informal consultation: influencing decision-making process in the parent company

! 4 Informal consultation: meetings with SB of the group to share standpoint WC

! 4 Informal consultation: memostructure with same consultation process for "non-important" decisions

! 4 Informal consultation: neg. input of the CWC not incorporated in request for advice/intended decision

! 4 Informal consultation: once a month DB and management

! 4 Informal consultation: Philosophy of early consultation

! 4 Informal consultation: Philosophy of early consultation: + less tension on the process and allowing room for questions

! 4 Informal consultation: Prior informal meetings BOD & WC before appointment of BOD members

! 4 Informal consultation: starting as early as possible prevents frustration and unneccesary waste of resources

! 4 Informal consultation: when informally and when formally?

! 4 Initiative CWC: (neg.) no proposals initiated by the COR

! 4 Initiative CWC: development-orietented annual assessment meetings (ontwikkelingsgericht functioneringsgesprekken)

! 4 Initiative CWC: influence on outsourcing by formulating a plan of action

! 4 Initiative CWC: Initiative of the COR on contracting

! 4 Initiative CWC: management asked CWC for an alternative solution; CWC developed own initiative in a short summary (2 pages)

! 4 Initiative CWC: possible if constructive

! 4 Initiative CWC: Pragmatic solution proposed by COR

! 4 Initiative CWC: proposal initiated by the COR

! 4 Initiative CWC: proposal initiated by the COR: validation through external consultancy

! 4 Initiative CWC: reacting on signal from the undertaking

! 4 Initiative CWC: Scenario development: Development of scenarios by COR
Linked Codes:
← is associated with – ! 4 Scenario development: Joint scenario development by CEO and WC

! 4 Initiative CWC: Social paragraph
Linked Codes:
← is associated with – ! 4 Initiative CWC: Social paragraph: added value

! 4 Initiative CWC: Social paragraph: added value
Linked Codes:
– is associated with → ! 4 Initiative CWC: Social paragraph

! 4 Initiative CWC: strategic use of the right to speak

! 4 Initiative CWC: works council's proposal for a phasing in of decisions

! 4 Input CWC: maangement uses input non-judgemental to improve; rational and constructive approach

! 4 Medezeggenschap 2.0: change towards team-based organisation --> change in EP structure necessary

! 4 Medezeggenschap 2.0: management consults CWC on changes to bring say and MZ in line

! 4 Mergers: works council only involved after the facts - once the AC is merged into the Dutch entity

! 4 Pre-advice: better decisions

! 4 Pre-advice: consensus oriented and matching intended decision and advice

! 4 Pre-advice: effectiveness (avoid implementation problems) and efficiency (flexibility, early input, fast formal trajectory)

! 4 Pre-advice: improved communication of decisions to the workforce (CWC involved in the process and knows the arguments) (manager!)

! 4 Pre-advice: shared with management prior to formal RfA

! 4 Problems – Absence of consultation: innovative startups without influence EP

! 4 Problems – Consultation: limitations - WC does not want to be consultated at a very early stage due to embargo and collective redundancies

! 4 Problems – Early consultation: risks of early involvement CWC

! 4 Problems – Pitfalls of modern process-oriented consultation

! 4 Problems Consultation: Disputes, legal proceedings and resolution mechanisms

! 4 Process-oriented consultation: (neg.) Con's pre-consultation model
Linked Codes:
– is associated with → ! 4 Process-oriented consultation: + RB: process with planning phase/draft phase - working group + management & short consultation phase

! 4 Process-oriented consultation: + "De meetlat" - consultation process planning tool
Linked Codes:
← is associated with – ! 4 Process-oriented consultation: + Input of OR is taken into consideration prior to start of the formal consultation

! 4 Process-oriented consultation: + Calculating time needed advice- traject: backwards from moment of implementation, including stand-still period (aanzegtermijn, afkoelingsphase art. 25(3) WOR e.d.)
Linked Codes:
– is associated with → ! 4 Process-oriented consultation: + RB: process with planning phase/draft phase - working group + management & short consultation phase

! 4 Process-oriented consultation: + Input of OR is taken into consideration prior to start of the formal consultation
Linked Codes:
– is associated with → ! 4 Process-oriented consultation: + "De meetlat" - consultation process planning tool

! 4 Process-oriented consultation: + Pro's of the pre-consultation phase
Linked Codes:
– is associated with → ! 4 Process-oriented consultation: + RB: process with planning phase/draft phase - working group + management & short consultation phase

! 4 Process-oriented consultation: + Process developed by COR checked by expert
Linked Codes:
– is associated with → ! 4 Process-oriented consultation: + RB: process with planning phase/draft phase - working group + management & short consultation phase

! 4 Process-oriented consultation: + RB: process with planning phase/draft phase - working group + management & short consultation phase
Linked Codes:
← is associated with – ! 4 Added value: Explaining the necessary steps to the works council
← is associated with – ! 4 Added value: Explaining the strategy to the works council & employees (must be able to explain it to be succesful)
← is associated with – ! 4 Process-oriented consultation: (neg.) Con's pre- consultation model
← is associated with – ! 4 Process-oriented consultation: + Calculating time needed advice-traject: backwards from moment of implementation, including stand-still period (aanzegtermijn, afkoelingsphase art. 25(3) WOR e.d.)
← is associated with – ! 4 Process-oriented consultation: + Pro's of the pre- consultation phase
← is associated with – ! 4 Process-oriented consultation: + Process developed by COR checked by expert
← is associated with – ! 4 Process-oriented consultation: + RFE phase: advice- request submitted to COR and personnel informed prior to formal consultation

← is associated with – ! 4 Process-oriented consultation: + Sticking to the EP proces: Let the management experience the failing of a dossier when not following the agreed upon process
← is associated with – ! 4 Process-oriented consultation: + Time effectiveness of pre-determined consultation process
← is associated with – ! 4 Process-oriented consultation: + Timing of meetings and access to information
← is associated with – ! 4 Process-oriented consultation: Townhall meetings (to explain the consultation process to constituencies)
← is associated with – ! 4 Process-oriented consultation: working group of the COR supports/develops consultation dossier with management

! 4 Process-oriented consultation: + RFE phase: advice-request submitted to COR and personnel informed prior to formal consultation
Linked Codes:
– is associated with → ! 4 Process-oriented consultation: + RB: process with planning phase/draft phase - working group + management & short consultation phase

! 4 Process-oriented consultation: + Sticking to the EP proces: Let the management experience the failing of a dossier when not following the agreed upon process
Linked Codes:
– is associated with → ! 4 Process-oriented consultation: + RB: process with planning phase/draft phase - working group + management & short consultation phase

! 4 Process-oriented consultation: + Time effectiveness of pre- determined consultation process
Linked Codes:
– is associated with → ! 4 Process-oriented consultation: + RB: process with planning phase/draft phase - working group + management & short consultation phase

! 4 Process-oriented consultation: + Timing of meetings and access to information
Linked Codes:
– is associated with → ! 4 Process-oriented consultation: + RB: process with planning phase/draft phase - working group + management & short consultation phase

! 4 Process-oriented consultation: added value Dutch model for Anglo- Saxon MNCs

! 4 Process-oriented consultation: added value for EP process planning (works council can also plan ahead; hiring experts, involving internal experts)

! 4 Process-oriented consultation: added value for RvB - CWC "sells" decision

! 4 Process-oriented consultation: added value of early pre-consultation

! 4 Process-oriented consultation: annual EP calendar with pre-agreed milestones

! 4 Process-oriented consultation: cross-functional consultation meetings (matrix structure)

! 4 Process-oriented consultation: dialogue model (Berenschot)

! 4 Process-oriented consultation: effectiveness

! 4 Process-oriented consultation: Employee participation statute (medezeggenschapsstatuut)

! 4 Process-oriented consultation: flexibility of this process

! 4 Process-oriented consultation: Monitoring of outcomes of consultation procedures

! 4 Process-oriented consultation: Phasing of the participation steps (pre-consultation, pre-advice, consultation, advice, decision)

! 4 Process-oriented consultation: pre-advice is discussed with CWC and input is implemented in final request for advice

! 4 Process-oriented consultation: Pre-consultation at the earliest possible moment: developing the solution together (CEO+CWC)

! 4 Process-oriented consultation: Pre-consultation: Management request prior to starting the consultation procedure a working group to develop a consultation dossier (adviesaanvraag)

! 4 Process-oriented consultation: Pre-consultation: no formal agreements on the process possible (case by case)

! 4 Process-oriented consultation: technical pre-consultation prior to formal consultations

! 4 Process-oriented consultation: Template for advices based on observations (not arbitrary, subjective)

! 4 Process-oriented consultation: temporary employee participation members (project-based)

! 4 Process-oriented consultation: temporary EP-members: added value

! 4 Process-oriented consultation: the process of formulating the RfA is the main source of influence for the WC

! 4 Process-oriented consultation: Townhall meetings (to explain the consultation process to constituencies)
Linked Codes:
– is associated with → ! 4 Process-oriented consultation: + RB: process with planning phase/draft phase - working group + management & short consultation phase

! 4 Process-oriented consultation: Umbrella RfA (request for advice)

! 4 Process-oriented consultation: WC handbook with model questions for consultation procedures

! 4 Process-oriented consultation: working group of the COR supports/develops consultation dossier with management
Linked Codes:
– is associated with → ! 4 Process-oriented consultation: + RB: process with planning phase/draft phase - working group + management & short consultation phase
← is associated with – ! 4 Process-oriented consultation: Working group: added value(s)
← is associated with – ! 4 Process-oriented consultation: Working group: managers of the unit concerned participate in the meetings

! 4 Process-oriented consultation: Working group: added value(s)
Linked Codes:
– is associated with → ! 4 Process-oriented consultation: working group of the COR supports/develops consultation dossier with management

! 4 Process-oriented consultation: working group: arbeidsvoorwaardencommissie (employment conditions committee)

! 4 Process-oriented consultation: Working group: management supports the use of working groups

! 4 Process-oriented consultation: Working group: managers of the unit concerned participate in the meetings
Linked Codes:
– is associated with → ! 4 Process-oriented consultation: working group of the COR supports/develops consultation dossier with management

! 4 Process-oriented consultation: Working group: problematic issue of delegation of powers

! 4 Process-oriented consultation: Working group: useful for very specific or very broad dossiers

! 4 Reorganisation: transition manager

! 4 Scenario development: Joint scenario development by CEO and WC
Linked Codes:
– is associated with → ! 4 Initiative CWC: Scenario development: Development of scenarios by COR

! 4 Strategy – (neg.) Formal consultation: Strategic decision making: Influence limited

! 4 Strategy – Formal consultation: Strategic decision making: CWC participates in thought-process/development of the corporate strategy

! 4 Strategy – Formal consultation: Strategic decision making: Influence CWC

! 4 Strategy – Formal consultation: Strategic decision making: works council informed and application locally shared by management

! 4 Strategy – Formal consultation: Strategy: resource planning discussed regularly with works council

! 4 Strategy – Formal consultation: Strategy: strategy and societal trends discussed jointly by CWC and management and translated into strategy for the MNC

! 4 Strategy: Covenant on Strategy 2020 + MZ 2.0 discussed during two- day workshop with MZ

! 4 Strategy: Dutch management cannot go against strategy but has the freedom to decide how to implement it

! 4 Strategy: MZ 2.0 signed by CWC, individ. works councils and the management

! 4 Strategy: MZ 2.0 working group of all WC chairmen, CWC chairman and management

! 4 Strategy: Strategy 2020 -> EP-strategy (MZ 2.0) in line with MNC strategy 2020

! 4 Strategy: strategy for the Netherlands is discussed

! 4 Strategy: strategy not discussed with CWC; but general anticipated trends are shared by the management

! 4 Strategy: WC members present in meetings of NL CEO with senior leaders

! 4 Time effectiveness: works council must be informed early to avoid delay, not WC fault

! 4 Translations: RfA's on investments are written in English for the parent company but the management summary for the CWC is in English

! 4 Urgent decisions: committee or working group gives advice or consent "unless..." (subject to conditions)

◈ 5 SUPERVISORY BOARD

102 Members:

! 5 Alternative SB Consultation: (lunch) meeting of (C)WC with SB and management after SB meeting (3 times a year or more often)

! 5 Alternative SB Consultation: rotating delegation CWC (3-4) meets with one SB-member (also rotating) after every SB-meeting

! 5 Alternative SB Consultation: SB agenda point (ca. 30 minutes) on WC --> CWC members present for this item during SB meeting (4-5 times a year)

! 5 Application structure regime
Linked Codes:
← is associated with – ! 5 Application structure regime: Now supervisory board instituted
← is associated with – ! 5 Problems SB: Application structure regime: No Supervisory Board

! 5 Application structure regime: Now supervisory board instituted
Linked Codes:
– is associated with → ! 5 Application structure regime

! 5 Concernfunctionarissen: "SB often not properly constituted (naar behoren samengesteld)"

! 5 Concernfunctionarissen: added value

! 5 Concernfunctionarissen: added value - members topmanagement as SB members to enable access to information/influence

! 5 Concernfunctionarissen: equal amount of external and internal members

! 5 Concernfunctionarissen: majority SB external

! 5 Concernfunctionarissen: majority SB semi-external ("member- farmers/ leden-veehouders")

! 5 Concernfunctionarissen: one active and one retired manager in the SB

! 5 Concernfunctionarissen: works council asked to refrain from recommending external candidate

! 5 Contacts topholding: Contacts RvC with topholding

! 5 Contacts topholding: two topmanagers in the SB of the Dutch subsidiary to allow for contacts in case of decisions at parent company- level

! 5 Contacts topholding: WC discusses remuneration policy with SB of the group

! 5 Election (neg.) : No direct influence COR on RvC profile

! 5 Election (neg.) : No use enhanced recommendation right (versterkt aanbevelingsrecht)

! 5 Election: (neg.) little added value of rec. SB member for the management (poppoenkastje, circus beperken)

! 5 Election: CWC profile for recommended SB members

! 5 Election: Enhanced recommendation right (versterkt aanbevelingsrecht)

! 5 Election: headhunter for selection of recommended candidate CWC

! 5 Election: Influence/input of COR on profile future RvC members

! 5 Election: Joint Committee of works council and management for a profile of the SB

! 5 Election: joint meeting of CWC, management and potential SB member (enhanced recommendation right)

! 5 Election: prior consultation CWC for EVERY new SB candidate

! 5 Election: Regular right of recommendation (gewoon aanbevelingsrecht)

! 5 Election: WC informed over progress regarding SB candidates' selection

! 5 formal consultation: 2-3 times a year CWC (DB) with voordrachtscommissaris

! 5 formal consultation: added value (rotating) participation SB members in OV meetings
Linked Codes:
– is associated with → ! 5 Formal Consultation: SB members present during OV meetings on a rotating basis

! 5 formal consultation: AGVZ meetings (art. 24 WOR)

! 5 formal consultation: CWC chairman joins SB meeting

! 5 formal consultation: CWC with voordrachtscommissaris on a regular basis

! 5 formal consultation: four times a year CWC with voordrachtscommissaris

! 5 Formal Consultation: recommended SB members present in OV meetings on a general basis (not the other SB members)

! 5 Formal Consultation: RvC members give input during OV meetings

! 5 Formal consultation: SB chairman once a year with DB of CWC

! 5 Formal Consultation: SB members present during OV meetings on a rotating basis
Linked Codes:
← is associated with – ! 5 formal consultation: added value (rotating) participation SB members in OV meetings

! 5 Formal Consultation: SB members present in OV meetings on a general basis

! 5 Formal consultation: Triangular meetings ("driehoeksoverleg")

! 5 Formal consultation: Triangular meetings with topmanagement present

! 5 Formal consultation: twice a year

! 5 Formal Consultation: twice a year CWC with (two) werknemerscommissarissen

! 5 Formal meetings with RvC on a regular basis
Linked Codes:
← is associated with – ! 5 Formal meetings: once a year with the entire SB and entire WC

! 5 Formal meetings: once a year with the entire SB and entire WC
Linked Codes:
– is associated with → ! 5 Formal meetings with RvC on a regular basis

! 5 Formal meetings: RvC gathers information from CWC for meetings with the management

! 5 Formal meetings: SB chairman with CWC chairperson or DB on a regular basis

! 5 Formal meetings: topical meetings with SB, management and CWC instead of AGVZ meetings/entire OV

! 5 General (neg.): No added value RvC

! 5 General – Consultation: better access to information by having a separate meeting with SB from regular consultation meetings

! 5 General – Consultation: SB discusses issues with management after meeting with CWC, if necessary.

! 5 General: Added value RvC in the structure regime

! 5 General: Composition RvC

! 5 General: independent member with veto rights to safeguard the take-over agreement (PE)

! 5 General: informally promotes emphasis on the importance of the OR and good OR members

! 5 General: Mediating role RvC

! 5 General: Mitigated structure regime

! 5 General: Neutral role of RvC (balancing of company and employee interests)

! 5 General: Raad van Toezicht

! 5 General: reasons application structure regime (management)

! 5 General: Role of the RvC

! 5 General: Shell: ex-CEO chairman of the SB

! 5 General: TWO supervisory boards

! 5 Informal consultation: ad hoc in case of important issues/business decisions

! 5 Informal consultation: End-of-the-year meeting of SB, CWC and management

! 5 Informal consultation: End-of-the-year meeting of SB, CWC and management: CEO gives a presentation

! 5 Informal consultation: Informal meetings with RvC on a regular basis

! 5 Informal consultation: meeting CWC with SB members on an irregular basis in addition to formal meetings

! 5 Informal consultation: meetings without management present possible

! 5 Informal consultation: monthly contact with recommended SB member

! 5 Informal consultation: on a regular basis with the (DB) of the CWC

! 5 Informal consultation: prior exchange of information prior to GM of shareholders with recommended SB members

! 5 Informal consultation: Prior informal meetings SB & WC before appointment of SB members

! 5 Informal consultation: prior to SB meetings (via telephone, email)

! 5 Informal consultation: recommended SB members present in CWC meetings on a quarterly basis

! 5 Informal consultation: SB informed by CWC on current SoA on shopfloor-level

! 5 Informal Consultation: SB members present during informal meetings on a rotating basis

! 5 Informal consultation: twice a year

! 5 Other: woman capital

! 5 Problems - Consultation: (neg.) no presence of SB members on a rotating basis

! 5 Problems SB: Application structure regime: budget by corporate does not allow for SB

! 5 Problems SB: Application structure regime: No Supervisory Board
Linked Codes:
– is associated with → ! 5 Application structure regime

! 5 Problems SB: Application structure regime: WC has no influence on SB composition (any more)

! 5 Problems SB: mismatch between organisational structure and structure regime (legal s.)

! 5 Problems: Corporate members SB - other: conflict of interest through ExCo and SB function as well as shareholdings

! 5 Problems: Reservations management re meetings SB-CWC: openness and feedback to management after meetings

! 5 Problems: role of the SB minimal (family undertaking)

! 5 Problems: SB Consultation: (neg.) presence of SB members during entire OV is inefficient

! 5 Problems: SB Formal consultation: (neg.) No triangular meetings ("driehoeksoverleg")

! 5 Professionalism CWC: dakpansgewijze opbouw needs improvement - capacity building and knowledge transfer through overlapping terms of CWC members

! 5 SB Access to information: all RfA are submitted to SB as well & meeting CWC-SB member takes place

! 5 SB access to Information: SB receives CWC newsletter

! 5 SB access to information: SB receives minutes of the CWC OV meetings

! 5 SB initiative CWC: SB introduced on the initiative of the works council

! 5 SB other: member-farmers

! 5 SB Other: Nationaal Register

! 5 SB Strategy: Check whether the strategy is shared with the OR and consultation has taken place

! 5 SB Strategy: Due dilligence of the strategy with the strategy-manager of the topholding

! 5 SB Strategy: making sure that the CWC has understood the strategy and intervene if necessary

! 5 SB Strategy: strategy for the Netherlands is discussed regularly

! 5 SE-works council: Dutch employee representative in the supervisory board of the MNC

! 5+6 Consultation: CWC informs SB on own action plan on a regular basis

◊ 6 PROFESSIONALISM CWC

82 Members:

! 6 Annual MZ day: Employee participation day (medezeggenschapsdag): Inviting management and WC members on a large-scale reorganisation

! 6 Annual MZ-day: Annual meeting of works council representatives

! 6 Committees (art. 15 commissies)

! 6 Elections: (neg.) CWC as escape due to lack of employability

! 6 Elections: (neg.) CWC does not reflect the workforce;

! 6 Elections: added value representative EP

! 6 Elections: combination of profile with project-based temporary EP-membership (to balance lack of candidates in elections)

! 6 Elections: dakpansgewijze opbouw - capacity building and knowledge transfer through overlapping terms of CWC members

! 6 Elections: management stimulates representative EP

! 6 Elections: Maximum term MC member: added value(s)
Linked Codes:
– is associated with → ! 6 Elections: Maximum terms for WC members (e.g. 3x 4 years)

! 6 Elections: Maximum terms for WC members (e.g. 3x 4 years)
Linked Codes:
← is associated with – ! 6 Elections: Maximum term MC member: added value(s)

! 6 Elections: profile for EP-members

! 6 Elections: representativeness of CWC

! 6 Elections: short movie of CEO and CWC chairman to promote candidacies

! 6 Input employees: 30 minutes update-meetings with section concerned in RfA

! 6 Input employees: Achterbanoverleg

! 6 Input employees: employees of the department concerned involved in the working group for an RfA procedure

! 6 Input employees: Interview responses by employees incorporated in consultation meetings

! 6 Input employees: Interviews conducted by COR with impacted staff

! 6 Input employees: Knowledge-base members (kennisbank-leden)

! 6 Input employees: Monitoring of effectiveness of EP among employees (employees as customer of EP)

! 6 Input employees: part-time WC members/"buitenleden"

! 6 Input WC's: involving members of WC's of the entities in a consultation traject

! 6 Internal strategy: agenda/priority list of the CWC

! 6 Internal strategy: proposal for a social paragraph (by the COR)

! 6 Internal strategy: stakeholder overview --> which relationships are important for the CWC (SB, unions, SER, politicians)

! 6 Internal strategy: Vision of the OR for the future development of the MNE

! 6 Internal strategy: works council and management address sustainable employment issues (duurzame inzetbaarheid) together

! 6 Newsletter: highlights translated into English for foreign colleagues

! 6 Proactive stance – Reorganisation: letter to the CEO indicating the implications on the NL undertaking

! 6 Proactive stance – Reorganisation: Own inititative on early involvement works councils

! 6 Proactive stance CWC: management values proactive stance CWC

! 6 Proactive stance: arguing in solutions as CWC instead of "I do not want this proposal"

! 6 Problems – Proactive stance CWC: (neg.) only a (small) group of CWC members is proactive

! 6 Problems – Proactive stance: (neg.) CWC still "in the past"

! 6 Problems – Proactive stance: (neg.) CWC very passive and only "tick the box"; no own initiatives

! 6 Problems – Professionalism COR: management reserved stance re professionalism COR

! 6 Problems – Professionalism: (neg.) CWC unprepared

! 6 Problems – Use of experts: neg. using legal advice too much

! 6 Problems – Use of experts: works council uses "in-house" contract lawyer (huisjurist) too (?) frequently

! 6 Problems Internal organisation: (neg.) difficult to address internal organisational changes within the EP-structure

! 6 Problems Internal strategy: poss. abuse of CWC membership: always meetings with two CWC-members present

! 6 Professionalism COR

! 6 Professionalism COR: action plan on "wenkend perspectief"

! 6 Professionalism COR: own initiative on a profile for a new CEO by means of an online-questionnaire

! 6 Professionalism COR: own inititative on ageing workforce

! 6 Professionalism COR: own inititative on statutes for SB

! 6 Professionalism_No negative impact of dispute on the relationship

! 6 Self-assessment: Assessment of works council work next to/as part of annual appraisal

! 6 Self-assessment: development-oriented assessment interviews (ontwikkelingsgericht functioneringsgesprekken) CWC

! 6 Self-assessment: Evaluation of COR work

! 6 Social innovation: meetings ("wenkend perspectief") organised jointly by management, SB and CWC present

! 6 Strategic non-use of WC rights

! 6 Strategy: giving feedback to the maangement on implementation of corporate strategy

! 6 Support base – multimedia: short clips for elections and for own initiatives CWC

! 6 Support base: Communication of proposed decisions to the workforce via interviews & walk-in hours by OR

! 6 Support base: Consultation process explained to constituencies

! 6 Support base: CWC meetings (ondernemingsraadvergaderingen) in principle open to all employees

! 6 Support base: explaining to employees the role of the EP together (CWC & management)

! 6 Support base: minutes of consultation meetings (CWC-management) made available to employees on the intranet

! 6 Training: Clustering of tranining for WCs with similar topics (onderdeelcommissies)

! 6 Training: I-We-Task model

! 6 Training: Individual coaching of COR members

! 6 Training: personal development plan

! 6 Training: training of new SB members by CWC (presentation of past EP)

! 6 Training: use of internal HR-academy (opleidingsinstituut)

! 6 Training: working group is trained on the specific topic

! 6 Training: Workshop for OR to determine own position on the profile of the RvC candidate(s)

! 6 Use of experts
Linked Codes:
← is associated with – ! 6 Use of experts: Reasons_use of external experts only

! 6 Use of experts: (neg.) management finds that too much external experts are used

! 6 Use of experts: added value for EP process

! 6 Use of experts: added value for management

! 6 Use of experts: external expert

! 6 Use of experts: internal exeperts - added value

! 6 Use of experts: internal experts for specific topic areas

! 6 Use of experts: internal experts participate in project groups for RfAs

! 6 Use of experts: Reasons_use of external experts only
Linked Codes:
– is associated with → ! 6 Use of experts

! 6 Working group: external consultant CWC participates in the working group

! 6 Working group: of the WC on strategy and finance, which analyses the financial results

! 6A Market conditions

! 6B Digitalisation

! 6C ZZP'er

◈ 7 EWC & FOREIGN CONTACTS

47 Members:

! 7 Alternative EU consultation: coordination committee (EP) + topmanagement visits nat. works councils in case of reorganisations

! 7 Alternative EU consultation: Employee forum (broader than EWC)

! 7 Alternative EU consultation: European Staff Council

! 7 Alternative forms: Information and consultation body

! 7 Alternative forms: Information and consultation body: informal contact with the EU CEO and CFO (benen-op-tafel gesprekken)

! 7 Alternative forms: Information and consultation body: meetings on a quarterly basis

! 7 Alternative forms: International consultation committee

! 7 Alternative forms: International email group

! 7 Communication EWC: Monthly conference call EWC

! 7 Consultation EWC
Linked Codes:
← is associated with – ! 7 Consultation EWC: executive committe (DB) EWC regularly meets with member of the topmanagement (BOD member on labour, Arbeitsdirektor)

! 7 Consultation EWC - Inviting managers to present (reorganisation) plans in the EWC, if one country is concerned

! 7 Consultation EWC: article 6 negotiated agreement with information and consultation (2x per year full EWC, 2x per year select comité)

! 7 Consultation EWC: Consultation model transferred from CWC to EWC with working groups and pre-consultation

! 7 Consultation EWC: executive committe (DB) EWC regularly meets with member of the topmanagement (BOD member on labour, Arbeitsdirektor)
Linked Codes:
– is associated with → ! 7 Consultation EWC

! 7 Consultation EWC: Management may inspect the draft opinion and change the wording without altering the content

! 7 Consultation EWC: Pro's (pre- &)consultation model on EU level

! 7 Consultation EWC: Publication of advice opinion

! 7 Consultation SE: combination of translators and language training

! 7 Consultation SE: Dutch EP represented in Konzernbetriebsrat and SE-WC in Germany

! 7 Consultation SE: learning process regarding the consultation structure

! 7 Consultation SE: majority SH is the CEO and is present at the consultation meeting

! 7 Country feedback EWC: every 2 month for all EU subsidiaries to the top-management
Linked Codes:
← is associated with – ! 7 Country feedback EWC: positive responses senior management
← is associated with – ! 7 Country feedback EWC: Role of the Dutch works council

! 7 Country feedback EWC: once a year by the country representatives

! 7 Country feedback EWC: positive responses senior management
Linked Codes:
– is associated with → ! 7 Country feedback EWC: every 2 month for all EU subsidiaries to the top-management

! 7 Country feedback EWC: Role of the Dutch works council
Linked Codes:
– is associated with → ! 7 Country feedback EWC: every 2 month for all EU subsidiaries to the top-management

! 7 cross-border EP network facilitating informal meetings of WCs and managers in the same division within the MNC

! 7 cross-border EP network: incidental contact with WC colleagues in other EU countries

! 7 CWC Relationship with the EWC

! 7 EWC – added value: platform to compare implementation of MNC policies (added value)

! 7 EWC - added value: Regular exchange of information with German counterpart (Konzernbetriebsrat)

! 7 EWC and Unions: Inviting Union reps to EWC plenary meetings

! 7 EWC: General facts

! 7 EWC: other

! 7 Information EWC: Chairman supervisory board present in EWC for a Q&A session

! 7 Information EWC: contact between EWC members and DB of the NL CWC

! 7 Mergers/Reorganisations EWC: Letter of comfort

! 7 Organisation EWC: ad-hoc representation for a specific issue

! 7 Organisation EWC: Coordination of actions via EWC prior to national steps to be taken

! 7 Organisation EWC: coordination of EP agenda

! 7 Organisation EWC: division of tasks

! 7 Organisation EWC: Function of EWC chairman defined and recognised as job within the organisation

! 7 Proactivity: dragons den (CGI tomorrow)

! 7 Problems – No EWC: reasons

! 7 Problems EWC: (neg.) no added value

! 7 Problems EWC: (neg.) cultural differences

! 7 Strategic changes: large reorganisations tabled in the EWC. Dutch CWC can raise national concerns

! 7 Strategic issues: Consultation in the EWC prior to nat. (implementing) consultation

◇ 8 FACILITIES

22 Members:

! 8 Assessment and valuation: EP work currently not assesed in appraisal meetings

! 8 Coordinator: Coordinator MZ (HR: link between management and COR)
Linked Codes:
← is a – ! 8 Coordinator: Labour Relations Manageer (link between COR and RvB)

! 8 Coordinator: Labor director: link between US topmanagement and EP

! 8 Coordinator: Labour Relations Manageer (link between COR and RvB)
Linked Codes:
– is a → ! 8 Coordinator: Coordinator MZ (HR: link between management and COR)

! 8 Coordinator: One Country Manager als general contact point

! 8 Dual employment for part-timers

! 8 Facilities

! 8 How to modernise EP

! 8 Investing in EP: money and qualified staff members in WC

! 8 Investing in EP: proactive campaigning among employees for WC elections by management

! 8 Ombudsman proposed by COR

! 8 Professional "change team" (veranderteam) --> by the management for a dialogue with the employee representation

! 8 Strategy sessions for WC with BoD (+ head HR) and SB present --> getting to know each other

! 8 Training and development plan for EP members --> coherent!

! 8 Training: provided for CWC in light of reorganisations

! 8 Work exemptions (vrijstelling)

! 8 Work exemptions: (neg.) no fixed agreement on work exemptions

! 8 Work exemptions: Flexible work exemptions for WC members (100% in peak times and less for BAU)

! 8 Work exemptions: importance of arrangements on this matter

! 8 Work exemptions: neg. comments management

! 8 Work exemptions: neg. implications work environment

! 8 Work exemptions: negative impact on assessment of reg. work

◈ 9 SOFT SKILLS

65 Members:

! 9 Added value: of the (recommended) SB member(s)

! 9 Added value: of the COR for the management

! 9 Added value: of the COR for the RvC

! 9 Added value: of the SB for the CWC

! 9 Added value: Raad van Toezicht

! 9 Attitude +: Positive stance CEO/management vis-a-vis COR

! 9 Attitude +: taking the CWC seriously

! 9 Attitude +: taking the RvT seriously

! 9 Attitude -: Negative/reserved stance CEO/management vis-a-vis COR

! 9 Attitude of the management

! 9 Attitude: (neg.) Formalistic attitude

! 9 Attitude: change in management resulted in open lines of communication

! 9 Attitude: Time and attentiveness (tijd en aandacht)

! 9 CEO present on training days of new COR members

! 9 Chemistry between WC and management: do not approach consultation too formalistic but pragmatic

! 9 Conduct: Specifying of policies on conduct together with COR

! 9 Confidentiality

! 9 Confidentiality: (neg.) misused to keep information from CWC

! 9 Confidentiality: (neg.) NDA can create irritations within the WC/MNC

! 9 Confidentiality: added value not using embargo (management)

! 9 Confidentiality: article 20 WCA versus NDA?

! 9 Confidentiality: financial market authorities / compliance may hinder sharing of information

! 9 Confidentiality: management does not use embargo --> information provided on the basis of trust

! 9 Constructivism: Constructive attitude CWC and management

! 9 Constructivism: Picking a point and working towards that point on the horizon together

! 9 Constructivism: Rational discussion of the issue at hand

! 9 Constructivism: Single method of measuring employee involvement developed together by COR and HR

! 9 Decent labour relations: leaving employees ambassadors of the MNE & CWC important

! 9 Directness

! 9 EWC: has to be taken seriously

! 9 Firm and direct on the subject and soft on the relationship

! 9 Listening skills and valuation of both parties

! 9 Openness: (CEO) Not lying to works council, but cannot provide all information sought

! 9 Openness: directors and managers seek advice of the works council for issues

! 9 Openness: downside of granting extensive access to CWC (management)

! 9 Openness: Open and truthful relationship

! 9 Perception: (CEO:) perception by Anglo-Saxon parent company of EP negative despite effectiveness

! 9 Primary role of the CWC for the management

! 9 Proactive WOR-chairman

! 9 Problems exchange info: information are not processed correctly though lines of communication ("Chinese whispers")

! 9 Problems Feedback: (neg.) WC not used as "sounding board" (klankbordgroop)

! 9 Problems Learning process: (neg.) Anglo-Saxon mother did not learn from EP in daugether companies

! 9 Relationship management: informal contact with new CEO to indicate constructive attitude

! 9 Relationship management: resulting in a dialogue/Rhineland model

! 9 Relationship management: the oil in the machinery

! 9 Respect: Mutual respect and understanding of cultural differences

! 9 Respect: Mutual respect management + WC

! 9 Transparency: added value of information symmetry

! 9 Transparency: making sure that all stakeholders are on the same "datapoint"

! 9 Transparency: No surprises and transparency; openness

! 9 Transparency: solving issues to create win-win synergies

! 9 Trust SORTED

! 9 Trust: [Het vetrouwen moet groeien] The trust in the proces grows over time and due to the failures of not following the developed consultation process/model

! 9 Trust: CEO and WC chair jointly address issues regarding trust – doing it together (management, process improvement)

! 9 Trust: CEO trusts CWC and SB

! 9 Trust: confidential information are not leaked by CWC

! 9 Trust: CWC would violate trust only if managment violates relationship

! 9 Trust: neg. mistrust CWC in management due to private equity takeover

! 9 Trust: neg. trustful relationship has been violated by the CWC

! 9 Trust: Not misusing trustful relationship (you may have something from me and then I can ask a favour of you)

! 9 Trust: Not violating the trustful relationship

! 9 Trust: preventing paranoia

! 9 Trust: trustful relationship facilitates dialogue

! 9 Understanding: Dutch employees do not perceive the importance of German parent

! 9 Understanding: Explaining the Dutch model to foreign (parent) corporations

10 GENERAL CHARACTERISTICS INTERVIEWEES

9 Members:

! 10 Chairman of the works council
Linked Codes:
– is associated with → ! 10 Position in the works council

! 10 Management: other functions/roles in the MNC

! 10 Official secretary (ambtelijk secretaris)
Linked Codes:
– is associated with → ! 10 Position in the works council

! 10 Position in the EWC

! 10 Position in the management team

! 10 Position in the supervisory board

! 10 Position in the works council
Linked Codes:
← is associated with – ! 10 Chairman of the works council
← is associated with – ! 10 Official secretary (ambtelijk secretaris)

! 10 Role of the chairman of the work council

! 10 Supervisory board member by nomination of the WC (voordrachtscommissaris)

11 Other

7 Members:

! 11 EP network: contacts of the respondent(s) outside the organisation

! 11 EP network: IVO

! 11 EP Network: WC's of large financial institutions

! 11 Leadership team meeting

! 11 Now, wow, how

! 11 Other forms of employee participation

! 11 ROON – regionaal overleg ondernemingsraden Noord-Limburg

Maastricht Law Series

The Maastricht Law Series is created in 2018 by Boom juridisch and Eleven International Publishing in association with the Maastricht University Faculty of Law. The Maastricht Law Series publishes books on comparative, European and International law. The series builds upon the tradition of excellence in research at the Maastricht Faculty of Law, its research centers and the Ius Commune Research School. The Maastricht Law Series is a peer reviewed book series that allows researchers an excellent opportunity to showcase their work.

Published in this series:

Volume 1: Reinhard Zimmermann, Does the Law of Succession Reflect Cultural Differences?, ISBN 978-94-6236-856-9

Volume 2: Anna Berlee, Access to personal data in public land registers, ISBN 978-94-6236-841-5

Volume 3: Marcus Meyer, The Position of Dutch Works Councils in Multinational Corporations, ISBN 978-94-6236-848-4